P9-EJI-866

OKANAGAN UNIV/COLLEGE LIBRARY

**01952803**

RC 489 .S63 O36 1995
Handbook of psychological
01952803

## DATE DUE

| | *Mar 3 l* |
|---|---|
| JAN 2 2 1996 | |
| SEP 2 8 1996 | |
| APR 2 1 1997 | |
| MAR 1 9 1998 | |
| NOV 2 8 1998 | |
| *UVBC 99050211* | |
| *due Mar 4/99* | |
| MAR 2 6 1999 | |
| FEB 1 6 2000 | |
| NOV 1 - 2000 | |
| | |
| | |
| | |
| | |
| | |
| | |
| | |

BRODART.                                        Cat. No. 23-221

# HANDBOOK OF PSYCHOLOGICAL SKILLS TRAINING

# RELATED TITLES OF INTEREST

**Handbook of Behavior Therapy with Children and Adults: A Developmental and Longitudinal Perspective**
Robert T. Ammerman and Michel Hersen (Editors)
ISBN: 0–205–14583–3

**Handbook of Prescriptive Treatments for Children and Adolescents**
Robert T. Ammerman, Cynthia G. Last, and Michel Hersen (Editors)
ISBN: 0–205–14825–5

**Managed Mental Health Care: A Guide for Practitioners, Employers, and Hospital Administrators**
Thomas R. Giles
ISBN: 0–205–14838–7

**Handbook of Psychotherapy with Children and Adolescents**
Thomas R. Kratochwill and Richard J. Morris (Editors)
ISBN: 0–205–14804–2

**Cognitive Therapy of Borderline Personality Disorder**
Mary Anne Layden, Cory F. Newman, Arthur Freeman, and Susan Byers Morse
ISBN: 0–205–14807–7

**Social Skills for Mental Health: A Structured Learning Approach**
Robert P. Sprafkin, N. Jane Gershaw, and Arnold P. Goldstein
ISBN: 0–205–14841–7

**Handbook of Sexual Dysfunctions: Assessment and Treatment**
William O'Donohue and James H. Geer (Editors)
ISBN: 0–205–14787–9

**Handbook of Behavior Therapy and Pharmacotherapy for Children: A Comparative Analysis**
Vincent B. Van Hasselt and Michel Hersen (Editors)
ISBN: 0–205–13949–3

# HANDBOOK OF PSYCHOLOGICAL SKILLS TRAINING: CLINICAL TECHNIQUES AND APPLICATIONS

**William O'Donohue**
*Northern Illinois University*

**Leonard Krasner**
*Stanford University*

**Editors**

**Allyn and Bacon**
*Boston   London   Toronto   Sydney   Tokyo   Singapore*

Copyright © 1995 by Allyn and Bacon
A Division of Paramount Publishing
160 Gould Street
Needham Heights, Massachusetts 02194

All rights reserved. No part of the material protected by this copyright
notice may be reproduced or utilized in any form or by any means, electronic
or mechanical, including photocopying, recording, or by any information
storage and retrieval system, without written permission from the
copyright owner.

**Library of Congress Cataloging-in-Publication Data**

O'Donohue, William
    Handbook of psychological skills training : clinical techniques
and applications / William O'Donohue, Leonard Krasner.
        p.   cm.
    Includes bibliographical references and index.
    ISBN 0–205–15261–9
    1. Social skills—Study and teaching.  2. Life skills—Study and
teaching.  3. Psychotherapy.  I. Krasner, Leonard
II. Title.
RC489.S63036   1995
158'.2'071—dc20                                          94–2728
                                                          CIP

ISBN 0-205-15261-9
H52616

Printed in the United States of America

10 9 8 7 6 5 4 3 2 1    98 97 96 95 94

*This volume is dedicated to my parents, William and Margery, with thanks for all their love, kindness and support.*

*W.O.*

*This volume is dedicated with love to all the Krasner family.*

*L.K.*

# CONTENTS

# ABOUT THE EDITORS

**William O'Donohue,** Ph.D., is an assistant professor of psychology at Northern Illinois University. He received a doctorate in clinical psychology from the State University of New York at Stony Brook and a master's degree in philosophy from Indiana University. He has co-edited several books, including *Theories of Human Sexuality, The Sexual Abuse of Children,* and *The Handbook of the Sexual Dysfunctions* (all with J. H. Geer). He has published in the areas of human sexuality and its problems, cognitive behavior therapy, clinical decision making, and the philosophy of psychology.

**Leonard Krasner** received his doctorate from Columbia University. He is a licensed clinical psychologist (California and New York) and has been involved in training clinical psychologists as scientists/practitioners in various academic and hospital settings. He has authored, co-authored, edited, or co-edited numerous books and articles. He is currently clinical professor, Department of Psychiatry and Behavioral Sciences, Stanford University.

# ABOUT THE CONTRIBUTORS

**Deborah R. Barclay** is a graduate student in child clinical psychology at Memphis State University and a clinical intern at the University of Mississippi Medical Center. Her current research is focused on how different parenting styles affect children's self-understanding.

**Douglas A. Bernstein** received his Ph.D. in 1968 from Northwestern University. Since then, he has been teaching graduate and undergraduate courses in psychology at the University of Illinois at Urbana-Champaign. He is currently director of the department's introductory psychology program. His research interests focus on techniques for the reduction of anxiety, cigarette smoking behavior, and other topics within the general realm of behavioral medicine. He has written (with T. D. Borkovec) *Progressive Relaxation Training* (1973) and *Introduction to Clinical Psychology* (1991, with M. T. Nietzel and R. Milich). He has also written an introductory psychology textbook with three other faculty members at Illinois (Houghton Mifflin, 1991).

**Margaret L. Box** received her bachelor's degree from Indiana University in Bloomington and has a master's degree in clinical psychology from Louisiana State University. Her interest area is behavior modification with developmentally delayed children.

**Charles R. Carlson** received his Ph.D. in clinical psychology from Vanderbilt University in 1983. He is currently a faculty member in the Department of Psychology at the University of Kentucky; prior to this appointment, he was on the faculty at Wheaton College until 1988. His research interests center on muscle pain disorders of the head and neck region.

**Eileen Gambrill** is professor of social welfare at the University of California at Berkeley. She is the au-

thor of several books, including *Critical Thinking in Clinical Practice, Behavior Modification: Handbook of Assessment, Intervention and Evaluation,* and *Taking Charge of Your Social Life* (with Cheryl Richey). She served as editor-in-chief of *Social Work Research and Abstracts* from 1984 to 1988 and serves on a number of editorial boards.

**Steven R. Gold** received his Ph.D. in clinical psychology from Purdue University. He is currently a professor of psychology and director of clinical training at Northern Illinois University. His research interests include sexual fantasy, sexual aggression, and consequences of child sexual abuse.

**Arnold P. Goldstein** is professor of special education and director, Center for Research on Aggression, at Syracuse University. His primary interests, as both practitioner and researcher, are interventions with juvenile delinquents, abusive parents, and other chronically aggressive individuals.

**John Gottman,** Ph.D. is a professor at the University of Washington Department of Psychology and a licensed clinical psychologist. He has published numerous books and articles on marriage, children's friendships, emotion, and research methodology. The American Association of Marriage and Family Therapists (AAMFT) gave him the 1989 Cumulative Contributions to Research in Family Therapy award. His most recent book, *What Predicts Divorce,* summarizes his research on marriage. A forthcoming book offers prescriptions for specific problems in marital communication.

**David A. F. Haaga** is an assistant professor of psychology at American University. He received a Ph.D. from the University of Southern California and postdoctoral training at the Center for Cognitive Therapy.

His research focuses on depression, cognitive assessment, and smoking. In 1992 he received the New Researcher Award from the Association for Advancement of Behavior Therapy.

**Arthur C. Houts** is professor, Department of Psychology, Memphis State University. He teaches child behavior therapy and has conducted research on the role of fathers in parent training. His research is supported by a grant from the National Institute of Child Health and Human Development (RO1 HD21736).

**Carolyn Hughes,** Ph.D. (University of Illinois, 1990) is an assistant professor at Vanderbilt University. Over the course of the past ten years, as a teacher and an advanced graduate student, Professor Hughes has been studying self-instructional strategies among persons with severe disabilities. Most recently, she has developed the Tennessee High School Model, which promotes the utilization of self-instructional strategies in the classroom and the community.

**Elizabeth J. Letourneau** received an M.A. in clinical psychology at Northern Illinois University, where she is currently completing her doctoral work, also in clinical psychology. Ms. Letourneau's research interests include different aspects of human sexuality, and she has published in the areas of male sex offender treatment and male and female sexual dysfunctions. Ms. Letourneau is currently researching aspects of female sexual arousal.

**Johnny L. Matson** received his Ph.D. in psychology in 1976. He has held positions at the University of Pittsburgh and Northern Illinois University. Currently, he is professor of psychology at Louisiana State University. Dr. Matson has served as a consultant to the U.S. Justice Department, the National Institute of Mental Health and the President's Committee on Mental Retardation. He was elected a fellow to the American Psychological Society, the American Psychological Association, and the American Association on Mental Retardation. Dr. Matson is the author of 280 publications, including 27 books.

**Cory F. Newman,** Ph.D., is clinical director of the Center for Cognitive Therapy and assistant professor of psychology in psychiatry at the University of Pennsylvania. Dr. Newman actively treats patients; supervises clinicians; lectures at the local, national, and international levels, and is author of two new

volumes, *Cognitive Therapy of Borderline Personality Disorder* and *Cognitive Therapy of Substance Abuse.*

**James Noll,** B.A., is a graduate student in the clinical psychology program at Northern Illinois University. His current research interests include operant choice behavior, behavior therapy, aging, and Alzheimer's disease.

**Raymond W. Novaco,** Ph.D., is a professor in the Department of Psychology and Social Behavior at the University of California, Irvine. His academic work has concerned clinically focused research on anger and aggression and also environmentally oriented studies of human stress and violence.

**Thomas W. Pierce** is currently an assistant professor of psychology at Radford University. Before that he was a postdoctoral fellow in the Center for the Study of Aging at Duke University Medical Center. He obtained his Ph.D. from the University of Maine and his B.A. from McGill University.

**Thomas E. Rudy** is associate professor of anesthesiology and psychiatry, and associate director, Pain Evaluation and Treatment Institute, University of Pittsburgh. He has published over 100 journal articles and chapters. His research has been funded by the National Institute of Dental Research and the National Institute of Arthritis and Musculoskeletal and Skin Diseases.

**Frank R. Rusch,** Ph.D. (University of Washington, 1977), is a professor of special education at the University of Illinois. He also directs the Transition Research Institute, which addresses youths' transition from school to adult life. Over the past fifteen years, Professor Rusch has studied self-mediated instructional strategies, including antecedent cue regulation, self-control, self-instructional strategies, and self-reinforcement. This work is in stark contrast to externally mediated strategies that are common in instructional settings.

**Regina Rushe,** B.S.N., A.M., is a graduate student at the University of Washington Department of Psychology and expects her Ph.D. in clinical psychology in 1994. Her baccalaureate degree, from the University of Pittsburgh, is in nursing and psychology. She is currently on internship at the Palo Alto Veteran's Administration in the Interdisciplinary Training Team Program. Together with Neil Jacobson, John Gottman, and colleagues, she is conducting a descriptive investigation of spouse abuse. Her dissertation will focus on verbal and nonverbal attempts at persuasion that distinguished abusive from nonabusive couples.

**Jay A. Sevin** is a psychology intern at the Kennedy Kreiger Institute of Johns Hopkins University Medical School. He has finished all his didactic work, including the dissertation in the Ph.D. program in clinical psychology at Louisiana State University. He is the author of a number of articles on mental retardation and developmental disabilities.

**Dr. Deborah Shanley** is presently dean of the School of Liberal Arts and Education and Medgar Evers College of the City University of New York. She served ten years as a public school teacher and has published numerous articles in the areas of special education and curriculum-based assessment, both here and abroad.

**Jeff Szymanski** received his B.S. in psychology from Northern Michigan University, and he is currently working on his M.A. in clinical psychology at Northern Illinois University. Mr. Szymanski plans to continue work toward a Ph.D. at Northern Illinois University, with a research emphasis on psychotherapy process variables.

**Peter Trower**, Ph.D., is head of Rehabilitation Psychology, Hon. Lecturer, Birmingham University, and Fellow the B.P.S. Has written, taught, researched and published widely in the areas of social skills training, cognitive behavioral approaches to interpersonal problems, and the psychopathology of social anxiety.

**Dennis C. Turk** is professor of psychiatry, anesthesiology, and behavioral science and director of the Pain Evaluation and Treatment Institute at the University of Pittsburgh. He has over 170 publications, including eight books: *Pain and Behavioral Medicine; Pain Management; Facilitating Treatment Adherence; Health, Illness, and Families; Psychosocial Assessment in Terminal Care; Reasoning, Inference, and Judgment in Clinical Psychology; Handbook of Pain Assessment;* and *Non-Invasive Approaches to Pain Control in the Terminally Ill.*

**Julie S. Vargas** is currently professor of behaviorology at West Virginia University. A former third- and fourth-grade teacher, she is author of three books and several articles in education. She is a past president of the Association for Behavior Analysis and is president of the B. F. Skinner Foundation.

**Philip G. Wilson**, Ph.D. (University of Illinois, 1991) is a visiting assistant professor at the University of Colorado–Denver. Over the past several years, Dr. Wilson has studied applications of self-instructional strategies among persons with severe mental retardation working and living in integrated settings.

# PREFACE

This book presents some recent developments in psychotherapy and demonstrates their close connections with one another, with an educative orientation, and in particular with behavioral psychology. These developments are influenced by the following core propositions: In pursuing their goals, individuals are confronted with a wide variety of tasks (e.g., communicating, relating to others). Their performance relative to environmental demands may be deficient in critical ways. These deficiencies may in themselves be regarded as psychological problems (e.g., unassertiveness), may cause other psychological problems (e.g., depression), or may exacerbate existing problems (e.g., marital difficulties). Therapy becomes focused on the learning of skills so that individuals come to behavior differently (i.e., more competently) when confronted with these tasks and therefore can more readily achieve their goals.

The historical development in twentieth-century clinical psychology of this educative, skill-based approach to psychological problems can be traced from the studies of Salter (1949) and Wolpe (1969) on relaxation and assertion training for anxiety problems; Skinner (1953) on self-control training; and Bandura (1969) on response acquisition through modeling. Other more recent influences have been Patterson's (1975) and Becker's (1971) research in child management training; Paul's (Paul & Lentz 1977) outcome studies of a wide variety of skill training with hospitalized schizophrenics; Gottman's (Gottman, Notarius, Gonso, & Markman, 1976) use of communication skills for marital problems; Novaco's (1975) development of a skill-based anger control intervention; Goldstein's (Goldstein, Sprafkin, Gershaw, & Klein, 1980) skill-based intervention with delinquent youths; Turk's (1976) development of pain management skills; Meichenbaum's (1975) development of stress inoculation skills; and McFall's (1976, 1982) skill analysis of a variety of psychological problems. This book attempts to provide a contemporary compendium of the legacy of this orientation toward psychological problems.

This is neither to say that the skill-based orientation to psychotherapy is universally accepted nor that it is without problems. Herink's (1980) survey indicated that there might be in excess of 350 "schools" of psychotherapy. Many of the core ideas of these schools are antithetical to the core ideas of this orientation. Part of the purpose of gathering the material for this book is to present the case for this approach—or, to address a paraphrase of Paul's (1969) classic question: What is the evidence that this therapeutic approach is effective for what type of client, with what problem, delivered by what kind of therapist, and why? Part of the value in doing this is to illustrate the various lacunae in our knowledge relevant to these questions, and thus to indicate important areas for future research. Another aspect of this undertaking is to present evidence—which we take to indicate that there is considerable merit—for currently pursuing this orientation with a substantial variety of clients and problems. Thus, consistent with the scientist-practitioner orientation, this book attempts to provide information relevant to implementing various *skill-based interventions* as well as presenting their research base and additional research questions.

## REFERENCES

Bandura A. (1969). *Principles of behavior modification.* New York: Holt, Rinehart and Winston.

Becker, W. C. (1971). *Parents are teachers.* Champaign, IL: Research Press.

Goldstein, A. P., Sprafkin, R. P., Gershaw, N. J., & Klein, P. (1980). *Skillstreaming the adolescent.* New York: Pergamon Press.

Gottman, J., Notarius, C., Gonso, J., & Markman, H. (1976). *A couple's guide to communication.* Champaign, IL: Research Press.

Herink, R. (Ed.). (1980). *The psychotherapy handbook.* New York: American Library.

Meichenbaum, D. H. (1975). A self-instructional approach to stress management: A proposal for stress inoculation training. In I. Sarason & D. Shapiro (Eds.), *Stress and anxiety* (Vol. 2). New York: Wiley.

McFall, R. M. (1976). *Behavioral training: A skill acquisition approach to clinical problems.* Morristown, NJ: General Learning Press.

McFall, R. M. (1982). A review and reformulation of the concept of social skills. *Behavioral Assessment, 4,* 1–33.

Novaco, R. W. (1975). *Anger control: The development and evaluation of an experimental treatment.* Lexington, MA: Heath.

Patterson, G. R. (1975). *Families: Applications of social learning to family life.* Champaign, IL: Research Press.

Paul, G. L., & Lentz, R. J. (1977). *Psychosocial treatment of chronic mental patients: Milieu versus social-learning programs.* Cambridge, MA: Harvard University Press.

Salter, A. (1949). *Conditioned reflex therapy.* New York: Creative Age.

Skinner, B. F. (1953). *Science and human behavior.* New York: Free Press.

Turk, D. C. (1976). *An expanded skills training approach for the treatment of experimentally induced pain.* Unpublished doctoral dissertation, University of Waterloo.

Wolpe, J. (1969). *The practice of behavior therapy.* New York: Pergamon Press.

## ACKNOWLEDGMENTS

We are indebted to many individuals for their help in producing this book. Of course, we owe a huge debt to the chapter authors. We should like to express our appreciation for their hard work. We would also like to acknowledge the kind and expert assistance of the late Jerry Frank in initiating this project. We wish to express our thanks to our current editor, Mylan Jai-xen, and his assistant, Sue Hutchinson, for their cooperation and support. Thank you to our reviewers, Arthur M. Nezu of Hahnemann University and Mitchell L. Schare of Hofstra University, for their criticisms and suggestions. Finally, we would like to thank our families—Jane, Katherine, Miriam, Wendy, David, Charles, and Stephanie.

# CHAPTER 1

# PSYCHOLOGICAL SKILLS TRAINING

William O'Donohue
Leonard Krasner

A consequential and controversial question concerns the fundamental nature of psychotherapy: What is the essential character of problems addressed in therapy, what are the basic aims of therapy, and what is of the role of the psychotherapist? For example, is therapy aimed at gaining cathartic insight through the therapist's interpretations, clarifications, and confrontations into problems that arise as a result of unacceptable unconscious impulses? Is therapy aimed at assisting the client to choose to live authentically through the therapist's creation of an empathic and unconditionally accepting relationship to overcome inauthentic conditions of worth? Or, rather, is therapy an attempt to help the client think and emote more rationally, through the therapist's instruction in logic and challenge of irrational ideas and other cognitive errors, in order to decrease irrational behavior caused by faulty thinking? Sometimes these radically different conceptualizations of therapy can be partially captured by a metaphor—humans as "budding flowers," "scientists," "logicians," "computers," "philosophers," "rats," "students," or "emotional children."

These are but a few of the numerous extant views of the essence of therapy. In fact, one author recently reviewed eighteen models of psychotherapy (Prochaska, 1984), and another has suggested that there are approximately four hundred schools (Herink, 1980). These differ radically in the conceptualization of the fundamental nature of psychological problems, the basic nature of the role of the therapist, and the type of mechanisms or conditions that produce change. In this chapter we describe one model of the therapeutic enterprise, psychological skills training. Like many other models of therapy, psychological skills training can be seen as independent of and even inconsistent with other models or, more eclectically, as somewhat consistent with other models and thus at times serving as an useful adjunct to other models of therapy.

## WHAT IS PSYCHOLOGICAL SKILLS TRAINING?

The phrase *psychological skills training* is borrowed from Goldstein (1982) and Goldstein and Krasner (1987) and is associated with the following claims:

1. Situations and problems arise regularly in which, in order to achieve some end (e.g., solve the problem, realize some personal goal), an individual must be able to respond in a competent, skilled manner.
2. Situations and problems create diverse demands (e.g., need to communicate, need to solve some problem, need to relax, need to interact successfully with others).
3. These diverse demands require diverse skills and capacities (e.g., communication skills, social skills, relaxation skills, problem-solving skills) for their resolution. Life has its "hidden curriculum" (Chan & Rueda, 1979).
4. Individuals vary in their abilities to execute various skills. All individuals have a range of potential abilities, although, as a result of certain conditions (e.g., genetic, physiological, or environmental/learning problems), individuals can have restricted potentials or restricted levels of achievement within a given potentiality.
5. Some individuals, at certain times and in certain situations, are deficient in skills necessary to meet some demand or achieve some end. The qualifiers in the previous sentence are there to indicate the situational specificity of performance deficits.
6. When situational demands arise that exceed the individual's skills, states of affairs may arise that may be variously described as lack of success, frustration, or even depression, psychophysiological illness, and the like. The manner in which these consequences are described has important implications concerning what appears to be a reasonable way to improve these states of affairs.
7. These individuals can often profit from an educational (psychoeducational) experience in which skill and performance deficits are directly addressed and remediated. Moreover, as McFall (1982) has stated,

> incompetence can be seen as the product of a mismatch between a person's performance abilities and the task demands imposed on the person. This discrepancy can be described, alternatively, as being due either to a deficit in skills, or to excessive performance demands. Psychological problems grow out of this imbalance between abilities and demands in the person–environment system; therefore, the reduction of psychological problems, which involves establishing a balance in the system, can be achieved either through increasing the person's abilities or through decreasing the environmental task demands imposed on the person. (p. 22)

Psychological skills training also can be clarified in part by a more precise definition of a "skill." The *Oxford English Dictionary* (1982) provides a relevant definition of *skill:* "to have discrimination or knowledge, esp. in a specified matter" (p. 2847). Competent performance in some skill may require declarative knowledge and/or procedural knowledge. Declarative knowledge concerns knowing that certain relevant propositions are true—for example, "Occasional eye contact with the speaker will increase the probability that the speaker will know that I am listening." Procedural knowledge is knowing *how* to do something—for example, knowing the knack of relaxing striated muscles. Egan and Cowan (1979, p. 8) define skills in a more molar and functional manner: "the competencies that are necessary for effective living." McFall (1982) defines "skills" as "the specific abilities required to perform competently at a task (pp. 12–13).

Goldstein (1982) has provided a succinct definition of psychological skills training:

> the planned, systematic teaching of the specific behaviors needed and consciously desired by the individual in order to function in an effective and satisfying manner, over an extended period of time, in a broad array of positive, negative and neutral interpersonal contexts. The specific teaching methods which constitute social skills training directly and jointly reflect psychology's modern social learning theory and education's contemporary pedagogic principles and procedures. (p. 3)

*Skills,* as described in this chapter and throughout this book, are often general classes of more circumscribed subskills. For example, the general class *social skills* may be construed to consist of more delimited skills such as paralinguistic skills, assertion skills, conversational skills, and affiliative skills. These, in turn, can be further refined to more specific classes of behavior such as maintaining eye contact, body orientation, expressing positives, and the like. Therefore, actual skills-training programs would translate, for example, the relatively abstract concept of "social skills" into various subskills, and these perhaps into further subskills, until a more elemental behavioral level is reached. It is these classes of behaviors that provide the actual content of skills-training programs.

An important distinction is that between skills, performance, and competence. The term *skills,* when used precisely, speaks only of the ability to perform in a certain manner. It does not directly address whether the individual actually does perform in this manner in relevant situations, nor does it refer to the effect of this responding. The term *skills* simply refers to the extent to which certain responses are in the individual's repertoire. Individuals may lack skills because they never learned the skills, because they learned competing inappropriate responses instead, or because previously acquired skills may have decayed as a result of disuse (e.g., dating skills in a newly widowed individual).

*Performance* refers to the individual's actual display of the behavior. Thus, an individual can have the skills to maintain a conversation but may not perform in this manner for some reason (e.g., anxiety or lack of a suitable conversation partner). Individuals may have problems recognizing the appropriate times and situations for the execution of certain skills. Individuals may also not execute skillful behavior because of erroneous beliefs that such behavior will not produce desired results or beliefs that they cannot perform the skills adequately. In fact, Bandura (1977) has long argued that self-efficacy (i.e., subjects' beliefs about their abilities) is a better predictor of outcomes than level of skill. Another important aspect of performance that needs to be assessed is the subject's collateral responding to his or her own skill performance. For example, if the subject performs a behavior but has a collateral reaction of anxiety, then this is important information, as anxiety may decrease the probability of future performance by decreasing the intrinsic reinforcement associated with this performance.

Finally, *competence* refers to the effects of the performance of skills on the individual's environment. If, for example, the individual maintains a conversation and, as a result, the individual and the conversation partner enjoy themselves, further their relationship, and converse more frequently in the future, it might be said that the individual's performance was competent in this skill area in this situation. Competent performance of some skill may be related to its effortlessness and to a high percentage of effectiveness and accuracy, as well as to the fact that additional practice results in little improvement (Colley & Beech, 1989). Goldfried and D'Zurilla (1969) have suggested that a skillful or competent response may be defined as one that resolves the immediate problems while minimizing the probability of future problems. Schlundt and McFall (1985) provide a useful explication of the notion of social competence, which may be extrapolated to other areas of skill competence:

When a behavior is called *socially competent,* this involves a value-based judgment by an observer concerning the effectiveness of an individual's performance in a specific task. Three aspects of this definition need to be stressed: First, competence is a judgment about behavior and not a judgment about some enduring characteristic of the performer; second, the judgment is based on an episode of behavior within a context, not merely on a single, isolated molecular act; and third the judge who evaluates the competence of a performance does so on the basis of certain implicit or explicit values. (p. 23; emphasis in the original)

The rating of competence by ecologically relevant social judges can give rise to certain problematic issues. For example, in all likelihood because of problematic sex roles, assertive women as compared to unassertive women or assertive men are often judged by both men and women to be less likable, intelligent, competent, and attractive (Solomon & Rothblum, 1985). At times, this can result in a dichotomy between ecological competence and what may be termed *normative competence*—that is performance that meets certain criteria that attempt to correct for problematic social judgments.

Moreover, part of the client's problem may be that the criteria on which the client's behavior is judged to be competent or incompetent may be unclear or unknown. An important part of therapy may be clarifying, explicating, and evaluating implicit competency criteria.

The goal of psychological skills training, therefore, is skill competence, and a goal of assessment is to ascertain at which level (skill, performance, or competence) the individual requires help. We will, however, follow conventional usage and use the more common phrase *skill training* when what is meant is, more precisely, "skill competence training."

Finally, as Phillips (1985) has pointed out, the term *skilled* or *competent behavior* as used in psychology departs from the more common use in which a salesperson who can sell people what they do not need is called "skilled" or in which a Don Juan who seduces women through the use of deception might be regarded as "skilled." *Skilled performance,* as used here, always refers to a reciprocal process in which a person behaves in a manner that helps fulfill his or her rights, needs, goals, or duties, *while simultaneously honoring the similar rights, needs, goals, and duties of others.* Performing a skill in a competent manner is never done at the expense of another but, by definition, is done in a manner that is reciprocally productive of mutual reinforcement. Rinn and

Markles's (1979) definition of social skills of children may be seen as a case in point:

> [Children's social skills are] a repertoire of verbal and nonverbal behaviors by which children affect the responses of other individuals (e.g., peers, parents, siblings, and teachers) in the interpersonal context. This repertoire acts as a mechanism through which children influence their environment by obtaining, removing, or avoiding desirable and undesirable outcomes in the social sphere. Further, the extent to which they are successful in obtaining desirable outcomes and avoiding or escaping undesirable ones *without inflicting pain on others* is the extent to which they are considered socially skilled. (p. 108, emphasis added)

## THE HISTORY OF PSYCHOEDUCATIONAL SKILLS TRAINING

Each chapter in this book starts with a brief history of the specific skills-training topic being covered. In this section we will put into a broader historical context the model from which the concept of skills training of all kinds has developed.

First, we will note some of the various labels that are used for the general model or paradigm implicit in the chapters on skills training: applied psychology, behavior modification, behavior therapy, cognitive-behavioral therapy, behavioral medicine, environmental design, and so on. The use of the descriptive category of *skills training* implies the description of an effective skillful behavior. Thus, the emphasis on overt behavior puts this approach clearly within the "behavioral" model.

Phillips (1985) places the history of the concept of *social skills* within the context of *social imitation learning,* traceable to the early research of Mary Cover Jones (1924). Bellack and Hersen (1977) trace the development of "social skills training techniques" to the earlier research of Salter (1949), Wolpe (1958), Lazarus (1971), and Zigler and Phillips (1960).

Another stream of social skills concepts is linked to research in England in the early 1960s in which behaviors labeled as "skills" were applied to the interaction of human beings with machines (Welford, 1966). In working with machine systems, human skills involved various information-processing procedures in the perception of the particular machine with which the individual was interacting.

This early research on skills analysis of human–machine systems culminated in the research of a British social psychologist, Argyle (1981), and the publication of the first book to include the term *social skills* in its title: *Social Skills and Mental Health* (Trower, Bryant, & Argyle, 1978). Trower and his group initiated research on a wide variety of specific social skills. They emphasized the need to analyze the specific "social skills" needs of individuals in *real-life situations* rather than approaching the individual's "social skills" on the basis of responses to *questionnaires.*

Phillips (1985) clearly, and appropriately, places the concept of social skills within the behavioral model that developed and flourished in the 1960s and 1970s. The very term *social skills* implies interactive behavior with other human beings. Such descriptive terms as "social reinforcement," "imitation," "modeling," "aversive consequences," and "assertiveness" are additional descriptions of positive and negative interactions between human beings. Thus, the social skills approach is one of the major developments in the history of the behavioral model. Krasner (1971) noted that fifteen streams of development within the "science" of psychology had come together during the 1950s and 1960s to form the approach to behavior change generally known as behavior therapy. One of these streams, the research applying *conditioning/learning* concepts to human behavior, included the early social skills work of Phillips (1956). In effect, researchers viewed the training of "social skills" as an adjunct to and even an effective alternative to psychotherapy.

Phillips (1985) aptly describes the social skills movement by noting: "It is a movement that properly places much maturation for change and development in the social matrix and not in intrapsychic development that allegedly unfolds despite the social circumstances. The variables are those relating to the person-environment exchange or interaction as with all behavior research and conceptualization" (pp. 16–17).

Phillips (1985) summarizes the history of the social skills movement in terms of seven major trends: social skills training research initiated in the 1930s; studies of social competence of individuals prior to hospitalization as indicators of how the individual would fare in the hospital and afterward; research on the relationship between human and machine system and human–human systems; derivation of social and moral behavior; the utilization of social skills training in the context of remedial assistance and thus away from the disease model of "abnormal" behavior; replacing "assertiveness" as a unifying concept with emphasis on situation-specific behavior; and focusing on the social matrix on which an individual functions rather than on the "cognitions" of the individual.

To further the historical perspective of "skills training," we will briefly mention the other streams of development within psychology that evolved into the behavior therapy model or paradigm (Krasner, 1990): the concept of *behaviorism* in experimental psychology (e.g., Hilgard & Marquis, 1940; Kantor, 1969); the *instrumental* (operant) *conditioning* research of Thorndike (1931), Skinner (1938, 1953, 1957), and Keller and Schoenfeld (1950); the development of the technique of *reciprocal inhibition* as a treatment procedure (Wolpe, 1958); the experimental studies of a group of investigators at Maudsley Hospital in London under the direction of H. J. Eysenck (1960, 1964); interpretations of psychoanalysis in learning theory terms (e.g., Dollard & Miller, 1950), which enhanced learning theory as a respectable base for clinical work; the concept of *classical conditioning* as the basis for explaining and changing both normal and deviant behavior (e.g., Pavlov, 1928); theoretical concepts and research studies of *social role learning* and *interactionalism* in social psychology and sociology (e.g., Homans, 1961; Mead, 1934; Sarbin, 1954); research in the field of developmental and child psychology (e.g., Baer, 1968; Bijou & Baer, 1961); social influence studies of *demand characteristics, experimenter bias,* and *placebo* (e.g., Frank, 1973; Rosenthal, 1966); an environmentally based *social learning* model as an alternative to the *disease* model of human behavior (e.g., Bandura, 1969; Krasner & Ullmann, 1965; Ullmann & Krasner, 1965); a movement within psychiatry away from the orthodox focus on internal dynamics and pathology toward concepts of human *interaction* and environmental influence; and a utopian emphasis on the planning of social environments to elicit and maintain the best of human behavior (e.g., Skinner, 1948).

The remainder of this chapter continues to expand on the concept of skills training within the historical/theoretical context. Each of the subsequent chapters places its particular procedures within the broader theoretical framework delineated in this chapter.

In recent years, skills-based interventions have been used with favorable results with a number of clinical problems. Table 1.1 briefly summarizes some of the major uses. Social skills training has led to the improvement of psychosocial functioning and reduc-

**Table 1.1.** A Selective Review of Types of Skills Training

Problem-solving skills

Social skills (for children, adults, schizophrenics)

Assertion skills

Relaxation skills

Anger control skills

Pain management skills

Sexual interaction skills

Parenting skills

Employment skills

Academic skills

Environmental design skills

Coping skills

Stress management skills

Scientific thinking skills (Kuhn, Amsel, & O'Loughlin, 1988)

Survival skills for urban women (Thurston, Dasta, & Greenwood, 1984)

Empathy skills (Goldstein & Michaels, 1985)

Communication skills (Gottman, Notarius, Gonso, & Markman, 1976)

Behavior modification skills (in professionals, Milne, 1982; in schoolchildren

tion of rehospitalization rates of schizophrenics (Hersen & Bellack, 1976; Liberman, DeRisi, & Mueser, 1989; Paul & Lentz, 1977). A skills-based curriculum has decreased the rule-violating and aggressive behavior of conduct-disordered adolescents (Goldstein, Sprafkin, Gershaw, & Klein, 1980; Goldstein, Chapter 18 this volume). Social skills training has had a remarkable effect on depression (Becker, Heimberg, & Bellack, 1987; Rehm, Fuchs, Roth, Kornblith, & Romano, 1979). Social, assertive, and problem-solving skills have had an impact on substance abuse (Monti, Abrams, Binkoff, & Zwick, 1986). Anger control skills have reduced physical abuse and marital problems (Novaco, 1975; Chapter 15 this volume). Relaxation skills, stress management skills, and social skills have improved anxiety problems (Carlson & Bernstein, Chapter 2 this volume; Trower, 1986; Twentyman & McFall, 1975). Communication skills have had an important impact on marital and family discord (Gottman & Rushe, Chapter 13 this volume; Gottman, Notarius, Gonso, & Markman, 1976). Vocational skills has led to improvements in the life situation of a variety of clients, especially the mentally handicapped (Black, Muehlenhard, & Massey, 1985; Rusch, Hughes, & Wilson, Chapter 17, this volume). Problem-solving skills have had positive results with problems such as schizophrenia, retardation, depression (Castles & Glass, 1986; Hansen, St. Lawrence, & Christoff, 1985; Kalfus, Hawkins, & Reitz, 1984; O'Donohue & Noll, Chapter 7 this volume).

Less traditional applications of skills training include teaching contingency management skills to children to improve teacher–student relationships (Sherman & Cormier, 1974), and teaching these skills to elderly nursing home patients to increase their satisfaction with their living situation (Fisher & Carstensen, 1990). Vealey (1988) has reviewed the contribution of psychological skills training, such as relaxation, imagery skills, attentional skills, and pain management skills, to athletic performance. Goldstein and Krasner (1987) have provided a review of the application of skills training in industrial, community, educational, and legal contexts, among others. This is obviously neither a comprehensive literature review of skills training nor a critical analysis of the actual efficacy of such an approach. The remainder of this book is largely concerned with these two topics. Rather, this list is meant to illustrate briefly some of the promise and the diversity of psychological skills training.

From this list, we can also see that social skills training is probably the most frequently used. In fact, L'Abate and Milan (1985) have claimed that social skills training "must be considered one of the most widely deployed intervention strategies for the delivery of mental health services" (p. xi). We have no evidence to evaluate this claim, which might be exaggerated. However, it does seem fair to say that social skills have become an increasingly frequently used mode of intervention for a variety of problems. This is probably due to the fact that humans are social animals, and thus depend on, and are relied on by, others in numerous ways. As pointed out by Ullmann and Krasner (1965), "the difference between normal and abnormal behavior is not intrinsic; rather it lies in a societal reaction" (p. 32). Thus, the impact of an individual's behavior on others and their judgments of this behavior have important roles in defining whether the individual's behavior is problematic and changeworthy. Hence, social skills training may be particularly useful, as it may most directly affect this "disturbing" social impact.

## RELATIONSHIP WITH OTHER STREAMS OF THERAPY

The role of psychological skills training in traditional psychotherapy can be interpreted in either a *strong* or a *weak* sense. In the strong sense, psychoeducational skills training is taken to be inconsistent with, and in intellectual competition with, alternative models of therapy and problems in living. For example, taken in the strong sense, the medical model is inconsistent with psychoeducational skills training. From the perspective of psychoeducational skills training, people are not patients who are afflicted with a mental disease, who can be cured by doctors through various medical and therapeutic cures. Rather, people are taken to be learners who have had various problems in learning or performing skills and who can be taught by educators to behave in a manner that is more effective and gratifying. In the psychological skills training model, the kinds of events that occur in a helping situation are not "abnormality (or illness) → diagnosis → prescription → therapy → cure" but, rather, "client dissatisfaction (or ambition) → goal setting → skills teaching → satisfaction or goal achievement" (Authier, Gustafson, Guerney, & Kasdorf, 1975). Theories that take much of human behavior to be the product of fixed traits are also inconsistent with psychological skills training. In the latter model, for example, shyness is regarded not as an immutable trait but, instead, as a situational social competence deficit that can be remediated by appropriately tailored social skills training and perhaps relaxation and other anxiety reduction skills. In the strong sense, a psychological skills orientation is taken to be strictly inconsistent with models of therapy and problems that have different views about the nature of the therapist's role, the nature of problems dealt with in therapy, the basic mechanisms of therapeutic change, and the fundamental aims of therapy.

In the weak sense of this phrase, psychological skills training is taken to be compatible with other therapeutic approaches and therefore may be used as an adjunct to these approaches. Here, the individual can be taken as suffering from a mental disorder due to problems other than skills deficits (e.g., poor self-insight) and thus as needing specialized experiences in psychotherapy such as accurate emotional insight into unconscious processes, while *also* needing improvement in certain skills, such as relaxation and social skills. Less radically, research has indicated that training in communication and problem-solving skills can add to the effectiveness of traditional exposure therapy for agoraphobia and panic disorder (Arnow, Taylor, Agras, & Telch, 1985; Kleiner, Marshall, & Spevack, 1987). Moreover, the view can be taken that mental disorders (American Psychiatric Association, 1987), for example, have a deleterious effect on developmental and learning processes and, therefore, can interfere with skill acquisition or performance. In this view, skills training might be a necessary adjunct of more traditional treatment. Liberman, DeRisi, and Mueser (1989) have suggested, for example, that schizophrenics may often profit from a continuity of care that includes social skills training, pharmacological treatment, crisis intervention, family therapy, supportive psychotherapy, self-help groups, medical care, day hospital care, and vocational treatment, among other services.

Moreover, it is interesting to note that certain problems, such as pain and headaches, that are traditionally thought to be the exclusive province of medicine and physiochemical interventions, are increasingly being thought of as amenable to skills remediation (e.g., pain management skills, stress management skills, and relaxation training skills; see Chapters 2, 14 and 16 in this volume). Furthermore, other medical problems, which are not remediable by skills training, seem to have consequences for which psychological skills training is relevant. For example, cancer and surgery bring on problems with anxiety that potentially can be helped by stress management and relaxation skills (Johnston, 1980).

There is also an increasing body of research to show that the psychological skills of the medical practitioner can play an important role in healing. For example, social skills are critical in patient satisfaction (e.g., Cunningham, Morgan, & McGucken, 1984); communication skills are a factor in treatment compliance (Ley, 1982); and both of these skills seem to be related to treatment outcome (Matthews & Ridgeway, 1984). Nichols (1985) has pointed out that certain skills for both medical providers and patients may be critical "in reducing the impact of known stresses imposed by the medical subculture and hospital regimes, as well as dealing with the stresses of illness itself" (p. 233).

These considerations give rise to the following possibility: The skills that individuals (clients) may need to manage their lives successfully may not be of a different order than the skills professionals need to help their clients. Helping professionals and clients alike need to communicate, assert their rights, func-

tion interpersonally, control anger, manage stress, and so on. Egan (1982) has been one of the most explicit writers on analyzing what skills an effective therapist or, in his terms, a "skilled helper" requires. Among the skills that Egan believes necessary are: verbal and nonverbal attending behavior; active listening; responding to the client from the client's internal frame of reference; constructive use of probing; summarizing to help identify recurring themes; appropriate challenging in order to help the client see things from an alternative and more constructive perspective; empathy; self-disclosure; and goal setting (for more on the role of skills in professional training and professional settings, see Dryden, 1985; Goldstein & Goedhart, 1973; Nichols, 1985; Weinman & Medlik, 1985).

How does an individual make an educated, rational choice between the strong and weak views of psychological skills training? The choice rests partly on the individual's values and, in particular, on the individual's general views of the human situation (Krasner & Houts, 1984; O'Donohue, 1989). Do humans develop primarily through learning and education? Does the notion of *skills* capture and do justice to all the subtleties, complexities, and content of the human experience and its problems? For example, does it capture the important human capacity for giving and receiving love, and the problems that arise therein? Does it capture what some individuals might call their search for meaning in life? Does it do justice to what individuals take to be important issues in their life, such as understanding and coping with problems emanating from their family of origin, coping with or overcoming their personal insecurities, or understanding and relating in a mutually satisfactory manner with others? The answers to these questions are no doubt complex and go to the heart of vitally important issues facing every individual. We are not so presumptuous as to pretend that we have the answers to these critical questions. We suggest, however, that the extent to which a psychological skills orientation can address these complex questions is an empirical question. Although the view presented here is admittedly unorthodox, we claim that it is not sufficient simply to assert that psychological skills training is too simplistic to conceptualize and treat these problems effectively. In the face of the accumulating body of evidence concerning the wide-ranging effectiveness of psychological skills training, it seems reasonable to expect the contrarian to offer arguments and evidence for such claims.

For example, what orientation produces the most effective (or cost-effective) results, a view that takes the child-abusing parent as a personality-disordered individual (perhaps antisocial) and in need of some sort of personality restructuring, or one that sees the parent as an individual who needs to be assessed and possibly educated in self-control skills, parenting skills, marital skills, anger control skills, and social skills? To what extent are adolescents who are violating a number of legal and ethical rules suffering from a mental disorder called conduct disorder and, therefore, in need of some sort of conventional psychotherapy, as opposed to the view that these are individuals who need to learn aggression management, feeling awareness, and problem-solving skills (Goldstein, Sprafkin, Gershaw, & Klein, 1980). Hamburg (1990) has developed a therapy and prevention program designed to teach adolescents five classes of what she believes are essential skills for the adolescent: nonviolent conflict resolution, friendship formation, peer resistance, assertiveness, and renegotiation of relationships with adults. The rationale of this approach is as follows: "Young adolescents (10–15) are *susceptible* to *high-risk* problem behaviors without certain life skills. Therefore, it is useful to specify *protective* life skills and how to *acquire* them" (p. iv; emphasis in the original).

McFall and Twentyman (1973) have labeled one component of the proposed model a "response acquisition approach" to treatment:

> Maladaptive behaviors are construed in terms of the absence of specific response skills. The therapeutic objective is to provide patients with direct training in precisely those skills lacking in their repertoires. Very little attention is given to eliminating existing maladaptive behavior; instead it is assumed that as skillful, adaptive responses are acquired, rehearsed and reinforced, the previous maladaptive responses will be displaced and disappear. (p. 139)

The psychological skills training model proposed here is similar to this model and is also similar to coping-skill models of psychotherapy (DeNelsky & Boat, 1986; Goldfried, 1980) and to problem-solving models of psychotherapy (D'Zurilla, 1986), although psychological skills training as described here typically includes a broader range of skills. It is probably most similar to and compatible with McFall's (1976) Behavioral Training, Goldstein's Structured Learning Therapy (Goldstein, Gershaw, & Sprafkin, 1975), and Skillstreaming (Goldstein, 1986). It has important commonalities with Gazda and Brooks's (1985)

life skills training. It is also highly compatible with behavior-analytic and cognitive behavioral models of psychotherapy. It has important commonalities with Ellis's rational emotive therapy, as can be seen in the following quote:

> RET assumes that one of the most constructivist and creative of humans' tendencies is their ability to attend to *new* knowledge imparted by therapists, teachers, and educational materials, to *consider* its plausibility, to *select* and *modify* parts of it for growth purposes and to *utilize* it for present and future change. If people were not able to creatively *use* the therapeutic (and other) teaching, psychotherapy would hardly exist. What we call *experience*—including therapeutic experience—largely consists of taking the direct and indirect instruction of others and selectively *making* parts of it our "own" percepts and precepts. (Ellis, 1990, p. 185, emphasis in the original)

## POTENTIAL ADVANTAGES

We have tried to be frank in explicating that a reasonable concern with psychoeducational skills training might be that it is too simple to deal adequately with many of life's complexities. However, a fair evaluation needs to include potential advantages as well as potential disadvantages. It should be stressed that these advantages are potential advantages and are based on plausibility considerations that await a more definitive empirical evaluation.

1. Psychological skills training relies on the mechanism of "learning" that is relatively well researched, clear, and understood instead of on less well researched, clear, and understood mechanisms such as cathartic insight or authentic living.

2. Psychological skills training relies on the notion of continua of skill abilities and competencies, as well as of situational demands determining what abilities are necessary to produce what ends. Therefore, by eschewing categorical pejorative judgments, psychological skills training construes problems in living in such a way as to decrease stigma associated with psychological difficulties. Reducing stigma is important because it can be an iatrogenic cost to help-seeking behavior.

3. Psychological skills training potentially decreases power differentials (and thereby potential abuses) between trainer and client in several ways. By stressing that the trainer relies on and can improve

on the same skills as the client, the trainer avoids creating a potentially invidious dichotomy in which the healthy (or rational) is helping the sick (or irrational). Clearly explication of goals gives the client a better basis for independently determining his or her own progress and status. Finally, explicating the content of training (e.g., assertion skills) puts the client in a better position to understand therapy.

4. Psychological skills training directly implies a course of remediation, unlike problems encountered when conceptualizing problems along the lines of the diagnoses found in the *Diagnostic and Statistical Manual of Mental Disorders,* third edition—revised (American Psychiatric Association, 1987), which have notorious problems in predicting what treatment will be recommended.

5. A psychological skills training model provides clear, testable hypotheses concerning the origin of psychological problems (e.g., deficiencies in exposure to skilled models at certain developmental periods). Skills deficits may represent a potentially important source of proximate causes of psychological problems. For example, social skills and problem-solving deficits may be an important proximate cause of depression (Becker, Heimberg, & Bellack, 1987; Lewinsohn, Mischel, Chaplin, & Barton, 1980); deficits in relaxation skills may lead to anxiety (Wolpe, 1958). McFall (1976) suggests that skills deficits themselves may arise from "lack of experience or opportunity to learn, faulty learning as a result of unrepresentative or faulty experiences, obsolescence of a previously adaptive response, learning disabilities resulting from biological dysfunctions, or traumatic events, such as injuries or diseases, that nullify prior learning or obstruct new learning" (p. 6). Thus, the etiological chain could be: One of McFall's factors → competency deficit → psychological sequelae (e.g., depression). This model would predict and therefore could be tested by the existence of a direct relationship between increased competency and decreased psychological problems. In fact, DeNelsky and Boat (1986) have recently advanced a model of psychological diagnosis and treatment in which problems are analyzed in terms of skill deficits rather than in terms of symptoms or pathologies.

6. Skill training may be an important method for the prevention of problems. For example, early training in basic competencies and application of certain skills at key developmental periods may lessen the degree of problems in adulthood. Building competence in skills may serve to buffer or obviate the negative effects of stress, conflict, and problems. Egan (1984) recounts an interesting fable relevant to this issue:

> A person walking beside a river sees someone drowning. This person jumps in, pulls the victim out, and begins artificial respiration. Then another drowning person calls for help. The rescuer jumps into the water again, and pulls the second victim out. This process repeats itself several times until finally, much to the amazement of the bystanders who have gathered to watch this drama, the rescuer, even though the screams of yet another victim can be clearly heard from the river, gets up from administering artificial respiration and begins to walk upstream. One of the bystanders calls out: "Where are you going? Can't you hear the cries of the latest victim?" The rescuer replies: "You take care of him. I'm going upstream to find out who's pushing all these people in and see whether I can stop it." He might have added: "I'm also going to find out why all these people can't swim and see whether I can teach them how." (p. 23)

Competencies in skills may reduce the threat of stress and psychobiological diatheses. For example, Liberman, DeRisi, and Mueser (1989) have suggested that skills training, especially social skills training, can improve psychosocial functioning and decrease the relapse rate among schizophrenics. Finally, to the extent that there are predictable developmental problems and tasks (Erikson, 1956; Havighurst, 1953), psychological skills training can be used across the life span to better enable individuals to handle these developmental tasks.

7. Problems are seen as arising from a discrepancy between an individual's capabilities and environmental demands. This interactive model is consistent with the literature (Mischel, 1976), which shows that the greatest portion of variance is accounted for by this interaction.

8. Psychological skills training avoids what may be called the "irrationalist's inconsistency" of certain models in which therapists are rational scientist-practitioners who weigh evidence in coming to their conclusions, but whose conclusions are that human behavior is controlled by irrational (e.g., unconscious sex and aggressive) forces. Helping professionals, as part of their specialized role, should be especially competent at problem-solving skills in domains relevant to their professional work, as

well as at scientific thinking skills (Kuhn, Amsel, & O'Loughlin, 1988).

9. Psychological skills training in providing clearly specified and focused topics and training goals is more amenable to scientific evaluation than more artful forms of psychotherapy that rely on less replicable and more idiosyncratic modes of therapeutic interaction. Replication is a key to the scientific study of a phenomenon.

10. Though consistent with a deficit model of intervention, psychological skills training also is consistent with a personal growth model in which individuals who are performing relatively competently strive for further improvement in various skill areas.

11. Goldstein, Gershaw, and Sprafkin (1985) have argued that traditional psychotherapy, with its emphasis on verbal abilities, insight, and middle-class values, is often inappropriate with lower SES clients, and that psychological skills training has advantages (e.g., it is shorter term, more concrete, and more directive) that are particularly useful for this population.

12. To the extent that similar component skills are necessary for topographically dissimilar tasks (e.g., pain management is necessary for both maintaining an exercise regimen and coping with chronic headaches), an independent measure of this component skill should allow more accurate prediction of behavior across similar (e.g., different episodes of headache coping) as well as dissimilar tasks (e.g., headache coping, maintaining a jogging regimen). As Schlundt and McFall (1985) have pointed out, prediction based on an assessment of component skills and task demands is potentially more useful than other models of behavioral assessment, which predict that similar behaviors will occur in similar situations.

13. Psychological skills training, to the extent that it teaches general skills such as problems solving, may enable the client to be in a better position to solve diverse problems and not only the problem that may have precipitated professional contact. As Larson (1984) has stated, "To treat [in traditional therapy] is to give a person a fish, to train [in skills] is to teach that person how to fish" (p. 9).

14. Larson (1984) has suggested that "the replicability, accessibility, portability, brevity, and efficiency of skills training approaches make them ideal

vehicles for extending training in helping skills beyond the circumscribed traditional population of mental health workers'' (p. 9). Kiesler (1980) has suggested that, given recent epidemiological data (Regier, Goldberg, & Taube, 1978), current supplies of professional helpers cannot meet current needs:

> If the nation used the whole 65 million hours of service delivery potentially available to it through licensed psychologists and psychiatrists, a total pool of approximately three hours per person needing treatment per year would be involved, for the *most optimistic estimates* of need. This would vary downward to 40 minutes per person per year at the most pessimistic estimate. (p. 1070)

Larson argues for the use of paraprofessionals, health care workers, self-help groups, parents, teachers, and other lay helpers as additional sources of trainers in psychological skills. This is in direct contrast to psychoanalytic models of professional helpers in which extensive training and perhaps years of individual psychotherapy are required before a position is ready to provide help to others.

## THE PROCESS OF PSYCHOEDUCATIONAL SKILLS TRAINING

This question becomes: If improvement in psychological skills is sought, how can this be best accomplished? Phrased more operationally: Under what conditions can improvement in this particular skill by this particular individual be taught by this particular therapist/trainer? Skills training should not operate under similar uniformity myths that have been argued as plaguing other forms of therapy (Kiesler, 1966). The possibility of complex interactions between the client, therapist, goal, and situation must be countenanced from the beginning.

Rude and Rehm (1991) have raised an interesting and important possibility from a review of treatments of deficits thought to be associated with depression. They concluded that there was little relationship between subject's initial deficit scores and treatment outcome. In fact, in many studies the reverse was found: The initially more skilled subjects showed more treatment gains than the initially less skilled. This, of course, is contrary to what would be expected from considerations such as regression to the mean or the law of initial values. Rude and Rehm suggest that extant skills training programs have been based on a compensation model of the client–treatment interaction (Cronbach & Snow, 1977). A *compensation effect* is said to occur when an individual with deficits benefits more from treatments that directly target, and presumably compensate for, these deficits. According to the compensation model, the best treatment would seem to be the one that most directly addresses the specific deficits. However, Rude and Rehm have suggested that the pattern of findings in the outcome literature better supports a *capitalization effect,* which is said to occur when subjects demonstrate more benefit from methods that capitalize on their strengths. According to this model, subjects will benefit most from therapy that seeks to improve skills in which they already show a great deal of proficiency. Clearly, this is a vitally important issue that warrants further research.

Davis and Butcher (1985) have suggested that the major questions faced by a professional designing a skills training curriculum are the following:

1. *Whom to teach?* This decision involves two questions: Who is going to be the trainer, and who will be the participants?
2. *What to teach?* This requires a careful assessment of the needs of the individual(s) to be taught. If Rude and Rehm (1991) are correct, for the treatment of depression it requires a careful assessment of the individual's strengths. A clear identification of goals is important both for the trainer and the participant.
3. *Reasons for teaching?* Why is it desirable for the participants to achieve a certain level of particular skills?
4. *Where and when to teach?* Should such skills be taught early in an attempt at primary prevention? Are they so critical that they should be taught in an important institutional setting, such as schools?
5. *How to teach?* What means and methods are available for achieving the desired ends? Considerations include beginning at a point already reached by the participant; working at an appropriate pace for the participant; arriving at clear, reasonable goals to which the client gives informed consent; setting shorter term goals; evaluating progress; and providing feedback and reward.
6. *Evaluation.* Davis and Butcher (1985) have correctly pointed out that, just as feedback is essential in training, so is feedback essential for the course designer and trainer. This is particularly important because feedback is essential in improving the intervention. Given the critical nature of feedback, Davis and Butcher have recommended that it be viewed as a vital and integral part of the course.

Larson (1984) has suggested that psychological skills training is characterized by the following:

1. They all involve the active participation of clients and trainees in the process.
2. There is a focus on specific behaviors (internal and external) and the mastery and maintenance of these behaviors.
3. The programs are based on established learning principles of observing, discriminating, reinforcing, and generalizing.
4. Each program includes both didactic and experiential emphases.
5. The programs are highly structured.
6. Goals are clear.
7. Progress is monitored.
8. Mystification is minimized. (p. 6)

Assessment should include the measurement of environmental demands, the individual's skill abilities, performance of these skills, and skill competence—that is, effectiveness of performance. The first and last dimensions require the assessment of the individual's environment. Assessment consists largely of gathering relevant samples of performance, demands, and competency evaluations. Schlundt and McFall (1985) have correctly pointed out that it is circular simply to infer skill deficits from incompetent performance without an independent means of assessing skill deficits. Skills assessment necessitates "independent methods for isolating and measuring each of the requisite skills underlying competent performance" (p. 23).

Schlundt and McFall (1985) also have proposed that tasks are useful units of analysis. According to McFall (1982):

> One must understand these important features of [a] task: its purpose, its constraints, its setting, the rules governing task performance, the criteria for distinguishing between successful and unsuccessful performance and how the task relates to other aspects of the person's life system. (p. 16)

McFall (1982) has provided a useful conceptual framework for skills training: (1) identifying and prioritizing relevant and critical life tasks for the individual or group; (2) providing a behavioral analysis of each task; (3) obtaining a representative sample of each individual's performance on each task; (4) establishing task-specific criteria of competent performance for each task; (5) evaluating performance samples; and (6) providing summarizations, integrations, and interpretations of the evaluation results.

Schlundt and McFall (1985) have also suggested that the concept of *life space* is useful for assessment in psychological skills training. An individual's life space is the totality of tasks that structure the individual's day-to-day activities. Similar individuals have similar life spaces. For example, all students are involved in academic and social tasks, among other tasks.

To date, much skills training has been taught in groups. This is determined in part by the potential cost-effectiveness of working with groups but is also done because a group setting allows certain distinct learning advantages, such as vicarious learning and generalization. Skills training relies heavily on the following procedures: goal setting, task analysis, instructions, modeling, role playing, prompting, self-monitoring, modifying interfering cognitions, performance feedback, shaping, practice, homework, overlearning, and transfer training. In all likelihood it is also critical for these specific techniques to be used in an interpersonal context in which the trainer displays empathy, warmth, respect, genuineness, appropriate self-disclosure, directiveness, concreteness, and immediacy. To date, much of the extant research in skills training has been outcome research; thus, information about process variables is scant. Research needs to be conducted to partial out the impact of each of these procedures and "nonspecifics" in order to understand the contribution and interactions of these as well as to identify the necessary and sufficient conditions of skill acquisition in various situations.

## FUTURE DIRECTIONS

More work needs to be done concerning the study of situational demands and related skills that are important across individuals as well as across situations. This will provide important base rate information that can be useful both in forming reasonable hypotheses to be explored in individual therapy and in developing more "canned" group programs that have a high probability of relevance for any given group of individuals (Curran, Wallander, & Farrell, 1985). Lovett and Harris (1987) provide one example of an approach to this problem. They interviewed mentally retarded adults and asked them what skills were most important to them. The subjects indicated vocation and social skills. Relatedly, more research needs to be conducted on what relevant judges take to be effective ways of responding to these tasks and the generality of such judgments (Schlundt & McFall, 1985).

Longitudinal research investigations of the role of skills training in preventing problems is also an important future direction for research. This research can be conducted with either high-risk individuals (e.g., children of schizophrenic parents) or the general population. Important questions also concern which skills to teach and when to teach them. By far, most of the extant work on skills training has been with adults (for notable exceptions to this, see Matson, Sevin, & Box, Chapter 3, this volume; Vargas & Shanley, Chapter 9, this volume). More research needs to be conducted on what level of skills children need at each developmental level.

Pyramidal models of skills training (Davis, 1985) need to be further researched. In this type of model, trainees eventually become trainers for the next generation of skill learners. This model can be particularly useful when there is a shortage of trainers but might also be useful in motivating trainees and in overlearning.

Integration of various more specific skills training programs into broader curricula also needs to be further researched (see Goldstein et al.'s work on curriculum formation, Chapter 18, this volume). An important related question concerns the sequence of skills training. Is it the case (with certain clients in certain situations) that the learning of one skill may facilitate the learning of other skills? More strongly, is it the case that learning one skill can be a prerequisite for learning another skills? Finally, can one skill interfere with or preclude the learning of another skill (e.g., negative assertion with affiliation)?

Finally, similarity across skill areas needs to be investigated. For example, McFall (1982) has proposed a model of social competence and social skills that analyzes these into more basic processing skills. There are three general classes of processing skill, with more specific skills assumed under these. Decoding skills (reception, perception, and interpretation) refer to processes in which incoming sensory information in received, stored, and construed in relation to the individual's meaning structures. Decision skills (response search, response test, response selection, repertoire search, and utility evaluation) concern the ability to generate possible responses; test and evaluate their utility with respect to the task at hand; and select these responses, if available, from the person's repertoire. Encoding skills (execution and self-monitoring) refer to executing the behaviors decided on in the previous stage in a coordinated manner and evaluating the effectiveness of their execution.

An interesting question becomes: To what extent does this model provide a generic model of subtasks involved in a wide variety of molar skilled performances? For example, do problem-solving, communication, and relaxation skills all involve similar sub-tasks? That is, do all of these require a decoding step (e.g., what is the problem, listening, and how tense are my muscles and what in the environment may be causing this to increase or decrease); a decision step (what are my possible verbal responses, how do these do with respect to various tests, which one should I select, and how useful will these be) and an encoding skill stage (how can I effectively execute this problem solution, this message, or this relaxation increasing response?) Prima facie, McFall's model seems to have such generality.

Finally in Table 1.2 we provide a summary of some major applications of skills training. We believe that this illustrates the diversity and promise of this approach.

**Table 1.2.** Major Applications of Skills Training

| DEVELOPERS | PROGRAM | TRAINERS | TRAINEES | TRAINING METHODS | SKILLS |
|---|---|---|---|---|---|
| Altmaier & Bernstein (1981) | Counseling skills training | Counselors | Counselors-in-training | Modeling, role playing, feedback, didactic and experiential homework assignments | Problem-solving skills Empathy skills Interviewing skills |
| Blechman, Tryon, Ruff, & McEnroe (1989) | Family skills training | Counselors | Parents | Instruction, feedback, in vivo role playing | Communication skills Listening skills Behavior management skills Problem-solving skills Self-disclosure Descriptive praise |
| Breidenbach (1984) | Behavioral skills training | Teachers | Elementary school children | "10-count relax" technique, self-instruction | Anger management skills Problem-solving skills Interactive skills |
| Brown, Kratochwill, & Bergan (1982); Duley, Cancelli, Kratochwill, Bergan, & Meredith (1983) | Motivational analysis interview skills | Counselors | Counselors-in-training | Audio/videotaped modeling, performance feedback, behavioral rehearsal | Interviewing skills Verbal skills |
| Curran, Faraone, & Graves (1988) | Family therapy | Diverse | Families in acute inpatient settings | Didactic instruction, videotaped and live modeling, group discussion, behavioral rehearsal and role playing, feedback, assignments | Communication skills Problem-solving skills Listening skills Conversation skills Giving and receiving feedback Assertiveness Making requests |
| Dickson, Hargie, & Morrow (1989); Hargie, Saunders, & Dickson (1987) | Communication skills | Counselors | Varied | Lectures, modeling, practice, feedback | Nonverbal skills Reinforcement Questioning Self-disclosure Listening skills Assertiveness skills |

*Continued*

Table 1.2 continued

| DEVELOPERS | PROGRAM | TRAINERS | TRAINEES | TRAINING METHODS | SKILLS |
|---|---|---|---|---|---|
| Fisher & Carstensen (1990) | Skills training for the elderly | Counselors | Elderly nursing home residents | Positive reinforcement, direct instruction, modeling, coaching, role playing, feedback | Conversation skills Requesting skills Social skills |
| Foxx, McMorrow, Bittle, & Fenlon (1985) | Social skills training | Counselors | Psychiatric inpatients | Response specific feedback, self-monitoring, individualized reinforcement, individualized performance criteria | Complimenting others Politeness Social confrontation Social interaction Questions/answers |
| Goldstein, Sprafkin, Gershaw, & Klein (1983) | Social skills training | Teachers | Adolescents and preacolescents | Modeling, role playing, performance feedback, transfer of training | Interpersonal skills Coping skills Planning skills Agression management |
| Hahlweg, Baucom, & Markman (1988) | Behavioral marital therapy | Counselors | Couples | Homework assignments, in vivo practice, instruction | Communication skills Problem-solving skills Negotiating Contracting Listening skills Self-disclosure Giving positive feedback |
| Hatzenbuehler & Schroeder (1982) | Assertiveness training | Counselors | Unassertive adult outpatients | Instruction, modeling behavioral rehearsal, feedback, and homework assignments | Assertiveness skills |
| Hawkins, Catalano, & Wells (1986) | Skills training intervention for drug abusers | Counselors | Drug abusers | Group discussions, modeling, role playing, and feedback | Assertiveness Problem-solving skills Stress management Giving and receiving praise Coping skills |
| Hazel, Schumaker, Sherman, & Sheldon (1982) | Social skills and problem solving | Counselors | Learning-disabled and non-learning-disabled adolescents | Modeling, behavioral rehearsal, feedback | Social skills Problem-solving skills Negotiation Giving feedback Receiving feedback Resisting peer pressure |
| Kelly (1985) | Group social skills training | Counselors | Unspecified | Modeling, rehearsal, feedback/shaping | Assertion Conversation skills Dating skills Job interviewing skills |
| Kettlewell & Kausch (1983) | Cognitive-behavioral treatment program | Counselors | Aggressive children | Coping skills training, behavioral rehearsal, self-instruction | Problem-solving skills |

| DEVELOPERS | PROGRAM | TRAINERS | TRAINEES | TRAINING METHODS | SKILLS |
|---|---|---|---|---|---|
| LaGreca (1983) | Interpersonal and social skills training | Teachers | Children | Lecture, modeling, group discussion, role-play, feedback | Smiling<br>Greeting others<br>Joining current peer activities<br>Conversation skills<br>Cooperating and sharing<br>Complimenting others<br>Physical grooming |
| LaGreca, Stone, & Bell (1983) | Vocational-interpersonal skill training | Counselors | Mentally retarded adults | Modeling, coaching, behavioral rehearsal | Interpersonal skills<br>Social competency skills |
| Liberman, DeRisi, & Mueser (1989) | Social skills training | Diverse | Psychiatric inpatients | Behavioral rehearsal, modeling, coaching, homework assignments, role plays | Communication skills<br>Social skills<br>Dating skills<br>Conversation skills<br>Problem-solving skills<br>Coping skills<br>Friendship skills |
| Lowry & Whitman (1989) | Parent training | Counselors | Mothers of developmentally delayed infants | Verbal instruction, modeling, feedback | Parenting skills<br>Teaching skills<br>Reinforcement skills |
| McAuley (1988) | Parent training | Counselors | Parents | Instruction, in vivo practice, paradoxical techniques, role reversal | Communication skills<br>Behavior management skills<br>Problem-solving skills |
| Mills (1987) | Interpersonal functioning | Counselors | Adolescents with learning and/or behavior problems | Relaxation training, magic circle activities, group discussions | Listening skills<br>Decision-making skills<br>Self-awareness skills<br>Conflict management skills |
| Rose (1987) | Social skills training | Counselors | Middle childhood | Rehearsal, instruction modeling, feedback, social rewards, assignments, group contingencies | Assertiveness<br>Empathy skills<br>Recognizing and expressing emotions<br>Requesting skills<br>Refusing requests<br>Conversation skills<br>Coping skills<br>Leadership skills |
| Sheridan & Smith (1987) | Stress intervention program | Teachers | High school students | Relaxed breathing, guided daydreams, tense–relax training, autogenic training | Stress management skills |
| Vealey (1988) | Psychological skills training for athletes | Sports psychologists and coaches | Athletes | Imagery, self-talk, goal setting, physical relaxation | Arousal control skills<br>Attentional control skills<br>Interpersonal skills<br>Life-style management skills |

# REFERENCES

Altmaier, E. M., & Bernstein, D. N. (1981). Counselor trainees' problem-solving skills. *Counselor Education and Supervision, 20,* 285–291.

American Psychiatric Association. (1987). *Diagnostic and Statistical Manual of Mental Disorders,* 3rd ed., rev. Washington, DC: American Psychiatric Press.

Arnow, B. A., Taylor, C. B., Agras, W. S., & Telch, M. J. (1985). Enhancing agoraphobia treatment outcome by changing couple communication patterns. *Behavior Therapy, 16,* 452–467.

Authier, J., Gustafson, K., Guerney, B., & Kasdorf, J. (1975). The psychological practitioner as a teacher: A theoretical-historical and practical review. *Counseling Psychologist, 5,* 31–50.

Baer, D. M. (1968). Some remedial uses of the reinforcement contingency. In J. M. Shlien (Ed.), *Research in psychotherapy* (Vol. 3, pp. 3–20). Washington, DC: American Psychological Association.

Bandura, A. (1969). *Principles of behavior modification.* New York: Holt, Rinehart & Winston.

Bandura, A. (1977). Self-efficacy: Toward a unifying theory of behavioral change. *Psychological Review, 84,* 191–215.

Becker, R. E., Heimberg, R. G., & Bellack, A. S. (1987). *Social skills training treatment for depression.* New York: Pergamon Press.

Bellack, A. S., & Hersen, M. (1977). *Behavior modifications: An introductory textbook.* Baltimore: Williams & Wilkins.

Bijou, S. W., & Baer, D. N. (1961). *Child development* (Vol. 1). New York: Appleton-Century-Crofts.

Black, J. L., Muehlenhard, C. L., & Massey, F. H. (1985). Social skills training to improve job maintenance. *Journal of Employment Counseling, 22,* 151–160.

Blechman, E. A., Tryon, A. S., Ruff, M. H., & McEnroe, M. J. (1989). Family skills training and childhood depression. In C. E. Schaefer & J. M. Briesmeister (Eds.), *Handbook of parent training: Parents as co-therapists for children's behavior problems.* New York: Wiley.

Breidenbach, D. C. (1984). Behavioral skills training for students: A preventive program. *Social Work in Education, 6,* 231–240.

Brown, D. K., Kratochwill, T. R., & Bergan, J. R. (1982). Teaching interview skills for problem identification: An analogue study. *Behavioral Assessment, 4,* 63–73.

Castles, E. E., & Glass, C. R. (1986). Training in social and interpersonal problem solving skills for mildly and moderately retarded adults. *American Journal of Mental Deficiency, 91,* 35–42.

Chan, K. S., & Rueda, R. (1979). Poverty and culture in education: Separate but equal. *Exceptional Children, 45,* 422–428.

Colley, A. M., & Beech, J. R. (1989). Acquiring and performing cognitive skills. In A. M. Colley & J. R. Beech (Eds.), *Acquisition and performance of cognitive skills.* New York: Wiley.

Cronbach, L. J., & Snow, R. E. (1977). *Aptitudes and instructional methods.* New York: Irvington.

Cunningham, C., Morgan, P., & McGucken, R. (1984). Down's syndrome: Is dissatisfaction with disclosure of diagnosis inevitable? *Developmental Medicine and Child Neurology, 26,* 33–39.

Curran, J. P., Faraone, S. V., & Graves, D. J. (1988). Acute inpatient settings. In I. R. H. Falloon (Ed.), *Handbook of behavioral family therapy.* New York: Guilford Press.

Curran, J. P., Wallander, J. L., & Farrell, A. D. (1985). Heterosocial skills training. In L. L'Abate & M. A. Milan (Eds.), *Handbook of social skills training and research.* New York: Wiley.

Davis, H. (1985). Training professionals in behavior modification. *British Journal of Medical Psychology, 58,* 241–248.

Davis, H., & Butcher, P. (1985). Sharing psychological skills. *British Journal of Medical Psychology, 58,* 207–216.

DeNelsky, G. Y., & Boat, B. W. (1986). A coping skills model of psychological diagnosis and treatment. *Professional Psychology: Research and Practice, 17,* 322–330.

Dickson, D. A., Hargie, O. D. W., & Morrow, N. C. (1989). *Communication skills training for health professionals.* London: Chapman and Hall.

Dollard, J., & Miller, N. E. (1950). *Personality and psychotherapy.* New York: McGraw-Hill.

Dryden, W. (1985). Teaching counseling skills to non-psychologists. *British Journal of Medical Psychology, 58,* 217–222.

Duley, S. M., Cancelli, A. A., Kratochwill, T. R., Bergan, J. R., & Meredith, K. E. (1983). Training and generalization of motivational analysis interview assessment skills. *Behavioral Assessment, 5,* 281–293.

D'Zurilla, T. J. (1986). *Problem-solving therapy: A social competence approach to clinical intervention.* New York: Springer.

Egan, G. (1982). *The skilled helper: Model, skills and methods for effective helping.* Monterey, CA: Brooks/Cole.

Egan, G. (1984). People in systems: A comprehensive model for psychosocial education and training. In D. Larson (Ed.), *Teaching psychological skills: Models for giving psychology away* (pp. 21–43). Monterey, CA: Brooks/Cole.

Egan, G., & Cowan, M. A. (1979). *People in systems: A model for development in the human-service professions and education.* Monterey, CA: Brooks/Cole.

Ellis, A. (1990). Is rational-emotive therapy (RET) "rationalist" or "constructivist"? *Journal of Rational-Emotive and Cognitive-Behavior Therapy, 8,* 169–193.

Erikson, E. H. (1956). Growth and crises of the "healthy personality." In C. Kluckhohn & H. A. Murray (Eds.), *Personality in nature, society and culture, 2nd ed.* New York: Knopf.

Eysenck, H. J. (1960). *Behavior therapy and the neuroses.* Oxford: Pergamon Press.

Eysenck, H. J. (Ed.). (1964). *Experiments in behavior therapy: Readings in modern methods of mental disorders derived from learning theory.* Oxford: Pergamon Press.

Fisher, J. E., & Carstensen, L. L. (1990). Generalized effects of skills training among older adults. *Mental Health in the Nursing Home, 9,* 91–107.

Foxx, R. M., McMorrow, M. J., Bittle, R. G., & Fenlon, S. J. (1985). Teaching social skills to psychiatric inpatients. *Behaviour Research and Therapy, 23,* 531–537.

Frank, J. D. (1973). *Persuasions and healing: A comparative study of psychotherapy,* rev. ed. Baltimore: Johns Hopkins University Press.

Gazda, G. M., & Brooks, D. K. (1985). Life skills training: The development of the social/life skills training movement. *Journal of Group Psychotherapy, Psychodrama, and Sociometry, 38*(1), 1–10.

Goldfried, M. R. (1980). Psychotherapy as coping skills training. In M. J. Mahoney (Ed.), *Psychotherapy process: Current issues and future directions.* New York: Plenum Press.

Goldfried, M. R., & D'Zurilla, T. J. (1969). A behavioral-analytic model for assessing competence. In C. D. Spielberger (Ed.), *Current topics in clinical and community psychology* (Vol. 1). New York: Academic Press.

Goldstein, A. P., Gershaw N. J., & Sprafkin, R. P. (1975). Structured learning therapy—Skill training for schizophrenics. *Schizophrenia Bulletin, 14,* 83–86.

Goldstein, A. P. (1982). *Psychological skill training: The structured learning technique.* New York: Pergamon Press.

Goldstein, A. P. (1986). Psychological skill training and the aggressive adolescent. In S. J. Apter & A. P. Goldstein (Eds.), *Youth violence: Programs and prospects.* Pergamon General Psychology Series, Vol. 135. Oxford: Pergamon Press.

Goldstein, A. P., Gershaw, N. J., & Sprafkin, R. P. (1985). Structured learning: Research and practice in psychological skill training. In L. L'Abate & M. A. Milan (Eds.), *Handbook of social skills training and research* (pp. 284–302). New York: Wiley.

Goldstein, A. P., & Goedhart, A. (1973). The use of structured learning for empathy enhancement in paraprofessional psychotherapist training. *Journal of Community Psychology, 1,* 168–173.

Goldstein, A. P., & Krasner, L. (1987). *Modern applied psychology.* New York: Pergamon Press.

Goldstein, A. P., & Michaels, G. Y. (1985). *Empathy: Development, training and consequences.* Hillsdale, NJ: Lawrence Erlbaum.

Goldstein, A. P., Sprafkin, R. P., Gershaw, N. J., & Klein, P. (1980). *Skillstreaming the adolescent.* Champaign, IL: Research Press.

Goldstein, A. P., Sprafkin, R. P., Gershaw, J., & Klein, P. (1983). Structured learning: A psychoeducational approach for teaching social competencies. *Behavioral Disorders, 8,* 161–170.

Gottman, J., Notarius, C., Gonso, J., & Markman, H., (1976). *A couples' guide to communication.* Champaign, IL: Research Press.

Hahlweg, K., Baucom, D. H., & Markman, H. (1988). Recent advances in therapy and prevention. In I. R. H. Falloon (Ed.), *Handbook of behavioral family therapy.* New York: Guilford Press.

Hamburg, B. A. (1990). *Life skills training: Preventive interventions for young adolescents.* New York: Carnegie Corporation.

Hansen, D. J., St. Lawrence, J. S., & Christoff, K. A. (1985). Effects of interpersonal problems solving training with chronic aftercare patients on problem-solving component skills and effectiveness of solutions. *Journal of Consulting and Clinical Psychology, 53,* 167–174.

Hargie, O., Saunders, C., & Dickson, D. (1987). *Social skills in interpersonal communication,* 2nd ed. London: Croom Helm.

Hatzenbuehler, L. C., & Schroeder, H. E. (1982). Assertiveness training with outpatients: The effectiveness of skill and cognitive procedures. *Behavioural Psychotherapy, 10,* 234–252.

Havighurst, R. J. (1953). *Human development and education.* New York: Longmans, Green.

Hawkins, J. D., Catalano, R. F., & Wells, E. A. (1986). Measuring effects of a skills training intervention for drug abusers. *Journal of Consulting and Clinical Psychology, 54,* 661–664.

Hazel, J. S., Schumaker, J. B., Sherman, J. A., & Sheldon, J. (1982). Application of a group training program in social skills and problem solving to learning disabled and non-learning disabled youth. *Learning Disability Quarterly, 5,* 398–408.

Herink, R. (Ed.). (1980). *The psychotherapy handbook.* New York: New American Library.

Hersen, M., & Bellack, A. S. (1976). A multiple-baseline analysis of social-skills training in chronic schizophrenics. *Journal of Applied Behavior Analysis, 9,* 239–245.A

Hilgard, E. R., & Marquis, P. G. (1940). *Conditioning and learning.* New York: Appleton-Century.

Homans, G. C. (1961). *Social behavior: Its elementary forms.* New York: Harcourt, Brace & World.

Johnston, M. (1980). Anxiety in surgical patients. *Psychological Medicine, 10,* 145–152.

Jones, M. C. (1924). The elimination of children's fears. *Journal of Experimental Psychology, 7,* 383–390.

Kalfus, G. R., Hawkins, R. P., & Reitz, A. L. (1984). A program for teaching problem solving in a school for disturbed-delinquent adolescent youth. *Journal of Child Development and Adolescent Psychotherapy, 1,* 26–29.

Kantor, J. R. (1969). *The scientific evolution of psychology* (Vol. 11). Granville, OH: Principia Press.

Keller, F. S., & Schoenfeld, W. N. (1950). *Principles of psychology: A systematic text in the science of behavior.* New York: Appleton-Century-Crofts.

Kelly, J. A. (1985). Group social skills training. *Behavior Therapist, 8,* 93–95.

Kettlewell, P. W., & Kausch, D. F. (1983). The generalization of the effects of a cognitive-behavioral treatment program for aggressive children. *Journal of Abnormal Child Psychology, 11,* 101–114.

Kiesler, C. A. (1980). Mental health policy as a field of inquiry for psychology. *American Psychologist, 35,* 1066–1080.

Kiesler, D. J. (1966). Some myths of psychotherapy research and the search for a paradigm. *Psychological Bulletin, 65,* 110–136.

Kleiner, L., Marshall, W. L., & Spevack, M. (1987). Training in problem-solving and exposure treatment for agoraphobics with panic attacks. *Journal of the Anxiety Disorders, 1,* 219–238.

Krasner, L. (1971). Behavior therapy. In P. H. Mussen (Ed.), *Annual review of psychology* (Vol. 22, pp. 483–532). Palo Alto, CA: Annual Reviews.

Krasner, L. (1990). History of behavior modification. In A. S. Bellack, M. Hersen, & A. E. Bellack (Eds.), *International handbook of behavior modification and therapy,* 2nd ed. (pp 3–25). New York: Plenum Press.

Krasner, L., & Houts, A. C. (1984). A study of the "value" systems of behavioral scientists. *American Psychologist, 39,* 840–850.

Krasner, L., & Ullmann, L. P. (Eds.). (1965). *Research in behavior modification: New developments and implications.* New York: Holt, Rinehart & Winston.

Kuhn, D., Amsel, E., & O'Loughlin, M. (1988). *The development of scientific thinking skills.* San Diego: Academic Press.

L'Abate, L., & Milan, M. A. (1985). Preface. In L. L'Abate & M. Milan (Eds.), *Handbook of social skills training and research* (pp. xi–xiii). New York: Wiley.

Lazarus, A. A. (1971). *Behavior therapy and beyond.* New York: McGraw-Hill.

LaGreca, A. M. (1983). Teaching interpersonal skills: A model for instruction in the schools. *School Psychology International, 4,* 109–112.

LaGreca, A. M., Stone, W. L., & Bell, C. R. (1983). Facilitating the vocational-interpersonal skills of mentally retarded individuals. *American Journal of Mental Deficiency, 88,* 270–278.

Larson, D. (1984). Teaching psychological skills: Models for giving psychology away. Monterey, CA: Brooks/Cole.

Lewinsohn, P. M., Mischel, W., Chaplin, W., & Barton, R. (1980). Social competence and depression: The role of illusory self-perceptions. *Journal of Abnormal Psychology, 89,* 203–212.

Ley, P. (1982). Satisfaction, compliance and communication. *British Journal of Clinical Psychology, 21,* 241–254.

Liberman, R. P., DeRisi, W. J., & Mueser, K. T. (1989). *Social skills training for psychiatric patients.* New York: Pergamon Press.

Lovett, D. L., & Harris, M. B. (1987). Important skills for adults with mental retardation: The client's point of view. *Mental Retardation, 25,* 351–356.

Lowry, M. A., & Whitman, T. L. (1989). Generalization of parenting skills: An early intervention program. *Child and Family Behavior Therapy, 11,* 45–65.

McAuley, R. (1988). Parent training: Clinical application. In I. R. H. Falloon (Ed.), *Handbook of behavioral family therapy.* New York: Guilford Press.

Mead, G. H. (1934). *Mind, self and society: From the standpoint of a social behaviorist.* Chicago: University of Chicago Press.

Matthews, A., & Ridgeway, V. (1984). Psychological preparation for surgery. In A. Steptoe & A. Matthews (Eds.), *Health care and human behaviour.* London: Academic Press.

McFall, R. M. (1982). A review and reformulation of the concept of social skills. *Behavioral Assessment, 4,* 1–33.

McFall, R. M. (1976). *Behavioral training: A skill-acquisition approach to clinical problems.* Morristown, NJ: General Learning Press.

McFall, R. M., & Twentyman, C. T. (1973). Four experiments on the relative contributions of rehearsal, modeling and coaching to assertion training. *Journal of Abnormal Psychology, 81,* 199–218.

Mills, M. C. (1987). An intervention program for adolescents with behavior problems. *Adolescence, 22,* 91–96.

Milne, D. (1982). A comparison of two methods of teaching behaviour modification to mental handicap nurses. *Behavioral Psychotherapy, 10,* 54–64.

Mischel, W. (1976). *Introduction to personality,* 2nd ed. New York: Holt, Rinehart & Winston.

Monti, P. M., Abrams, D. B., Binkoff, J. A., & Zwick, W. R. (1986). Social skills training in substance abuse. In C. R. Hollin & P. Trower (Eds.), *Handbook of social skills training* (Vol. 2, pp. 111–142). New York: Pergamon Press.

Nichols, K. A. (1985). Psychological care by nurses, paramedical and medical staff: Essential developments for the general hospitals. Special Issue: Sharing psychological skills: Training nonpsychologists in the use of psychological techniques. *British Journal of Medical Psychology, 58*(3), 231–240.

Novaco, R. W. (1975). *Anger control.* Lexington, MA: D.C. Heath.

O'Donohue, W. (1989). The (even) bolder model: The clinical psychologist as metaphysician-scientist-practitioner. *American Psychologist, 44,* 1460–1468.

Oxford University Press (1982). *The compact edition of the Oxford English dictionary.* Oxford: Oxford University Press.

Paul, G. L., & Lentz, R. J. (1977). *Psychosocial treatment of chronic mental patients: Mileau vs. social learning program.* Cambridge, MA: Harvard University Press.

Pavlov, I. P. (1928). *Lectures on conditioned reflexes* (W. H. Grant, trans.). New York: International Publishers.

Phillips, E. L. (1956). *Psychotherapy: A modern theory and practice.* Englewood Cliffs, NJ: Prentice-Hall.

Phillips, E. L. (1985). Social skills: History and prospect. In L. L'Abate & M. A. Milan (Eds.), *Handbook of social skills training and research* (pp. 3–21). New York: Wiley.

Prochaska, J. O. (1984). *Systems of psychotherapy.* Homewood, IL: Dorsey.

Reiger, D. A., Goldberg, I. D., & Taube, C. A. (1978). The de facto U.S. Mental health services system. *Archives of General Psychiatry, 35*(6), 685–693.

Rosenthal, R. (1966). *Experimenter effects in behavioral research.* New York: Appleton-Century-Crofts.

Rude, S. S., & Rehm, L. P. (1991). Response to treatments for depression: The role of initial status on targeted cognitive and behavioral skills. *Clinical Psychology Review, 11,* 493–514.

Rehm, L. P., Fuchs, C. Z., Roth, D. M., Kornblith, S. J., & Romano, J. M. (1979). A comparison of self-control and assertion skills treatments of depression. *Behavior Therapy, 10,* 429–442.

Rinn, R. C., & Markle, A. (1979). Modification of social skills deficits in children. In A. S. Bellack & M. Hersen (Eds.), *Research and practice in social skills training.* New York: Plenum Press.

Rose, S. R. (1987). Social skills training in middle childhood: A structured group approach. *Journal for Specialists in Group Work, 12,* 144–149.

Salter, A. (1949). *Conditioned reflex therapy.* New York: Farrar Strauss.

Sarbin, T. R. (1954). Role theory. In G. Lindzey (Ed.), *Handbook of social psychology* (pp. 223–258). Cambridge, MA: Addison-Wesley.

Schlundt, D. G., & McFall, R. M. (1985). New directions in the assessment of social competence and social skills. In L. L'Abate & M. A. Milan (Eds.), *Handbook of social skills training and research.* (pp. 22–49). New York: Wiley.

Sheridan, C. L., & Smith, L. K. (1987). Stress and academic achievement in teenagers: Assessment and intervention. *International Journal of Psychosomatics, 34,* 20–24.

Sherman, T. M., & Cormier, W. H. (1974). An investigation of the influence of student behavior on teacher behavior. *Journal of Applied Behavior Analysis, 7,* 11–21.

Skinner, B. F. (1938). *The behavior of organisms: An experimental analysis.* New York: Appleton-Century-Crofts.

Skinner, B. F. (1948). *Walden two.* New York: Macmillan.

Skinner, B. F. (1953). *Science and human behavior.* New York: Macmillan.

Skinner, B. F. (1957). *Verbal behavior.* New York: Appleton-Century-Crofts.

Solomon, L. J., & Rothblum, E. D. (1985). Social skills problems experienced by women. In L. L'Abate & M. Milan (Eds.), *Handbook of social skills training and research* (pp. 303–325). New York: Wiley.

Thorndike, E. L. (1931). *Human learning.* New York: Century.

Thurston, L. P., Dasta, K., & Greenwood, C. R. (1984). *Journal of Community Psychology, 12,* 192–196.

Trower, P. (1986). Social skills training and social anxiety. In C. R. Hollin & P. Trower (Eds.), *Handbook of social skills training* (Vol 2). Oxford: Pergamon Press.

Trower, P., Bryant, B., & Argyle, M. (Eds.). (1978). *Social skills and mental health.* London: Methuen.

Twentyman, G. T., & McFall, R. M. (1975). Behavioral training of social skills in shy males. *Journal of Consulting and Clinical Psychology, 43,* 384–395.

Ullmann, L. P., & Krasner, L. (1965). *Case studies in behavior modification.* New York: Holt, Rinehart & Winston.

Vealey, R. S. (1988). Future directions in psychological skills training. *The Sport Psychologist, 2,* 318–336.

Weinman, J. and Medlik, L. (1985). Sharing psychological skills in the general practice setting. *British Journal of Medical Psychology, 58,* 223–230.

Welford, A. T. (1960). The ergonomic approach to social behavior. *Ergonomics, 9,* 357–369.

Wolpe, J. (1958). *Psychotherapy by reciprocal inhibition.* Stanford, CA: Stanford University Press.

Zigler, E., & Phillips, L. (1960). Social effectiveness and symptomatic behaviors. *Journal of Abnormal and Social Psychology, 61,* 231–238.

# CHAPTER 2

# RELAXATION SKILLS TRAINING: ABBREVIATED PROGRESSIVE RELAXATION

Charles R. Carlson
Douglas A. Bernstein

Self-control is a virtue encouraged throughout the world. The restoration of self-control is among the principal tasks for the helping professions when dealing with persons in crisis. One of the most basic levels of self-control is control over physical and emotional responding. Progressive relaxation has emerged as one of the primary tools for enabling persons to respond to life events with a measure of physical and emotional self-control. In this chapter we present an introduction to the theoretical and practical application of progressive relaxation skills training for enhancing self-regulation.

## OVERVIEW

In the early part of this century, psychologist and physician Edmund Jacobson began to explore the processes by which tension disorders could be resolved through the application of relaxation skills (Jacobson, 1970, 1977). Until his death in 1983 at the age of 94, he continued to pursue an understanding of self-control procedures. His interest in relaxation formally began in 1910 with his dissertation on the influence of relaxation on the startle response. Over the next seventy years, his ideas regarding relaxation methods and theories stimulated the development of a broad range of clinical treatment protocols.

Jacobson conceptualized relaxation as a mechanism for the conservation of adenosine triphosphate (ATP), one of the body's principal energy sources. Excessive muscle tension results not only in excessive energy expenditure, but also in excessive wear and tear on many body systems. For Jacobson, relaxation was a means of controlling both the physical deterioration and the extra energy expenditure associated with overactive skeletal muscles. Through the consistent application of relaxation skills, Jacobson believed that fatigue could be reduced and optimal functioning of body systems maintained.

Progressive relaxation training involves learning how to regulate ongoing muscle tension through the systematic tensing and releasing of major muscle groups throughout the body. Jacobson (1970) also introduced the concept of "self-operations control." Self-operations control involves making conscious decisions about the level of ongoing muscle activity.

This concept has a meaning similar to that of the concept of self-regulation in today's cognitive-behavioral vocabulary. Jacobsonian progressive relaxation centers on teaching a person to recognize even minute amounts of muscle tension and then to quickly eliminate that tension. Originally, training in progressive relaxation required from 40 to 60 individual sessions; in the later years of his life, however, Jacobson (1977) noted that control of some disorders could be accomplished with as few as six or seven sessions of muscle relaxation training.

In the years following Jacobson's pioneering work, many variants of progressive relaxation appeared. A review of the relaxation literature through 1979 identified at least 28 different approaches (Hillenberg & Collins, 1982). One recent example is stretch-based relaxation training (cf. Carlson et al., 1990). The emphasis in this technique is on the stretching of muscles to foster relaxation rather than the tensing of muscles. Another approach, called behavioral relaxation (Poppen, 1988), involves assuming a series of postural positions while breathing at a controlled rate. Similarities across many relaxation methods suggest common underlying mechanisms by which relaxation is achieved. Indeed, the rationale underlying progressive relaxation invites procedural variations, including the abbreviated progressive relaxation procedures outlined by Bernstein and Borkovec (1973), on which this chapter focuses.

## THEORETICAL RATIONALE FOR THE USE OF PROGRESSIVE RELAXATION

The research work of Gellhorn and colleagues (Gellhorn, 1958; Gellhorn & Loofbourrow, 1963; Gellhorn & Kiely, 1962) implicated overactivation of the autonomic nervous system—and, more specifically, of the sympathetic branch—as the underlying cause of excessive skeletal muscle tension. Sympathetic activation in response to perceived stressors leads to increases in skeletal muscle activity. The activation of the sympathetic nervous system is mediated by the ascending reticular activation system (ARAS) and hypothalamus. These two brain regions are also responsive to negative feedback information from skeletal muscle tissue proprioceptors. When skeletal muscle activity is reduced, there is a corresponding reduction in neural input from the muscle proprioceptors to the ARAS and hypothalamus areas. Lack of proprioceptive feedback information to the ARAS and hypothalamus is believed to assist in

quieting the autonomic nervous system and reducing emotional reactivity.

Experimental evidence for the overactivation model has been found in animal studies (Gellhorn, 1958; Gellhorn & Loofbourrow, 1963), but direct evidence from human studies has been sparse. Most human studies have provided evidence for a decrease in sympathetic nervous system activity through progressive relaxation procedures only by measuring such indirect variables as blood pressure, heart rate, respiration rate, and skin temperature (cf. King, 1980; Lehrer, 1982).

Wolpe (1958) proposed that progressive relaxation activates the parasympathetic branch of the autonomic nervous system. Increased parasympathetic activity then prompts reduced sympathetic activity. More recently, Benson (1975) proposed that relaxation, or more specifically the "relaxation response," is characterized by a generalized reduction in sympathetic nervous system activity and a corresponding increase in parasympathetic activation. These effects are achieved through a common mechanism involving focused attention, a quiet posture and environment, and a passive attitude. Benson's theory emphasizes the importance of increased parasympathetic activity as a result of relaxation; however, it is not clear whether parasympathetic activity in general, or just some subset of physiological responses, is involved during relaxation.

The ideas of early investigators like Jacobson and Gellhorn represent a "peripheralist" perspective consistent with the views of James (1890). The peripheralist position holds that thoughts and/or emotions have physiological consequences in peripheral organ systems like the skeletal muscles. On the other hand, Davison (1966) proposed that inhibition of efferent activity from the cortex downward may be the central mechanism by which relaxation operates. From this perspective, relaxation is a "top-down" phenomenon in which cognitive factors play a controlling role. Research by Obrist (1982) has suggested that cardiovascular and musculo-skeletal events may be linked by a common central mechanism and offers support for Davison's position. Moreover, focused attention appears to be an important component in the relaxation process (Davidson & Schwartz, 1976). The role of positive emotion generated with the progressive relaxation procedures may also be a valuable contributor to the relaxation process. The importance of these phenomena has convinced many that the strict peripheralist view of relaxation is incomplete.

In summary, the exact physiological and psychological mechanisms through which relaxation operates are still not well understood. There is general agreement, however, that progressive relaxation procedures effectively reduce autonomic activation and give the individual a means of controlling maladaptive physiological activation.

## CLIENT EVALUATION FOR PROGRESSIVE RELAXATION TRAINING

Effective clinical treatment, regardless of the problem or professional discipline, begins with attention to diagnostic evaluation. Without careful assessment, treatment may not match client needs. The potential for such mismatches is the principal concern associated with relaxation tapes and programs that are available to the public without professional consultation. As discussed later, for example, relaxation procedures can have negative side effects. Furthermore, negative experiences with relaxation might impede resolution of presenting problems and might even discourage people from seeking appropriate professional help. There are, in fact, some persons for whom relaxation methods are likely to fail. Jacobson (1977) believed that if a person could not learn to observe and report on muscle tension, relaxation skills could not be acquired.

The clinical interview is the primary basis for evaluating the appropriateness of relaxation training, though for many clinicians, multimodal methods, including psychophysiological techniques, are possible; indeed, our coverage will focus on a multimodal evaluation approach. Blanchard and colleagues (Blanchard et al., 1982) have explored the predictive utility of pretreatment evaluation and found that treatment outcomes can be related to specific client variables. Information from the client as well as from significant others is useful in developing a picture of the client's level of activation.

The evaluation process is concerned primarily with whether or not the presenting complaints are related to tension, anxiety, or excessive emotional and/or physical activation. Client behaviors in the consulting room that may be related to this issue include, but are not limited to, breathing patterns (e.g., rapid/shallow rate and/or chest versus abdominal; Fried, 1987), frequency of body movements and/or ''tense'' mannerisms, irritability, and alterations in speech patterns that suggest memory failure or other disruptions in information processing. Reports of sleep disruptions,

increased use of drugs or alcohol, adherence to rituals, withdrawal from others, change in appetite, sexual dysfunction, interpersonal conflict, and a tendency to overwork may also suggest autonomic overactivation.

Other manifestations of overactivation should also be noted during the interview. Typical indicators of anxiety and excessive tension include complaints of feeling overwhelmed, panicky, jittery, moody, fatigued, depressed, faint, forgetful, and in pain. Inability to concentrate and/or an excessive narrowing of attentional focus may also appear. Reports of increased heart rate and blood pressure, excessive sweating, elevated muscle activity, muscular hyperresponsivity/pain, gastrointestinal upset, genitourinary dysfunctions, and low hand and foot temperatures may be associated with tension and anxiety. Interview data should yield converging evidence that the individual is experiencing anxiety, tension, or inappropriate emotional activation.

Another important area for evaluation includes possible reasons for the client's apparent overactivation (Turkat & Wolpe, 1985). Clinicians should be alert to the circumstances surrounding initial episodes of tension and anxiety, because these may provide significant clues to etiology and maintenance factors such as acute and chronic stressors, and lack of social support. During the evaluation process, the clinician should strive to build a composite picture of the development of the dysfunctions by evaluating the events surrounding the onset of symptoms.

The major target in the exploration of the bases for overactivation are the consequences—including ''secondary gains''—of the individual's tension-related behaviors and cognitions. If overactivation has been ongoing (i.e., six months or more), adaptations may have occurred that can interfere with the development of relaxation skills. It is not uncommon, for example, that sustained tension and anxiety come to interfere with sleep and physical activity. Because both sleep and activity level can influence physiological activation levels, it is important to evaluate these issues with the client. Careful analysis of a client's behaviors and cognitions (and their consequences) is necessary to determine whether or not relaxation skills training is appropriate.

Another element in determining the appropriateness of relaxation training is the identification of any medical basis for presenting symptoms, especially when tension disorders are accompanied by physical complaints. As a general principle, before beginning relaxation training, the client should have a medical evaluation to rule out such primarily organic bases for the presenting complaints as metabolic disorders (e.g., hyperthyroidism), neurologic disorders (e.g., nerve root compression), and cardiovascular disorders (e.g., mitral valve prolapse, hypertension). In short, clients should have medical approval for relaxation-based therapy.

A final phase of the initial assessment process involves working with the client to determine the appropriate treatment goals. If tension and anxiety are primarily learned responses to specific life events, relaxation may help the client "unlearn" these dysfunctional behaviors. On the other hand, if tension and anxiety are primarily the result of social skill deficits or dysfunctional cognitive styles, then treatment goals may also include social skills development or cognitive restructuring. The clinician should remain sensitive to the unique needs of each client and recognize that relaxation-based therapy should sometimes be postponed while development of other client competencies takes center stage. Relaxation training alone is not likely to be effective unless any deficits contributing to the initiation and maintenance of tension are addressed.

## DIAGNOSTIC EVALUATION MEASURES

Decisions regarding the appropriateness of progressive relaxation training can be influenced by the use of standardized evaluation instruments and psychophysiological profiles. The use of standardized psychological measures provides the clinician with additional information on which to base treatment recommendations, but the use of these instruments presupposes professional training in their application. One instrument commonly used to supplement clinical interview data is the Minnesota Multiphasic Personality Inventory-2 (MMPI-2; Hathaway & McKinley, 1989). The MMPI-2 offers a comprehensive review of potential problem areas in personal functioning. MMPI-2 data may suggest areas requiring further exploration via interviews.

Measures of emotion-based dimensions such as anxiety and depression can also provide useful information. The State-Trait Anxiety Inventory (STAI; Spielberger, Gorsuch, & Lushene, 1970) provides reliable (coefficient alpha = +.90) qualitative and quantitative data about the client's anxiety level. The Beck Depression Inventory (BDI; Beck et al., 1978) assesses level of depression and serves as an additional screening tool for suicidal ideation. Occasion-

ally, there may be a need to evaluate emotional reactivity or other emotion-related variables not assessed by the STAI or the BDI. The Emotional Assessment Scale (Carlson et al., 1989; split-half reliability = .94) is designed for such tasks.

There are several standardized instruments that explore behavioral styles. These instruments include the Miller Behavioral Style Scale (MBSS; Miller, 1987), the Health Locus of Control Scale (HLC; Wallston, Wallston, Kaplan, & Maides, 1976), and the Cognitive Somatic Anxiety Scale (CSA; Schwartz, Davidson, & Goleman, 1978). The MBSS provides an index of an individual's tendency to monitor or attend to internal and/or external events, as compared to his or her tendency to avoid or blunt sensory information. Coefficient alpha for the monitoring subscale is .79; coefficient alpha for the blunting subscale is .69. Because relaxation training specifically focuses the individual toward internal sensations, information from the MBSS may help identify persons for whom such activities will be difficult to carry out. The HLC affords a rapid and reliable (coefficient alpha = .54) assessment of the client's beliefs about personal influence on health outcomes; such information can be quite useful when discussing with the client the potential utility of relaxation training and the active role he or she must play in it. Finally, the CSA provides information concerning the cognitive and somatic components of anxiety the patient may be experiencing. Such information can be useful in preparing the client for a treatment program and also in identifying potential treatment targets.

It may also be desirable to ask the client to self-monitor muscle tension or anxiety. Visual analog rating scales provide one method for doing this (Carlson et al., 1990). The visual analog scale is a 10-centimeter line anchored at the left endpoint with a descriptor such as "least possible muscle tension" and at the right endpoint with the term "highest possible muscle tension." The client periodically rates the level of muscle tension experienced by placing a mark somewhere on the line to represent his or her judgment of the level of muscle tension, and these ratings provide a profile of subjective levels of tension throughout the course of everyday events. The use of muscle tension ratings prior to, during, and after relaxation training can also provide an index of clients' progress that can motivate continued skill development.

Psychophysiological evaluation also plays an important role in documenting the degree to which an individual displays excessive physical and emotional reactivity. With the increased availability of modular physiological equipment interfaced with a personal computer, it is reasonable for most clinicians who routinely use progressive relaxation training to consider investing in physiological recording equipment. Basic systems often have at least four physiological channels, most commonly including two electromyograph (EMG) channels to measure electrical activity in muscles and two channels to measure skin temperatures. Physiological recordings also provide objective indices of the client's relaxation ability prior to, during, and after training.

Psychophysiological evaluation consists of two phases. The static phase involves sampling and recording the resting activity of muscle groups believed to play a significant role in the individual's stress response pattern (Cram, 1988). This phase involves briefly scanning and recording the resting activity of the target muscle groups while the individual sits and stands quietly. The dynamic phase involves monitoring "target" muscle groups identified during the static phase as overactive; activity in the muscles is continuously recorded while the client engages in several structured activities (e.g., resting quietly, performing mental arithmetic, or attempting to relax).

In the dynamic phase of the profiling procedure (Blanchard & Andrasik, 1985), the client is typically seated in a comfortable chair while EMG activity in several "target" muscles is recorded during three distinct periods. The first period establishes a baseline for the muscle activity. The second period usually involves a 1- to 10-minute stressor task such as subtracting by 13 from a four-digit number. In the final phase, the client is asked to relax. This protocol gives the clinician useful information about the client's physiological vulnerabilities as well as information about pretreatment relaxation ability. (For more detailed information about the use of physiological measurement in clinical practice, consult such resources as Blanchard & Andrasik, 1985).

One of the purposes of conducting an evaluation is to rule out any potential contraindications for relaxation treatment. Relaxation is an active procedure for altering physiological, behavioral, cognitive, and emotional functioning. Its use must be carefully considered and, as already noted, in some cases medical consultation may be necessary before undertaking relaxation training. If the client is taking regular medication, for example, relaxation training may alter the amount of medication needed for physiological control. An inability to focus attention, follow instruc-

tions, or engage in home practice would be a contraindication for relaxation training. A client who is unable to discriminate muscle tension may also not be well suited for relaxation training. Clients whose backgrounds might make relaxation frightening should be given special screening (cf. Borkovec, 1987; Borkovec et al., 1987). Once the evaluation process has been completed and the results have been discussed with the client, decisions regarding the implementation of relaxation training can be made. Many different relaxation training methods are available (e.g., Smith, 1985), although the remainder of this chapter will focus on abbreviated progressive relaxation training (APR).

## PRESENTATION OF ABBREVIATED PROGRESSIVE RELAXATION TRAINING

### The Core Program

Abbreviated progressive relaxation training consists of six phases: an introduction, presentation of basic techniques, consolidation of muscle groups, relaxation by recall, relaxation via recall and counting, and relaxation by counting alone.

### Introduction

The first step in the training process is to explain to the client the APR procedures and rationale. As part of this initial explanation, it should be emphasized that relaxation skills enable the client to reduce the effects of tension and anxiety and thus help to manage the presenting complaints more effectively. The clinician should ensure that this rationale is clearly understood by the client, since the client's motivation for training and home practice often depends on it. The time taken to develop the client's understanding and acceptance of the rationale for APR is likely to pay long-term dividends.

The essential points to cover in discussing the background and rationale for APR include (1) a brief historical overview of the techniques; (2) the notion that development of relaxation skill is very similar to the development of other physical skills, such as piano playing or tennis; (3) the importance of regular at-home practice of the skills learned in the consulting room, and (4) the fact that APR involves learning skills that are under the client's control, rather than something the clinician does "to" the client.

An example of the presentation of APR's history and rationale follows (adapted from Bernstein & Borkovec, 1973). Each clinician should adapt this presentation to his or her own delivery style.

The procedures I have been discussing in terms of reducing your tension are collectively called "progressive relaxation training." They were first developed in the 1930s by a psychologist and physician named Jacobson, and in recent years we have modified his original techniques in order to make them simpler and easier to learn. Basically, progressive relaxation training consists of learning to . . . tense and then to relax various groups of muscles all through the body, while at the same time paying very close and careful attention to the sensations and feelings associated with both tension and relaxation. That is, in addition to teaching you how to relax, I will also be encouraging you to learn to recognize and pinpoint tension and relaxation as they appear in everyday situations, as well as in our sessions here.

You should understand quite clearly that learning relaxation skills is very much like learning any other kind of skill such as swimming, or golfing, or riding a bicycle; thus, in order for you to get better at relaxing, you will have to practice doing it just as you would have to practice other skills. It is very important that you realize that progressive relaxation training involves learning on your part; there is nothing magical about the procedures. I will not be doing anything to you; I will merely be introducing you to the techniques and directing your attention to various aspects of them, such as the presence of certain feelings in the muscles. Thus, without your active cooperation and regular practicing of the things you will learn, the procedures are of little use.

Now I mentioned earlier that I will be asking you to tense and then to relax various groups of muscles in your body. You may be wondering why, if we want to produce relaxation, we start off by producing tension. The reason is that, first of all, everyone is always at some level of tension during the waking hours; if people were not tense to some extent, they would simply fall down. The amount of tension actually present in everyday life differs, of course, from individual to individual, and we say that each person has reached some "adaptation level," the amount of tension under which he or she operates day to day.

The goal of progressive relaxation training is to help you learn to reduce muscle tension in your body far below your adaptation level at any time you wish to do so. In order to accomplish this, I could ask you to focus your attention, for example, on the muscles in your right hand and lower arm and then just to let them relax. Now you might think you can let these muscles drop down below their adaptation level just by "letting them go" or whatever, and to a certain extent, you probably can. However, in progressive relaxation, we want you to learn to produce larger and very much more noticeable reductions in tension, and a good way to do this is first to produce a lot of tension in the muscle group (i.e., to raise the tension well above adaptation level) and then release that tension quickly. Tensing the muscle prior to letting it relax and then quickly relaxing it can help the muscle become deeply relaxed.

Another important advantage to creating and releasing tension is that it will give you a good chance to focus your attention upon and become clearly aware of what tension really feels like in each of the various groups of muscles we will be dealing with today. In addition, the tensing procedure will make a vivid contrast between tension and relaxation and will give you an excellent opportunity to compare the two directly and appreciate the difference in feeling associated with each of these states.

Do you have any questions about what I've said so far?[1]

## Presentation of Techniques

When questions regarding the rationale and basic procedures have been answered satisfactorily, the therapist is ready to present the basic techniques to the client. In the initial phase of skill development, relaxation training focuses on 16 basic muscle groups. These 16 muscle groups and one means of tensing each of them are as follows:

1. Dominant hand and forearm—make a tight fist.
2. Dominant upper arm—push elbow down against chair.
3. Nondominant hand and forearm—same as dominant.
4. Nondominant upper arm—same as dominant.
5. Forehead—raise eyebrows as high as possible.
6. Upper cheeks and nose—squint and wrinkle nose.
7. Lower face and jaw—clench teeth and pull back corners of mouth.
8. Neck—pull chin toward chest and try to raise it simultaneously.
9. Chest, shoulders, upper back—pull shoulder blades together.
10. Abdomen—make stomach hard.
11. Dominant upper leg—tense muscles on upper side and lower side.
12. Dominant calf—pull toes toward head.
13. Dominant foot—point toes downward, turn foot in, and curl toes gently.

[1]Adapted by permission of Research Press, Champaign, Illinois, from *Progressive Relaxation Training* by D. A. Bernstein and T. D. Borkovec (1973, pp. 19–23).

14. Nondominant upper leg—same as dominant.
15. Nondominant calf—same as dominant.
16. Nondominant foot—same as dominant.

The client should be instructed to tense the muscle for 5 to 7 seconds, to release the tension quickly, and to allow the muscle to relax for 30 to 40 seconds. It is important to remind the client to avoid tensing muscles to the point of pain or discomfort. Care should be taken to ensure that the client can perform each of the exercises without discomfort. Should there be a problem with any of the tensing procedures, the therapist and client will need to work together to develop appropriate tension-release strategies. In some cases, preexisting injuries or pain may make it necessary to substitute or omit selected muscle groups. It is prudent to review each of the exercises in the same order as they will be presented to the client in order to give consistency to the training. It is a good idea, as well, for the clinician to demonstrate each of the tension-release procedures, not only in order to clarify them, but also to reduce client concerns about "making faces" or performing other "odd" tension procedures.

In the typical case, the client should be resting in a reclined position with adequate support for head and spine. A recliner chair works well for this purpose; so does a physical therapy table with several pillows. Sometimes an initial adjustment behind the head, neck, lower back, or knees with an extra pillow or rolled towel can improve client comfort considerably. Instructions to the client regarding the elements of a relaxed position (Poppen, 1988) are also quite useful in helping the client rest comfortably. Poppen has noted ten postures and behaviors indicative of relaxation:

1. Head supported and centered in the mid-line of the body
2. Eyes closed with smooth eyelids and smooth forehead
3. Lips slightly apart with tongue resting gently in the mouth
4. No throat movements
5. No vocalizations
6. Shoulders lowered and even—no movement
7. No trunk movement except for rhythmic breathing
8. Breathing is slow and regular
9. Fingers curled in relaxed position
10. Toes pointing away from each other at a 45 to 90 degree angle

These characteristics provide the clinician with a set of cues by which to gauge the level of relaxation the client is experiencing. Indeed, an important element in relaxation training is the therapist's ability to "read" the client's nonverbal cues and adapt the procedures in a manner that maximizes training effectiveness.

After the tension-release instructions have been reviewed, the following instructions (adapted from Bernstein & Given, 1984) should be presented:

1. I will be instructing you to focus your attention on one muscle group at a time. Please pay attention only to what I am saying and to the sensations you are experiencing in that muscle group, allowing the rest of your body to remain relaxed. I will ask you to tense and relax each of the muscle groups in the same order as when we practiced the tensing procedures.

2. When I ask you to tense a group, I will say, for example, "Tense the muscles in your forehead by raising your eyebrows, now." "Now" will be the cue word for you to tense the muscles. Keep your muscles relaxed until I say "now." But remember not to tense the muscles to the point that you would feel pain, discomfort, or cramping.

3. When I want you to relax a muscle group, I will say "O.K., relax the muscles in your forehead." When I say that, let all the tension go all at once, not gradually.

4. I will ask you to tense and relax each muscle group twice. After the second time, I will ask you to signal if the muscle group is completely relaxed. Please signal by raising the index finger on your right hand, but do not signal unless the muscles feel completely relaxed.

5. During the session, try not to move any more than is necessary to remain comfortable. In order to gain the most benefit from relaxation, it is preferable not to move any muscles that have already been relaxed. This reduces the likelihood that tension will reappear in those muscles.

6. In order to maintain as much relaxation as possible, I am going to ask you not to talk to me during our session unless it is absolutely necessary. We will mainly use your finger signal as a means of communication. We will talk about how the session went and any questions you may have after we finish today.

7. Our session will take about 45 minutes, so if you would like to use the restroom before we start, please do so. Also, if you are wearing contact lenses, you may want to remove them as well.

8. Now I would like to have you remove or loosen any items of clothing (such as belts, buttoned

collars, or tight cuffs) that may cause discomfort during the session.

9. Do you have any further questions? Is there anything that is unclear?

10. All right, get in a comfortable, relaxed position—fine. Now please close your eyes and keep them closed during the session. I will dim the lights now to minimize visual stimulation.[2]

At this point the relaxation training begins using the same sequence of muscle groups as presented to the client. It is helpful to encourage the client to breathe slowly and regularly throughout the relaxation procedures and not to hold the breath during the tension phases, unless it may be specifically useful, such as when tensing the chest, shoulders, and upper back. Breath holding may foster muscle tension and interfere with general relaxation. Rhythmic, relaxed breathing is an important element of the procedure, and the therapist may be able to coordinate tension-release instructions with the client's breathing pattern, creating tension in the muscle group as inhalation occurs and cueing release of the muscle group at exhalation.

Once the client is in a comfortable position and regular breathing has been established, the therapist's instructions should focus the client's attention on the first muscle group to be relaxed. The client is then instructed to tense the muscle group at the cue word "now." During the tension phase, the client is encouraged to focus attention on the sensations in the muscles. Tension should be maintained for 5 to 7 seconds (remember to shorten this time in areas in which tension could produce pain or cramping, especially in the feet) then quickly released using the cue phrase, "O.K., relax." The muscles should be allowed to relax for 30 to 40 seconds, during which time the client is instructed to focus attention on the changing sensations in the muscles. During the relaxation period, the therapist should remain quiet, except for phrases given at the beginning of the phase to focus the client's attention on feelings in the muscles; excessive therapist comments during this period may be distracting and could hinder the client's learning self-relaxation skills. (The client's reactions to and comfort with therapist comments should be discussed at the end of the session.) Relaxation "patter" (Bernstein & Borkovec, 1973) that encourages the client

to focus attention on relaxation may include statements like "Let the muscles become quiet and relaxed," "Just allow the muscles to relax," "Relax," and "Continue to allow relaxation to occur."

After the first relaxation phase, the muscle group is tensed again in the same way as before, followed by a relaxation phase of 45 to 60 seconds. Once the second relaxation phase is completed, the client is asked to signal with a finger if the muscle group feels relaxed. If relaxation is achieved, training progresses to the next muscle group. If the client does not signal relaxation, the tense–release–relax procedures are repeated a third time. If relaxation is not achieved this third time, the techniques are repeated again; if relaxation is not accomplished after four or five attempts, the therapist should consider an alternative strategy such as returning to the muscle group after relaxation of all other muscle groups is completed (see Bernstein & Borkovec, 1973).

The following is an example of the therapist's comments for one muscle group:

Next we're going to tense the muscles of the upper cheeks and nose by squinting the eyes and wrinkling the nose. Go ahead, *now,* and squint the eyes and wrinkle the nose. That's right, hold the tension and notice what it feels like. Hold it; O.K., now relax the muscles. Just let the muscles be quiet and without tension.

Notice the difference between the muscles being tense and now being relaxed. Focus your attention on the sensations in the muscles relaxing. Let your breathing be slow and regular as you continue to let the muscles relax, . . . relax. [After 30 to 40 seconds, repeat the tense–release–relax procedure.]

O.K., I would like you to tell me by raising your index finger if the muscles in the central area of your face are as relaxed as the muscles in the forehead [for comparison, use the muscle group that was previously relaxed]. All right, just continue letting the muscles relax.

Once relaxation has been completed for all 16 muscle groups, the client should be encouraged to continue noticing the sensations of relaxation and allowing the muscles to stay relaxed. After a few moments, the therapist should ask the client to signal if he or she is feeling completely relaxed. If the response is affirmative, the client is encouraged to continue relaxing and enjoying the sensations of relaxation. If the client does not respond, care should be taken to ensure that the client has not fallen asleep. If

---

[2]Adapted by permission of Guilford Press, New York, from *Principles and Practice of Stress Management* by R. Woolfolk and P. Lehrer (Eds.) (1984, pp. 52–53).

the client has fallen asleep, the therapist should not touch the client, but should simply give instructions to conclude the session; sometimes these instructions must be repeated in a gradually louder voice to awaken the client. If the therapist is certain that nonresponding is due to muscle tension, the client should be asked to signal which muscle groups are still tense as the therapist names each of them. When tense muscle groups are identified, the relaxation procedures are repeated for those groups until the client reports no muscle tension, until the available time has expired, or until the therapist judges that there are problems that require discussion.

Typically, a relaxation session is concluded as follows:

> In a moment we will conclude our session. I'm going to count backwards from 5 to 1. With each number, you will gain increasing awareness of your surroundings. When I reach "1," you should be fully alert and ready to resume your normal activities just as if you had had a relaxing nap. 5—gently move your feet and legs. 4—move your arms and hands. 3—move your head and shoulders. 2—open your eyes. 1—you should now be alert, refreshed, and ready to resume normal activities.

At this point, the clinician should explore in an open-ended manner the client's reactions to the training session. Questions such as "How was that?" or "How do you feel?" are appropriate ways to begin. In addition, it may be helpful to have the client provide a subjective rating of relaxation using a scale of 0 to 10, where "0" represents no relaxation and "10" represents the most relaxation possible. During the debriefing session, it is also important to discuss any problems with relaxation that might have occurred. Common problems include difficulty in tensing or relaxing a particular muscle group, intrusive thoughts, or pain sensations. The clinician should take time to discuss potential ways to deal with these problems.

Finally, there should be a discussion of plans for at-home practice sessions. The client should practice the procedures twice a day for 15 to 20 minutes each time; regular practice is essential for skill acquisition. Attention should focus on identifying not only times for practice but also a place to practice. The setting for relaxation should be a quiet, comfortable one that protects the client from distractions and interruptions. The client should be encouraged to enlist the help of significant others in arranging for these conditions. Detailed discussion about the place and times for relaxation greatly increases the probability that practice will take place as agreed.

## Combining Muscle Groups

After about three training sessions, most clients will report an ability to achieve deep relaxation using the 16-muscle-group procedure. Additional indications of developing relaxation ability include reports of regular practice and deep relaxation with two or fewer tense–release–relax cycles, reductions in levels of tension or anxiety, clearer postural signs of relaxation during training sessions, improved sleep, appearance of deep relaxation before the entire training session is completed, and a feeling of drowsiness at the end of the relaxation. When the client demonstrates improved relaxation ability with the 16-muscle-group method, a shorter 7-muscle-group procedure can be introduced.

In the 7-group method, the original 16 muscle groups are combined so that several groups of muscles are tensed and relaxed simultaneously. The muscle groups are combined as follows:

1. Dominant hand, forearm, and upper arm
2. Nondominant hand, forearm, and upper arm
3. All muscles in the face
4. Neck
5. Chest, shoulders, upper back, and abdomen
6. Dominant upper leg, calf, and foot
7. Nondominant upper leg, calf, and foot

If, for some reason, these combinations are not well suited to the needs of the client, the clinician should develop suitable alternatives. The method for conducting the relaxation sessions is the same as for the 16 muscle groups. After about two weeks of practice, most clients are able to achieve a deep state of relaxation using the 7-muscle-group procedure. If problems arise, the clinician should identify which combinations of muscle groups are contributing to the problem and separate them into their original components for more practice before returning to the combined approach.

When practice and skill acquisition proceed smoothly, training continues by combining the 7 muscle groups into 4. The 4-muscle-group method employs:

1. Both arms and both hands
2. Face and neck
3. Chest, shoulders, back, and abdomen
4. Both legs and feet

Relaxation practice with the 4-group method should take approximately 10 minutes. Again, the client is encouraged to practice twice daily until he or she is able to relax the muscles deeply using the 4-group procedure.

## Relaxation by Recall

The purpose of APR is to provide the client with skills that can be used in almost any situation to control elevated levels of muscle tension and arousal. In order to accomplish this, relaxation training can be advanced still further so that the client can relax muscles quickly and unobtrusively, without tension-release cycles, simply by recalling the feelings associated with previously learned relaxation procedures.

Relaxation by recall is accomplished by having the client focus attention on the first group of muscles in the 4-group procedure. The client is then instructed to use the cue words "O.K., relax" while recalling the sensations in the muscles as the tension is released and the muscles begin to relax. The relaxation phase, accompanied by the standard relaxation "patter," continues for 30 to 45 seconds. After the relaxation phase, the client is asked to indicate whether or not the target muscles are relaxed. If relaxation has occurred, training proceeds to the next muscle group. If the client does not indicate the muscles are relaxed, the procedure is repeated. The client is encouraged to focus attention on the problematic muscles and attempt to relax the muscle tension.

In the early stages of relaxation by recall, the muscles sometimes do not relax well. In such circumstances, it is useful to reinstitute a tense–release–relax procedure during the training session to foster relaxation. However, the client should be encouraged to use the relaxation-by-recall approach during at-home practice sessions. The relaxation-by-recall sessions end in a manner similar to the other training sessions by giving the client an opportunity to explore feelings associated with the session and to plan for home practice sessions.

## Recall with Counting

Once relaxation by recall is well developed, the therapist can add a counting procedure to enhance the depth of relaxation. The counting procedure is used near the end of the training session, after relaxation by the recall method is signaled. It simply involves counting slowly from 1 to 10. With each number, the client is encouraged to relax more deeply. The therapist uses the client's breathing pattern to time the counting—one number at each exhalation. In addition, the therapist uses a variety of relaxation phrases

(such as "relaxing more and more") with each number to assist the client in further relaxation. The counting procedure can also be used by the client in at-home practice to deepen the level of relaxation.

## Counting-Alone Procedure

After sufficient practice with relaxation by recall and counting, the client is ready to be introduced to relaxation by counting alone. This aspect of training capitalizes on the learned associations between deepening feelings of relaxation and the counting procedure. The relaxation-by-recall steps are dropped, and the client is encouraged to relax as the therapist counts from 1 to 10. Again, the therapist should include relaxation patter and time the count to coincide with the client's breathing pattern. Each count is given as the client exhales.

If relaxation is not signaled when the counting is completed, relaxation by recall can be employed. In some cases, it may even be necessary to employ one or more tense–release–relax cycles to achieve relaxation. Once the client is able to relax by counting alone, relaxation skills will have reached criterion and the client may reduce the frequency of practice sessions to once a day. However, the client should continue these practice sessions to maintain relaxation skills.

## FACTORS INFLUENCING OUTCOMES OF RELAXATION TRAINING

### Therapist–Client Relationship

As in any clinical endeavor, the therapist–client relationship is an important ingredient in the development of a client's relaxation skills. In particular, as noted earlier, the therapist should communicate support, information, confidence, and encouragement, but should also be cautious not to suggest that he or she is "doing something" to the client. To the contrary, the therapist should emphasize the importance of developing self-control through relaxation training.

As the client learns how to use relaxation skills, the therapist may find that the training serves as a bridge to help the client consider other therapeutic issues. Effective relaxation training often reduces unwanted anxiety. As anxiety diminishes, the client may become aware of other interpersonal issues. Success in relaxation training often builds the client's self-efficacy for making other changes in thought and action patterns (cf. Burish, Carey, Krozely, & Greco, 1987; Reynolds & Coats, 1986). The demeanor of the clinician during relaxation training is important in setting the stage for the client's potential growth and change.

## Environmental Considerations

The physical environment for conducting relaxation training should be chosen carefully to contribute to the process of skill acquisition. The room should be well ventilated and quiet; freedom from outside noises and distractions enables the client to focus on internal feelings and sensations. Room decor should reflect a soothing environment; bright colors or unusual artwork can divert attention from relaxation training. It is also helpful to be able to dim the lights and close draperies. Bright lights can be an impediment to relaxation training.

Seating for both client and therapist should also be thoughtfully planned. A recliner chair that supports the client firmly and comfortably is generally the best option. However, care should be taken to help the client adjust him- or herself with additional pillows or support if the recliner chair does not provide optimal comfort. The consulting room and the client's chair should be large enough to create the impression of a relaxed, uncluttered setting that fosters freedom of movement. A comfortable chair for the therapist helps encourage relaxed, well-paced instructions and a minimum of fidgeting. Constructing an effective therapeutic environment also includes preventing distractions by placing a "Do Not Disturb" sign on the door and switching off the phone. (The client should be urged to take similar precautions during at-home practice.) One final environmental factor involves the therapist's verbal style during the training program. The volume and pace of the therapist's voice should be at a normal level when training sessions begin. As the session progresses and relaxation occurs, the therapist should lower the volume and slow the rate of speech. Then, as the session concludes, the volume and rate should be gradually returned to a normal level.

## Timetable for Presentation of Relaxation Skills

In general, relaxation skills are developed within a training program that requires about ten sessions. The exact number depends, of course, on each individual's responses to training and the diligence of his or her at-home practice. In experimental research using relaxation training, the average number of sessions is five or fewer (Borkovec & Sides, 1979; Hillenberg & Collins, 1982). Burish and colleagues (Burish et al., 1987; Carey & Burish, 1987), for example, routinely have demonstrated significant reductions in anticipatory anxiety related to cancer chemotherapy by using a five-session program. The experimental literature thus highlights the importance of clinicians modifying the training structure to meet individual needs. The standard ten-session training program follows the timetable presented below:

| | |
|---|---|
| Sessions 1, 2, and 3 | Training in 16 muscle groups |
| Sessions 4 and 5 | Training in 7 muscle groups |
| Sessions 6 and 7 | Training in 4 muscle groups |
| Session 8 | Training in 4 muscle groups with recall |
| Session 9 | Training in 4 muscle groups with recall and counting |
| Session 10 | Training with counting |

## Measurement of Outcomes

The recent development of objective behavioral methods to evaluate levels of relaxation (Poppen, 1988) provide the clinician with an important means to monitor client progress in APR training. Scores on this 10-item behavioral relaxation checklist used by the therapist can be charted for each practice session. However, client self-report is probably the most important source of information regarding relaxation progress. Self-ratings of relaxation after practice sessions can be useful, as can periodic self-ratings of muscle tension during the client's daily activities. Reports of at-home practice frequency, the time it takes to achieve deep relaxation, and client reports of satisfaction with the training program also serve as indices of progress.

Standardized evaluation instruments used in the initial assessment provide another option for evaluating the progress of relaxation training. Such instruments, especially when combined with physiological indices of relaxation—such as decreased EMG or resting blood pressure levels—provide converging evidence for the efficacy of treatment. Finally, of course, the resolution or attenuation of presenting complaints also suggests the effectiveness of relaxation.

## ADVERSE EFFECTS AND PROBLEMS POTENTIALLY ASSOCIATED WITH RELAXATION TRAINING

### Adverse Effects

Adverse effects of relaxation training appear infrequently in the general clinical population (Edinger & Jacobsen, 1982; Heide & Borkovec, 1983); they are more common among persons with generalized anxiety disorders (Borkovec & Mathews, 1988; Braith, McCullough, & Bush, 1988; Heide & Borkovec, 1983; Ley, 1988; Norton, Rhodes, Hauch, & Kaprowy, 1985). The negative effects most commonly described are fear of losing control, increased tension, and increased symptoms of anxiety. These negative side effects have been labeled relaxation-induced anxiety (RIA) and relaxation-induced panic (RIP) (Adler, Craske, & Barlow, 1987).

Relaxation-induced anxiety is used to describe a gradual increase in the behavioral, physiological, and psychological elements of arousal/anxiety during a relaxation session. As the name suggests, relaxation-induced panic is associated with the rapid onset of severe anxiety during the session. Ley (1988) has proposed that persons prone to hyperventilation (due to chronic sympathetic nervous system responses to stress) have an increased risk for hyperventilation episodes during relaxation. Two mechanisms may be at work: First, relaxation can increase the inspiratory volume slightly, thus creating panic in persons who are prone to hyperventilation. Second, small reductions in metabolic rate because of reduced activation during relaxation may result in a decrease in carbon dioxide production from metabolism. If carbon dioxide production drops in a person prone to hyperventilation, then hypocapnia (low concentrations of carbon dioxide in the blood plasma) can develop. The primary symptoms of hyperventilation/hypocapnia are breathlessness, rapid heart rate, and palpitations. Thus, Ley (1988) suggests that relaxation-induced anxiety or panic events are in reality episodes of hyperventilation brought on by behavioral and physiological changes during relaxation.

Other mechanisms for RIA/RIP have also been proposed. These include fear of relaxation sensations (Borkovec, 1987; Borkovec et al., 1987), fear of losing control (Bernstein & Borkovec, 1973; Carrington, 1977), and interoceptive conditioning (Adler et al., 1987). Further research on these and other causal mechanisms associated with RIA/RIP is necessary, but the clinician should be sensitive to the potential for RIA/RIP and the factors that may underlie them.

### Common Problems

Bernstein and Borkovec (1973) presented a list of common problems encountered during relaxation training, including client coughing and/or sneezing, excessive movement, muscle cramps or spasms, and sleep. Anxious thoughts, laughter, talking, and sexual arousal were also mentioned. In a survey by Edinger and Jacobsen (1982) of the actual frequency of specific problems during relaxation training, 116 clinicians—who had conducted relaxation training with an estimated 17,542 clients—identified intrusive thoughts as the most frequent (15%) problem encountered, followed by fear of losing control (9%), disturbing sensory experiences (4%), muscle cramps or spasms (4%), and sexual arousal (2%).

#### Coping with Physical Problems

Clients who are prone to coughing (e.g., smokers) or sneezing (e.g., those with colds or allergies) may require special attention during relaxation training. Adjustments in body position or decreases in the depth and pace of breathing may be necessary for smokers in order to control coughing during the training. Persons with allergy attacks or seasonal colds may need to postpone relaxation training.

If muscle cramps associated with tension cycles are frequent, it may be necessary to reduce the length of time the muscles are tensed. Tensing of muscle groups most likely to cramp (i.e., feet and toes) may have to be restricted or even skipped, if cramping is frequent. Muscle spasms are often a natural consequence of deep muscle relaxation. Helping clients to interpret muscle spasms as an indication of deepening relaxation rather than tension can have a positive influence on their motivation to practice.

When clients begin to relax deeply, it is not uncommon for them to fall asleep, especially in the early stages of training. One indication that the client has fallen asleep is a failure to respond to the questions regarding level of relaxation. As noted earlier, if the client is sleeping, it can be useful to increase gradually the loudness of instructions or questions. Experienced therapists find that if they pace the relaxation carefully and modulating voice qualities (volume, inflection, etc.) most clients can remain awake while learning relaxation. Excessive client movement during the training sessions should be discouraged. Often, simply reminding the client of the need to remain in a quiet position will control this problem.

## Coping with Cognitive Problems

Client talking or laughing during relaxation training can also often be prevented by reminding clients of the ground rules for the training session. Occasional talk or laughter should be ignored; a discreet comment may be necessary if it continues.

Clients who experience intrusive thoughts during relaxation should be encouraged to focus attention on the therapist's voice as a means of controlling distractions. Another strategy is to plan with the client a clear, pleasant image or scene to focus on should unwanted thoughts intrude. A third alternative is to encourage the client to focus attention on some physical sensation, such as air moving down the back of the throat during inhalation. Intrusive thoughts can also be controlled by instructing the client to pace his or her breathing rate by counting slowly during both inhalation and exhalation. Finally, the therapist can assist in the management of intrusive thoughts by increasing the amount and variety of relaxation patter.

Occasionally, the low level of lighting, quiet environment, soft voice of the therapist, and pleasant feelings of relaxation can contribute to feelings of sexual arousal in the client. The therapist should be sensitive to this possibility and willing to discuss the matter. Acceptance of the client's feelings and reassurance that such feelings usually fade as relaxation skill develops are generally enough to deal with the problem. If sexual feelings persist over several relaxation sessions, the therapist obviously should explore their meaning and possible function. This exploration might best be done during a session that does not involve relaxation training in order to help the client maintain objectivity. The possibility of sexual arousal during relaxation training is another reason for not touching the client during training sessions. A therapist's touch during relaxation can be misinterpreted and may interfere with the client's skill development.

## REPRESENTATIVE APPLICATIONS OF RELAXATION TRAINING

Progressive relaxation techniques are effective in decreasing physiological activation associated with a wide variety of disorders (cf. Borkovec & Sides, 1979; Lehrer, 1982; Lehrer & Woolfolk, 1984). Typically included in the lists of treatment targets appropriate for APR are insomnia, generalized anxiety, specific anxieties or phobias, hypertension, and tension headache. Within the last five years, a number of well-designed experimental studies using APR as a primary treatment modality have appeared in the literature. These studies represent a growth in the sophistication of experimental evaluation of treatment outcomes; in addition, the outcomes have added to our understanding of the processes underlying the effectiveness of APR.

Abbreviated relaxation procedures have been used in the treatment of generalized anxiety disorders for some time. Borkovec's (Borkovec et al., 1987; Borkovec & Mathews, 1988) recent program of research has demonstrated the clinical efficacy of several treatments for nonphobic anxiety; a principal component of the successful treatment packages developed by Borkovec is APR. Even though APR is a common ingredient of the treatment programs developed by Borkovec, a well-controlled evaluation of a treatment package using only APR for generalized anxiety disorder has not as yet appeared. However, Reynolds and Coats (1986) explored the effectiveness of relaxation training alone in a small-group treatment format with moderately depressed adolescents. The study also included a group cognitive-behavioral treatment and a wait-list control group. Results indicated that both cognitive-behavioral and relaxation-only treatments resulted in reduction of depressive symptoms; there were no differences in effectiveness between the active treatment conditions. These results suggest that relaxation alone can be an effective therapeutic tool, although the lack of a placebo control group and long-term follow-up requires that the results be interpreted with caution.

Halonen and Passman (1985) assessed the influence of APR on the treatment of depression among postpartum women. They compared APR alone to conditions in which women were given APR and stress management training, stress management training only, and an attention control group. The results indicated that persons experiencing the APR only or APR and stress management reported lower levels of depression than persons assigned to the other two groups. These results again suggest that APR may be an appropriate component of intervention programs for depression.

The use of APR in the treatment of conditioned side effects associated with cancer chemotherapy has received considerable attention (e.g., Lyles, Burish, Kroxely, & Oldham, 1982; Burish et al., 1987; Carey & Burish, 1987; Redd & Andrykowski, 1982). In

Burish's program of research, APR was administered over a five-session format using the methods described in Bernstein and Borkovec's (1973) manual. Burish has found that relaxation training not only helps in the amelioration of conditioned nausea and vomiting (Lyles et al., 1982), but also can prevent the onset of these symptoms with certain forms of chemotherapy (Burish et al., 1987).

Methodological issues related to the delivery of APR training in a clinical setting have also been a focus of research. Carey and Burish (1987) compared the effectiveness of relaxation training delivered by professionals (i.e., psychologists or senior graduate students), trained paraprofessionals, or an audiotape, with a no-treatment control. The results showed that professionally delivered relaxation training was effective in reducing both distress and physiological activation among patients undergoing chemotherapy; the audiotape and paraprofessional training was no more effective than the no-treatment control condition. These findings suggest that the role of the professional in relaxation training is important in determining the outcomes of treatment. However, future research is needed to clarify specific therapist behaviors that may contribute to the effectiveness of APR-based treatments.

Abbreviated progressive relaxation has been found to enhance immunocompetence in a geriatric population (Kiecolt-Glaser et al., 1985). As compared to a group of elderly persons receiving social contact (periodic visitation) or a no-contact control condition, elderly persons who were trained in APR showed better immunocompetence, as indicated by increased numbers of natural killer cells and herpes antibodies. Moreover, the persons in the APR condition also reported less overall distress than persons assigned to the other two conditions. These results are particularly intriguing because of the potential for APR to enhance immune system functioning in chronic illnesses. However, additional data are not available at present to address this question.

The role of APR in the treatment of hypertension has been discussed for at least the last ten years. Two recent studies evaluated the effects of APR on blood pressure. Hoelscher, Lickstein, and Rosenthal (1986) found that APR presented individually or in groups was effective in lowering both systolic and diastolic blood pressure as compared to no-treatment controls. However, Chesney, Black, Swan, and Ward (1987) conducted a study evaluating the efficacy of APR with 158 hypertensive individuals in the workplace. They found that APR was no more effective than a program of regular blood pressure monitoring for reducing systolic and diastolic blood pressures. Chesney et al.'s findings raise an important question concerning the efficacy of APR programs for the reduction of blood pressure in moderate hypertensives. Although their results suggest caution in the application of APR procedures for hypertension reduction, it certainly would be helpful to see a replication of these findings. This study does set an important standard of comparison for future studies of blood pressure reduction by including a blood pressure monitoring–only condition.

Abbreviated relaxation methods have also been used to alleviate the discomfort and severity of symptoms associated with spasmodic dysmenorrhea (Sigmon & Nelson, 1988). In this study, using a sample of 40 women reporting frequent problems with spasmodic dysmenorrhea, they compared APR with an activity-scheduling program and a wait-list control condition. The results indicated that both APR and training in activity scheduling reduced self-reports of symptom severity and discomfort associated with spasmodic dysmenorrhea. These results were maintained at a one-month follow-up evaluation.

Finally, the research of Blanchard over the past fifteen years (Blanchard et al., 1990; Blanchard et al., 1988; Attanasio, Andrasik, & Blanchard, 1987) exemplifies the controlled evaluation of relaxation-based treatments for muscle contraction headache. In a recent study, Blanchard et al. (1990) found that, in comparison with headache monitoring only, cognitive treatment with relaxation training, and a placebo control condition, both relaxation training alone and relaxation training in combination with cognitive therapy were equally effective in reducing headache symptoms. These results are consistent with an emerging pattern of evidence suggesting that APR alone can be a potent therapeutic tool as well as an important component of larger treatment packages.

Ultimately, however, appropriate application of APR depends on the clinician's ability to identify whether or not clients may benefit from them. A recent meta-analysis of relaxation training (Hyman, Feldman, Harris, Levin, & Malloy, 1989) suggested that effect sizes for relaxation training range from .43 to .66. Treatment of headache, insomnia, and hypertension consistently showed positive effects according to their analyses. On the other hand, treatment of chronic pain and anxiety showed low to moderate effectiveness. These results highlight the importance of clarifying patient expectations for treatment before training is begun. Relaxation training may not, and often does not, provide the complete symptom relief the client is seeking. Helping the client set reasonable expectations for the effectiveness of relaxation training is an important part of the training process. Effective relaxation training requires much of the clinician in order to adapt the basic APR procedures to the unique needs and experiences of the client seeking to enhance self-control.

## REFERENCES

Adler, C. M., Craske, M. G., & Barlow, D. H. (1987). Relaxation-induced panic (RIP): When resting isn't peaceful. *Integrative Psychiatry, 5,* 94–112.

Attanasio, V., Andrasik, F., & Blanchard, E. B. (1987). Cognitive therapy and relaxation training in muscle contraction headache: Efficacy and cost-effectiveness. *Headache, 27,* 254–260.

Beck, A., Ward, C. H., Mendelson, M., Mock, J., & Erbaugh, J. (1978). An inventory for measuring depression. *Archives of General Psychiatry, 4,* 561–571.

Benson, H. (1975). *The relaxation response.* New York: William Morrow.

Bernstein, D. A., & Borkovec, T. D. (1973). *Progressive relaxation training: A manual for the helping professions.* Champaign, IL: Research Press.

Bernstein, D. A., & Given, B. A. (1984). Progressive relaxation: Abbreviated methods. In R. Woolfolk & P. Lehrer (Eds.), *Principles and practice of stress management.* New York: Guilford Press.

Blanchard, E. B., & Andrasik, F. (1985). *Management of chronic headaches: A psychological approach.* New York: Pergamon Press.

Blanchard, E. B., Andrasik, F., Neff, D. F., Arena, J. G., Ahles, F. A., Jurish, S. E., Pallmeyer, J. P., Saunders, N. L., Teders, S. J., Barron, K. D., & Rodichok, L. D. (1982). Biofeedback and relaxation training with three kinds of headache: Treatment effects and their prediction. *Journal of Consulting and Clinical Psychology, 50,* 562–575.

Blanchard, E. B., Appelbaum, K. A., Guarnieri, P., Neff, D. F., Andrasik, F., & Jaccard, J. (1988). Two studies of the long-term follow-up of minimal therapist contact treatments of vascular and tension headache. *Journal of Consulting and Clinical Psychology, 56,* 427–432.

Blanchard, E. B., Appelbaum, K. A., Radnitz, C. L., Michultka, D., Morrill, B., Kirsch, C., Hillhouse, J., Evans, D. D., Guarnieri, P., Attanasio, V., Andrasik, F., Jaccard, J., & Dentiger, M. P. (1990). Placebo-controlled evaluation of abbreviated progressive muscle relaxation and of relaxation combined with cognitive therapy in the treatment of tension headache. *Journal of Consulting and Clinical Psychology, 58,* 210–215.

Borkovec, T. D. (1987). Commentary. *Integrative Psychiatry, 5,* 104–106.

Borkovec, T. D., & Mathews, A. M. (1988). Treatment of nonphobic anxiety disorders: A comparison of nondirective, cognitive, and coping desensitization therapy. *Journal of Consulting and Clinical Psychology, 56,* 877–884.

Borkovec, T. D., Mathews, A. M., Chambers, A., Ebrahimi, S., Lytle, R., & Nelson, R. (1987). The effects of relaxation training with cognitive or nondirective therapy and the role of relaxation-induced anxiety in the treatment of generalized anxiety. *Journal of Consulting and Clinical Psychology, 55,* 883–888.

Borkovec, T. D., & Sides, J. K. (1979). Critical procedural variables related to the physiological effects of progressive relaxation: A review. *Behavior Research and Therapy, 17,* 119–125.

Braith, J. A., McCullough, J. P., & Bush, J. P. (1988). Relaxation-induced anxiety in a subclinical sample of chronically anxious subjects. *Journal of Behavior Therapy and Experimental Psychiatry, 19,* 193–198.

Burish, T. G., Carey, M. P., Krozely, M. G., & Greco, F. A. (1987). Conditioned side effects induced by cancer chemotherapy: Prevention through behavioral treatment. *Journal of Consulting and Clinical Psychology, 55,* 42–48.

Carey, M. P., & Burish, T. G. (1987). Providing relaxation training to cancer chemotherapy patients: A comparison of three delivery techniques. *Journal of Consulting and Clinical Psychology, 55,* 732–737.

Carlson, C. R., Collins, F. L., Nitz, A. J., Sturgis, E. T., & Rogers, J. L. (1990). Muscle stretching as an alternative relaxation training procedure. *Journal of Behavior Therapy and Experimental Psychiatry, 21,* 29–38.

Carlson, C. R., Collins, F. L., Stewart, J. F., Porzelius, J., Nitz, J. A., & Lind, C. O. (1989). The assessment of emotional reactivity: A scale development and validation study. *Journal of Psychopathology and Behavioral Assessment, 11,* 313–325.

Carrington, P. (1977). *Freedom in meditation.* New York: Doubleday.

Chesney, M. A., Black, G. W., Swan, G. E., & Ward, M. M. (1987). Relaxation training for essential hypertension at the worksite: I. The untreated mild hypertensive. *Psychosomatic Medicine, 49,* 250–263.

Cram, J. R. (1988). Surface EMG recordings and pain-related disorders: A diagnostic framework. *Biofeedback and Self-Regulation, 13,* 123–138.

Davidson, R. J., & Schwartz, G. E. (1976). The psychobiology of relaxation and related states: A multi-process theory. In D. I. Mostofsky (Ed.), *Behavior control and modification of physiological activity.* Englewood Cliffs, NJ: Prentice-Hall.

Davison, G. C. (1966). Anxiety under total curarization: Implications for the role of muscular relaxation in the desensitization of neurotic fears. *Journal of Nervous and Mental Disease, 143,* 443–448.

Edinger, J. D., & Jacobsen, R. (1982). Incidence and significance of relaxation treatment side effects. *Behavior Therapist, 5,* 137–138.

Fried, R. (1987). *The hyperventilation syndrome.* Baltimore: Johns Hopkins University Press.

Gellhorn, E. (1958). The influence of curare on hypothalamic excitability and the electroencephalogram. *Electroencephalography and Clinical Neurophysiology, 10,* 697–703.

Gellhorn, E., & Kiely, W. F. (1962). Mystical states of consciousness: Neurophysiological and clinical aspects. *Journal of Nervous and Mental Disease, 154,* 399–405.

Gellhorn, E., & Loofbourrow, G. N. (1963). *Emotions and emotional disorders: A neurophysiological study.* New York: Harper & Row.

Halonen, J. S., & Passman, R. H. (1985). Relaxation training and expectation in the treatment of postpartum distress. *Journal of Consulting and Clinical Psychology, 53,* 839–845.

Hathaway, S. R., & McKinley, J. C. (1989). *Minnesota Multiphasic Personality Inventory-2.* Minneapolis: University of Minnesota Press.

Heide, F. J., & Borkovec, T. D. (1983). Relaxation-induced anxiety: Paradoxical anxiety enhancement due to relaxation training. *Journal of Consulting and Clinical Psychology, 51,* 171–182.

Hillenberg, B., & Collins, F. (1982). A procedural analysis and review of relaxation training research. *Behaviour Research and Therapy, 20,* 251–260.

Hoelscher, T. J., Lickstein, K. L., & Rosenthal, T. L. (1986). Home relaxation practice in hypertension treatment: Objective assessment and compliance induction. *Journal of Consulting and Clinical Psychology, 54,* 217–221.

Hyman, R. B., Feldman, H. R., Harris, R. B., Levin, R. F., & Malloy, G. B. (1989). The effects of relaxation training on clinical symptoms: A meta-analysis. *Nursing Research, 38,* 216–220.

Jacobson, E. (1970). *Modern treatment of tense patients.* Springfield, IL: Charles C Thomas.

Jacobson, E. (1977). The origins and development of progressive relaxation. *Journal of Behavior Therapy and Experimental Psychiatry, 8,* 119–123.

James, W. (1890). *Principles of psychology.* New York: Henry Holt.

Kiecolt-Glaser, J. K., Glaser, R., Williger, D., Stout, J., Messick, G., Sheppard, S., Ricker, D., Romisher, S. C., Briner, W., Bonnell, G., & Donnerberg, R. (1985). Psychosocial enhancement of immunocompetence in a geriatric population. *Health Psychology, 4,* 25–41.

King, N. J. (1980). Abbreviated progressive relaxation. In M. Hersen, R. M. Eisler, & P. M. Miller (Eds.), *Progress in behavior modification.* New York: Academic Press.

Lehrer, P. M. (1982). How to relax and how not to relax: A reevaluation of the work of Edmund Jacobson—I. *Behavior Research and Therapy, 20,* 417–428.

Lehrer, P. M., & Woolfolk, R. L. (1984). Are stress reduction techniques interchangeable, or do they have specific effects? A review of the comparative empirical literature. In R. L. Woolfolk & P. M. Lehrer (Eds.), *Principles and practice of stress management.* New York: Guilford Press.

Ley, R. (1988). Panic attacks during relaxation and relaxation-induced anxiety: A hyperventilation interpretation. *Journal of Behavior Therapy and Experimental Psychiatry, 19,* 253–259.

Lyles, J. N., Burish, T. G., Kroxely, M. G., & Oldham, R. K. (1982). Efficacy of relaxation training and guided imagery in reducing the adverseness of cancer chemotherapy. *Journal of Consulting and Clinical Psychology, 50,* 509–529.

Miller, S. M. (1987). Monitoring and blunting: Validation of a questionnaire to assess two styles of information-seeking under threat. *Journal of Personality and Social Psychology, 52,* 345–353.

Norton, G. R., Rhodes, L., Hauch, J., & Kaprowy, E. A. (1985). Characteristics of subjects experiencing relaxation and relaxation-induced anxiety. *Journal of Behavior Therapy and Experimental Psychiatry, 16,* 211–216.

Obrist, P. A. (1982). Cardiac-behavioral interactions: A critical appraisal. In J. T. Cacioppo & R. E. Petty (Eds.), *Perspectives in cardiovascular psychophysiology.* New York: Guilford Press.

Poppen, R. (1988). *Behavioral relaxation training and assessment.* New York: Pergamon Press.

Redd, W. H., & Andrykowski, M. A. (1982). Behavioral intervention in cancer treatment: Controlling aversion reactions to chemotherapy. *Journal of Consulting and Clinical Psychology, 50,* 1018–1029.

Reynolds, W. M., & Coats, K. I. (1986). A comparison of cognitive-behavioral therapy and relaxation training for the treatment of depression in adolescents. *Journal of Consulting and Clinical Psychology, 54,* 653–660.

Schwartz, G. E., Davidson, R. J., & Goleman, D. J. (1978). Patterning of cognitive and somatic processes in the self-regulation of anxiety: Effects of meditation versus exercise. *Psychosomatic Medicine, 40,* 321–328.

Sigmon, S. T., & Nelson, R. O. (1988). The effectiveness of activity scheduling and relaxation training in the treatment of spasmodic dysmenorrhea. *Journal of Behavioral Medicine, 11,* 483–495.

Smith, J. C. (1985). *Relaxation dynamics: Nine world approaches to self-relaxation.* Champaign, IL: Research Press.

Spielberger, C., Gorsuch, R., & Lushene, R. (1970). *The State-Trait Anxiety Inventory.* Palo Alto, CA: Consulting Psychologists Press.

Turkat, I. D., & Wolpe, J. (1985). Behavioral formulation of clinical cases. In I. D. Turkat (Ed.), *Behavioral case formulation.* New York: Plenum Press.

Wallston, B. S., Wallston, K. A., Kaplan, G. D., & Maides, S. A. (1976). Development and validation of the health locus of control scale. *Journal of Consulting and Clinical Psychology, 44,* 580–585.

Wolpe, J. (1958). *Psychotherapy by reciprocal inhibition.* Stanford, CA: Stanford University Press.

# CHAPTER 3

# SOCIAL SKILLS IN CHILDREN

Johnny L. Matson
Jay A. Sevin
Margaret L. Box

Social skills training began in the adult psychopathology literature with assertiveness training. Early studies dealt with dating skills of college students (McFall & Littlesand, 1971; McFall & Marston, 1970) and then with serious emotional disorders, most notably schizophrenia (Hersen & Bellack, 1976). Early successes with these approaches were noteworthy. Only later did researchers begin to focus on social skills training with children. Thus, social skills training with children has mirrored other treatments and has been extrapolated from therapies for emotional problems of adults. Efforts with children have been promising, however, and are the focus of this chapter.

Although various childhood problems have been acknowledged for centuries, the value of treating childhood psychopathology was not fully recognized until the twentieth century in the United States. Since then, the study and treatment of aggression, conduct, and learning problems have become cornerstones in the development of the field of mental health for young people. The study of social behavior in children grew with the realization that a range of skills were important both for childhood and for later adult adjustment (Frame & Matson, 1987). In Chicago, William Healy founded the Institute for Juvenile Research in 1909 to learn more about the causes and prevention of juvenile delinquency. Healy emphasized the role of social behavior in childhood problems. Lightner Witmer, another early leader in the field, also emphasized the necessity of a psychosocial approach in treating children (Peterson & Burbach, 1988). These early developments helped begin the momentum that has led to the current widespread interest in psychological interventions for children.

## IMPORTANCE OF SOCIAL SKILLS WITH CHILDREN

There is growing consensus that many social behaviors are learned primarily in the context of peer relationships (French & Tyne, 1982). It is likely that socialization leading to adaptive behavior patterns is heavily dependent on normal peer interactions (Hartup, 1976). Thus, social skills problems, which may lead to a child's exclusion from peer interactions and friendships, may limit social learning opportunities, leading to a cyclical pattern of peer rejection or isolation (Oden, 1980).

Social skills problems have been related to a wide range of childhood disorders. Accordingly, effective early treatment may head off a range of difficulties that become more severe with age. Social skills problems have been related to juvenile delinquency (Roff, Sells, & Golden, 1972), school maladjustment (Gronlund & Anderson, 1963), dropping out of school (Ullman, 1957), dishonorable military discharge (Roff, 1961), and mental health problems in later life (Cowen et al., 1973), including adult suicide (Stengel, 1971). In the mentally retarded population, social skills have important implications for determining severity of mental retardation (Grossman, 1983) and readiness for mainstreaming (Gresham, 1982a). Additionally, social skills problems have been linked to general maladjustment with peers at school and home (Wahler, 1976). A person's overall personality seems to be markedly affected by social problems. Kagan and Moss (1962) concluded that anxiety disorders, social interaction problems, and patterns of aberrant sexual behavior were related to social excesses and deficits. As noted before, these problems are compounded further by the negative stereotypes toward children that develop as a result of their social deficiencies (Barclay, 1966; Brown, 1954; Guinouard & Rychlak, 1982). Therefore, social skills are very important if one is to get along at school, at home, in the workplace, and in social leisure contexts outside the family unit.

The magnitude of social skills problems in childhood is considerable. Gronlund (1959) found that 12% of children in regular classrooms reported having only a single friend. Of these children, 6% stated that they had no friends. In their review, French and Tyne (1982) reported that 5% to 15% of elementary school students experience significant problems with interpersonal relationships. Strain, Cooke, and Apolloni (1976) found that 14% to 30% of a child clinical sample were referred for counseling services in connection with demonstrated low rates of social performance. Furthermore, social withdrawal is reported in 15% of referred children under the age of 6 (Gilbert, 1957). Given the widespread nature of these problems, it is no wonder that social skills training (SST) for children has become such a popular area of study for researchers.

## DEFINING THE PROBLEM

Despite general consensus regarding the importance of social skills in normal childhood development, researchers have failed to adopt a uniform way of defining social skills problems. In sociometric definitions, the degree of a child's acceptance in a peer group is taken as an indication of the child's level of social skills (Gresham, 1982a). Libet and Lewinsohn (1973) (cited in Gresham, 1981) defined social skills as behaviors that increase the probability that an individual will be reinforced and decrease the probability that the individual will be punished. Matson and Ollendick (1988) proposed that the socially skilled person is one who should be able to adapt well to his or her environment, avoiding both verbal and physical conflict through communication with others. Numerous other conceptualizations of social skills and social skills deficits have been presented in the literature. A few of the more prominent definitional systems will be reviewed in this section.

McFall (1982), in a well-known and often cited review paper, discussed the useful distinction between *trait* models and *molecular-behavioral* models. In trait models, social skills are considered to be an underlying personality characteristic. Observable social behavior is only a reflection of an underlying response predisposition. McFall (1982) all but dismissed trait approaches due to poor agreement between trait measures of social skills and difficulty in establishing construct validity. Also, trait measures have little relationship to performance in real-life scenarios (Bellack, Hersen, & Lamparski, 1979). Other authors have noted critically that trait approaches have not contributed to the development of effective interventions for social skills problems (Matson & Ollendick, 1988).

In molecular-behavioral models, by contrast, social skills are broken down into observable, operationally defined components. Social skills problems are diagnosed when a person exhibits inappropriate interpersonal behaviors or does not exhibit specific appropriate behaviors. Thus, social skills problems are defined in terms of specific behavioral excesses or deficits. A molecular approach allows for ease of both measurement and training. Also, behavioral models have contributed to the development of effective SST packages, which have typically come out of a tradition of operant conditioning and social learning theory (Matson & Ollendick, 1988). Although they have generally proved more useful than trait models,

McFall (1982) noted that molecular approaches also have their problems. For instance, they fail to define the most appropriate units of analysis. Also, when issues of social validity are not considered, purely molecular approaches can fail to define targets for intervention that are socially meaningful.

To address these problems, McFall (1982) presented an alternative two-tiered model in which social *skills* are differentiated from social *competence.* Social skills refer to specific behaviors or abilities that must be contained in the behavioral repertoire if one is to perform a given social task competently. Social competence refers to an *evaluation* of the adequacy of the *performance* of a social skill in a particular social context. Competence is not presented as a trait; rather, evaluations of competence are always task specific. McFall's (1982) system has parallels in several of the conceptualizations that are discussed later on (e.g., Gresham, 1982a; Oden, 1980).

Similar ideas are noted by Oden (1980). Social competence might be evaluated according to the child's knowledge of appropriate skills for various social situations and how skillfully the child applies that knowledge. Oden (1980) placed less emphasis on the evaluative nature of social competence, highlighted in McFall (1982). Instead, she highlighted the importance of taking personal status characteristics (race, sex, age, having an unusual name, etc.) into consideration when evaluating social skills. Personal status characteristics can influence peer rejection, which may limit an individual's opportunities to participate in social contexts. Thus, a child's acceptance does not directly correspond to social knowledge and skills. Rather, group acceptance is a function of social knowledge, skill in applying knowledge, and personal status characteristics.

In a different light, French and Tyne (1982) have suggested that children with peer relationship problems might be usefully classified as either *neglected* or *rejected* on the basis of peer nominations. Socially neglected children receive few positive nominations and few, if any, negative nominations. Socially rejected children also receive few positive peer nominations but receive a large number of negative nominations. Thus, both groups may have social skills deficits (e.g., seldom socially reinforce other children). Rejected children, however, also exhibit excesses of socially unacceptable behaviors (e.g., aggression). Some empirical support for this distinction exists (Green, Vosk, Forehand, & Beck, 1979; Gronlund & Anderson, 1957; Hartup, 1970; Hartup,

Glazer, & Chartsworth, 1967). This distinction may have important implications for treatment.

Kratochwill and French (1984) discussed an additional dimension to social skills problems in children, namely anxiety withdrawal. These authors, echoing the distinction made by French and Tyne (1982), focused on the important distinction between social withdrawal and conduct disorder. Social withdrawal may be associated with anxiety disorders, schizoid disorder, or elective mutism. Although socially withdrawn children may have difficulty establishing adult social relationships, they are less at risk for serious mental illness (e.g., schizophrenia) than are children with conduct disorders (Kohlberg, LaCrosse, & Ricks, 1972).

Cavell (1990) conceptualized social competence according to three factors: (1) social attainment, (2) peer acceptance, and (3) global judgments of social competence. *Social attainment* consists of physical health, adequate IQ, academic or occupational achievement, and appropriate level of motivational and emotional variables such as locus of control and self-esteem. *Peer acceptance* is the extent to which individuals are popular among their peers. The final factor, *global judgments,* includes molar behaviors such as leadership, aggression, and withdrawal. Cavell's (1990) model is representative of more comprehensive theoretical systems that have attempted to link specific, molecular skills with broader social constructs.

Puttalaz and Gottman (1982) highlighted the importance of using social validation to establish empirically the specific social behaviors that should be considered crucial to the concept of social skills. Previous models of social skills have been hampered by being overly theoretical. Specific behavioral deficits should be treated only if empirical evidence suggests that treatment of these target behaviors is warranted. In a review of empirical studies dealing with peer acceptance and childhood friendships, the authors noted six general dimensions that incorporate most of the skills considered to be important: (1) overall positiveness, (2) ability to resolve conflicts or disagreements, (3) awareness of group norms or social rules, (4) ability to communicate accurately, (5) ability to establish a common bond between oneself and others, and (6) positive self-perception.

Finally, Gresham (1988) suggested that social competence represents a multidimensional construct that includes adaptive behavior (e.g., independent functioning, vocational activity) as well as social skills. Social skills might be subclassified as academic performance, cooperative behaviors, social initiation behaviors, assertive behaviors, peer reinforcement behaviors, communication skills, problem-solving skills, and social self-efficacy. Social skills problems can be delineated into three basic types: skills deficits, performance deficits, and self-control deficits (Gresham, 1982a). A child has a social skills deficits if important social behaviors are not in the child's repertoire. This is similar to Bandura's (1977) notion of a learning deficit. When a child knows how to perform a given behavior but does not perform the behavior at acceptable levels, a performance deficit is diagnosed. The concept of a performance deficit is similar to McFall's (1982) concept of social competence. Performance deficits may emerge as a result of stimulus control problems—that is, when there are insufficient environmental cues or opportunities to perform a task. Also, performance deficits may emerge when reinforcement and punishment contingencies are insufficient to motivate appropriate social behavior. With self-control deficits, children may have social skills in their repertoire but fail to perform these skills because of *interfering behaviors.* Interference can take the form of response-inhibiting anxiety (e.g., phobic behavior), embarrassment (e.g., social anxiety), impulsivity (as in attention deficit disorder), or anger control problems. The concept of interfering behaviors is an important one. It highlights the frequent concordance of social skills problems and emotional disorders, which will be discussed in greater detail in the next section.

As is evident from the foregoing review, a uniform conceptualization of social skills has not been adopted in the literature. However, the studies cited here suggest several useful guidelines. At this time there is little evidence to support the utility of trait definitions (McFall, 1982). Molecular-behavioral definitions, which operationalize discrete behaviors for study and take into account situational specificity, appear to have greater merit in terms of facilitating assessment and treatment. However, molecular conceptualizations should also take into account the complex interplay of social and environmental events, setting variables, and the like that affect interpersonal behaviors. Also, concepts of social skills should include interaction effects of social behavior and variations in behavior based on the responses of others (Matson & Ollendick, 1988). The differentiation of skills versus performance deficits appears to be useful and has been adopted in some form by various authors (Gresham, 1982a; Matson & Ollendick, 1988; McFall, 1982; Oden, 1980). Also, personal status characteristics and self-control deficits frequently deserve attention in assessment and treatment of social skills problems. Further subdivisions of social skills problems offered in the literature (e.g., Gresham, 1988; Puttalaz & Gottman, 1982) have face validity but need further study. Future conceptualizations of social skills should focus on behaviors that predict important long-term social outcomes for children. Definitions will evolve with our understanding of relationships between specific deficits and risk for future problems (Putallaz & Gottman, 1982). The empirically establishment of the social significance of behavioral goals for social skills training should receive greater emphasis (Gresham, 1982b).

## RELATIONSHIP TO EMOTIONAL PROBLEMS

The importance of social skills might be further highlighted by examining the relationship between emotional disorders and social behavior. We have noted that social behavior is related to various problems of adjustment in children. Chief among these are disorders of *conduct.* Conduct disorders represent one-third to one-half of all family and school referrals for child mental health services (Gardner & Cole, 1986). It is generally accepted that conduct disorder is primarily a social phenomenon, characterized by persistent patterns of socially unacceptable behaviors and violations of societal norms (American Psychiatric Association, 1987). These considerations are important given that antisocial behaviors, unlike internalizing problems, are more likely to persist in adulthood (Campbell, 1989). Social skills training frequently represents a significant component in therapies for disorders of conduct (Baum, 1989).

Social adjustment problems are in fact exacerbated when a child is prone to emotional disorders. In discussions of social skills problems in children, depression is the most frequently noted of these disorders. Helsel and Matson (1984), for example, found greater social skills deficiencies in depressed children relative to the general population. These data are corroborated by research with adults on interrelationships of social and emotional disorders. Relationships between stressful life events (Brown & Harris, 1978), social support and family environment (Monroe, Bromet, Connell, & Steiner, 1986), and social coping skills (Billings & Moos, 1984) have been investigated in numerous studies.

Confirmation of these relationships has occurred recently in studies with adolescents. Hops, Lewinsohn, Andrews, and Roberts (1990) found that being prone to depression was related to perceptions of quality of familial relations and perceived social support. Familial interaction patterns appeared to be important in the formation of self-consciousness in social situations, negative body-self evaluations, and the ability to cope with major life stressors. Thus, the family may serve as a source for the development or lack of development of social skills that are preventative agents for serious emotional problems.

In addition to depression, correlations between social skills deficits and numerous other types of childhood psychopathology have been reported. In examining the Anxiety Disorders of childhood and adolescence, it is clear that several of these disorders have a strong social component. For instance, Separation Anxiety, at least in more severe cases, can be incapacitating, affecting relationships with parents and limiting interactions with almost everyone else. (The possibility of reverse causality also exists.) A social skills factor is even more evident in Avoidant Disorder of Childhood, which is characterized by serious impairment of social functioning in peer relationships. Also, Elective Mutism is characterized by various degrees of social withdrawal. Kagan and Moss (1962) concluded that Gender Identity Disorders and patterns of sexual behavior are often related to social skills problems. Also, it is consistently reported that many children with Attention Deficit Hyperactivity Disorder have problems with interpersonal relationships that may persist in adolescence and even adulthood (Whalen, 1989). In addition, social skills deficits have been termed a defining characteristic of mental retardation (Grossman, 1983) and are also being increasingly recognized as problematic in children with sensory impairments (Matson, Heinze, Helsel, & Kapperman, 1986; Matson & Ollendick, 1988).

Thus, although social isolation may occur in the absence of emotional disorders, social skills problems also frequently represent a significant component in most types of childhood psychopathology. The current interest in developing effective methods of assessing and treating social skills deficits is warranted given these data. The need for effective social skills training and psychosocial interventions is likely to persist even with the advent of effective drugs for emotional problems. Psychotropic drugs eliminate some problems; but they cannot train new skills nor otherwise teach a child how to deal with conflict situations, problems that often trigger or exacerbate emotional disorders.

## ASSESSMENT

Effective intervention depends on reliable and valid detection of behaviors for intervention. In the last two decades, numerous methods have been developed for assessing social skills in children. Early assessment strategies had numerous shortcomings, emphasizing face validity over generalizability, psychometric factors, and social validity (Bellack, 1983). However, the assessment of social skills in children has become much more sophisticated in the last few years.

Gresham (1988) offers several general guidelines for the assessment process. First, the primary goal of assessment should be the collection of information needed for intervention planning. An assessment strategy should be employed with an individual child only if it contributes unique or corroborative data to problem analysis and treatment planning. Thus, a *specific problem-solving* approach is recommended over the standard assessment battery approach. Second, assessment might be loosely described as serving three functions: problem classification, intervention planning, and evaluation of intervention effects. The examiner should know which of these functions various assessment strategies serve. In general, "intervention" strategies serve more critical roles than "classification" strategies. Third, a strategy can be classified as an "intervention" method to the extent that it contributes to the *functional analysis* of behavior. That is, assessment strategies that provide data on the antecedents, sequences, and consequences of social behaviors are most important for effective treatment. Fourth, different assessment strategies frequently tap different dimensions of social behavior. Therefore, multimodal assessment is typically recommended. Several of the most frequently used methods of assessing social skills in clinical research and practice will be briefly reviewed in the remainder of this section.

### Sociometric Ratings

In early studies, the most common methods for evaluating childhood social competence were sociometric strategies (Moreno, 1934). Sociometric methods include *peer nominations* and *peer ratings*. Peer nominations can be positive or negative. In positive nominations, children in a social group (e.g., a classroom) are asked to list their best friends in the group (usually limited to three or five friends). Similarly, in negative nominations, children are asked to list the children in the social group whom they do not like. The number of nominations a child receives is thought to reflect his or her relative peer status within the group. In peer ratings, children are asked to rate *each child* in the social group according to some specified social or interpersonal dimension. Likert scale scoring is typically employed here.

There are several advantages to using sociometric ratings. Sociometrics directly utilize peer information. They provide a good indication of a child's peer status. They provide important information on how peers see each other. Also, they can be easily adapted for use with younger children by using pictures of classmates rather than lists of names. Several researchers have reported good psychometric properties of sociometric methods, including good temporal stability (Busk, Ford, & Schulman, 1973), internal consistency (Gresham, 1981), criterion validity (Asher & Hymel, 1981), and social validity (Gresham, 1982b). There is some evidence that peer ratings show greater temporal stability than nominations and that positive nominations are more stable than negative nominations (French & Tyne, 1982). These three methods probably tap slightly different dimensions. Peer ratings may tap overall peer acceptance, whereas nominations tap the extent to which children are best friends with or least liked by peers (Asher & Hymel, 1981). As discussed previously, the use of positive and negative nominations in conjunction may allow the differentiation of neglected versus rejected children (French & Tyne, 1982; Hymel & Asher, 1977). Peer nominations also allow one to assess reciprocity of relationships—that is, whether children are nominated by the children whom they nominate.

There are also several disadvantages to using sociometric techniques. The information provided is fairly global in nature. Sociometric data generally serve the function of classification. Although they have been used occasionally to assess treatment outcome (e.g., Bierman, Miller, & Stabb, 1987), sociometric ratings provide little information regarding antecedents and consequences of social behavior, availability of social cues, and the like. Thus, they are seldom useful in functional analyses. Not surprisingly, a lack of correspondence between sociometric and direct observational/behavioral data is frequently reported (Bierman et al., 1987, Van Hasselt, Hersen, Whitehill, & Bellack, 1979). Finally, using sociometrics to collect repeated measures data is typically impractical.

## Social Skills Checklists

The last decade has seen the advent of a few standardized social skills rating scales for children. This section will focus on two such scales, the Matson Evaluation of Social Skills with Youngsters (MESSY; Matson, Rotatori, & Helsel, 1983) and the Teacher's Rating of Social Skills (TROSS-C; Clark, Gresham, & Elliott, 1985).

The Matson Evaluation of Social Skills with Youngsters (Matson et al., 1983) has received a good deal of attention as a checklist to assess social skills. It is the most heavily researched standardized social skills checklist for children (Matson & Ollendick, 1988). The MESSY consists of 62 items on the self-report version and 64 items on the teacher/parent report. Items are rated using a five-point Likert scale. Typical items include: (1) "I tell people they look nice"; (2) "I ask if I can be of help"; (3) "I get into fights a lot"; (4) "I become angry easily"; (5) "I am bossy"; (6) "I laugh at other people's jokes and funny stories"; (7) "I join in games with other people"; and (8) "I slap or hit when I am angry." The initial sample for the MESSY consisted of 744 children and youths between 4 and 18 years of age from schools in the Midwest (Matson et al., 1983). Good interrater and test–retest reliability have been established, and the MESSY has been factor-analyzed.

Emergent factors on the self-report version include: (1) appropriate social skills; (2) inappropriate assertiveness; (3) impulsivity/recalcitrance; (4) overconfidence; and (5) jealousy/withdrawal. The MESSY has also proved useful in studying social skills deficits in handicapped children. For example, using the MESSY, Macklin and Matson (1985) found that hearing-impaired children were typically less assertive than nonhandicapped peers. This finding corresponds to research demonstrating that persons with sensory handicaps are more likely to evince social inactivity. These data are not surprising given the typical lack of verbal communication skills in this group.

Another measure of social skills with children is the TROSS-C (Clark et al., 1985). The scale consists of 52 items filled out by the child's teacher. Typical items are: (1) completes classroom assignments within required time; (2) uses free time in an acceptable manner; (3) interacts with peers; (4) invites peers to play; (5) displays sense of humor; (6) invites peers to join an ongoing activity or group; and (7) praises peers. This scale compliments the MESSY by emphasizing school-related problems, obviously a major concern with children. Psychometric data are promising (Clark et al., 1985). The standardization sample of 250 children from four diagnostic groups included children with behavior disorders, learning disabilities, and mental retardation as well as nonhandicapped children (Gresham, Elliot, & Black, 1986).

The MESSY and TROSS-C represent important additions to the social skills assessment literature, given their focuses on interpersonal behaviors in children. Advantages of using checklists include: (1) they are quick and easy to use; (2) they allow the collection of quantifiable data; (3) they allow the evaluation of a wide range of social behaviors; and (4) they have potential utility as outcome measures in treatment programs (Van Hasselt et al., 1979). Checklists might also be used to assess appropriate targets for intervention. Disadvantages include their total reliance on informant data. Also, checklists provide little information regarding the specific antecedents and consequences of social behaviors. Therefore, it is recommended that checklists be used in conjunction with direct observational data.

## Behavioral Observations

Direct observational data are an essential component of any behavioral assessment. Typically, a number of specific social behaviors are selected as targets for intervention. These behaviors are carefully operationally defined to enhance interrater reliability. Dimensions of recording may include event recording, frequency counts, time sampling, or assessment of duration of target behaviors. Common examples of target behaviors in social assessments from the literature include frequency of peer and teacher interactions, duration of social contact and frequency of verbal acknowledgements (Kratochwill & French, 1984).

In some respects, direct observation is the simplest method for assessing social behaviors in children. It is certainly the most direct method of measuring behavior. Social behavior can be measured in naturalistic settings where they are actually occurring (Gresham, 1988). Also, direct measures of behavior are less prone to memory errors (Gresham, 1982a). Additional advantages include the fact that direct observations provide essential data for functional analyses of behavior. Antecedents and consequences of social events and interpersonal behaviors can be directly observed. Direct observational data are also sensitive to the effects of social skills training (Strain et al., 1976). Oden (1980) has cautioned that direct

observations should be conducted in multiple settings given the situational specificity of many appropriate and inappropriate social behaviors. Moreover, when multiple setting observations are accomplished, important questions regarding the nature of interpersonal deficits can often be answered. Does the child have a skills deficit or a performance deficit? Does the child evidence the target skill in some settings but not others? If so, are there insufficient cues or opportunities in settings where social skills appear to be absent? Can skill performance be increased by providing additional or more salient cues? Are the reinforcement contingencies different in different settings or with different peer groups? Does the child have problems primarily with peer relationships in group situations or in dyadic relationships? Direct observational data often play a critical role in answering these questions.

Despite these advantages, there are also numerous difficulties encountered in conducting direct observations of social behaviors. Van Hasselt et al. (1979) note that there is tremendous variability in the complexity and types of behavior observation systems employed by different researchers. The examiner must choose the level at which observations will be made. Focusing on global, molar behaviors may be of little use in planning interventions (Bellack, 1983). Working at too molecular a level may obscure the big picture (Matson & Ollendick, 1988), failing to take into account complex interactions between environmental and behavioral events. Bellack (1983) recommends working at an intermediary level. Also, the examiner must take into account possible effects caused by expectancies, reactivity to the observational process, rater drift, instructions to clients, various situational contexts, variations in confederate behavior across sessions, and the like (Bellack, 1983; Sattler, 1988; Van Hasselt et al., 1979). Collecting interrater reliability data on a percentage of rated sessions is recommended to offset some of these problems (Reid, 1970).

## Behavioral Role-Plays

Direct observations of target responses may be employed in role-plays. Role-play scenes are typically based on critical incidents of problem behavior. For example, a situation might unfold as follows: (Narrator) "You are talking with a friend when Billy the brat comes over and says . . ." (Role-model prompt) "You are a real dummy." (Child's Response) "_____." The child's response would then be scored on a Likert rating of 1 (bad) to 5 (very good) or based on a rating of occur/does not occur. Target behaviors might include eye contact (looking at the person's eyes), verbal content (what the person says in response to the role-model prompt), tone of voice (affect appropriate to the situation including happy, sad, angry), and so on.

Role-plays are particularly useful for assessing behaviors that are difficult to observe in naturalistic settings because of low frequency of occurrence. Also, role-plays may represent the only viable alternative when it is impossible in the naturalistic setting to manipulate the social stimuli that lead to target responses. In addition, role-plays allow exposure of the client to multiple trials of the target scenario in a small amount of time. That is, they have the advantage of being more controlled and more concentrated.

Serious disadvantages to using role-play formats have also been reported in the literature. The chief concern regards external validity (Matson & Ollendick, 1988; Van Hasselt et al., 1979). Several authors have reported that role-plays typically show low correlations with social behaviors exhibited in naturalistic settings (Gresham, 1982a). It is possible that role-plays assess knowledge of appropriate social behavior rather than typical performance. Gresham (1982b) also discussed problems regarding social validity and noted that there is little evidence that role-play performance correlates with performance on other social tasks that predict socially important outcomes. Results from studies with psychiatric patients and college students have also indicated that external validity may be a problem (Bellack, Hersen, & Turner, 1978; Van Hasselt et al., 1979). Bellack (1983) noted that in some children skills deficits may become apparent only when they are persistently thwarted or when they are faced with an uncooperative environment. Because a child's initial response may be appropriate, single-prompt role-plays may be insufficient to detect problems. Thus, at the very least, multiple-prompt role-plays may be necessary.

## General Measures of Adjustment

Several general measures of child psychopathology include subscales that measure social behaviors. An example of this is the Child Behavior Checklist (CBCL; Achenbach & Edelbrock, 1983). The CBCL is one of the most prominent rating scales for measuring child behavior problems (Schneider & Byrne, 1989). It includes three scales labeled as measures of social competence: activities, social, and school. For two subscales, activities and social, weight is given to time spent in socially relevant activities. The items are indirect measures of social behavior because emphasis is placed on outcomes versus the social behaviors that promote successes in this area. Thus, doing well in sports and extracurricular activities is emphasized. Other general measures containing social skills subscales include the Behavior Problem Checklist (Quay & Peterson, 1975), the Vineland Adaptive Behavior Scale (Sparrow, Balla, & Cicchetti, 1984), and the AAMD Adaptive Behavior Scale (Lambert, Windmiller, Thoringer, & Cole, 1975).

In our view, general measures of psychopathology and adaptive behavior have limited utility in assessing social skills problems. They rarely measure interpersonal behaviors in great enough detail to contribute to functional analyses of behavior or treatment planning. However, given that social skills problems represent significant components in many types of childhood psychopathology, general screening measures might be incorporated into larger assessment batteries. From a research standpoint, general measures may be useful for studying relationships between social skills deficits and emotional and behavioral disorders. They may also be used for assessing anxiety, impulsivity, and other behaviors that may interfere with social skills performance (Gresham, 1982a).

## Behavioral Interviews

Behavioral interviews can represent an important component of the assessment process. Gresham (1988) noted that behavioral interviews can provide information critical to functional analyses of behavior. Oden (1980) commented that interviews with children may provide information regarding knowledge of social norms and whether the child realizes that he or she has problems relating to peers. Interviews with parents and teachers may help detect receptivity to various interventions as well as unrealistic expectations regarding therapy (Gresham, 1982a). With a few exceptions, however, (e.g., Senatore, Matson, & Kazdin, 1982), researchers have seldom used behavioral interviews to study social skills in children systematically.

## Additional Considerations

On the basis of visual inspection, several of the assessment measures described here appear to tap different dimensions of social behavior in children.

This has, in fact, been corroborated in empirical studies. Bierman and her colleagues conducted two studies relevant to this topic. In the first (Bierman & Furman, 1984), children were assigned to one of four treatment groups: conversational skills training, a goal-oriented group experience, a treatment combination condition, or no treatment. Children with skills training improved on measures of conversational skills, the peer involvement group enjoyed an improved status in sociometric ratings, and children in combined conditions improved on both measures. The lack of concordance between measures indicates that sociometrics and behavioral measures were tapping different dimensions of social behavior.

In the second study (Bierman et al., 1987), children were assigned to either (1) a social instructions condition focusing on positive social behaviors, (2) a prohibition condition to reduce negative behaviors, or (3) combined treatments. Again, different treatments resulted in different improvements on the various measures of social competence. Sociometric status changed only for children in the combined treatment group.

Additional support for the notion that different measures tap different dimensions of social behavior can be found in a study by Matson, Esveldt-Dawson, and Kazdin (1983). Children were assessed using multiple social skills measures, including performance on behavioral role-play tests, peer nominations, teacher ratings of popularity, the MESSY, and structured interviews. Peer nominations and teacher ratings were significantly correlated ($r = .62$). However, role-play performance failed to correlate significantly with either child or teacher ratings. In an additional study (Kazdin, Matson, & Esveldt-Dawson, 1984), data on role-play performance, knowledge of social skills, self-efficacy, and overt social behavior were collected for 38 psychiatric inpatient children. Role-play data correlated poorly with overt measures of social behavior. Measures completed by informants did converge and delineated diagnostic groups of children. Taken together, these studies highlight the importance of multimodal assessment. Single measures may not provide the range of data necessary to produce a broad-band assessment that provides a clear picture of social strengths and weaknesses.

As noted before, a second important point relates to the limited roles a particular assessment strategy may serve. Sociometrics, checklists, and general measures of psychopathology, which provide comparison data, are useful in broadly identifying and classifying social skills problems. Checklists, direct observations, and behavioral interviews can assist in target behavior selection and treatment planning. Direct observational data and behavioral interviews are most critical for conducting functional analyses of behavior. Sociometrics, checklists, and direct observations are useful for evaluating treatment outcome. In general, assessment strategies that lend themselves to easy repeated measures over time are important here. General measures of psychopathology are useful in assessing broader based problems that may have an impact on social behavior.

A third important point relates to social validity. Assessment and treatment should focus on behaviors that predict important social outcomes. Gresham (1982b) categorized social skills assessment strategies according to their social validity properties. Type I measures included direct measures of socially valued goals. These included sociometrics, teacher or parent ratings, and some school archival data. Type II measures had straightforward construct validity and demonstrated empirical relationships with Type I measures. These included direct observations of overt social behavior, role-play tests, self-report inventories, and behavioral interview data. Type III measures, which are the least socially valid strategies, included behavioral role-play measures, social problem-solving scales, and performance on social cognition tasks.

Given the frequent concurrence of social skills problems and child psychopathology, a fourth point relates to the importance of broad-based assessment. In assessing social skills deficits, the examiner should be aware of possible concomitant problems including anxiety, depression, hyperactivity, elective mutism, and the like (Kratochwill & French, 1984). These conditions may have a direct bearing on a child's social skills problems. In some children, treatment efficacy may hinge on whether these additional issues are taken into consideration.

Formerly, the goal of assessment was classification and diagnosis. The primary focus has shifted to identification of target behaviors for intervention and evaluation of the effectiveness of specified treatment plans. This linkage between assessment and intervention is no better utilized than in the social skills literature.

## TREATMENT

The remainder of this chapter will focus on the treatment of social skills problems in children. Research and clinical efforts in this area have been very positive and are likely to be of considerable value in ameliorating a range of problems. Intervention strategies are typically classified as operant conditioning procedures, coaching, social learning therapies, cognitive-behavioral therapies, social skills curricula, or self-instructional strategies. (Throughout this discussion, the reader will note that most social skills training packages actually include components from more than one of these categories.) Given the rapid growth of research in this area, a comprehensive review is beyond the scope of this chapter. However, each of these topics will be briefly reviewed, and representative studies will be discussed. Following this, treatment comparison studies and general summaries of the social skills treatment literature will be presented. The reader is referred to Gresham (1985), Matson and Ollendick (1988), and Schneider and Byrne (1985) for reviews of additional studies.

## Operant Conditioning Procedures

Operant methods, derived from the applied behavior analysis literature, were the first techniques used to treat social skills problems in children. Operant training packages typically include components such as reinforcement, punishment, shaping, chaining, and related behavior management procedures. Target behaviors are typically operationally defined, overt, molecular social behaviors such as eye contact, greeting responses, sharing behaviors, peer initiations, or aggression.

Several authors have reported marked changes in social behaviors accomplished using simple contingency management programs. Typical of these studies was a paper by Hart, Reynolds, Baer, Brawley, and Harris (1968). The authors worked with a 5-year-old girl in her preschool classroom. The primary aim of the study was increasing cooperative play (pulling a child in a wagon, sharing, helping the child during play, etc.). Treatment, administered by the child's teacher, consisted of contingent reinforcement of approximations of appropriate play behaviors. Initially, these included simple verbalizations to children who were playing. Later, actual playing was reinforced. Proximity to children was also targeted. Treatment resulted in dramatic increases in target responses.

Social skills deficits in mentally retarded children have also been a frequent focus in the literature. Hopkins (1968) used a reinforcement-based approach consisting of edibles and social interactions. Smiling was increased in two children using an established reinforcement schedule. Ball playing of two mentally retarded boys was treated in a similar fashion by Whitman, Mercurio, and Caponigri (1970). However, in addition to edible and social reinforcers, physical prompts and verbal instructions were used.

With emotionally disturbed and developmentally disabled children, the combination of reinforcement and punishment methods is common. Typically, differential reinforcement methods are combined with overcorrection, time out, or similar methods to deal with aggression and/or noncompliance. For example, Azrin and Powers (1975) used overcorrection and reinforcement to eliminate classroom disturbances of emotionally disturbed children.

In almost every study of contingency management and social skills, the role of reinforcement contingencies in increasing appropriate social behaviors has been demonstrated (e.g., Allen, Hart, Buell, Harris, & Wolf, 1964; Buell, Stoddard, Harris, & Baer, 1968; Whitman et al., 1970). In addition, in classroom or group settings, treatment gains are often found to generalize to nontreated peers (Strain & Timm, 1974; Strain et al., 1976). Despite reported successes, however, several authors have commented on the relative lack of generalization and maintenance data in studies employing operant techniques alone (Marchetti & Campbell, 1990; Van Hasselt et al., 1979).

## Coaching

Several social skills training packages have been loosely classified as "coaching" procedures. Coaching usually consists of specific verbal instructions regarding a social behavior. Following instructions, the child is given the opportunity to practice the target behavior with another child. Typically, coaching is used in conjunction with verbal feedback and contingent reinforcement. In a typical study, Oden and Asher (1977) targeted play behaviors in third and fourth graders. Target behaviors included game participation, sharing, communicating (e.g., talking and listening), and supportive behaviors (e.g., giving attention or help). Treatment included verbal instructions, active rehearsal, and postplay review sessions. Treatment resulted in improved sociometric status for children in the coaching condition. These gains were maintained for most subjects at one-year follow-up.

In a second study, Ladd (1979) used a similar treatment package employing direct guided rehearsal with gradual fading of prompts with third graders. Target behaviors included asking positive questions, offering useful suggestions, and being helpful to others. Treatment resulted in marked improvements in target behaviors. Peer acceptance and specific social skills continued to improve at one-month follow-up.

Coaching strategies have proved useful in several additional studies (Gresham, 1985; Kratochwill & French, 1984). However, the frequent inclusion of instructions, active rehearsal, feedback, and reinforcement makes it difficult to determine which components of therapy are essential for promoting social gains.

## Social Learning Approaches

Social learning approaches became popular in the 1970s through the work of McFall (1982) and associates, who described their approach as assertion training, and that of Hersen and Bellack (1976), who used social skills training to remediate many problems exhibited by schizophrenic adults. Social learning strategies are characterized by their emphasis on modeling or role playing. In actual practice, social learning packages typically include some combination of instructions, modeling, role playing, behavioral rehearsal, performance feedback, and social or material reinforcement. Social learning strategies have become perhaps the most popular social skills training approaches, especially for children without serious intellectual impairments.

Serna, Schumaker, and Hazel (1986) demonstrated the utility of social learning strategies for training numerous interactional behaviors. Targeted skills included giving and accepting criticism and giving and following instructions. Specifically, several behaviors were taught, including facing a speaker, maintaining eye contact, keeping a neutral facial expression, maintaining straight posture, getting a person's attention by calling his or her name, stating instructions in the form of a request, being specific about a request, giving a rationale for the request, asking if listeners understood the instructions that were given, and explaining the instructions further if they were not understood. A sequence of responses were also trained, including nonverbal behaviors such as appropriate eye contact, facial expression, body posture, and head nods.

In a recent study, Matson, Fee, Coe, and Smith (1991) used a social learning package to train appropriate social skills (e.g., greeting responses, requests for toys) and decrease inappropriate social behaviors (e.g., tantrums, aggression, grabbing toys). Subjects included 28 4- and 5-year-old children with developmental disabilities. Treatment consisted of modeling, role playing, instructions, and reinforcement of target behaviors. Also, instructions were explained using puppets, given the children's limited attention spans

for didactic training. Significant differences were noted between treatment and control groups on specific target behaviors. Gains were not noted in social play, which was not directly taught in the training program, suggesting the importance of treating individually each behavior of concern.

Social skills training has proven to be applicable for a range of serious problems of adolescents. In a study by Warzak and Page (1990), two sexually active female adolescents were taught refusal skills. Eye contact, refusal, and specifying the unacceptability of sexual behavior were trained. Role playing, modeling, behavioral rehearsal, feedback, and reinforcement were employed. Reports by staff responsible for the care of subjects confirmed reduced rates of sexual activity, although there are obvious potential problems with the reliability of the dependent measures. Nonetheless, the potential utility of this type of intervention for such extreme social problems would appear to warrant further study.

Other studies have confirmed the utility of modeling and other social learning strategies for teaching social skills to children and adolescents (Gottman, 1977; Keller & Carlson, 1974; Matson & Ollendick, 1988; O'Connor, 1969, 1972). As with coaching procedures, however, the multicomponent nature of most social learning packages makes evaluating essential intervention components difficult. The relative effectiveness of modeling strategies will be further discussed later on.

## Cognitive-Behavioral Strategies

Cognitive therapy is a loosely defined group of techniques that take into account specific "internal events." Emphasis is placed on the client's participation in treatment. Common training focuses include decision making, problem-solving skills, knowledge of social norms, perspective taking, self-reinforcement, and other self-regulatory methods. The assumption is that increased social knowledge and improved problem-solving skills will translate into social effectiveness. Restated, changing problem-solving processes is thought to result in behavioral changes in naturalistic settings. Several authors have questioned these assumptions (e.g., Gresham, 1985). Nevertheless, cognitive-behavioral strategies are frequently used in social skills training with adolescents. As with previous treatments, cognitive-behavioral packages typically employ a mix of strategies, including cognitive, behavioral, and social learning components.

Sarason and Sarason (1981) developed a social skills training package for students in a high school with high dropout and delinquency rates. Subjects included 127 adolescents. Treatment focused on: (1) increased awareness of the consequences of an action, (2) available alternatives in a situation, (3) the effects of one's behavior on another/perspective taking, and (4) communication skills. Research was carried out in class sessions as part of a regular course. Treatment included role-plays, live and videotaped modeling of both cognitions and behaviors, and feedback. Sessions dealt with job interviews, resisting peer pressure, asking for help in school, asking questions in class, getting along with parents, dealing with job frustration, and other topics. Subjects in the social skills training group were able to generate more and better solutions to conflict situations and also handled themselves better in job interviews. At one-year follow-up, treatment subjects showed lower rates of tardiness, absences, and behavior referrals. Furthermore, the treatment was cost-effective, in that it was administered to large groups of children in a classroom setting.

A second illustrative study focused on increasing social skills of six shy adolescents (Christoff, Scott, Kelley, Schlundt, & Kelly, 1985). Problem-solving skills, conversational skills (e.g., self-disclosures, positive opinions), and self-esteem measures were included. In problem-solving training, adolescents practiced recognizing problems, generating solutions, and evaluating solutions. Conversational training included modeling and active rehearsal as well as therapist feedback. Treatment resulted in subjects' ability to solve peer relationship problems more effectively. Also, conversational skills showed improvements on various dependent measures. Moreover, global ratings of ease of social interacting and conversing with others were made by parents and teachers. Thus, this study is also noteworthy for its inclusion of several social validity measures that corroborated the social importance of treatment gains.

## Social Skills Curricula

Several social skills training curricula have been used with children and adolescents. Also in line with this approach is the use of games. Foxx, Faw, and Nisbett (1991), for example, used the latter approach with emotionally disturbed children averaging 11 years of age. Their game was a commercially available one, *Sorry*. This was incorporated with the *Stacking the Deck* social skills training program

(Foxx & McMorrow, 1983). A specially designed twelve-card deck containing social situations was substituted for the regular *Sorry* card deck. Each card contained a situation designed to elicit a complex verbal response before a subject's game piece could be moved. On the basis of answers to these cards: (1) the trainer provided responses specific to verbal feedback (e.g., good answer, a better answer might be . . . ); (2) clients were allowed to move game pieces only when they responded correctly; (3) clients self-monitored by recording their number of correct responses; and (4) $1.00 was given to those who met their individualized performance criteria. Finally, a client could earn a $1.00 bonus for surpassing these criteria. This approach proved to be very effective. The additional structure of the curriculum/game seems to be becoming more popular as a treatment method. A more detailed step-by-step twelve-week curriculum (Ollendick, 1982), addressing multiple social and classroom skills, is outlined in Matson and Ollendick (1988).

## Self-Instructional Training

In the last few years, a trend in the literature has emerged emphasizing teaching children to be more independent and to assume more responsibility for their problems. In line with this trend, a few social skills training studies have begun to incorporate self-instructional components into their treatment batteries.

For example, Dougherty, Fowler, and Paine (1985) treated playground behavior of two children, 9 and 10 years of age, with mild and moderate mental retardation. Target behaviors included negative interactions (e.g., criticisms, name calling, rough bodily contact, property destruction), positive interactions (social behaviors directed towards a peer and not rated as negative), rule infractions (e.g., leaving the playground), and others. Treatment included an adaptation of the RECESS program by Walker et al. (1978). Initially, adult monitoring and a point system were used to decrease negative interactions exhibited by the first child. In later sessions, reductions were maintained first by peer monitoring and then by self-monitoring. In the next phase of the study, the first subject was trained to serve as a peer monitor for the second subject. Authors reported adaptation of the point system for peer monitors and self-monitors without loss of effectiveness. Also, serving as a peer monitor for another child had additional benefits for the first subject.

In a second study, Matson and Adkins (1980) used a self-instructional training package to teach social skills to two mentally retarded institutionalized young adults. Target behaviors included initiating conversations, making compliments, and making appropriate requests or responses to requests. Several inappropriate social behaviors (e.g., cursing, making unreasonable requests) were also targeted for reduction. Training included having subjects listen to social skills audiotapes. Following this, active rehearsal of social behaviors, which had been discussed on the tapes, was conducted in sessions with a therapist. Treatment resulted in marked increases in appropriate verbal interactions and decreases in inappropriate responding. In addition, it was cost-effective, requiring less staff time than standard social skills training packages.

Initial studies have indicated the potential utility of self-instructional components in social skills training. Chief advantages include their cost-effectiveness and face validity. However, few studies employing these interventions have been conducted. Additional studies appear warranted.

## Treatment Comparison Studies

Given the demonstrated effectiveness of social skills training packages for children, a few researchers have begun to evaluate the relative effectiveness of different training procedures. Treatment comparison studies represent a major step in the elucidation of critical components for effective therapy.

Gresham and Nagle (1980) conducted the first treatment comparison of coaching versus modeling procedures. Subjects included 40 socially isolated third and fourth graders. Children were assigned to coaching, modeling, mixed abbreviated modeling and coaching, or control conditions. Dependent measures included sociometric rating scales, peer nomination measures, and behavioral observations of specific social skills. Coaching and modeling conditions both included multiple behavioral and social learning components and differed primarily in the use of live verbal instructions versus videotaped models. Coaching and modeling were both effective and generally equivalent for teaching social skills to subjects, as measured by sociometric and behavioral indices. Combined treatment was not superior to either the modeling or the coaching condition.

Matson and Senatore (1981) conducted the first study comparing social skills training and traditional

psychotherapy with mildly mentally retarded individuals. Subjects ($n = 35$) were randomly assigned to social skills training, traditional psychotherapy, or no-treatment/control conditions. Traditional therapy emphasized establishing group cohesion and expressing feelings. Social skills training included active rehearsal of specific social behaviors, feedback, social reinforcement, and role-plays. Social skills training was significantly more effective than traditional psychotherapy and no-treatment for improving interpersonal behaviors. Gains included both increases in appropriate and reductions in inappropriate verbal statements.

Bierman and Furman (1984) studied variations in social skills training packages. Subjects included 56 fifth and sixth graders. Children were randomly assigned to: (1) conversational skills training (individual coaching), (2) peer involvement under superordinate goals (group experience), (3) combined treatments, or (4) a control condition. Several interesting group differences were noted. Children who received individual coaching showed marked long-term improvements in conversation skills during dyadic and small-group interactions. These conclusions were based on data from multiple measures. In contrast, children in the peer involvement group primarily showed marked but temporary gains in sociometric status. Only children in the combined condition shared general sustained improvements in peer acceptance in addition to social skills and peer interaction rates. The study suggested that different treatments may be associated with gains in different dimensions of social behavior.

In a separate study, Bierman and her colleagues evaluated the relative effectiveness of the components of an operant/coaching treatment package (Bierman et al., 1987). Six- to 10-year-old boys ($n = 32$) were assigned to: (1) instructions to promote positive social skills, (2) prohibitions to reduce negative social behaviors, (3) combined treatment, or (4) a no-treatment condition. The instruction condition included verbal instructions and practice of several social skills (e.g., sharing, helping others). The prohibition condition included a response cost procedure for negative conduct, but prosocial behaviors were not rewarded. As in the aforementioned study, only children in the combined treatment condition received improved sociometric ratings from nontarget peers. Children in the prohibition group showed decreased negative behaviors but only temporary increases in peer acceptance. Children in the instruction condition improved on specific social targets. Improvements were less immediate but more stable at six-week follow-up. The study suggests the importance of targeting both appropriate social gains and negative behavior reductions.

The final treatment comparison study involved adults but is equally relevant to this topic. Senatore, Matson, and Kazdin (1982) treated interpersonal behaviors of 35 mentally retarded adults. Subjects were assigned to one of three treatment conditions. The first condition was a standard social skills training (SST) package including instructions, modeling, performance feedback, reinforcement, and role-plays. The second condition was identical to SST with the addition of an active rehearsal component in which subjects overtly practiced social behaviors with the assistance of therapist prompts. The third group consisted of a no-treatment/control condition. Both treatment groups showed improvements in interpersonal behaviors. However, active rehearsal led to significantly greater improvements than SST alone on both role-play and behavioral interview measures. These differential improvements were maintained at six-month follow-up. The data suggest that active rehearsal may be an important treatment component, at least with individuals with intellectual impairments.

## Review Studies

We conclude the section on treatment of social skills by briefly discussing two large-scale review studies that are important for summarizing the literature. In the first study, Gresham (1985) reviewed 33 studies on the treatment of social skills in children. Studies were generally classified as modeling, coaching, treatment packages, or social problem solving. Studies were critically evaluated according to subject characteristics, treatment specification, outcome measures, statistical analyses, experimental design, generalization, and cost-effectiveness. The following conclusions were noted:

1. Interactions between subject characteristics and treatment outcomes have been generally ignored in the literature. There is some minimal evidence that children benefit from having models who are culturally or racially similar.
2. Coaching and modeling procedures are generally effective for treating social skills problems in children. Neither procedure has demonstrated superiority over the other. However, there is little evidence that cognitive elements result in gains over and above operant and social learning strategies.

3. Most SST packages have demonstrated increases in specific targeted behaviors. However, few studies have concerned themselves with empirically establishing that changes in targeted behaviors lead to socially important outcomes for children. Social validity has received little emphasis. This is particularly a problem in the cognitive-behavioral training literature.
4. More studies are needed focusing on the generalization and maintenance of social gains.
5. Of the four types of therapies reviewed, modeling was judged to be the most cost-effective, followed by coaching. Social problem-solving programs generally required larger amounts of time.

In the second review paper, Schneider and Byrne (1985) conducted a meta-analysis of 51 studies dealing with the treatment of social skills deficits in children. Interventions were classified as modeling, coaching, operant, or social-cognitive. The following were among the conclusions reported by the authors:

1. Effect sizes were greatest where direct reinforcement of social skills was the intervention procedure. Similarly, large effect sizes were obtained for modeling and coaching studies. Effect sizes for cognitive interventions were significantly smaller than those in operant studies.
2. Effect sizes were larger for studies that utilized direct observational data or other measures with high reliability.
3. SST was more effective for preschoolers and adolescents than for elementary-age children. Also, SST was more effective for withdrawn than for aggressive children.
4. It was suggested that long-term effectiveness of SST and training of socially important outcomes is in need of further study. The reader is referred to the original article for additional findings.

In conclusion, the treatment literature has demonstrated the general utility of social skills training for remediating a host of social deficits and excesses in children. There is surprising consistency across several large-scale reviews regarding recommendations for future study:

1. The literature has largely ignored the role of subject characteristics (Gresham, 1985; Oden, 1980; Schneider & Byrne, 1985).
2. Operant procedures, coaching, and social learning strategies have all proved effective in treating so-

cial skills problems in children (Gresham, 1985; Gresham & Nagle, 1980; Matson & Ollendick, 1988; Schneider & Byrne, 1985; Van Hasselt et al., 1979). There is little evidence regarding additional benefits of using cognitive or self-instructional components (Gresham, 1985; Hobbs, Moquin, Tyroler, & Lahey, 1980; Lahey & Strauss, 1982; Schneider & Byrne, 1985). Also, given the multicomponent nature of most treatment packages, it is difficult to establish the separate and combined impact of different strategies (Schneider & Byrne, 1985; Van Hasselt et al., 1979). More treatment comparison studies are needed.

3. Social validity should be increasingly emphasized in the assessment and treatment literature (Puttalaz & Gottman, 1982). This includes evaluations of the socially perceived importance of the targets of SST, treatment acceptability, and most importantly, the social or clinical significance of trained social gains for long-term behavioral outcomes (Gresham, 1988).

4. Researchers should continue to address the issues of generalization and maintenance (Marchetti & Campbell, 1990; Van Hasselt et al., 1979).

## SUMMARY

The literature on social skills training with children has grown considerably during the last two decades. Despite the relative newness of the field, important advances in assessment, treatment, and conceptualizations of social skills have occurred. The study of these topics has been motivated in part by the prevalence of social skills problems in children and adolescents. Also, there has been increased recognition that social skills deficits represent important components in the most prevalent childhood disorders, including depression, anxiety disorders, hyperactivity, and disorders of conduct.

Earlier, simpler conceptualizations of social skills are being replaced by complex operational definitions that take into account broader social contextual issues. Researchers continue to evaluate and understand the unique advantages and disadvantages of various assessment strategies, including sociometrics, checklists, behavioral observations, behavioral interviews, role-plays, and general measures of psychopathology. Although more work is needed, the effectiveness of various treatment strategies, including reinforcement, coaching, and modeling, has been reliably demonstrated. Furthermore, as outlined previously, there is general consensus among investigators

regarding critical future directions for social skills research. The complex nature and importance of social behavior in children continue to intrigue and challenge researchers. Early successes represent promising starting points.

## REFERENCES

Achenbach, T. M., & Edelbrock, C. (1983). *Manual for the Child Behavioral Checklist and Revised Child Behavior Profile.* Burlington: University of Vermont, Department of Psychiatry.

Allen, K. E., Hart, B., Buell, J. S., Harris, T. R., & Wolf, M. M. (1964). Effects of social reinforcement on isolate behavior of a nursery school child. *Child Development, 35,* 511–518.

American Psychiatric Association. (1987). *Diagnostic and statistical manual of mental disorders,* 3rd ed., revised. Washington, DC: American Psychiatric Press.

Asher, S. R., & Hymel, S. (1981). Children's social competence in peer relations: Sociometric and behavioral assessment. In J. D. Wine & M. D. Smye (Eds.), *Social competence.* New York: Guilford Press.

Azrin, N. H., & Powers, M. A. (1975). Eliminating classroom disturbances of emotionally disturbed children by positive practice procedures. *Behavior Therapy, 6,* 525–534.

Bandura, A. (1977). *Social learning theory.* Englewood Cliffs, NJ: Prentice-Hall.

Barclay, J. R. (1966). Interest patterns associated with measures of social desirability. *Personality Guidance Journal, 45,* 56–60.

Baum, C. G. (1989). Conduct disorders. In T. H. Ollendick & M. Hersen (Eds.), *Handbook of child psychopathology,* 2nd ed. New York: Plenum Press.

Bellack, A. S. (1983). Recurrent problems in behavioral assessment of social skills. *Behavior Research and Therapy, 21,* 29–41.

Bellack, A. S., Hersen, M., & Lamparski, D. (1979). Role-play tests for assessing social skills: Are they valid? *Journal of Consulting and Clinical Psychology, 47,* 335–342.

Bellack, A. S., Hersen, M., & Turner, S. M. (1978). Role play tests for assessing social skills: Are they valid? *Behavior Therapy, 9,* 448–461.

Bierman, K. L., & Furman, W. (1984). The effects of social skills training and peer involvement on the adjustment of adolescents. *Child Development, 55,* 151–162.

Bierman, K. L., Miller, C. L., & Stabb, S. D. (1987). Improving the social behavior and peer acceptance of rejected boys: Effects of social skills training with instructions and prohibitions. *Journal of Consulting and Clinical Psychology, 55,* 194–200.

Billings, A. G., & Moos, R. H. (1984). Coping, stress, and social resources among adults with unipolar depression. *Journal of Personality and Social Psychology, 46,* 877–891.

Brown, C. (1954). Factors affecting social acceptance of high school students. *School Review, 62,* 151–155.

Brown, G. W., & Harris, T. (1978). *Social origins of depression.* London: Free Press.

Buell, J., Stoddard, P., Harris, F. R., & Baer, D. M. (1968). Collateral social development accompanying reinforcement of outdoor play in a preschool child. *Journal of Applied Behavior Analysis, 1,* 167–173.

Busk, P. L., Ford, R. C., & Schulman, J. L. (1973). Stability of sociometric response in classrooms. *Journal of Genetic Psychology, 123,* 69–84.

Campbell, S. B. (1989). Developmental perspectives. In T. H. Ollendick & M. Hersen (Eds.), *Handbook of child psychopathology, 2nd ed.* New York: Plenum Press.

Cavell, T. A. (1990). Social adjustment, social performance and social skills: A tri-component model of social competence. *Journal of Clinical Child Psychology, 19,* 111–122.

Christoff, K. A., Scott, W. O. N., Kelley, M. L., Schlundt, D., & Kelly, J. A. (1985). Social skills and social problem-solving training for shy young adolescents. *Behavior Therapy, 16,* 468–477.

Clark, L., Gresham, F. M., & Elliott, S. N. (1985). Development and validation of a social skills assessment measure: The TROSS-C. *Journal of Psychoeducational Assessment, 4,* 347–358.

Cowen, E. L., Pederson, A., Babjian, H., et al. (1973). Long-term follow-up of early detected vulnerable children. *Journal of Consulting and Clinical Psychology, 43,* 438–446.

Dougherty, B. S., Fowler, S. A., & Paine, S. C. (1985). The use of peer monitors to reduce negative interactions during recess. *Journal of Applied Behavior Analysis, 18,* 141–153.

Foxx, R. M., Faw, G. D., & Nisbett, I. (1991). Social skills training for inpatient emotionally disturbed children: An analysis of generalization. *Child and Family Behavior Therapy, 12,* 11–37.

Foxx, R. M., & McMorrow, M. J. (1983). *Stacking the Deck: A social skills game for mentally retarded adults.* Champaign, IL: Research Press.

Frame, C. L., & Matson, J. L. (1987). *Handbook of assessment in childhood psychopathology: Applied issues in differential diagnosis and treatment evaluation.* New York: Plenum Press.

French, D. C., & Tyne, T. F. (1982). The identification and treatment of children with peer-relationship difficulties. In J. P. Curran & P. M. Monti (Eds.), *Social skills training.* New York: Guilford Press.

Gardner, W. I., & Cole, C. L. (1986). Conduct disorders. In C. Frame & J. L. Matson (Eds.), *Handbook of assessment in childhood psychopathology: Applied issues in differential diagnosis and treatment evaluation.* New York: Plenum Press.

Gilbert, G. M. (1957). A survey of "referral problems" in metropolitan child guidance centers. *Journal of Clinical Psychology, 13,* 37–42.

Gottman, J. M. (1977). The effects of a modeling film on social isolation in preschool children: A methodological investigation. *Journal of Abnormal Child Psychology, 5,* 69–78.

Green, K. D., Vosk, B., Forehand, R., & Beck, S. (1979). *An examination of differences among sociometrically identified accepted, rejected, and neglected children.* Unpublished manuscript, University of Georgia.

Gresham, F. M. (1981). Assessment of children's social skills. *Journal of School Psychology, 19,* 120–133.

Gresham, F. M. (1982a). *Social skills: Principles, procedures, and practices.* Des Moines: State of Iowa Department of Public Education.

Gresham, F. M. (1982b). Social validation of assessment of children's social skills: Establishing standards for social competency. In *Social skills: Principles, procedures, and practices.* Des Moines: State of Iowa Department of Public Education.

Gresham, F. M. (1985). Utility of cognitive-behavioral procedures for social skills training with children: A critical review. *Journal of Abnormal Child Psychology, 13,* 411–423.

Gresham, F. M. (1988). Social skills: Conceptual and applied aspects of assessment, training, and social validation. In J. Witt, S. Elliott, & F. Gresham (Eds.), *Handbook of behavior therapy and education.* New York: Plenum Press.

Gresham, F. M., Elliot, S. N., & Black, F. L. (1986). *Factor structure replication and bias investigation of the teacher rating of social skills.* Unpublished manuscript, Louisiana State University.

Gresham, F. M., & Nagle, R. J. (1980). Social skills training with children: Responsiveness to modeling and coaching as a function of peer orientation. *Journal of Consulting and Clinical Psychology, 48,* 718–729.

Gronlund, N. E. (1959). *Sociometry in the classroom.* New York: Harper & Row.

Gronlund, H., & Anderson, C. (1957). Personality characteristics of socially accepted, rejected, and neglected junior high school pupils. *Educational Administration and Supervision, 43,* 329–338.

Gronlund, H., & Anderson, L. (1963). Personality characteristics of socially accepted, rejected, and neglected junior high school pupils. In J. Seiderman (Ed.), *Educating for mental health.* New York: Crowell.

Grossman, H. J. (1983). *Classification in mental retardation.* Washington, DC: American Association on Mental Retardation.

Guinouard, D. E., & Rychlak, J. F. (1982). Personality correlates of sociometric popularity in elementary school children. *Personnel and Guidance Journal, 40,* 438–442.

Hart, B. M., Reynolds, N. J., Baer, D. M., Brawley, E. R., & Harris, F. R. (1968). Effect of contingent and noncontingent social reinforcement on the cooperative play of a preschool child. *Journal of Applied Behavior Analysis, 1,* 73–76.

Hartup, W. W. (1970). Peer interaction and social organization. In P. H. Mussen (Ed.), *Carmichael's manual of child psychology*. New York: Wiley.

Hartup, W. W. (1976). Peer interaction and the behavioral development of the individual child. In E. Schopler & R. J. Reichler (Eds.), *Psychopathology and child development*. New York: Plenum Press.

Hartup, W. W., Glazer, J. A., & Charlsworth, R. (1967). Peer reinforcement and sociometric status. *Child Development, 38,* 1017–1024.

Helsel, W. J., & Matson, J. L. (1984). The assessment of depression in children: The internal structure of the Child Depression Inventory (CDI). *Behavior Research and Therapy, 22,* 289–298.

Hersen, M., & Bellack, A. S. (1976). A multiple baseline analysis of social skills training in chronic schizophrenics. *Journal of Applied Behavior Analysis, 9,* 239–245.

Hobbs, S. S., Moguin, L. E., Tyroler, M., & Lahey, B. B. (1980). Cognitive behavior therapy with children: Has clinical utility been demonstrated? *Psychological Bulletin, 87,* 147–165.

Hopkins, B. L. (1968). Effects of candy and social reinforcement instructions, and reinforcement schedule learning on the modification and maintenance of smiling. *Journal of Applied Behavior Analysis, 2,* 121–129.

Hops, H., Lewinsohn, P. M., Andrews, J. A., & Roberts, T. E. (1990). Psychosocial correlates of depressive symptomatology among high school students. *Journal of Clinical Child Psychology, 19,* 211–220.

Hymel, S., & Asher, S. R. (1977). *Assessment and training of isolated children's social skills.* Paper presented at the biennial meeting of the Society for Research in Child Development, New Orleans.

Kagan, L., & Moss, H. A. (1962). *Birth to maturity: A study in psychological development.* New York: Wiley.

Kazdin, A. E., Matson, J. L., & Esveldt-Dawson, K. (1984). The relationship of role-play assessment of children's social skills to multiple measures of social competence. *Behavior Research and Therapy, 22,* 129–139.

Keller, M. F., & Carlson, P. M. (1974). The use of symbolic modeling to promote social skills in preschool children with low levels of social responsiveness. *Child Development, 45,* 912–919.

Kohlberg, L., LaCrosse, J., & Ricks, D. (1972). The predictability of adult mental health from childhood behavior. In B. Wolman (Ed.), *Manual of child psychology.* New York: McGraw-Hill.

Kratochwill, T. R., & French, D. C. (1984). Social skills training for withdrawn children. *School Psychology Review, 13,* 331–338.

Ladd, G. W. (1979). *Social skills and peer acceptance: Effects of a social learning method for training verbal social skills.* Paper presented at the biennial meeting of the Society for Research in Child Development, San Francisco.

Lahey, B. B., & Strauss, C. C. (1982). Some considerations in evaluating the clinical utility of cognitive behavior therapy with children. *School Psychology Review, 11,* 67–74.

Lambert, N., Windmiller, M., Thoringer, D., & Cole, L. J. (1975). AAMD Adaptive Behavior Scale, rev. ed. Washington, DC: American Association on Mental Deficiency.

Libet, J. M., & Lewinsohn, P. M. (1973). Concept of social skill with special reference to the behavior of depressed persons. *Journal of Consulting and Clinical Psychology, 40,* 301–312.

Macklin, G. F. & Matson, J. L. (1985). A comparison of social behaviors among non-handicapped and hearing-impaired children. *Behavior Disorders, 1,* 60–65.

Marchetti, A. G. & Campbell, V. A. (1990). Social skills. In J. L. Matson (Ed.), *Handbook of behavior modification with the mentally retarded.* New York: Plenum Press.

Matson, J. L., & Adkins, J. (1980). A self-instructional social skills training program for mentally retarded persons. *Mental Retardation, 18,* 245–248.

Matson, J. L., Esveldt-Dawson, K., & Kazdin, A. E. (1983). Validation of methods for assessing social skills in children. *Journal of Clinical Child Psychology, 12,* 174–180.

Matson, J. L., Fee, V. E., Coe, D. A., & Smith, D. (1991). A social skills program for developmentally delayed preschoolers. *Journal of Clinical Child Psychology, 20,* 428–433.

Matson, J. L., Heinze, A., Helsel, W. J., & Kapperman, G. (1986). Assessing social behaviors in the visually handicapped: The Matson Evaluation of Social Skills with Youngsters (MESSY). *Journal of Clinical Child Psychology, 15,* 78–87.

Matson, J. L. & Ollendick, T. H. (1988). *Enhancing children's social skills: Assessment and treatment.* New York: Pergamon Press.

Matson, J. L., Rotatori, A. F., & Helsel, W. J. (1983). Development of a rating scale to measure social skills in children: The Matson Evaluation of Social Skills with Youngsters (MESSY). *Behaviour Research and Therapy, 21,* 335–340.

Matson, J. L., & Senatore, V. (1981). A comparison of traditional psychotherapy and social skills training for improving interpersonal functioning of mentally retarded adults. *Behavior Therapy, 12,* 369–382.

McFall, R. M. (1982). A review and reformulation of the concept of social skills. *Behavioral Assessment, 4,* 1–33.

McFall, R. M., & Littlesand, D. B. (1971). Behavior rehearsal with modeling and coaching in assertion training. *Journal of Abnormal Psychology, 77,* 313–323.

McFall, R. M., & Marston, A. R. (1970). An experimental investigation of behavior rehearsal in assertive training. *Journal of Abnormal Psychology, 76,* 295–303.

Monroe, S. M., Bromet, E. J., Connell, M. M., & Steiner, S. C. (1986). Social support, life events, and depressive symptoms: A one-year prospective study. *Journal of Consulting and Clinical Psychology, 54,* 424–431.

Moreno, J. L. (1934). *Who shall survive? A new approach to the problem of human interrelations.* Washington, DC: Nervous and Mental Disease Publishing Company.

O'Connor, R. D. (1969). Modification of social withdrawal through symbolic modeling. *Journal of Applied Behavior Analysis, 2,* 15–22.

O'Connor, R. D. (1972). Relative effects of modeling, shaping, and combined procedures for modification of social withdrawal. *Journal of Abnormal Child Psychology, 79,* 327–334.

Oden, S. (1980). A child's social isolation: Origins, prevention, intervention. In G. Carteledge & J. F. Milburn (Eds.), *Teaching social skills to children.* New York: Pergamon Press.

Oden, S., & Asher, S. R. (1977). Coaching children in social skills for friendship making. *Child Development, 48,* 495–506.

Ollendick, T. H. (1982). *The Social Competence Project.* Unpublished manuscript, Virginia Polytechnic Institute and State University, Blacksburg.

Peterson, L., & Burbach, D. J. (1988). Historical trends. In J. L. Matson (Ed.), *Handbook of treatment approaches in childhood psychopathology.* New York: Plenum Press.

Puttalaz, M., & Gottman, J. (1982). Conceptualizing social competence in children. In P. Karoly & J. J. Steffen (Eds.), *Improving children's competence.* Lexington, MA: D. C. Heath.

Quay, H. C., & Peterson, D. R. (1975). *Manual for the Behavior Problem Checklist.* Unpublished.

Reid, J. B. (1970). Reliability assessment of observation data: A possible methodological problem. *Child Development, 41,* 1143–1150.

Roff, M. (1961). Childhood social interactions and young adult bad conduct. *Journal of Abnormal and Social Psychology, 63,* 333–337.

Roff, M., Sells, B., & Golden, M. M. (1972). *Social adjustment and personality development in children.* Minneapolis: University of Minnesota Press.

Sarason, I. G., & Sarason, B. R. (1981). Teaching cognitive and social skills to high school students. *Journal of Consulting and Clinical Psychology, 49,* 908–918.

Sattler, J. M. (1988). *Assessment of children,* 3rd ed. San Diego: Author.

Schneider, B. H., & Byrne, B. M. (1985). Children's social skills training: A meta-analysis. In B. Schneider, K. Rubin, & J. Ledingham (Eds.), *Children's peer relations: Issues in assessment and intervention.* New York: Springer.

Schneider, B. H., & Byrne, B. M. (1989). Parents rating children's social behavior: How focused the lens? *Journal of Clinical Child Psychology, 18,* 237–241.

Senatore, V., Matson, J. L., & Kazdin, A. E. (1982). A comparison of behavioral methods to train social skills in mentally retarded adults. *Behavior Therapy, 13,* 313–324.

Serna, L. A., Schumaker, J. B., Hazel, J. S. (1986). Teaching reciprocal social skills training to parents and their delinquent adolescents. *Journal of Clinical Psychology, 15,* 64–77.

Sparrow, S. S., Balla, D. A., & Cicchetti, D. V. (1984). *The Vineland Adaptive Behavior Scales.* Circle Pines, MN: American Guidance Services.

Stengel, E. (1971). *Suicide and attempted suicide.* New York: Penguin.

Strain, P. S., Cooke, R. P., & Apolloni, I. (1976). *Teaching exceptional children: Assessing and modifying social behavior.* New York: Academic Press.

Strain, P. S., & Timm, M. A. (1974). An experimental analysis of social interaction between a behaviorally disordered preschool child and her classroom peers. *Journal of Applied Behavior Analysis, 7,* 583–590.

Ullman, C. (1957). Teachers, peers, and tests as predictors of adjustment. *Journal of Educational Psychology, 48,* 257–267.

Van Hasselt, V. B., Hersen, M., Whitehill, M. B., & Bellack, A. S. (1979). Social skill assessment and training for children: An evaluative review. *Behaviour Research & Therapy, 17,* 413–437.

Wahler, R. G. (1976). Deviant child behavior within the family: Development of speculations and behavior change strategies. In H. E. Leitenberg (Ed.), *Handbook of behavior modification and behavior therapy.* Englewood Cliffs, NJ: Prentice-Hall.

Walker, H. M., Street, A., Garrett, B., Crossen, J., Hops, H., & Greenwood, C. R. (1978). *RECESS: Reprogramming environmental contingencies for effective social skills.* Center at Oregon for Research in Behavioral Education for the Handicapped.

Warzak, W. F., & Page, T. J. (1990). Teaching refusal skills to sexually active adolescents. *Journal of Behavior Therapy and Experimental Psychiatry, 21,* 133–139.

Whalen, C. K. (1989). Attention deficit and hyperactivity disorders. In T. H. Ollendick & M. Hersen (Eds.) *Handbook of child psychopathology, 2nd ed.* New York: Plenum Press.

Whitman, T. L., Mercurio, J. R., & Caponigri, V. (1970). Development of social responses in two severely retarded children. *Journal of Applied Behavior Analysis, 3,* 133–138.

# CHAPTER 4

# ADULT SOCIAL SKILLS: STATE OF THE ART AND FUTURE DIRECTIONS

Peter Trower

Relationships bear on virtually every facet of ordinary life. Indeed, life seems almost inconceivable without them. Yet recent research shows that difficulty in forming relationships is surprisingly widespread. Surveys ranging from Japan to Germany to the United States reveal that at least 30% of young people everywhere consider themselves too shy, and more than 70% say that at some time in their lives shyness has hampered them socially (Jones, Cheek, & Briggs, 1986). Loneliness, one of the consequences of excessive shyness, is also widespread: 25% of U.S. subjects reported recent loneliness in a nationwide survey (Rubenstein & Shaver, 1982). Lonely people are more likely to be psychiatric casualties, to be problem drinkers, to have psychosomatic disorders, to be prone to suicide, to have self-deprecatory beliefs, and to be unhappy and pessimistic (Peplau & Perlman, 1982). Lack of satisfactory long-term relationships is also associated with more physical illness in general and with higher mortality (Argyle & Henderson, 1985).

There is a wealth of research showing these and other deleterious effects of poor relationships on psychosocial adjustment, especially when they come early in life. A major predictor of poor prognosis in a number of psychiatric disorders such as schizophrenia is an early history of social isolation and few or poor relationships.

The weight of evidence of this kind on the importance of relationships, and on the effect of the lack of or disruption of relationships on psychopathology, attests to the urgent need for further development of relationship-enhancing social policies, services, and therapies. Social skills training is one of the therapies that has been developed to meet just such a need. In this chapter I shall review current theory and practice and explore possible future directions.

The first section focuses on models of social skills. After reviewing currently accepted models, I ask whether a further reformulation is needed and outline a number of alternatives that adhere to the "interpersonal paradigm."

The second section reviews the characteristic social problems of the three major diagnostic groups for whom social skills training has been most widely applied: shyness-social phobia, depression, and schizophrenia.

The third section describes current assessment and training practice for the aforementioned three client groups and selectively reviews the evidence for their efficacy.

The final section returns to the question of the possible need for a further reformulation and adoption of an interpersonal perspective, and outlines a possible agenda for future practice that such a shift might imply.

## CURRENT AND ALTERNATIVE MODELS FOR SOCIAL SKILLS TRAINING: A CASE FOR FURTHER REFORMULATION?

In this section I will briefly review well-known and currently widely accepted information-processing models of social skills that guide assessment and training in practice. I will then describe a number of alternative theories that fall within the interpersonal paradigm and ask whether a further reformulation is needed.

### Current Theories of Social Skill

A number of theories of social skills are now well accepted and can be described broadly as information-processing models (Argyle & Kendon, 1967; Carver & Scheier, 1984; McFall, 1982; Trower & Turland, 1984; Wallace, 1982).

One way of making clear the role of these models in social skills training is to make a distinction between social skills components—behavioral components or repertoire of actions—and social *skill*—the process of generating skilled behavior (Trower, 1980, 1982).

Social *skills* (i.e., the components) are the actual normative behaviors—single elements (looks, nods, conventional linguistic phrases, etc.) or identifiable sequences of elements (greetings, partings, segments of discourse)—that a person may use in a given subculture and that conform to social rules in general and situation rules in particular. Such components form the individual's behavioral repertoire and are usually run off automatically, without conscious monitoring of the constituent parts.

On the other hand, social *skill* (i.e., the process) is the individual's ability to generate skilled behavior according to rules and goals and in response to social feedback. The information-processing models try to account for how this process works. The models use somewhat different terminology but refer to similar stages, such as decoding, decision making, and response selection (McFall, 1982) or in Wallace's (1982) terminology, to receiving, processing, and sending.

In one of the early theories, Argyle and Kendon (1967) describe the process as functionally similar to the process underlying the acquisition of serial motor skills. The individual goes through the *process* of monitoring the immediate situation and continually adjusting his behavior in the light of feedback. In this model, too, there are three stages. Given some goal-state to be achieved, the first includes the perception of cues from the environment, the second is the (cognitive) translation of these into plans for action, and the third is the motor response that entails performing the chosen action. The outcome is the consequent change in the environment. The process is cyclic in that external changes are picked up as feedback at the perceptual level and the process is repeated. Because so much social behavior is predictable, repeating sequences once learned (by trial and error or by observation) can be stored in memory in symbolic form and run off as a "skilled" sequence when required (Bandura, 1977). Later models elaborate on the stages of cognitive processing. For example, in McFall's (1982) model, decoding skill includes reception, perception, and interpretation; decision-making skill includes response search, response test, response selection, repertoire search, and utility evaluation; and encoding skill includes execution and self-monitoring.

Failure in social behavior can be described in terms of component skills deficits and/or process skill deficits. There is a good deal of evidence that a wide range of psychiatric patients exhibit patterns of deficiency in component skills.

There is less research on processing skill, but the research that has been done clearly indicates that this is a major problem area. Typical process failures include distortions such that people misinterpret incoming information at the decoding level, leading them to select dysfunctional actions or no actions, leading in turn to the execution and thereby the learning of dysfunctional skills or no skills, and to the inevitable failure to achieve goals. Indeed, cognitive distortions may give rise to dysfunctional goals in the first place. Decoding skill deficiency, particularly in the area of facial-affect recognition skills, has been an area of increasing research interest in recent years (Feinberg, Rifkin, Schaffer, & Walker, 1986). The treatment of process skills problems draws on two traditions, problem solving (D'Zurilla & Goldfried,

1971; Spivack, Platt, & Shure, 1976) and cognitive-behavioral therapy. Both approaches are drawn upon in current social skills training programs described later in this chapter.

## Alternative Theories for Social Skill

The information-processing models are a considerable advance on earlier models that focused more or less exclusively on components of social behavior—such as the skills deficit model—that did not take account of the perceptual, cognitive, and performance process. The process models have provided the guidelines and stimulus for more comprehensive skills training programs.

Despite their strengths, these models do not explicitly contain an interpersonal theory within them. I now raise the question whether there is a need for a further reformulation of the model that has an interpersonal theory at its center and that is also rooted in the evolved biology of human beings. A biopsychosocial framework of this kind has been put forward by Gilbert (1989). In this section I will review some theories of this kind that may provide us with alternative models for social skills.

The basis of a more interpersonal approach would recognize that relationships were fundamental to the survival of the person. Indeed, I would make the radical claim that the concept of the individual apart from other persons is a myth; a person's self has no existence apart from others.

If such a radical view seems to be going too far, it is worth pointing out that such a view is by no means new. Similar assertions about the essential social and interpersonal nature of human beings were written several generations ago by two "Establishment" figures in psychiatry and sociology, Sullivan (1953) and Cooley (1902).

Is such radicalism justified? This is an important question because it implies relationships are universally the most important human psychological need; that relationship needs should go to the top of our therapeutic agenda; and that research, assessment, and training practices should be changed in a number of ways.

So neglected was this interpersonal paradigm in psychology, psychiatry, and other social sciences that Anchin and Kiesler (1982) and Harre and Secord (1972), among others, felt the need in the early 1980s to lay out in separate ways the case for a paradigm shift, the former in the form of "The Interpersonal Manifesto" (Kiesler, 1982) and the latter in the form

of the "ethogenic" approach, which rejected virtually all the fundamentals of the "science" of social psychology at the time.

Inevitably, the theory and practice of social skills, though in some ways a refreshing departure from the asocial emphasis on the decontextualized "sick" and malfunctioning individual, nonetheless was influenced by the paradigm of the individual. Many of the problems encountered in the development of social skills training in the earlier years can be traced to this "parametric" paradigm (as Harre and Secord termed it) (Trower, 1984).

Despite some progress in the past decade, a number of authors have said that the hoped-for paradigm shift has in the main not taken place. Safran (1990) shows, for example, that neither cognitive therapy nor cognitive psychology—the conceptual breakthroughs of the 1980s—have endorsed the interpersonal nature of humans, and he puts forward his own interpersonal theory in an attempt to rectify the deficit.

What, then, are the interpersonal theories? Next, I list a number of key concepts from writers and researchers in the "interpersonal" school, with a view to their possible use as "potential" new theories for social skills training.

### 1. The Interpersonal Manifesto

In his "Interpersonal Manifesto," Kiesler (1982) develops a number of fundamental assumptions. The first of these is that the basic unit of study should be interpersonal transactions, not the behavior of individuals. He criticizes the normal practice of studying individuals in isolation and says that the basic level of human reality is transactional. This principle is well stated by Carson (1969): Personality is "inconceivable other than in the context of interpersonal relations" (Carson, 1969, p. 25) and "personality is nothing more (or less) than the patterned regularities that may be observed in an individual's relations with other persons, who may be real in the sense of actually being present, real but absent and hence 'personified' or illusory" (p. 26). Put another way, the basic unit of analysis is the dyad, not the individual. The dyad is a system, a two-person process, not one person at a time interacting with another.

A second principle is that the concept of self is theoretically central and that the "self" is entirely social, interpersonal, and transactional. Swensen (1973) summarizes the position: "Literally to exist as a person, to have a self, to be a personality, one must have others to interact with. If there is no one around to interact with, no self, no personality, no human being, as we usually think of the concept, can exist." (p. 6). One of the main functions of the self-system involves the self-presentations we make to others. Through self-presentations, people seek confirmation of their preferred self and attempt to "pull" social responses from others that are complementary to the behavior presented. For example, care eliciting pulls caregiving.

A third principle is that there is a limited set of interpersonal transactions and therefore of self-presentations. Leary (1957) developed the most influential model in his Interpersonal Circle with the two major orthogonal dimensions of dominance–submission and love–hate, giving rise to a range of combinations of transactional styles.

A fourth principle is that interpersonal transactions reflect a reality of circular rather than linear causality. New methodologies are necessary to measure the basic circular aspects of transactions identified by Danziger (1976): feedback (two individuals are simultaneously the causes and effects of each other's behavior), redundancy (dyadic behavior shows a patterned, predictable ordering) and nonsummativity (meaning lies in the temporal sequence of elements, not the elements themselves). For Leary, redundancy (or what he called complementarity) was shown by "reciprocity" on the dominance–submissiveness axis (the one, dominance, invokes the opposite, submissiveness) and by "correspondence" on the love–hate axis (the one, love or hate, invokes the equivalent in the other).

A fifth principle is that the vehicle for human transactions is verbal and nonverbal communication, and the evidence shows that nonverbal communication is the language of emotion, of relationship, and most important of self-presentation, whereas social skills, as I shall argue, are the building blocks of self-presentation.

## 2. Self-Presentation

A central component of the interpersonal framework outlined by Kiesler is self-presentation. Virtually all social behavior is influenced by self-presentation needs, and it is relevant at this point to explore the self-presentation model, originated by Goffman (1959) and developed by Schlenker and Leary (1982), as an explanatory model for social anxiety. Self-presentation refers to the behavioral projections of self-images that make up a person's

identity. It is a goal-directed act designed to influence how others perceive and treat the actor. "Social anxiety arises when people are motivated to make a particular impression on others but doubt that they will do so, because they have expectations of unsatisfactory impression-relevant reactions from others" (Schlenker & Leary, 1982, p. 645). Poor social skills are clearly a major factor contributing to low expectations, but the crucial variables are cognitive ones: The individual must believe he or she lacks the skills necessary to create the desired impression and must also believe it is important or essential to succeed in creating such an impression. I am referring here to such dysfunctional beliefs as "A person must be competent to be worthwhile but I am totally inadequate." Given the central role of self-presentation in relationships, it is important that we incorporate this concept in social skills research.

## 3. Interpersonal Theory

The foregoing principles provide an important framework for the social skills approach, but the picture is not yet complete because it is clear now that social skills theory must incorporate a further dimension, from cognitive therapy, given that dysfunctional beliefs play a crucial role in blocking or disrupting the acquisition and performance of social skills (Trower & Dryden, 1991). Building on Kiesler's model, Safran (1990) provides just such a theory, which embraces the interpersonal dimension. He argues from an ecological perspective that humans have a wired-in propensity for maintaining relatedness to others and that this propensity plays an important role in the survival of the species. As part of this propensity, a person develops an internal working model representing interpersonal interactions, or, in Safran's terms, an interpersonal schema: a generic knowledge structure based on previous self–other interactions, which contains information relevant to the maintenance of interpersonal relatedness. The interpersonal schema serves to guide subsequent perceptual selection and behavior and, therefore, gives shape to the characteristic self-presentations of that individual. Schemata activate and are maintained by interpersonal cycles in which people evoke schema-consistent responses from others. Clearly, Safran's model could be developed to incorporate the information-processing models of Argyle and Kendon (1967), McFall (1982), and Wallace (1982); but it goes beyond these in placing interpersonal schemata at the core. Trower and Turland (1984) offered a model that to some extent incorporates both views.

In summary, I have argued that interpersonal schemata play a crucial role in the production of social behavior, and we should incorporate them in our approach to social skills assessment and training.

## 4. Evolutionary Biology: The Fourth Dimension

So far we have argued that relationships are basic to, and even definitional of, persons; that relationships are of four primary kinds; that self-presentation is the basic vehicle for relating; and that the interpersonal schema is the mechanism for the production of self-presentational behavior. Social skills are clearly the behavior building blocks in this framework of concepts.

There remains what may be called a fourth dimension, underpinning all these themes. This is the view that comes from evolutionary biology, which I would interpret as follows:

1. Social relating is fundamental to individual and species survival.

2. As a result of millions of years of evolutionary pressure, human beings and other primates have become biologically equipped to an extremely advanced degree for social interaction—that is, have this propensity ''wired in.''

3. The main *forms* of relationships are also biologically prepared for. Likewise, humans and primates are genetically endowed with the ability to create certain *modes* of social structure in which to interact. This endowment for conspecific (own-species) relating is genetically open in humans, allowing for maximum adaptation through learning, but still marks the boundaries of possibilities—both the potential and the limits.

4. According to evolutionary biology theory, each individual is endowed with a genetic repertoire of *competencies* (also described elsewhere as mentalities, archetypes, etc.), each open to varying amounts of modification by learning. By *competency* is meant a complex module of cognitive, emotive, and behavioral patterns (together with the anatomical, physiological, and electrochemical substrates that underpin them) that enable an individual to perform a role in response to external or internal needs—for example,

flight or appeasement. A competency is an appraisal-response system of the kind outlined in the various information-processing models of social skills referred to earlier, except that, in the present theory, there are a variety of discrete and specific competencies. In our present terminology, a competency consists of a selected appraisal of the situation (which in turn consists of selective perception, an interpersonal schema and a mood or feeling state, and a specific response choice that is best fitted to deal with the situation in a self- or kin-enhancing way). The competency may operate automatically or under conscious control.

Although the basic repertoire of competencies is said to be innate, they are open to modification by learning. In particular, individuals must have relevant cognitive-social learning experiences before they can turn these potentialities into social skills that they can utilize in social interaction.

These competencies can be grouped into the following three categories:

1. Phylogenetically the oldest are a cluster of competencies that are reptilian in origin and originally evolved for dealing with predator threat. They include threat display, fight, flight, freeze, faint, camouflage, and territorial checking. The typical sequence begins with a threat display to a competitor, during which a judgment is made about relative strength, speed, and the like (social comparison), followed by fight or flight depending on the outcome, with flight being followed by permanent retreat to another territory.

2. The second group of competencies are paleo-mammalian in origin and emerged as a result of the evolution of true social grouping. They include competing, dominating, submitting and appeasing; reverted escape (a modification of the flight response in which the animal returns to the source of danger); and braced readiness (a state of vigilant high arousal). The typical sequence may again begin with the threat display, but in this case the loser does not flee but submits and thereby remains in the social group, and maintains a subordinate relationship with the now-dominant animal by means of continuing submissiveness.

3. There are also competencies that are both paleo- and neomammalian in origin and consist of those behaviors that evolved alongside warm-blood-

edness and the rearing of young. These include caregiving (by the parent) and care eliciting and play (by the offspring), and those behaviors that evolved with the emergence of the hunter-gatherer and include attractiveness display, reassurance giving, and cooperating.

Gilbert (1989) suggests that all competencies can be understood as functioning within a defense or safety system, and proposes that the first two categories of competencies function as part of the defense system where threat is high, and enable individuals to respond to threat and danger from conspecifics in a way that minimizes injury and maximizes social cohesion. The defense system operates mostly within a social structure that Chance (1984) describes as the agonic mode, characterized by ranked power hierarchies and dominant–subordinate relationships. The third category of competencies includes those that function within a safety system where threat is low or nonexistent and that enable the individual to explore, be creative, form alliances, mate, and so on. The safety system operates mostly within the hedonic mode (Chance, 1984), a social structure characterized by networks rather than hierarchies, power sharing, and mutual caring and cooperation. Thus, the major relationship categories of dominant–submissive and love–hate identified by Leary (1957) map onto the major evolved relationship competencies, a point thoroughly explored by Gardner (1988) and Gilbert (1989).

From the social skills point of view, the focus of interest in the present model is social behavior, particularly self-presentation behavior. Self-presentations, the main social behavioral products of the competencies, are used for establishing relationships such as in threat and attractiveness displays, and in maintaining relationships such as in dominant and submissive behavior, cooperative and caring behavior, and the like. Problems arise when people are stuck in one kind of self-presentation, which may be inappropriate for certain situations, or when they perform self-presentations poorly and for various other reasons prove incapable of flexible adaptation. For example, social phobics often exhibit submissive rather than, say, cooperative self-presentations, with negative effects on their self-esteem, failure in friendship and other cooperative relationships, and other consequences (Trower & Gilbert, 1989).

It is clear that the "healthiest" individuals utilize category three competencies in hedonic mode societies. The greater the degree of threat and insecurity within the individual and/or within the society, the more likely it is that the individual will recruit more primitive defensive competencies. This implies that most psychopathology will relate to defense system responses, such that medium severity will be marked by agonic dominance or submissive behavior (the latter including low self-esteem, high anxiety, and negative self-evaluation) and the most severe marked by reptilian behavior such as fight and flight, depression, social isolation, fragility of self-identity and ego boundaries, and the like. We have worked out how the present theory can account for social phobia (Trower & Gilbert, 1989), and it would be useful to carry out the same exercise for other problems, such as schizophrenia. It is interesting to note here the relationship between marginalization of schizophrenics and the severity and chronicity of the disorder in Western society compared to the contrasting integration and low levels of severity and chronicity in Third World countries, (Warner, 1985). The reason for this difference, I would argue, is that in Third World countries "schizophrenics" are valued members of ordinary "hedonic" groups and are not thrust into the most subordinate strata of society.

In summary, I have reviewed a number of current information-processing models and alternative theories that together form an interpersonal paradigm, and have raised the question of whether a further reformulation incorporating the interpersonal perspective should be considered. I shall return to this question in the last section of this chapter, after reviewing current perceptions of client needs and the state of the art in assessment and training.

## TRAINING FOR WHOM AND FOR WHAT?

There are few client groups that do not have social and interpersonal problems as part of the syndrome, and for whom some version of SST might not be appropriate. To limit the scope of this section, however, I will review the social problem profiles of the three main diagnostic groups for whom SST has been most well developed: shyness/social phobia, depression, and schizophrenia.

### Shyness/Social Phobia

Two research traditions in the area of social anxiety have developed separately and have only recently been brought together and recognized as a common concern (Leitenberg, 1990). One, concerned with the everyday shyness or "communication apprehension," has been sponsored by social and developmental psychologists and educators (Crozier, 1990; Jones, Cheek, & Briggs, 1986). The second, concerned with the "clinical" problem of social anxiety/phobia and developed by clinical psychologists and psychiatrists, has been a neglected area until recently (Heimberg, 1989a, 1989b). Social skills and training have been a major preoccupation with both research groups.

Shyness researchers found that the experience of shyness is remarkably common, with less than 10% of a cross-cultural survey reporting they had never felt shy (Zimbardo, 1977). A three-component model of shyness has been generally accepted as most appropriate (Cheek & Melchior, 1990). The first component concerns emotional arousal and physiological complaints such as pounding heart, sweating, and blushing; research shows 40% to 60% suffer such complaints. The second cognitive component is concerned with public self-consciousness, self-deprecating thoughts, and worries about being evaluated negatively by others. Between 60% and 90% of shy students reported such thoughts in a variety of studies. The third component is concerned with social competence, where the results are mixed—some shy people appear to be socially unskilled, others not so. We return to this point later.

Shyness is strongly related to loneliness. Shy people usually report being lonely, and the two constructs share many features, including negative affect (depression, anxiety, hostility, etc.) and social inhibition (few friends, low dating frequency, and ineffective interpersonal style). There is some evidence that shyness precedes and predicts subsequent loneliness.

In contrast to shyness, social phobia has been a comparatively neglected topic in psychiatric research (Barlow & Wolfe, 1981; Liebowitz, Gorman, Fyer, & Klein, 1985). Only recently has this neglected problem been fully recognized (American Psychiatric Association, 1987; Heimberg, 1989a, 1989b). One of the main diagnostic criteria for social phobia in the *Diagnostic and Statistical Manual of Mental Disorders,* third edition, revised (DSM-III-R; American Psychiatric Association, 1987) is a persistent fear of one or more situations in which the person is exposed to possible scrutiny by others. The main component is the fear of acting in a way that is embarrassing or humiliating. There are, however, problems with differential diagnosis with regard to other disorders, avoidant personality disorder in particular; and social phobia also coexists with other disorders, particularly panic disorder, agoraphobia, depression, and schizophrenia.

Social phobics vary considerably in the level of social skills deficits shown. A majority of studies have shown highly anxious people to be less skilled than low anxious people at the level of general impressions (e.g., Halford & Foddy, 1982), but the picture with regard to specific behavioral differences is mixed, with some studies showing differences in, for example, amount of speaking, response latency, amount of looking, and general avoidant behavior, but other studies not showing such differences. At the cognitive level, socially anxious subjects have various negative beliefs that disrupt the performance of social skills (e.g., Alden & Cappe, 1981). For example, they see themselves as less skillful than others see them, endorse perfectionistic standards, attribute failure to themselves and successes to situational causes, and endorse other irrational beliefs. In a well-designed study, Beidel, Turner, and Dancu (1985) not only confirmed these findings across several social-evaluative situations but found higher physiological arousal, in particular higher blood pressure and heart rate readings, in subjects with clinical levels of social anxiety.

This confusing picture may be clarified if it could be established that there are different types of social anxiety/phobia and/or personality disorder. One possibly important distinction is made in DSM-III-R between specific social phobia and generalized social phobia, the latter being closely related to, if not identical with, avoidant personality disorder. There is some evidence that the latter group are more socially unskilled and avoidant, more sensitive interpersonally, and fearful of more situations (Turner, Beidel, Dancu, & Keys, 1986).

Despite the growing body of clinical research on social anxiety, there is little that addresses the issues of interpersonal relationships and self-presentation. I shall therefore return to this topic in the final section.

## Depression

Traditionally, depression has been conceptualized as a disorder of the individual. This tendency persists in more recent developments, such as cognitive therapy. However, a number of authors have been critical of this narrow view (Coyne, 1990) on the basis that there is now compelling research evidence that quality of relationships plays an integral role in the onset, maintenance, and recovery of depression. These authors have put forward more broad based interpersonal (Coyne, 1976; Gotlib & Colby, 1987) and biopsychosocial (Gilbert, 1992) models of depression.

Early studies found that depressives had less verbal output, fewer initiations, and a lower rate of positive/ reinforcing behavior (e.g., Libet & Lewinsohn, 1973). Gotlib and Robinson (1982) found that they made fewer statements of direct support, made a greater number of negative content statements, had more monotonous speech, smiled less frequently, engaged in gestures not related to their speech, and had less positive facial expressions. In drawing together the results of several studies (e.g., Gotlib & Meltzer, 1987), it appears that such behavior does not lead conversation partners to judge the depressed person as less socially skilled so much as to judge *themselves* as less socially skilled than they would normally. This effect on others now seems fairly robust and supports Coyne's (1976) original finding that ordinary subjects who had telephone conversations with depressives felt more depressed, anxious, and hostile, and rejected opportunities for future contact. There was evidence from this and two other studies (Hammen & Peters, 1978; Howes & Hokanson, 1979) that it is the content of what is said—that is, intensely personal and negative self-disclosure—that creates such impressions and reactions, leading to a negative spiral of rejection and further depression.

Depression has been one of the most studied problems from a cognitive therapy perspective (Beck, Rush, Shaw, & Emery, 1979), and characteristic cognitions of depressed people have been well documented (Teasdale, 1983), but there has been little work to date connecting the pattern of depressive cognitions with the interpersonal style of depressed people. The likelihood is that the two (cognitions and behavioral style) combine to produce a self-fulfilling prophesy (beliefs affect social actions, which in turn affect beliefs).

## Schizophrenia

Unlike the two previous groups, where there is considerable debate about the level of social skill deficiency, there are no such doubts about schizophrenia. Severe impairment of social functioning is one of the key features of schizophrenia, and deterioration of social relations is a defining diagnostic criteria in DSM-III-R. Long-stay institutionalized schizophrenic patients are among the most deficient in skills of all psychiatric groups (Sylph, Ross, & Kedward, 1978), and it has been long established that level of social competence plays a major role in the etiology and prognosis of the disorder (e.g., Zigler & Phillips, 1961).

Recently, Bellack and his colleagues (Bellack, Morrison, Wixted, & Mueser, 1990), in a rigorously designed and conducted study, found strong support for the contention that schizophrenics have pronounced deficits in social competence. They were substantially impaired on verbal, nonverbal, and overall ratings of social skill and on interview ratings of role functioning. They scored significantly worse than nonpatient controls on each measure. They were also rated as more impaired than affective disorder patients. This study also produced evidence that social dysfunction was not simply a by-product of negative or positive symptoms, and supported the hypotheses that social competence is an independent component of schizophrenia, orthogonal to both positive and negative symptoms, although all three undoubtedly interact in deleterious ways. And it is clear that both positive (such as disorders of thought and perception, mannerisms and posturing, inappropriate or incongruous affect) and negative symptoms (lack of energy and motivation, social withdrawal) create extreme difficulty in initiating and maintaining social interactions.

Partly because of their social difficulties and partly because of totally inadequate community care, most persons with schizophrenia lead lives of extremely poor quality (Warner, 1985). Roughly half of U.S. schizophrenics are in institutions, in inadequate community settings, in jail, in prison, or on the streets. Most lead lives of social isolation. Most studies have shown that patients have networks of social contacts that are much more restricted than is usual in our society. Schizophrenics are found to have close contacts with only one-third to one-fifth the number of people that is average for the community. One-third of the chronically mentally ill have no friends at all. Relationships tend to be more one-sided, dependent, and lacking in complexity of content and diversity of interconnections. Social isolation has been repeatedly shown to be associated with poor outcome. Finally, disturbed family relations are common and are among the main causes of relapse of schizophrenics (Falloon, Boyd, & McGill, 1984).

## SOCIAL SKILLS ASSESSMENT, TRAINING, AND OUTCOME: GENERAL ASSESSMENT APPROACHES

In this section I will describe social skills assessment and training approaches that have been developed in general and for each of the problem areas identified herein—shyness/social phobia, depression, and schizophrenia—and will briefly review some other approaches that may complement these. I will also selectively review the outcome literature pertinent to each area.

## Dimensions of Assessment

The development of assessment methods to describe social skills problems and evaluate the effectiveness of training has been no easy task, given the complexity of the subject and the difficulty of defining valid criterion variables. There are a number of different ways that assessment of social skill problems has been developed, including the clinical interview, self-report measures, self-monitoring, behavioral observation, peer and "expert" rating, and physiological monitoring.

Assessment measures can be grouped in various ways. One way is to group them into trait versus state measures; another related way is to group them into molar versus molecular measures. There have been considerable debates about the validity and appropriateness of these different emphases; for example, trait measures are in danger of invoking internal dispositions that do not actually exist, and state or molecular (behavioral) measures may focus on behavioral elements that do not correspond to true social skills. Another problem has been that behavioral measures do not correlate very well with judgments of social skill and are very cumbersome to use clinically, whereas trait measures—which do correlate well with overall judgments and are quick to administer—are not informative about actual behavior.

However, intermediate measures (ratings based on the subjective impression of behaviors rather than on measures of the actual behaviors) have held greater promise in that they relate to both global and molecular levels of measurement and are more clinically useful (Boice & Monti, 1982).

## Sources of Measurement

Another way of distinguishing measures is in terms of the source of measurement. There are three different sources: (1) actor's self-report, (2) partner's or co-actor's judgment of actor and, (3) third-party observation. There is a preference to obtain all three sources of judgment, particularly as there are usually considerable differences between the three, and all three are required for research and clinical purposes. A comprehensive sourcebook of such measures is provided in Spitzberg and Cupach (1989), who divide the material into the content domains of assertiveness, empathy and role taking, motivation (including anxiety), fundamental social/behavioral competence, and children's competence.

The self-report measures—of which there are many dozens in the SST literature—include questionnaires, checklists, rating scales, and self-monitoring devices. These measures are designed to assess a variety of variables, including general personality dispositions, specific behavioral categories, cognitive and emotional reactions to stimuli and situations, performance of skills at global and specific levels, and monitoring of these reactions over time and situations. These measures vary greatly in their degree of psychometric acceptability, with more recent research showing an improvement over earlier ones.

One of the criticisms of behavioral measures has been that the basic assumptions about the nature of social interaction are too simplistic and do not take account of the context, interaction, or linguistic structure of discourse (Trower, 1983). However, recent developments are encouraging—for example, the application of discourse analysis from the field of linguistics (Gervasio, 1987) and the growth of more appropriate experimental and statistical procedures for analyzing sequences of social interaction (e.g., Bakeman & Gottman, 1986; Schlundt & McFall, 1985).

## Assessment of Process Variables

Assessment of process variables, including social perception, cognition, and emotion, and the skills that underlie these has been one of the fastest growing areas. For example, Riggio (1989) has developed a self-report measure of expressivity (skill in sending), sensitivity (skill in receiving), and control (skill in influencing communication processes) (discussed later). Assessment of cognitions is acknowledged as a particularly difficult area. However, there is some progress in this area, and there are now a number of psychometrically sound measures. For example, Heimberg, Nyman, and O'Brien (1987) found considerable support for the validity of the thought-listing technique, in which subjects are requested to provide spoken or written records of their cognitive responses to specific stimuli. Similarly, Glass and Furlong (1990) demonstrated satisfactory reliability and validity of their Social Interaction Self-Statement Test (discussed later). Shepherd (1984) has adapted the Personal Questionnaire, which is a method for scaling and grading difficulties expressed in the client's own words. After construction of the questionnaire, the client selects the statement that best describes the intensity of the difficulty at the time, ranging from "very" to "not at all." This questionnaire provides a check on the internal reliability of each item. It has high test–retest reliability and is simple and direct. Another approach of this type is, of course, the long-established but comparatively little used repertory grid technique (Bannister & Fransella, 1985), one of the few psychometrically sound formats that allows clients to express their own thoughts and feelings.

Objective, laboratory-type tests of the perception of social cues have also been developed recently. A number of authors have used the Stroop color-naming task, in which subjects are asked to name the ink colors of words related to physical (e.g., disease, fatal), social threat (e.g., foolish, criticized), or neutral control words. A number of studies have now shown that clients, for example those with social phobia (Hope, Rapee, Heimberg, & Dombeck, 1990), show more extensive perceptual processing of threat-related cues than do controls. Another area is the assessment of affect recognition (particularly facial) by presentation of stimulus materials (e.g., posed facial expressions) and identification by the client of the emotions expressed. Morrison, Bellack, and Mueser (1988) are critical of studies using these latter techniques on the grounds of ecological and criterion validity, and have made useful suggestions about their use in future research.

## Role-Play Tests

Measures of social behavior and process variables require social situations in which the performance takes place. Real-life situations are clearly the best but also usually the least practical, and researchers and clinicians alike have for long been compelled to adopt laboratory-type role-play simulations. Two main alternatives have been used. The first is a staged "naturalistic" interaction—for example, observing a social skills trainee's behavior in a waiting room situation, while the trainee is unaware that assessment is taking place (Gutride, Goldstein, & Hunter, 1973). More commonly, however, a structured role-play is used, where the trainee acts out a response to a set scene. There are at least four different types of role-play test, some of which have been heavily criticized as lacking in "ecological" (real-life) validity, to such an extent that Bellack (1983) has urged that

the use of single-prompt role-play and taped role-play tests should be abandoned. Other types have more promise and have been endorsed by several authors (Kern, Miller, & Eggers, 1983). Merluzzi and Biever (1987) found that structured and unstructured role-plays had some validity when social skills were rated on molar scales. Pettit, McClaskey, Brown, and Dodge (1987) also found validity for molar ratings but not molecular ratings in a laboratory simulation of social interactions among children. Bellack, Morrison, Wixted, and Mueser (1990) found in their role-play test of a range of subjects (schizophrenics, those with affective disorder, and nonpatient controls) that role-play behavior "provides an excellent reflection of overall social functioning in the community" (p. 817).

## GENERAL TRAINING APPROACHES

Many training manuals and videotapes are available for social skills training that deal with general and specific aspects of training. We refer to several of these in the following pages. Most such manuals have advice on working with individuals versus groups, mix of clients, use of equipment, and preparation and presentation of material. The training *procedure* generally consists of the following components:

1. *Instruction.* A particular skill or skills theme is taken, and its function in social interaction is described. The skill is then broken down into a sequence of behavioral elements so that the trainee can see exactly what has to be done.

2. *Modeling.* Learning by observing others, or modeling, is a very efficient way of acquiring complex new skills, because the trainee can see the entire sequence carried out as a whole and can judge for himself its effectiveness (Bandura, 1977). The best method is to get a model who is similar to the trainee in age, sex, and social class and who gives a coping rather than a mastery performance. All these factors help the trainee to associate himself with the model and encourage emulation.

3. *Rehearsal.* After instruction and modelling, the trainee is ready to try the new skill in role-play with a role-partner. As in rehearsing lines for a play, each successive attempt should approximate more closely the final desired effect. Sometimes trainers get their clients to practice covert rehearsal first—

that is, to go through the behavioral sequence in imagination.

4. *Coaching, feedback, and reinforcement.* In the ongoing process of rehearsal, trainees obtain information on how they are doing so that they can rectify their performance. Feedback can be given via audio or video replay and verbally. Skillful handling of feedback is vital to successful training and should be based on positive reinforcement.

5. *Homework.* Training is preparation, and the next step is for the client to implement the new skill in the problem situation. Homework assignments are set very concretely, and subsequent training sessions spend a good deal of time dealing with homework implementation difficulties.

The training *contents* are dictated by the type of problem being dealt with and are referred to in the following pages in connection with the clients under focus.

## Shyness/Social Phobia

*Assessment*

In current assessment approaches to shyness and social phobia, the main elements of information on which the therapist focuses fall into three main areas: (1) social skills; (2) experienced and expressed anxiety, including avoidance behavior and physiological responding; and (3) perceptual/cognitive processing, including dysfunctional beliefs. From this information, a tailored treatment program can be designed and decisions taken whether to include social skills training, cognitive therapy, exposure or other anxiety-reducing procedure, or a combination of any of these.

*Prior to interview,* information in all three areas can be obtained by self-report measures. Guidance on selection of measures can be obtained from a number of published reviews. For example, Scholing and Emmelkamp (1990) give a critical and useful review which is divided according to the three-system approach—verbal-cognitive, behavior-motoric, and psychophysiological.

I have selected five representative self-report questionnaires—a screening instrument, an internal dialogue test, a social skills measure, a social situations questionnaire, and an interpersonal questionnaire.

The first is a screening measure—the Social Phobia and Anxiety Inventory (SPAI), a 32-item self-report measure developed by Turner, Beidel, Dancu, and Stanley (1989). This discriminates social phobics from other anxiety groups and matches DSM-III-R criteria better than other measures.

The second measure is the Social Interaction Self Statement Test (SISST) (Glass, Merluzzi, Biever, & Larsen, 1982), a measure of internal dialogue. Thoughts of extremely socially anxious subjects measured on the SISST were related to irrational beliefs and fear of negative evaluation, social anxiety, and global behavioral ratings by interaction partners and judges (Glass & Furlong, 1990). This measure is of particular interest because it is strongly predictive of social skills. Judges were more interested in talking to and predicted greater comfort interacting with subjects who had a more positive and less negative internal dialogue on the SISST. Similarly, subjects with this score profile were rated by confederates as more socially skilled, warm, dominant, poised, and rewarding, and as less socially anxious, passive, and difficult.

The third instrument recommended is the Social Situations Questionnaire (SSQ) (Trower, Bryant, & Argyle, 1978), which assesses degree of anxiety in and frequency of encountering a range of common social situations.

Fourth, I would recommend a measure of social skills. The Social Performance Survey Schedule (SPSS) (Lowe & Cautela, 1978) is a useful behavioral measure containing 50 positive and 50 negative statements of social behaviors whose frequency can be rated on a five-point scale.

Interpersonal questionnaires will be discussed in the final section.

The *interview phase* can contain a diagnostic component and a social assessment component. The first can be structured using the Anxiety Disorders Interview Schedule (ADIS-R) (Di Nardo et al., 1985) if a clear differential diagnosis is required. For the second, I suggest the following format:

1. Begin with a traditional open invitation to the client to talk about past or current social relationships.
2. Ask the client to describe any difficulties in each of two main skills areas: affiliativeness (problems on the warm–cold dimension relating to lack of casual conversation and the expression of friendliness and intimacy) and assertiveness (problems on the dominant–submissive dimension relating to lack of appropriate positive and negative assertion).

3. Using answers to the SSQ as a prompt, ask the client to describe difficulties in the foregoing areas in each of three situation domains: work, leisure, and home.

4. Ask the client to choose a specific situation that typifies one of the most important difficulties. Then ask:

   When and where did it happen?
   Who was involved?
   What did they (and you) say and do?
   What led up to this?
   What was the consequence of this?
   What did you feel before, during, and after the event?
   What were you thinking before, during, and after the event?

5. Carry out a role-play simulation of the event, and videotape the role-play.

6. Finally, play back the video and, together with the client, rate the client's performance on a rating scale, such as the Social Skills Rating Scale (Trower, Bryant, & Argyle, 1978), which covers verbal and nonverbal elements of social behavior and global impressions. Negotiate agreed ratings and use these as performance baselines for future training sessions. In effect, the ratings can become a personal profile for identifying performance targets.

Steps 4, 5, and 6 can be repeated with examples of difficulties identified in other situation domains.

### Interventions

*Skills training.* When assessment reveals a *skills deficit* as part of the profile of problems, then clearly a skills training approach is indicated. The format of social skills training is now well known, and on this assumption the following description will be kept very brief. The general principle is that the client is taught the skills in laboratory-based practice sessions and then uses them in the situations where the difficulties occur.

The *content* of training can be entirely tailored to an individual's specific difficulties, or it can take the form of a more or less structured course, for example for a group of 6 to 8 clients with common problems. Research shows that people with shyness problems share a common core of difficulties. One of these common core problems is basic conversation, and the package developed by Trower, Bryant, and Argyle (1978) is an example of this type of training. The steps are as follows:

1. Session 1 is an introductory training exercise, which involves practicing a brief five-point conversation, starting with a greeting, ending with a farewell, and including the essential verbal and nonverbal components.

2. Session 2 deals with observation skills and includes exercises and guidance on obtaining information about situations and other people.

3. Session 3 involves listening skills such as verbal and nonverbal reflections, minimal "encouragements" such as head nods and "mhmms," listener commentary, and questions.

4. Session 4 covers speaker skills with guidance on things to talk about, how to gain experience and knowledge, and how to remember information. Advice is also given on self-disclosure and the nonverbal accompaniments of speech.

5. Session 5 deals with meshing skills, including the continuity of conversation themes, the timing of utterances, and cues for managing speaking turns.

6. Session 6 focuses on the mainly nonverbal expression of interpersonal attitudes, especially warmth and assertiveness.

7. Session 7 covers everyday social routines such as greeting and parting; giving compliments, praise, and other kinds of support; apologizing; excusing; and saving face. This session also includes assertive routines such as insisting on rights and refusing.

8. Session 8 moves on to problem-solving skills, including choosing alternative responses and deciding on general strategies of behavior, such as being rewarding and controlling and presenting the self.

9. Session 9 gives some general guidance on situation training—the rules that apply to particular situations such as parties, dance clubs, and restaurants.

More recently, van der Molen (1984) and van der Molen and Trower (1991) have developed an integrated program for shy people that divides skills into *receiving* (listening, responding) and *sending* (asserting). The skills are organized as follows:

*Listening-Receiving Skills*
   Attending behavior
   Minimal encouragements
   Asking questions
   Paraphrasing content
   Reflecting feelings
*Sending-Asserting Skills—Active*
   Self-disclosure

Asking favors
Disagreeing
Expressing feelings
Expressing negative feelings (anger)
Expressing positive feelings (affection)
*Sending-Asserting Skills—Reactive*
Refusing requests
Responding to disagreement
Responding to negative feelings
Responding to positive feelings

Finally, a useful skill for dealing with potential conversation breakdowns is:

Meta-conversation (talking about talking)

*Cognitive therapy with exposure.* When assessment of the socially anxious shows *dysfunctional cognitions* as the main problem, then the treatment of choice may be cognitive restructuring with exposure to feared social situations without an explicit SST component.

An example of this approach comes from Heimberg, Dodge, Hope, Kennedy, Zollo, and Becker (1990). This group has a program that is administered by two co-therapists to five or six patients with social phobia in 12 weekly sessions and comprises several components:

1. Developing a cognitive-behavioral explanation of social phobia
2. Training patients in the skills of identification, analysis, and disputation of problematic cognitions through the use of structured exercises
3. Exposing patients to simulations of anxiety-provoking situations in the context of the treatment group
4. Using cognitive-restructuring procedures, such as those mentioned in step 2, to teach patients to control their maladaptive thinking before and during the ''exposure simulations'' described in step 3
5. Using similar procedures to teach patients to engage in rational self-analysis rather than negative self-evaluation after the conclusion of an exposure simulation
6. Assigning homework in which patients would expose themselves to real anxiety-provoking events after they have confronted these events in exposure simulations
7. Teaching patients a self-administered cognitive-restructuring routine so that they may engage in

cognitive preparation for homework assignments and in rational self-analysis after their completion.

If avoidance behavior is more prominent than dysfunctional thinking or lack of skills, then exposure in vivo may need to be the core therapy. The client is encouraged to stay in the feared situation until anxiety diminishes, and then to tackle increasingly difficult situations. Examples of feared situations given by Scholing and Emmelkamp (1990) are:

1. Go to an electronics store and let a clerk inform you extensively about color television sets. Inquire about the advantages and disadvantages of the different makes, the longevity, the price, the guarantee, and so on.
2. Go into a bar and start a conversation with a stranger.
3. Stand in line at the supermarket and give the person in front of you a compliment.

Useful procedures for exposure in vivo with social phobics include the following:

1. Make several exposure hierarchies, each centered around one common theme (e.g., working while observed by others, informal contacts with other people, or heterosocial situations).
2. Instead of staying long enough for anxiety to reduce, an alternative is to increase the frequency of entering similar situations.
3. Get the client to identify and give up using subtle avoidance behavior tactics, such as sitting back in a group, not asking questions in a meeting, and excusing oneself when there is no need for it. The links with skills training are obvious here.

In a study evaluating their multicomponent approach, Heimberg et al. (1990) found that there were significant gains on the main measures, both immediately and at six-month follow-up, compared to a credible placebo control group.

In two evaluation studies (Mattick & Peters, 1988; Mattick, Peters, & Clarke, 1988) the treatment that combined exposure and cognitive restructuring was superior on the main measures to all other treatment groups (exposure alone, cognitive restructuring alone, and waiting list control)—a difference that tended to increase at follow-up.

*Combined intervention.* Few programs have been developed that incorporate comprehensively all the approaches described. The program of van der Molen (1984) and van der Molen and Trower (1991) add cognitive restructuring and relaxation to the basic social skills training. The present author is also in the process of preparing a program that incorporates the interpersonal dimension, particularly the modification of actual to preferred self-presentation and "manipulation" styles, and focusing on the skills of expressivity, sensitivity, and control identified by Riggio (1989).

## Outcome

Social anxiety is a problem par excellence where a combination of social skills training (SST) and cognitive psychotherapy would theoretically be more effective than either treatment alone. This is because social anxiety is simultaneously a social problem and one where a belief-based fear of negative evaluation is a defining characteristics. SST acts as an appropriate form of exposure as well as helping with new skills, whereas cognitive psychotherapy is designed to change dysfunctional self-evaluative beliefs that would otherwise be expected to block the acquisition of skills or undermine the benefit of exposure. As Butler (1989) reports, for example, the fear of being negatively evaluated, criticized, or rejected appears not to decrease after exposure alone and points up the need for cognitive strategies to facilitate realistic appraisals and thereby help patients find out whether or not their expectations were erroneous.

Most of the earlier outcome studies on SST did not include a cognitive psychotherapy component, nor did they include evaluations of whether cognitive changes were taking place as well as behavioral ones. There are a number of reviews of these studies, including Arkowitz (1977); Curran (1977); Marzillier (1978); and Twentyman and Zimering (1979). Another, more recent set of reviews included some evaluations of cognitive psychotherapy, and more studies based on clinical cases (including Curran, Wallander, & Farrell, 1985; Emmelkamp, 1982; Heimberg & Barlow, 1988; Shepherd, 1983; Stravynski & Shahar, 1983).

A considerable proportion of the studies in this first set of reviews were judged to be flawed methodologically, and it was difficult to draw any conclusions from them. However, conclusions that *were* drawn included the following:

1. SST could produce behavioral change in the short term compared to no-treatment control groups,

and there was *some* evidence that it was superior to viable alternative treatments such as systematic desensitization and discussion groups.

2. There was little convincing evidence that changes were durable or generalized to real-life settings.

Twentyman and Zimering (1979) found that both SST and systematic desensitization produced equally effective results with socially anxious clients.

Some of the findings from the second set of reviews were as follows:

1. A majority view that SST and cognitive restructuring together produce the most promising results for socially anxious clients (Emmelkamp, 1982; Heimberg & Barlow, 1988, but not Stravynski & Shahar, 1983).
2. SST is superior to no-treatment controls and to a number of viable treatment alternatives including short-term psychotherapy, group discussion, sensitivity training, and bibliotherapy (Stravynski & Shahar, 1983).
3. There is *some* evidence that effects are maintained, but evidence on generalization remains weak.
4. The full package of SST components works better than any single component.

The authors also noted that there were still far too many methodological weaknesses in studies.

Two studies found that cognitive interventions added nothing to SST or exposure. Stravynski and Shahar (1983) found that SST alone and SST combined with cognitive modification based on rational-emotive therapy were equally effective in increasing social interaction with reduced anxiety, reduced depression, and reduced irrational beliefs, but cognitive modification did not enhance the effectiveness of SST. A study by Biran, Augusto, and Wilson (1981) found that cognitive restructuring added nothing to exposure in therapeutic change in patients whose main problem was "scriptophobia" (fear of writing in the presence of others). However, Heimberg and Barlow (1988) argue that these studies may have administered cognitive procedures in a way that would not be deemed acceptable by cognitive therapists, and did not take account of recent developments in knowledge of the cognitive processes involved in social phobia.

Cognitive interventions have been found effective in several studies, both as independent treatments (Emmelkamp, Mersch, Vissia, & van der Helm,

1985; Jerremalm, Jansson, & Ost, 1986; Kanter & Goldfried, 1979) or in combination with exposure or SST (Butler, Cullington, Munby, Amies, & Gelder, 1984; Heimberg et al., 1990; Mattick & Peters, 1988).

In a recent review of cognitive-behavioral interventions for social phobia, Heimberg (1989a) calls for greater differentiation between diagnostic subtypes, more investigation of specific responses to specific treatments or combinations of treatments, and more study of the mechanisms of change.

## Depression

*Assessment*

In this section I shall draw mainly upon the assessment and training framework developed by Becker, Heimberg, and Bellack (1987), with some recommended additions and deletions. The three components of assessment are diagnosis/mood, social behavior and situational factors affecting behavior, and perceptual and cognitive processes.

Prior to the main social skills assessment, self-report questionnaires and a clinical interview to establish diagnosis and severity of disturbed mood are recommended. As a minimum, the Beck Depression Inventory (Beck, Wald, Mendelson, Mock, & Erbaugh, 1961) should be used to establish initial severity and monitor mood during the course of training. The most popular structured clinical interview instrument is the Schedule for Affective Disorders and Schizophrenia (SADS) (Endicott & Spitzer, 1978). If it is important to distinguish between Major Depressive Disorder and Dysthymic Disorder, then the Hamilton Rating Scale for Depression (Hamilton, 1960) is perhaps the best discriminator (SST appears to be equally effective for both, as will be discussed).

Following Becker et al. (1987), the main skills assessment commences with an interview schedule structured as follows:

1. History of reinforcement and punishment from others
2. Client's perception of consequences of own social behaviors and evaluation of naturally occurring reinforcement and punishment history
3. Situational control factors—that is, situation-specific factors that influence behavior such as age, sex, status, and other partner variables, and work, home, and other setting variables

4. Client's self-evaluation and self-reinforcement regarding own social behavior
5. Client's perceived difficulties with three major skill areas ("performance classes"), namely, (a) positive assertion, (b) negative assertion, and (c) conversational skill

The therapist aims to get a list of problematic situations, persons, or skills, rank-ordered for difficulty level, for subsequent role-play simulations.

After the interview, the next step is role-play simulations of 12 situations, divided into three types: (1) scenes requiring negative versus positive assertion, (2) familiar versus less familiar partners, and (3) male versus female partners. Each scene is presented with a narrative description of the situation, followed by a prompt from the therapist and a signal for the subject to respond. The client's response is then coded on social skill scales, both molecular (paralinguistic and nonverbal elements) and molar (ratings of positive and negative assertion). Poor responses to such artificial scenes may be due to lack of conceptual knowledge of situation variables.

These scenarios are supplemented with "extended" role-plays tailored to the individual and designed to evaluate if clients detect "dynamic" social cues from others regarding turn-taking, topic changing, ambivalence, emotional expression, and the like, and whether they modify their behavior as a result.

Other assessment methods used include self-monitoring in the form of a homework log sheet and self-report measures of assertion, particularly the Rathus Assertiveness Scale, which appears to have the best psychometric properties.

*Training*

In the Becker et al. (1987) program, the first stage (following assessment) is direct behavioral training. This focuses on specific problem situations and involves approximately the steps of instruction, modeling, role-play, and rehearsal already outlined. The clinician instructs the client both in the specifics of behavioral performance and in the reasons that the target behavior is important. Several role-play rehearsals of the problem situations are conducted. This part of training also includes "flexibility" training, which aims, among other things, at facilitating transfer of new skills to other situations by varying the situational content.

The second stage is practice and generalization, in which homework assignments are set so that newly acquired skills may be put into practice in everyday life.

The third stage is social perception training, which focuses on the *where's* and *when's* of adaptive responding rather than the *how's*. Attention is paid to the context in which a response occurs—appropriate times, places, and reasons for a response; the historical context; and the impact of recent interactions. Again, role-play is a major aid to learning. A number of target areas are worked upon, and these include the following:

1. Floor shifts (cues for taking speaking turns) and topic changes (cues for smooth transition between topics)
2. Clarifying the other's communications (attending, summarizing, and verifying)
3. Recognizing ambivalence and being persistent (recognizing verbal and nonverbal cues that indicate ambivalence on the part of the listener)
4. Detecting the other's emotional state (recognizing the verbal and nonverbal components of behavior that are usually indicative of positive and negative emotional states)
5. Reinforcing and punishing (positive and negative reciprocity)

The fourth stage is self-evaluation and self-reinforcement training. This tackles negative beliefs that may block the acquisition and implementation of better social skills. For example, clients are helped to modify perfectionistic standards (by which they judge their performances as "failures") by such questions as: (1) What could make the response acceptable? (2) Is this modification realistically attainable? (3) What standard might be more adaptive?

*Outcome*

We will first look at some of the conclusions that have been drawn in reviews of the outcome literature (e.g., Williams, 1986) on the comparative effects of SST, cognitive-behavioral therapy and other therapies. First, controlled studies consistently show that SST alleviates depression, and maintains and even enhances such improvements at follow-up (e.g., Sanchez, Lewinsohn, & Larson, 1980). A form of SST that included cognitive-behavioral components was equal in effectiveness to amitriptyline and psychodynamic psychotherapy, but no more so (Bellack, Hersen, & Himmelhoch, 1983). Second, SST combined with cognitive-behavioral therapy does have a specific effect, in changing interpersonal skills as opposed to other aspects of depression. For example, Hersen, Bellack, Himmelhoch, and Thase (1984) found a variety of significant differences and trends on behavioral skills (e.g., speech duration, voice tone, gaze, and assertiveness) favoring cognitive-behavioral SST compared with drugs and psychotherapy, such differences being maintained at six-month follow-up. However, Williams (1986) argues that such changes in skills are also produced by other therapies that are not specifically geared to change skills per se, such as cognitive therapy combined with pleasant events scheduling (Zeiss, Lewinsohn, & Munoz, 1979) or self-control training (Fuchs & Rehm, 1977), and raises the question whether social skill improvements may be no more than a correlate of increased general motivation and increased motor activity that comes about as a result of any effective treatment. General conclusions about the effect of SST alone or SST plus CBT on depression (and, indeed, on other disorders) are limited because insufficient research has been done to indicate which subtypes and symptoms of depression do best with which treatment. Research of the recommended kind includes the study of McKnight, Nelson, Hayes, and Jarrett (1984), which compared the effects of SST and cognitive therapy in reducing depression. They found that the effectiveness of treatment is greatly enhanced when the treatment is related to the findings of the initial assessment. They found, for example, that social skills deficits improved with SST, and cognitive deficits with cognitive therapy. A problem with interpreting the literature is that it is not always entirely clear whether SST procedures included cognitive therapy components.

Despite these limitations, it is encouraging that cognitive-behavioral SST has been shown to be effective in alleviating depression and that it has the benefit (1) of having a much lower dropout rate than, for example, drugs (Bellack et al., 1983); (2) of having no known side effects; (3) of working with clients who do not respond to drugs; and (4) of being reasonably cost-effective. It is noteworthy that this tradition of research has not drawn on the literature referred to in the assessment section earlier on the connection between depressive cognitions and the interpersonal style of depressed individuals.

## Schizophrenia

Early disappointing results with SST for longer term clients, including those with schizophrenia and personality disorders, has led researchers in more recent years to the insistence that assessment and training must be embedded in a total package of care if it is to work. An example is that outlined by Bellack (1989), consisting of four components:

1. *Treatment,* including medication, family therapy, social skills training, medical care, and crisis intervention
2. *Rehabilitation,* including housekeeping, nutrition, hygiene, job training, and transportation
3. *Social services,* including income support, housing, social support, and recreation
4. *Continuity of care,* involving the active coordination of these services

I would also add to this list schemes that empower patients (and would have a significant bearing on SST) including advocacy, patients' councils, and consumer-led planning of services.

*Assessment*

In this section I draw mainly on Liberman, DeRisi, and Mueser (1989), with some modifications. The approach to training is substantially different from that for other diagnostic groups and is affected by symptoms, and therefore it is important to establish the diagnosis and symptomatology. The recommended, standardized structured interviews include the SADS (Endicott & Spitzer, 1978), mentioned earlier, the Structured Clinical Interview for DSM-III (SCID) (Spitzer & Williams, 1985), and the Present State Examination (PSE) (Wing, Cooper, & Sartorius, 1974).

Liberman et al. (1989) offer an assessment approach that takes account of the difficulties specific to this population, who often have difficulty in communicating. Their assessment methods are necessarily opportunistic, informal as well as formal, and broad-based in terms of informants. The procedure is also complex and can best be summarized in the following steps:

| Step | Procedure |
|---|---|
| 1. Determine ability of patient to follow instructions, pay attention. | Rule out severe incoherence and conceptual disorganization in schizophrenic or organic disorders. Use lowest effective dose of psychotropics. Try structured activity to displace intrusive and bizarre symptoms. |
| 2. Do initial assessment of | Use checklist of criteria for setting interpersonal goals |
| patient's social skills before starting training. | (supplied by authors). Examine histories and assessments in medical record. Talk to caregivers, family, responsible clinicians. Use results of assessment instruments. Observe patient yourself. |
| 3. Evaluate patient's affiliative and instrumental abilities. | Set up a "dry run" with two or three helpers (staff or other patients). Help patient put problems in interpersonal context. |
| 4. Check stressors in patient's life: time-limited events, ongoing tensions, conflicts. | Look for big changes, overstimulation, overinvolvement of family, caregiver, drugs, alcohol use. |
| 5. Check coping skills. | Ask what changes patient would make, what situations make for lack of confidence, social anxiety. See if there are constructive activities in which patient can engage to displace symptoms. |
| 6. Identify tentative goals and scenes for role playing and training. | Involve patient as much as possible, and use all other sources of assessment data. |
| 7. Use structured instruments for further assessment. | Focused behavioral interview. Do naturalistic observation. Do role-play test. Examine permanent products of patient's social life. |
| 8. Obtain as many details as possible for the scenes you will use first. | Ask "Who?" "What?" "Where?" "When?" and "How often?" Get descriptions of physical setting, people, and events. |
| 9. Be sure goals are positive, attainable, specific, functional, high-frequency, consistent with rights and responsibilities, chosen by patient as likely to occur. | Use these criteria to be sure goals, situations will be useful and productive in training. |

## Training

Liberman et al. (1989) have developed a training program based on a three-stage model of social interaction similar to that of Argyle and Kendon (1967), which formed the basis of the program of Trower, Bryant, and Argyle (1978). Stage 1 is *receiving*, which includes the skills necessary for accurate perception of social information. Stage 2 is *processing*, including the steps necessary for choosing the most effective skills for the situation. Stage 3 is *sending*, the actual behavioral skills involved in the social transaction.

On the basis of this model, Liberman et al. (1989) offered a detailed 20-step procedure for carrying out a training session: These steps are summarized as follows:

1. Give introduction to social skills training.
2. Introduce new patients.
3. Solicit orientation from experienced patients who can explain social skills training to new patients.
4. Reward patients for their contributions to the orientation. Use praise liberally.
5. Check homework assignments—details of actual performance, obstacles to generalization.
6. Help each patient pinpoint an interpersonal problem, goal, and scene for this session.
7. Target scene and interpersonal situation for dry run role-play.
8. Set up the scene.
9. Give instructions for the scene.
10. Run the scene as a dry run.
11. Give positive feedback. Get everyone to participate.
12. Assess receiving, processing, sending skills. Ask:
    What did the other say?
    What was the other feeling?
    What were your short-term goals?
    What were your long-term goals?
    What other alternatives could you use?
    Would an alternative help reach your goals?
13. Use a model selected for similarity to real person in patient's life.
14. Ensure patient has assimilated the skills. Ask to report on model's performance.
15. Use another model if there is time.
16. Give instructions for next rehearsal or rerun. Concentrate on one or two behaviors selected by the patient.
17. Rerun scene using coaching, including hand signals and whispered prompts and praise.
18. Give immediate positive feedback.
19. Give real-life assignment.
20. Choose another patient for the training sequence and return to step 1.

Having described their training procedure, Liberman et al. (1989) then described the content of their training, which is very detailed and behaviorally precise. The training is organized into a series of modules, which include training in Medication Self-Management, Conversation Skills, Friendship and Dating Skills, Recreation for Leisure, Symptom Self-Management, and Grooming and Self-Care. Each module consists of a number of skills areas. For example, the Friendship and Dating Skills Module consists of

Initiating conversations with strangers
Recognizing and expressing emotions
Making friends
Going on a date

Each skill area is further subdivided into components. For example, the skill area Making Friends is subdivided into giving compliments, receiving compliments, compromising and negotiation, finding activities to do together, and expressing affection. Each of these in turn is broken down into steps. For example, Receiving Compliments consists of:

1. Look at person.
2. Thank him or her for compliment.
3. Acknowledge the compliment by:
   (a) Saying how it makes you feel, or
   (b) Saying how you feel about the item that was complimented.

These authors pay particular attention to the difficulties of carrying out training with this client group. For example, they have an attention-focusing procedure for highly distractible institutionalized chronic schizophrenic patients. It consists of multiple, discrete, relatively short training trials, and a closely structured training situation with careful manipulation of the teaching components. Continuous prompting and vigorous reinforcement are given.

## Outcome

Many studies, using both single-case design and control group designs, were carried out, mainly in the 1970s, and there are a number of reviews of these early studies (Hersen, 1979; Marzillier & Winter,

1978; Shepherd, 1981; Wallace et al., 1980). The general consensus of the reviews was similar to that of SST in other areas—that SST could produce behavioral change in the short term, but evidence that such changes were maintained or generalized was equivocal, and the relevance of some of the target behaviors as well as inappropriate training goals and procedures was questioned.

More recently, several large-scale clinical trials have documented that schizophrenics can acquire and maintain new skills, and that social skills training can have a significant effect on relapse (Bellack, Turner, Hersen, & Luber, 1984; Hogarty et al., 1986; Wallace & Liberman, 1985). As a result of this accumulating body of research, SST is now regarded as one of the most important psychosocial components of a comprehensive treatment program for schizophrenia. In a recent review, however, Halford and Hayes (1991) conclude that despite the large volume of research, it is still not known if SST effects generalize to the day-to-day social behavior of schizophrenic patients.

More recently, there has been a marked shift in emphasis in SST research with schizophrenia, with more attention paid to understanding the causes and effects of poor social skills on symptoms and relapse, and a more functional and person-centered approach to implementing training programs (Shepherd, 1986). This has been fueled by a concern to reduce the factors that lead to relapse in schizophrenia—a considerable problem, with 50% to 60% of discharged schizophrenics readmitted within two years (Brown, 1982). Liberman and his colleagues (Liberman, Neuchterlein, & Wallace, 1982) suggest a two-way model of relapse—namely, that relapse is a function of too much stress and too few social coping skills. This led to the development of two applications of SST, one aimed at improving the social skills of patients directly and ensuring that these skills generalized and were maintained, the second aimed at improving relationships within the family.

With regard to direct training and the problem of generalization, one recent shift has been to integrate SST better into ongoing rehabilitation programs, such as partial hospitalization. For example, Bellack et al. (1984) treated 44 chronic schizophrenic patients in a 12-week day hospital program supplemented by comprehensive SST and compared the results with those for an equivalent group of 20 who received only day hospital treatment. Although both groups showed improvement immediately following treatment, the SST group continued to improve or maintained their gains on most measures during a six-month follow-up,

compared to the non-SST group, which either maintained gains or lost them. However, half the patients in both groups were hospitalized again in the year following treatment. There was also a 50% attrition rate of subjects by follow-up. More promising results in generalization and maintenance were obtained in two studies by Liberman and his colleagues. In the first study, patients were given highly task- and situation-relevant SST (Liberman, Lillie, Falloon, Harpin, Hutchinson, & Stoute, 1984). The authors obtained significant increases in skilled behavior across situations—hospital, family and community, and evidence of spontaneous generalization. In the second study (Liberman, Mueser, & Wallace, 1986; Wallace & Liberman, 1985), patients who received intensive (12 hours per week) SST as inpatients showed better functioning, spent less time in hospital, and had fewer relapses two years after treatment than did a group receiving a "holistic health" control treatment.

Hansen et al. (1984) used a social validation approach in which target behaviors and criterion levels were established from an assessment of the social skills of "normal" persons in the community. Following training, the frequency of component behaviors increased to the socially validated criterion levels, and training effects generalized to unfamiliar, nonpsychiatric conversational partners and were maintained throughout a seven-month follow-up.

With regard to SST applied to the family, families high in expressed emotion (high EE, which refers to overemotional, usually hostile forms of interaction), a major trigger of relapse (Hooley, 1985), were taught better communication skills (Falloon et al., 1984). They found fewer symptoms and less relapse following family training. These results led to a considerable research program and widespread use of such family training. Reviewing family psychoeducation (FP) in general, Halford and Hayes (1991) concluded that these procedures were clearly superior to no treatment in reducing relapse when patients and relatives are treated as a family group, and overall much stronger evidence of clinical impact than has been demonstrated with SST. Interestingly Hogarty et al. (1986) found that SST and FP combined were twice as effective as when applied singly, and reduced relapse to 0% at twelve-month follow-up and 25% at two-year follow-up (Hogarty, Anderson, & Reiss, 1987).

A further development concerns the design of the "community" into which patients are discharged. Shepherd (1986) criticizes the notion of SST as prescribed therapy irrespective of the environment, as well as the associated outcome studies based on this approach. Designing environments means attempting to ensure that patients have opportunities to function in as normal a social context as possible, where normal social behavior is indeed the norm. Then, instead of starting with the skills and hoping they will generalize, we should start with the role setting and work out which skills are necessary: "This is like turning the social skills model upside down. By trying to start from the place where we hope to end up, we might achieve more significant improvements in 'real' social adaptation" (Shepherd, 1986, p. 31). If FP is regarded as a form of intervention in the social environment, then we may speculate that Shepherd is right, given the greater impact of FP alone compared to SST alone, and the powerful interaction effect of the two combined.

## TOWARD AN INTERPERSONAL REFORMULATION

There is no doubt that social skills theory, research, and practice have had a major impact on approaches to psychopathology and, in particular, to the problem areas reviewed in this chapter. The effect of this impact has been to focus attention on the fundamentally interpersonal nature of psychiatric disorders, and to provide a unique assessment and therapeutic technology to help meet the identified need. A continuous cycle of research interrogation and advancement has led to improvements in the models and the subsequent practice—for example, from a simple behavioral components approach to more sophisticated information-processing models. We should consider whether a further reformulation is now appropriate, which would embrace more explicitly the interpersonal paradigm outlined in the first part of this chapter. Such a reformulation would imply at least the following agenda:

1. The adoption of an explicitly person-centered philosophy of assessment and training. The interpersonal approach emphasizes the need for an understanding of the individual's unique view of himself in relation to others, evaluation of his current social behavior, expectations of others' reactions, and social goals and preferred interpersonal style.
2. An emphasis on the centrality of relationship building and the employment of skills assessment and training to help achieve this end.

3. The identification and assessment of vital interpersonal competencies that appear to be absent or blocked and that would better meet the person's social goals. Gilbert (1989) argues that there are a number of evolved social roles or competencies that are vital for social adaptation and integration, and even for survival (Warner, 1985), but which an individual may not utilize well or at all because of inhibitory learning experiences. Gilbert lists cooperating, competing, caregiving, and care eliciting as the four basic "biosocial goals."
4. To focus skills training on self-presentation behavior appropriate to the interpersonal competencies identified. Each interpersonal competency is characterized by a pattern of self-presentation—for example, dominance by dominant behavioral displays that signal to and try to elicit a reciprocal response from the other.
5. To focus on all other parts of any interpersonal competency that becomes the focus of training—for example, social perception, interpersonal schema, and emotion/physiological arousal, as well as behavior.

Current research and practice undoubtedly deal with some of these issues. Most molecular skills training deals with behaviors that form part of self-presentation behavior. Training programs now include social perception training and interventions that are aimed at cognitive processing. However, it is rare that the interpersonal approach and the five agenda points listed are made an explicit and structured part of assessment and training. How, then, might programs be modified?

### Interpersonal Assessment

Despite the proliferation of measures, there are few that are currently familiar to and used by SST researchers and practitioners that would meet the needs of an interpersonal approach. This is not to deny that many existing measures tap information that an interpersonal approach would draw on, such as self-report measures (assertiveness, dating), observation of behavioral elements, and the like. But the interpersonal approach would also need to assess the person's blocked competencies, perhaps at the behavioral level by assessing limitations in the person's repertoire of self-presentations (for example, for competing and for cooperating), and at the cognitive level by measuring distortions in their interpersonal schema.

An early method of assessing social impressions was the use by independent judges of seven-point semantic differential scales, the choice of which were guided by Leary's Interpersonal Circle and related literature, and which included warm–cold, dominant–submissive, passive–active, socially skilled–unskilled (Trower, Bryant, & Argyle, 1978).

A number of authors have developed measures based on variants of Leary's Interpersonal Circle (a comprehensive review of such methods of assessment is provided by Kiesler, 1990). Horowitz and his colleagues (Horowitz, Rosenberg, Baer, Ureno, & Villasenor, 1988) conducted a content analysis of the presenting complaints of psychiatric outpatients and developed the Inventory of Interpersonal Problems (IIP), a measure that focuses solely on interpersonal behavior and assesses a wide range of interpersonal problems (Horowitz, 1979). The IIP has been shown to have good test–retest reliability and to be correlated in a meaningful way with other interpersonal measures and with clinicians' ratings of clients' behavior (Horowitz et al., 1988). Recently Alden, Wiggins, and Pincus (1990) have further developed this measure for depressed and socially anxious people whose main underlying problem is interpersonal. Principal components analyses yielded two dimensions they labeled Domineering versus Nonassertive and Overly Nurturant versus Cold. Scales were developed to mark eight octants relative to these two dimensions. The structure and thematic content of the eight octant scales were cross-validated on a large ($N = 970$) university sample and on a sample of psychiatric outpatients.

Another group, Safran, Hill, and Ford (1988) developed the Interpersonal Schema Questionnaire (ISQ), which assesses the expectations clients would have of other people's responses to their own interpersonal behavior. No psychometric data were reported, except insofar as administrations of the questionnaire to three independent samples yielded essentially similar results; that is, high symptomatic subjects expected significantly more negative interpersonal responses from significant others than did low symptomatic subjects.

Finally Buss, Gomes, Higgins, and Lauterbach (1987), developed self- and observer-report versions of their Tactics of Manipulation measure to look at the tactics people use to influence the behavior of others. No specific psychometric statistics were cited, although their study showed high correlations across a range of other data sources, including personality questionnaires and behavior ratings.

Another body of work reviewed by Spitzberg and Cupach (1989) is concerned with assessing what they term "relational competence." The assessment focus includes the quality and extent of relationship networks, the skills needed to develop intimacy, to understand relational partners, knowledge of friendship rules, ability to employ "secret tests" about the status of a relationship, and so on. A novel assessment strategy is the Social Relations Model (Kenny & LaVoie, 1984), which is designed to identify three components—an actor effect (actor's relational competence), a partner effect (a measure of the actor's eliciting style on others) and a relationship effect (the degree to which the actor adapts his behavior to the partner). Psychometric data are not cited for these or for the other assessments reviewed by Spitzberg and Cupach's otherwise excellent handbook.

Yet another focus for assessment would be to examine an individual's style of interpersonal relating from a cognitive viewpoint. Safran, Segal, Hill, and Whiffen (1990) have suggested how a methodology could be developed for assessing a person's interpersonal schema—in particular, expectations and beliefs about other people (e.g., "People are uncaring and rejecting"), beliefs about self (e.g., "I am unlovable") and beliefs about the "way one must be in order to maintain relatedness" (e.g., "I must be strong at all times"). One method is to obtain the client's descriptions of key interactions and examine the way recall is biased by the persons' interpersonal schema.

The interpersonal approach also gives a vital new role to personality assessment. Traditionally, psychiatric disorders were differentially diagnosed into either mental disorders or personality disorders, but the advent of the multiaxial evaluation system with DSM-III introduced the idea that people may have both a mental disorder and a personality disorder (as well as other coexisting problems). Interpersonal assessment should, therefore, look more at the personality profiles and interpersonal styles of clients. For example Biran (1989) showed that socially anxious students were heterogeneous with regard to personality. The two main types (as measures on the Millon Clinical Multiaxial Inventory; Millon, 1984) were narcissistic personality and avoidant personality, but there were also compulsive and histrionic types.

The kinds of measures described here can produce very revealing information. For example, Alden and Phillips (1990) looked at the interpersonal self-perceptions of subjects who were socially anxious *and* of subjects who were both depressed and socially anxious. Both groups scored low on the vertical domineering–nonassertive pole, and the anxious group scored high on social avoidance. These findings support the theory put forward by Trower and Gilbert (1989) that socially anxious people characteristically have interpersonal schemata that lead them to see relationships structured in terms of dominance hierarchies, and perceive themselves as low rankers (inferior, appeasing, nonassertive, etc.) or in danger of becoming low rankers within such relationships. A large body of research is reviewed that supports this notion.

Finally, an interpersonally oriented approach to assessing behavioral social skills has been developed by Riggio (1989). He was interested in identifying the skill dimensions that were crucially involved in the development of relationships, and came up with six dimensions, as follows:

1. *Emotional expressivity:* A general skill in nonverbal sending, reflecting ability to express emotion, attitudes, and cues of interpersonal orientation
2. *Emotional sensitivity:* A general skill in receiving, showing ability to decode others' emotions rapidly and accurately
3. *Emotional control:* A general ability to regulate and moderate nonverbal communication
4. *Social expressivity:* General speaking ability and skill in engaging others in social interaction
5. *Social sensitivity:* An ability to comprehend verbal communication, and knowledge of social norms and conventions
6. *Social control:* A general skill in social self-presentation, acting, and role-playing.

With regard to the psychometric properties of the SSI, factor analysis of the SSI lends support for this multidimensional structure of social skill (Riggio, 1989). In addition, Riggio has established reasonable test–retest reliability ($r$ = .81 to .96) and internal consistency (alpha = .62 to .87) and has demonstrated reasonable convergent and discriminant validity (reported in Riggio, 1989).

## Interpersonal Training

I am not aware of any directly interpersonally oriented versions of social skills training. How would such training be undertaken?

Training would need to be rather more closely informed by interpersonal assessment than traditional forms of skills training. A possible protocol might be as follows:

1. The therapist might need to help the client see what kind of response his present, habitual, and probably dysfunctional self-presentation behavior is likely to invoke in others—in other words, to understand his current ''tactic of manipulation.'' In a socially anxious client, his self-presentation style might be self-debasing, appeasing behavior, which triggers in others a tendency to be arrogant and self-assured.
2. The client learns that a repertoire of basic self-presentation strategies that he inherently possesses—such as competing, cooperating, giving, or eliciting care—is needed for social survival, and he may have to realize that he actually uses only one or none of these.
3. The client focuses on one strategy that is most obviously underutilized or lacking and would better meet his social needs, and commences at this point a traditional skills training program.
4. The intention is that the client should learn that the new style evokes a quite different response; for example, considerate cooperativeness evokes the parallel response in the majority of people.
5. The client learns the pattern of others' behavior that would trigger his dysfunctional (appeasing) style, such as loud voice and dominant posture, and uses this as a cue to utilize the alternative style.

A natural laboratory where dysfunctional interpersonal styles occur is, of course, in the family, and it may be useful to draw on family therapy models—particularly behavioral family therapy and traditional systems-based family therapy—as a resource for interpersonal training.

One version of behavioral family therapy (Falloon, Boyd, & McGill, 1984) explicitly uses SST to try to change the high levels of criticism and hostility directed to the patient by the relative, and which often triggers relapse in schizophrenia. This is done by such skills as active listening, assertive communication, problem definition, and problem solving. It is not difficult to reconceptualize this process within an interpersonal framework. In our current terminology, this might then be described as the teaching of a cooperative interpersonal style, which evokes a corresponding response from the client, leading to a virtuous cycle of increasing affiliation. The cooperative style can be seen as replacing the previous hostile–dominant pattern, which presumably (though this is unresearched) invokes an opposite response from the client, of appeasement, abasement, subservience, or a more primitive fight, flight, or disengagement from relating altogether. Such low-ranking behavior is associated with stress and low self-esteem (Gilbert, 1989), which are in turn associated with relapse. The fact that behavioral family therapy has a better track record of success than traditional SST (Halford & Hayes, 1991), might indicate that interpersonal training has some promise, too.

The second family therapy model is the "interpersonal systems approach," which Gotlib and Colby (1987) have developed for depression. It combines systems theory with components of cognitive-behavioral therapy.

The systems theory part of this approach clearly involves the marital partner or the whole family. It includes:

1. Joining, which is conceptually similar to the therapeutic alliance
2. Reframing, which involves reinterpreting (e.g., the depression) in such a way that the family members relinquish their previous entrenched conceptualizations of the problem
3. Restructuring, which allows the family to alter dysfunctional patterns of interaction
4. Altering boundaries, which is designed to help break down subgroup barriers that separate family members

The cognitive-behavioral component has the two goals of (1) helping the individual understand the effect of his depression on those around him and (2) attenuating the depressed person's increased accessibility to negative stimuli. Techniques for the latter task include monitoring thoughts and perceptions more accurately by use of a daily thought record, especially at the time of critical incidents; recording positive events and the behaviors and reactions of others, both positive and negative; and increasing the number of pleasurable activities and incorporating these into a daily activities schedule. Gotlib and Colby (1987) reports that a number of studies using this approach have shown promising results, but more empirical work is required. However, this approach may provide a framework for developing a more general interpersonal training approach.

# REFERENCES

Alden, L., & Cappe, R. (1981). Nonassertiveness: Skill deficit or selective self-evaluation. *Behavior Therapy, 12,* 107–114.

Alden, L. E., & Phillips, N. (1990). An interpersonal analysis of social anxiety and depression. *Cognitive Therapy and Research, 14,* 449–512.

Alden, L. E., Wiggins, J. S., & Pincus, A. (1990). Construction of the IIP Circumplex Scales. *Journal of Personality Assessment, 55,* 34–45.

American Psychiatric Association. (1987). *Diagnostic and statistical manual of mental disorders,* 3rd ed. revised Washington, DC: American Psychiatric Press.

Anchin, J. C., & Kiesler, D. J. (Eds.). (1982). *Handbook of interpersonal psychotherapy.* New York: Pergamon Press.

Argyle, M., & Henderson, M. (1985). The rules of friendship. *Journal of Social and Personal Relationships, 1,* 211–37.

Argyle, M., & Kendon, H. (1967). The experimental analysis of social performance. In L. Berkowitz (Ed.), *Advances in experimental social psychology* (Vol. 3). New York: Academic Press.

Arkowitz, H. (1977). Measurement and modification of minimal dating behavior. In M. Hersen, R. Eisler, & P. M. Miller (Eds.), *Progress in behavior modification.* New York: Academic Press.

Bakeman, R., & Gottman, J. (1986). *Observing interaction.* New York: Cambridge University Press.

Bandura, A. (1977). *Social learning theory.* Englewood Cliffs, NJ: Prentice-Hall.

Bannister, D., & Fransella, F. (1985). *Inquiring man.* London: Croom Helm.

Barlow, D. H., & Wolfe, B. E. (1981) Behavioral approaches to anxiety disorders: A report on the NIMH-SUNY, Albany Research Conference. *Journal of Consulting and Clinical Psychology, 49,* 448–454.

Beck, A. T., Rush, A. J., Shaw, B. F., & Emery, G. (1979) *Cognitive therapy of depression.* New York: Guilford Press.

Beck, A. T., Ward, C. H., Mendelson, M., Mock, J., & Erbaugh, J. (1961). An inventory for measuring depression. *Archives of General Psychiatry, 4,* 561–571.

Becker, R. E., Heimberg, R. G., & Bellack, A. S. (1987) *Social skills training treatment for depression.* New York: Pergamon Press.

Beidel, D. C., Turner, S. M., & Dancu, C. V. (1985) Physiological, cognitive and behavioral aspects of social anxiety. *Behaviour, Research and Therapy, 23,* 109–11

Bellack, A. S. (1983). Recurrent problems in the behavioral assessment of social skill. *Behaviour Research and Therapy, 21,* 29–42.

Bellack, A. S. (1989). A comprehensive model for treatment of schizophrenia. In A. S. Bellack (Ed.), *A clinical guide for the treatment of schizophrenia.* New York: Plenum Press.

Bellack, A. S., Hersen, M., & Himmelhoch, J. M. (1983). A comparison of social skills training, pharmacotherapy and psychotherapy for depression. *Behaviour Research and Therapy, 21,* 101–107.

Bellack, A. S., Morrison, R. L., Wixted, J. T., & Mueser, K. T. (1990). An analysis of social competence in schizophrenia. *British Journal of Psychiatry, 156,* 809–818.

Bellack, A. S., Turner, S. M., Hersen, M., & Luber, R. F. (1984). An examination of the efficacy of social skills training for chronic schizophrenic patients. *Hospital and Community Psychiatry, 35,* 1023–1028.

Biran, M. (1989). *Outcome of cognitive-behavioral treatment for speech-anxiety and basic personality patterns.* Paper presented at the World Congress of Cognitive Therapy, Oxford, England, June–July.

Biran, M., Augusto, F., & Wilson, G. T. (1981). In vivo exposure vs. cognitive restructuring in the treatment of scriptophobia. *Behaviour Research and Therapy, 19,* 525–532.

Boice, R., & Monti, P. M. (1982) Specification of nonverbal behaviors for clinical assessment. *Journal of Nonverbal Behavior, 2,* 79–94.

Brown, M. (1982). Maintenance and generalization issues in skills training with chronic schizophrenics. In J. P. Curran & P. M. Monti (Eds.), *Social skills training: A practical handbook for assessment and treatment.* New York: Guilford Press.

Buss, D. M., Gomes, M., Higgins, D. S., & Lauterbach, K. (1987). Tactics of manipulation. *Journal of Personality and Social Psychology, 52,* 1219–1229.

Butler, G. (1989). Issues in the application of cognitive and behavioral strategies to the treatment of social phobia. *Clinical Psychology Review, 9,* 91–106.

Butler, G., Cullington, A., Munby, M., Amies, P., & Gelder, M. (1984). Exposure and anxiety management in the treatment of social phobia. *Journal of Consulting and Clinical Psychology, 52,* 642–650.

Carson, R. C. (1969). *Interaction concepts of personality.* Chicago: Aldine.

Carver, C. S., & Scheier, M. F. (1984). A control theory approach to behaviour, and some implications for social skills training. In P. Trower (Ed.), *Radical approaches to social skills training.* London: Croom Helm.

Chance, M. R. A. (1984). Biological systems synthesis of mentality and the nature of the two modes of mental operation: Hedonic and agonic. *Man-environment systems, 14,* 143–157.

Chance, M. R. A. (1988). (Ed.). *Social fabrics of the mind.* Hove, Sussex: Lawrence Erlbaum.

Cheek, J. M., & Melchior, L. A. (1990). Shyness, self-esteem, and self-consciousness. In H. Leitenberg (Ed.), *Handbook of social and evaluation anxiety.* New York: Plenum Press.

Cooley, C. H. (1902). *Human nature and the social order.* New York: Charles Scribner's Sons.

Coyne, J. C. (1976). Depression and the response of others. *Journal of Abnormal Psychology, 85,* 186–193.

Coyne, J. C. (1990). Interpersonal processes in depression. In G. I. Keitner (Ed.), *Depression and families.* Washington DC: American Psychiatric Press.

Crozier, W. R. (1990). *Shyness and embarrassment.* Cambridge: Cambridge University Press.

Curran, J. P. (1977). Skills training as an approach to the treatment of heterosexual-social anxiety: A review. *Psychological Bulletin, 84,* 140–157.

Curran, J. P., Wallander, J. L., & Farrell, A. D. (1985). Heterosocial skills training. In L. L'Abate & M. A. Milan (Eds.), *Handbook of social skills training and research.* New York: Wiley.

Danziger, K. (1976). *Interpersonal communication.* Chicago: Aldine.

Di Nardo, P. A., Barlow, D. H., Cerny, J. A., Vermilyea, B. B., Himadi, W. D., & Waddell, M. T. (1985). *Anxiety disorders interview schedule revised (ADIS-R).* Albany, NY: Center for Stress and Anxiety Disorders.

D'Zurilla, T. J., & Goldfried, M. R. (1971). Problem solving and behavior modification. *Journal of Abnormal Psychology, 78,* 197–226.

Emmelkamp, P. M. G. (1982). *Obsessions and Phobias.* New York: Plenum Press.

Emmelkamp, P. M. G., Mersch, P. P., Vissia, E., & van der Helm, M. (1985). Social phobia: A comparative evaluation of cognitive and behavioral interventions. *Behaviour, Research and Therapy, 23,* 365–369.

Endicott, J., & Spitzer, R. L. (1978). A diagnostic interview: The schedule for affective disorders and schizophrenia. *Archives of General Psychiatry, 35,* 837–844.

Falloon, I. R. H., Boyd, J. L., & McGill, C. W. (1984). *Family care of schizophrenia.* New York: Guilford Press.

Feinberg, T. E., Rifkin, A., Schaffer, C., & Walker, E. (1986). Facial discrimination and emotional recognition in schizophrenia and affective disorders. *Archives of General Psychiatry, 43,* 276–279.

Fuchs, C. Z., & Rehm, L. P. (1977). A self-control behavior therapy program for depression. *Journal of Consulting and Clinical Psychology, 45,* 206–215.

Gardner, R. (1988). Psychiatric syndromes as infrastructure for intra-specific communication. In M. R. A. Chance (Ed.), *Social fabrics of the mind.* Hove, Sussex: Lawrence Erlbaum.

Gervasio, A. H. (1987). Assertiveness techniques as speech acts. *Clinical Psychology Review, 7,* 105–119.

Gilbert, P. (1989). *Human nature and suffering.* London: Lawrence Erlbaum.

Gilbert, P. (1992). *Depression: The evolution of powerlessness.* Hove, Sussex: Lawrence Erlbaum.

Glass, C. R., & Furlong, M. (1990). Cognitive assessment of social anxiety: Affective and behavioral correlates. *Cognitive Therapy and Research, 14,* 365–384.

Glass, C. R., Merluzzi, T. V., Biever, J. L., & Larsen, K. H. (1982). Cognitive assessment of social anxiety: Development and validation of a self-statement questionnaire. *Cognitive Therapy and Research, 6,* 37–55.

Goffman, E. (1959). *The presentation of self in everyday life.* New York: Doubleday Anchor.

Gotlib, I. H., & Colby, C. A. (1987). *Treatment of depression: An interpersonal systems approach.* New York: Pergamon Press.

Gotlib, I. H., & Meltzer, S. J. (1987). Depression and the perception of social skill in dyadic interaction. *Cognitive Therapy and Research, 11,* 41–54.

Gotlib, I. H., & Robinson, L. A. (1982). Responses to depressed individuals: Discrepancies between self-report and observer-rated behavior. *Journal of Abnormal Psychology, 91,* 231–240.

Gutride, M. E., Goldstein, A. P., & Hunter, G. F. (1973). The use of modeling and role-playing to increase social interaction among asocial psychiatric patients. *Journal of Consulting and Clinical Psychology, 40,* 408–415.

Halford, K., & Foddy, M. (1982). Cognitive and social skills correlates of social anxiety. *British Journal of Clinical Psychology, 21,* 17–28.

Halford, W. K., & Hayes, R. (1991). Psychological rehabilitation of chronic schizophrenic patients: Recent findings on social skills training and family psychoeducation. *Clinical Psychology Review, 11,* 23–44.

Hamilton, M. (1960). A rating scale for depression. *Journal of Neurology, Neurosurgery, and Psychiatry, 23,* 56–62.

Hammen, C. L., & Peters, S. D. (1978). Interpersonal consequences of depression: Responses to men and women enacting a depressed role. *Journal of Abnormal Psychology, 87,* 322–332.

Harre, R., & Secord, P. F. (1972). *The explanation of social behaviour.* Oxford: Blackwell.

Heimberg, R. G. (1989a). Cognitive and behavioral treatments for social phobia: A critical analysis. *Clinical Psychology Review, 9,* 107–128.

Heimberg, R. G. (1989b). Social phobia: No longer neglected. *Clinical Psychology Review* (Special Issue: Social Phobia), *9,* 1–2.

Heimberg, R. G., & Barlow, D. H. (1988). Psychosocial treatments for social phobia. *Psychosomatics, 29,* 27–37.

Heimberg, R. G., Dodge, C. S., Hope, D. A., Kennedy, C. R., Zollo, L., & Becker, R. E. (1990). Cognitive behavioral group treatment of social phobia: Comparison to a credible placebo control. *Cognitive Therapy and Research, 14,* 1–23.

Heimberg, R. G., Nyman, D., & O'Brien, G. T. (1987). Assessing variations of the thought-listing technique: Effects of instructions, stimulus intensity, stimulus modality and scoring procedures. *Cognitive Therapy and Research, 11,* 13–24.

Hersen, M. (1979). Modification of skill deficits in psychiatric patients. In A. S. Bellack & M. Hersen (Eds.), *Research and practice in social skills training.* New York: Plenum Press.

Hersen, M., Bellack, A. S., Himmelhoch, J. M., & Thase, M. E. (1984). Effects of social skills training, amitriptyline, and psychotherapy in unipolar depressed women. *Behavior Therapy, 15,* 21–40.

Hogarty, G. E., Anderson, C. M., Reiss, D. J., Kornblith, S. J., Greenwald, D. P., Javna, C. D., & Madonia, M. J. (1986). Family psycho-education social skills training and maintenance chemotherapy: I. One year effects of a controlled study on relapse and expressed emotion. *Archives of General Psychiatry, 43,* 633–642.

Hogarty, G. E., Anderson, C. M., & Reiss, D. J. (1987). Family psychoeducation, social skills training and medication in schizophrenia: The long and the short of it. *Psychopharmacology Bulletin, 23,* 12–13.

Hooley, J. M. (1985). Expressed emotion: A review of the critical literature. *Clinical Psychology Review, 5,* 119–139.

Hope, D. A., Rapee, R. M., Heimberg, R. G., & Dombeck, M. J. (1990). Representations of the self in social phobia: Vulnerability to social threat. *Cognitive Research and Therapy, 14,* 177–189.

Horowitz, L. M. (1979). On the cognitive structure of interpersonal problems treated in psychotherapy. *Journal of Consulting and Clinical Psychology, 47,* 993–998.

Horowitz, L. M., Rosenberg, S. E., Baer, B. A., Ureno, G., & Villasenor, V. S. (1988). The inventory of interpersonal problems: Psychometric properties and clinical applications. *Journal of Consulting and Clinical Psychology, 56,* 885–892.

Howes, M. J., & Hokanson, J. E. (1979). Conversational and social responses to depressive interpersonal behaviour. *Journal of Abnormal Psychology, 88,* 625–634.

Jerremalm, A., Jansson L., & Ost, L. G. (1986). Cognitive and physiological reactivity and the effects of different behavioral methods in the treatment of social phobia. *Behaviour, Research and Therapy, 24,* 171–180.

Jones, W. H., Cheek, J. M., & Briggs, S. R. (Eds.). (1986). *Shyness: Perspectives on research and treatment.* New York: Plenum Press.

Kanter, N. J., & Goldfried, M. R. (1979). Relative effectiveness of rational restructuring and self-control desensitization in the reduction of interpersonal anxiety. *Behavior Therapy, 10,* 472–490.

Kenny, D. A., & La Voie, L. (1984). The social relations model. *Advances in Experimental Social Psychology, 18,* 141–182.

Kern, J. M., Miller, C., & Eggers, J. (1983). Enhancing the validity of role-play tests: A comparison of three role-play methodologies. *Behavior Therapy, 14,* 482–492.

Kiesler, D. J. (1982). Interpersonal theory for personality and psychotherapy. In J. C. Anchin & D. J. Kiesler (Eds.), *Handbook of interpersonal psychotherapy.* Elmsford, NY: Pergamon Press.

Kiesler, D. J. (1990). Interpersonal methods of assessment and diagnosis. In C. R. Snyder & D. R. Forsyth (Eds.), *Handbook of social and clinical psychology.* New York: Pergamon Press.

Leary, T. (1957). *Interpersonal diagnosis of personality.* New York: Ronald Press.

Leitenberg, H. (1990). *Handbook of social and evaluation anxiety.* New York: Plenum Press.

Liberman, R. P., DeRisi, W. J., & Mueser, J. T. (1989). *Social skills training for psychiatric patients,* New York: Pergamon Press.

Liberman, R. P., DeRisi, W. J., & Mueser, R. T. (1989). *Social skills training for psychiatric patients,* New York: Pergamon Press.

Liberman, R. P., Lillie, F., Falloon, I. R. H., Harpin, R. E., Hutchinson, W., & Stoute, B. (1984). Social skills training with relapsing schizophrenics. *Behavior Modification, 8,* 155–179.

Liberman, R. P., Mueser, K. T., & Wallace, C. J. (1986). Social skills training for schizophrenic individuals at risk for relapse. *American Journal of Psychiatry, 143,* 523–526.

Liberman, R. P., Neuchterlein, K. H., & Wallace, C. J. (1982). Social skills training and the nature of schizophrenia. In J. P. Curran & P. M. Monti (Eds.), *Social skills training: A practical handbook of assessment and treatment.* New York: Guilford Press.

Libet, J., & Lewinsohn, P. M. (1973). The concept of social skill with special reference to the behaviour of depressed persons. *Journal of Consulting and Clinical Psychology, 40,* 30 4–12.

Liebowitz, M. R., Gorman, J. M., Fyer, A. J., & Klein, D. F. (1985). Social phobia. *Archives of General Psychiatry, 42,* 729–736.

Lowe, M. R., & Cautela, J. R. (1978). A self-report measure of social skill. *Behavior Therapy, 9,* 535–544.

McFall, R. M. (1982). A review and reformulation of the concept of social skills. *Behavioral Assessment, 4,* 1–33.

McKnight, D. L., Nelson, R. O., Hayes, S. C., & Jarrett, R. B. (1984). Importance of treating individually assessed response classes in the amelioration of depression. *Behavior Therapy, 15,* 315–335.

Marzillier, J. S. (1978). Outcome studies of skill training: A review. In P. Trower, B. M. Bryant, & M. Argyle (Eds.), *Social skills and mental health.* London: Methuen.

Marzillier, J. S., & Winter, K. (1978). Success and failure in social skills training: Individual differences. *Behaviour Research and Therapy. 16,* 67–84.

Mattick, R. P., & Peters, L. (1988). Treatment of severe social phobia: Effects of guided exposure with and without cognitive restructuring. *Journal of Consulting and Clinical Psychology, 56,* 251–260.

Mattick, R. P., Peters, L., & Clarke, J. C. (1988). *Exposure and cognitive restructuring for severe social phobia: A controlled study.* Manuscript submitted for publication.

Merluzzi, T. V., & Biever, J. (1987). Role-playing procedures for the behavioral assessment of social skill: A validity study. *Behavioral Assessment, 9,* 361–378.

Morrison, R. L., Bellack, A. S., & Mueser, K. T. (1988). Deficits in facial-affect recognition and schizophrenia. *Schizophrenia Bulletin, 14,* 67–83.

Peplau, L. A., & Perlman, D. (Eds.) (1982). *Loneliness: A sourcebook of current theory, research and therapy.* New York: Wiley.

Pettit, G. S., McClaskey, C. L., Brown, M. M., & Dodge, K. A. (1987). The generalizability of laboratory assessments of children's socially competent behavior in specific situations. *Behavioral Assessment, 9,* 81–96.

Riggio, R. E. (1989). *Manual for the social skills inventory.* Palo Alto, CA: Consulting Psychologists Press.

Rubenstein, C., & Shaver, P. (1982). *In search of intimacy: Surprising conclusions from a nationwide survey on loneliness and what to do about it.* New York: Delacorte Press.

Safran, J. D. (1990). Towards a refinement of cognitive therapy in light of interpersonal theory: I. Theory. *Clinical Psychology Review, 10,* 87–106.

Safran, J. D., Hill, C., & Ford, C. (1988). *A self-report measure of the interpersonal schema.* Unpublished manuscript.

Safran, J. D., Segal, Z. V., Hill, C., & Whiffen, V. (1990). Refining strategies for research on self-representations in emotional disorders. *Cognitive Therapy and Research, 14,* 143–160.

Sanchez, V., Lewinsohn, P. M., & Larson, D. W. (1980). Assertion training: Effectiveness in the treatment of depression. *Journal of Clinical Psychology, 36,* 526–529.

Schlenker, B. R., & Leary, M. R. (1982). Social anxiety and self-presentation: A conceptualization and model. *Psychological Bulletin, 92,* 641–669.

Schlundt, D. G., & McFall, R. M. (1987). Classifying social situations: A comparison of five methods. *Behavioral Assessment, 9,* 21–42.

Scholing, A., & Emmelkamp, P. M. G. (1990). Social phobia: Nature and treatment. In H. Leitenberg (Ed.), *Handbook of social and evaluative anxiety.* New York: Plenum Press.

Shepherd, G. (1981). *A review of social skills training with psychiatric patients,* 1970–1980. Unpublished manuscript, Department of Psychology, Institute of Psychiatry, University of London.

Shepherd, G. (1983). Social skills training with adults. In S. Spence & G. Shepherd (Eds.), *Developments in social skills training.* London: Academic Press.

Shepherd, G. (1984). Assessment of cognitions in social skills training. In P. Trower (Ed.), *Radical approaches to social skills training.* London: Croom Helm.

Shepherd, G. (1986). Social skills training and schizophrenia. In C. R. Hollin & P. Trower (Eds.), *Handbook of social skills training.* Oxford: Pergamon Press.

Spitzberg, B. H., & Cupach, W. R. (1989). *Handbook of interpersonal competence research.* New York: Springer-Verlag.

Spitzer, R. L., & Williams, J. B. W. (1985). *Instructional manual for the structured clinical interview for DSM-III.* New York: Biometrics Research, New York State Psychiatric Research Institute.

Spivack, G., Platt, J. J., & Shure, M. B. (1976). *The problem-solving approach to adjustment.* San Francisco: Jossey-Bass.

Stravynski, A., & Shahar, A. (1983). The treatment of social dysfunction in nonpsychotic psychiatric outpatients: A review. *Journal of Nervous and Mental Diseases, 171,* 721–728.

Sullivan, H. S. (1953). *The interpersonal theory of psychiatry.* New York: W. W. Norton.

Swensen, C. H. (1973). *Introduction to interpersonal relations.* Glenview, IL: Scott Foresman.

Sylph, J. A., Ross, H. E., & Kedward, H. B. (1978). Social disability in chronic psychiatric patients. *American Journal of Psychiatry, 134,* 1391–1394.

Teasdale, J. D. (1983). Negative thinking in depression: Cause, effect or reciprocal relationship? *Advances in behaviour, research and therapy, 5,* 3–25.

Trower, P. (1980). Situational analysis of the components and processes of behavior of socially skilled and unskilled patients. *Journal of Consulting and Clinical Psychology, 30,* 526–537.

Trower, P. (1982). Towards a generative model of social skills: A critique and synthesis. In J. P. Curran & P. M. Monti (Eds.), *Social skills training: A practical handbook for assessment and treatment.* New York: Guilford Press.

Trower, P. (1983). Social skills and applied linguistics. In R. Ellis & D. Whittington (Eds.), *New directions in social skills training.* London: Croom Helm.

Trower, P. (Ed.). (1984). *Radical approaches to social skills training.* London: Croom Helm.

Trower, P., Bryant, B. M., & Argyle, M. (1978). *Social skills and mental health.* London: Methuen.

Trower, P., & Dryden, W. (1991). Interpersonal problems. In W. Dryden & R. Rentoul (Eds.), *Adult clinical problems: A cognitive-behavioural approach.* London: Routledge.

Trower, P., & Gilbert, P. (1989). New theoretical conceptions of social anxiety and social phobia. *Clinical Psychology Review, 9,* 19–35.

Trower, P., & Turland, D. (1984). Social phobia. In S. M. Turner (Ed.), *Behavioral theories and treatment of anxiety.* New York: Plenum Press.

Turner, S. M., Beidel, D. C., Dancu, C. V., & Keys, D. J. (1986). Psychopathology of social phobia and comparison to avoidant personality disorder. *Journal of Abnormal Psychology, 95,* 389–394.

Turner, S. M., Beidel, D. C., Dancu, C. V., & Stanley, M. A. (1989). An empirically derived inventory to measure social fears and anxiety: The Social Phobia and Anxiety Inventory. *Psychosocial Assessment: A Journal of Consulting and Clinical Psychology, 1,* 35–40.

Twentyman, C. T., & Zimering, R. T. (1979). Behavioral training of social skills: A critical review. In M. Hersen, R. M. Eisler, & P. M. Miller (Eds.), *Progress in behavior modification* (Vol. 7). New York: Academic Press.

van der Molen, H. T. (1984). *Aan verlegenheid valt iets te doen: Een cursus in plaats van therapie.* Deventer, Netherlands: Van Loghum Slaterus.

van der Molen, H. T., & Trower, P. E. (1991). *Social skills training for shy people.* Unpublished manual, Birmingham University.

Wallace, C. J. (1982). The social skills training project of the mental health clinical research center for the study of schizophrenia. In J. P. Curran & P. M. Monti (Eds.), *Social skills training: A practical handbook.* New York: Guilford Press.

Wallace, C. J., & Liberman, R. P. (1985). Social skills training for patients with schizophrenia: A controlled clinical trial. *Psychiatry Research, 14,* 239–247.

Wallace, C. J., Nelson, C. J., Liberman, R. P., Aitchison, R. A., Lukoff, D., Elder, J. P., & Ferris, C. (1980). A review and critique of social skills training with schizophrenic patients. *Schizophrenia Bulletin, 6,* 42–63.

Warner, R. (1985). Recovery from schizophrenia: Psychiatry and political economy. London: Routledge & Kegan Pane.

Williams, J. M. G. (1986). Social skills and depression. In C. R. Hollin & P. Trower (Eds.), *Handbook of social skills training.* Oxford: Pergamon Press.

Wing, J. K., Cooper, J. E., & Sartorious, N. (1974). *The measurement and classification of psychiatric symptoms.* Cambridge: Cambridge University Press.

Zeiss, A. M., Lewinsohn, P. M., & Munoz, R. F. (1979). Nonspecific improvement effects in depression using interpersonal skills training, pleasant events schedules, or cognitive training. *Journal of Consulting and Clinical Psychology, 45,* 543–551.

Zigler, E., & Phillips, L. (1961). Social competence and outcome in psychiatric patients. *Journal of Abnormal and Social Psychology, 63,* 264–271.

Zimbardo, P. G. (1977). *Shyness: What it is and what to do about it.* New York: Jove.

# CHAPTER 5

# ASSERTION SKILLS TRAINING

Eileen Gambrill

There has been a long-term interest in assertion training in the field of behavior therapy (see, e.g., Rakos, 1991; Ruben, 1985). The aim of assertion training is to enhance interpersonal effectiveness and comfort in social situations. Assertive skills are essentially effective social influence skills that are acquired through learning. A lack of effective social behavior has been implicated in a wide range of problems, including marital discord, unsafe sex behaviors, depression, sexual dysfunction, dependency, antisocial aggressive behavior, and substance abuse (see, e.g., Gottman & Krokoff, 1989; Barbaree & Davis, 1984; St. Lawrence, 1986; Marlatt & Gordon, 1985; Yesmont, 1992; Van Hasselt, Hersen, & Bellack, 1984). Assertive individuals have been found to have fewer health problems (Williams & Stout, 1985). Opportunities are lost and unpleasant events tolerated because of ineffective social skills. A coveted promotion may be foregone because of an inability to ask an employer for the higher position. The opportunity to meet someone interesting may be lost because of discomfort with the thought of approaching the person and starting a conversation. Resentment and anger may accumulate until, finally, one more pre-cipitating event sets off an inappropriately strong reaction. Behavior that reduces anxiety, disappointment, or anger may occur, such as drinking, social isolation, or attention to physical symptoms. The role of anxiety and skill deficits in interpersonal situations has long been recognized in the behavioral literature. Salter (1949) was the first to note the range of situations in which interpersonal anxiety may occur and to point to the inhibitory role of conditioned anxiety reactions on effective behavior. Wolpe (1958) considered effective social behavior to be related to well-being and emphasized the inhibiting role of anxiety and the role of assertion in inhibiting anxiety. Nonassertive behavior was viewed as resulting from the conditioning of anxiety to specific cues. Assertive behavior was assumed to reciprocally inhibit dysfunctional anxiety created by past histories of punishment.

Assertion training has been used with clients across the age spectrum, including children (Bornstein, Bellack, & Hersen, 1977; Rotheram, Armstrong, & Booraem, 1982; Tanner & Holliman, 1988); adolescents (Fodor, 1992; Horan & Williams, 1982; Huey & Rank, 1984; Ollendick & Hersen,

1979; Sarason & Ganzer, 1973; Schinke & Gilchrist, 1984; Van Hasselt, Hersen, Kazdin, Simon, & Mastantuono, 1983; Wehr & Kaufman, 1987; Werner et al., 1975); and the elderly (Gambrill, 1985; Ruben, 1987) as well as with various groups of adults, including women (Gambrill & Richey, 1980; Goldstein-Fodor & Epstein, 1983; Linehan, 1984), and social welfare clients (Arnold & Parrott, 1978; Galinsky, Schopler, Satir, & Gambrill, 1978). It has been used with clients who stutter (Schloss, Espin, Smith, & Suffolk, 1987); the physically disabled (Dunn & Herman, 1982); developmentally disabled individuals (Downing, 1987; Kirkland & Caughlin-Carver, 1982; Senatore, Matson, & Kazdin, 1982); psychiatric patients (Benton & Schroeder, 1990; Donahoe & Dreiksenga, 1988; Liberman, DeRisi, & Mueser, 1989), parents (Clifford, 1987; Landau & Paulson, 1977); individuals labeled mentally retarded (Bregman, 1984); athletes (Connelly, 1988); coaches (Miller, 1982); couples (Epstein, DeGiovanni, & Jayne-Lazarus, 1978); mothers and daughters (Fodor & Wolfe, 1977); depressed clients (Dobia & McMurray, 1985; Sanchez, Lewinsohn, & Larson, 1980), and men who batter (Edelson & Tolman, 1992). Assertion training has been used to alter physical problems such as benign vocal nodules (Gray, England, & Mahoney, 1965), as well as to decrease heterosexual anxiety (Burgess, 1969), explosive or aggressive behavior (Eisler, Hersen, & Miller, 1974), facial tics (Mansdorf, 1986), substance abuse (Callner & Ross, 1976; Chaney, O'Leary, & Marlatt, 1978; Williams, Hadden, & Marcavage, 1983), and obsessive-compulsive behavior (Walton & Mather, 1963).

Assertive behavior facilitates compliance with medical treatment (see, e.g., Ary, Toobert, Wilson, & Glasgow, 1986). Assertion training is included in many package programs such as Goldstein's program designed to reduce delinquency (Goldstein, Glick, Irwin, Pask-McCartney & Rubama, 1989). *Asset* (Hazel, Schumaker, Sherman & Sheldon-Wilden, 1981), Marlatt and Gordon's (1985) relapse prevention program, and programs designed to enhance social support systems of abusive or neglectful parents (see, e.g., Richey, Lovell & Reid, 1991, and Kinney, Haapala, Booth, & Levitt, 1991). In the Richey et al. program, the focus was on giving and receiving compliments, handling criticism, expressing disagreement, and sharing negative concerns. These behaviors are also included in some programs designed to help shy, socially anxious, or lonely adults increase enjoyable social contacts (see Chapter 12). Assertion training has been found to result in changes in real-life as well as role-played situations and in positive changes in self-concept and locus of control (Workman, Boland, Grafton, & Kester, 1986–1987) (for reviews of assertion training, see, for example, Heimberg, Montgomery, Madson, & Heimburg, 1977; Galassi & Galassi, 1978; Rakos, 1991.)

Perhaps more than any other behavioral method, assertion training has been popularized in books (e.g., MacNeilage & Adams, 1982; Alberti & Emmons, 1970; (see also later editions) Bloom, Coburn, & Pearlman, 1975; Bower & Bower, 1976; Butler, 1981; Dickson, 1982; Doty, 1987; Drury, 1984; Emmons, Richardson, & Frost, 1981; Fensterheim & Baer, 1975; Gambrill & Richey, 1988; Jakubowski & Lange, 1978; Morton, Richey, & Kellett, 1981; Osborn & Harris, 1975; Phelps & Austin, 1975; Smith, 1975). Assertion training caught on especially with women who were interested in increasing their options, including both professionals such as health care providers (see, e.g., Herman, 1977; Morton, Richey, & Kellett, 1981; Sundel & Sundel, 1980) and clients. MacDonald (1982) argues that women encounter more situations requiring assertion. Rakos (1991) notes that the kinds of work and marital concerns raised by women in assertion training suggest that stereotyped sex-role expectations are important factors. Popularized versions of assertive training sometimes bring in themes that are not seen in academic research–oriented reports, such as the idea that there is a real "self" to be discovered (see, e.g., *Assertion Training: How to Be Who You Really Are* (Rees & Graham, 1991).

## WHAT IS ASSERTIVE BEHAVIOR?

More than twenty different definitions of assertiveness were discussed by St. Lawrence (1987). Laypeople and professional trainers differ in their definitions (see Wilson & Gallois, 1993). Fundamental to the concept of assertion is a concern with basic human rights (see the later discussion of the value stance included in assertion training). The appropriate expression of emotion is emphasized. Wolpe (1958) used the word *assertion* broadly to refer to the expression of both negative and positive feelings in social situations. He defined assertive behavior as "the proper expression of any emotion other than anxiety toward another person" (Wolpe, 1973, p 81). Assertion training is designed to increase clients influence over their social environments by increasing the expression of both positive and negative feelings as well as by increasing comfort in social situa tions. Wolpe and Lazarus (1966) viewed any of the following as assertive: "A polite refusal to accede to an unreasonable request, a genuine expression of endearment, appreciation, or respect, an exclamation of joy, irritation, adulation or disgust" (p. 39). Most definitions combine a concern for basic rights of all involved individuals and emotional expression. For example, Lange and Jakubowski (1976) state, "Assertion involves standing up for personal rights and expressing thoughts, feelings and beliefs in direct, honest, and appropriate ways which do not violate another person's rights" (p. 7). Alberti and Emmons (1970) define assertive behavior as "Behavior which enables persons to act in her own best interests, to stand up for himself without undue anxiety, to express his honest feelings comfortably, or to exercise his own rights without denying the rights of others" (p. 2). These are broad definitions of *assertion.* Other investigators use the term more narrowly to refer to situations that involve standing up for one's rights, expressing disagreement, being persistent and firm, asking for clarification, expressing complaints, refusing unwanted requests, and dealing with aggression (Argyle, Furnham, & Graham, 1981, p. 328). Argyle, et al. (1981) point out, "It seems that several constructs are usually included under the general heading of assertion, such as defense of one's own rights and the restriction and rejection of unjust demands, social competency, independence, capacity to take control of various situations, skills of initiating, communication of positive feelings and personal experiences" (p. 50).

Clear verbal communication is central to assertive behavior. Descriptions of assertive behavior emphasize the characteristics of directness, clarity, and respect (Rakos, 1991). *Respect* refers to following norms of politeness. This emphasis complements the value placed on the expression of rights through the sharing of desires, feelings, or opinions. "I" statements, in contrast to "you" statements connoting blame and accusations, are encouraged. "I" statements encourage speakers to accept responsibility for expressing their own feelings, desires, or opinions. Direct statements avoid apologies, lies, or excuses. Recently, attention has been given to assertive behavior as speech acts (as discourse). Assertive compared to nonassertive speech has been found to be stylistically more complex and less dominated by feeling verbs than the assertion training literature would lead one to expect (Gervasio, Pepinsky, & Schwebel, 1983; Gervasio, 1987).

There is a clear functional concern in the clinical literature describing the use of assertion training in developing behaviors that are effective in addressing real-life complaints (see, e.g., Wolpe, 1958, 1973; Wolpe & Lazarus, 1966). Thus, the social effectiveness of assertive behavior is emphasized. Assertive behavior is effective social behavior. This is also true of much of the research literature. For example, phrases used by researchers include "skill in maintaining and enhancing reinforcement" (Rich & Schroeder, 1976); "expressions which cause others to take them into account" (MacDonald, 1974). Some early studies, however, focused on the form of assertive behavior rather than on its function (effects in real-life settings). For example, the behaviors of individuals rated high and low on assertion were examined. A focus on the form of behavior rather than its function may result in encouraging behaviors that have negative rather than positive social consequences.

This chapter offers an overview of assertion training. The relationship between assertion and social skills training is first discussed. The value stance inherent in assertion training is then addressed, followed by a description of the traditional tripartite division of behavior into assertive, aggressive, and passive reactions and the reasons that this division has declined in popularity among researchers. Examples of behaviors that have received attention are then described. Assessment issues and sources of assessment data are reviewed, followed by a description of intervention methods designed to enhance assertive behavior. The effectiveness of assertion training is then discussed, as are common factors related to less-than-hoped-for success.

## HOW DOES ASSERTION TRAINING DIFFER FROM SOCIAL SKILLS TRAINING?

Similar techniques are used in assertion and social skills training, and similar assessment, intervention, and evaluation skills are required on the part of counselors. These include skills in effective use of a variety of assessment tools, familiarity with and skill in correctly implementing a variety of intervention methods, and skill in selecting relevant and clear progress indicators. In both assertion training and social skills training, cognitive, behavioral, and affect management skills may be in need of refinement or development. As research related to many kinds of social behavior increased, the terms *assertive behavior* and *assertive training* have often been replaced by the terms *effective/competent social behavior* and *so-*

*cial skills training.* Sometimes the specific skill addressed is described with no mention of assertive behavior (e.g., Warzak & Page, 1990). Some researchers continue to use the term *assertive behavior* to refer to a circumscribed set of behaviors-in-situations, such as refusing requests. For example, in the cognitive-behavioral intervention program for socially phobic clients developed by Heimberg (see Chapter 12), the category "assertive behavior" is used to refer to refusing requests. One problem with the term *assertive behavior* is confusion of *assertion* with *aggression.* Another disadvantage is encouragement of a trait approach to social behavior that obscures the situational specificity of behavior. For example, in early studies, assessment of assertive behavior covered a range of different kinds of situations, and an overall assertiveness rating was often given. In a study of two male chronic schizophrenic patients, overall assertiveness was rated on a scale ranging from 1 (very unassertive) to 5 (very assertive) (Hersen & Bellack, 1976). A client may be appropriately assertive in one situation (e.g., initiating conversations), passive in others (e.g., refusing favors), and aggressive in other contexts (e.g., requesting changes in behavior). Assertion training differs from social skills training in emphasizing individual rights and obligations and encouraging participants to alter norms and stereotypes that limit options. For example, an advantage of the phrase *assertive behavior* for some groups, such as women, is the emphasis on taking the initiative to improve social and other opportunities. There is often an activist stance, as discussed in the next section. It is identical to social skills training in encouraging social behaviors that enhance positive social consequences. Assertive behavior is essentially effective social behavior.

## THE VALUE STANCE INVOLVED IN ASSERTION TRAINING

A value stance as well as an intervention strategy is associated with assertion training. The most popular book in the area, which sold over two million copies, is called *Your Perfect Right* (Alberti & Emmons, 1970). It is assumed that people have a right to express their feelings in a manner that subjugates neither others nor themselves, and that well-being includes this expression (Wolpe & Lazarus, 1966). It is thus for the overly reticent as well as for those who are overly aggressive in their encounters. The former group fail to assert their rights, whereas the latter group achieve their goals at someone else's expense.

Wilson and Gallois (1993) highlight the tension between expressing personal feelings and the value of maintaining positive social relationships. Research shows that the latter is important to people, and both have been emphasized by writers such as Wolpe (1969); that is, the expression of personal preferences should enhance positive relationships. Individual rights and obligations are emphasized in a context of increasing positive gains for both oneself and others. Such training implies that it is adaptive to express oneself in appropriate ways, to be able to distinguish situations in which restraint is called for from those in which assertion would be most adaptive, and to act in such a manner. It is considered unadaptive and unfair to be taken advantage of, to allow oneself to be imposed on unduly, and to be intimidated. It is assumed that life will be more enjoyable if one is active in constructing one's own social environment. Steps are taken to deal with anxiety about possible negative reactions through the development of positive self-instructions and effective social and relaxation skills, as needed. Assessment calls for a careful descriptive analysis of relevant interpersonal relationships. If this analysis indicates that assertion will have unavoidable negative effects—as it may have, for example, in abusive relationships (O'Leary, Curley, Rosenbaum, & Clarke, 1985)—then this approach would not be recommended; other intervention methods would be explored (see also the later section on cautions).

The value stance emphasized in assertion training, sometimes to the point of being a guideline for life, emphasizes individual rights and obligations. These obligations and rights may be viewed differently by clients, trainers, and researchers (Wilson & Gallois, 1993). Obligations include the requirement to consider the rights of other people. Thus, clients are encouraged to consider not only their own rights and obligations in a given situation but those of other participants as well. What is viewed as a right or an obligation varies in different cultures and ethnic groups, and counselors will have to be careful not to impose their cultural standards on groups for whom these are not appropriate; otherwise, negative consequences and/or loss of positive consequences may result (see, e.g., Chan, 1993; Delamater & McNamara, 1986). Soto (1983) found that sex-role traditionalism in Puerto Rican women in New York was inversely related to assertiveness. The emphasis in assertion training on maintaining individual rights will not be appropriate in some groups or cultures. The finding in U.S. studies that the greatest difficulty is created by situations in which a person is annoyed or angry because his or her rights have been ignored or violated may not be replicated in other countries or cultures. Wood and Mallinckrodt (1990) point out that ethnic minority clients may need to acquire skills valued within the majority culture if they want to be more effective in this culture as well as to acquire assertive responses appropriate in their ethnic culture. The values of assertion training may also conflict with religious beliefs (Bolsinger & McMinn, 1989).

It is both a strength and a weakness of assertion training that responsibility for change is placed on the individual. It is a strength in enhancing individual options. It is a weakness in offering false promises of what can be achieved through individual change. Political, social, and economic factors that may limit options are not addressed (Gambrill, 1990). Women writing about assertion training for women often point out this weakness when discussing sex-role stereotyping and sexual discrimination that influences social behavior (see, e.g., Goldstein-Fodor & Epstein, 1983; Linehan, 1984; MacDonald, 1982). The ideology that each person can improve the quality of his or her life through individual effort is integral to assertion training, and this ideology is part of what Weiss (1969) calls *The American Myth of Success.* Some current versions of the self-made man (and, more recently, woman) emphasize the power of the mind: the ability to think one's way to success. This mentalistic focus is not characteristic of assertion training as originally presented (Wolpe, 1958).

## THE TRIPARTITE DIVISION OF ASSERTIVE, PASSIVE, AND AGGRESSIVE BEHAVIOR

Effective social skills (assertive behaviors) are differentiated from both aggressive and submissive behaviors. Aggression is defined as the "hostile expression of preferences by words or actions in a manner which coerces others to give in to these preferences; any act which suppresses or take away the rights of another person" (MacDonald, 1974, p. 32) (see Figure 5.1). The aggressive person "puts down," hurts, or humiliates people and achieves goals at the expense of causing bad feelings in others (Alberti & Emmons, 1974). Anger is expressed at the other person rather than at the situation, and reactions express intention of hostile action. Punitive or aggressive responses may involve ridicule, disparagement, shouting, violent gestures, or other threatening or belligerent body expressions (Hollandsworth, 1977) (see Table 5.1). Research on anger shows that inappropriate expression of anger usually results in negative feelings on the part of the expressor and often decreases the chance of attaining valued goals (Averill, 1982). Submission is defined as "the act of allowing one's rights to be ignored, as any act which yields humbly to the preferences of another person" (MacDonald, 1974, p. 32). The submissive person allows others to choose for him. He does not achieve desired goals. His reactions

**Figure 5.1.** This "academy" confuses assertion with aggression.

MAXINE Comix © Copyright Marian Henley. Reprinted by permission of the artist.

**Table 5.1.** Comparison of Passive, Assertive, and Aggressive Styles

| | PASSIVE | AGGRESSIVE | ASSERTIVE |
|---|---|---|---|
| Behavior patterns | Does not express feelings and preferences. | Critical expression of expectations and feelings, explosiveness, unpredictability | Clear, direct expression of preferences and feelings |
| | Makes indirect and apologetic statements of views. | Blaming and judgmental criticisms | Descriptive rather than judgmental criticisms |
| | Makes complaints to the wrong person. | Attribution of negative intentions to others. | Persistence |
| | Does not address problems. | Muscle tension | Willingness to listen |
| | Gives up soon, little persistence. | Acts on problems too quickly | Negotiates and compromises |
| | Vague agreements. | Unwilling to listen | |
| | | Refusal to negotiate and compromise | |
| Verbal behavior | Minimizing words | Loaded words | Neutral, nonjudgmental language |
| | Apologetic statements | Accusatory "you" statements | Concise, clear statements |
| | Statements made about people in general rather than in reference to a specific person | "Always" or "never" statements | Personalized statements: "I . . ." |
| | General instead of specific descriptions | Demands instead of requests | Specific descriptions |
| | Statements disguised as questions | Judgments disguised as questions | Words reflecting cooperation |
| | | | Requests instead of demands |
| | | | No statements disguised as questions |
| Voice characteristics and nonverbal behavior | Pleading or questioning tone | Sarcastic, judgmental | Even, audible voice tone |
| | Hesitations | Interrupts others | Eye contact |
| | Little eye contact | "Looking-through" eye contact | Erect posture but relaxed |
| | Slumped posture | Tense posture | Match between words and nonverbal behavior |
| | Lack of match between words and nonverbal behavior | | |
| Results | Has rights violated; is taken advantage of. | Violates other people's rights; takes advantage of others. | Respects own rights as well as those of others. |
| | Not likely to achieve goals. | Achieves goals at the expense of others. | Achieves desired goals without hurting others. |

*Sources:* Adapted from R. E. Alberti & M. L. Emmons, *Your Perfect Right* (San Luis Obispo, CA: Impact Press, 1974), and S. S. Drury, *Assertive Supervision: Building Involved Teamwork* (Champaign, IL: Research Press, 1984).

indicate that he is in the wrong and that the other person is right.

Assertion is defined as "the open, calm, confident expression of preferences by words or actions in a manner which causes others to take them into account" (MacDonald, 1974, p. 32) (see also the earlier discussion of assertive behavior). It is assumed that it is best to express oneself in as positive a way as possible. Let us look at the following

possible reactions to a statement from a waiter in a restaurant:

*Waiter:* Please sit over here.
*Patron 1:* Well, O.K. (Agrees even though he does not want to.)
*Patron 2:* No, its my right to sit anywhere I want. I'm sitting over here.
*Patron 3:* I would prefer to sit over here. Could we?

Patron 1 readily submits without even voicing his preferences. Unless the waiter is unusually perceptive and has a high desire to please his patrons, he may not notice or respond to the hesitation reflected in the first response. Patron 2 is overly confrontational and may be inaccurate in assuming that he can sit anywhere, because some tables may be reserved. Rather than state his preference, he gives an ultimatum, which is likely to put off others. Patron 3 states his preference and asks if it can be granted. He could also have indicated a reason. This is an example of an assertive response. A preference is stated in a polite but firm manner. The individual is neither overly confrontive nor overly submissive. Some efforts have been made to determine how specific populations categorize various behaviors in a given situation (e.g., MacDonald, 1974).

Assertive behavior is behavior that is socially effective. What is judged to be competent today may not be so in the near or distant future as, for example, expected roles of men and women change. Definitions of social competence differ in terms of (1) their clarity; (2) the degree to which both long- and short-term consequences are considered; (3) the degree to which personal goals and outcomes (e.g., comfort, self-esteem) as well as social goals and consequences (effects on others) are considered; (4) the degree to which societal standards are appealed to; (5) whether negative as well as positive consequences are considered; and (6) whether they focus on process and/or outcomes (Gambrill & Richey, 1987). Examples of definitions include the following:

Social skill is "the complex ability both to emit behaviors that are positively or negatively reinforced and not to emit behaviors that are punished or extinguished by others" (Libet & Lewinsohn, 1973).

Effective behavior is a response or pattern of responses to a problematic situation which alters the situation so that it is no longer problematic and, at the same time, produces a maximum of other positive consequences and a minimum of negative ones (Goldfried & D'Zurilla, 1969, p. 158).

Possession of necessary skills to produce the desired effects on other people in social situations (Argyle, 1980).

Those responses that elicit reinforcing consequences from a given social interaction, in a manner that is socially acceptable and does no harm to others (Spence, 1982, pp. 159–160).

Assertive behavior does not necessarily win friends. For example, assertive female speakers are viewed as less likable, friendly, and pleasant than nonassertive female speakers (Kelly, Kern, Kirkley, Patterson, & Keane, 1980; see also Falbo, Hazen & Linimon, 1982). Friends may accept refusals more readily than strangers, but refusals hurt friends more (Lewis & Gallois, 1984). This highlights the importance of careful consideration of both long- and short-term personal and social goals (Nezu & D'Zurilla, 1979), the particular relationship involved, the "rules" of the situation, and the value of including "elaborations" such as offering compromises and empathic statements together with direct statements (see later discussion of negative assertion). The perception of some assertive behavior as aggressive may be due to the difference between social conventions and assertive prescriptions. That is, assertive behavior may involve rule breaking. Rule breaking may be required to alter usual patterns of behavior that limit options. For example, Gervasio (1987) notes that it may be more socially acceptable to put off a request than to refuse it. The addition of certain response components, such as empathic responses, may soften a direct refusal and thereby increase the compatibility between social conventions and recommendations for assertive behavior (see review in Wilson & Gallois, 1993). Framing of interests as common goals and noting the unique contributions each person can make may be the most effective way to make requests (Gervasio, 1987).

## THE SITUATIONAL NATURE OF INEFFECTIVE SOCIAL BEHAVIOR

Ineffective social behavior is typically situational. That is, clients usually experience difficulty only in certain situations. For example, they may express positive feelings appropriately, but encounter difficulty when trying to express negative feelings. The situational nature of assertive behavior is supported by factor analyses of self-report measures showing a number of separate factors (see, e.g., Gambrill & Richey, 1975). Some people experience anxiety when trying to express themselves in intimate relationships but have no discomfort in service situations with store clerks and waitresses. A variety of factors may affect social competence, including (1) the degree of intimacy involved; (2) whether the feeling to be expressed is positive or negative; (3) various characteristics of relevant people, including status, age, and sex; (4) perceived status of self in the situation; and

(5) number of people present (MacDonald, 1974). The situational nature of assertive behavior is illustrated in a study in which 32 assertive situations were presented to 60 hospitalized male psychiatric patients (Eisler, Hersen, Miller, & Blanchard, 1975). Half required the expression of negative assertion, and the other half required positive reactions. The partners in the situations were either male or female and either familiar or unfamiliar. Behavior varied as a function of the social context presented. Responses to negative scenes were characterized by longer replies, increased eye contact, greater affect, more speech volume, and increased latency of response. Subjects tended to talk longer to other men than to women. The men were significantly more assertive with women than with men.

Clients may have difficulty asserting themselves as a function of the particular social power base involved in an exchange, such as attraction or coercive power (French & Raven, 1960). Ineffective behavior may occur only in interactions with people in positions of authority, such as supervisors at work. British writers especially highlight an individual's power or status as the most important determinant of assertiveness (see, e.g., Argyle, Furnham, & Graham, 1981). Power may be based on social class, age, gender, or position in an organizational hierarchy. In general, it seems that it is more difficult to be assertive with people with greater power, a more dominant role, and a higher status than it is with people of lower power who are less dominant or of a lower status. This is probably due to differential histories of reinforcement with these different individuals reflecting real differences in consequences (both negative and positive) that may be delivered. Competence in performing a task affects degree of assertiveness. Argyle et al. (1981) suggest that people are assertive and assume positions of leadership when they are more competent at a task, or know more about a topic being discussed than do others present.

Women tend to be less aggressive and less dominant than men and goals reported by women in social exchanges often differ from those of men: Women often pursue interpersonal goals rather than task completion (see review in Wilson & Gallois, 1993). Women participate less in mixed-sex task-oriented group discussions (Lewittes & Bem, 1983). "The traditional feminine sex role dictates that the ideal woman act in a nonassertive or passive manner. A women who fits the feminine stereotype is oriented toward other people, seeking to nurture them and to receive her satisfactions through their accomplishments"

(Linehan, 1984, p. 143). The less clear the rules in a situation, the more difficult it may be to act effectively. Cultural norms influence the nature of the behavior that will be successful in given situations.

As our society becomes increasingly ethnically diverse, it will be increasingly important for clinicians to be sensitive to gender and cultural differences that influence the effectiveness of given behaviors-in-situations (see, e.g., Sue & Sue, 1990). Differences among groups are highlighted by research showing the different antecedents reported for different emotions. For example, encounters with strangers are a more common antecedent for anger in Japan than in the United States and Europe, whereas reactions to injustice are not as common an antecedent for anger in Japan as they are in the United States and Europe (Scherer, Wallbott, Matsumoto, & Kudoh, 1988).

## THE COMPONENTS OF EFFECTIVE SOCIAL BEHAVIOR

The particular goals each client wishes to pursue are important to consider in selecting response options. Both long-term and short-term personal and social goals should be considered (Nezu & D'Zurilla, 1979). An assertive reaction may have positive short-term outcomes but negative long-term ones. The effects on the particular relationship involved should be considered (Wolpe, 1969). Negotiating conflicting goals in social situations can be challenging, and there is increasing evidence that lack of skill in this area is related to ineffective social behavior (see, e.g., Dodge, Asher & Parkhurst 1989). There are objective goals (e.g., not accepting an unwanted invitation), relationship goals (maintaining a positive relationship or avoiding a negative encounter with a stranger), and self-esteem goals (preserving a positive image of oneself) (Linehan, 1984) (see also earlier definitions of social competence). Goals of maintaining positive relationships and expressing preferences may clash.

The specific components of effective social behavior depend on the situation involved (see, for example, Pitcher & Meikle, 1980). Various approaches have been taken to identify effective responses. One approach is to use judges and base decisions on majority opinion. Another is a contrasted group approach in which differences between groups (e.g., assertive and unassertive individuals) are identified. The most valid approach is to determine what behaviors are most effective in attaining specific outcomes in real-life situations. Patients rated high in overall assertiveness speak louder, respond more rapidly, give longer replies, evidence more profound affect, show less compliance, and request more changes in the other person's behavior than do patients rated low in assertiveness (Eisler, Miller, & Hersen, 1973). Nonverbal behaviors such as eye contact and body posture oriented toward the other person are important (Serber, 1972). One of the major deficiencies in the assertion training literature is lack of valid task analyses in specific situations indicating what behaviors-in-situations and their sequences are effective and the range of behaviors that will be effective in a situation in attaining a given outcome (i.e., what is the operant class). In place of descriptive and functional analyses, a priori clinical judgments are often used.

The components of assertive behavior can be divided into three main areas: (1) content (what is said), (2) paralinguistic features (how it is said), and (3) nonverbal behaviors such as eye contact and posture. Timing and persistence are often important. Effective timing requires self-management skills as well as selection of facilitating contexts. Verbal content is examined for directness, clarity, and respect. There is an emphasis on the use of "I" statements that acknowledge responsibility for feelings and opinions, such as "I believe that . . ." The use of "I" statements is associated with evaluations of assertion, whereas the use of "you" statements is associated with aggressiveness (Kolotkin, Wielkiewicz, Judd, & Wieser, 1984). Reliance on "I" statements not only recognizes responsibility but also tends to avoid negative reactions that may result from accusatory "you" statements. There is an emphasis on the use of the "minimally effective response." This refers to behavior that is successful in accomplishing goals with a minimum of effort and negative emotion (and a small likelihood of negative consequences) (Rimm & Masters, 1974). The minimal effective response reflects mild language and an absence of threats and blame. Norms of politeness are followed, and negative labels are avoided (see Table 5.1).

Verbal responses can be examined for appropriate escalation of responses, which is required when initial assertive reactions are not effective. For example, a request may be refused in a more direct manner, or greater firmness of voice may be used. Persistence is often necessary. This may require repeating an initial statement. Maintaining focus on the key issue (or goal) is a key aspect of effective persistence.

Both paralinguistic and nonverbal components of behavior contribute to overall judgments of assertion (Linehan & Walker, 1983). Paralinguistic components include response latency, duration, fluency, voice volume, intonation, affect, and pitch. Reactions associated with assertiveness include firmness and intermediate levels of volume, latency, and duration. Here, too, what will be effective will depend on the particular situation. In general, extremes should be avoided. Nonverbal behaviors include eye contact, facial expression, gestures, and posture. Both facial expression and eye contact contribute to evaluations of assertive behaviors (Kolotkin et al., 1984; Romano & Bellack, 1980). Timing has also been found to be important (Fischetti, Curran, & Wessberg, 1977). As with other kinds of behavior, it is often the pattern that is critical.

## The Relationship between Thoughts and Assertive Behavior

There has been a movement away from a component model of social skills, in which attention is focused on specific verbal or nonverbal behaviors, toward a process model, in which cognitions such as goal setting and knowledge of rules are considered integral aspects of social competence (see, e.g., Argyle, Furnham, & Graham, 1981; Trower, O'Mahony, & Dryden, 1982). Cognitive surfeits and/or deficits may interfere with use of social skills. These repertoires are developed largely through unique histories of reinforcement. Cognitive-behavioral therapists emphasize the role of dysfunctional attributions, negative self-statements, and unrealistic expectations in inhibiting effective social behavior, including the role of such thoughts in preventing corrective exposure to feared situations. The finding that the addition of cognitive treatment methods to social skills training improves success supports the value of addressing interfering thoughts (see, e.g., Wolfe & Fodor, 1977). McFall (1982) uses an information-processing model emphasizing the importance of (1) decoding skills (the reception, perception, and interpretation of social stimuli); (2) decision-making skills (used to generate and select an appropriate response); and (3) enacting skills (translating the chosen alternative into action (execution) and following the impact of the response (self-monitoring). The information obtained in the last phase is used to adjust future behavior. A number of factors may negatively influence the decoding stage, including distractions, misinterpretations (faulty discriminations), unrealistic expectations, and faulty attributions. Expectations may function as rules that may increase or decrease effective behavior (Poppen, 1989). An interest in saving time and pressures to act may result in rule-based learning that does not mirror real-life contingencies. In the decision-making stage, possible response options are reviewed and the consequences of each evaluated. One response is selected, and the repertoire is scanned to determine if it is available. Affective excesses or deficits may disrupt performance at all three stages. For example, excessive anger may result in the misinterpretation of social signals, the decision to use an aggressive response option, the enactment of an aggressive response, and misinterpretation of the effect of the action as positive (when it is negative). A potential disadvantage of an information-processing view of social competence is the possibility of overlooking related contingencies of reinforcement. A reluctance to refuse unreasonable requests may be due to a past history of punishment for such refusals. An information-processing perspective may encourage a focus on collateral effects of contingencies (such as thoughts and feelings) rather than on altering the contingencies responsible for these.

Accurate perception and translation of social cues is required for effective social behavior. People who are ineffective in social situations are not as sensitive as others are to social cues (Trower, Bryant, & Argyle, 1978). The steps of generating behavioral alternatives, selecting one that will be effective, trying it out, and evaluating the outcome are components of social problem-solving models (see, e.g., Goldfried & D'Zurilla, 1969; Nezu & D'Zurilla, 1979). People who are not assertive have deficits in problem recognition, and assessment, as well as in selection of appropriate responses (Chiauzzi & Heimberg, 1986).

Differences have been found between assertive and nonassertive individuals in what these people say to themselves (see Stefanek & Eisler, 1983). These "differences" can be viewed as by-products of past histories of reinforcement. Unassertive individuals often have unrealistic expectations—"Everyone should like me," "I should never make mistakes," "Other people should do what I want them to." They are overly self-critical and inaccurately label aggressive and assertive behavior (see, e.g., Alden & Cappe, 1981; Alden & Safran, 1978). Assertive compared to nonassertive individuals have an internal locus of control (see, e.g., Schwartz & Higgins, 1979). Schwartz and Gottman (1976) found that less assertive men had more negative self-statements and fewer positive self-statements than did more assertive men but did not differ from more assertive men in

their knowledge of appropriate behaviors. Other studies have found differences in content knowledge between high- and low-assertion subjects (Bruch, 1981). Even though observers indicated no differences among assertive and nonassertive individuals, nonassertive compared to assertive college students rated themselves as less assertive, less effective, and more anxious, and were more likely to endorse irrational beliefs than were assertive students (Alden & Cappe, 1981). Beliefs may result in distortion of social feedback. For example, if an individual believes she is not worth knowing, she may interpret social signals and positive feedback as negative. Excessive fears of negative evaluation increase scanning for negative cues. People who differ in assertion also differ in their predictions about the consequences of different courses of action. Fiedler and Beach (1978) found that people who decided not to act assertively predicted more bad consequences and fewer positive consequences from assertion than did people who decided to act assertively. Compared to subjects rated low in assertion, subjects rated high in assertion expect more positive reactions from others and have less of a discrepancy between what they think they should do and what they actually do (Eisler, Frederiksen, & Peterson, 1978).

Assertive individuals expected positive outcomes to follow refusal of requests compared to nonassertive individuals, who expected positive outcomes to follow compliance (Kuperminc & Heimberg, 1983). The opposite pattern was found in relation to negative consequences. However, there were also differences in the values given to positive and negative consequences in these two different groups. The positive consequences of refusal were rated as more desirable and the negative consequences of compliance were evaluated as more undesirable by assertive than by nonassertive clients. Thus, differences in behavior between assertive and nonassertive individuals may reflect value differences in outcome as well as differences in the judged reasonableness of requests (Chiauzzi & Heimberg, 1983). Failure to obtain data regarding the value of specific goals in specific situations to each subject or client makes it difficult to judge the effectiveness of behavior from the client's point of view.

In summary, differences in assertive behavior have been found to be related to a variety of cognitive behaviors, including perception and translation of social cues, interpersonal problem solving, self-monitoring, affect regulation, use of positive self-statements, and expectations and beliefs.

# DIFFERENT KINDS
# OF ASSERTIVE BEHAVIOR

Some social behaviors occur in response to an overture by another person. Others require initiative—for example, responding to someone initiating a conversation, in contrast to initiating a conversation oneself (Gambrill, 1977). A second variable is the valence of the affect involved: Is it negative or positive? Situations involving negative assertion include refusing requests, responding to criticism, discouraging unwanted interactions, requesting a change in someone else's behavior, disagreeing with others, and resisting interruptions. In each case, difficulties may occur only in relation to specific individuals (strangers, acquaintances, intimates) or contexts (service-related—as in stores and restaurants— authority, family). Situations involving negative assertion have received greater emphasis in the literature than those involving positive assertion. For example, in his recent book *Assertive Behavior* (1991), Rakos devotes chapters to conflict assertion (see also Wilson & Gallois, 1993). Positive assertion includes initiating and maintaining conversations, making small talk, giving and receiving compliments, and expressing positive emotions (Schroeder, Rakos, & Moe, 1983. See also Twardosz, Schwartz, Fox, & Cunningham, 1979). Socially valid data describing what specific behaviors are necessary and sufficient to achieve certain goals in specific social situations are often absent. This lack is the most outstanding problem in the area of assertion training. The effect of a given behavior will often differ depending on the unique relationship involved (see Wilson & Gallois, 1993). Relationships involve a pattern of behavior, and the unique pattern involved may substantially influence the outcome of a given reaction.

## Negative Assertion in Response to Someone Else Taking the Initiative

Behaviors in this category include refusing requests and responding to criticisms. Beliefs related to ineffective reactions in such situations are described.

### Refusing Unwanted Requests

Failure to refuse unwanted requests makes life difficult for many people, and this behavior has received a great deal of research attention. McFall and his colleagues lead the way in investigating this particular behavior. An example of a situation used in

this early work together with examples of refusal responses is found in McFall and Bridges (1970, p. 121).

> Your roommate is constantly borrowing dimes from you in order to buy Cokes, candy, and so on but never seems to pay you back. You are getting rather annoyed at this and have decided to stop lending money. Now your roommate comes up to you and says, "Hey, can I borrow a dime for a Coke?" What would you say?

> 1. "No, you've never paid me back in the past, and I'm tired of losing money."
> 2. "No, sorry, you owe me too many dimes already."

Rarely are response alternatives selected on the basis of their effectiveness in real-life situations. Opinions of judges are typically used in place of a functional analysis of behaviors of interest. Although clients are often encouraged to include the word "No" in their refusal statements, this may violate rules of social convention (Gervasio, 1987). Requests can be refused without including the word "No." "Elaborations," such as explaining the reason for a refusal, may increase the effectiveness of a response. For example, an empathic response could be made, such as "I know you . . . but . . ." Empathic assertions contain explanations, acknowledge other people's feelings, offer compromises, show appreciation, or offer praise (Rakos, 1986). Here, too, what will be effective depends on the situation. The kind of responses just described may be more appropriate in an ongoing continuing relationship than in interactions with strangers and salespeople in which elaborations may result in an unwanted continuation of an exchange. Offering compromises and alternatives, acknowledging the feelings of other individuals, and describing reasons for one's response were evaluated as important components of effective refusal behavior (Romano & Bellack, 1980).

Clients can be trained to handle different kinds of persuasion efforts that may follow a refusal. These include (1) attempted flattery—"I always thought you were a generous person"; (2) criticism— "You really have a problem"; (3) the "poor-soul" routine—"I wouldn't ask you unless I was down to my last penny"; (4) the "once-in-a-lifetime" request—"I've never asked you before and I promise I'll never ask again"; (5) the promise of "nevermore"—"This is the last time I'll ever ask"; (6) a guilt-induction attempt—"I really feel bad that you turned me down." These may be countered (1) by repeating the refusal or (2) by saying, "That may be true, but I won't lend you the money" (the first part of this reply has been called *fogging* (Smith, 1975). This permits the deflection of manipulative criticism while keeping decision making in one's own hands.

### Refusing Tempting Requests

Another type of request that may prove problematic occurs when we are asked to do something that for certain reasons we might like to do but, for other reasons, would prefer not to do. This involves behaviors related to self-control that are influenced by associated consequences (see, e.g., Skinner, 1953). Anticipation of future undesirable consequence, such as returning to jail or tipping the scale at a higher weight, as well as the positive consequences of refusal, may be covertly reviewed or imagined in an effort to increase the probability of refusal. Probation may be violated because of lack of skill in how to say no to peers who tempt a teenager to engage in activities that may violate the conditions of his probation. A training program to offer such skills was designed by Sarason and Ganzer (1973). Youth learned how to use deflecting techniques. For example, when asked to "hit" a gas station that they happen to be passing, the youth might suggest getting a beer first to talk it over. Response components described earlier are also included here, including directness, empathy, self-disclosure (e.g., "I just got off probation"), repeating the statement, and negative inquiry. The latter refers to prompting of criticism in order to use the information offered or to exhaust the criticism (Smith, 1975). The goal is to avoid doing or accepting something that the youth does not wish to do (see also Goldstein et al., 1989). Training clients how to resist pressure to drink or use drugs is a key part of relapse prevention programs (Marlatt & Gordon, 1985).

Common misconceptions related to a reluctance to refuse unwanted requests include the belief that one has to please everyone; that it is awful to hurt or disappoint other people and that this should be avoided at all cost; that others have more of a right than the client does to determine what he or she will and will not do; and that there is no polite way to say no. Fears related to saying no include the concern that the exchange will escalate (the other person will become abusive) or that others will be disapproving. Assertion training should provide a repertoire of effective reactions to negative escalation.

### Responding to Criticism

Some clients are overly sensitive to criticism from others and demonstrate poor skills in responding to it. As with any behavior, reactions may differ in different situations. A client may effectively handle criticism from his wife but may have trouble responding in authority relationships at work when criticized. Fogging may be used to defuse a detractor; the possibility that the criticism may have some foundation can be admitted. A client might say, "That may be true, but . . ." An empathic reaction could be included, such as, "I can see how you might feel that way, but . . ." Clients are encouraged to avoid hostile or defensive reactions and are encouraged to agree with any truthful aspects of the criticism. A variety of misconceptions may be related to extreme sensitivity to criticism and a lack of appropriate reactions, including the belief that one must never make a mistake, that it is a terrible thing to be criticized, or that making a mistake reflects negatively on overall self-worth (see Drury, 1984, for further detail).

## Negative Assertion Involving Taking the Initiative

Successful social exchanges require skills in taking the initiative in influencing one's social environment. This may include requesting a change in an annoying behavior, disagreeing with someone, resisting interruption, ending an unwanted exchange, or apologizing.

### Requesting a Change in an Annoying Behavior or Negative Event

Just as it is important to be able to refuse requests, it is also important to make requests of others. Responses are examined for the following qualities: Was there a clear request for a behavior change? Was the change requested clearly described? Was there an avoidance of attack on the other person? Was a reason stated? An example of making a request for a behavior change is shown as follows (Galassi & Galassi, 1974, p. 9):

> You have gone to dinner at a nice restaurant. You decided to splurge this evening and ordered a steak dinner. You ordered a rare steak. However, when you cut into the steak, you find it is well done.

*You:* Waiter, I'd like to see you a moment.
*Waiter:* Is everything OK?

*You:* No, I ordered a rare steak and this is well done.

*Waiter:* OK. (Begins to walk off.)

*You:* One moment; I would like you to return this steak and bring me a rare one.

*Waiter:* I distinctly remember you ordering a well-done steak, sir.

*You:* That's impossible. I always order my steak rare.

*Waiter:* I have it written down right here on my slip.

*You:* You must have misunderstood me, then. Would you please return this steak and get me a rare one?

*Waiter:* All right, I'll be back in a few minutes.

*You:* Thank you.

Here, too, what will be effective will be influenced by the particular situation and relationship involved (e.g., power differences). Elaborations and empathic responses may increase effectiveness in ongoing relationships but may not be appropriate in transitory exchanges. A five-step procedure could be used in ongoing relationships, as follows:

• *I feel* angry . . .
• *when* you interrupt me before I am finished talking . . .
• *because* I lose track of what I am saying.
• *I would prefer* it if you would wait until I am finished talking.
• *That would* allow me to relax and finish what I am saying.

Requests for behavior change are more likely to be effective if they are made at an appropriate time. Thus, the timing of requests should be discussed. Requests could be preceded by recognition of the positive aspects of a relationship.

Beliefs related to a reluctance to express preferences include the belief that one does not have a right to request changes of others or that it is better simply to let things go and not say anything. If a behavior or event is quite bothersome, not saying anything usually will have long-term negative effects. Teaching clients effective, positive ways to request changes as well as to respond to different kinds of reactions will challenge their belief that requests can be made only in an unpleasant manner. Fear of negative reactions may prevent a client from requesting changes. The likelihood of such reactions should be explored. Offering skills in handling a variety of responses may be effective in avoiding or neutralizing negative reactions. Severe negative reactions may occur no matter how skilled the performance (for example, with an abusive partner). In such instances, other intervention methods should be selected (see later discussion). Clients should be coached to reinforce people for making requested changes (St. Lawrence, Hansen, Cutts, Tisdelle, & Irish, 1985).

### Disagreeing with Others

Clients may have difficulty expressing opinions that differ from those of others. They may not express these at all or may do so in an offensive manner, such as by saying, "You don't know what you're talking about." Or they may disagree without elaborating on the reason for disagreement, which will decrease effectiveness. The use of the personal pronoun *I* is encouraged, as is the use of elaborated opinion statements, such as, "I think there is another way to look at the issue, because . . ." (Gambrill & Richey, 1988). Interest in the other person can be shown by following this with a question such as "Have you ever looked at it from that angle?" Clients may wait too long to express disagreement, allowing anger and annoyance to build up. They are encouraged to express their disagreement at an early point without interrupting others unless they are forced to do this. Differing opinions may not be shared because a client believes that her opinions are less valuable than those of others, that people will not like her if she disagrees with what they say, or that one has to be abusive to differ with others.

### Apologizing

Social interaction inevitably involves mishaps that require making amends or apologizing (Argyle, et al., 1981). Apologizing often requires taking the initiative, although at times clients may be confronted with a misdeed and asked for an apology. A statement of apology may include an empathic statement. Difficulty in offering apologies is sometimes related to the belief that one must never make mistakes.

### Ending Interactions

Many clients complain that they get trapped in conversations that they do not wish to have or continue. Fifty-four percent of a sample of elderly adults reported that ending conversations was difficult for them (see Gambrill, 1985). Often, when clients report that they would like to end conversations, observation of their behavior shows that they continue to reinforce talking by looking, smiling, nodding, and asking questions. Many clients believe it is impolite to interrupt another person to make a bid to end the conversation. However, this may be necessary when others are insensitive to cues that indicate a desire to speak or to leave, such as a decrease in eye contact, a shift of body posture away from the person, or an attempt to speak. If no natural pause is provided in an exchange, it will be necessary to break into the conversation. One might say, "Excuse me, I'm sorry to interrupt you, but I have to leave now." It is not necessary to offer an excuse, although a reason for departure may be offered. Statements of interest in leaving may have to be repeated.

## Positive Assertion in Response to Someone Else Taking the Initiative

Relevant situations include responding to compliments and overtures from others. Ineffective response to overtures may result in lost opportunities for enjoyable social contacts (see Chapter 12 in this volume).

## Positive Assertion Involving Taking the Initiative

This category includes initiating and maintaining conversations, arranging future contacts, admitting personal shortcomings (asking for help and making certain kinds of self-disclosures), asking favors, complimenting others, expressing positive emotions such as showing affection, and giving compliments. The latter two categories have been referred to as commendatory responses (Schroeder, et al., 1983). Expressing opinions could also be included in this category. (See Chapter 12 for additional discussion.)

### Asking Favors

Some clients find it difficult to ask favors of others. Some people incorrectly assume that others should know what they want and become resentful when this is not the case. As with any social behavior that requires an initiation, the attention of the other person must be gained through effective verbal and nonverbal behavior, including appropriate loudness of voice, eye contact, and body positioning. Words should match nonverbal behavior. Being clear as to exactly what is desired, as well as stating the reason for asking the favor, may increase the chance of compliance. Some clients report that they do not ask favors because they feel crushed when turned down. They may believe that being turned down is "awful"

or that they will be obligated to the other person or that they have no right to ask for favors. However, in assertion training it is assumed that, just as others have a perfect right to say no, the client has a perfect right to ask.

### Complimenting Others

Here, too, beliefs may get in the way of effective behavior. For example, a man may feel it is "unmanly" to express compliments. Possible misconceptions should be addressed. As with other assertive behaviors, nonverbal behavior should match verbal behavior, and the client's "compliment-giving repertoire" should be checked to make sure that verbal compliments are not diluted by incongruent nonverbal behavior, such as looking away or frowning.

## ASSESSMENT

Goals of assessment are to determine personally relevant objectives for each client; the exact changes that are required in the client's repertoire (behaviors, feelings, and/or thoughts) to remove presenting complaints and attain valued objectives; the situations in which these should occur, the personal and environmental factors that may facilitate or hinder achievement of objectives; and environmental changes that should be made, such as altering the reactions of significant others (see Table 5.2). What behaviors occur too seldom or too often? Goals selected should be reviewed carefully to determine if they serve to maintain or decrease unwanted stereotypes and limited options. Involvement of clients in selecting goals is important for both ethical and practical reasons. Participation of clients in making decisions has been shown to enhance positive outcomes (see, e.g., Langer & Rodin, 1976) and is supported by the ideology of assertion training.

Many factors may be related to a lack of assertive behavior, including skill deficits, anxiety, behavior excesses such as aggressive responses that interfere with the acquisition and use of effective skills, lack of practice, lack of discrimination among various response alternatives, dysfunctional cognitions such as excessive attention to potential negative consequences, and lack of self-management skills (Gambrill, 1977) (see Table 5.3). The variety of factors that may be related to a lack of assertive behavior in specific situations highlights the need for an individualized assessment, including identification of cognitive, emotional, and behavioral responses that inter-

**Table 5.2.** Key Questions to Be Answered

1. What specific outcomes are desired by the client?

2. What skills are required to attain these outcomes?

3. What social settings are involved?

4. Does the client have the skills required to attain these outcomes?

5. If not, what specific skills must be acquired or refined, and in what situations must these occur?

6. What cognitive, emotional, or behavioral responses interfere with the acquisition and/or performance of available skills?

7. Should significant others be involved in intervention?

8. How can opportunities to use valued skills be increased? Can Social settings be arranged to encourage helpful social behaviors?

9. What prompts (self-presented and environmental) can be arranged to encourage desired behaviors and discourage interfering responses?

10. What consequences (self-presented and environmental) can be arranged to encourage desired behaviors and discourage interfering responses?

11. What intervention formats are most likely to be effective at a minimal cost in time, effort, and discomfort?

12. What can be done to maximize generalization and maintenance of valuable skills?

fere with the acquisition or use of assertive behaviors (Gresham, 1988). The distinction between skill deficits and performance deficits has a long history in psychology. Depression as well as anxiety may interfere with use of skills. It cannot be assumed that clients do not know how to perform assertive behaviors simply because they do not do so. A number of investigators have noted that people who are unassertive do have knowledge about effective behavior. For example, Brockway (1976) found that professional women usually did have assertive skills available but did not display these because of anxiety.

Research shows that women compared to men are particularly prone to negative thoughts in situations requiring assertion. This may be a result of their socialization to be more self-critical of their actions and because of their tendency to place more importance on social than self-approval (Wolfe & Fodor, 1978). Socialization messages may include ''think of others first,'' ''Be modest,'' ''Don't complain,'' ''Don't be demanding'' (Lange & Jakubowski, 1976). Studies investigating gender-related influences on assertive behavior shows that gender does

indeed influence consequences (see, e.g., Hess, Bridgewater, Bornstein, & Sweeney, 1980). Assertive behaviors may be available but not used because of a past history of punishment and/or extinction. Lack of reinforcement as well as punishing consequences may contribute to social anxiety. Only through a careful assessment can the possible contribution of behavior deficits, lack of social opportunities, conditioned anxiety, faulty cognitions, and lack of practice be determined. Goals of value to each client should be determined. Too often, clinicians and researchers select goals on a priori grounds that reflect their own beliefs and interests rather than those of clients (Gambrill & Richey, 1987) (see also description of goals in Wilson & Gallois, 1993).

Assessment involves identifying the specific situations in which assertive difficulties occur, the persons involved, the client's goals in each situation, and the moments that are most difficult. Indications of a lack of assertive behavior and its relationship to a presenting problem may be gained from data gathered in the natural environment as well as from data gathered during interviews. Sources of information include self-report in behavioral interviews or paper-and-pencil inventories, self-monitoring, role-play, direct observation in the natural environment, and reports from significant others (Rich & Schroeder, 1976; St. Lawrence, 1987). Measures obtained from different sources may present different views of skills, as discussed in the following sections. Careful attention should be paid to rules related to specific social behaviors in specific situations (Argyle & Henderson, 1985). Variables influencing what will be effective include type of message, response class, target person, and sex of receiver and sender, as well as power and status (Wilson & Gallois, 1993).

## The Behavioral Interview

Clients may express an interest in increasing assertive behavior, perhaps stimulated by the popularization of assertion training. The relevance of a lack of assertive behavior to presenting problems is often revealed during the interview through descriptions of interactions (or the avoidance of these). For example, a 67-year-old female client who complained of chronic fatigue revealed on inquiry that she was ''forced'' to remain awake at night by her housemate who ''made her'' watch television, including the commercials, after she took her sleeping pill. Clients may display an undue deference to the counselor, offer examples of interactions that indicate a lack of

**Table 5.3.**  Presenting Problems and Related Interventions

| PROBLEM | INTERVENTION |
| --- | --- |
| Behavior deficits | Develop required skills through use of model presentation, coaching, instructions, practice, and feedback. |
| Faulty discriminations | Provide information about when to use skills; provide prompts and incentives to encourage use of skills in context in which they will be reinforced. |
| Inaccurate beliefs about the nature of social relationships | Provide accurate information. Discuss benefits of accurate beliefs; address unrealistic expectations. |
| Excessive fear of negative evaluation (high social discomfort) | Decrease concern with negative evaluation through success experiences in real-life contexts as well as by cognitive restucturing tailored to nature of dysfunctional thoughts or systematic desensitization. |
| Failure to use available skills | Encourage use of skills by rehearsal, giving assignments; arrange prompts and incentives; provide self-management training. |
| Behavior surfeits such as aggressive reactions | Depends partially on whether there is a deficit of appropriate social behaviors. Replace with positive alternative behaviors; address and alter related cognitions, anger management training, increase social problem-solving skills. |
| Few opportunities to use social skills | Encourage indentification of available opportunities; create new contexts for meeting people. |
| Unrealistic expectations, such as excessively high performance standards | Encourage use of realistic performance standards; this may require identifying and challenging irrational assumptions. |
| Significant others who will punish assertive behaviors | Involve significant others in counseling; identify interests common to clients and significant others. |
| Low sense of worth; low self-esteem; hopelessness | Hard to say; depends on cause. Offering positive social experiences may alter these problems, or a variety of methods may be required including helping the client to understand the learning experiences related to beliefs. |

effective expression, or interact with significant others in an unassertive manner in the office. Examples that point to ineffective behavior may be offered when the client is asked about what happens right before and after events of interest. A client may report that it is only after his supervisor unjustly criticizes him or his wife arranges social events without asking him that he starts to feel depressed.

The interview can be used to determine the range of situations in which interpersonal difficulties are experienced, the models to which the client has been exposed in the past, and the consequences that follow both effective and ineffective behaviors. Descriptions of exactly what is done and said, thought, and felt in relevant situations should be obtained including consequences that occur. Examples of situations of concern to a 30-year-old man who requested help in controlling physical and verbal aggressive outbursts on his job as a police officer included the following:

1. You are at a party. A man confronts you and tells you about two policemen who beat up his son. He says, "Don't you cops have anything better to do than go around beating up kids?"
2. You see a person go through a red light. You pull him over and he complains that the light was yellow and not red. He says, "What, are you blind?"
3. A woman is parked illegally. You ask her to move her car and she says, "Don't you cops have anything better to do than hassle people?"
4. You are sitting at home with the curtains closed. Your wife comes in and opens them. She says, "You know I like the curtains open."
5. You go to investigate a prowler. When you get to the dorm you see a female student. You go up to her and ask if she has any information. (Rahaim, Lefebvre, & Jenkins, 1980, p. 5)

It is useful to check the client's report against that of involved others when possible; clients may not accurately identify important deficits or surfeits in their social behavior or may misinterpret the reactions of others. For example, they may think that others disapprove of their actions, when, in fact, this is not the case.

## Standardized Measures

There are a number of self-report paper-and-pencil inventories designed to assess assertive behavior. Scales developed differ in their established reliability and validity (St. Lawrence, 1987). For example, the Children's Assertive Behavior Scale (CABS) can distinguish popular from unpopular boys but does not predict actual behavior (Waas & French, 1989). Social desirability may influence responses (see, e.g., Kiecolt & McGrath, 1979). Scales include the Wolpe-Lazarus Assertiveness Schedule, which contains 30 true–false items (Wolpe & Lazarus, 1966), the 30-item Rathus Assertiveness Schedule (Rathus, 1973), the 50-item Galassi College Self-Expression Scale (Galassi, DeLeo, Galassi & Bastien, 1974; see also Gay, Hollandsworth, & Galassi, 1975), and the 40-item Assertion Inventory (Gambrill & Richey, 1975). The Assertion Inventory provides an overview of degree of comfort in various interpersonal situations, as well as information as to how situations are usually handled. Respondents indicate degree of discomfort (on a scale from 1 to 5), as well as how likely they are to carry out the behavior if the opportunity arises (on a scale from 1 to 5), in relation to each situation. Responses to clusters of related items (as determined by factor analysis) can be reviewed. These two scales are also used in the 50-item scale for Interpersonal Behavior developed by Arrindell et al. (1990). These authors view assertion as a sub-construct of shyness.

Content and correlational analysis of assertion inventories indicate a predominance of items dealing with negative assertion (Furnham & Henderson, 1984). Correlation among five commonly used inventories ranged from .24 to .80. Self-report assertion measures have been developed for children (Ollendick, 1984), adolescents (Conner, Dann, & Twentyman, 1983; Lindsay & Lindsay, 1982), and professionals (Gripton & Valentich, 1977). Standardized paper-and-pencil inventories such as the Assertion Inventory are screening devices that may point to the relevance of certain areas. More specific information must be gained via other assessment methods, such as behavioral interviews, self-monitoring, role-play, and observation in the natural environment. One limitation of many self-report measures is failure to distinguish between assertive and aggressive individuals (DeGiovanni & Epstein, 1978).

Other self-report inventories, such as the 30-item Conflict Resolution Inventory, concentrate on more discrete situations, such as refusing requests (McFall & Bridges, 1970, p. 5). Examples from this inventory include the following:

> You have volunteered to help someone, whom you barely know, to do some charity work. He/she really needs your help but when he/she calls to arrange a time, it turns out that you are in the middle of exams.

> You are studying for an exam but your best friend asks you to go to a concert with him/her. He/she makes you feel that if you were a true friend you would go.

Response alternatives include (1) "I would refuse and would not feel uncomfortable about doing so"; (2) "I would refuse but would feel uncomfortable doing so": (3) "I would not refuse but would feel uncomfortable because I didn't"; (4) "I would not refuse even though I might prefer to, but would not feel particularly uncomfortable because I didn't"; and (5) "I would not refuse because it seems a reasonable request." Warren and Gilner (1978) developed a measure of positive assertive behaviors (The Behavioral Test of Tenderness Expression) (see also Twardoz et al., 1979). A Discrimination Test has been developed to assess the extent to which a person can select the appropriate alternative (assertive, aggressive, or nonassertive behavior) in a series of 60 items (see Lange & Jakubowski, 1976). Other tests have been designed to assess knowledge of assertive behavior, such as the Written Assertiveness Knowledge Test (Bruch, 1988). Lack of sufficient data regarding reliability and validity is a concern with these tests of knowledge. A number of self-report instruments assess self-statements in social situations. Here, too, some focus on a specific kind of situation, such as those calling for refusal of a request (Schwartz & Gottman, 1976; Fiedler & Beach, 1978). Others apply to a broader class of situations (Heimberg, Chizuzzi, Becker, & Madrazo-Peterson, 1983). Scales have been designed to assess irrational beliefs related to social behavior, such as The Irrational Beliefs Test (Alden & Safran, 1978) and The Irrational Beliefs About Assertion Questionnaire (Craighead, 1979).

## Self-Monitoring

Clients may be requested to keep a log of relevant situations in the natural environment, noting the situation, what was said and done, satisfaction with responses, subjective ratings of discomfort, what they would have liked to say or do, and what they thought and felt. It is also helpful to ask clients to write down what an effective response would be. Problems with self-monitoring include reactive effects that compromise reliability and validity (Ciminero, Nelson, & Lipinski, 1986). An example of a client-gathered log is shown in Table 5.4. We can see from the right-hand column that this client was able to come up with an effective reaction for some situations. She clearly had difficulty in saying no as well as in initiating conversations. Data gathered over the rest of the week supported the hypothesis that these were two areas of difficulty for her. She also had difficulty in making reasonable requests of her secretary, which had the consequence of often making her seem unreliable to others, because letters would not be answered on time. Data may be collected by recording relevant incidents on audiotape. Praise should be offered for effective behaviors that are noted. As with any self-monitoring assignment, successful participation is more likely if clear instructions are given, an easy format for recording is provided, recording is not overly intrusive, and clients understand the rationale for self-monitoring. Self-monitored data could be summarized in a variety of ways to assess progress such as percentage of opportunities acted on.

## Role-Play

Clients can be requested to role-play relevant behavior in the office. Reciprocal roles could be assumed by the counselor after finding out how significant others are likely to act, or these may be played by other people (e.g., secretaries who may be available). Clients may also be observed during structured role-plays with confederates or significant others in the office. A variety of role-play tests have been designed. Some are related to specific kinds of responses, such as the Behavioral Role-Playing Assertion Test, which mainly assesses refusal responses (McFall & Lillisand, 1971). Other role-play tests assess behavior in a range of situations. The Behavioral Assertiveness Test (Eisler, Miller, & Hersen, 1973) consists of 16 potentially difficult social situations presented on audiotape. A male or female confederate in the room with the client states the phrase to which the client responds in relation to each situation. Behaviors evaluated include latency of response, loudness of speech, compliance, requests for new behavior, and affect. The Diabetes Assertiveness Test (Gross & Johnson, 1981) contains situations that confront preadolescent diabetics. Variations in the mode of presentation of scenes (for example, live or

tape-recorded confederate), as well as other variables such as responses required of subjects, influence performance (see Galassi & Galassi, 1976). Video- or audiotape can be used to record role-played interactions. Role-plays should be made as lifelike as possible, with careful description of the environmental context.

If a client is having difficulty expressing a complaint to his employer, the role-play should be initiated with the client leaving the room and then reentering it so that his posture, eye contact, and gait can be assessed when he first presents himself. Perhaps he avoids looking at the counselor, enters the room with drooped shoulders, and shuffles his feet in an uncertain way. Both verbal and nonverbal behaviors in need of change should be identified. Nonverbal behaviors, such as eye contact, gestures, smiles, body positioning, and facial expression, influence the impact of communications. Paralinguistic (speech disturbances, temporal patterning) and nonverbal behaviors have often been found to be the best predictors of ratings of overall performance (see, e.g., Romano & Bellack, 1980) (for a review of nonverbal behavior and communication, see, for example, Siegman & Feldstein, 1987).

Relevant behaviors and situations should be clearly defined so they are easily discernible, allowing determination of exactly what changes should be made to increase social effectiveness. Global ratings offer little or no information about the specific behaviors and their sequence and timing that are related to these ratings. Specific behaviors judges identify as related to global ratings may not accurately reflect cues that in fact influence their behavior (Nisbett & Ross, 1980). *Looking* has been defined as the client turning his head 45 degrees toward his partner with his eyes focused between the top of the head and the chin; *smiling* has been defined as a 45-degree crease in the client's cheek, with his teeth showing (Eisler, Hersen, & Agras, 1973). Some responses, such as reinforcing comments, may not permit this type of precision. However, the kinds of statements that fall into a class can be identified—for example, approval, agreement, and signs of interest. Appearance may have to be addressed because physical attractiveness influences behavior in a variety of contexts (Patzer, 1985).

Voice qualities are reviewed; these include tone, pitch, clarity, speech disturbances, and loudness, as well as the match between these qualities and both nonverbal behavior and content (Trower, Bryant, & Argyle, 1978). Nonverbal behaviors should match verbal behavior; for example, smiling when refusing

**Table 5.4.** Example of a Client-Gathered Log

| DATE | TIME | | SITUATION | WHO IS INVOLVED | WHAT YOU SAID OR DID | WHAT HAPPENED | WHAT YOU DID | WHAT YOU WOULD HAVE LIKED TO DO |
|------|------|--|-----------|-----------------|---------------------|---------------|-------------|--------------------------------|
| 9/13 | 9:00 | A.M. | Work | Secretary | Request that urgent letter be typed | She said she did not have time. | Said "O.K." | Repeat request and try to convey urgency: "This is a really important letter. Do you think there is some other way we could get it typed?" |
| 9/13 | 11:30 | A.M. | Work | Colleague | | Asked if I could talk. | Said "O.K." | Say no, because I was really into work and it was not urgent that we talk: "Gee, I have to finish this now. Could we talk later this afternoon?" |
| 9/13 | 12:00 | P.M. | Work | Colleague | | Asked to have lunch with me. | Said "Yes" | Say no, because I really find this person a bore. |
| 9/13 | 7:00 | P.M. | Home | Friend | | Telephoned and asked if he could come over. | Said "Yes" | Say no—really felt like being alone. |
| 9/14 | 3:00 | P.M. | Faculty meeting | New man | Nothing | Nothing | | Would have liked to go over and start a conversation with him. |

*Source:* E. D. Gambrill, *Behavior Modification: Handbook of Assessment, Interventions and Evaluation* (San Francisco: Jossey-Bass, 1977).

a request would not usually be appropriate. *How* the client says things is as important as *what* is said, including latency of response and loudness and fluency of speech. The client's reactions are examined to see, for example, whether eye contact was adequate, whether words were stated loudly and clearly enough to be understood, whether there was a relative absence of hesitations and stammers, and whether timing of responses was appropriate. In each situation, the particular components and their sequence that make up an effective reaction may be somewhat different. Situations may be presented by film, audiotape, or videotape and the client's responses observed and recorded for assessment purposes. Films for assessment of assertive behavior have been developed (see, e.g., Gervasio, 1988). Asking the client to describe his thoughts and feelings during role-played interactions, as well as beliefs about what the other person was thinking and feeling, will help to identify useful and dysfunctional feelings and thoughts.

Behavior during role-plays may not reflect behavior in real-life situations (Bellack, 1983; Bellack, Hersen & Lamparski, 1979). Some clients will not be able to become involved in role plays; others may be too anxious to participate. Some clients respond more effectively in role-plays than they do in real-life situations because they know that negative consequences will not really occur (Bellack, Hersen, & Turner, 1979). Knowledge about effective behavior does not necessarily reflect what is done in either role-plays or real-life situations. Correspondence between knowledge and behavior appears to be greater for high-assertive than for low-assertive subjects (Eisler, Frederiksen, & Peterson, 1978). Reactions during role-play may be influenced by specific response sets, reinforcement for competent performance, description of the specific behaviors to be assessed; and the kind of prompts used (e.g., live or taped) (see Rakos, 1991, for a review). Available skills may be identified by asking the client to respond as she thinks one ideally should respond.

## Observation in Real-Life Situations

Role-playing methods are artificial and may not reflect behavior in real life. For this reason, role playing may be supplemented by observation of the client interacting with significant others in real-life settings. For example, a person who has difficulty in service situations could be unobtrusively accompanied to a store and his behavior observed to identify effective and ineffective components. As with simulated situations, asking clients to write down their thoughts before, during, and after interactions of interest will aid in identifying helpful and dysfunctional thoughts. This should be done as soon as convenient after relevant exchanges.

## Physiological Measures

Physiological arousal prior to a task is common with both nonphobic individuals and social phobics (see Barlow, 1987, for further discussion). As in other areas, there may be little relationship between physiological reactions and overt behavior (Lehrer & Leiblum, 1981; St. Lawrence, 1987). Many individuals are "anxious performers"; that is, they act in an assertive manner even when they are anxious (Gambrill & Richey, 1975). Performance despite anxiety is a feature of social phobia. Physiological measures may be useful when clients cannot accurately report changes in arousal that accompany their anxiety. Self-report could be used in place of physiological measures; for example, a client could rate degree of anxiety during social encounters. However, self-report data may not yield the same information as may physiological measures.

In summary, there are a variety of sources of assessment information that may be used. The possible inaccuracy of any one, such as self-report, can be overcome by use of multiple sources. Lack of correlation between different sources may offer valuable information. For example, effective behavior accompanied by high anxiety may indicate a need for desensitization of anxiety reactions. The question of concern during assessment is whether the client displays ineffective social behavior in relation to situations of concern. The effect of this is determined in relation to both client-presented problems and others noted by the counselor. An important part of assessment is determining whether needed skills are available. If they are present, intervention will address factors that interfere with their display, such as oversensitivity to negative reactions. If the client does not possess needed skills, intervention procedures that will establish or refine them, such as model presentation and behavior rehearsal, would be selected.

## MOTIVATING CLIENTS
## TO BE MORE ASSERTIVE

Forming a conceptualization of effective social behavior as important is a component of assertion training. Attention is devoted to enhancing the discrimination between submissive, assertive, and aggressive behavior; to encouraging the belief that people have a perfect right to express feelings, both negative and positive, in ways that do not harm or diminish others; to pointing out the losses involved in a lack of assertion; and to highlighting the relationship of unassertive behavior to presenting problems if this is not evident to the client. Discussion centers around the disadvantages of ineffective social behavior and the potential benefits of effective behavior. Although this tripartite division of social behavior overlooks variations within the three categories, it is often helpful in highlighting the fact that valued consequences may be lost both by submissive as well as aggressive reactions. Specific situations are selected in which nonassertive behavior has occurred, and these are carefully reviewed, pointing out what befell the person both in terms of negative consequences such as doing things he did not wish to do, aggravating others unnecessarily, losing opportunities, and having unpleasant feelings such as anxiety and resentment.

It may be helpful to illustrate to clients how their behavior appears to others. This can be done by assuming the role of a client and duplicating his or her usual nonassertive behavior, perhaps even exaggerating it, to highlight how this behavior strikes others. This enactment often surprises people and frequently is followed by statements such as "No wonder no one ever listens to me." Statements may also be made indicating new awareness of specific actions. A client may realize, for example, that he infrequently looks at others during exchanges. The negative consequences of a lack of assertive behavior are often made apparent during assessment. For example, a client may realize, by keeping a log, that she rarely states her preferences but, instead, expects others to know what she wants. The client comes to recognize the losses that result from ineffective behavior and the relationship of such behavior to presenting problems (which may include marital discord, loneliness, inappropriate anger, depression, or substance abuse). Possible detrimental effects on others are also revealed through assessment.

Clients often have beliefs that interfere with a willingness to become more assertive, and discussion may be necessary to alter them. Various beliefs may have to be challenged, such as the belief that one should never hurt people's feelings and that, therefore, one should never criticize others or complain; that it is childish or inappropriate to express positive emotions; that one is indebted to another person and must suffer silently whatever impositions the

other wishes to inflict; or that one must always please others. Lange and Jakubowski (1976) describe socialization messages women may receive that interfere with performing assertive behavior. There is a rebalancing of risks toward increased concern about lost opportunities for positive experiences and decreased concern about avoiding unpleasant consequences.

The client may initially feel that to be assertive is to be aggressive; that he will hurt other people's feelings; that they will not like him; and that he has no right to impose his preferences on others. The role of assertive responses in inhibiting anxiety is described, drawing on examples from the client's history as well as current examples (Wolpe & Lazarus, 1966), and the cueing and motivating role of the client's emotional reaction, whether positive or negative, is pointed out (Wolpe, 1973). If, for example, a client is angry about poor service in a restaurant, the anger can serve as a cue and motivator for assertive behavior. The benefits of effective social behavior may be highlighted by requesting the client to observe models of effective behavior in real-life settings and to note what happens after such behavior.

Realistic and unrealistic anticipated consequences are clarified through discussion, and the client is prepared for possible negative ones by providing skills in responding to these and through encouraging positive self-instructions and self-reinforcement. In addition, training focuses on the use of positive responses and the minimally effective response. Convincing clients of the inaccuracy of some of their concerns can be encouraged by asking them to observe effective models in real-life settings and to note what happens after effective social behavior, as well as what happens after their own successful behaviors. If negative as well as positive consequences are likely to follow assertive reactions, the short- and long-term benefits and costs of assertive behavior should be discussed, and the client must choose his preferred alternative. Some authors recommend that training begin with commendatory assertion (compliments, small talk, expressing positive feelings) in order to increase the likelihood of positive effects (Delameter & McNamara, 1986; St. Lawrence, Hansen, Cutts, Tisdelle, & Irish, 1985). Knowledge about the pattern of interaction in which an assertive behavior occurs is important in predicting its short- and long-term effects. This contextual analysis is a hallmark of a behavioral approach.

One strategy that may be effective in altering interfering beliefs is to ask the client whether she thinks it fair for a person to be treated in such a manner and whether she would treat someone else this way. Often the answer is no, the reason being that it would be unfair to do so. Thus, the client states that he would not inflict on others what he readily bears himself. If the client already recognizes the inequalities in his relationships, highlighting them further offers additional incentives for participation in the steps necessary to alter behavior. The counselor stresses the manner in which unexpressed feelings such as anger and resentment build up, create anxiety, and hinder positive relationships.

If the problem lies in the other direction, antisocial aggression, the negative consequences of this, as well as the beneficial effects of assertive behavior, are emphasized. Here, too, clients learn to influence their social environment in more effective ways.

## ASSERTION TRAINING

Assertion training usually consists of a variety of components, including instruction, model presentation, behavior rehearsal, feedback, programming of change, and homework assignments. Other procedures that may also be used include self-instruction training, relaxation training, cognitive restructuring (e.g., modification of unrealistic expectations or beliefs), and interpersonal problem-solving training. Textual material may be used to offer instructional information. For example, clients could be asked to read portions of *Your Perfect Right* (Alberti & Emmons, 1974) to clarify differences between aggressive, assertive, and submissive behavior. With undergraduates, instructions and guided practice (coaching and behavior rehearsal) have been sufficient to increase assertive behavior (McFall & Twentyman, 1973). With other populations, such as psychiatric patients and more complex social behaviors, modeling has been required with behaviors such as resisting pressure. Duration of assertion training is usually brief (7 to 12 weekly sessions).

Many clients anticipate negative consequences from being more assertive. They may fear that others will scream at them, perhaps even assault them, and certainly put them in their "place." Some people anticipate negative consequences that are indeed likely. For example, requesting behavior changes or refusing unwanted requests of an abusive partner may increase abuse (O'Leary, Curley, Rosenbaum, & Clarke, 1985). An employer may not be at all pleased when an employee requests changes in relation to his work, no matter how diplomatically the request is made. Ideally, however, the results of assertion are

positive both for the client and for significant others, in the short as well as in the long term, in that assertion encourages mutual respect, removes feelings of resentment, and facilitates positive encounters. Exploring the consequences of a lack of assertion often helps to point out the disadvantages both to clients as well as to other involved individuals of nonassertive behavior. For example, not taking steps to equalize participation in conversations may result in the "listener" starting to dislike and to avoid the "talker."

Once clients accept the goal of changing their behavior and agree to try out more effective reactions, specific instructions concerning types of responses to use as well as when to use them is usually provided. Reactions that will result in positive exchanges are encouraged, even in situations involving an initial negative reaction toward a client. An example is the empathic assertion advocated by Lazarus (1973), in which one tries to empathize with the other person's situation—for example, by saying to a snappish clerk, "It looks like you're very busy today." Selection of intervention methods should depend on the nature of the client's cognitive, emotional, and behavioral deficits and surfeits in relation to relevant goals and situations, as well as likely consequences and options for rearranging the environment. Thus, the selection of procedures should flow directly from assessment (see Table 5.3). If appropriate behaviors exist but are not performed because of anxiety, intervention may focus on enhancing anxiety management skills. If needed social skills are absent, a procedure designed to develop them, such as model presentation and behavior rehearsal, can be selected. Discrimination training is required when skills are available but are not used at appropriate times. Assessment often reveals effective behaviors that simply have to be placed under new stimulus control—that is, prompted in other situations. For example, effective ways of saying no to a spouse may be of value in work situations also but may not be used there. Training may be carried out individually or in a group setting (see later discussion of the use of groups). A session may focus on developing effective behavior in one situation or on increasing a specific behavior of value in a range of similar situations.

### Instructions

Instructions concerning effective behavior may be given verbally or presented in textual, audiotape, or filmed form (see Table 5.5). This is often blended with model presentation and coaching during role-plays (see for example Hersen, Eisler, Miller, Johnson & Pinkston, 1973). Specific behaviors are identified to increase, decrease, stabilize, or vary, and their relationship to desired goals is described. Instructions may be given concerning only one behavior at a time, which is then role-played; or more than one behavior may be reviewed depending on the entering repertoires of each client. What not to do (e.g., smile or giggle while requesting a change in an annoying behavior) as well as what to do (look at the person, face the person) are described. Intervention may consist of instructions given in a book. This self-help format is known as *bibliotherapy*. Consideration of individual differences is a key problem in this format and the majority of self-help books on assertion training have not been evaluated in terms of effectiveness (Gambrill, 1992).

**Table 5.5.** Instructional Aids and Related Handout for Cognitive-Behavioral Assertion Training

### PRINCIPLES OF ASSERTIVE BEHAVIOR

*Guidelines for effective delivery: My appearance*

Nonverbal behavior: How do I look?

| | |
|---|---|
| _____ Eye contact? | 1. Keep good eye contact; look at person I'm talking to instead of down at the floor or off to the side. Lean forward slightly. |
| _____ Relaxed posture? | 2. Try to keep my body relaxed, not rigid or tense. Breathing deeply may help to relax me. |
| _____ Still? | 3. Don't fidget and move around excessively, wring hands, change feet, etc. |
| _____ No fists or pounding? | 4. Don't clench fists, hit, or pound on things. If I get angry, express it directly instead of indirectly by clenching fists, etc. |
| _____ Serious? | 5. Act serious; avoid laughing or inappropriate smiling when someone is trying to jeopardize my rights. |

*Tone of voice: How do I sound?*

| | |
|---|---|
| _____ Firm? | 1. Speak in a definitive and firm voice as if I really mean what I say. |
| _____ No whining? | 2. No whining, pleading, or apologetic voice. |
| _____ No stammering? | 3. No stammering, undue hesitance, mumbling, or extraneous words (e.g., *er, ah, mmmm.*). |
| _____ No sarcasm or hostility? | 4. No sarcasm, hostility, or yelling. If I am angry, express it directly rather than indirectly by a hostile, sarcastic, or "cold" voice. |
| _____ Calm? | 5. When I am talking to someone who is speaking rapidly in a loud voice, keep my voice low and speak slowly. |
| _____ Steady? | 6. Maintain my voice at a steady volume. When my voice becomes lower at the end of a request or refusal, I may sound as if I am unsure. |

*Guidelines for effective content: What I say*

Nonthreatening situations: Dealing with everyday situations

| | |
|---|---|
| _____ Comments concise? | 1. Keep what I say concise and to the point; say what I want directly instead of beating around the bush. |
| _____ Message clear? | 2. Be sure and state clearly the message I want the other person to hear, instead of expecting them to infer it from other things I say. |
| _____ Statement of wishes? | 3. Try to use phrases "I want," "I don't want," instead of "I need," "You should," or "I can't," perhaps one statement of why. |
| _____ No apologetic behavior? | 4. Perhaps give one factual reason, but not apologetic behavior or long-winded excuses. |
| _____ No "shoulds"? | 5. No "shoulds" or inappropriate demands; don't tell others what they "should" do, feel, want, etc. |
| _____ No threats or attacks? | 6. When angry, express it directly rather than by attacking or threatening. |

*Source:* M. M. Linehan, "Structured Cognitive-Behavioral Treatment of Assertion Problems," in P. C. Kendall and S. D. Hollon (Ed.), *Cognitive-Behavioral Interventions.* (New York: Academic Press, 1979), pp. 228–229.

## Model Presentation

Instruction, model presentation, rehearsal, and coaching can be used when clients lack requisite behaviors in certain situations or when there is a need to refine behaviors. The need to use modeling will be influenced by the complexity of the skill to be acquired and nature of the entering repertoire. The greater the complexity of the skill and the more deficient the entering repertoire, the greater the need for model presentation is likely to be (see Rakos, 1991, for more detail). There are a number of studies showing that instructions alone (without modeling) are not sufficient to develop appropriate social behaviors with psychiatric patients (see, e.g., Eisler, Blanchard, Fitts, & Williams, 1978). An advantage of model presentation is that an entire chain of behavior can be illustrated and the client then requested to imitate it. Nonverbal behaviors can be demonstrated as well as verbal behaviors, and the client's attention drawn to those that are especially important. The effectiveness of model presentation in establishing new behaviors, in decreasing avoidance behaviors, and in facilitating behaviors is well documented (Bandura, 1969, 1986). Pentz and Kazdin (1982) found that modeling alone improved the assertive behavior of both passive and aggressive adolescents. Models are more effective if they are similar to the client in sex and age, if they are perceived to have a high status, if their reactions are followed by positive consequences, and if the client's attention is directed toward desired response elements (Bandura, 1986). A client can be asked to notice the model's eye contact, hand motions, and posture. Models of both effective and ineffective behavior may be presented. For example, aggressive, passive, and assertive methods of dealing with each of eight situations, such as refusing requests and requesting behavior changes, were shown to male clients with spinal cord injuries (Dunn, Van Horn, & Herman, 1981). The model may verbalize helpful positive thoughts during the role-play if effective social skills are hampered by negative thoughts. Appropriate self-statements can at first be shared aloud by the client when imitating the model's behavior, and then, by instruction, gradually moved to a covert level. Models who display coping responses (for example, they become anxious and cope effectively with this) are more effective than models who display mastery response (i.e., do not experience any difficulty in a situation) (Meichenbaum, 1972). The effects of modeling are enhanced if the observer has an opportunity to practice the observed behavior and is asked to identify important components of, and general rules associated with, the modeled behavior. For example, observers who summarized a model's behavior learned and retained more information than those who did not (see, e.g., Bandura, Grusec, & Menlove, 1966). Following model presentation, the client is requested to practice (rehearse) the modeled behavior. Praise is offered for effective behaviors or approximations to them, and coaching is provided as needed. Models and instructions are represented as needed, and rehearsal, prompts, and feedback are continued until desired responses and comfort levels are demonstrated.

Effective behaviors may be modeled by the counselor, or written scripts, audiotape, videotape, or film may be used. The advantage of written material is that it can be referred to on an as-needed basis. Essential elements of various responses can be highlighted and written models offered. A checklist can be provided for each situation so that clients can check their behavior, thoughts, and feelings against it to assess their responses in relation to outcomes. The client may be instructed to watch people with effective behavior who are in similar roles and to write down the situation, what was done, and what happened. This increases exposure to a variety of effective models, offers examples to use during rehearsal, increases discrimination as to when to use certain behaviors, and offers opportunities for vicarious extinction of anxiety reactions through observation of positive outcomes following assertive behavior. The opportunity to see how negative reactions can be handled may be provided as well. Client observations are discussed, noting effective elements as well as other situations in which assertive behaviors may be usefully employed.

McFall and Lillesand (1971) used model presentation coaching and rehearsal to increase refusal of unreasonable requests. Assessment included noting responses to nine prerecorded stimulus situations. During training, a tape-recorded narrator first described a scene. The student responded covertly or overtly to the scene, listened to one male and one female assertive model, and was coached regarding the components of an assertive reaction. Further feedback was offered, and the entire sequence was then repeated. Covert rehearsal produced greater improvement than did overt rehearsal. The imagery of the client can be checked during covert modeling by asking the client to share out loud what he is imagining (Kazdin, 1976). Imagining multiple models and favorable consequences is more effective than imagining only one model or a lack of positive effects. Adding overt rehearsal and homework assignments adds to the effects of covert modeling (Kazdin & Mascitelli, 1982).

## Behavior Rehearsal

Role playing during assessment may reveal that the client has many effective components of needed skills, and it may be decided that instructions and prompts during rehearsal will be sufficient to develop and refine needed repertoires. Not only does behavior rehearsal provide for learning new behaviors, but it also allows their practice in a safe environment and so serves to reduce discomfort. Rehearsal may be particularly effective when skills are available or involved behaviors are simple rather than complex. The value of rehearsal is emphasized by a study that found significant effects after only 12 minutes of rehearsal (Lawrence, 1970). The situations employed during role playing should be explicitly described and should closely resemble real-life conditions. Rehearsal involves exposure to feared situations, and this exposure is considered to be the key factor in decreasing social anxiety, especially if people remain in the situation even when they are anxious and succeed in performing despite their discomfort (see Chapter 12 in this book). Changes in beliefs and attitudes often follow changes in performance, making cognitive restructuring unnecessary.

Instructions or signals can be used to prompt specific responses. They can be used prior to practice or model presentation as well as during rehearsal. Instructions are given before the client practices a behavior, thus ''prompting'' him to engage in certain behaviors rather than others. Perhaps he did not look at his partner during the role-play and is coached to look at the other person while he (the client) is speaking. Care must be taken to identify *specific* behaviors. Checklists may be given to clients as reminders about effective behaviors. Covert modeling or rehearsal in which the client imagines himself or someone else dealing effectively in social situations may also be used (see e.g. Kazdin, 1976, 1982). Home sessions in which the client engages in covert rehearsal can be used to supplement office sessions.

A hierarchy of scenes graduated in accord with the client's anxiety can be used for role playing. Each situation can be placed on a card, and these can be arranged in order of their individual SUD (subject units of anxiety) ratings. Role playing is initiated with scenes that induce low levels of discomfort.

Clients who are reluctant to engage in role playing can be requested to read from a prepared script. As comfort increases, role playing can be introduced. If a client is too anxious to read from a script, relaxation training may be offered as a prelude to role playing. When there are many deficits, one behavior at a time may be focused on (see example discussed in next section). Role-plays should involve scenes related to real-life situations; each role-play may be repeated until required levels of skill and comfort are demonstrated. For example, in a case reported by Eisler (1976) six scenes were enacted ten times in various random orders, focusing on one behavior at a time such as eye contact, and feedback was offered after each performance. After obtaining a stable increase in one behavior, instructions were then given concerning the next behavior. Sixty rehearsals were provided over five sessions.

## Feedback

Corrective feedback is offered following each rehearsal. Specific positive aspects of the client's performance are first noted and praised. The focus is on improvements over baseline levels. Thus, approximations to final behaviors are reinforced. Critical comments, such as ''You can do better'' or ''That wasn't too good,'' should be avoided. The client is encouraged to develop behaviors that are most likely to result in positive consequences. Instructions and rapid performance feedback were successful in increasing the assertive behaviors of two patients who were residents of a veterans administration hospital (Eisler, Hersen, & Miller, 1974). One patient, a 28-year-old house painter, had been admitted after he fired a shotgun into the ceiling of his home. His history revealed periodic rages following a consistent failure to express anger in social situations. His behavior was assessed by asking him to role-play situations in which he was unable to express anger. These included being criticized by a fellow employee at work, disagreeing with his wife about her inviting company to their home without checking with him first, and having difficulty refusing requests made by his 8-year-old son. An assistant played the complementary role (wife, son, or fellow employee) in each situation. The client's reactions were videotaped and also observed through a one-way mirror. Review of data collected revealed expressive deficits in four components of assertion: (1) eye contact (he did not look at his partner when speaking to him), (2) voice loudness (one could barely hear what he said), (3) speech duration (responses consisted of one- or two-word replies), and (4) requests (he did not ask his partner to change his or her behavior).

Twelve situations that were unrelated to the client's problem areas but that required assertive behavior were used during training. Each was role-played five times in different orders over sessions. Instructions were given to the client through a miniature radio receiver (Bug-in-the-Ear—Farrall Instrument Company, P.O. Box 1037, Grand Island, NE 68801). Instructions related to only one of the four responses at any one time. Thus, during the initial scenes, he was coached to look at his partner when speaking to him, and during the second series he was coached to increase the loudness of his voice but received no instructions concerning any other response. During the fourth series, he was coached to speak longer and, during the last, instructed to ask his partner for a behavior change. Feedback was provided concerning his performance after each role-play. This procedure permitted a multiple-baseline analysis of the four behaviors. Each response increased after specific instructions regarding this were given and effects generalized to the specific situations that were problematic for this client. Ratings of his behavior were made by reviewing videotapes of his performance.

A similar procedure was successful in increasing the assertive behavior of a 34-year-old man with a history of alcoholism. His current admission had been related to an inability to handle increased responsibility at work after he was promoted to a managerial position at a small motel. It was difficult for him to confront those who worked for him when they performed poorly; he complied with unreasonable demands made on him by his employer as well as by motel guests; and he was unable to resist pressure from salespersons. More rapid gains for both clients might have occurred if training had been directly concerned with their specific problematic situations.

Feedback in the form of praise that does not specify particular behaviors may be ineffective in altering behavior in positive directions. This kind of general praise does not help clients to identify specific ways in which behavior could be refined to achieve greater success.

## Programming of Change

Specific goals should be established for each session. Perhaps only one or two behaviors will be focused on in any one session, or the initial repertoire might be such that all needed verbal and nonverbal behaviors can be practiced. Assessment of the client's behavior in relation to given situations will reveal available behaviors and training should build on this entering repertoire. Thus goals are established individually for each client during each session. (This may be difficult to do in group settings. See later discussion of the use of groups.) Ideally, reinforcement for improvement should always be in relation to a client's past performance rather than in terms of comparisons with other people. Any improvements, even small ones, are noted and praised. This process offers the client a model of how to alter his own behavior (to identify specific changes to be made, practice them, and offer positive feedback for improvements).

Hierarchies ranked in terms of the degree of anxiety or anger that situations induce can be used to establish assertive skills gradually. Rehearsal starts with situations inducing a small degree of anger or anxiety; as these are mastered, higher level scenes are introduced. Escalation of scenes is programmed in accordance with the skill and comfort level of the client. A hierarchy used with a 22-year-old man who engaged in destructive acts concerned making requests of the nursing staff (Wallace, Teigen, Liberman, & Baker 1973). Eight scenes were included that varied staff responses (yes or no) and the latency of the reply (five seconds to no response at all).

## Homework Assignments

After needed skill and comfort levels are attained, assignments can be agreed on that will be carried out in the natural environment. Homework has been found to contribute to the maintenance and generalization of assertion (Kazdin & Mascitelli, 1982). Prior preparation may be required if negative reactions are anticipated. Assignments are selected that offer a high probability of success at a low cost in terms of discomfort. An adequate understanding of various relationships in which assertive behavior is proposed is needed in order to maximize the likelihood of positive consequences and minimize the likelihood of negative outcomes (Wolpe, 1958). New assertive behaviors will not always immediately change the behavior of others in a positive way. The behavior of significant others may change only slowly, and more effective behavior may initially create negative feelings and actions. In these instances, coping skills should be developed to handle such reactions before asking the client to carry out new behaviors. Ideally, significant others should be involved in the counseling process so that they may facilitate change efforts, but this will not always be possible.

With some behaviors, such as assertive behaviors in service situations, unknown individuals may be involved. Here, the client is trained to identify situations in which a positive reaction to assertive behaviors is likely. For example, if a problem exists in service situations, clients can first select clerks who appear friendly and who smile at them rather than ones who scowl and look as if they have had a bad night. Homework assignments cards may help to prompt task completion (Liberman, King, DeRisi, & McCann, 1975). These indicate the date the assignment was given, description of the assignment, when it is to be completed, and the date completed. When effective social behavior occurs without difficulty in easy situations, more difficult ones are then attempted. Clients are instructed to offer positive self-statements for effective behavior. The first instance of effective behavior may not be an exact replica of one that has been rehearsed. Practice, coaching, and model presentation provide instruction concerning the essential elements of effective behavior, and clients are encouraged to vary their reactions in appropriate ways. As with any other assignment, a check is made at the next meeting to find out what happened. Client logs provide a daily record of progress and guide selection of new assignments. Information reviewed may include what was said and done; when it was said and done; how the client felt before, during, and after the exchange; whether positive self-statements were provided for trying to influence one's social environment even though the attempt might have failed; and what consequences followed the client's behavior. Positive feedback is offered for effective behaviors, additional instructions given as necessary, and further relevant assignments agreed on. If an ineffective response was given in a situation, the client can be asked to write down one that he thinks would have been more effective. This will provide added practice in selecting effective behaviors.

## Cognitive Restructuring—Changing What Clients Say to Themselves

Cognitive skills relevant to assertive behavior include helpful attributions, realistic expectations, helpful rules, self-reinforcement, interpersonal problem-solving skills, and accurate perception and translation of social cues. In addition, cognitive skills are involved in the regulation of affect (e.g., anger and anxiety). Unrealistic beliefs and other kinds of thoughts, such as negative self-statements, that get in the way of assertive behavior should be identified and

replaced by helpful self-statements and beliefs. This process is initiated during assessment and continues during intervention. Discussion of beliefs about what is proper social behavior and who has a right to do what should be addressed during assessment in the process of selecting goals. Cognitive restructuring may include altering unrealistic expectations, attitudes about personal rights and obligations, and/or self-instruction training in which clients learn to identify negative self-statements related to ineffective social behavior and to replace them with positive self-statements. Clients with low levels of dysfunctional attitudes seem to do equally well with either skills training or skills training combined with rational relabeling (Hammen, Jacobs, Mayol, & Cochran, 1980). Cognitive-behavioral methods such as those developed by Beck (1990) and Novaco (1975) may be used to help clients identify unrealistic expectations or anger-provoking cues that hinder effective social behavior and to replace these with facilitating self-instructions. Clients could be encouraged to conduct mini–cost–benefit analyses in situations of concern.

## The Self-Management Aspects of Assertive Behavior

Self-management aspects of assertive behavior include identifying situations in which assertion is called for (and those in which it is not), monitoring the effect of assertion, and offering appropriate self-feedback (Kanfer, 1970). The process of generating effective social behaviors can be enhanced by the use of questions that function as cues (What's happening? What are my choices? What might happen if . . . ? Which choice is better? How could I do it? How did I do? (Park & Gaylord-Ross, 1989). Self-management skills such as use of precommitment strategies may be used to encourage assertive behaviors (see Watson & Tharp, 1988, for an example of such strategies). Self-monitoring may enhance generalization and maintenance of assertive behaviors (Jacobs & Cochran, 1982).

## Anxiety Reduction Methods

Relaxation training could be provided if anxiety interferes with use of social skills (see also Chapter 12 in this book). The specific method selected to alter anxiety will depend on the cause(s) of anxiety (e.g., negative thoughts, a past history of punishing consequences because of lack of skills, and/or unrealistic expectations (everyone must like me). Exposure methods may be used to decrease social anxiety (see Chapter 12 in this book). If intervention is successful, anxiety is lessened in interpersonal situations and assertive responses are used only when a client believes that these would be of value in attaining personal and social goals. Clients may be indifferent to situations that previously caused discomfort, such as minor digs and slights; the misconception of many situations as rejecting, which occurred previously as a result of oversensitivity, should be removed. On the other hand, discussion of limiting effects of stereotyping and role expectations may result in greater sensitivity to certain reactions (such as belittling sexist remarks) and greater likelihood of assertive reactions in such situations.

## THE USE OF A GROUP CONTEXT

Assertion training is often carried out in groups. A group offers a number of advantages, including a variety of models, multiple sources of support, normalization and validation of concerns, and the availability of many people to participate in role plays (Alberti & Emmons, 1974; Rose & Edleson, 1987). Assertion training in groups has been carried out with a variety of individuals, including college students (Galassi, Galassi, & Litz, 1974); Mexican-American mothers (Landau & Paulson, 1977); public welfare clients (Galinsky, Schopler, Satir, & Gambrill, 1978), severely disturbed hospitalized patients (Field & Test, 1975), men who batter (Edleson & Tolman, 1992), and women (Wolfe & Fodor, 1978; Osborn & Harris, 1975). Group training may be especially important for women. Because of their socialization, women, compared to men, may require more social support and more opportunities to observe assertive women in order for them to express their preferences. Assertion-training groups usually include from five to ten sessions lasting one and a half to two hours each. Duration of training has been found to be related to effects achieved (Bander, Russell & Weiskott, 1978). Criteria should be established to select participants. These may include motivation to change, skills in participation in a group context and willingness to share relevant information. Decisions must be made about how to structure group sessions (for example, each session could be structured around a specific kind of assertive reaction). Groups differ in their degree of structure, ranging from highly structured to more free flowing. Structured programs have been found to be more effective than simpler programs containing less information (Schulman & Bai-

ley, 1983). Both experiential and didactic content are included.

## ENCOURAGING GENERALIZATION AND MAINTENANCE

A number of steps can be taken to increase the likelihood of generalization and maintenance of assertive behaviors. These include recruiting natural reinforcers (e.g., involving significant others), reinforcing generalization (e.g., via self-reinforcement), and using a variety of examples and situational variations during training (Stokes & Osnes, 1989). Variations that may occur in real life that influence assertive behavior should be included in practice examples. For example, a woman may have difficulty refusing unwanted requests in a number of situations (with friends as well as supervisors at work). If so, practice should be given with all these different situations. Self-reinforcement can be used to encourage the development and maintenance of new behaviors (Rehm & Marston, 1968). Such reinforcement may be of special relevance in maintaining behaviors that are sometimes followed by punishing consequences. Clients can be encouraged to reward themselves for making efforts to exert more effective influence over their social environment, even though these are not always successful. If a woman tries to speak up more during a meeting and fails to gain the floor, she still should reward herself for trying. Rehm and Marston (1968) instructed their subjects to award themselves between one to three points, depending on the degree of assertiveness. Generalization and maintenance can be encouraged by use of homework assignments (Kazdin & Mascitelli, 1982). Some studies suggest that covert modeling can also be useful, especially if combined with elaboration of imagery and summary coding of modeled events (see, e.g., Kazdin, 1979, 1980). Self-monitoring may also enhance generalization and maintenance (Warrenfeltz-Rodney, 1981) Assertion training programs can be examined to determine the extent to which procedures to enhance generalization and durability of gains have been included.

## WHEN DIRECT ASSERTION FAILS OR MAY HAVE NEGATIVE CONSEQUENCES

Direct assertion may have negative effects or may have been tried and failed. Thus, a client's concern about becoming more assertive may have a realistic basis. Watzlawick, Weakland, and Fisch (1974) describe an example in which in-laws persisted in offering unwanted help to a young couple. The in-laws visited four times a year for visits of about three weeks each, and took over all household responsibilities during their stays. Resistance to these attempts were interpreted as ingratitude, and frequent scenes in public occurred over who was going to pay the check. The husband said that tangible proof of achieving his goal of greater independence from his parents would consist of his father telling him of his own accord, "You are now grown up; the two of you have to take care of yourselves and must not expect that mother and I are going to pamper you indefinitely" (Watzlawick, Weakland, & Fisch, 1974, p. 118). A way was sought to provide the in-laws an opportunity to be "good parents" in a way that would also decrease their "helping behaviors." The couple was instructed to allow the house to become dirty and the laundry to pile up prior to their next visit and to allow the in-laws to carry out household chores, repairs, and responsibilities without any suggestion that they not engage in these tasks. The in-laws cut the visit short, and the father told his son "that he [the son] and his wife were much too pampered, that they had gotten much too accustomed to being waited on and supported by the parents, and that it was now high time to behave in a more adult fashion and to become less dependent on them" (p. 119). The in-laws could now be good parents by "weaning" their son. Women who live with abusive partners are unassertive with their abusing spouses, and their partners are also unassertive (Morrison, Van Hasselt, & Bellack, 1987). Focusing on increasing assertive behavior of these abused women toward their partners may be inappropriate (O'Leary et al., 1985). Other methods may be called for. Or assertive training could be offered to women who live in shelters for battered women in order to help them to terminate an abusive relationship (Meyers-Abell & Jansen, 1980).

If someone is very upset or if the slight or annoyance is minor, it may be best for all concerned to remain quiet or to select another time to express oneself (Alberti & Emmons, 1974). Expressing negative feelings to a person who is already upset may result in a rapid negative escalation and thus entail more cost in terms of emotion than one wishes to endure. Minor annoyances are best left unmentioned. Asking someone to change his behavior is an implied criticism, and a more effective way to alter behavior may be to reinforce desired alternatives (e.g., by offering verbal approval). If a person can't change a behavior, why bother trying?

## IS ASSERTION TRAINING EFFECTIVE?

Both single-case and group designs have been used to evaluate the success of assertion training. Single-case designs are uniquely suited for evaluating progress with individual clients. Multiple baseline designs across behaviors have often been used (see, e.g., Hersen & Bellack, 1976). Comparison of the effectiveness of assertion training in different studies is often hampered by the use of different criteria for selection of subjects, different kinds of training programs, and different criteria for assessing progress. Evaluation is sometimes limited to changes in self-report or role-play measures, leaving unanswered the question of whether beneficial changes occur in real life. Follow-up has usually been conducted only over brief periods. Generalization has been a persistent problem; that is, new behavior does not generalize to other situations, including real-life situations (Scott, Himadi, & Keane, 1983). Responses to situations requiring negative assertion do not necessarily generalize to those requiring positive assertion (Kirschner, 1976). Guidelines for increasing generalization are often ignored (Trower, 1982; Stokes & Osnes, 1989). Packaged programs are often used, leaving the question: "What are the effective ingredients of assertion training?" unanswered. The use of packaged programs may also be a waste of time and effort in including unneeded components.

Programs focused on altering cognitions believed to be related to ineffective behavior have sometimes been found to be as effective as those focused on altering overt behavior, yielding the conclusion that there is an equivalence of effect across cognitive methods and assertion training (Stefanek & Eisler, 1983). There are indications that a combination of methods is most effective (see, e.g., Linehan, Goldfried, & Goldfried, 1979). Trower, Yardley, Bryant, and Shaw (1978) found that socially unskilled patients responded more to social skills training than they did to anxiety reduction methods. Phobic patients responded equally well to both methods. Rehearsal does not necessarily decrease situational anxiety (Wolfe & Fodor, 1977) and cognitive methods do not necessarily increase appropriate assertive behavior (Moon & Eisler, 1983). Studies that purport to show that cognitive methods are as effective as social skills training in enhancing social skills often do not include individual assessment of specific socially validated entry-level skills and design of individually tailored programs based on this assessment (Rosenfarb, Hayes, & Linehan, 1989). This may underestimate the potential value of skills training. Global self-report measures are often used to assess change in specific areas, resulting in an underestimation of success of intervention programs.

Thus, despite clear evidence that assertion training is effective with a number of different types of clients with a number of different kinds of presenting problems, it is also clear that success could be enhanced by reliance on a thorough behavioral analysis and selection of validated intervention programs. For maximum effect, intervention should be individually tailored to the unique goals and related cognitive, emotional, and behavioral entering repertoires of each client. The important question is not whether there is a significant change, but what are the maximum gains that could be made. Assertion training will do little to alter political, social, and economic sources of inequity. Such training is individually focused and encourages people to take responsibility for the quality of their social exchanges. There is the danger of blaming clients for problems that do not originate with them (Gambrill, 1990). Hollin and Trower (1988) note, "potential environmental influences are being minimized if not ignored, and individual training slips toward a 'medical model' in which the person is to be 'cured' rather than the environment modified . . . an accurate behavior analysis would make such issues clear" (p. 1983). The ideology of success through mind power that is especially prevalent in the United States (Weiss, 1969), where assertion training flowered, requires vigilance for discouraging programs that may offer only the illusion of greater influence.

## COMMON REASONS FOR FAILURE

There are a number of ways to decrease the effectiveness of assertion training (see, e.g., Ruben & Ruben, 1989; Goldstein-Fodor & Epstein, 1983). Almost all result from failure to complete an individually tailored behavioral analysis, including identification of factors that interfere with the acquisition and/or performance of useful skills and selection of intervention methods based on this analysis. Reliance on a priori clinical judgments in place of socially valid data for selection of behaviors to alter is a common source of error. Studies finding no difference in reactions to assertive behavior on the part of men and women as assessed in role-plays (e.g., So-

lomon, Brehony, Rothblum, & Kelly, 1983) may not reflect what occurs in real life when social desirability may play less of a role in influencing responses. Although most studies carefully specify the goals sought, these are often selected by the researcher or clinician rather than by the clients (Gambrill & Richey, 1987). Another reason for less than desired success is neglect of contingencies that influence the outcome of assertion (Goldstein-Fodor & Epstein, 1983; Wolpe, 1958). That is, information about the specific setting events, antecedents, and consequences that will influence success in real-life settings is not gained. This encourages the structural error—focusing on behavior alone rather than behaviors-in-situations. Consequences that directly influence assertive behavior are often provided by significant others. Success may require their involvement in counseling. Another error that will compromise effectiveness is to rush into intervention without carefully reviewing clients' beliefs about altering their behavior. Additional causes of failure of assertion training with women described by Goldstein-Fodor and Epstein (1983) include failure to prepare clients for new roles, failure to counter real discrimination, and placement of the burden of change on the individual. Not attending training sessions and carrying out homework assignments may compromise success. St. Lawrence (1981) found that a money deposit contingency ($20.00) resulted in higher attendance, participation in more exercises during sessions, and completion of more extra-session self-monitoring logs. Not planning for generalization and maintenance of desired behavior is yet another reason for failure.

## THE FUTURE

As with most efforts to discover global dispositions, the search for cross-situational consistency for people labeled "assertive" or "unassertive" has not resulted in success, and this is not surprising. The phrase *assertive behavior,* as used broadly, refers to a huge array of behaviors-in-situations. Focus on specific kinds of problematic social situations (such as refusing unwanted requests, initiating conversations) is more likely to offer helpful information in relation to specific situations of concern; the skills required to do well in each; common cognitive, behavioral, and affective excesses and deficits; and environmental constraints and options. Although systematic approaches have been described for some time suggesting useful ways to obtain helpful information (e.g., Goldfried & D'Zurilla, 1969), these have often been ignored. A more systematic developmental approach should yield a bank of programs related to specific social goals. Modules related to each would include not only textual material, but also audiotape and videotape models of effective and ineffective behavior and an interactive computer program to help with assessment, intervention, and evaluation tasks. The development of interactive computer programs to aid in skills training will no doubt be one of the main developments of the future.

Has the term *assertive behavior* outlived its usefulness? As a term connoting a traitlike approach to behavior, it has. As a term that is often confused with the idea of aggressive reactions, it has not been helpful. But as a term that highlights social inequities and stereotypes that limit options and the need for changes to correct these inequities and remove limiting stereotypes, it has been helpful.

## SUMMARY

Assertion training is designed to increase competence in social interactions. It may be carried out either individually or in group meetings. Both broad and narrow definitions of assertive behavior have been used, ranging from definitions that restrict the term to behaviors such as refusing unwanted requests and broad definitions that include a wide range of behaviors involving the expression of both positive and negative feelings. The distinction between assertive, passive, and aggressive behavior is made with assertion referring to effective behavior. Assertion training caught on with the public, and many popular books are available. Assertion training differs from social skills training in its emphasis on personal rights and obligations. There is a philosophy or ideology that accompanies assertion training that does not accompany social skills training.

Careful assessment is required to determine what cognitive and behavioral skills are needed; to identify relevant situations; to determine whether there are discrimination problems in relation to when certain behaviors can most profitably be displayed; to identify unrealistic beliefs or expectations that may interfere with assertive behavior, and to determine whether negative self-statements or lack of affect management skills interfere with effective behavior. Sources of assessment data include the behavioral interview, self-monitoring, self-report measures, role playing, observation in the natural environment, and physiological measures.

A number of procedures are usually involved in assertion training, including instructions, model presentation, behavior rehearsal and coaching, feedback, programming of change, homework assignments, and the cultivation of attitudes and beliefs that encourage assertive behavior. The more outstanding the behavior deficits and need for behavior refinement, the more likely that instructions and model presentation will be required. Intervention may also include efforts to replace negative thoughts with positive self-instructions. Homework assignments graded in accordance with client comfort and skill levels are a component of assertion training, and client-recorded logs describing relevant behaviors and the situations in which they occur can be reviewed to offer feedback and to encourage use of skills.

Studies of the effectiveness of assertion training differ greatly in rigor, ranging from poorly controlled studies to rigorous single-case and group studies. Recently, greater attention has been given to cognitive behavior related to assertion. Research to date indicates that assertion training is effective in relation to a wide variety of outcomes, including enhancing self-esteem, as well as in increasing positive consequences in real-life settings. However, assertion training is individually focused. Following this individually tailored route will not redress political, social, and economic inequities that may impede change. Planning for generalization and maintenance will be required to increase the likelihood that desired behaviors will occur in appropriate situations and will be durable.

## REFERENCES

MacNeilage, L., & Adams, K. (1982). *Assertiveness at work: How to increase your personal power on the job.* Englewood Cliffs, NJ: Prentice-Hall.

Alberti, R. E., & Emmons, M. L. (1970). *Your perfect right.* San Luis Obispo, CA: Impact Press. (See also later editions, 6th Ed. 1990).

Alden, L., & Cappe, R. (1981). Nonassertiveness: Skill deficit or selective self-evaluation? *Behavior Therapy, 12,* 107–114.

Alden, L., & Safran, J. (1978). Irrational beliefs and nonassertive behavior. *Cognitive Therapy and Research, 2,* 357–364.

Argyle, M. (1980). Interaction skills and social competence. In P. Feldman & J. Orford (Eds.) *Psychological Problems: The social context.* New York: Wiley.

Argyle, M., Furnham, A., & Graham, J. A. (1981). *Social situations.* Cambridge: Cambridge University Press.

Argyle, M., & Henderson, M. (1985). *The anatomy of relationships*. London: Heinemann.

Arnold, B. R., & Parrott, R. (1978). Job interviewing: Stress management and interpersonal-skills training for welfare-rehabilitation clients. *Rehabilitation Counseling Bulletin, 22*, 44–52.

Arrindell, W. A., Sanderman, R., Hageman, W. J. J. M., Pickersgill, M. J., Kwee, M. G. T., Van der Molen, H. T., & Lingsma, M. M. (1990). Correlates of assertiveness in normal and clinical samples: a multidimensional approach. *Advances in Behavior Research and Therapy, 12*, 153–282.

Ary, D. V., Toobert, D., Wilson, W., & Glasgow, R. E. (1986). Patient perspective on factors contributing to nonadherence to diabetes regimen. *Diabetes Care, 9*, 168–172.

Averill, J. (1982). *Anger and aggression: Implications for theories of emotion*. New York: Springer-Verlag.

Bander, R. S., Russell, R. K., & Weiskott, G. N. (1978). Effects of varying amounts of assertiveness training on level of assertiveness and anxiety reduction in women. *Psychological Reports, 43*, 144–146.

Bandura, A. (1969). *Principles of behavior modification*. New York: Holt, Rinehart & Winston.

Bandura, A. (1986). *Social foundations of thought and action*. Englewood Cliffs, NJ: Prentice-Hall.

Bandura, A., Grusec, J. E., & Menlove, F. L. (1966). Observational learning as a function of symbolization and incentive set. *Child Development, 37*, 499–506.

Barbaree, H. E., & Davis, R. B. (1984). Assertive behavior, self-expectations, and self-evaluations in mildly depressed university women. *Cognitive Therapy and Research, 8*, 153–171.

Barlow, D. H. (1987). *Anxiety and its disorders: The nature and treatment of anxiety and panic*. New York: Guilford Press.

Beck, A. T. (1990). *Anxiety disorders and phobias: A cognitive perspective*. New York: Basic Books.

Bellack, A. S. (1983). Recurrent problems in the behavioural assessment of social skill. *Behavior Research and Therapy, 21*, 29–42.

Bellack, A. S., Hersen, M., & Lamparski, D. (1979). Role play tests for assessing social skills: Are they valid? Are they useful? *Journal of Counseling and Clinical Psychology, 47*, 335–342.

Bellack, A. S., Hersen, M., & Turner, S. M. (1979). Relationship of role playing and knowledge of appropriate behavior to assertion in the natural environment. *Journal of Consulting and Clinical Psychology, 47*, 670–678.

Benton, M. K., & Schroeder, H. E. (1990). Social skills training with schizophrenics: A meta-analytic evaluation. *Journal of Consulting and Clinical Psychology, 58*, 741–747.

Bloom, L. Z., Coburn, K., & Pearlman, J. (1975). *The new assertive woman*. New York: Delacorte.

Bolsinger, S. A., & McMinn, M. R. (1989). Assertiveness training and Christian values. *Counseling and Values, 34*, 21–32.

Bornstein, M. R., Bellack, A. S., & Hersen, M. (1977). Social skills training for unassertive children: A multiple baseline analysis. *Journal of Applied Behavior Analysis, 10*, 183–195.

Bower, S. A., & Bower, G. H. (1976). *Asserting yourself: A practical guide for positive change*. Reading, MA: Addison-Wesley.

Bregman, S. (1984). Assertiveness training for mentally retarded adults. *Mental Retardation, 22*, 12–16.

Brockway, B. S. (1976). Assertion training with professional women. *Social Work, 21*, 498–505.

Bruch, M. A. (1981). A task analysis of assertive behavior revisited: Replication and extension. *Behavior Therapy, 12*, 217–230.

Bruch, M. A. (1988). Written assertiveness knowledge test. In M. Hersen & A. S. Bellack (Eds.), *Dictionary of behavioral assessment*. New York: Pergamon Press.

Burgess, E. P. (1969). Elimination of vomiting behavior. *Behavior Research and Therapy, 7*, 173–176.

Butler, P. (1981). *Self-assertion for women*. New York: Harper & Row.

Callner, D. A., & Ross, S. M. (1976). The reliability and validity of three measures of assertion in a drug addict population. *Behavior Therapy, 7*, 559–567.

Chan, D. W. (1993). Components of assertiveness: their relationships with assertive rights and depressed mood among Chinese college students in Hong Kong. *Behaviour Research and Therapy, 31*, 529–538.

Chaney, E. F., O'Leary, M. R., & Marlatt, G. A. (1978). Skill training with alcoholics. *Journal of Consulting and Clinical Psychology, 46*, 1092–1104.

Chiauzzi, E., & Heimberg, R. G. (1986). Legitimacy of request and social problem-solving: A study of assertive and non-assertive subjects. *Behavior Modification, 10*, 3–18.

Ciminero, A. R., Nelson, R. O., & Lipinski, D. P. (1986). Self-monitoring procedures. In A. R. Ciminero, K. S. Calhoun, & H. E. Adams (Eds.), *Handbook of behavioral assessment*. New York: Wiley.

Clifford, T. (1987). Assertiveness training for parents. *Journal of Counseling and Development, 65*, 552–554.

Connelly, D. (1988). Increasing intensity of play of nonassertive athletes. *The Sport Psychologist, 2*, 255–265.

Connor, J., Dann, L., & Twentyman, C. (1982). A self-report measure of assertiveness in young adolescents. *Journal of Clinical Psychology, 38*, 101–106.

Craighead, L. W. (1979). Self-instructional training for assertive-refusal behavior. *Behavior Therapy, 10*, 529–542.

DeGiovanni, S., & Epstein, N. (1978). Unbinding assertion and aggression in research and clinical practice. *Behavior Modification, 2*, 173–192.

Delamater, R. J., & McNamara, J. R. (1986). The social impact of assertiveness: Research findings and clinical implications. *Behavior Modification, 10*, 139–158.

Dickson, A. (1982). *A woman in your own right*. London: Quartet Books.

Dobia, B., & McMurray, N. E. (1985). Applicability of learned helplessness to depressed women undergoing assertiveness training. *Australian Journal of Psychology, 37*, 71–80.

Dodge, K. A., Asher, S. P., & Parkhurst, J. T. (1989). Social life as "goal-coordination task." In C. Ames & R. Ames (Eds.), *Research on motivation in education* (Vol. 3). New York: Academic Press.

Donahoe, C. P., & Dreisenga, S. A. (1988). A review of social skills training with chronic mental patients. In M. Hersen & P. M. Miller (Eds.), *Progress in behavior modification* (Vol. 23). Newbury Park, CA: Sage.

Doty, L. (1987). *Communication and assertive skills for older persons*. New York: Hemisphere.

Downing, J. (1987). Conversational skills training: Teaching adolescent with mental retardation to be verbally assertive. *Mental Retardation, 25*(3), 147–155.

Drury, S. S. (1984). *Assertive supervision: Building involved teamwork*. Champaign, IL: Research Press.

Dunn, M. E., & Herman, S. H. (1982). Social skills and physical disability. In D. M. Doleys, R. L. Meredith, & R. Ciminero (Eds.), *Behavioral psychology in medicine: Assessment and treatment strategies*. New York: Plenum Press.

Dunn, M. E., Van Horn, E., & Herman, S. H. (1981). Social skills and spinal cord injury: A comparison of three training procedures. *Behavior Therapy, 12*, 153–164.

Edleson, J. L., & Tolman, R. M. (1992). *Intervention for men who batter: An ecological approach*. Newbury Park, CA: Sage Publications.

Eisler, R. M. (1976). Assertive training in the work situation. In J. D. Kimmboltz & C. E. Thoresen (Eds.), *Counseling methods*. New York: Holt, Rinehart and Winston.

Eisler, R. M., Blanchard, E. B., Fitts, H., & Williams, J. G. (1978). Social skill training with and without modeling for schizophrenic and non-psychotic hospitalized psychiatric patients. *Behavior Modification, 2*, 147–172.

Eisler, R. M., Frederiksen, L. W., & Peterson, G. L. (1978). The relationship of cognitive variables to the expression of assertiveness. *Behavior Therapy, 9*, 419–427.

Eisler, R. M., Hersen, M., & Agras, W. S. (1973). Effects of videotape and instructional feedback on nonverbal marital interaction: An analogue study. *Behavior Therapy, 4*, 551–558.

Eisler, R. M., Hersen, M., & Miller, P. M. (1973). Effects of modeling on components of assertive behavior. *Journal of Behavior Therapy and Experimental Psychiatry, 4*, 1–6.

Eisler, R. M., Hersen, M., & Miller, P. M. (1974). Shaping components of assertive behavior with instructions and feedback. *American Journal of Psychiatry, 131*, 1344–1347.

Eisler, R. M., Hersen, M., Miller, P. M., & Blanchard, E. B. (1975). Situational determinants of assertive behaviors. *Journal of Consulting and Clinical Psychology, 43*, 330–340.

Eisler, R. M., Miller, P. M., & Hersen, M. (1973). Components of assertive behavior. *Journal of Clinical Psychology, 29*, 295–299.

Emmons, M. L., & Alberti, R. E. (1983). Failure: Winning at the losing game in assertiveness training. In E. B. Foa & P. M. C. Emmelkamp (Eds.), *Failures in behavior therapy*. New York: Wiley.

Emmons, M. L., Richardson, D., & Frost, M. (1981). *Assertive Christian*. New York: Harper & Row.

Epstein, N., DeGiovanni, I. S., & Jayne-Lazarus, C. (1978). Assertion training for couples. *Journal of Behavior Therapy and Experimental Psychiatry, 9*, 149–157.

Falbo, T., Hazen, M. D., & Linimon, D. (1982). The costs of selecting power bases or messages associated with the opposite sex. *Sex Roles, 8*, 147–157.

Fensterheim, H., & Baer, J. (1975). *Don't say yes when you want to say no*. New York: McKay.

Fiedler, D., & Beach, L. R. (1978). On the decision to be assertive. *Journal of Consulting and Clinical Psychology, 46*, 537–546.

Field, G. D., & Test, M. A. (1975). Group assertive training for severely disturbed patients. *Journal of Behavior Therapy and Experimental Psychiatry, 6*, 129–134.

Fischetti, M., Curran, J. P., & Wessberg, H. W. (1977). Sense of timing: A skills deficit in heterosexual socially anxious males. *Behavior Modification, 1*, 179–194.

Fodor, I. G. (1992). *Adolescent Assertiveness and Social Skills Training: A Clinical Handbook*. New York: Springer.

Fodor, I. G., & Wolfe, J. L. (1977). Assertiveness training for mothers and daughters. In R. Alberti (Ed.), *Assertiveness: Innovations, applications, and issues*. San Luis Obispo, CA: Impact Press.

French, J. R. P., & Raven, B. (1960). The bases of social power. In D. Cartwright & A. Zander (Eds.), *Group dynamics, research and theory*. Evanston, IL: Row Peterson.

Furnham, A., & Henderson, M. (1984). Assessing assertiveness: A content and correlational analysis of five assertiveness inventories. *Behavioral Assessment, 6*, 550–561.

Galassi, J. P., & Galassi, M. D. (1974). *Session by session assertive training procedures*. Unpublished manuscript. University of North Carolina, Chapel Hill.

Galassi, M. D., & Galassi, J. P. (1976). The effects of role play variations on the assessment of assertive behavior. *Behavior Therapy, 7*, 343–347.

Galassi, M. D., & Galassi, J. P. (1978). Assertion: A critical review. *Psychotherapy, 15*, 16–29.

Galassi, J. P., DeLo, J. S., Galassi, M. D., & Bastien, S. (1974). The college self-expression scale: A measure of assertiveness. *Behavior Therapy, 5*, 165–171.

Galassi, J. P., Galassi, M. D., & Litz, M. C. (1974). Assertive training in groups using video feedback. *Journal of Counseling Psychology, 21*, 390–394.

Galinsky, M. J., Schopler, J. H., Satir, E. J., & Gambrill, E. D. (1978). Assertive training for public welfare clients. *Social Work With Groups, 1,* 365–379.

Gambrill, E. D. (1977). *Behavior modification: A handbook of assessment, intervention, and evaluation.* San Francisco: Jossey-Bass.

Gambrill, E. D. (1985). Social skill training with the elderly. In L. L'Abate & M. A. Milan (Eds.), *Handbook of social skills training and research.* New York: Wiley.

Gambrill, E. D. (1990). *Critical thinking in clinical practice.* San Francisco: Jossey-Bass.

Gambrill, E. D. (1992). Self-help books: Pseudo science in the guise of science? *Skeptical Inquirer, 16,* 389–399.

Gambrill, E. D., & Richey, C. A. (1975). An assertion inventory for use in assessment and research. *Behavior Therapy, 6,* 547–549.

Gambrill, E. D., & Richey, C. A. (1988). *Taking charge of your social life.* Berkeley, CA: Behavioral Options.

Gambrill, E. D., & Richey, C. A. (1980). Assertion training for women. In C. L. Heckerman (Ed.), *The evolving female: Psychosocial perspectives.* New York: Human Sciences Press.

Gambrill, E. D., & Richey, C. H. (1987). Gender issues related to group social skills training. *Social Work with Groups, 6,* 51–66.

Gay, M. L., Hollandsworth, J. G., Jr., & Galassi, J. P. (1975). An assertiveness inventory for adults. *Journal of Counseling Psychology, 4*(22), 340–344.

Gervasio, A. H. (1987). Assertiveness techniques as speech acts. *Clinical Psychology Review, 7,* 105–119.

Gervasio, A. H. (1988). Linguistic analysis of an assertiveness training film. *Psychotherapy, 25,* 294–304.

Gervasio, A. H., Pepinsky, H. B., & Schwebel, A. I. (1983). Stylistic complexity and verb usage in assertive and passive speech. *Journal of Counseling Psychology, 30,* 546–556.

Glass, C., Gottman, J., & Shmurak, S. (1976). Response acquisition and cognitive self-statement modification approaches to dating skills training. *Journal of Counseling Psychology, 23,* 520–526.

Goldfried, M. R., & D'Zurilla, T. J. (1969). A behavior-analytic model for assessing competence. In C. D. Spielberger (Ed.), *Current topics in clinical and community psychology* (Vol. 1). New York: Academic Press.

Goldstein-Fodor, I., & Epstein, R. C. (1983). Assertiveness training for women: Where are we failing? In E. B. Foa & P. M. G. Emmelkamp (Eds.), *Failures in behavior therapy* (pp. 137–152). New York: Wiley.

Goldstein, A. P., Glick, B., Irwin, M. J., Pask-McCartney, & Rubama, I. (1989). *Reducing Delinquency: Intervention in the Community.* New York: Pergamon Press.

Gottman, J. M., & Krokoff, L. J. (1989). Marital interaction and satisfaction: A longitudinal view. *Journal of Consulting and Clinical Psychology, 57,* 47–52.

Gray, B., England, G., & Mahoney, J. (1965). Treatment of benign vocal nodules by reciprocal inhibition. *Behavior Research and Therapy, 3,* 187–193.

Gresham, F. M. (1988). Social skills: Conceptual and applied aspects of assessment, training and social validation. In J. C. Witt, S. N. Elliot, & F. M. Gresham (Eds.), *Handbook of behavior therapy in education.* New York: Plenum Press.

Gripton, J., & Valentich, M. (1977). Development of a work assertiveness scale for social workers. *The Social Worker (Le Travailleur Social), 45,* 15–20.

Gross, A. M., & Johnson, W. G. (1981). Diabetes assertiveness test: A measure of social coping skills in preadolescent diabetics. *The Diabetes Educator, 7,* 26–27.

Hammen, C. L., Jacobs, M., Mayol, A., & Cochran, S. D. (1980). Dysfunctional cognitions and the effectiveness of skills and cognitive behavioral assertion training. *Journal of Consulting and Clinical psychology, 48,* 685–695.

Hazel, J. S., Schumaker, J. B., Sherman, J. A., & Sheldon-Wildgen, J. (1981). *Asset: A social skills program for adolescents.* Champaign, IL: Research Press.

Heimberg, R. G., & Montgomery, D., Madsen, C. H., Jr., & Heimberg, J. S. (1977). Assertion training: A review of the literature. *Behavior Therapy, 8,* 953–971.

Heimberg, R. G., & Becker, R. E. (1981). Cognitive and behavioral models of assertive behavior: Review, analysis and integration. *Clinical Psychology Review, 1,* 353–373.

Heimberg, R. G., Chiauzzi, E. J., Becker, R. E., & Madrazo-Peterson, R. (1983). Cognitive mediation of assertive behavior: An analysis of the self-statement patterns of college students, psychiatric patients, and normal adults. *Cognitive Therapy and Research, 7,* 455–464.

Herman, S. J. (1977). Assertiveness: One answer to job dissatisfaction for nurses. In R. E. Alberti (Ed.), *Assertiveness: Innovations, applications, issues.* San Luis Obispo, CA: Impact Press.

Hersen, M., & Bellack, A. S. (1976). A multiple baseline analysis of social-skills training in chronic schizophrenics. *Journal of Applied Behavior Analysis, 9,* 239–246.

Hersen, M., Eisler, R., Miller, P., Johnson, M., & Pinkston, S. (1973). Effects of practice, instructions, and modeling on components of assertive behavior. *Behaviour Research Therapy, 11,* 443–451.

Hess, E. P., Bridgwater, C. A., Bornstein, P. H., & Sweeney, T. M. (1980). Situational determinants in the perception of assertiveness: Gender-related influences. *Behavior Therapy, 22,* 49–58.

Hollandsworth, J. G. (1977). Differentiating assertion and aggression: Some behavioral guidelines. *Behavior Therapy, 8,* 347–352.

Hollandsworth, J. G., & Wall, D. (1977). Sex differences in assertive behavior: An empirical investigation. *Journal of Counseling Psychology, 24,* 217–222.

Hollin, C. R., & Trower, P. (1988). Development and applications of social skills training: A review and critique. In M. Hersen, R. Eisler, & P. Miller (Eds.), *Progress in behavior modification* (Vol. 22). New York: Academic Press.

Horan, J. J., & Williams, J. M. (1982). Longitudinal study of assertion training as a drug abuse prevention strategy. *American Educational Research Journal, 19,* 341–351.

Huey, W. C., & Rank, R. C. (1984). Effects of counselor and peer-led group assertive training on Black adolescent aggression. *Journal of Counseling Psychology, 31,* 95–98.

Jacobs, M. K., & Cochran, S. D. (1982). The effects of cognitive restructuring on assertive behavior. *Cognitive Therapy and Research, 6,* 63–76.

Jakubowski, P., & Lange, A. J. (1978). *The assertive option: Your rights and responsibilities.* Champaign, IL: Research Press.

Kanfer, F. H. (1970). Self-monitoring: Methodological limitations and clinical applications. *Journal of Consulting and Clinical Psychology, 35,* 148–152.

Kazdin, A. E. (1976). Effects of covert modeling, multiple models, and model reinforcement on assertive behavior. *Behavior Therapy, 7,* 211–222.

Kazdin, A. E. (1979). Effects of covert modeling and coding of modeled stimuli on assertive behavior. *Behaviour Research and Therapy, 17,* 53–61.

Kazdin, A. E. (1980). Covert and overt rehearsal and elaboration during treatment in the development of assertive behavior. *Behaviour Research and Therapy, 18,* 191–210.

Kazdin, A. E. (1982). The separate and combined effects of covert and overt rehearsal in developing assertiveness. *Journal of Consulting and Clinical Psychology, 50,* 250–258.

Kazdin, A. E., & Mascitelli, S. (1982). Covert and overt rehearsal and homework practice in developing assertiveness. *Journal of Consulting and Clinical Psychology, 50,* 250–258.

Kelly, J. A., Kern, J. M., Kirkley, B. G., Patterson, J. N., & Keane, T. M. (1980). Reactions to assertive versus unassertive behavior: Differential effects for males and females and implications for assertive training. *Behavior Therapy, 11,* 670–682.

Kiecolt, J. K., & McGrath, E. (1979). Social desirability responding in the measurement of assertive behavior. *Journal of Consulting and Clinical Psychology, 47,* 640–642.

Kinney, J., Haapala, D., Booth, C. (1991). *Keeping families together.* New York: Aldine de Gruyter.

Kirkland, K. & Caughlin-Carver, J. (1982). Maintenance and generalization of assertive skills. *Education and Training of the Mentally Retarded, 17,* 313–318.

Kirschner, N. M. (1976). Generalization of behaviorally oriented assertive training. *The Psychological Record, 26,* 117–125.

Kolotkin, R. A., Wielkiewicz, R. M., Judd, B., & Wieser, S. (1984). Behavioral components of assertion: Comparison of univariate and multivariate assessment strategies. *Behavioral Assessment, 6,* 61–78.

Kuperminc, M., & Heimberg, R. G. (1983). Consequence probability and utility as factors in the decision to behave assertively. *Behavior Therapy, 14,* 637–646.

Landau, P., & Paulson, T. (1977). Group assertion training for Spanish speaking Mexican-American mothers. In R. E. Alberti (Ed.), *Assertiveness: Innovations, applications, and issues.* San Luis Obispo, CA: Impact Press.

Lange, A. J., & Jakubowski, P. (1976). *Responsible assertive behavior: Cognitive/behavioral procedures for trainers.* Champaign, IL: Research Press.

Langer, E., & Rodin, J. (1976). The effects of choice and enhanced personal responsibility: A field experiment in an institutional setting. *Journal of Personality and Social Psychology, 34,* 191–198.

Lawrence, P. S. (1970). The assessment and modification of assertive behavior. Doctoral dissertation, Arizona State University. (University Microfilms 396-B, No. 70–11, 888).

Lazarus, A. A. (1973). On assertive behavior: A brief note. *Behavior Therapy, 4,* 697–699.

Lehrer, P. M., & Leiblum, S. R. (1981). Physiological, behavioral, and cognitive measures of assertiveness and assertion anxiety. *Behavioral Counseling Quarterly, 1,* 261–274.

Lewis, P. N., & Gallois, C. (1984). Disagreements, refusals, or negative feelings: Perception of negatively assertive messages from friends and strangers. *Behavior Therapy, 15,* 353–368.

Lewittes, H. J., & Bem, S. L. (1983). Training women to be more assertive in mixed-sex task-oriented discussions. *Sex Roles, 9,* 581–596.

Liberman, R. P., DeRisi, W. J., & Mueser, K. T. (1989). *Social skills training for psychiatric patients.* Elmsford, NY: Pergamon Press.

Liberman, K. P., King, L. W., DeRisi, W. J., & McCann, M. (1975). *Personal effectiveness: Guiding people to assert themselves and improve their personal skills.* Champaign, IL: Research Press.

Libet, J., & Lewinsohn, P. M. (1973). The concept of social skill and special reference to the behaviour of depressed persons. *Journal of Consulting and Clinical Psychology, 40,* 304–312.

Lindsay, W., & Lindsay, J. (1982). A self-report questionnaire about social difficulty for adolescents. *General Psychiatry, 42,* 729–736.

Linehan, M. M. (1979). Structured cognitive behavioral treatment of assertion problems. In P. C. Kendall & S. D. Hollon (Eds.), *Cognitive-behavioral interventions: Theory, research, and procedures.* New York: Academic Press.

Linehan, M. M. (1984). Interpersonal effectiveness in assertive situations. In E. A. Bleckman, *Behavior modification with women.* New York: Guilford Press.

Linehan, M. M., Goldfried, M. R., & Goldfried, A. P. (1979). Assertion therapy: Skill training or cognitive restructuring. *Behavior Therapy, 10,* 372–388.

Linehan, M. M., & Walker, R. O. (1983). The components of assertion: Factor analysis of a multimethod assessment battery. *British Journal of Clinical Psychology, 22,* 277–281.

MacDonald, M. L. (1974). *A behavioral assessment methodology applied to the measurement of assertion.* Unpublished doctoral dissertation, University of Illinois at Urbana.

MacDonald, M. L. (1982). Assertion training for women. In J. P. Curran & P. M. Monti (Eds.), *Social skill training: A practical guide for assessment and treatment.* New York: Guilford Press.

Mansdorf, I. J. (1986). Assertiveness training in the treatment of a child's tics. *Journal of Behavior Therapy and Experimental Psychiatry, 17,* 29–32.

Marlatt, G. A., & Gordon, J. R. (1985). *Relapse prevention: Maintenance strategies in addictive behavior change.* New York: Guilford Press.

McFall, R. M. (1982). A review and reformulation of the concept of social skills. *Behavioral Assessment, 4,* 1–33.

McFall, R. M., & Bridges, D. V. (1970). *Behavior rehearsal with modeling and coaching in assertive training: Assessment and training stimuli.* Unpublished manuscript. University of Wisconsin–Madison.

McFall, R. M., & Lillesand, D. B. (1971). Behavior rehearsal with modeling and coaching in assertion training. *Journal of Abnormal Psychology, 7,* 313–323.

McFall, R. M., & Twentyman, C. T. (1973). Four experiments on the relative contribution of rehearsal, modeling, and coaching to assertion training. *Journal of Abnormal Psychology, 81,* 199–218.

Meichenbaum, D. H. (1972). Examination of model characteristics in reducing avoidance behavior. *Journal of Behavior Therapy and Experimental Psychiatry, 3,* 225–227.

Meyers-Abell, J. E., & Jansen, M. A. (1980). Assertive therapy for battered women: A case illustration. *Journal of Behavior Therapy and Experimental Psychiatry, 11,* 301–305.

Miller, T. W. (1982). Assertiveness training for coaches: The issue of healthy communication between coaches and players. *Journal of Sport Psychology, 4,* 107–114.

Moon, J. R., & Eisler, R. M. (1983). Anger control: An experimental comparison of three behavioral treatments. *Behavior Therapy, 14,* 493–505.

Morrison, R. L., Van Hasselt, V. B., & Bellack, A. S. (1987). Assessment of assertion and problem-solving skills in wife abusers and their spouses. *Journal of Family Violence, 2,* 227–238.

Morton, J. C., Richey, C. A., & Kellett, M. (1981). *Building assertive skills: A practical guide to professional development for allied dental health providers.* St. Louis: Mosby.

Nezu, A., & D'Zurilla, T. J. (1979). An experimental evaluation of the decision-making process in social problem solving. *Cognitive Therapy and Research, 3,* 269–277.

Nisbett, R., & Ross, L. (1980). *Human inference: Strategies and shortcomings of social judgement.* Englewood Cliffs, NJ: Prentice-Hall.

Novaco, R. W. (1975). *Anger control: The development and evaluation of an experimental treatment.* Lexington, MA: D. C. Heath.

O'Leary, K. D., Curley, A., Rosenbaum, A., & Clarke, C. (1985). Assertion training for abused wives: A potentially hazardous treatment. *Journal of Marital and Family Therapy, 11,* 319–322.

Ollendick, T. H. (1984). Development and validation of the children's assertiveness inventory. *Child and Family Behavior Therapy, 5,* 17–24.

Ollendick, T. H., & Hersen, M. (1979). Social skill training for juvenile delinquents. *Behaviour Research and Therapy, 17,* 547–554.

Osborn, S. M., & Harris, G. G. (1975). *Group assertive training for women.* Springfield, IL: Charles C Thomas.

Park, H. S., & Gaylord-Ross, R. (1989). A problem solving approach to social skills training in employment settings with mentally retarded youth. *Journal of Applied Behavior Analysis, 22,* 373–380.

Patzer, G. L. (1985). *The physical attractiveness phenomenon.* New York: Plenum Press.

Pentz, M. A., & Kazdin, A. E. (1982). Assertion modeling and stimuli effects on assertive behavior and self-efficacy in adolescents. *Behaviour Research and Therapy, 20,* 365–371.

Phelps, S., & Austin, N. (1975). *The assertive woman.* San Luis Obispo, CA: Impact Press.

Pitcher, S. W., & Meikle, S. (1980). The topography of assertive behavior in positive and negative situations. *Behavior Therapy, 11,* 532–547.

Poppen, R. L. (1989). Some clinical implications of rule-governed behavior. In S. Hayes (Ed.), *Rule governed behavior: Cognition, contingencies and instructional control.* New York: Plenum Press.

Porter, N., & Geis, F. (1981). Women and nonverbal leadership cues: When seeing is not believing. In C. Mayo & N. M. Henley (Eds.), *Gender and non-verbal behavior.* New York: Springer-Verlag.

Rahaim, S., Lefebvre, C., & Jenkins, J. O. (1980). The effects of social skills training on behavioral and cognitive components of anger management. *Journal of Behavior Therapy and Experimental Psychiatry, 11,* 3–8.

Rakos, R. F. (1986). Asserting and confronting. In O. Hargie (Ed.), *A handbook of communication skills.* London: Croom Helm.

Rakos, R. F. (1991). *Assertive behavior: Theory, research and training.* New York: Routledge.

Rathus, S. A. (1973). A 30-item schedule for assessing assertive behavior. *Behavior Therapy, 4,* 398–406.

Rees, S., & Graham, R. (1991). *Assertion training: How to be who you really are.* London: Routledge.

Rehm, L. P., & Marston, A. R. (1968). Reduction of social anxiety through modification of self-reinforcement. *Journal of Consulting and Clinical Psychology, 32,* 565–574.

Rich, A. R., & Schroeder, H. W. (1976). Research issues in assertiveness training. *Psychological Bulletin, 83,* 1081–1096.

Rimm, D. D., & Masters, J. C. (1974). *Behavior therapy: Techniques and empirical findings.* New York: Wiley.

Romano, J. M., & Bellack, A. S. (1980). Social validation of a component model of assertive behavior. *Journal of Consulting and Clinical Psychology, 48,* 478–490.

Rose, S. D., & Edleson, J. L. (1987). *Working with children and adolescents in groups.* San Francisco: Jossey-Bass.

Rosenfarb, I. S., Hayes, S. C., & Linehan, M. M. (1989). Instructions and experimental feedback in the treatment of social skills deficits in adults. *Psychotherapy, 26,* 242–251.

Rotheram, M. J., Armstrong, M., & Booraem, C. (1982). Assertiveness training in fourth- and fifth-grade children. *American Journal of Community Psychology, 10,* 567–582.

Ruben, D. H. (1985). *Progress in assertiveness, 1973–1983.* Metuchen, NJ: Scarecrow Press.

Ruben, D. H. (1987). Improving communication between the elderly and pharmacies: A self-initiative training program. *Journal of Alcohol and Drug Education, 32,* 7–12.

Ruben, D. H., & Ruben, M. J. (1989). Why assertiveness training programs fail. *Small Group Behavior, 20*(3), 367–380.

St. Lawrence, J. S. (1981). Efficacy of a money deposit contingency on clinical outpatient's attendance and participation in assertive training. *Journal of Behavior Therapy and Experimental Psychiatry, 12,* 237–240.

St. Lawrence, J. S. (1986). Assessment and treatment of social dysfunction in chronic schizophrenics. *The Behavior therapist, 9,* 85–86.

St. Lawrence, J. S. (1987). Assessment of assertion. In M. Hersen, R. M. Eisler, & P. M. Miller (Eds.), *Progress in behavior modification* (Vol. 12, pp. 152–190). Newbury Park, CA: Sage.

St. Lawrence, J. S., Hansen, D. J., Cutts, T. F., Tisdelle, D. A., & Irish, J. D. (1985). Situational context: Effects on perceptions of assertive and unassertive behavior. *Behavior Therapy, 16,* 51–62.

Salter, A. (1949). *Conditioned reflex therapy.* New York: Creative Age.

Sanchez, V., Lewinsohn, P. M., & Larson, D. W. (1980). Assertion training: Effectiveness in the treatment of depression. *Journal of Clinical Psychology, 36,* 526–529.

Sarason, I. G., & Ganzer, V. J. (1973). Modeling and group discussion in the rehabilitation of juvenile delinquents. *Journal of Counseling Psychology, 20,* 442–449.

Scherer, K., Wallbott, H. G., Matsumoto, D., & Kudoh, J. (1988). Emotional experience in cultural contact: A comparison between Europe, Japan and the United States. In K. R. Scherer (Ed.), *Facets of emotion: Recent research.* Hillsdale, NJ: Lawrence Erlbaum.

Schinke, S. P., & Gilchrist, L. D. (1984). *Life skills counseling with adolescents.* Baltimore: University Park Press.

Schloss, P. J., Espin, C. A., Smith, M. A., & Suffolk, D. R. (1987). Developing assertiveness during employment interviews with young adults who stutter. *Journal of Speech and Hearing Disorders, 52,* 30–36.

Schroeder, H. E., Rakos, R. F., & Moe, J. (1983). The social perception of assertive behavior as a function of response class and gender. *Behavior Therapy, 14,* 534–544.

Schulman, J. A. & Bailey, K. G. (1983). An information feedback program for the development of assertive behavior. *Psychotherapy: Theory, Research and Practice, 20,* 220–231.

Schwartz, R. M. & Gottman, J. M. (1976). Toward a task analysis of assertive behavior. *Journal of Consulting and Clinical Psychology, 44,* 910–920.

Schwartz, R. D. & Higgins, R. L. (1979). Differential outcome from automated assertive training as a function of locus of control. *Journal of Consulting and Clinical Psychology, 47,* 686–694.

Scott, R. R., Himadi, W., & Keane, T. M. (1983). A review of generalization in social skills training: Suggestions for future research. In M. Hersen, R. M. Eisler, & P. M. Miller (Eds.), *Progress in behavior modification* (Vol. 15). New York: Academic Press.

Senatore, V., Matson, J. L., & Kazdin, A. E. (1982). A comparison of behavioral methods to train social skills to mentally retarded adults. *Behavior Therapy, 13,* 313–324.

Serber, M. (1972). Teaching the nonverbal components of assertion training. *Journal of Behavior Therapy and Experimental Psychiatry, 3,* 179–183.

Siegman, A. W., & Feldstein, S. (1987). *Nonverbal behavior and communication,* 2nd ed. Hillsdale, NJ: Lawrence Erlbaum.

Skinner, B. F. (1953) *Science and human behavior.* New York: Macmillan.

Smith, M. J. (1975). *When I say no I feel guilty.* New York: Dial.

Solomon, L. J., Brehony, K. A., Rothblum, E. D., & Kelly, J. A. (1983). Corporate managers' reactions to assertive social skills exhibited by males and females. *Journal or Organizational Behavior Management, 4*(3–4), 49–63.

Soto, E. (1983). Sex-role traditionalism and assertiveness in Puerto Rican women living in the United States. *Journal of Community Psychology, 11,* 346–354.

Spence, S. H. (1982). Social skills training with young offenders. In P. Feldman (Ed.), *Developments in the study of criminal behavior: Vol. I. The prevention and control of offending.* Chichester: Wiley.

Stefanek, M. E., & Eisler, R. M. (1983). The current status of cognitive variables in assertiveness training. In M. Hersen, R. M. Eisler, & P. M. Miller (Eds.), *Progress in behavior modification* (Vol. 15). New York: Academic Press.

Stokes, T. F., & Osnes, P. G. (1989). An operant pursuit of generalization. *Behavior Therapy, 20,* 337–355.

Sue, D. W., & Sue, D. (1990). (2nd Ed.) *Counseling the culturally different: Theory and practice,* 2nd ed. New York: Wiley.

Sundel, S. S., & Sundel, M. (1980). *Be assertive: A practical guide for human service workers.* Newbury Park, CA: Sage.

Tanner, V. L., & Holliman, W. B. (1988). Effectiveness of assertiveness training in modifying aggressive behaviors in young children. *Psychological Reports, 62,* 39–46.

Trower, P. (1980). Situational analysis of the components and processes of behavior of socially skilled and unskilled patients. *Journal of Consulting and Clinical Psychology, 48,* 327–339.

Trower, P. (1982). Toward a generative model of social skills: A critique and synthesis. In J. P. Curran & P. M. Monti (Eds.), *Social skills training.* New York: Guilford Press.

Trower, P., Bryant, B., & Argyle, M. (1978). *Social skills and mental health.* Pittsburgh: University of Pittsburgh Press.

Trower, P., O'Mahony, J. F., & Dryden, W. (1982). Cognitive aspects of social failure: Some implications for social skills training. *British Journal of Guidance and Counseling, 10,* 177–184.

Trower, P., Yardley, K., Bryant, B. M., & Shaw, P. (1978). The treatment of social failure: A comparison of anxiety-reduction and skills-acquisition procedures on two social problems. *Behavior Modification, 2*(1), 41–60.

Twardosz, S., Schwartz, S., Fox, S., & Cunningham, J. L. (1979). Development and evaluation of a system to measure affectionate behavior. *Behavioral Assessment, 1,* 177–190.

Van Hasselt, V. B., Hersen, M., & Bellack, A. S. (1984). The relationship between assertion and sociometric status of children. *Behaviour Research and Therapy, 22,* 689–696.

Van Hasselt, V. B., Hersen, M., Kazdin, A. E., Simon, J., & Mastantuono, A. K. (1983). Training blind adolescents in social skills. *Journal of Visual Impairment and Blindness, 77,* 413–437.

Waas, G. A., & French, D. C. (1989). Children's social problem solving: Comparison of the Open Middle Interview and Children's Assertive Behavior Scale. *Behavioral Assessment, 11,* 219–230.

Wallace, C. J., Teigen, J. R., Liberman, R. P., & Baker, V. (1973). Destructive behavior treated by contingency contacts and assertive training: A case study. *Journal of Behavior Therapy and Experimental Psychiatry, 4,* 273–274.

Walton, D., & Mather, M. D. (1963). The application of learning principles to the treatment of obsessive-compulsive states in the acute and chronic phases of illness. *Behavior Research and Therapy, 1,* 163–174.

Warren, N. J., & Gilner, F. H. (1978). Measurement of positive assertive behaviors: The behavioral test of tenderness expression. *Behavior Therapy, 9,* 178–184.

Warrenfeltz-Rodney, B. (1981). Social skills training of behavior disordered adolescents with self-monitoring to promote generalization to a vocational setting. *Behavior Disorders, 7,* 18–27.

Warzak, W. J., & Page, T. J. (1990). Teaching refusal skills to sexually active adolescents. *Journal of Behavior Therapy and Experimental Psychiatry, 21,* 133–139.

Watson, D. L., & Tharp, R. G. (1988). *Self-directed behavior: Self-modification for personal adjustment,* 5th ed. Pacific Grove, CA: Brooks/Cole.

Watzlawick, P., Weakland, J., & Fisch, R. (1974). *Change: Principles of problem formulation and problem resolution.* New York: Norton.

Wehr, S. H., & Kaufman, M. E. (1987). The effects of assertive training on performance in highly anxious adolescents. *Adolescence, 22,* 195–205.

Weiss, R. (1969). *The American myth of success: From Horatio Alger to Norman Vincent Peale.* New York: Basic Books.

Werner, J. S., Minkin, N., Minkin, B. L., Fixsen, D. L., Phillips, E. L., & Wolfe, H. M. (1975). "Intervention package." An analysis to prepare juvenile delinquents for encounters with police officers. *Criminal Justice and Behavior, 2,* 55–84.

Williams, J. M., & Stout, J. K. (1985). The effect of high and low assertiveness on locus of control and health problems. *Journal of Psychology, 119,* 169–173.

Williams, J. M., Hadden, K., & Marcavage, E. (1983). Experimental study of assertion training as a drug prevention strategy for use with college students. *Journal of College Student Personnel, 24,* 201–206.

Wilson, K., & Gallois, C. (1993). *Assertion and its social context.* New York: Pergamon Press.

Wolfe, J. L., & Fodor, I. G. (1977). Modifying assertive behavior in women: A comparison of three approaches. *Behavior Therapy, 8,* 567–574.

Wolfe, J. L., & Fodor, I. G. (1978). A cognitive/behavioral approach to modifying assertive behavior in women. In J. M. Whiteley & J. V. Flowers (Ed.), *Approaches to assertion training.* Monterey, CA: Brooks/Cole.

Wolpe, J. (1958). *Psychotherapy by reciprocal inhibition.* Stanford, CA: Stanford University Press.

Wolpe, J. (1973). *The practice of behavior therapy,* 2nd ed. New York: Pergamon Press. See also later eds.

Wolpe, J., & Lazarus, A. (1966). *Behavior therapy techniques.* New York: Pergamon Press.

Wood, P. S., & Mallinckrodt, B. (1990). Culturally sensitive assertiveness training for ethnic minority clients. *Professional Psychology: Research and Practice, 21*(1), 5–11.

Workman, J. F., Boland, P. A., Grafton, C. L., & Kester, D. L. (1986–1987). Changes in self-concept, locus of control, and anxiety among female college students as related to assertion training. *Educational Research Quarterly, 11*(2), 21–28.

Yesmont, G. A. (1992). The relationship of assertiveness to college students' safer sex behaviors, *Adolescence, 23,* 253–272.

# CHAPTER 6

# COGNITIVE SKILLS TRAINING

Cory F. Newman
David A. F. Haaga

The cognitive model of psychopathology and psychotherapy developed by Beck and his collaborators (e.g., Beck, 1976; Beck, Emery, & Greenberg, 1985; Beck, Freeman, & Associates, 1990; Beck, Rush, Shaw, & Emery, 1979) views negatively biased thinking patterns as significant factors in many kinds of psychological distress. Originally, this model was developed on the basis of clinical observations and empirical research on depression (e.g., Beck, 1967). More recently, cognitive theory and therapy have been applied to a host of other disorders, including but not limited to social phobia (e.g., Heimberg, 1989), panic disorder (e.g., D. M. Clark, 1988; Newman, Beck, Beck, & Tran, 1990), eating disorders (e.g., Edgette & Prout, 1989), marital distress (e.g., Epstein & Baucom, 1989), substance abuse (e.g., Beck & Emery, 1977) and personality disorders (Beck et al., 1990; Young, 1990).

Although biases in cognitive process and content are not viewed as the sole causes of these disorders (Beck, 1987), they may help maintain the disorders and therefore represent fruitful points of intervention. Relevant cognitive features are believed to vary across disorders. To take just a few examples, the depressed client often selectively attends to negative feedback and memories of the self, thus perhaps exacerbating and prolonging depression (Blaney, 1986; Haaga, Dyck, & Ernst, in press). Similarly, the anxious client overestimates the probability of danger and risk in the environment while underestimating his or her own coping resources, thus remaining excessively fearful and avoidant (Beck & Clark, 1988). In like fashion, the client who suffers from panic attacks makes catastrophic interpretations about unusual physical or mental symptoms and thus goes to great lengths to avoid situations that are associated with such symptoms (D. M. Clark, 1988). This then leads to needless restrictions in the client's life and anxious hypervigilance to internal signs of distress. Analogous misinterpretations of internal bodily cues, coupled with obsessive thoughts of food and distortions of body image, are evident in the eating disorders (Clark, Feldman, & Channon, 1989).

Cognitive therapists propose that altering such cognitive dysfunctions provides a powerful means of treatment (Segal & Shaw, 1988). However, the goal of cognitive therapy (CT) is not merely to cajole, exhort, or otherwise persuade clients into thinking in ways that conform to the therapist's cognitive style! Rather, a goal is to teach clients a set of durable skills that will help them to think more objectively and more flexibly rather than being locked into one rigid cognitive set. Moreover, clients are taught to view their thoughts as testable hypotheses, as opposed to reaching negative conclusions through the use of faulty "shortcut" heuristics (Barber & DeRubeis, 1989; Hollon & Kriss, 1984; Nisbett & Ross, 1980). This goal of teaching empiricism in cognitive processing is mixed with a healthy dose of optimism. Haaga and Davison (in press) note that the "motto" of CT might be seen as " 'a positive is a positive; a negative is a chance to gather information and practice the techniques.' " To be sure, CT does not endeavor to teach clients to engage in idle positive thinking. In colloquial terms, the cognitive therapist attempts to train clients to exercise "good judgment" in their daily lives.

Although cognitive therapists are likely to impart information during treatment that will alter the *content* of the client's thinking (Beutler & Guest, 1989) (e.g., positive feedback may therapeutically alter the content of client's thinking about themselves), it is most important that the clients learn an improved *process* of thinking. We are speaking of a process that helps clients to make fewer faulty inferences about themselves, their lives, and their futures, and that helps them to think through their problems more methodically. Baron, Baron, Barber, and Nolen-Hoeksema (1990) depict "actively open-minded" thinking (p. 295) as desirable and rational. Here clients refrain from wishful thinking and remain open to (indeed, actively search for) other possible conclusions or evidence relevant to their hypotheses. This is in stark contrast to the kinds of impulsive and/or superstitious thinking that lead to repeated patterns of mistakes in life and ineffective coping.

Clearly, to use methodical procedures for testing one's beliefs will not guarantee a life free of psychological distress. By the same token, there is ample evidence that nondisordered populations also use faulty heuristics in reaching decisions and conclusions (Nisbett & Ross, 1980; Tversky & Kahneman, 1974). In fact, it may be that improvement in cognitive therapy entails initially learning to think in ways that are more optimal than is actually typical of the usual functioning of "normal" people. Evans and Hollon (1988) speculated that "the primary detectable changes produced by cognitive therapy will prove to be the introduction of formal reality-testing

procedures that go beyond those in which most people typically engage" (p. 370).

It is the primary goal of this chapter to describe and explicate the means by which cognitive therapists train their clients to develop, enhance, and maintain such cognitive skills. Case examples will be employed to illustrate these procedures, and data on the efficacy of these methods will be reviewed. However, we will begin with a review of the *assessment* of cognitive skills, a critical issue for both therapy and research.

## COGNITIVE ASSESSMENT

Testing cognitive theory and implementing cognitive therapy require reliable and valid means of assessing cognitions. Segal and Shaw (1988) highlight three levels of analysis: (1) cognitive products (or content), (2) cognitive processes, and (3) cognitive structures. Cognitive *content* refers to conscious thoughts or images; this level of cognition is the most easily accessed, as it involves the kinds of statements that clients emit spontaneously in sessions. Cognitive *processes* refer to the client's characteristic procedures for transforming input from the environment and drawing inferences about its meaning. For example, cognitive theory holds that depressed people tend to show biased processes of drawing inferences from data, such as arbitrary inference, selective abstraction, or overgeneralization (Beck, 1976). The most inferential level of study is the examination of cognitive *structures,* or "schemata," a construct that has suffered from inexact definition in the clinical literature. This terminology is currently used, for instance, to refer to both the hypothesized structure of thought (e.g., in the form of a filter or template that guides the processing of information) and the hypothesized content of latent core beliefs (Ingram & Kendall, 1986).

In the current practice of CT, the term *schema* usually pertains to the latter (see Beck et al., 1990, for examples of schemata associated with each of the DSM-III-R personality disorders, which are intended to guide the therapist's conceptualizations of such cases). The schemata are hypothesized to influence insidiously a client's interpretation of incoming information so that it subtly conforms to the cognitive status quo. It has also been proposed that these schemata lead a client to act on the environment in such a way as to confirm their veracity (Freeman & Leaf, 1989), a phenomenon commonly referred to as the "self-fulfilling prophecy."

## Standardized Questionnaire Assessment Methods

Most standardized methods of cognitive assessment are questionnaires measuring the cognitive contents associated with a particular disorder (e.g., unipolar depression, panic disorder). In this subsection, we review three of the more widely used inventories, which measure depressive thinking.

The Automatic Thoughts Questionnaire (ATQ; Hollon & Kendall, 1980) comprises 30 negative self-statements found to discriminate between depressed and nondepressed criterion groups (identified by self-reported symptoms). Clients indicate on a five-point Likert scale how frequently each thought occurred to them during the past week. A number of studies of clinical samples indicate that the internal consistency and concurrent validity of the ATQ are high (e.g., Dobson & Shaw, 1986; Eaves & Rush, 1984; Harrell & Ryon, 1983; Ross, Gottfredson, Christensen, & Weaver, 1986). It is significantly correlated with other measures of depressive cognition as well as multiple indices of depression (Merluzzi & Boltwood, 1989). The ATQ also demonstrates sensitivity to variations in the level of depressed affect (whether in the context of a primary disorder of major depression or depression that is secondary to other disorders, such as substance abuse). On a scale ranging from 30 to 150, depressive groups have obtained means from the 80s to as high as 126, with standard deviations in the 20s. Means for normal control groups have been found to range from 39 to 48, and standard deviations from 10 to 17 (Merluzzi & Boltwood, 1989).

Another major scale in the field of cognitive assessment of depression is the Dysfunctional Attitude Scale (DAS; Weissman & Beck, 1978). This 40-item scale attempts to tap into clients' deeper and more fundamental maladaptive beliefs. Each item is scored on a Likert scale of 1 (totally disagree) to 7 (totally agree), with higher scores indicating the endorsement of more dysfunctional attitudes. The DAS has shown good reliability (Dobson & Breiter, 1983; Dobson & Shaw, 1986) and satisfactory validity as a measure of depressive beliefs (e.g., Dobson & Breiter, 1983; Dobson & Shaw, 1986; Hamilton & Abramson, 1983). In general, scores decline when depressive symptoms remit (Parks & Hollon, 1988). Whether or not the DAS can identify a client's vulnerability to future depressive episodes, as the theory would predict, is an open question (Hollon, DeRubeis, & Evans, 1987). At the same time, an item-by-item review of a client's DAS responses can be used clinically to explore "the extent and nature of dysfunctional beliefs held by a depressed [client] at the onset and throughout the course of treatment" (Merluzzi & Boltwood, 1989, p. 259).

The Attributional Style Questionnaire (ASQ: Seligman, Abramson, Semmel, & von Bayer, 1979) was designed to test the reformulation of the learned-helplessness hypothesis (Abramson, Seligman, & Teasdale, 1978), which predicts that depressed clients will tend to attribute negative life events to internal, stable, and global factors. The questionnaire consists of six positive and six negative hypothetical situations, with an equal distribution of items that concern achievement and interpersonal relations. Respondents are asked to imagine themselves in each of the situations and to generate the one primary cause of the event if it had actually happened to them. They then rate that cause on each attributional dimension (internality, stability, globality) via the use of seven-point Likert scales. Higher scores for internality, stability, and globality of attributions for the negative situations are hypothesized to be associated with depression.

Like the DAS, the ASQ is intended to measure a cognitive phenomenon that leads to, and not simply coincides with, depression; therefore, correlations with measures of the syndrome of depression are only moderately high (Peterson & Seligman, 1984). However, most studies have found the ASQ to discriminate depressed from nondepressed subjects (e.g., Eaves & Rush, 1984; for a review, see Robins, 1988). Consistent with the theory, Metalsky, Abramson, Seligman, Semmel, and Peterson (1982) found that an *interaction* of depressive attributional style and a subsequent negative life event produced depressive symptoms.

ASQ subscales show only modest reliability (Peterson et al., 1982). However, a noteworthy strength of the ASQ is that it primes the respondent with examples of negative life events to which they respond (Parks & Hollon, 1988). Furthermore, clients are asked to generate their own causal explanations, rather than simply selecting from among choices that are provided for them. Noting the importance of schema activation in assessment and treatment procedures (Beck et al., 1990; Riskind & Rholes, 1984), Parks and Hollon make their own positive attribution, that data supporting the ASQ's utility are a "consequence of the fact that it primes subjects for depressotypic thinking" (p. 178).

The DAS, ATQ, and ASQ are often administered to clients periodically over the course of therapy. In the spirit of the $n$ = one experimental research design (Kazdin, 1980), therapists and clients can examine the sequence of scores in order to determine their correlation with symptom relief and behavioral change, and to chart the stability and durability of such changes as an index of the progress of therapy. That is, to the extent that dysfunctional thinking is decreased, this would suggest that CT is having a positive effect, and it would be expected that the client will independently report an improvement in affect.

Much of the recent literature on the cognitive assessment of depression has involved these measures, but numerous other cognitive assessment inventories have been developed for use in studying depression and other disorders (for comprehensive reviews, see Merluzzi & Boltwood, 1989; Parks & Hollon, 1988).

## Alternative Cognitive Assessment Methods

Although the structured questionnaire has been the most frequently used cognitive assessment strategy (D. A. Clark, 1988), such measures are limited insofar as they tell us more about cognitive content than about the skills that clients employ in order to think more objectively, methodically, and positively. Consequently, it may be difficult to assess the degree to which symptomatic improvement results from the cognitive skills training aspect of the therapy per se, as opposed to other therapeutic factors. Numerous alternative cognitive assessment formats have therefore been developed, including think-aloud methods, free association, thought-listing (Cacioppo & Petty, 1981), thought sampling (Hurlburt, 1980), and inferential methods drawn from basic cognitive research, such as feature analysis in categorization processes (e.g., Rosch, 1978), and the mapping of cognitive space via multidimensional scaling (Goldfried, Padawer, & Robins, 1984; Landau & Goldfried, 1981; McDermut, Haaga, & Shayne, in press).

In feature analysis, clients are asked to evaluate a general category (e.g., a ''good'' job) by generating attributes or features that they consider to make up the essence of that general category (e.g., high salary, flexible hours, intellectual stimulation). In this manner, idiosyncratic and possibly maladaptive ways of defining the general category can be assessed. Multidimensional scaling analyses of cognitive structure have typically been based on data generated when clients are asked to engage in a card-sorting task requiring them to group features of categories or objects into separate piles, each representing items that subjectively seem to belong together. Scaling analyses then spatially represent clients' perceptions of the relationships among these items. For example, Goldfried et al. (1984) found that non–socially anxious men made cognitive distinctions between academic-related interactions with women and dating interactions with women, whereas socially anxious men did not. Socially anxious subjects appeared to view both types of situations as representing potentially threatening encounters.

Some of these procedures (notably, multidimensional scaling) are too cumbersome and time-consuming for therapists to use regularly. More popular in the clinical practice of CT are event recording, imagery assessment, and unstructured interview methods of cognitive assessment.

### Event Recording

Event recording is a form of self-monitoring in which clients are taught to attend to their thoughts at critical times, such as when they notice an increase in negative emotionality or engage in maladaptive behaviors (e.g., avoiding going to work, yelling at a significant other, taking an illicit drug). Identification of the client's thoughts and implicit beliefs at such times can suggest potent cognitive interventions. Furthermore, if clients become adept at this type of self-monitoring, they can begin to recognize excellent opportunities to practice cognitive intervention skills at critical points.

Although event recording is subject to the reactivity associated with self-monitoring procedures (Ciminero, Nelson, & Lipinski, 1977), it provides rich information about the thought processes surrounding maladaptive behaviors (Parks & Hollon, 1988). Event recording is used extensively in the cognitive-behavioral therapies of depression (Beck et al., 1979), anxiety (Beck et al., 1985; Goldfried, Decenteceo, & Weinberg, 1974), anger (Novaco, 1979), and alcohol abuse (Marlatt & Gordon, 1985).

### Imagery Assessment

Imagery assessment is another potentially fruitful area of clinical investigation. For example, a client who is having difficulty articulating his or her thoughts about a given situation may be able to describe an image of the event. As the therapist asks for more imaginal details (e.g., "Who are you talking to?" "What is he saying to you?" "Describe how you feel." "What are you noticing around you?" "What is going through your mind as this happens?"), the client may be able to recollect thoughts that ordinarily would be difficult to access.

Unfortunately, the majority of standardized imagery inventories measure imagery ability, rather than the clinical content of imagery. Therefore, such widely used imagery questionnaires as the Imaginal Processes Inventory (Singer & Antrobus, 1972) and the Minnesota Paper Form Board (Likert & Quasha, 1970) generally are not applicable to the clinical setting. "Thus, there is a need for a research program geared toward the development of assessment tools designed to assess imagery within the therapeutic context" (Parks & Hollon, 1988, p. 172).

*Unstructured Clinical Interviewing*

The clinical interview is perhaps the single most common form of cognitive assessment. This type of questioning is typically employed in a functional analytic fashion, in which the client is asked to specify antecedents and consequences of various emotions, behaviors, thoughts, and physiological reactions. Ideally, the result of such structured questioning is a model of the client's overall functioning, often in the form of a flow chart that specifies hypothesized causal routes between the emotions, behaviors, thoughts, and physiological responses, as well as the reactions of others and other environmental consequences.

Important cognitions can often be revealed simply by asking the client for his or her thoughts at important times during the course of the therapy session. These might be marked by shifts in emotionality or behavior (e.g., a talkative client suddenly becomes very quiet, a client grimaces in response to a therapist's comment, or begins to weep, or changes the topic when the therapist asks a particular type of question). In like fashion, the client can be taught to use his or her own negative emotionality as a cue to ask, "What am I saying to myself right now that could be contributing to my being upset?" (Goldfried & Davison, 1976).

Many authors have discussed the importance of eliciting these "hot" (affect-laden) cognitions (e.g., Greenberg & Safran, 1989; Safran, Vallis, Segal, & Shaw, 1986) "since the more important cognitive processes may be accessible only in the affective state that is characteristic of the client when he/she is experiencing his/her problems" (Safran et al., 1986, p. 521). This consideration suggests that it can actually be counterproductive to teach clients immediately to utilize coping self-statements in a palliative fashion. Clients who do so could become "reasonable" and "sensible" at the expense of ever really coming to grips with their feelings and the deeper beliefs that drive maladaptive strategies in living (Safran & Greenberg, 1982).[1]

In order to uncover hypothesized deeper beliefs or schemata, therapists assist clients in evaluating a representative sample of their thoughts in order to look for common themes. Once such themes are posited, it is possible to examine clients' behaviors in terms of their consistency with the themes. The validity of the assessment of tacit beliefs would be estimated by the extent to which it helps predict behavior in the situations in which the beliefs are expected to be activated.

## COGNITIVE SKILLS TRAINING AND APPLICATIONS

In this section, we describe procedures for training some of the core cognitive skills clients learn in CT. The differentiation of cognitive skills training from cognitive assessment is somewhat artificial in that identification of problematic cognitions shades into the realm of intervention. Indeed, the first skill to be described in this section is clients' learning to assess their own maladaptive thinking. Succeeding subsections describe training procedures for the skills of (1) rational reevaluation of dysfunctional thoughts, (2) manipulation of attentional focus, and (3) use of guided imagery as a means of altering maladaptive thinking.[2]

### Self-Assessment of Maladaptive Cognition

One of the most basic skills that the cognitive therapist teaches the client is to reflect actively on his or her own thoughts—in other words, to engage in metacognition. The first step in this process involves questioning clients about their thoughts at times of emotional upset and then instructing them to begin doing this for themselves. Clients are told that their distress need not involve gratuitous pain, that in fact their experiences of distress can be used as opportunities to learn about themselves and, in particular, to learn to notice and modify their biased, pathogenic perceptions. If the client complains that such self-

examination of upsetting thoughts exacerbates their
discomfort, the therapist can explain further that it is
vital to understand the specific individualized manner
in which they interpret the environment in order to be
able to devise cognitive interventions tailor-made to
the problem. Besides the straightforward method of
asking, "What am I saying to myself right now that
could be making me feel worse?" when feeling upset, clients can be taught to ask themselves additional,
more specific questions tapping the "cognitive triad"
(Beck, 1970):

- "What am I thinking about *myself* right now?"
- "What do I expect will happen in the *future,* based
  on my impressions right now?"
- "What am I thinking about the state of my *life* (my
  world) right now?"

To take this process a step further, the therapist
trains the client to apply the "downward-arrow"
technique to assess his or her own deeper beliefs or
schemata (Beck et al., 1979). In other words, once the
client ascertains an automatic thought[3] associated
with an episode of upset, he or she writes it down on
the top of a page and then asks the question: "Why is
this distressing to me?" A proposed answer is written
below (with an arrow pointing down toward the answer from the thought listed above). The process is
repeated until an underlying belief is elucidated. This
process can be quite a revelation for the client, who
then comes to understand more fully why he or she
reacted so strongly to objectively nonthreatening
situations.

For example, June is a young woman who escaped
a physically abusive home situation to live with her
aunt and cousins. She told her therapist that she was
very upset to find that her aunt had left her a note on
the kitchen table, asking her to please clean up after
herself before going out. She realized that her first
thought was "Aunt Bonnie thinks I'm a slob," which
June found upsetting. But at the time she read the
note, she began to shiver and break into uncontrollable sobbing, a reaction that seemed to her an overreaction, but one that she could not stop. She reported
that she then retreated to her room and began writing
her thoughts on a sheet of paper. Starting with the
initial automatic thought listed above, June used the
downward-arrow technique by finishing the sentence
"This is upsetting to me because it means that . . ."
The sequence of thoughts she identified was as
follows:

Aunt Bonnie thinks I'm a slob.

. . . which means that . . .          ↓

She's displeased with me in
general.

. . . which means that . . .          ↓

She's sorry she took me in to live
here.

. . . which means that . . .          ↓

She'll probably ask me to leave.

. . . which means that . . .          ↓

I'll be all alone, unwanted, and
with nowhere to go.

June took this exercise a step further, applying
downward-arrow questions directly addressing each
element of the cognitive triad.

What does all of this make me think of myself?
   —"that I'm an undesirable person who isn't worthy of love"
What does all of this make me think of my life
situation?
      —"that nobody cares about me, and nobody
      is capable of really understanding my situa-
      tion or helping me to get my life on track"
What does all of this make me think of my future?
      —"that I'll never be appreciated or loved,
      but rather I'll be negatively judged, dis-
      liked, and mistreated for all my life"

June then understood why she was so shaken by
this note. Using reevaluation techniques to be described shortly, she then was able to decatastrophize
the meaning of the event, putting it in a less threatening perspective. She reported that her crying stopped,
and, while she was still somewhat perturbed, she was
able to go about her business without significant
emotional interference. She cleaned up after herself
and later was able to interact with her aunt in a
sincerely friendly way.

In this manner, June had taken tremendous strides
toward developing cognitive coping skills. In session,
when she presented this episode (and her therapeutic
responses), June and the therapist proceeded to explore her beliefs about her unlovability, aloneness,
and hopelessness in the context of her abusive up-
bringing. This legitimized and acknowledged her
pain, thus bolstering the therapeutic relationship,
while also setting the stage for June to use cognitive
skills to make a break from the past, including current
situations (e.g., the note) that would otherwise evoke
schemata formed long ago.

## Rational Reevaluation

The identification of automatic thoughts and schemata, as highlighted above, is followed by the client's attempts to modify those thoughts and schemata therapeutically. Cognitive therapists teach their clients to engage in the cognitive skill of objective self-reflection via the use of a series of questions to themselves.

One particularly useful format for organizing, concretizing, and recording this self-help process is the Daily Thought Record, or "DTR" (see Newman & Beck, 1990). The DTR is probably the best known exemplar of the written application of cognitive skills. Its clinical popularity is based on its being both an excellent teaching tool and a useful recording device.

The standard format of the DTR is presented in Figure 6.1. Clients are presented with five columns, in which they are to write about problematic situations, concomitant emotions, automatic thoughts associated with these emotions, rational responses to the previous automatic thoughts, and the outcome of the DTR exercise in terms of resultant emotions and residual belief in the dysfunctional automatic thoughts.

This is a formidable task. Blackburn and Eunson (1989) have written about the difficulty of training clients to use DTRs properly. At the same time, they state that the teaching of the appropriate use of the DTR is a tremendous boon to educating clients about the cognitive model of psychopathology and to increasing their sense of mastery in applying the model to everyday problems. One method of facilitating this process involves initially teaching clients the use of the first three columns only. In this phase, the primary task is the identification and differentiation of problematic situations, emotions, and automatic thoughts.

An important part of this process is that clients are instructed to rate degrees of emotionality and of belief in their automatic thoughts. For example, rather than simply indicating that he or she feels angry, a client would produce a rating between 0 and 100 that would reflect the subjective level of this emotion. Right away, this task begins to discourage the maladaptive habit of all-or-none perceptions. Similarly, the rating of *belief* in the automatic thought begins to teach the client that thoughts are not equivalent to incontrovertible facts or dogma. For example, a client who is frustrated in completing an important task may have the automatic thought, "I can't do it and I don't even care anymore!" Left unchecked, this thought may reinforce a dysfunctional desire to quit.

Upon second reflection via the use of the DTR, however, the client may realize that he or she does not really believe completely that he or she "doesn't even care anymore." The degree of belief in this thought may be only, say, 70%. Thus, the process of reevaluation has already begun. If there is only 70% belief in an automatic thought, there must be 30% doubt as well, which implies that there are other ways to view the situation and to approach the problem. Later, this will lead nicely into the fourth and fifth columns of the DTR, where constructive alternatives for thinking, acting, and feeling are delineated and evaluated.

Another way to facilitate the clients' learning of the use of the DTR is to work on one collaboratively during the therapy session. Taking a problem that arises naturally during the session, therapists can walk clients through the various columns and provide instant feedback. For example, therapists may note when clients mistakenly list thoughts in the "Emotions" column (e.g., writing "I felt like I was being totally rejected"). In like fashion, therapists can help clients distinguish between factual situations and their resultant thoughts. For instance, a client might record in the "Situation" column that "I was being stood up," which is a cognitive interpretation of the situation of being kept waiting by a date.

Additionally, therapists can help clients generate responses to each column if the clients have difficulty doing so on their own. If a client cannot remember what was going through his or her mind while feeling depressed about a given situation, the therapist can prompt the client via open-ended questioning or multiple-choice questioning. As an example of open-ended questioning, the therapist might ask, "If you were to be in that situation now, what might you be saying to yourself about what's going on around you?" or, "Have you been in similar situations in the past? If so, what impressions did you have about those experiences?" If the therapist chooses multiple-choice questioning, he or she would provide the client with a number of possible responses and would ask the client to indicate which one(s) rings most true. It would be appropriate to state at such times that an important goal will be that the client eventually learn to do this for himself or herself.

### Questioning the Automatic Thought

Depending on how fast the client is catching on, the therapist then teaches her or him to finish columns 4 and 5 of the DTR. The fourth column, "Ra-

**Figure 6.1.** Daily Record of Dysfunctional Thoughts

| DATE | SITUATION<br><br>Describe:<br>1. Actual event leading to unpleasant emotion, or<br>2. Stream of thoughts, daydream, or recollection, leading to unpleasant emotion. | EMOTION(S)<br><br>1. Specify sad/ anxious/angry etc.<br>2. Rate degree of emotion, 1-100. | AUTOMATIC THOUGHT(S)<br><br>1. Write automatic thought(s) that preceded emotion(s).<br>2. Rate belief in automatic thought(s), 0-100%. | RATIONAL RESPONSE<br><br>1. Write rational response to automatic thought(s).<br>2. Rate belief in rational response, 0-100%. | OUTCOME<br><br>1. Re-rate belief in automatic thought(s), 0-100%.<br>2. Specify and rate subsequent emotions, 0-100. |
|------|------|------|------|------|------|
|  |  |  |  |  |  |
|  |  |  |  |  |  |

*Explanation:* When you experience an unpleasant emotion, note the situation that seemed to stimulate the emotion. (If the emotion occurred while you were thinking, daydreaming, etc., please note this.) Then note the automatic thought associated with the emotion. Record the degree to which you believe this thought: 0% = not at all; 100% = completely. In rating degree of emotion: 1 = a trace; 100 = the most intense possible.

tional Responding,'' can be best taught via the use of four questions for the client to ask regarding an automatic thought.

1. *What's the evidence?* The first question is, ''What is the evidence that supports and/or refutes this automatic thought or belief?'' In answering this question, the client eschews the use of hunches, intuition, or gut feelings, all of which are typically laden with faulty inferences (Newman & Beck, 1990). The cognitive therapist encourages the client to reflect on factual, independently verifiable information (rather than conjecture or out-of-context observations) in order to address this question appropriately (Newman, 1989). To return to the example of June, she first would examine the evidence for and against her automatic thought that ''Aunt Bonnie thinks I'm a slob.'' Replies such as, ''I just know it,'' and, ''I can tell by the tone of the note'' would be rejected as evidence by virtue of their being based on pure conjecture and unverified observation, respectively. Responses such as, ''Aunt Bonnie said to me, 'June, you're just like your father. He was always a slob,' '' or, ''She has complimented me many times previously for my help in keeping the house looking clean and neat'' would be good examples of evidence pertinent to a rational reevaluation of the automatic thought. It frequently requires a great deal of practice for clients to master the skill of gathering ''admissible evidence.'' The therapist can assist in this process by guiding the client's attention toward relevant memories, current life assets (such as friends, talents, and material resources), direct feedback from other people, and historical records (e.g., old photos, letters, academic transcripts).

2. *Alternative perspectives?* A second question, ''Are there any other ways to look at this situation?'' is geared to help the client to think divergently or to become more flexible in considering alternative appraisals. If clients have difficulty in learning to apply this question, they can be asked to answer as if they were someone else—for example, ''How would my best friend explain my situation?'' Another aid in generating alternative perspectives is to ask, ''How might this initially upsetting event actually be a blessing in disguise?'' In any event, clients are encouraged to brainstorm possible answers, not to censor potential responses on the basis of initial pessimism and incredulity. In the case of June, she would be asked to come up with alternative hypotheses for her aunt's note, other than its meaning that she is thought of as a slob. One such answer might be: ''I know that Aunt Bonnie likes to write reminder notes, especially when she will not be around to supervise the household. She might just be giving me instructions so that she feels in control of things around here. There may be no personal attack meant at all.'' It is important that clients learn the value of generating multiple answers to this question, lest they misuse the technique by getting into the habit of producing dichotomous all-or-none interpretations.

3. *Worst case scenario?* A third useful question is, ''Realistically, what is the worst thing that could happen in this situation, and how would it affect my life?'' This question provokes an earnest analysis of the degree of seriousness of the situation or feeling, which may help clients decatastrophize their thoughts (Newman & Beck, 1990). Our client June might answer this question by saying that in reality the worst that will happen is that she will have to do extra work around the house in order to stay in Aunt Bonnie's good graces. This might not be fun, but it is not the personal disaster that she originally thought it might be (as demonstrated by her downward arrow assessment).

4. *Action implications?* A fourth question is important for practical purposes and for building self-efficacy: ''Even if there is reason to believe that my negative viewpoint is warranted, what can I do to help remedy this situation?'' This approach combats the client's sense of helplessness and hopelessness, and serves as a call to constructive action. For example, June may answer this question by choosing to have a heart-to-heart talk with her aunt, by pledging to herself to be more responsible around the house, or by choosing to ignore the note if she already had every intention of cleaning up.

Figures 6.2 through 6.5 demonstrate simulated rational responses to a set of automatic thoughts, using each of the four questions.

For the sake of simplicity and practicality, cognitive therapists frequently rely on just these four questions. In principle, however, the number of potentially useful ones is unlimited. Depending on the circumstance, for instance, one might evaluate an automatic thought by asking oneself (1) ''How is it to my benefit or detriment to think this way?'' or (2) ''What will I have to gain or lose by trying to look at things another way?''

**Figure 6.2.** Daily Record of Dysfunctional Thoughts: Questioning the Evidence

| DATE | SITUATION<br><br>Describe:<br>1. Actual event leading to unpleasant emotion, or<br>2. Stream of thoughts, daydream, or recollection, leading to unpleasant emotion. | EMOTION(S)<br><br>1. Specify sad/anxious/angry, etc.<br>2. Rate degree of emotion, 1-100. | AUTOMATIC THOUGHT(S)<br><br>1. Write automatic thought(s) that preceded emotion(s).<br>2. Rate belief in automatic thought(s), 0-100%. | RATIONAL RESPONSE<br><br>1. Write rational response to automatic thought(s). | OUTCOME<br><br>1. Re-rate belief in automatic thought(s), 0-100%.<br>2. Specify and rate subsequent emotions, 0-100. |
|---|---|---|---|---|---|
| 8/9 | I went to Peggy's house to take her out to dinner, as prearranged. However, she was not there. | hurt 75%<br><br>sad 100%<br><br>depressed 90% | 1. She hates me.  80%<br><br>2. She wants to get rid of me.  95%<br><br>3. It's all over.  100%<br><br>4. I must have done something wrong.  90%<br><br>5. I always screw up.  80%<br><br>6. This always happens to me.  100%<br><br>7. I'll never have anyone to love.  90% | Hold on a minute. I don't know for sure that she hates me. She probably wouldn't have gone out with me eight times in the past month unless she was interested in me.<br><br>And it isn't like Peggy to end a relationship by standing the guy up. She's fairly assertive and I think she'd tell me, instead.<br><br>In thinking back to our last date, I can't think of anything horrible that I might have done. In fact, she seemed to be having a good time.<br><br>It's not true that this always happens to me. With Janice, I was the one who ended the relationship. | *Emotions*<br>hurt          25%<br>sad           15%<br>depressed  30%<br><br>*Automatic Thoughts*<br>1. 20%<br>2. 40%<br>3. 50%<br>4. 15%<br>5. 10%<br>6. 10%<br>7. 10% |

*Explanation:* When you experience an unpleasant emotion, note the situation that seemed to stimulate the emotion. (If the emotion occurred while you were thinking, daydreaming, etc., please note this.) Then note the automatic thought associated with the emotion. Record the degree to which you believe this thought: 0% = not at all; 100% = completely. In rating degree of emotion: 1 = a trace; 100 = the most intense possible.

**Figure 6.3.** Daily Record of Dysfunctional Thoughts: How Else Can I View This Situation?

| DATE | SITUATION | EMOTION(S) | AUTOMATIC THOUGHT(S) | RATIONAL RESPONSE | OUTCOME |
|---|---|---|---|---|---|
| | Describe: 1. Actual event leading to unpleasant emotion, or 2. Stream of thoughts, daydream, or recollection, leading to unpleasant emotion. | 1. Specify sad/anxious/angry, etc. 2. Rate degree of emotion, 1-100. | 1. Write automatic thought(s) that preceded emotion(s). 2. Rate belief in automatic thought(s), 0-100%. | 1. Write rational response to automatic thought(s). | 1. Re-rate belief in automatic thought(s), 0-100%. 2. Specify and rate subsequent emotions, 0-100. |
| 8/9 | I went to Peggy's house to take her out to dinner, as prearranged. However, she was not there. | hurt 75% <br><br> sad 100% <br><br> depressed 90% | 1. She hates me.  80% <br><br> 2. She wants to get rid of me.  95% <br><br> 3. It's all over.  100% <br><br> 4. I must have done something wrong.  90% <br><br> 5. I always screw up.  80% <br><br> 6. This always happens to me.  100% <br><br> 7. I'll never have anyone to love.  90% | Maybe Peggy's not showing up for our date isn't intentional on her part. Maybe she forgot, or thought our date was for Saturday, not Friday night. Maybe she had a last-minute emergency with one of her clients and couldn't get to a phone. <br><br> If she did try to call me, she probably would have had trouble getting through because I was on the phone up until the time I left. <br><br> Even if she did stand me up to get rid of me, it doesn't mean I did something wrong. A person who'd do something like that has problems of her own. <br><br> In any case, I won't know until I ask her. | *Emotions* <br> hurt     25% <br> sad      15% <br> depressed 40% <br><br> *Automatic Thoughts* <br> 1. 20% <br> 2. 50% <br> 3. 50% <br> 4. 20% <br> 5. 20% <br> 6. 40% <br> 7. 10% |

*Explanation:* When you experience an unpleasant emotion, note the situation that seemed to stimulate the emotion. (If the emotion occurred while you were thinking, daydreaming, etc., please note this.) Then note the automatic thought associated with the emotion. Record the degree to which you believe this thought: 0% = not at all; 100% = completely. In rating degree of emotion: 1 = a trace; 100 = the most intense possible.

129

**Figure 6.4.** Daily Record of Dysfunctional Thoughts: Decatastrophizing—What's the Worst That Could Happen?

| DATE | SITUATION<br><br>Describe:<br>1. Actual event leading to unpleasant emotion, or<br>2. Stream of thoughts, daydream, or recollection, leading to unpleasant emotion. | EMOTION(S)<br><br>1. Specify sad/anxious/angry, etc.<br>2. Rate degree of emotion, 1-100. | AUTOMATIC THOUGHT(S)<br><br>1. Write automatic thought(s) that preceded emotion(s).<br>2. Rate belief in automatic thought(s), 0-100%. | RATIONAL RESPONSE<br><br>1. Write rational response to automatic thought(s). | OUTCOME<br><br>1. Re-rate belief in automatic thought(s), 0-100%.<br>2. Specify and rate subsequent emotions, 0-100. |
|---|---|---|---|---|---|
| 8/9 | I went to Peggy's house to take her out to dinner, as prearranged. However, she was not there. | hurt 75%<br><br>sad 100%<br><br>depressed 90% | 1. She hates me.   80%<br><br>2. She wants to get rid of me.   95%<br><br>3. It's all over.   100%<br><br>4. I must have done something wrong.   90%<br><br>5. I always screw up.   80%<br><br>6. This always happens to me.   100%<br><br>7. I'll never have anyone to love.   90% | Let's say she does hate me and wants to get rid of me. It's not the end of the world. I still have my friends, my house, and my career.<br><br>It doesn't mean I'll never have another relationship. There have been women in the past who have loved me. So there's no reason to think there won't be someone in the future.<br><br>Even if it is over, I'll be hurt and upset for awhile, but I'll survive. | *Emotions*<br>hurt            25%<br>sad             15%<br>depressed   25%<br><br>*Automatic Thoughts*<br>1. 20%<br>2. 40%<br>3. 50%<br>4. 15%<br>5. 10%<br>6. 10%<br>7. 5% |

*Explanation:* When you experience an unpleasant emotion, note the situation that seemed to stimulate the emotion. (If the emotion occurred while you were thinking, daydreaming, etc., please note this.) Then note the automatic thought associated with the emotion. Record the degree to which you believe this thought: 0% = not at all; 100% = completely. In rating degree of emotion: 1 = a trace; 100 = the most intense possible.

**Figure 6.5.** Daily Record of Dysfunctional Thoughts: Generating Options—What Can I *Do* about This?

| DATE | SITUATION<br><br>Describe:<br>1. Actual event leading to unpleasant emotion, or<br>2. Stream of thoughts, daydream, or recollection, leading to unpleasant emotion. | EMOTION(S)<br><br>1. Specify sad/ anxious/angry, etc.<br>2. Rate degree of emotion, 1-100. | AUTOMATIC THOUGHT(S)<br><br>1. Write automatic thought(s) that preceded emotion(s).<br>2. Rate belief in automatic thought(s), 0-100%. | RATIONAL RESPONSE<br><br>1. Write rational response to automatic thought(s). | OUTCOME<br><br>1. Re-rate belief in automatic thought(s). 0-100%.<br>2. Specify and rate subsequent emotions, 0-100. |
|---|---|---|---|---|---|
| 8/9 | I went to Peggy's house to take her out to dinner, as prearranged. However, she was not there. | hurt 75%<br><br>sad 100%<br><br>depressed 90% | 1. She hates me. 80%<br><br>2. She wants to get rid of me. 95%<br><br>3. It's all over. 100%<br><br>4. I must have done something wrong. 90%<br><br>5. I always screw up. 80%<br><br>6. This always happens to me. 100%<br><br>7. I'll never have anyone to love. 90% | Even if I have made a mistake and she wants to end it, I may be able to make it up to her. Maybe I can change her mind.<br><br>Even if I can't change her mind, I have options: My married friends are always offering to fix me up with single women they know. I could call up a friend and go to a nightclub—that's how I met Peggy in the first place. I could join a singles' club or take a cooking class.<br><br>Losing Peggy wouldn't be the end of the world. | *Emotions*<br>hurt 25%<br>sad 15%<br>depressed 5%<br><br>*Automatic Thoughts*<br>1. 20%<br>2. 30%<br>3. 50%<br>4. 15%<br>5. 10%<br>6. 5%<br>7. 0% |

*Explanation:* When you experience an unpleasant emotion, note the situation that seemed to stimulate the emotion. (If the emotion occurred while you were thinking, daydreaming, etc., please note this.) Then note the automatic thought associated with the emotion. Record the degree to which you believe this thought: 0% = not at all; 100% = completely. In rating degree of emotion: 1 = a trace; 100 = the most intense possible.

131

Finally, clients use column 5 to reevaluate their feelings and thoughts with the help of rating scales. Important goals include a reduction of the level of belief in the initial automatic thoughts and a reduction in the level of emotional distress. Additionally, it is hoped that the rational responses from column 4 will produce more positive feelings and will generate new constructive ways to handle the situation listed in column 1.

Although the ultimate goal for the CT client is to become capable of mentally walking through the steps of rationally reevaluating automatic thoughts, especially in difficult situations, it is vital that clients learn these skills initially through *active writing and recording* on the DTR. Our clinical experience suggests that such active writing is associated with quicker and more complete acquisition of cognitive skills. Although this link between written practice and skill acquisition might reflect only the influence of a common third variable, such as higher client motivation, it might also reflect a causal connection. That is, clients may be better able to concretize a problem and remember a solution when the visual-motoric-verbal information-processing modalities involved in writing are activated all at once than when learning techniques are used that involve only one information-processing modality at a time.

Rational reevaluation of automatic thoughts as practiced via the DTR may be the most difficult yet most important cognitive skill to be mastered in CT, as many other interventions are offshoots of this structured tool. To set the appropriate level of expectations, we often tell our clients that a great deal of practice in doing DTRs is required before positive effects will accrue. We urge them to persevere through the learning phase and to feel free to ask us for assistance and feedback during this process. We add that as they become more proficient in the use of this technique, they will gain a sense of increased mastery in helping themselves to feel better and think more open-mindedly and constructively. For the clinician, a running assessment of the client's skill in using the DTR may be one of the best barometers of cognitive skill acquisition.

Among the skills and techniques that are offshoots of the use of the DTR are (1) identifying the category of cognitive error, (2) turning an automatic thought expectation into a hypothesis to be tested, and (3) utilizing preselected rational responses in order to cope with anticipated difficult situations.

### Identifying the Cognitive Error

Identification of specific cognitive errors can orient the client to the process of reevaluating dysfunctional thoughts. Such errors[4] are presented in Beck et al. (1979) and in more colloquial terminology in Burns (1980). Although it is not always necessary that clients reliably categorize their automatic thoughts, it is potentially important that they recognize when they are engaging in such high-frequency errors as all-or-none thinking, overgeneralization, jumping to conclusions, mind-reading, and disqualifying the positive. Although we do not propose that all negative automatic thoughts fall into one of these categories (that would be an example of all-or-none thinking on *our* part), the covariation of these types of faulty inferences with depression (Blackburn & Eunson, 1989) suggests the importance of identifying them as a part of cognitive skills training.

We have found that clients often enjoy spotting their cognitive errors and giving them category names, especially when this task is presented in the form of an intellectual game. When clients are so engaged in this process, compliance and practice time are increased, thus further solidifying the skills. As a caveat, it is important for the therapist to make certain that the client does not misconstrue this task as an indication that he or she is "stupid" or is an "irrational person." Instead, the task is presented as an intellectual way to take the emotional sting out of pathogenic thinking by reducing it to an identifiable, manipulable problem.

As a clinical example, one of our clients, "Gerald," made it a point to note each time during the week that he made all-or-none statements to himself. His success in the task enabled him to intercept numerous automatic thoughts before they were translated into feelings of low self-esteem. In one particularly memorable session, he excitedly reported to one of us (CFN) that the application of this skill "turned my week around." He had been experiencing a creative block in his work on an advertising campaign and noticed himself saying, "I can't do anything right. I just don't have what it takes to succeed in this business." He responded to this all-or-none automatic thought by going through his files to review (and revel in) numerous previous successful projects. This action disabused him of his completely bleak self-evaluation and led to a creative reinvigoration. This led to the timely completion of his work, an outcome that greatly relieved him and gave him a tremendous sense of mastery over his thoughts, moods, and situational adversity.

## Making Testable Predictions

When clients list automatic thoughts revealing negative expectancies, it is possible to turn these into opportunities for naturalistic experimentation. Rather than engaging only in speculation, clients can actively *test* the veracity of these automatic thoughts in the real world.

As an example, "Brenda" had reluctantly accepted an invitation to spend an upcoming weekend afternoon shopping with her sister. She had agreed against her better judgment, as she knew that there was a great deal of work to which she had to attend at home (including her graduate school applications, which were nearing their deadlines for submission). Brenda became irritated with her sister and with herself when she accepted the invitation; she thought, "I'll never be able to get my work done." As Brenda and her therapist began to work on solving this problem, it was suggested that one alternative was to tell her sister in an assertive, caring, respectful way that she simply did not have time to spend with her that weekend. However, Brenda dismissed this potential solution with the automatic thought: "She'll be very upset with me. She won't understand. She'll think I'm selfish, and she'll cry about it to our mother, which will in turn lead my mother to call me and give me an earful. I don't need the aggravation!" This was a very upsetting thought to Brenda, as it reinforced her belief that she was emotionally trapped in the situation and that she would always have to subjugate her own needs in order to placate her sister and mother. Although Brenda's family system was in fact dysfunctional and there was a kernel of rationality to what Brenda was thinking, there was also an opportunity to try to make some changes in the family by experimenting with being assertive. Brenda agreed to try to implement the assertive approach (which was practiced via role-play in session) and to see for herself what her sister's response would be.

The above intervention can be presented as a "no-lose" proposition. That is, if her sister were to respond in a more benign fashion than anticipated, then Brenda (1) would have concrete evidence to dispute her negative thoughts, (2) would have more time for her work, and (3) would have set the stage for future alteration of an enmeshed family system. If, instead, her sister responded in the expected negative way, then Brenda could test the implications of her assertiveness. The benefits of attending to her work, for instance, might outweigh any negative reaction on the part of her sister and mother. In any event, she will have set a healthy precedent that may be more easily repeated in the future.

## Preparing and Overlearning Rational Responses

Another important skill is the use of preparatory rational responses. Often clients will generate excellent rational responses in situation A, only to forget them entirely when in the midst of problematic situation B. Panic disorder clients in particular often seem to forget their cognitive skills when in the throes of an attack. A long-run solution is to develop the ability to think clearly even in such dire circumstances. Therapists can address this aim, for instance, by inducing panic in the safety of the office (e.g., via hyperventilation exercises; Beck & Greenberg, 1988) to provide opportunities for practice of coping skills in response to strong feelings, but in a nonthreatening environment. In the meantime, clients can get around the problem of forgetting their skill in stressful situations by keeping a cumulative written record of their most effective rational responses in the form of flashcards. One client humorously likened this to keeping an archives of "The Best of Johnny Carson" or "The Best of Saturday Night Live" episodes. These cards (usually 3 × 5 index cards) can be carried in the client's purse, wallet, automobile glove compartment, or the like. Clients quickly come to appreciate the well-known fact that recognition memory is easier than free recall. Clinically, this translates into a readier application of efficacious rational responses in difficult situations—responses that might otherwise be forgotten in the heat of the moment.

"Roy," a client who suffered from panic attacks, kept a number of such cards in the glove compartment of his car, where he most frequently experienced his attacks. He learned to read these cards before starting the car to boost his confidence and inoculate himself against intrusive automatic thoughts that would exacerbate his symptoms. These cards, generated in session and from homework assignments, contained such statements as these:

- "Remember, you've made this drive dozens of times, and never had an accident, even when your symptoms seemed unbearable."

- "I'm not weak and helpless. I take care of myself and my business quite well. I just happen to have some hypersensitive cognitive and bodily reactions to stress. I can work on these."
- "If I start to feel anxious, I'll just focus on the task at hand, which is driving. I will not start to worry about every little reaction which takes place inside of me."

Roy's regular use of these flashcards led to his eventual memorization of their contents, even in the midst of panic symptoms. When he would memorize one batch, he would then work on a new set, until he accumulated an impressive array of easily accessed rational responses for use at critical moments. In this manner, Roy averted becoming trapped in the vicious cycle of "closed-system" information processing that is common in panic disorder clients (Beck & Greenberg, 1988).

## Manipulation of Attentional Focus

Another frequently useful cognitive skill is that of focusing attention away from intrusive automatic thoughts. It is important to bear in mind that this is a skill that should be taught only to those clients who are prone to catastrophizing and other forms of excess negative thinking. Those clients who are adept at avoiding upsetting cognitions to the point of being in denial are already all too willing to focus attention away from such automatic thoughts. It is critical that these clients be trained to be skilled attenders to their automatic thinking.

When it is appropriate to help clients focus away from the self, as is commonly the case in treating depression (Ingram, Lumry, Cruet, & Sieber, 1987) or panic disorder (Beck & Greenberg, 1988), clients are instructed either to attend to an instrumental task (e.g., writing a report or letter, cleaning one's apartment, giving a speech) or to distract themselves with an array of benign thoughts. The latter technique may involve something as simple as noticing visual stimuli in the environment (e.g., the wall is painted light blue; the clock is digital), as "silly" as playing mind games (e.g., "If I think of all my friends and relatives, how many middle names and birthdays can I accurately identify?"), or as meaningful as trying to remember some of the most intensely positive moments of one's life to date. With regard to these positive memories, we often have clients generate these for homework as a useful exercise in its own right, as it is all too common for distressed clients to overlook many positive life events that otherwise would serve to lift mood and enhance the client's view of his or her life. Once these memories are painstakingly uncovered and discussed, they can be listed on paper and used as positive distractors during times of distress.

## Guided Imagery

The use of guided imagery can be a powerful alternative to the verbal and action-based methods discussed previously for assessing and changing thoughts and beliefs (Edwards, 1989). For example, clients who find it difficult to articulate their upsetting thoughts verbally may be able instead to call up an image about the distressing situation. In such instances, the evoked image may elegantly tie together "the often intricate relationships between specific facts, beliefs, and assumptions that may be isolated in verbal representation" (Edwards, 1989, p. 283). An example of the power of imagery (in this case, the negative power) can be found in Sylvia Plath's autobiographical novel, *The Bell Jar* (1971). The protagonist of the novel perceived herself to be detached from the world around her, as if she were encased in a scientist's observational bell jar. This visual representation of her life had much to do with the character's depression and suicidality.

By simply requesting that clients close their eyes, or by using a relaxation induction, therapists can assist clients in manipulating their images so that more *positive* metaphors for the self, the world, and the future are achieved. "Wendy," a histrionic, depressed client, despaired over others' negative reactions to her overstimulating interpersonal style. Her initial image of herself was that of a poor, lonely, starving, homeless waif whom everyone treated with indifference or downright cruelty. This view reinforced her sense of worthlessness, as well as her view of others as malevolent. The therapist, having conceptualized this client's problem as involving the inappropriate overuse of self-presentation behaviors borne of a desperate desire to be noticed and appreciated, helped her to adopt a new image. In place of the waif, Wendy was to imagine herself as being embodied by her favorite symphony (Mahler's Fifth) played at an ear-splitting 200 decibels! The message was clear—she possessed beautiful qualities, but her volume was far too high for others to appreciate them; instead, they felt pain and abandoned her. One important implication of this image was that Wendy would have to exert more control over her "volume lever."

In practice, when she would perceive that others were not responding favorably to her, she would invoke the image (and audition) of Mahler's Fifth and would imagine lowering the volume on her "internal stereo system." Results were far more effective than verbal cognitive restructuring methods alone had been.

Clients can be taught to utilize a variety of images to counteract distressing thoughts. For example, a client who fears interacting with his boss may call up an image of the employer wearing children's pajamas, so as to make him or her seem vulnerable, silly, and less threatening. Another application of imagery is goal rehearsal, in which clients picture themselves solving a current problem and note the steps taken to achieve the goal. In the use of coping imagery, clients imagine dealing with a range of possible outcomes of a situation (from best to worst) (Weishaar & Beck, 1986). Alternatively, clients may simply tune into a mind's-eye view of their releasing their tensions (and/or inhibitory automatic thoughts) and naturally allowing themselves to complete a task successfully. Such an approach is very popular among athletes, as typified by Gallwey's *The Inner Game of Tennis* (1974), a book that has gained widespread notice as a treatise on maximizing one's potential in tennis and in life through constructive changes in state of mind.

Yet another imaginal technique is "time projection," in which the client is instructed to imagine life months or years in the future, so as to gain some emotional distance and perspective about the current upsetting event (Weishaar & Beck, 1986). "Ron," a client who was suicidal over his divorce, practiced imagining himself ten years into the future, happily married to someone new, and saying to himself: "Man, I thought my whole world was gone when I got divorced. I'm glad I didn't go through with killing myself, because I would have cheated myself out of what I have today." This time-projected image alone did not cure Ron of depression, but it effectively motivated him to want to stick around to see what his future would really be like.

# Special Issues in Cognitive Skills Training

## Affective Deficits

Up to this point we have discussed cognitive skills training as though clients' affective problems are invariably excesses of negative emotions. That is,

increasing negative emotions, though perhaps a useful vehicle for assessing "hot cognitions," has not typically been seen as an end in itself. Surely, however, there are cases in which this generalization would not hold. For a client who evidences a maladaptive deficit in negative emotionality—for example, a husband who does not feel remorse when he repeatedly deceives his wife—cognitive therapists would try to help him increase negative mood by focusing on the deleterious consequences of his actions for his marriage. Such an intervention would be appropriate to provide motivation to change. At the same time, the client might be taught cognitive skills oriented toward diminishing his exaggerated anger towards his wife.

Cognitive therapy can also be used in order to facilitate the experience and expression of affect when clients are suffering a diminished quality of life as a result of their restricted emotionality (Newman, 1991). For example, a client who shies away from giving or receiving expressions of love and intimacy would be encouraged to evaluate the pros and cons of maintaining or changing this mode of operation. Furthermore, the client would be encouraged to take risks in sharing words and acts of caring with significant others. Conversely, the client's fears involved in such undertakings would be assessed and treated so that these inhibitory thoughts and feelings would diminish.

## Compliance

The common denominator of the cognitive assessment and skills training procedures described in this chapter is that they all require extensive cooperation from clients and hard work on their part, both in and out of session. Such may not, of course, be invariably forthcoming. Some guidelines for maximizing compliance with homework in CT, summarized by Haaga and Davison (in press), include: (1) regularly offering a rationale for assignments, (2) mentioning to the client that research suggests a link between homework completion and clinical improvement (see below), (3) eliciting a verbal commitment to complete the assignment, (4) writing down the assignment, (5) shaping compliance by starting with easier tasks and gradually increasing the level of difficulty, (6) collaborating with the client in setting the terms and details of the task, and (7) trouble-shooting in advance the potential problems that might interfere with completion of the assignment. Results of a study on compliance in counseling (Worthington, 1986) underscore the importance of introducing regular homework assignments early in the treatment process and monitoring the rate of compliance in order to communicate its importance; in other words, "... when counselors directly asked about it, compliance was greatest. This confirms Shelton and Levy's (1981) assertion that homework should be followed up in subsequent sessions" (p. 128).

If noncompliance is forthcoming despite application of these procedures and seems related to more general personality difficulties (e.g., passive-aggressive personality disorder), it is often possible to gain important cognitive information by soliciting complaints or doubts about the course of therapy or the therapeutic relationship itself. Such queries can elicit material that may illuminate maladaptive ways that such clients idiosyncratically construe other important life tasks and relationships.

## EMPIRICAL EVALUATIONS OF COGNITIVE SKILLS TRAINING

### Outcome Studies of Cognitive Therapy

Although some recent studies have indicated promising results regarding the efficacy of CT for such syndromes as eating disorders (Garner, 1987) and bipolar disorder (Chor, Mercier, & Halper, 1988), it nevertheless remains true that most CT outcome studies have concerned depression or anxiety. This body of research has indicated rather consistently that improvements are substantial and are maintained beyond the end of treatment to a greater degree than is shown by psychotropic medication groups (e.g., Blackburn, Eunson, & Bishop, 1986; Simons, Murphy, Levine, & Wetzel, 1986; for reviews, see Dobson, 1989; Hollon & Najavits, 1988).

A major exception to these findings concerns the end-of-treatment results of the National Institute of Mental Health (NIMH) Treatment of Depression Collaborative Research Program (Elkin, et al., 1989); CT was not found to be significantly more effective than a minimal-treatment-plus-pill-placebo group. Hollon and Najavits (1988) note that the adequacy with which CT was executed in this study may have been undermined by the therapists' off-site training and infrequent supervision (once per month for study cases). More detailed analysis of the relationship between the quality of CT interventions and treatment outcome promise to shed light on this account of the findings.

*Cognitive versus Behavioral Components*

In evaluating outcome data on CT, it is important to note that most of these studies tested the complete package of CT, which includes an array of behavioral interventions. Therefore, it is difficult to assess the degree to which cognitive skills training alone contributes to therapeutic improvements. Some studies of the treatment of anxiety disorders have attempted to separate the cognitive component from the behavioral component of cognitive-behavioral therapies (e.g., Kanter & Goldfried, 1979; Mattick & Peters, 1988). In general, these studies suggest that cognitive interventions make a unique contribution to treatment efficacy.

Although these are promising findings, it may be argued that a great deal more such "dismantling" research is needed to determine the absolute and relative contributions to therapeutic outcome made by cognitive versus behavioral treatment components. However, a strong case can be made against investing time, money, and energy in such projects, as it is extremely tricky to design interventions that are either purely cognitive or purely behavioral. For example, a behavioral intervention such as activity scheduling involves more than just action—it involves planning as well as assessing the mastery and pleasure experienced in each activity (Beck et al., 1979) requires a cognitive appraisal of the value of taking part in the task. Likewise, even a prototypically "behavioral" treatment such as covert systematic desensitization involves the client's use of imagery, clearly a cognitive component.

Other behavioral interventions, such as social skills training, often necessitate attention to cognitive factors, especially when the client's objective skills are intact but are impeded by inhibitory thoughts and beliefs. Problem-solving skills (D'Zurilla & Goldfried, 1971; Nezu, Nezu, & Perri, 1989; O'Donohue & Noll, Chapter 7, this volume) involve significant cognitive components, including identification and definition of a problem, generation of possible solutions (a direct carryover from the fourth rational response question, "What can I *do* about this situation?"), and evaluation of the advantages and disadvantages of each possible solution.

Conversely, cognitive interventions such as reevaluation of automatic thoughts via use of the DTR often necessitate the client's becoming active in writing and sometimes lead to enactment of behavioral experiments to test these thoughts.

Although it is theoretically possible, then, to devise and study "pure" forms of cognitive interventions, doing so may fail to represent the actual practice of CT. It seems to us (see also Beck, in press; Haaga & Davison, 1989) more instructive to study ecologically valid interventions even if this entails some overlap between the cognitive and behavioral domains.

## Role of Skill Development in CT Outcome

Barber and DeRubeis (1989) argue that the effectiveness of CT lies in its teaching clients to use compensatory skills. In other words, clients' *primary* appraisals of self, world, and future may not be fundamentally altered, but they learn to apply skills that lead to more constructive *secondary* appraisals.

### Homework and Outcome

If this is indeed the case, it suggests that the between-session practice of such compensatory skills would be vital to the success of CT. Curiously, little research has focused on the impact of homework compliance in CT (Primakoff, Epstein, & Covi, 1986).

Some evidence, though, indicates that homework is indeed a curative factor in CT. Neimeyer, Twentyman, and Prezant (1985), and Persons and Burns (1985) found that depressed clients receiving CT with homework assignments made more progress than did those not receiving homework. Neimeyer and Feixas (1990) reported that a CT group receiving homework assignments only slightly (albeit significantly so with respect to clinician ratings of depression) outperformed a group that did not include homework. The results of these experimental comparisons are consistent with a view that cognitive skill development (presumably enhanced by homework assignments) contributes to CT outcome. However, they are open to alternative interpretations as well, inasmuch as no comparisons were made with nonspecific homework groups investing equivalent time in treatment-related activities but without focusing directly on cognitive skill training.

Further indication that homework is an active ingredient in CT comes from Persons, Burns, and Perloff (1988), who found that homework compliance was a significant predictor of end-of-treatment depression scores. Again, there is a plausible alternative, noncausal explanation for these results—namely, that the third variable of client motivation causes both homework compliance and improvement in therapy. Despite the limitations of these studies,

their results converge, which lends credence to the hypothesis that homework (and the practicing of cognitive skills in general) is positively related to outcome.

### Cognitive Mediation of Improvement in CT

What remains unresolved is the extent to which the beneficial impact of CT is mediated by improvements in cognitive skills. As noted earlier in reviewing standardized cognitive assessment procedures, some of the fault for this state of ambiguity may stem from difficulties in developing apt measures of such skills. Popular measures such as the DAS, ATQ, and ASQ tell us how much the client has improved in terms of depressive cognitive content but are less informative regarding the development of skills the client has used to arrive at a healthier affective/cognitive state.

This measurement issue comes to the fore when CT clients and antidepressant medication clients evidence similar changes on cognitive measures (Segal & Shaw, 1986). In one respect, this is a curious finding, as we would expect cognitive assessments to be more responsive to CT than to pharmacotherapy. In another respect, these findings simply tell us that recovered depressives think more positively, no matter what treatment achieved this end. That CT clients seem to maintain their therapeutic gains more than do medicated clients (e.g., Simons et al., 1986) encourages the speculation that CT is teaching cognitive skills useful for promoting constructive thinking during subsequent episodes of stress, but that these skills are not tapped by existing measures.

Progress in this area is highlighted by a recent study indicating that depressed clients who showed the greatest skill in the use of the DTR by the end of treatment showed superior maintenance of therapeutic gains at six-month follow-up (Neimeyer & Feixas, 1990). These authors concluded that long-term improvement can be expected only for those clients who consolidate skills through active practice within and between CT sessions, noting that ". . . [clients'] abilities to utilize cognitive self-monitoring and rational restructuring skills may be especially important following therapy termination, when . . . therapist assistance . . . [is] no longer available" (p. 289). A caution regarding their measure of cognitive skill is that DTRs were rated across all five columns via the use of a rudimentary three-point scale (0, 1, or 2) of proficiency. The restricted range of this scale might limit its utility for detecting substantial associations between level of skill in completing the DTR (or perhaps specific aspects of it, such as the "Rational Response" column) and therapeutic outcome. An important challenge for empirical research on CT is to refine further and validate measures of cognitive skill acquisition in order to test their hypothesized influence on therapy outcome.

### Evolving Perspectives on Measurement of Cognitive Skills

Understanding more precisely the role of cognitive skills training in therapeutic change might therefore require the design of more specific skills assessments. For example, in the same way that cognitive therapists are rated for competency on the Cognitive Therapy Scale (Young & Beck, 1980), so too could clients be rated on their abilities to solve cognitive dilemmas. This may be done either naturalistically (by videotaping a therapy session and rating the client's verbal content, behavior, and mood) or in the form of a "take-home test." Such measures ideally should simulate personally meaningful, quite stressful situations, for it seems likely that resistance to relapse is proportional to the level of skills one can employ at times of highest vulnerability (Haaga, 1990). For example, a student who becomes anxious and depressed during exam periods, then remits during summer vacation, cannot be said to be truly improved until she or he successfully applies coping skills during exams the following semester. To the extent that the cognitive therapist can test the client's skills by arranging for the client to be exposed to simulated and/or real high-risk stressors, a more definite assessment can be made of the client's resilience against relapse.

Toward this end, the Articulated Thoughts during Simulated Situations (ATSS; Davison, Robins, & Johnson, 1983) paradigm for cognitive assessment requires clients to *generate* responses (by thinking aloud) to simulated, experimentally controllable stimulus situations presented via audiotape. Recent research using this paradigm supported the view that depressed clients were more likely than a non-depressed psychiatric control group to verbalize thoughts indicative of the cognitive errors or biases (e.g., overgeneralization) predicted by cognitive theory in a negative, stressful simulated situation only (not in neutral or positive situations) (White, Davison, Haaga, & White, 1990). The situational specificity of this group difference lends support to the notion that laboratory simulations of stressful situations can provide a credible stimulus and thereby afford a useful assessment of cognitive responses to stress.

Similarly, the Ways of Responding Questionnaire (WOR; Barber & DeRubeis, 1989) has been developed in order to assess the quality of the client's cognitive coping responses to a series of standardized stressful events, in this case presented in writing. Research in progress is testing the relationship between WOR responses and short-term mood enhancement as well as long-term treatment outcome. The WOR, used perhaps in conjunction with a comprehensive scale for assessing proficiency in the use of the DTR, might shed more light on the actual cognitive processes in which CT clients are engaging in order to cope.

Ideally, measures such as the ATSS and WOR would be applied at times and in situations that are most salient to the client's problems. This calls to mind the importance of eliciting hot cognitions during the course of treatment, as well as the importance of formulating a detailed and idiographic case conceptualization for each client.

It is important to bear in mind the difference between having skills and using them. A critical, difficult first step is the development of more useful measures of the cognitive skills clients possess after CT, but we also need research on the determinants of their implementing these skills. Drawing on work in other areas of research (Bandura, 1986), Kavanagh and Wilson (1989) hypothesized that a critical determinant will be self-efficacy for using cognitive skills. That is, at any given level of skill development, clients who are more confident of their ability to use cognitive coping skills will persist more in trying to use these tactics and be more successful. Although the literature on prediction of response to CT suggests that positive findings are often difficult to replicate (Haaga, DeRubeis, Stewart, & Beck, in press), it is nevertheless grounds for cautious optimism that a self-efficacy measure developed by Kavanagh and Wilson (1989) was positively associated with maintenance of improvement in their study of CT for depression.

## CONCLUSIONS

In this chapter we have described the assessment and training of cognitive skills from the standpoint of Beck's cognitive therapy, and we have briefly reviewed research on these issues. It is reasonably well established that cognitive therapy can be a durably effective treatment program, and there is encouraging preliminary evidence that the skills training procedures discussed in this chapter contribute meaningfully to this effectiveness. Reaching a more definitive conclusion on the relevance of these skills will necessitate further developments in their assessment and further research on the mediation of change in cognitive therapy.

Besides such treatment research, we hope to see research on cognitive skills training as a preventive approach. If such an approach were to prove useful, more people may have the opportunity to develop the psychological wherewithal to cope with future stressors that could otherwise lead to full-blown disorders.

Finally, although it is appropriate to be cautious in interpreting the empirical status of cognitive skills training, we wish to conclude by conveying our enthusiasm for the immense potential power of such skills acquisition. Development of cognitive skills can open new doors to enhancing productivity and happiness for clients. Information that was once inaccessible (regarding new points of view, new ways of solving problems, and the like) is now readily available. There is less need to enlist the help of others, as these skills can be applied on one's own. The skills are highly generalizable in that people are capable of thinking virtually all the time in all situations. In this sense, the learning of cognitive reevaluation through the use of the DTR (for instance) need not remain merely an esoteric technique for use only in circumscribed situations. Rather, it can become virtually a way of life, a helpful resource for use during times of upset or indecision. Some clients even gain a feeling of status from learning "how to think like a scientist." Although the specific techniques involved in many skills-training approaches can seem mundane, logical analysis and empirical testing of the validity of one's perceptions strike many clients as being special learning opportunities that inspire motivation and lead to personal growth.

## NOTES

1. The virtues of eliciting hot cognitions notwithstanding, excessive negative affect can *interfere* with the application of higher order cognitive skills. Such difficulties are most vividly observed in borderline clients who self-mutilate in response to emotional pain. In such cases, it may be necessary to train the client assiduously to apply cognitive coping skills as *preparation* for the remaining work of therapy.

2. It is essential to note that these procedures do not constitute CT in its entirety. To the contrary, cognitive skills are likely to prove most helpful if taught in the context of (1) the behavioral skills often considered in CT (e.g., problem solving, social skills), (2) a healthy, positive therapeutic relationship in which the client perceives the therapist as empathic (Beck et al., 1979; Persons, Burns, & Perloff, 1988); and (3) a comprehensive case conceptualization (Persons, 1989; Safran, Vallis, Segal, & Shaw, 1986) to facilitate individually tailored, purposeful application of cognitive skills rather than the more undirected approach that can result if an adequate case conceptualization is lacking.

3. An automatic thought is a spontaneous, discrete thought associated with a situation the client perceives as upsetting. Often these thoughts are experienced as unintended and as compelling. Upon reevaluation, however, they may be found to be biased and unnecessarily contributing to emotional distress. Newman and Beck (1990) provide detailed suggestions regarding how to explain automatic thoughts to clients and how to train them to self-monitor automatic thoughts.

4. The notion that psychopathology is routinely associated with errors or distortions in thinking has been questioned on the basis of research suggesting that depression may actually correspond to *greater* accuracy in perceiving feedback from the environment (Alloy & Abramson, 1979, 1988). Evans and Hollon (1988) noted, however, that the "depressive" samples on which these "depressive realism" findings are based (relatively dysphoric students) may not resemble the more severely depressed clients commonly seen in clinical practice. This latter group may be the only ones showing negatively biased or distorted thinking.

Moreover, it is important to note that many relevant cognitions cannot readily be identified as accurate versus erroneous, for they concern matters (such as the client's future prospects for happiness) about which an objective reality is, for practical purposes, currently unknowable. In any event, it can be clinically productive to frame—for instance, jumping to a negative conclusion about such topics without considering other possibilities as an "error," even if a rigorous theoretical analysis would reveal such usage as imprecise.

## REFERENCES

Abramson, L. Y., Seligman, M. E. P., & Teasdale, J. (1978). Learned helplessness in humans: Critique and reformulation. *Journal of Abnormal Psychology, 87,* 49–74.

Alloy, L. B., & Abramson, L. Y. (1979). Judgment of contingency in depressed and non-depressed students: Sadder but wiser? *Journal of Experimental Psychology: General, 108,* 441–485.

Alloy, L. B., & Abramson, L. Y. (1988). Depressive realism: Four theoretical perspectives. In L. B. Alloy (Ed.), *Cognitive processes in depression* (pp. 223–265). New York: Guilford Press.

Bandura, A. (1986). *Social foundations of thought and action: A social cognitive theory.* Englewood Cliffs, NJ: Prentice-Hall.

Barber, J. P., & DeRubeis, R. J. (1989). On second thought: Where the action is in cognitive therapy for depression. *Cognitive Therapy and Research, 13,* 441–457.

Baron, J., Baron, J. H., Barber, J. P., & Nolen-Hoeksema, S. (1990). Rational thinking as a goal of therapy. *Journal of Cognitive Psychotherapy: An International Quarterly, 4,* 293–302.

Beck, A. T. (1967). *Depression: Clinical, experimental, and theoretical aspects.* New York: Hoeber.

Beck, A. T. (1970). The core problem in depression: The cognitive triad. In J. H. Masserman (Ed.), *Depression: Theories and therapies* (pp. 47–55). New York: Grune & Stratton.

Beck, A. T. (1976). *Cognitive therapy and the emotional disorders.* New York: International Universities Press.

Beck, A. T. (1987). Cognitive models of depression. *Journal of Cognitive Psychotherapy: An International Quarterly, 1,* 5–37.

Beck, A. T. (1991). Cognitive therapy as *the* integrative therapy: Comments on Alford and Norcross. *Journal of Psychotherapy Integration, 1,* 191–198.

Beck, A. T., & Clark, D. A. (1988). Anxiety and depression: An information processing perspective. *Anxiety Research, 1,* 23–36.

Beck, A. T., & Emery, G. (1977). *Cognitive therapy of substance abuse.* Philadelphia: Center for Cognitive Therapy.

Beck, A. T., Emery, G., & Greenberg, R. L. (1985). *Anxiety disorders and phobias: A cognitive perspective.* New York: Basic Books.

Beck, A. T., Freeman, A., & Associates (1990). *Cognitive therapy of personality disorders.* New York: Guilford Press.

Beck, A. T., & Greenberg, R. L. (1988). Cognitive therapy of panic disorder. In A. J. Frances & R. E. Hales (Eds.), *American Psychiatric Press Review of Psychiatry* (Vol. 7, pp. 571–583). Washington, DC: American Psychiatric Association.

Beck, A. T., Rush, A. J., Shaw, B. F., & Emery, G. (1979). *Cognitive therapy of depression.* New York: Guilford Press.

Beutler, L. E., & Guest, P. D. (1989). The role of cognitive change in psychotherapy. In A. Freeman, K. M. Simon, L. E. Beutler, & H. Arkowitz (Eds.), *Comprehensive handbook of cognitive therapy* (pp. 123–142). New York: Plenum Press.

Blackburn, I. M., & Eunson, K. M. (1989). A content analysis of thoughts and emotions elicited from depressed patients during cognitive therapy. *British Journal of Medical Psychology, 62,* 23–33.

Blackburn, I. M., Eunson, K. M., & Bishop, S. (1986). A two-year naturalistic follow-up of depressed patients treated with cognitive therapy, pharmacotherapy, and a combination of both. *Journal of Affective Disorders, 10,* 67–75.

Blaney, P. (1986). Affect and memory: A review. *Psychological Bulletin, 99,* 229–246.

Burns, D. D. (1980). *Feeling good: The new mood therapy.* New York: William Morrow.

Cacioppo, J. T., & Petty, R. E. (1981). Social psychological procedures for cognitive response assessment: The thought-listing techniques. In T. V. Merluzzi, C. R. Glass, & M. Genest (Eds.), *Cognitive assessment* (pp. 309–342). New York: Guilford Press.

Chor, P. N., Mercier, M. A., & Halper, I. S. (1988). Use of cognitive therapy for treatment of a patient suffering from a bipolar affective disorder. *Journal of Cognitive Psychotherapy: An International Quarterly, 2,* 51–58.

Ciminero, A. R., Nelson, R. O., & Lipinski, D. P. (1977). Self-monitoring procedures. In A. R. Ciminero, K. S. Calhoun, & H. E. Adams (Eds.), *Handbook of behavioral assessment* (pp. 195–232). New York: Wiley.

Clark, D. A. (1988). The validity of measures of cognition: A review of the literature. *Cognitive Therapy and Research, 12,* 1–20.

Clark, D. A., Feldman, J., & Channon, S. (1989). Dysfunctional thinking in anorexia and bulimia nervosa. *Cognitive Therapy and Research, 13,* 377–387.

Clark, D. M. (1988). A cognitive model of panic attacks. In S. Rachman & J. D. Maser (Eds.), *Panic: Psychological perspectives* (pp. 71–89). Hillsdale, NJ: Lawrence Erlbaum.

Davison, G. C., Robins, C., & Johnson, M. K. (1983). Articulated thoughts during simulated situations: A paradigm for studying cognition in emotion and behavior. *Cognitive Therapy and Research, 7,* 17–40.

Dobson, K. S. (1989). A meta-analysis of the efficacy of cognitive therapy for depression. *Journal of Consulting and Clinical Psychology, 57,* 414–419.

Dobson, K. S., & Breiter, H. J. (1983). Cognitive assessment of depression: Reliability and validity of three measures. *Journal of Abnormal Psychology, 92,* 107–109.

Dobson, K. S., & Shaw, B. F. (1986). Cognitive assessment with major depressive disorders. *Cognitive Therapy and Research, 10,* 13–29.

D'Zurilla, T. J., & Goldfried, M. R. (1971). Problem solving and behavior modification. *Journal of Abnormal Psychology, 78,* 107–126.

Eaves, G., & Rush, A. J. (1984). Cognitive patterns in symptomatic and remitted unipolar major depression. *Journal of Abnormal Psychology, 93,* 31–40.

Edgette, J. S., & Prout, M. F. (1989). Cognitive and behavioral approaches to the treatment of anorexia nervosa. In A. Freeman, K. M. Simon, L. E. Beutler, & H. Arkowitz (Eds.), *Comprehensive handbook of cognitive therapy* (pp. 367–384). New York: Plenum Press.

Edwards, D. J. A. (1989). Cognitive restructuring through guided imagery: Lessons from Gestalt therapy. In A. Freeman, K. M. Simon, L. E. Beutler, & H. Arkowitz (Eds.), *Comprehensive handbook of cognitive therapy* (pp. 283–298). New York: Plenum Press.

Elkin, I., Shea, M. T., Watkins, J. T., Imber, S. D., Sotsky, S. M., Collins, J. F., Glass, D. R., Pilkonis, P. A., Leber, W. R., Docherty, J. P., Fiester, S. J., & Parloff, M. B. (1989). National Institute of Mental Health Treatment of

Depression Collaborative Research Program: General effectiveness of treatments. *Archives of General Psychiatry, 46,* 971–982.

Epstein, N., & Baucom, D. H. (1989). Cognitive-behavioral marital therapy. In A. Freeman, K. M. Simon, L. E. Beutler, & H. Arkowitz (Eds.), *Comprehensive handbook of cognitive therapy* (pp. 491–513). New York: Plenum Press.

Evans, M. D., & Hollon, S. D. (1988). Patterns of personal and causal inference: Implications for the cognitive therapy of depression. In L. B. Alloy (Ed.), *Cognitive processes in depression* (pp. 344–377). New York: Guilford Press.

Freeman, A., & Leaf, R. C. (1989). Cognitive therapy applied to personality disorders. In A. Freeman, K. M. Simon, L. E. Beutler, & H. Arkowitz (Eds.), *Comprehensive handbook of cognitive therapy.* New York: Plenum Press.

Gallwey, W. T. (1974). *The inner game of tennis.* New York: Random House.

Garner, D. M. (1987). Psychotherapy outcome research with bulimia nervosa. *Psychotherapy and Psychosomatics, 48,* 129–140.

Goldfried, M. R., & Davison, G. C. (1976). *Clinical behavior therapy.* New York: Holt, Rinehart & Winston.

Goldfried, M. R., Decenteceo, E. T., & Weinberg, L. (1974). Systematic rational restructuring as a self-control technique. *Behavior Therapy, 5,* 247–254.

Goldfried, M. R., Padawer, W., & Robins, C. (1984). Social anxiety and the semantic structure of heterosocial interaction. *Journal of Abnormal Psychology, 93,* 87–97.

Greenberg, L. S., & Safran, J. D. (1989). Emotion in psychotherapy. *American Psychologist, 44,* 19–29.

Haaga, D. A. F. (1990). Issues in relating self-efficacy to smoking relapse: Importance of an ''Achilles' heel'' situation and of prior quitting experience. *Journal of Substance Abuse, 2,* 191–200.

Haaga, D. A. F., & Davison, G. C. (1989). Slow progress in rational-emotive therapy outcome research: Etiology and treatment. *Cognitive Therapy and Research, 13,* 495–508.

Haaga, D. A. F., & Davison, G. C. (1991). Cognitive change methods. In F. H. Kanfer & A. P. Goldstein (Eds.), *Helping people change: A textbook of methods,* 4th ed. (pp. 298–308). Elmsford, NY: Pergamon Press.

Haaga, D. A. F., DeRubeis, R. J., Stewart, B. L., & Beck, A. T. (1991). Relationship of intelligence with cognitive therapy outcome. *Behaviour Research and Therapy, 29,* 277–281.

Haaga, D. A. F., Dyck, M. J., & Ernst, D. (1991). Empirical status of cognitive theory of depression. *Psychological Bulletin, 110,* 215–236.

Hamilton, E. W., & Abramson, L. Y. (1983). Cognitive patterns in major depressive disorder: A longitudinal study in a hospital setting. *Journal of Abnormal Psychology, 92,* 173–184.

Harrell, T. H., & Ryon, N. B. (1983). Cognitive-behavioral assessment of depression: Clinical validation of the Automatic Thoughts Questionnaire. *Journal of Consulting and Clinical Psychology, 51,* 721–725.

Heimberg, R. G. (1989). Cognitive and behavioral treatments for social phobia: A critical analysis. Special issue: Social phobia. *Clinical Psychology Review, 9,* 107–128.

Hollon, S. D., DeRubeis, R. J., & Evans, M. D. (1987). Causal mediation of change in treatment for depression: Discriminating between nonspecificity and noncausality. *Psychological Bulletin, 102,* 139–149.

Hollon, S. D., & Kendall, P. C. (1980). Cognitive self-statements in depression: Development of an automatic thoughts questionnaire. *Cognitive Therapy and Research, 4,* 383–395.

Hollon, S. D., & Kriss, M. R. (1984). Cognitive factors in clinical research and practice. *Clinical Psychology Review, 3,* 35–76.

Hollon, S. D., & Najavits, L. (1988). Review of empirical studies of cognitive therapy. In A. J. Frances & R. E. Hales (Eds.), *American Psychiatric Press Review of Psychiatry* (Vol. 7, pp. 643–666). Washington, DC: American Psychiatric Press.

Hurlburt, R. T. (1980). Validation and correlation of thought sampling with retrospective measures. *Cognitive Therapy and Research, 4,* 235–238.

Ingram, R. E., & Kendall, P. C. (1986). Cognitive clinical psychology: Implications of an information-processing perspective. In R. E. Ingram (Ed.), *Information processing approaches to clinical psychology* (pp. 3–21). Orlando, FL: Academic Press.

Ingram, R. E., Lumry, A. E., Cruet, D., & Sieber, W. (1987). Attentional processes in depressive disorders. *Cognitive Therapy and Research, 11,* 351–360.

Kanter, N. J., & Goldfried, M. R. (1979). Relative effectiveness of rational restructuring and self-control desensitization in the reduction of interpersonal anxiety. *Behavior Therapy, 10,* 472–490.

Kavanagh, D. J., & Wilson, P. H. (1989). Prediction of outcome with group cognitive therapy for depression. *Behaviour Research and Therapy, 27,* 333–343.

Kazdin, A. E. (1980). *Research design in clinical psychology.* New York: Harper and Row.

Landau, R. J., & Goldfried, M. R. (1981). The assessment of schemata: A unifying framework for cognitive, behavioral, and traditional assessment. In P. C. Kendall, & S. D. Hollon (Eds.), *Assessment strategies for cognitive-behavioral interventions* (pp. 363–399). New York: Academic Press.

Likert, R., & Quasha, W. H. (1970). *Revised Minnesota Paper Form Board Test.* New York: The Psychological Corporation.

Marlatt, G. A., & Gordon, J. R. (Eds.). (1985). *Relapse prevention: Maintenance strategies in the treatment of addictive behaviors.* New York: Guilford Press.

Mattick, R. P., & Peters, L. (1988). Treatment of severe social phobia. Effects of guided exposure with and without cognitive restructuring. *Journal of Consulting and Clinical Psychology, 56,* 251–260.

McDermut, W., Haaga, D. A. F., & Shayne, V. T. (1991). Schemata and smoking relapse. *Behavior Therapy, 22,* 423–434.

Merluzzi, T. V., & Boltwood, M. D. (1989). Cognitive assessment. In A. Freeman, K. M. Simon, L. E. Beutler, & H. Arkowitz (Eds.), *Comprehensive handbook of cognitive therapy* (pp. 249–266). New York: Plenum Press.

Metalsky, G. I., Abramson, L. Y., Seligman, M. E. P., Semmel, A., & Peterson, C. (1982). Attributional styles and life events in the classroom: Vulnerability and invulnerability to depressive mood reactions. *Journal of Personality and Social Psychology, 43,* 612–617.

Neimeyer, R. A., & Feixas, G. (1990). The role of homework and skill acquisition in the outcome of group cognitive therapy for depression. *Behavior Therapy, 21,* 281–292.

Neimeyer, R. A., Twentyman, C. T., & Prezant, D. (1985). Cognitive and interpersonal group therapies for depression: A progress report. *The Cognitive Behaviorist, 7,* 21–22.

Newman, C. F. (1989). Where's the evidence? A clinical tip. *International Cognitive Therapy Newsletter, 5,* 4, 8.

Newman, C. F. (1991). Cognitive therapy and the facilitation of affect: Two case illustrations. *Journal of Cognitive Psychotherapy: An International Quarterly, 5,* 305–316.

Newman, C. F., & Beck, A. T. (1990). Cognitive therapy of the affective disorders. In B. Wolman & G. Stricker (Eds.), *Depressive disorders: Facts, theories, and treatment methods.* New York: Wiley.

Newman, C. F., Beck, J. S., Beck, A. T., & Tran, G. Q. (1990). *Efficacy of cognitive therapy in reducing panic attacks and medication.* Paper presented at the Annual Meeting of the Association for the Advancement of Behavior Therapy, San Francisco.

Nezu, A. M., Nezu, C. M., & Perri, M. G. (1989). *Problem-solving therapy for depression: Theory, research, and clinical guidelines:* New York: Wiley.

Nisbett, R. E., & Ross, L. (1980). *Human inference: Strategies and shortcomings of social judgement.* Englewood Cliffs, NJ: Prentice-Hall.

Novaco, R. W. (1979). The cognitive regulation of anger and stress. In P. C. Kendall & S. D. Hollon (Eds.), *Cognitive-behavioral interventions: Theory, research, and procedures* (pp. 241–285). New York: Academic Press.

Parks, C. W., Jr., & Hollon, S. D. (1988). Cognitive assessment. In A. S. Bellack, & M. Hersen (Eds.), *Behavioral assessment: A practical handbook,* 3rd ed. (pp. 161–212). Elmsford, NY: Pergamon Press.

Persons, J. B. (1989). *Cognitive therapy in practice: A case formulation approach.* New York: W. W. Norton.

Persons, J. B., & Burns, D. D. (1985). Mechanisms of action of cognitive therapy: The relative contribution of technical and interpersonal interventions. *Cognitive Therapy and Research, 9,* 539–551.

Persons, J. B., Burns, D. D., & Perloff, J. M. (1988). Predictors of dropout and outcome in cognitive therapy for depression in a private practice setting. *Cognitive Therapy and Research, 12,* 557–575.

Peterson, C., & Seligman, M. E. P. (1984). Causal explanations as a risk factor for depression: Theory and evidence. *Psychological Review, 91,* 347–374.

Peterson, C., Semmel, A., von Baeyer, C., Abramson, L. Y., Metalsky, G. I., & Seligman, M. E. P. (1982). The Attributional Style Questionnaire. *Cognitive Therapy and Research, 6,* 287–299.

Plath, S. (1971). *The bell jar.* New York: Bantam Books.

Primakoff, L., Epstein, N., & Covi, L. (1986). Homework compliance: An uncontrolled variable in cognitive therapy outcome research. *Behavior Therapy, 17,* 433–446.

Riskind, J. H., & Rholes, W. S. (1984). Cognitive accessibility and the capacity of cognitions to predict future depression: A theoretical note. *Cognitive Therapy and Research, 8,* 1–12.

Robins, C. J. (1988). Attributions and depression: Why is the literature so inconsistent? *Journal of Personality and Social Psychology, 54,* 880–889.

Rosch, E. (1978). Principles of categorization. In E. Rosch & R. B. Lloyd (Eds.), *Cognition and categorization.* Hillsdale, NJ: Lawrence Erlbaum.

Ross, S. M., Gottfredson, D. K., Christensen, P., & Weaver, R. (1986). Cognitive self-statements in depression: Findings across clinical populations. *Cognitive Therapy and Research, 10,* 159–166.

Safran, J. D., & Greenberg, L. S. (1982). Cognitive appraisal and re-appraisal: Implications for clinical practice. *Cognitive Therapy and Research, 6,* 251–258.

Safran, J. D., Vallis, T. M., Segal, Z. V., & Shaw, B. F. (1986). Assessment of core cognitive processes in cognitive therapy. *Cognitive Therapy and Research, 10,* 509–526.

Segal, Z. V., & Shaw, B. F. (1986). Cognition in depression: A reappraisal of Coyne and Gotlib's critique. *Cognitive Therapy and Research, 10,* 671–693.

Segal, Z. V., & Shaw, B. F. (1988). Cognitive assessment: Issues and methods. In K. S. Dobson (Ed.), *Handbook of cognitive-behavioral therapies* (pp. 39–81). New York: Guilford Press.

Seligman, M. E. P., Abramson, L. Y., Semmel, A., & von Baeyer, C. (1979). Depressive attributional style. *Journal of Abnormal Psychology, 88,* 242–247.

Shelton, J. L., & Levy, R., and contributors (1981). *Behavioral assignments and treatment compliance: A handbook of clinical strategies.* Champaign, IL: Research Press.

Simons, A. D., Murphy, G. E., Levine, J. L., & Wetzel, R. D. (1986). Cognitive therapy and pharmacotherapy for depression: Sustained improvement over one year. *Archives of General Psychiatry, 43,* 43–48.

Singer, J. L., & Antrobus, J. S. (1972). Daydreaming, imaginal processes, and personality: A normative study. In P. W. Sheehan (Ed.), *The function and nature of imagery* (pp. 175–202). New York: Academic Press.

Tversky, A., & Kahneman, D. (1974). Judgment under uncertainty: Heuristics and biases. *Science, 185,* 1124–1131.

Weishaar, M. E., & Beck, A. T. (1986). Cognitive therapy. In W. Dryden & W. Golden (Eds.), *Cognitive-behavioral approaches to psychotherapy* (pp. 61–91). London: Harper & Row.

Weissman, A. N., & Beck, A. T. (1978). *Development and validation of the Dysfunctional Attitudes Scale: A preliminary investigation.* Paper presented at the Annual Meeting of the American Educational Research Association, Toronto, Canada.

White, J., Davison, G. C., Haaga, D. A. F., & White, K. (1990). *Cognitive bias in the articulated thoughts of depressed and nondepressed psychiatric patients.* Paper presented at the Annual Meeting of the Association for Advancement of Behavior Therapy, San Francisco.

Worthington, E. L. (1986). Client compliance with homework directives during counseling. *Journal of Counseling Psychology, 33,* 124–130.

Young, J. (1990). *Cognitive therapy for personality disorders: A schema-focused approach.* Sarasota, FL: Professional Resource Exchange.

Young, J., & Beck, A. (1980). *Cognitive Therapy Scale: Rating manual.* Unpublished manuscript. Philadelphia: Center for Cognitive Therapy.

# CHAPTER 7

# PROBLEM-SOLVING SKILLS

William O'Donohue
James Noll

In recent years the construct of problem solving has sparked a great deal of interest in many contexts. Within psychology, cognitive psychologists (e.g., Simon, 1955; Sternberg, 1985) have studied problem solving in an attempt to understand intelligent human behavior as well as to create systems capable of artificial intelligence. Interestingly, Sternberg (1982) in an attempt to understand what nonpsychologists (i.e., subjects sampled from supermarkets and subway stations) take "intelligence" to be, found that individuals tended to rate practical problem solving (i.e., "sizing up the situation accurately," "getting to the heart of the problem," and "reasoning logically") as one of the most important components of intelligence. Clinical psychologists (e.g., Blechman, 1976; D'Zurilla, 1986; Jacobson & Anderson, 1980; Kanfer & Busemeyer, 1982) have attempted to explicate and apply models of problem solving in an attempt to remediate deficits in this skill that seem to be implicated in diverse clinical problems such as depression, obesity, marital problems, agoraphobia, and conduct disorders. This chapter will review some of the basic theory, research, and applications regarding problem solving and will focus on the clinical applications of problem solving. This literature is quite large, and therefore what follows will only be a selective sampling and not an exhaustive review.

## THE INTELLECTUAL CONTEXT OF PROBLEM SOLVING

### Evolution, Physiology, and Problem Solving

Increasingly, psychologists are explicating the relevance of neo-Darwinian evolutionary theory for understanding human behavior (Campbell, 1987; Skinner, 1984; Staddon, 1983; Symons, 1987). Neo-Darwinian evolutionary theory is interpreted as indicating that all organisms have faced, been shaped by, and continue to face and be shaped by two principal problems: survival and reproduction. These overarching problems give rise to a number of subproblems, such as finding food, extracting nutrients, avoiding predators, and finding mates, which, in turn, give rise to further subproblems.

A major implication of neo-Darwinian theory is that the human body and its functioning and behav ioral dispositions are complex problem-solving attempts that have evolved through the process of natural selection (Popper, 1979):

> Animals, and even plants, are problem-solvers. And they solve their problems by the method of competitive tentative solutions and the elimination of error. The tentative solutions which animals and plants incorporate into their anatomy and their behaviour are biological analogues of theories; and vice versa: theories correspond (as do many exosomatic products such as honeycombs, and specially exosomatic tools, such as spiders' webs) to endosomatic organs and their ways of functioning. Just like theories, organs and their functions are tentative adaptations to the world we live in. . . . New behavior or organs may also lead to the emergence of new problems. And in this way they may influence the further course of evolution. (p. 145)

From this evolutionary perspective, biological and behavioral dispositions are construed as having arisen as a result of their problem-solving value. The characteristics of things that contain nutrients pose problems that have been resolved by, for example, the structure, variety, and placement of teeth; the problem of speedy responses to potential threats (e.g., orientation, focused attention, and quick energy for flight or fight) by the orienting reflexes and the diverse effects of the autonomic nervous system; the problems of locating food and predators, and avoiding impenetrable objects, which have been resolved by photosensitivity (e.g., photosynthesis and phototropisms in plants, and sight in humans). Campbell (1987) and Wachtershauser (1987) have suggested that we respond to only a very small range (roughly 400–700 nanometers) of the electromagnetic spectrum because evolutionarily this range has produced a new source of food and this is the only range in which photosynthesis can occur (longer wavelengths have insufficient energy to fuel the photochemical reaction, and shorter wavelengths destroy proteins and DNA). Moreover, in a fortuitous convergence, it is this range in which the transparent generally coincides with the penetrable, and therefore the selective advantages of distance reception and the avoidance of impenetrable objects occur.

Staddon (1983) has surveyed the manners in which simple orientation mechanisms such as geotropisms (i.e., movement influenced by gravity), phototropisms (movement influenced by light), and chemotaxes (movement with respect to a chemical gradient) assist relatively simple organisms such as plants, bacteria, and paramecia to solve problems such as finding food and escaping from noxious stimulation. More complex organisms, constitutive of this complexity, have other physiologically based mechanisms (other reflexes, and the abilities to be conditioned) to solve these and other problems. Thus, an understanding of evolution and its problem context can serve as an important source of information for understanding the physical structure, functioning, abilities, and constraints for humans. This is also important as physiologically based dispositions that were once selectively advantageous (e.g., a sweet tooth—or, somewhat more technically, the propensity for sweet substances to function as primary reinforcers) may now, for organisms that are in new (food-rich) environments (a relatively unusual evolutionary situation), likely lead to new problems (e.g., obesity).

Skinner (1984) has suggested that these contingencies of survival provide ultimate explanations; that is, they explicate remote parts of the causal chain. Skinner, in his later writings (e.g., Skinner, 1984), also has suggested that the ability to be conditioned is itself an evolutionary product retained because of its selective advantages. Moreover, operant conditioning (i.e., environmental selection by consequences) is a homologue of natural selection that is advantageous because selection occurs in shorter time frames and is more plastic than neo-Darwinian selection.

Thus, in an important sense, all living organisms are simply complex attempts to solve a variety of problems. This evolutionary problem solving provides a valuable perspective for understanding why we are the way we are and how we came to be this way. An important implication of this view is that we should expect that there are additional problems that need to be addressed. The ubiquity of problems comes from several sources. First, natural selection does not require perfect solutions but merely solutions that are not significantly worse than the competition and are sufficient to resolve the threat to survival or reproduction. Thus, problem "solutions" with significant error (e.g., color blindness, cavities) can endure and give rise to further problem-solving needs. Second, problems endure because the environment keeps changing, and therefore new selective mechanisms and problems arise. Food-rich environments now may be selecting out (e.g., through coronary heart disease) those who possess a good deal of proficiency in energy storage. Again, new problems emerge. Finally, problems exist because evolution is fundamentally competitive: Organisms are competing for scarce resources (e.g., healthy mates), and therefore this competition creates problems, such as how to "win" over competitors for the attraction of a good mate. The problems that clients present to helping professionals can be seen in part as problems that are produced and can be ultimately understood by this evolutionary context.

According to Popper (1979), the major difference between the problem solving of humans and that of subhumans is that for animals death and suffering constitute the major feedback in problem solving and error elimination, whereas humans can advance theories and arrange experiments (error-eliminating attempts) so that our (mistaken) theories and hypotheses can die in our stead. Of course, in order for this to happen, humans must actively seek criticism of their theories and beliefs and must test these critically—that is, attempt to falsify them. This leads us now to a discussion of problem solving and science.

## Science as Problem Solving

Although consilences in philosophy must be cautiously drawn and interpreted (O'Donohue & Smith, 1992), there is an important stream of modern philosophy of science that takes science to be essentially a problem-solving activity (Kuhn, 1970; Lakatos, 1970; Laudan, 1977; Popper, 1979). These philosophers, of course, differ in important respects regarding the details of this problem-solving process, but nonetheless agree that to understand science one must understand problem solving. This development is important not only because as psychologists and mental health professionals we commonly view ourselves as producing and consuming science and thus should understand science properly, but also because it is important to understand the exact nature of science given that, in recent years, several influential clinical theorists (e.g., Beck, 1976; Mahoney, 1977) have attempted to teach clients to think more scientifically as a form of therapy for psychological problems. This move could be defended in part on the grounds that science has produced a historically unprecedented efficient and productive method for solving intellectual, technical, and practical problems; therefore, it might be prudent to attempt to learn its essence and apply its methods to more personal problems of living. To be valid, however, any such application would have to capture the essence of science. As we shall see, this is no easy task, as there is fundamental disagreement about this important matter.

Popper (1979) was the first philosopher of science to suggest that science is essentially a problem-solving activity. According to the neo-Popperian philosopher of science, Koertge (1980):

> Scientific problems arise when our expectations are violated, when what we consider to be regularities call for a deeper explanation, when two previously disparate fields look as if they could be unified, or when a good scientific theory clashes with our familiar metaphysical framework. (p. 347)

Popper stated that the growth of science could be represented by the following scheme: $P_1 \rightarrow TS \rightarrow EE \rightarrow P_2$. An initial problem ($P_1$) gives rise to a tentative solution (TS), which gives rise to error-eliminating tests (EE), which give rise to a new problem ($P_2$). Popper (1963) has stated that science begins and ends with problems. It begins with problems in that:

> The belief that we can start with pure observations alone, without anything in the nature of a theory is absurd. . . . Twenty five years ago I tried to bring home the same point to a group of physics students in Vienna by beginning a lecture with the following instructions: "Take pencil and paper; carefully observe, and write down what you have observed." They asked of course, *what* I wanted them to observe. . . . Observation is always selection. It needs a chosen object, a definite task, an interest, a point of view, a problem. (p. 46)

Good scientific inquiry influences problems to evolve into different and deeper problems. According to Popper, good scientific inquiry proceeds by conjecturing a solution to a problem, clearly specifying what possible empirical observations would falsify the conjecture, and then performing observations to determine if these empirical results actually obtain.

Thomas Kuhn (1970), Imre Lakatos (1970), and Larry Laudan (1977) are three other influential philosophers and historians of science who have accounts that construe science as a problem-solving activity. Kuhn found fault with Popper's emphases on falsification and "revolution in permanence." According to Kuhn, these notions do not adequately capture what Kuhn took to be the historical fact of relative stability in science. Kuhn (1970) spoke of "puzzles" rather than problems and defined *puzzles* as "that special category of problems that can serve to test ingenuity or skills in solution" (p. 36). Interestingly, Kuhn assumes that it is highly likely for puzzles to have solutions and states: ". . . the really pressing problems, e.g., a cure for cancer or the design of a lasting peace, are often not puzzles at all, largely because they may not have any solution'' (pp. 36–37). Here we see a distinction of potential importance to clinical psychology that we will address later: the estimated probability that a problem can be solved.

In brief, Kuhn (1970) maintains that normal or paradigmatic science emerges from a immature or preparadigmatic period when there is agreement about what are legitimate and well-formed problems, proper methods of inquiry, and acceptable standards of solution. Normal science emerges after some notable puzzle solution, and subsequent normal science consists of using this puzzle solution as an exemplar for the solution of other puzzles. Revolutions occur and paradigms change when the anomalies of the old paradigm (i.e., puzzles that have resisted solution) appear able to be resolved using a new paradigm and new exemplars of puzzle solving. Kuhn's conception of science has been extremely influential on psychologists (Coleman & Salamon, 1988), but the reader is referred to Gholson and Barker (1985), Lakatos and Musgrave (1970), and O'Donohue (1993) for a critical evaluation of Kuhn.

Lakatos's (1970) account of science can be taken as an attempt to save the historical accuracy of Kuhn and at the same time the value of the normative claims of Popper's falsifactory account. Lakatos argues that scientific pursuits are conducted within a research program. Research programs consist of a hard core of metaphysical and theoretical postulates that are defended against contradictory findings, as well as a positive heuristic, which is a rough plan for making increasingly sophisticated models of the phenomena to be explained. Lakatos appraises research programs by whether there are progressive or degenerating problemshifts. A theoretically progressive problemshift occurs when a new theory has some excess empirical content over its predecessor, and an empirically progressive problemshift occurs when that excess empirical prediction is corroborated. A degenerative problemshift occurs when the new theory is ad hoc (not derived from the positive heuristic) and when it makes no new predictions.

Finally, Laudan (1977) suggests that the goal of science is to solve two basic types of cognitive problems—empirical and conceptual. Theories are evaluated according to their effectiveness at problem solving, which is a function of both the number and the importance of the problems solved as well as a negative function of the number of empirical

anomalies or conceptual problems generated. Laudan (1977) defines an empirical problem as ''anything about the natural world which strikes us as odd, or otherwise in need of explanation'' (p. 15). Conceptual problems concern ambiguity, circularity, self-contradiction, inconsistency with putative facts or valued methodology or accepted world views, and, finally, problems created by interests in theory unification and reduction. Progress is defined as an increase in problem-solving effectiveness. Laudan's account should be directly contrasted with a more positivistic account that takes the aim of science to be acquiring knowledge or truth.

## Summary

Thus, several influential philosophers of science view science as essentially a problem-solving activity. As science has been associated with an historically unprecedented growth of knowledge, clinical psychologists (Beck, 1976; Mahoney, 1977) have plausibly hypothesized that teaching clients to think scientifically might help these individuals with their problems in living. These therapies are, according to these accounts of science, essentially problem-solving skill interventions. If these philosophers of science are correct, then an important part of the content of these interventions should be explicit training in problem solving. Although we have reviewed the roles of problem solving in evolution and in science, we have yet to discuss the specifics of how problem solving occurs. Part of the scientist-practitioner model indicates that clinical practice should be influenced by and informed from basic science. We turn now to more specific accounts of problem solving largely developed within experimental psychology.

## THE EXPERIMENTAL PSYCHOLOGY OF PROBLEM SOLVING

In examining the vast experimental literature on problem solving, four principal approaches will be explicated: the Gestalt approach, the computational approach, the behavior-analytic approach, and the subjective probability approach.

## The Gestalt Approach

The earliest systematic experimental analysis of problem solving began with the Gestalt psychologists in the late 1920s, and extending until the early 1960s (e.g., Dunker, 1945; Koffka, 1931; Kohler, 1927; Wertheimer, 1959). This approach emphasized the organizational properties of cognitive activity involved in problem solving (Greeno, 1978). The Gestalt psychologists approached problem solving in the same manner in which they approached perception; that is, the solution of a problem involves the repeated combination of the problem elements until the integrated solution, or Gestalt, results (Best, 1992). According to the Gestalt psychologists, problem solving occurs in stages, in which the perception of the problem set changes and is discontinuous with that of previous stages. Citing Wallas (1926), Best (1992, p. 443) outlined the stages of problem solving that the Gestalt psychologists recognized:

1. *Preparation.* In the preparation stage of problem solving, the solver has recognized that a problem exists, and some preliminary attempts at understanding and solving the problem have been made.
2. *Incubation.* If the preliminary attempts fail, the solver may then put the problem aside for a while. At least on a conscious level, the thinker is no longer working on the task. However, at some unconscious level, work proceeds.
3. *Illumination.* Illumination refers to the famous flash of *insight* that ends the unconscious work and brings the answer to the surface of consciousness.
4. *Verification.* The verification stage refers to the confirmation of the insight. Generally, this stage is the least complicated and is usually nothing more than a simple checking to make sure that the insight has worked.

The solution of a problem involves the progression through these four stages in a linear and nonrecursive manner.

Of these four stages of problem solving, the incubation stage has received perhaps the most empirical attention. An early example is Katona's (1940) study. In this experiment, subjects were presented familiar ''matchstick'' puzzles in which the subjects were asked to rearrange patterns of matchsticks into a desired grouping. The subjects were divided into three groups: (1) a memory group, which was given the answer to the problem and told to memorize it; (2) an insight group, which was given special hints to solve the problem; and (3) a control group, which was not given any assistance. Subjects were tested at one week and three weeks after training. The results showed that the insight group performed much better than the memory group on novel trials. This was taken to indicate that the subjects in the insight group acquired an understanding of the problem structure and were able to achieve insight on novel trials.

Gestalt psychologists also emphasized the importance of problem representation in problem solving (Best, 1992). Problem-solving ability, then, is a function of good or efficient problem representation. This notion was echoed in later research on expert systems and in the computational approach. For example, de Groot (1966) exposed a chess configuration to novice and expert chess players for five seconds. The results indicated that the expert chess players were able to correctly recall the configurations 91% of the time, while the novice chess players could recall the correct configuration only 41% of the time. In addition, the expert players reproduced the configuration in ''chunks'' of four to five pieces at a time, whereas the novice players did not.

Although the importance of problem representation has survived, many of the Gestalt constructs involved in problem solving have not, and other criticisms have relegated the Gestalt approach to the wayside. Foremost is the lack of empirical support and the failure to produce a general model of human problem solving (e.g., Best, 1992; Greeno, 1978; Rachlin, 1989). Others had difficulty with the notion of necessary (unconscious) incubation and resulting illumination stage. Green (1966) stated this position quite succinctly:

> The salient feature of the model is incubation followed by inspiration. If a problem is solved in a straightforward manner by the solver, there is neither incubation nor inspiration, and the model is empty. Further, the nature of incubation is obscure. If incubation is merely leaving the problem, we have all incubated many problems that have never hatched. Probably the subject must return to the problem intentionally, and cases of unconscious inspiration are exaggerated. (p. 12)

Furthermore, more recent researchers and theorists have eschewed the discontinuous nature of Gestalt problem-solving stages and have, in turn, espoused and provided evidence for the continuous nature of problem solving performance (Best, 1992).

## The Computational Approach

The failure of Gestalt psychology to produce a successful model of human problem solving led to the dominance of behavioral and computational models of problem solving in the 1950s. The information-processing approach to problem solving began when Newell, Shaw, and Simon (1958) described a theory of problem solving based on concepts derived from computer operations. In viewing problem solving as a continuous process, this approach posited that problem solving occurs through a set of, though not necessarily successive, stages. In the most general case, problem solving consists of the transformation of a situation from an initial state to an end, or goal, state by means of a set of operations (e.g., Cohen, 1983). The first stage consists of problem definition or representation. In this stage, the "problem space" is defined; this involves the delineation of the initial and goal states. Cognitive psychologists also distinguish between well-defined problems and ill-defined problems (Reitman, 1964). A well-defined problem begins with a clearly specified start state and clearly defined goals. If one or both of these are not precisely defined, then the problem is said to be ill defined.

One representation called "task environment" attempts to explicate an array of all possible representations of the problem in a neutral way. According to Newell and Simon (1972), the task environment consists of the subject's representation of the problem in the problem space. In complex problem situations, the problem space is often a subset of the task environment. The problem space consists of a collection of nodes that stand for particular states of knowledge. The nodes are linked by operators that convert one node into another. Thus, in this model, problem solving consists of moving through the nodes of the problem space. Effectiveness is determined by two major variables: the quality of the problem space and the mode of search. The problem solver is searching for a solution path—a series of knowledge states— that leads through the problem space. In their empirical work, Newell and Simon suggest that solvers tend to work forward, moving from the initial knowledge state to the goal state, and use two general heuristics, means–end analysis and subgoal analysis.

In the second stage of the computational model, operators are selected. The operators, or operations, are chosen because they are believed to transform the initial state or to produce the goal state. In the third stage, operators chosen during the second stage are affected. In the final stage, the current state is evaluated against the goal state. If the current state is congruent with the goal state, a solution is surmised; otherwise, stages 2 and 3 are reimplemented. According to Greeno (1978), the major advantage of an information-processing approach to problem solving, especially over a behavioral approach, is the detailed analysis of the problem-solving performance and the more detailed understanding of the cognitive processes involved.

The computational approach is a derivative of the information-processing approach (e.g., Ernst & Newell, 1969; Newell & Simon, 1972; Simon, 1979). The computational approach is similar to the information-processing approach, but draws more heavily from computer modeling. The computational approach considers strategies, knowledge base, representation, and production systems (Cohen, 1983). Strategies involve the expansion of the diversity of problem-solving tactics. There are two principal types of strategies involved in problem solving: algorithms and heuristics. An *algorithm* is defined as a procedure that guarantees the solution of a problem. Each possible operation is attempted until the solution is found. In human problem solving, algorithms are rarely used, even when start states and goal states are well defined. For example, from the initial arrangement, chess has $10^{40}$ different potential outcomes, which precludes the production of an algorithm even by present-day computers (Best, 1992). Thus, algorithms may ensure problem solution, but they are highly inefficient and are only rarely found.

*Heuristics,* or loose guidelines for problem solution, on the other hand, are more efficient but do not guarantee problem solution. Much work on heuristics has been conducted by Newell and Simon (Newell & Simon, 1972; Simon, 1979). Heuristics are efficient to the extent that they represent the problem accurately. Although Newell and Simon proposed several ways in which people move through nodes (heuristics), two principal heuristics will be presented.

Subgoal analysis is a heuristic that involves dissecting the goal state into a number of component goal states. Creating subgoals affords a decrease in the amount of possible solutions each time a subgoal is met. Thus, if a problem has $m$ alternatives at each state and requires a series of $n$ levels in order to reach a solution, the problem has $m^n$ possible actions (Best, 1992). Knowing correctly the solution at one subgoal state reduces the possible number of actions to $m^{n/2}$.

A second heuristic is means–end analysis. In this heuristic, actions are taken such that the action selected brings the problem solver closer to the solution relative to other possible actions. In the terms of subgoal analysis, the operation of a means–end analysis would elicit the selection of an action that took the problem solver to the fifth level of a ten-level problem if the other potential actions lead the problem solver to, say, the third or fourth level. As with subgoal analysis, means–end analysis reduces the number of potential actions relative to the initial problem space.

The recognition of the knowledge base has emphasized the importance of previous learning experience and background information on current problem solving. The discussion of chunking in the previous section is relevant here. A good knowledge base allows the problem solver to recognize more and larger knowledge states. Chunking has the effect of reducing the number of potential actions to be taken as well as increasing the speed of recall.

Representation involves the recognition of isomorphic problems in order to expedite problem solution—that is, to identify heuristics. Thus, when problems are recognized as being similar or isomorphic, the selection of actions will be in accordance to actions that led to problem solution in the past. Again, the effect is to reduce the possible number of actions to be taken. However, humans often find it difficult to perceive isomorphic problem representations (Cohen, 1983).

The computational approach is not without its problems (Best, 1992). First, it has been argued that humans do not have access to higher mental operations such as problem-solving processes (Nisbett & Wilson, 1977). Second, much of the work conducted by Newell and Simon has employed artificial tasks that may not generalize to everyday problem solving in humans.

## The Behavior-Analytic Approach

Shortly after the computational approach to problem solving developed, learning theorists became interested in more complex behavior (Green, 1966). Behavioral analyses emphasized behavioral variability, in that raising the probability of improbable responses, by definition, is required for successful problem solving (Greeno, 1978). Most learning theorists posited that problem solving is simply a form of discrimination learning. This viewpoint was held, for example, by Skinner (1966). According to Skinner (1974):

> A person has a problem when some condition will be reinforcing but he lacks a response that will produce it. He will solve the problem when he emits such a response. . . . Solving a problem is, however, more than *emitting* the response which is the solution; it is a matter of taking steps to make that

response more probable, usually by changing the environment. (p. 123)

In general, Skinner (1966) posited that problem solving involved a change of behavior such that subjects must directly change either their behavior or their environment.

The explanation of problem solving as discrimination learning seems too general and, thus, empty. Although Skinner (1966) did not appear to be concerned about this difficulty, he recognized that "an exhaustive analysis of [problem-solving] techniques would coincide with an analysis of behavior as a whole" (pp. 225–226). In this passage, Skinner appears to be implying that all behavior is problem-solving behavior. We will return to this point shortly.

Skinner (1966) posited that problem solving involves the construction of useful discriminative stimuli. Indeed, Skinner held that verbal discriminative stimuli were easier to construct and were ultimately more useful. According to Skinner, most "statements of fact" could be reduced to a relation between stimuli and reinforcement. In any case, contingency-shaped and rule-governed problem solving are similar in that each involves the construction of discriminative stimuli that set the occasion for "solving" behavior to be emitted.

If problem solving involves the construction of useful discriminative stimuli, then one possible way to solve problems is behavior chaining (Skinner, 1966). A *behavior chain* is defined as a sequence of responses in which one response serves to set the occasion for the next response; that is, the response serves as a discriminative stimulus, in which the probability of the following response is increased (e.g., Ferster & Skinner, 1958).

Applied behavior analysts have used the concept of the behavior chain in producing complex forms of behavior through task analysis. Task analysis involves three steps (Cooper, Heron, & Howard, 1987). First, the task is analyzed such that the behavioral sequence is broken down into constituent units, after which its validity is assessed. Second, a baseline is conducted in which the subject's mastery of each component is assessed. Third, behavioral chain training is conducted in which the subject is taught the order of the component behaviors.

A common example of task analysis is the study conducted by Horner and Keilitz (1975). In this study, a developmentally disabled individual was taught to brush his teeth. The researchers first analyzed the task by observing the toothbrushing of staff and developmentally disabled individuals in order to produce the following behavioral components of toothbrushing:

1. Pick up and hold the toothbrush.
2. Wet the toothbrush.
3. Remove the cap from the toothpaste.
4. Apply the toothpaste to the brush.
5. Replace the cap on the toothpaste.
6. Brush the outside surfaces of the teeth.
7. Brush the biting surfaces of the teeth.
8. Brush the inside surfaces of the teeth.
9. Fill the cup with water.
10. Rinse the mouth.
11. Wipe the mouth.
12. Rinse the toothbrush.
13. Rinse the sink.
14. Put the equipment away.
15. Discard the disposables.

At this point, a distinction between judgment, decision, and choice may be beneficial. A decision always involves a judgment, although different theories place the locus at different places (Rachlin, 1989). Cognitive theories place the locus of judgment on internal processes. However, a judgment ultimately is a function of more global decision factors, in which a judgment may be an incomplete analysis of a problem (Rachlin, 1989). This is not to say that judgments are inconsequential, but that they occur early in the problem-solving sequence (Rachlin, 1989). In turn, choice may be construed to involve a consideration of alternative decisions. To the extent that problem solving involves weighing decisions, problem solving involves choice.

The early work of the Gestalt psychologists may, in some sense, be considered studies of choice behavior. Gestalt analyses of problem solving were at a molar level, similar to that of Tolman (1932, 1938; Rachlin, Battalio, Kagel, & Green, 1981). Skinner's (1966) analysis of problem solving was based on a molecular analysis of the contiguity between response and reinforcement. In 1961, however, Herrnstein provided evidence, consistent with the Gestalt studies, which indicated that behavioral regularities may be found at a molar level in the relationship between absolute response and reinforcement frequencies, as described in the following equation:

$$\frac{R_1}{R_2} = \frac{r_1}{r_2}, \tag{7.1}$$

where $R$ represents the absolute response frequencies to choice alternatives 1 and 2 and $r$ represents the absolute reinforcement frequencies associated with alternatives 1 and 2. One problem with equation 7.1 is that it cannot describe instances in which the choice is not to respond (e.g., Rachlin et al., 1981). Herrnstein (1970) demonstrated that equation 7.1 may be modified to account for this criticism and, hence, for single-alternative environments. This assertion is shown in the following equality:

$$R = \frac{kr}{r + r_e}, \tag{7.2}$$

where $R$ is the response rate; $r$ is the reinforcement rate; and the constant, $k$, is an empirically fit parameter. Herrnstein (1970) interpreted $k$ as the asymptotic response rate, or the behavioral capacity of the organism. The parameter $r_e$ was interpreted by Herrnstein as the reinforcement rate associated with extraneous sources. Equation 7.2, or matching relation, then, implies that all behavior is a function of choice or preference. This is similar to Skinner's (1966) conclusion that all behavior is problem-solving behavior. By transitivity, therefore, choice behavior is problem-solving behavior when more than two alternatives are present, a point to which Skinner (1974, pp. 124–126) later alluded.

In the typical "matching" experiment, a subject is presented two response alternatives, which are associated with variable interval schedules of reinforcement operating continuously and independently. Research has indicated that subjects generally allocate responses and time spent responding in the same proportion as the proportion of reinforcement obtained for responding on the response alternatives (for a review, see Davison & McCarthy, 1988; de Villiers, 1977). Thus, subjects "solve" the problem of behavior allocation by matching reinforcement proportions.

Equation 7.2 implies that even when reinforcement rates for a given behavior are held constant, response rates will differ as a function of extraneous reinforcement rates (e.g., McDowell, 1988). Thus, environments that are associated with high extraneous reinforcement rates will require higher rates of reinforcement for a desired behavior relative to that behavior in an environment associated with low rates of extraneous reinforcement. Because equation 7.2 is hyperbolic in form, environments with low rates of extraneous reinforcement will reach its asymptotic response rate much more quickly relative to environments with high rates of extraneous reinforcement, when $R$ is equal to $k$. Thus, behavior allocation is not solely a function of contingent reinforcement, but of extraneous reinforcement as well. Contingent reinforcement may produce high or low response rates depending on the amount of extraneous reinforcement associated with the environment under investigation. In terms of problem solving, problem solution rates may be affected by extraneous sources of reinforcement despite constant reinforcement rates for problem solution.

Most basic research with humans has used lever pulling or button pushing as the operant with monetary reinforcement (e.g., Bradshaw, Szabadi, & Bevan, 1976). Conger and Killeen (1974) extended matching research with humans by conducting experimental sessions in a discussion group. Subjects were told that they were participating in a study examining attitudes toward drug abuse in a videotaped group discussion format. Two planted discussants delivered reinforcement consisting of verbal approval contingent upon the emission of a verbal response from the subject. The results showed that the subjects matched response rates to reinforcement rates as delivered by the planted discussants with 81% of the variance accounted for. These results were taken to indicate that the verbal behavior of subjects come under control of the reinforcement contingencies in a social situation.

Applied researchers have begun to use the matching law to modify human behavior. Although not an intervention study, McDowell (1981) cited previous work in which the self-injurious scratching of an 11-year-old boy was examined. Equation 7.2 was applied to the data obtained from the functional analysis and 99.7% of the data was accounted for. Similarly, Martens and Houk (1989) demonstrated that equation 7.2 could be applied to the behavior of a developmentally disabled girl in a classroom setting. Equation 7.2 accounted for 83% of the variance in disruptive behavior and 44% of the variance in on-task behavior.

## The Subjective Probability Approach

The subjective probability approach first began by considering how decisions are evaluated. The expected value of a given event may be expressed as the sum of the cross-products of component outcome probabilities and values:

$$E[V] = P_1 V_1 + P_2 V_2 + \ldots + P_n V_n,$$

where $P$ is the probability of outcome $n$, and $V$ is the value of outcome $n$. The formation of expected values is clearly seen when probabilities are known and values are monetarily based. For example, the

expected value of a coin toss would be zero if $5 is won when heads show and $5 is lost when tails show. According to the expected value model, then, the best decisions are those with the highest expected values. The selection of decisions based on the highest expected values have been used to define rationality (Smyth, Morris, Levy, & Ellis, 1987).

However, numerous studies have indicated that human decision making does not conform to the expected-value model, with the implication that humans behave irrationally. Decisions may be affected by not only the value assigned to individual outcomes, but by the evaluations of the objective probabilities as well. Kahneman and Tversky (1973, 1979, 1982) suggested that humans make decisions or solve problems on the basis of subjective probabilities or decision weights. Thus, internal representations of objective event probabilities are more important than the objective probabilities per se (Rachlin, 1989). These researchers found that humans make predictions that are not consistent with statistical probabilities. For example, Kahneman and Tversky (1982) presented personal descriptions to undergraduates with no statistical coursework and graduate students with statistical coursework. Subjects were asked to estimate which alternative had the highest probability: that the person was, for example, a bank teller, or that the person was a bank teller *and* active in the feminist movement. Approximately 86% of the undergraduates and 50% of the graduate students endorsed the latter. However, according to probability theory, the chances of the individual being a bank teller and active in the feminist movement cannot exceed the chances of the individual being a bank teller alone, regardless of the probabilities assigned to each. This is expressed in the following equation:

$$P[E_1 \text{ and } E_2] = P[E_1] \times P[E_2].$$

Thus, if the probability of the individual being a bank teller is .9 and the probability of the individual being active in the feminist movement is .5, the probability that the individual is both is .45. However, when the undergraduates were presented an abstract verbal statement similar to the preceding equation, 86% of the subjects endorsed it. Hence, although humans may understand probability theory at some level in the abstract, they fail to apply it in concrete situations. The subjective probability approach attempted to investigate the factors involved in this discrepancy.

The researchers promoting the subjective probability approach suggested that, in general, humans ignore antecedent probabilities and make predictions based on the operation of heuristics. When a individual judges a stimulus to be a member of one class or another based on prototypical stimulus properties, a representative heuristic is being employed. For example, Kahneman and Tversky (1973) demonstrated that the estimated odds of an individual being an engineer or a lawyer were affected by manipulating hobbies and interests as detailed in personal descriptions. Thus, decisions about the individual being an engineer or a lawyer were based on the knowledge of stimuli associated with prototypical engineers and lawyers.

When a subject is influenced by his or her own knowledge of stimulus classes, an availability heuristic is being employed (e.g., how many engineers or lawyers he or she has known). For example, Kahneman and Tversky (1973) asked subjects to evaluate the odds that a word begins with the letter $k$ and the odds that a word contains $k$ as a third letter. Subjects estimated the proportion of words beginning with the letter $k$ as being much higher than the proportion of words with $k$ as their third letter. However, the reverse is true, in a ratio of approximately 3 to 1. In addition, Kahneman and Tversky found that the availability heuristic is also affected by the ease with which probability estimates are computed. Events in which probability estimates are more easily computed are judged to be more common than events in which probability estimate computations are more difficult.

Decision-making processes may be manipulated by raising the availability and representativeness associated with the outcome. Kahneman and Tversky (1982) called this manipulation "framing." In other words, the way a problem is presented can affect decision making by causing outcomes to be more available or representative. Kahneman and Tversky presented a scenario to subjects in which they were informed that there was an outbreak of an unusual Asian disease that would claim 600 lives and that two programs had been proposed. In the first condition, the adoption of Program A would lead to saving 200 people. If Program B were adopted, there was a ⅓ probability that 600 people would be saved and a ⅔ probability that nobody would be saved. In this condition, approximately 75% of the subjects chose Program A. In the second condition, the subjects were informed that the adoption of Program A would lead to 400 deaths and that, if Program B was adopted, there was a ⅓ probability that nobody would die and a ⅔ probability that 600 people would die. In this condition, approximately 75% of the subjects chose Program B.

The use of availability and representativeness heuristics may be efficient when objective probabilities are not known. However, the use of objective probabilities, or base rates, implies an integration with previous knowledge and experience. Even when base rates are available, their integration with previous knowledge may be difficult. Kahneman and Tversky (1973) again presented personal descriptions and asked subjects to estimate the probability that the individual was an engineer or a lawyer. This time, hobbies and interests were neutral. However, before the descriptions were presented, subjects were informed that the descriptions were randomly drawn from a sample of 100 engineers and lawyers, in a ratio of 70 to 30. Hence, base rates were provided to the subjects. The results indicated that the subjects estimated the probability of the individual being an engineer or lawyer at .5. Thus, even when the objective or antecedent probabilities were supplied, subjects did not estimate group membership probabilities accurately.

## CLINICAL PSYCHOLOGY AND PROBLEM SOLVING

The relationship between the research in experimental psychology on problem solving and clinical applications of problem solving is tenuous. None of these models has been directly extrapolated to the clinical setting. Rather, at best, a looser, family resemblance exists between these experimental models and clinical interventions. Part of the distinctiveness of clinical applications of problem solving might be that clinical approaches are prescriptive and normative; that is, they seek to optimize problem solving, while experimental models are generally descriptive in that they seek to describe how organisms solve problems, including all the flaws in these attempts. Another part of the distinctiveness comes from the different kinds of problems encountered in the two domains. Experimental studies of problem solving usually are based on well-defined problems and problems for which the solution is usually known in advance by the research psychologist. Clinical problems are more often ill defined, they have no clear correct answer, and the best solution usually is not known by the clinician ahead of time. Therefore, the generalizability of models from experimental psychology is limited. However, what aspects of these models might be profitably applied to the clinical domain is an important open question.

Clinical applications of problem solving view problem solving as a learnable skill and attempt to teach clients to perform this skill more proficiently in important real-life problem situations. The focus in therapy is not only on the presenting problem (e.g., feelings of dysphoria or marital dissatisfaction) or on problems that emerge between sessions (e.g., arguments with spouse); rather, a great deal of attention is paid to these as specific examples of problems that can be used as exemplars to learn and apply more general problem-solving skills. A premise of this therapy is that the client will continually experience a large number and a wide variety of problems (after all, that's life) and that it is beneficial for the client to learn positive attitudes toward problem solving, to learn skills in problem solving, and to develop habits in which these problem-solving skills are routinely applied to real-life problems. Another part of the rationale is that recidivism and lack of generalizability have plagued psychotherapy; thus, a more generic approach to problem solving might result in more transfer than a more focused treatment of a specific set of problems.

These clinical applications also tend to view problem solving as occurring in stages and view these stages as possessing their own domain of subproblems and subskills. For example, D'Zurilla (1986) maintains that normative problem solving occurs in five stages:

1. Problem orientation (perceiving that there is a problem and that a problem-solving stance is worthwhile)
2. Problem definition and formulation (gathering information about the problem, understanding the problem, setting goals, identifying the "real" problem)
3. Generation of alternative solutions (brainstorming to maximize possible problem solutions; possibly seeking advice regarding options from others)
4. Decision making (comparing and judging the possible solutions to select the best for implementation)
5. Solution implementation and verification (performing the chosen problem solution and judging the degree to which it is effective).

This general model, with various minor revisions, is the model adopted in most clinical interventions. The reader is referred to D'Zurilla (1986) for a fuller treatment of the details of these stages. Next we will list additional considerations and discuss some important subproblems associated with these stages.

## Problem Orientation

In the first stage, the client is taught the importance of taking a problem-solving stance. A perspective like the following is emphasized: "I don't like this situation. How can I change it and perhaps how can I learn to be a better problem solver in doing this? Can I look at the current problem as well as other problems as interesting challenges or opportunities to grow and learn? Can I even enjoy being creative and come up with a novel solution to this problem?"

In this initial stage, barriers and resistance to problem solving are identified and modified. The client is helped to achieve an attitude in which he or she views the situation with some optimism, with an appropriate work ethic, and with a willingness to devote some time and effort. Of central importance is that the client view the current problem as well as other problems as under some degree of personal control. The clinician should assess the person's degree of confidence in his or her general and specific problem-solving abilities and whether the client approaches or avoids problems in general and this problem in specific. The clinician should assess whether the individual attempts to avoid solving problems personally by inappropriately relying on others. This stage is based on the belief that continuing problems may be due not only to a lack of knowledge but also to interfering emotional and attitudinal factors.

## Problem Definition and Formulation

That something is a problem is a matter of judgment. The quality of this judgement can be evaluated. A critical question becomes: Why is this state of affairs judged to be problematic? A *problem* may be defined as a discrepancy between the current state of affairs and some desired state of affairs. Clients will tend to identify the critical difficulty as the current state of affairs, but the "real" problem may be what the client desires. For example, the first author once saw a client who dressed her 5-year-old daughter in white dresses as play clothes. The mother then desired that the daughter should keep these dresses perfectly clean while playing. Thus, the problem could have been (incorrectly) defined as: How can we intervene with the child to keep her white dresses clean while playing (i.e., how can we change the current state of affairs to the desired state of affairs?). It was clear, however, that the problem lay with the mother's definition of the desired state of affairs. This "problem" was quickly resolved when the mother's views about appropriate play clothes for a 5-year-old changed.

Defining a problem is itself a problem. Therefore, in a reflexive fashion it is often worthwhile to appling problem-solving strategies to this problem. A critical question becomes: What are alternative problem statements? Or, in Simon's terminology: What is the problem space? A helpful question may be: What is a way of stating the problem that will maximize the range of benefits to the client and to significant others while minimizing unacceptable costs? This question is important as some problem statements may be superficial and miss the real substance of the problematic state of affairs. For example, in the play clothes case, the "problem" was not simply a lack of knowledge that jeans, for example, make better play clothes than white dresses; rather, the "deeper" problem was the mother's rigid ideas about gender roles (i.e., girls should only wear dresses). Thus, an important manner of criticizing and understanding problem statements is by scrutinizing their deeper presuppositions.

The clinician also needs to keep in mind that the client may have more than one problem. For example, in this case there were also significant marital problems. Thus, the clinician needs to ask: Is this problem a specific instance of a more general problem, or a sign of a significant probability of a related problem?

There is always a triage problem involving scarce resources that can be allocated to problem solving. Thus, problems need to be prioritized and decisions need to be made regarding the amount of resources it is justifiable to spend on a problem. Kant has said that it is *wisdom* that has the merit of selecting, from among the innumerable problems that present themselves, those whose solution is important to humankind. Similarly, in the absence of specific research concerning the fecundity of problem prioritization, it may be wisdom that is responsible for an appropriate prioritization of problems in the individual case. Classic situations of misprioritizing problems include the fact that many individuals spend few resources on significant problems such as hypertension, while spending too many resources on "problems" such as wrinkles. The clinician and the client should understand the nature of the demand that a solution be found. Does this problem pose a risk to life or health? If so, how serious a threat? Whose psychological well-being depends on this problem? What exactly is the nature of this well-being? Is this problem of such a nature that a "Buddhist" solution—learning

to give up the desired state of affairs—is the best option?

Other important ways of understanding problems include understanding the history of the problem and how deep and interconnected (with other problems or important aspects of life) is a given problem. What background information is needed to understand this problem? Is this background information accurate and complete? A problem may be unanswerable given the prevailing belief system. One should attempt to gain some estimate of the probability that the problem can be solved and of the degree to which the problem can be resolved. Other important questions at this stage include: What are the facts of the situation and the context of the problem? What are the presuppositions of the problem, and are these problematic? Is this problem highly dynamic and highly likely to change? Is this a problem of ends (i.e., which goals to pursue) or one of means (i.e., once a particular goal is chosen, what causes can be instantiated to bring about this goal)?

All this can be a very difficult task given the omnipresence of a great variety of problems. Thus, an important and interesting question for further research becomes: Do successful, happy people work on different kinds of problems than unhappy individuals? For example, the miser works on the problem of resource preservation and cost containment. It may be, however, that happy individuals work much less on this problem and more on the problem of income expansion. Karl Popper (1957) has suggested that problems of removing pain (negative-utilitarianism) should take precedence over problems of increasing pleasure because it is easier to agree on what is bad than on what is good. More research needs to be conducted on how to find and identify problems. Can this partly be done actuarially? For example, first-time parents might be an actuarial category that might productively and efficiently provide a list of clients' problems.

## Generation of Alternative Solutions

During this stage, critical questions include: What problem solutions has the client tried in the past, and how good have these been? What are the constraints (e.g., scarce resources) on possible problem solutions? A very important question is: What are the barriers that need to be overcome to resolve this problem? These barriers may be personal (e.g., a lack of communication skills) or environmental (e.g., a lack of employment opportunities). Should the problem-solving attempt be collaborative? Do others have a vested interest in solving this problem and therefore, perhaps, a willingness to help? Or, alternatively: Do others have a vested interest in *not* solving this problem, and therefore might they be unwilling to help? What solutions have others tried for this kind of problem, and how good were these? What heuristics or procedures might be useful in resolving this problem? What background information is needed to generate alternative solutions? Is the background information accurate and complete?

## Decision Making

Critical issues include: What information is needed to evaluate and choose among these possibilities? Should I seek the opinion and advice of others (e.g., experts)? What evaluative criteria should be used and how should these be weighed? What are the probabilities that each possible solution will produce the desired end state? How can these probabilities be reliably estimated? What is the cost of each alternative (including potential negative side effects)? Is the

**Table 7.1.** Applications of Problem-Solving Skills

| PROBLEM | CITATION |
| --- | --- |
| Marital problems | Jacobson & Anderson (1980) |
| Depression | Nezu & Perri (1989) |
| Alcoholism | Chaney, O'Leary, & Marlatt (1978) |
| Borderline personality disorder | Stone (1988) |
| Social skills deficits | Maag (1990) |
| Anger control | Dangel, Deschner, & Rasp (1989) |
| Social anxiety | DiGuiseppe et al. (1990) |
| Social withdrawal | Christoff et al. (1985) |
| Agoraphobia | Kleiner, Marshall, & Spevack (1987) |
| Headaches | Lascelles, Cunningham, McGrath, & Sullivan (1989) |
| Rheumotoid arthritis | McCracken (1991) |
| Bulemia | Johnson, Corrigan, & Mayo (1987) |
| Obesity | Black (1987) |
| Relapse in schizophrenics | Sullivan et al. (1990) |
| Neglectful mothers | Dawson, de-Armas, McGrath, & Kelly (1986) |
| Wife-beating | Maiuro (1991) |
| Primary prevention of smoking | Shaffer, Beck, & Boothroyd (1983) |
| Parent–adolescent conflict | Robin (1979) |
| Family conflict | Foster, Prinz, & O'Leary (1983) |
| Test anxiety | Stevens & Pihl (1983) |
| Problems of old age | Garland (1985) |
| Academic problems | Richards (1981) |
| Increase informed consent to therapy | Tepper & Kaslow (1981) |
| Classroom management | Frisby (1990) |
| Improve collaboration between parents and teachers | Bauer & Sapona (1988) |
| Improve behavior of closed-head injured adults | Foxx, Martella, & Marchand-Martella (1989) |
| Coping with stress | Meichenbaum & Cameron (1983) |
| Indecisiveness | Mendonca & Seiss (1976) |

value of the goal worth this cost? Should I try a cheap and easy solution first or, simultaneously, a package of solutions? If the first alternative does not work, do I have a contingency plan? If the alternative does not work, can it provide me with some important information about the nature of the problem that perhaps may be useful in deciding on an alternative solution?

## Solution Implementation and Verification

In this stage, it might be useful to have a continuing fallabilistic orientation—that is, no problem solution is perfect; therefore, what are the errors and problems with this solution, and can this be improved? Here the desired attitude is: "I can always improve and I need to learn from error."

Also in this stage, the quality of the implementation might need to be assessed. The client might have decided on the "correct" solution but implemented it unskillfully (or for some reason sabotaged it), and therefore the new problem may be to intervene with the client so that the client can implement this solution in a more skillful, forthright manner.

An important possibility is that increased proficiency at any one of these steps may be therapeutic in its own right. For example, the client, in becoming more optimally problem oriented, might experience diverse benefits. More process research is needed to evaluate the independent contribution of each of these steps.

We have listed in Table 7.1 the variety of problems treated by a problem-solving intervention. The variety of problems treated through problem-solving skills training is remarkable and is perhaps a reflection of the notion that the most general feature of a clinical concern is that it is a *problem*. Two other features are noteworthy:

1. The clinician is also in the clinical situation and has to function as a problem solver, and several studies have attempted to teach professionals problem-solving skills to enhance their effectiveness.
2. A problem-solving skills orientation has a fundamentally different orientation than a more traditional therapy model. In the more traditional therapy model, the attempt is to solve the client's immediate problems, but little or no attention is typically devoted to teaching clients general problem-solving strategies that they can apply to other ongoing problems or to problems that arise in the future.

Thus, a goal of problem-solving therapy is to ensure that the skills taught in therapy generalize across time and across problems. Thus, in problem-solving therapy, the first order of discussion is the client's immediate problem, and the second order of discussion is problem solving itself. This has led some to look at problem-solving therapy as a metacognitive pursuit. An illustration of the importance of this second-order or meta perspective is the following: Knowing how to solve a problem is not identical with *knowing* that one knows how to solve a problem.

## CONCLUSION

Training in problem-solving skills has been attempted as an intervention for a wide variety of clinical problems with a significant amount of success. The importance of this perspective may lie in the general fact that life is a problem-solving process. The survival of the species and that of the individual suggest that the individual has some proficiency at this skill. However, as with any skill the individual can improve on this skill, and this may be necessary because evolution does not result in perfect problem solutions or in solutions to all problems. Evolution is a slow process, and there are advantages to a certain amount of plasticity in behavior to respond to problems that are variable, dynamic, or completely novel.

Scientific thinking may be an especially efficient method of problem solving. Several very influential philosophers of science have viewed science as essentially a problem-solving process. Thus, following clinicians such as Beck (1976) and Mahoney (1977), the process of scientific behavior needs to be accurately understood (no easy task) and, when understood sufficiently, may be profitably applied as a method of problem solving relevant to clinical problems. There is a certain divorce—one that is understandable but nonetheless unfortunate—between the experimental psychology of problem solving and the clinical applications of problem solving. Future research should focus on the relevance and value of constructs such as those in clinical pursuits.

Finally, although there is a significant amount of outcome research on the efficacy of a problem-solving skill perspective for a wide array of clinical problems, there is very little process research regarding the variables that contribute to outcome. To date, most interventions have adopted a sequential stage model of normative problem solving. Each of these stages has its subproblems, and more research is needed to address a paraphrase of Paul's (1969) classic question: What model of problem solving works

best with what type of client, with what type of
problem, provided by what type of therapist, and
how?

# REFERENCES

Bauer, A., & Sapona, R. (1988). Facilitation and problem
   solving: A framework for collaboration between coun-
   selors and teachers. *Elementary School Guidance and
   Counseling, 23*(1), 5–9.
Beck, A. T. (1976). *Cognitive therapy and the emotional
   disorder.* New York: International Universities Press.
Best, J. B. (1992). *Cognitive psychology,* 3rd ed. St. Paul,
   MN: West.
Black, D. (1987). A minimal intervention program and a
   problem-solving program for weight control. *Cognitive
   Therapy and Research, 11*(1), 107–120.
Blechman, E. A. (1976). The Family Contract Game: Tech-
   nique and case study. *Journal of Consulting and Clinical
   Psychology, 44,* 449–455.
Bradshaw, C. M., Szabadi, E., & Bevan, P. (1976). Behav-
   ior of humans in variable-interval schedules of reinforce-
   ment. *Journal of the Experimental Analysis of Behavior,
   26,* 135–141.
Campbell, D. T. (1987). Evolutionary epistemology. In G.
   Radnitzky & W. Bartley (Eds.), *Evolutionary epistemol-
   ogy, rationality, and the sociology of knowledge.* LaSalle,
   IL: Open Court.
Chaney, E. F., O'Leary, M. R., & Marlatt, G. A. (1978).
   Skill training with alcoholics. *Journal of Consulting and
   Clinical Psychology, 46,* 1092–1104.
Christoff, K. A., Scott, W. O. N., Kelley, M. L., Schlundt,
   D., Baer, G., & Kelly, J. A. (1985). Social skills and
   social problem-solving training for shy young adoles-
   cents. *Behavior Therapy, 16,* 468–477.
Cohen, G. (1983). *The psychology of cognition,* 2nd ed.
   New York: Academic Press.
Coleman, S. R., & Salamon, R. (1988). Kuhn's *Structure of
   Scientific Revolutions* in the psychological journal litera-
   ture, 1969–1983: A descriptive study. *Journal of Mind
   and Behavior, 9,* 415–446.
Conger, R., & Killeen, P. (1974). Use of concurrent oper-
   ants in small group research: A demonstration. *Pacific
   Sociological Review, 17,* 399–416.
Cooper, J. O., Heron, T. E., & Howard, W. L. (1987).
   *Applied behavior analysis.* Columbus, OH: Merrill.
Dangel, R., Deschner, J., & Rasp, R. (1989). Anger control
   training for adolescents in residential treatment. Special
   Issue: Empirical research in behavioral social work. *Behavior Modification, 13*(4), 447–458.
Davison, M., & McCarthy, D. (1988). *The matching law: A
   research review.* Hillsdale, NJ: Lawrence Erlbaum.
Dawson, B., de-Armas, A., McGrath, M., & Kelly, J.
   (1986). Cognitive problem-solving training to improve
   the child-care judgment of child neglectful parents. *Journal of Family Violence, 1*(3), 209–221.

de Groot, A. (1966). Perception and memory versus
   thought: Some old ideas and recent findings. In B. Kleinmuntz (Ed.), *Problem solving: Research, method, and
   theory* (pp. 19–50). New York: Wiley.
de Villiers, P. (1977). Choice in concurrent schedules and a
   quantitative formulation of the law of effect. In W. K.
   Honig & J. E. R. Staddon (Eds.), *Handbook of operant
   behavior* (pp. 233–287). Englewood Cliffs, NJ: Prentice-
   Hall.
Dunker, K. (1945). On problem solving. *Psychological
   Monographs, 58* (Whole No. 270).
D'Zurilla, T. J. (1986). *Problem solving therapy.* New
   York: Springer.
Ernst, G. W., & Newell, A. (1969). *GPS: A case study in
   generality and problem solving.* New York: Academic
   Press.
Ferster, C. B., & Skinner, B. F. (1958). *Schedules of rein-
   forcement.* Englewood Cliffs, NJ: Prentice-Hall.
Foster, S. L., Prinz, R. J., & O'Leary, K. D. (1983). Impact
   of problem-solving communication training and general-
   ization procedures on family conflict. *Child and Family
   Behavior Therapy, 5,* 1–23.
Foxx, R., Martella, R., & Marchand-Martella, N. (1989).
   The acquisition, maintenance, and generalization of
   problem-solving skills by closed head-injured adults. *Behavior Therapy, 20*(1), 61–76.
Frisby, C. (1990). A teacher inservice model for problem-
   solving in classroom discipline: Suggestions for the
   school psychologist. *School Psychology Quarterly, 5*(3),
   211–232.
Garland, J. (1985). Adaptation skills in the elderly, their
   supporters and careers. Special Issue: Sharing psychological skills: Training non-psychologists in the use of
   psychological techniques. *British Journal of Medical
   Psychology, 58*(3), 267–274.
Gholson, B., & Barker, P. (1985). Kuhn, Lakatos, and
   Laudan: Applications in the history of physics and psychology. *American Psychologist, 40,* 755–769.
Green, B. F. (1966). Current trends in problem solving.
   In B. Kleinmuntz (Ed.), *Problem solving: Research,
   method, and theory* (pp. 3–18). New York: Wiley.
Greeno, J. G. (1978). Natures of problem-solving abilities.
   In W. K. Estes (Ed.), *Handbook of learning and cognitive
   processes: Human information processing* (Vol. 5, pp.
   239–270). Hillsdale, NJ: Lawrence Erlbaum.
Herrnstein, R. J. (1970). On the law of effect. *Journal of the
   Experimental Analysis of Behavior, 13,* 243–266.
Horner, R. D., & Keilitz, I. (1975). Training mentally retarded adolescents to brush their teeth. *Journal of Applied
   Behavior Analysis, 8,* 301–309.
Jacobson, N. S., & Anderson, E. A. (1980). The effects of
   behavior rehearsal and feedback on the acquisition of
   problem-solving skills in distressed and nondistressed
   couples. *Behaviour Research and Therapy, 18*(1),
   25–36.
Johnson, W., Corrigan, S., & Mayo, L. (1987). Innovative
   treatment approaches to bulimia nervosa. Special Issue:

Recent advances in behavioral medicine. *Behavior Modification, 11*(3), 373–388.

Kahneman, D., & Tversky, A. (1973). On the psychology of prediction. *Psychological Review, 80,* 237–251.

Kahneman, D., & Tversky, A. (1979). Prospect theory: An analysis of decision under risk. *Econometrica, 47,* 263–291.

Kahneman, D., & Tversky, A. (1982). Subjective probability: A judgement of representativeness. In D. Kahneman, P. Slovic, & A. Tversky (Eds.), *Judgement under uncertainty: Heuristics and biases.* Cambridge: Cambridge University Press.

Kanfer, F. H., & Busemeyer, J. R. (1982). The use of problem solving and decision making in behavior therapy. *Clinical Psychology Review, 2,* 239–266.

Katona, G. (1940). *Organizing and memorizing.* New York: Columbia University Press.

Kleiner, L., Marshall, W. L., & Spevack, M. (1987). Training in problem-solving and exposiure treatment for agoraphobics with panic attacks. *Journal of Anxiety Disorders, 1,* 291–238.

Koertge, N. (1980). Methodology, ideology, and feminist critiques of science. *Philosophy of Science Association, 2,* 346–359.

Koffka, K. (1931). *The growth of the mind.* New York: Harcourt Brace.

Kohler, W. (1927). *The mentality of apes.* New York: Harcourt Brace.

Kuhn, T. S. (1970). *The structure of scientific revolutions,* 2nd ed. Chicago: University of Chicago Press.

Lakatos, I. (1970). Falsification and the methodology of scientific research programmes. In I. Lakatos & A. Musgrave (Eds.), *Criticism and the growth of knowledge* (pp. 91–196). Cambridge, England: Cambridge University Press.

Lakatos, I., & Musgrave, A. (Eds.). (1970). *Criticism and the growth of knowledge.* Cambridge, England: Cambridge University Press.

Lascelles, M., Cunningham, S., McGrath, P., & Sullivan, M. (1989). Teaching coping strategies to adolescents with migraine. *Journal of Pain and Symptom Management, 4*(3), 135–145.

Laudan, L. (1977). *Progress and its problems.* Berkeley: University of California Press.

Maag, J. (1990). Social skills training in schools. *Special Services in the Schools, 6*(1–2), 1–19.

Mahoney, M. J. (1977). Personal science: A cognitive learning therapy. In A. Ellis & R. Grieger (Eds.), *Handbook of rational emotive therapy.* New York: Springer-Verlag.

Maiuro, R. (1991). The evaluation and treatment of anger and hostility in domestically violent men. *Revista Intercontinental de Psicologia y Educacion, 4*(1), 165–189.

Martens, B. K., & Houk, J. L. (1989). The application of Herrnstein's law of effect to disruptive and on-task behavior of a retarded adolescent girl. *Journal of the Experimental Analysis of Behavior, 51,* 17–27.

McCracken, L. (1991). Cognitive-behavioral treatment of rheumatoid arthritis: A preliminary review of efficacy and methodology. *Annals of Behavioral Medicine, 13*(2), 57–65.

McDowell, J. J. (1981). On the validity and utility of Herrnstein's hyperbola in applied behavior analysis. In C. M. Bradshaw, E. Szabadi, & C. F. Lowe (Eds.), *Quantification of steady-state operant behaviour* (pp. 311–324). Elsevier North Holland: Biomedical Press.

McDowell, J. J. (1988). Matching theory in natural human environments. *Behavior Analyst, 11,* 95–109.

Meichenbaum, D. K., & Cameron, R. (1983). Stress inoculation training: Toward a general paradigm for training coping skills. In D. Meichenbaum & M. E. Jaremko (Eds.), *Stress reduction and prevention.* New York: Plenum Press.

Mendonca, J. D., & Siess, T. F. (1976). Counseling for indecisiveness: Problem solving and anxiety in management training. *Journal of Counseling Psychology, 23,* 330–347.

Newell, A., Shaw, J. C., & Simon, H. A. (1958). Elements of a theory of general problem solving. *Psychological Review, 65,* 151–166.

Newell, A., & Simon, H. A. (1972). *Human problem solving.* Englewood Cliffs, NJ: Prentice-Hall.

Nezu, A., & Perri, M. (1989). Social problem-solving therapy for unipolar depression: An initial dismantling investigation. *Journal of Consulting and Clinical Psychology, 57*(3), 408–413.

Nisbett, R. E., & Wilson, T. D. (1977). Telling more than we can know: Verbal reports on mental processes. *Psychological Review, 84,* 231–259.

O'Donohue, W. (1993). The spell of Kuhn on psychology: An exegetical elixir. *Philosophical Psychology, 6,* 267–287.

O'Donohue, W., & Smith, L. D. (1992). Philosophical and psychological epistemologies in behaviorism and behavior therapy. *Behavior Therapy, 23,* 173–194.

Paul, G. (1969). Behavior modification research: Design and tactics. In C. M. Franks (Ed.), *Behavior therapy: Appraisal and status.* New York: McGraw-Hill.

Popper, K. R. (1963). *The poverty of historicism.* London: Ark.

Popper, K. R. (1979). *Objective knowledge.* Oxford, England: Oxford University Press.

Rachlin, H. (1989). *Judgment, decision, and choice: A cognitive/behavioral synthesis.* New York: Freeman.

Rachlin, H., Battalio, R., Kagel, J., & Green, L. (1981). Maximization theory in behavioral psychology. *Behavioral and Brain Sciences, 4,* 371–417.

Reitman, W. (1964). Heuristic decision procedures, open constraints, and the structure of ill-defined problems. In M. W. Shelley & B. L. Bryan (Eds.), *Human judgments and optimality.* New York: Wiley.

Richards, C. (1981). Improving college students' study behaviors through self-control techniques: A brief review. *Behavioral Counseling Quarterly, 1*(3), 159–175.

Robin, A. L. (1979). Problem-solving communication training: A behavior approach to the treatment of parent-adolescent conflict. *The American Journal of Family Therapy, 7,* 69–82.

Shaffer, H., Beck, J., & Boothroyd, P. (1983). The primary prevention of smoking onset: An inoculation approach. *Journal of Psychoactive Drugs, 15*(3), 177–184.

Simon, H. A. (1955). A behavioral model of rational choice. *Quarterly Journal of Economics, 69,* 99–118.

Simon, H. A. (1979). Information processing models of cognition. *Annual Review of Psychology, 30,* 363–396.

Skinner, B. F. (1966). An operant analysis of problem solving. In B. Kleinmuntz (Ed.), *Problem solving: Research, method, and theory* (pp. 225–257). New York: Wiley.

Skinner, B. F. (1974). *About behaviorism.* New York: Vintage Books.

Skinner, B. F. (1984). Selection by consequences. *Brain and Behavioral Sciences, 7,* 477–510.

Smyth, M. M., Morris, P. E., Levy, P., & Ellis, A. W. (1987). *Cognition in action.* London: Lawrence Erlbaum.

Staddon, J. E. R. (1983). *Adaptive behavior and learning.* Cambridge: Cambridge University Press.

Sternberg, R. J. (Ed.). (1982). *Advances in the psychology of human intelligence* (Vol. 1). Hillsdale, NJ: Lawrence Erlbaum.

Sternberg, R. J. (Ed.). (1985). *Human abilities: An information processing approach.* San Francisco: Freeman.

Stevens, R., & Pihl, R. O. (1983). Learning to cope with school: A study of the effects of a coping skill training program with test-vulnerable seventh-grade students. *Cognitive Therapy and Research, 7,* 155–158.

Stone, M. (1988). Toward a psychobiological theory of borderline personality disorder: Is irritability the red thread that runs through borderline conditions? *Dissociation Progress in the Dissociative Disorders, 1*(2), 2–15.

Sullivan, G., Marder, S., Liberman, R., Donahoe, C., et al. (1990). Social skills and relapse history in outpatient schizophrenics. *Psychiatry, 53*(4), 340–345.

Symons, D. (1987). An evolutionary approach: Can Darwin's view of life shed light on human sexuality? In J. Geer & W. O'Donohue (Eds.), *Theories of human sexuality.* New York: Plenum Press.

Tepper, A., & Kaslow, F. (1981). Informed decision-making capacity: A patient's ability to participate in treatment determinations. *Law and Psychology Review, 6,* 49–67.

Tolman, E. C. (1932). *Purposive behavior in animals and men.* New York: Century.

Tolman, E. C. (1938). The determiners of behavior at a choice point. *Psychological Review, 45,* 1–41.

Wachtershauser, G. (1987). Light and life: On the nutritional origins of sensory perception. In G. Radnitzky & W. Bartley (Eds.), *Evolutionary epistemology, rationality, and the sociology of knowledge.* LaSalle, IL: Open Court.

Wallas, G. (1926). *The art of thought.* New York: Harper & Row.

Wertheimer, M. (1959). *Productive thinking.* New York: Harcourt Brace Jovanovich.

# CHAPTER 8

# SELF-APPRAISAL SKILLS

Jeff Szymanski
William O'Donohue

When an infant grows out of the initial stage, described by William James (1890, 1950, p. 16) as a "blooming, buzzing confusion," an important new skill that the infant acquires and employs is to individuate. The child both distinguishes itself from all else (i.e., develops a concept of self) and recognizes that other particular things are themselves individuals (i.e., Fluffy the cat is a different thing than Spunky the cat, although both are the same kind of thing). A recognition that there are things—including oneself—that exist as separate, indivisible entities is perhaps the foundation stone on which the entire cognitive edifice is built.

The construct of the self has played a central role in both Western and Eastern thought. In Western thought the self has appeared in the Delphi oracle relating to the supreme goal in life—"Know thyself," in Descartes' epistemological fulcrum for defeating radical skepticism—"Cogito, ergo sum," and in more recent existential, phenomenological, and hermeneutic philosophies. In Eastern thought, the goal of Buddhistic enlightenment is the elimination of self in a blending with some sort of universal consciousness.

I know I have an "I-feeling" (Preyer, 1889)—an immediate awareness of an unique point of view, an immediate experience of a personal agency, a private consciousness that is aware of and is at times both the subject and the object of feelings, hopes, desires, and intentions. To the extent that the problem of other minds can be overcome, most of us are willing to generalize our immediate perception of our own "I-feelings" and claim that others, also, have an immediate sense of self.

The notion of *self,* however, has had a controversial history within psychology. Some have given this construct a central role in their account of human behavior. James (1907–1983) spent a great deal of time developing an account of the self in which the many competing selves within a person could still form a single, coherent personal identity. Freud (1948) spoke a lot about the self, its hidden aspects, and its conflicting components. Others, such as Kelly (1955), Kohut (1977), and Allport (1955) have been labeled as self-psychologists. Recently, such contemporary movements within psychology as hermeneutics (Woolfolk, Sass, & Messer, 1988) and object relations theory (Fairbairn, 1952) give the "experiencing self" and its perception of "the other" a central role. Carl Rogers (1951) developed a theory of psychological health and disturbance that rested on constructs such as real self, ideal self, and self-actualization. Also, in recent years, cognitive-behavioral therapists have begun to focus on various constructs related to the self, such as self-efficacy, self-control, self-esteem, self-representation, self-management, self-interest, and self-statements (see the special issue of *Cognitive Therapy and Research,* 1990, Volume 14).

The controversy concerning the construct of the self and the reluctance of behavior therapists to utilize this construct is probably due to two thorny issues regarding the scientific study of the self: (1) the self, because of its first-person, phenomenological nature, is difficult to measure objectively (i.e., intersubjectively) and accurately (as a result of all sorts of problems related to indirect measurement, to self-report, and to limits on knowledge of internal entities (Nisbett & Wilson, 1977), and (2) the self in notions of personal agency (i.e., as an originating cause) creates tensions with another notion that is usually a presupposition of science—namely, that all events have prior determining causes. Moreover, internal causes have been particularly controversial within behavioral psychology. Skinner (1953), for example, has argued that covert causal constructs are eliminable in a scientific account because, in his deterministic view, all covert events (e.g., a feeling of selfhood) are lawfully related to both environmental antecedents and consequences. Therefore, they can be replaced by the more functional (i.e., manipulable) laws that state relations between environmental antecedents and consequences. Skinner argues that notions of the self as the cause of behavior are dangerous explanatory fictions that falsely divert attention from the true environmental causes of behavior. Thus, it seems fair to say that although the existence of the experience of self is fairly uncontroversial, others have been concerned about whether the self can be known in a scientifically useful manner.

Despite these controversies, currently certain clinical disorders are at least partially *defined* by the *Diagnostic and Statistical Manual of Mental Disorders,* third edition, revised (DSM-III-R; American Psychiatric Association, 1987) by direct or indirect reference to the self and errors and distortions related to this construct. Thus, anorexics have a distorted image of their body; bipolars have a grandiose view of self; social phobics fear negative evaluation of the

self; depressives have low self-esteem; psychogenic amnesics cannot recall important information about the self; schizophrenics can have delusional self-representations; transsexuals have a gender self-identity that differs from their anatomical identity; individuals suffering from depersonalization disorder have a degraded experience of self; narcissistic personalities are overly concerned with, and attach too much importance to, the self; and multiple personalities simply have too many selves.

Moreover, clinical researchers have recently provided empirical evidence that the construct of self and errors and distortions in this construct are implicated in a wide array of psychological problems. For example, Beck (1976) and others (e.g., Segal & Vella, 1990) have found that a view of the self as inadequate or worthless is related to depression. Other researchers have found that individuals suffering from anxiety disorders have self-representations that emphasize personal vulnerability and other negative self-statements (Hope, Rapee, Heimberg, & Dombeck, 1990; Ingram & Kendall, 1987; Mathews & MacLeod, 1985). Meicher (1986) found that adolescents who engaged in delinquent behavior had developmentally delayed self-representations compared to adolescents who did not engage in such behavior. As a final example, Gibbons et al. (1985) explained that self-focused attention tended to exacerbate negative affect in clinical populations.

It is assumed in this chapter that individuals appraise themselves on multiple dimensions. They make judgments concerning what they are like (self-concept); they evaluate what they are like and react emotionally to this evaluation (self-esteem); finally, they appraise what they are capable of accomplishing (self-efficacy). Clinically, it is noted that errors and deficits in these appraisal processes can result in a number of psychological problems. It is also assumed in this chapter that individuals can learn to appraise themselves and their abilities in a more accurate manner and in a manner that leads to a number of positive consequences. Therefore, this chapter includes theories from the self-concept, self-esteem, self-efficacy, and social comparison literature. The theories that will be discussed represent some of the most comprehensive and thoroughly researched in their fields. First, the theories and the empirical research supporting them will be discussed. Next, a variety of assessment tools will be described and evaluated in terms of their psychometric properties. Finally, suggestions for interventions are outlined.

# A THEORY OF SELF-CONCEPT

Prior to 1980, a variety of theories, definitions, and models of self-concept appeared in the literature. Although there continues to be an abundance of new theories in this area, the model proposed by Shavelson, Hubner, and Stanton (1976) stands out. Shavelson et al. (1976) referred to self-concept broadly as a person's perceptions of himself or herself. They hypothesized these perceptions being formed through an individual's experience with, and interpretations of, his or her environment; and they argued that environmental reinforcements, evaluations by significant others, and attributions of one's own behavior are particularly influential (Marsh, 1990b; Shavelson et al., 1976). After reviewing the current literature on self-concept, Shavelson et al. (1976) proposed that there are six aspects that comprise self-concept. First, self-concept is multifaceted, as opposed to unidimensional. That is, individuals categorize the information they have about themselves and relate these categories to one another. The second aspect of the model proposes that the different facets of self-concept are hierarchically organized. In other words, general self-concept, at the apex of the hierarchy, is divided into an academic self-concept and a nonacademic self-concept, which serve as the second level in the hierarchy. The academic self-concept is then broken down into specific lower level subsets such as academic subjects (e.g., English and math); and the nonacademic self-concept could be broken down into social, emotional, and physical components. The final level in the hierarchy would be made up of individual experiences in particular situations. The third aspect contends that self-concept can be differentiated from other constructs (e.g., academic achievement). The fourth aspect of the model is that self-concept has both a descriptive and evaluative dimension. Fifth, the facets of self-concept become increasingly independent as one gets older. Finally, general self-concept is stable—that is, resistant to change—but its subdivisions (e.g., verbal self-concept) are increasingly less stable moving down the hierarchy.

## RESEARCH SUPPORTING THE SHAVELSON ET AL. MODEL

Since the original proposal of their self-concept model (Shavelson et al., 1976), a number of studies have been conducted to evaluate (and modify) its many components. The proposal that self-concept is multifaceted seems to be the strongest aspect of their model, receiving support from a variety of studies (e.g., Byrne & Shavelson, 1986; Fleming & Watts, 1980; Marsh, 1990c; Marsh, Byrne, & Shavelson, 1988; Marsh & Shavelson, 1985; Marsh, Smith, & Barnes, 1983; Mboya, 1989; Shavelson & Bolus, 1982; Zorich & Reynolds, 1988). These studies have basically shown that different facets of self-concept are distinguishable from one's general sense of himself or herself and in some cases are only weakly related to one's general self-concept. The accuracy of this assertion, a multidimensional self-concept versus a unidimensional self-concept, has important implications for assessment and intervention. For example, if one argues that self-concept is unidimensional, then interventions will be aimed at changing this. If, however, one is attempting to improve something specific, such as a child's social skills, is it more effective to focus on improving his or her general sense of well-being or to focus on improving the child's social skills directly? This will be discussed in more detail later.

Research on the idea that self-concept is organized in a hierarchy has led to a reconceptualization of the hierarchy originally proposed by Shavelson et al. (1976). Support for the hierarchical model has been found with second through fifth graders (Marsh & Hocevar, 1985; Marsh & Shavelson, 1985), fifth and sixth graders (Marsh, Relich, & Smith, 1983), and seventh and eighth graders (Shavelson & Bolus, 1982). However, these results have also demonstrated that the hierarchy is much more complicated than was originally thought (Marsh & Shavelson, 1985; Marsh, Relich, & Smith, 1983; Marsh, Byrne, & Shavelson, 1988). For example, Shavelson et al. (1976) originally proposed that academic self-concept and nonacademic self-concept should be second-order facets of self-concept (i.e., occupy the second level in the hierarchy, just below general self-concept). However, Marsh and Shavelson (1985) found that if academic self-concept was split into a reading/academic self-concept and a math/academic self-concept, and if these served as second-order facets—as opposed to having one unified facet called academic self-concept at the second level—and if these second-order facets both loaded onto a lower order general school self-concept facet, this would fit the data better (definitely more complicated!). They also found more intercorrelations among the facets of self-concept than was originally thought.

Support for the third contention of the model, that self-concept can be differentiated from other constructs, has been discussed by Marsh (1990b). For example, he argued that a construct such as academic achievement needs to have a stronger relationship with academic self-concept than with nonacademic self-concept or general self-concept. This is supported by the Shavelson and Bolus (1982) study, which showed a correlation of general self-concept with English self-concept of .26, with math self-concept of .34, and with science self-concept of .30, compared to .52, .62, and .73 for correlations with academic self-concept. Marsh (1990b) concluded, based on the studies he reviewed, that, "... general self-concept is nearly uncorrelated with academic achievement" (p. 117). This supports the contention that a construct such as academic achievement can be differentiated from general self-concept. Marsh (1990b) also reviewed longitudinal studies demonstrating that prior academic self-concept, as measured by the Self-Description Questionnaire (Marsh, 1988), affected subsequent school grades (i.e., academic achievement).

Although a great deal of research has been done on the other components of this model, the assertion that self-concept is both descriptive and evaluative has not been tested directly. This appears to have important implications. For example, Hughes (1984) pointed out that in many studies, self-concept and self-esteem are interchangeable, and that when a distinction is made between the two, self-concept is defined as the descriptive perceptions of the self, whereas self-esteem is defined as the evaluative assessment of those descriptions. This is in conflict with Shavelson et al. (1976), but not with Coopersmith's model (1967).

With respect to the final two aspects of the model, Marsh's (1990b) review of the literature pointed to a lack of support for the assertion that the aspects of self-concept become increasingly differentiated with age, which points to a more general criticism of the research done on this model: its apparent dependence on educational settings for subjects. And finally, Shavelson and Bolus (1982) failed to find support for the increased stability of self-concept as one moved up the hierarchy.

## ASSESSING SELF-CONCEPT

A variety of approaches have been used for assessing self-concept (Marsh & Shavelson, 1985). Marsh (1990b) outlined four of these: (1) an agglomerate self-concept, (2) a unidimensional self-concept, (3) a weighted average, and (4) a higher order self-concept. The agglomerate approach, probably the most common, consists of summing a person's responses to questions, which are based on the different facets of the self, for a total score. This score represents the general self-concept. According to Marsh (1990b), "A more justifiable use of general-self" (p. 95) is to develop a scale that measures a unidimensional construct superordinate to the specific facets of self-concept. Items in these types of scales do not reflect the different aspects of self, but instead imply a general sense of self-worth or self-confidence. Third, the weighted-average approach assumes that some aspects of the self are more important or better predictors of general self-concept and, therefore, should count for more when adding the total, general self score. Marsh (1986), however, found that importance ratings assigned to the different facets by an entire group of subjects, by diverse subgroups, and even by individual ratings did not contribute to the prediction of global self-concept over the unweighted approach. Marsh (1990b) explained:

> This research has led me increasingly to the conclusion that general self-concept—no matter how it is inferred—is not a particularly useful construct. General self-concept does not reflect adequately the diversity of specific self facets. If the role of self-concept is to better understand the complexity of self in different contexts, to predict a wide variety of behaviors, to provide outcome measures for diverse interventions, and to relate self-concept to other constructs, then the specific facets of self-concept are more useful than a global indicator. (p. 100).

Therefore, Marsh (1990b) advocated the use of the higher order approach to measuring self-concept. This approach, based on the multidimensional theory of self-concept, uses items that represent the different facets of self-concept as well as items representing general self-concept (the items for general self-concept being similar to the superordinate approach described above). Items based on each of the facets are grouped into subscales that receive their own scores, in addition to a score for general self-concept. In contrast to the other approaches, the scores for the different subscales are as important as (possibly more important than) the overall self-concept score. This is a critical distinction: Marsh (1990b) has found that instruments designed in this fashion indicate that "responses to the General-self scale ... have surprisingly low correlations with many of the more specific facets of self" (p. 95). This has important implications for interventions, as will be discussed.

Keeping these considerations in mind, a description of some of the most commonly used assessment devices will now be outlined. The Piers-Harris Children's Self-Concept Scale (Piers, 1984) is an 80-item self-report scale with a yes/no response format, intended for use by children in grades 4 through 12. Piers (1984) reported six cluster scales: behavior, intellectual and school status, physical appearance and attributes, anxiety, popularity, and happiness and satisfaction. Piers (1984) also reported internal consistency coefficients for the total scale ranging from .88 to .93, and from .73 to .81 for the subscales. Cooley and Ayres (1988) found similar coefficients for these subscales (.74 to .83). Test–retest reliability coefficients reported by Piers (1984) ranged from .42 (over an eight-month interval) to .96 (over a three- to four-week interval) with a median coefficient of .73. Piers (1984) also provided evidence from a variety of studies supporting this scale's convergent validity, but evidence for discriminant validity is mixed. Finally, using the Self-Description Questionnaire (Marsh, 1988) and the Perceived Competence Scale for Children (Harter, 1979), Marsh (1990a) provided more evidence for convergent validity but also concluded that the scale had weak divergent validity.

Beck, Steer, Epstein, & Brown (1990) constructed the Beck Self-Concept Scale (BST), a 25-item self-report instrument developed using 550 psychiatric outpatients diagnosed primarily with mood or anxiety disorders. Respondents are instructed to describe themselves on 25 traits by comparing themselves to others whom they know. They reported good internal consistency of this scale (coefficient alpha = .82), and good test–retest reliability ($r = .88$ after one week, $r = .65$ after three months). The BST demonstrated both construct validity (e.g., $r = .38$ with the Beck Depression Inventory) and concurrent validity ($r = .51$ with the Rosenberg Self-Esteem Scale). The authors also report that the BST displayed discriminant and convergent validities with respect to measures of psychopathology. They caution, however, that this scale has not been thoroughly tested in normal adult populations.

The Self-Description Questionnaire (SDQ), designed by Marsh (1988), uses the higher order approach to measuring self-concept. The SDQ is a 76-item scale designed to measure seven specific facets of self: physical abilities, physical appearance, peer relationships, parent relationships, reading/verbal, mathematics, and school, as well as a global dimension of overall self-concept using a five-point true/false rating system. This questionnaire was devel-

oped for use with preadolescents, and other questionnaires have been developed for use with older populations (see Marsh, 1990b). Marsh (1990b), in a recent review, found strong factor-analytic support for all of these subscales. Marsh, Relich, and Smith (1983) found that correlations between the seven subscales ranged from zero to .4, and internal consistency reliabilities of the seven scales are in the .80s and .90s. The SDQ has also demonstrated convergent and discriminant validity (Marsh, 1990a) and construct validity (Marsh, Relich, & Smith, 1983).

Finally, some researchers have taken the approach of measuring only one facet of self-concept (e.g., social self-concept). An example of this would be the Social Self-Concept Scale (Zorich & Reynolds, 1988). This scale differentiated social self-concept from general and academic self-concept effectively and demonstrated both convergent and discriminant validity, as well as internal consistency ($r = .95$). No test–retest reliability data were reported, however.

## ISSUES AND CONCERNS INVOLVING STRATEGIES FOR IMPROVING SELF-CONCEPT

As with assessments, different approaches, based on the particular researcher's theoretical framework, have been developed for improving an individual's self-concept. On one side are researchers who focus on changing global self-concept and, therefore, develop interventions aimed at this goal; on the other side are those who focus on changing specific aspects of self-concept rather than concentrating on self-concept in general.

Marsh (1990b) disagreed with the global approach to self-concept interventions citing Scheirer and Kraut's (1979) review article. These authors concluded that evidence from academic intervention studies attempting to improve self-concept as a way to improve academic achievement have been largely ineffective (i.e., they failed to improve either self-concept or academic achievement). In support of the faceted approach to changing self-concept, Marsh, Relich, and Smith (1983) found that mathematical achievement, for example, correlated .55 with mathematical self-concept and .54 with academic self-concept, but only .33 with general self-concept and .01 with nonacademic self-concept. In addition to this, Mboya (1989) found that academic self-concept and academic achievement were more strongly correlated than were global self-concept and academic achievement. On the basis of these findings, these researchers argue that since global self-concept is correlated to a lesser degree with important variables such as academic achievement, the focus of the interventions should be on the lower order self-concepts (i.e., academic self-concept), rather than on changing an individual's global self-concept. Mboya (1989), for example, suggested that "Educational intervention strategies geared to raise academic achievement would probably be more likely to succeed if they were to focus on enhancement of academic self-concept rather than on global self-concept" (pp. 43–44). In addition, Marsh (1990b) remarked, "Thus, it is possible that an experimental intervention can have a substantial effect in one area of self-concept even if it has little effect on overall self-concept" (p. 154).

One example of the faceted approach to improving self-concept is the Outward Bound Standard Course (Marsh, Richards, & Barnes, 1986b). This program was designed to improve nonacademic self-concept. The subjects in this study ($N$ = 361) were organized into cooperative groups, and participated in personalized physical fitness programs that included strenuous activities such as rock climbing and cross-country running. Overt, external competition was deemphasized. Although there was a strong emphasis on the physical component, physical fitness was not the primary goal. Other goals of the program included improving awareness of self and others; increasing self-confidence, cooperation, self-reliance, and initiative; taking responsibility for oneself; and mastering stressful situations. Results of the study confirmed the original hypothesis: The program primarily affected nonacademic components of self-concept and had less of an impact on academic facets of self. An eighteen-month follow-up conducted by Marsh, Richards, and Barnes (1986a) showed no reduction in the gains made during the program. A similar intervention was developed to have an impact primarily on academic self-concept (Marsh & Richards, 1988).

Marsh and Peart (1988) used a more narrowly focused intervention aimed at changing only physical fitness self-concept. This study, using 11- to 14-year-old junior high school girls, compared the effectiveness of a cooperatively focused physical fitness program, a competitively focused physical fitness program, and a control group. For the control group, the girls participated in unstructured volleyball games. In the two fitness groups, the girls participated in aerobics training over a six-week period (fourteen 35-minute sessions). In both programs, the girls formed teams that competed against each other. The groups differed with respect to the amount of cooperation needed to perform the exercises (exercises in the cooperative group *required* the cooperation of two girls to perform them successfully, whereas exercises in the competitive group were individually oriented) and the types of verbal cues the girls received from the instructors (instructors for the cooperative group were encouraging and emphasized improvement, whereas instructors for the competitive group emphasized winning and being the best). The results indicated that both the competitive and the cooperative groups significantly enhanced physical fitness compared to the control group. Also, the cooperative group enhanced self-concept of physical ability and physical appearance, whereas the competitive group lowered had lower scores on these dimensions. Finally, the results of this study showed that these interventions had no significant effect on any other facet of self-concept, supporting its independent and multidimensional nature.

Barrett (1985) employed behavioral skills training for 28 normal children referred for deficits in social skills. He used cognitive-behavioral modification (e.g., strategies for approaching other children or groups of children, taking leave, and coping with rejection), modeling, role playing, and token reinforcement to improve the children's social skills. The role playing was utilized for modeling and practicing the skills. Results showed that significant improvements occurred only in the social ratings of self-concept. Finally, Craven, Marsh, and Debus (1991) used internally focused feedback and attributional feedback for improving reading and math self-concepts. Findings showed that other facets of self-concept were not affected by the intervention.

Critical questions arise at this point. For example, given that many professionals, such as authors of the *Diagnostic and Statistical Manual of Mental Disorders,* third edition, revised, (DSM-III-R), attach a significant amount of importance to the construct of *self-concept,* how does one go about integrating "self-concept improvement" into a treatment plan? Does this need to be done directly, or is it already implicit in many types of therapy? Should we as a profession continue to find specific treatments for each cluster of disorders or, instead, focus on intervening at a more generic and yet specific level (i.e., that of self-concept)? Finally, should the lower order facets of self-concept be addressed, as the Shavelson et al. (1976) model contends, or should we focus on a person's general sense of self and how that relates to his or her difficulties?

When reviewing the current literature on self-concept, it becomes apparent that few specific suggestions are given for techniques to improve someone's self-concept. At a more general level, persuasive arguments have been made that one should focus more on the specific facets of self-concept that are relevant than on global self-concept, and that focusing on competition among one's peers seems to be more detrimental than helpful. These are helpful guidelines but do not provide specific techniques for improving self-concept. When specific techniques are provided (e.g., self-awareness, physical activity, skills training), it is difficult to determine what elements of these interventions have been successful in improving self-concept.

A possible solution to this lacuna is to utilize findings from the self-efficacy literature. Although Bandura does not work directly in the area of self-concept, his proposed intervention strategies for enhancing self-efficacy may be appropriate for improving self-concept. In fact, one could argue that increases in self-efficacy lead to changes in self-concept. Strategies for increasing self-efficacy, and how they relate to self-concept, will be discussed later in this chapter.

## THEORY AND RESEARCH ON SELF-ESTEEM

Coopersmith (1967) defined *self-esteem* as an *evaluation* an individual makes and maintains about him- or herself. In this self-evaluation process, the individual examines his or her performance, capabilities, and attributes according to personal standards and values and makes a decision about his or her own worthiness. Thus, self-esteem expresses an attitude of approval or disapproval, and it indicates to what extent the individual believes that he or she is competent, significant, successful, and worthy. The attitudes one holds toward oneself, Coopersmith explained, carry affective loadings and have motivational consequences. Also, this definition focuses primarily on the relatively enduring level of self-esteem rather than on situational/transitory attitudes toward oneself.

Because self-esteem is defined as evaluative attitudes one holds about one's "self," it is important to discuss Coopersmith's (1967) definition of the "self." The *self* is an abstraction of the object Coopersmith refers to as the *person*. The self, then, develops as an individual observes his or her own behavior and observes the way other people respond to the individual's appearance, attitudes, and performance. Coopersmith also explained that the concept of *self* develops from a variety of diverse experiences and that, once formed, it is relatively resistant to change (a contention similar to that of the Shavelson model of general self-concept).

After reviewing the work of past theorists and researchers, Coopersmith (1967) determined that there are four factors that contribute to the development of self-esteem. The first factor refers to the amount and quality of treatment one receives from the significant others in the individual's life. In other words, we value ourselves as we are valued by others. This was supported by Coopersmith's (1967) study. For example, he pointed out three of the most important things parents can do for their children, with regard to self-esteem, are to accept them, to define clearly and enforce limits, and to respect their individual actions within those limits. Coopersmith (1967) also commented:

> In effect, we can conclude that the parents of children with high self-esteem are concerned and attentive toward their children, that they structure the worlds of their children along lines they believe to be proper and appropriate, and that they permit relatively great freedom within the structures they have established, (p. 236).

Although Coopersmith (1967) initially proposed that a person's record of past successes and his or her status in society was a second factor important in contributing to self-esteem, the results of his study did not confirm this. Instead, he pointed out that the use of general public standards for understanding how a person appraises him- or herself is of limited value. Paying attention to the person's immediate interpersonal environment appears to be more important in how a person evaluates him- or herself as successful:

> It is from a person's actions and relative position within this frame of reference that he comes to believe that he is a success or failure, and *not* in the far broader and more abstract context of general sociocultural standards. (Coopersmith, 1967, p. 243; emphasis in the original)

This is clearly supported by the social comparison literature discussed later in this chapter.

Third, Coopersmith (1967) proposed that one's values and aspirations determine how one appraises one's experiences (i.e., one's experiences are not judged objectively but, instead, are filtered through and perceived in relation to one's personal goals and values). For example, he argued that people are more likely to value doing well in one particular area of their life because they are good at it. Results of his study, however, did not support this contention (Coopersmith, 1967). Instead, he found that persons of all levels of self-esteem employ fairly similar standards to judge their worth. That is, everyone values being intelligent or having good social skills, not just those who excel in these areas. The results also showed, however, that persons with higher self-esteem set significantly higher personal goals than did those with medium or low self-esteem.

Finally, Coopersmith (1967) proposed that how individuals respond to devaluation affects their evaluation of "self": Do they minimize, distort, or ignore demeaning actions from others? Do they reject the right of others to judge them? Are they highly sensitive to praise or criticism of others? The results supported this assertion (Coopersmith, 1967). He found that persons with high-self esteem are less anxious, have fewer psychosomatic symptoms, are less likely to have marked problems, and are less sensitive to criticism. Persons of low self-esteem are described by Coopersmith (1967) as reporting feelings of inadequacy, unworthiness, helplessness, and inferiority. They report feeling incapable of improving their situations, and they feel they lack the resources to tolerate or reduce the pressures of everyday life. Coopersmith also observed that although persons with low self-esteem desire success, they have lower expectations that such successes will occur. They conclude that their actual achievements are of little importance and that, unless they can attain the goals they have set for themselves (realistic or not), they are unsuccessful and unworthy. Persons of high self-esteem, on the other hand, regard themselves as more effective in meeting environmental demands, feel they are better able to defend themselves against distress, and report being happier than those with low self-regard.

One of the assets of Coopersmith's theory is that he integrated prior research to form a comprehensive theory of self-esteem. Along with this theoretical formulation, he has also provided the results of an extensive research project aimed at validating his hypotheses. A possible drawback, however, is that most of the data Coopersmith reported is correlational and therefore must be viewed with caution. Also, it appears that most of the research done since 1967 has centered around his Self-Esteem Inventory rather than validating the theory underlying the scale.

A final point needs to be made with regard to this theory. Coopersmith (1967) stated that although the concept of self is probably multidimensional (as Shavelson et al. argued), he decided to focus only on the evaluative dimension. This is an important point. Most researchers, like Coopersmith, theorize, investigate, and write about self-esteem as a *separate* construct or in isolation from self-concept. Indeed, these two lines of research rarely converge. Shavelson et al. (1976) commented:

> As far as we know, the distinction between self-description and self-evaluation has not been clarified either conceptually or empirically. Accordingly, the terms self-concept and self-esteem have been used interchangeably in the literature. (pp. 414–415)

This has not changed very much since 1976. Shavelson's model appears to have made a place for self-esteem (one of the contentions of the model is that self-concept has both descriptive and evaluative components) but does not deal with it explicitly. One is left with questions such as: Are these two different processes or constructs? Are they two different aspects of the same process (i.e., different facets of the same construct)? Is self-esteem a secondary consideration when dealing with self-concept, or is it a primary concern? Also, if one agrees with the arguments of Marsh (e.g., 1990b) and his colleagues (e.g., Shavelson et al., 1976) with regard to the facets of self-concept, would this translate to facets of self-esteem? Would these facets be as important? If a clinician were attempting to assess a person's self-esteem or develop interventions for increasing self-esteem, should the clinician aim at altering global self-esteem or facets of self-esteem? For that matter, should interventions and assessments be aimed at both self-concept and self-esteem, or should they be treated separately? In summary, research on clearing up the conceptual ambiguities of the self-concept and self-esteem constructs appears to be a necessity in this field.

## ASSESSING SELF-ESTEEM

Coopersmith (1967) designed the Self-Esteem Inventory to measure evaluative attitudes toward the self in areas including social, academic, personal, and family. Form A includes 58 items, 8 of which make up a lie scale. Responders are to indicate whether an item is "Like me" or "Unlike me." Coopersmith (1967) reported a split-half reliability of .9. Johnson, Redfield, Miller, and Simpson (1983) reported a Cronbach alpha of .86, and Spatz and Johnston (1973) reported KR-20 internal reliabilities of .81, .86, and .80 for fifth, ninth, and twelfth grades, respectively.

For test–retest reliability, Coopersmith (1967) reported .88 for 30 fifth-grade children after a five-week period and .70 for a different sample of 56 children after a three-year interval. Byrne (1983) found a test–retest reliability of .63 over a six-month interval for 929 high school students, while Drummond, McIntire, and Ryan (1977) found test–retest reliabilities ranging from .52 to .60 for ninth through twelfth graders over six months. Byrne (1983) and Hughes (1984), both having conducted reviews of the literature, reported several studies providing evidence for convergent and discriminant validity of this scale. Finally, Johnson et al. (1983) reported internal consistency reliabilities ranging from .61 to .71 for the subscales. However, Hughes (1984) cautions against the use of the subscales, reporting that a substantial amount of factorial instability has been found in other studies.

Form B of the SEI, the short form, contains only 25 items. Bedeian, Teague, and Zmud (1977) found test–retest reliabilities of .80 for male and .82 for female college students over a five-week period ($N$ = 103). They also reported internal consistency KR-20 coefficients of .73 and .71. Also, Bedeian (1976) found concurrent validity for the short form but did not find strong support for convergent validity (Bedeian & Zmud, 1977).

A second self-esteem scale has been developed by Rosenberg (1965). His Self-Esteem Scale (SES) was originally developed as a unidimensional measure of global self-concept to use with high school students. This scale has ten items, which require respondents to use a four-point Likert scale ranging from "strongly agree" to "strongly disagree." In his original study, Rosenberg (1965) reported a test–retest reliability of .92 with 5,024 high school students. Byrne (1983), however, found a much lower reliability coefficient ($r$ = .62) with 929 high school students over a six-month period. Byrne's (1983) study also provided evidence for convergent validity (.59 correlation with Coopersmith's Self-Esteem Inventory) as well as discriminant validity.

## COOPERSMITH'S SUGGESTIONS FOR INCREASING SELF-ESTEEM

According to the results of the study conducted by Coopersmith (1967), when working with persons with low self-esteem it is important to keep two things in mind:

1. Explicitly define the criteria for success and failure.
2. The use of modeling is helpful.

Coopersmith (1967) pointed out that children who come from families with high self-esteem had clearly defined limits and rules that allowed the child to know when he or she had failed, by how much, and what he or she needed to do to be successful. The absence of these specified standards according to Coopersmith (1967), leaves the person "uncertain of his success and failure and lessens the likelihood that he will judge his performance as successful" (p. 246). It is also important that the rules be set at an appropriate level and be realistic for the individual. These conclusions are based on interview and questionnaire data with both the subjects and their mothers (Coopersmith, 1967).

The importance of using a model, as pointed out by Coopersmith (1967), is that

> the individual may observe how an effective individual deals with anxiety, resolves ambiguities, and makes decisions. He may observe how the person deals with insults and failures, handles money, and makes friends; the individual may thus learn alternative ways of action that confer a greater sense of power and control than he has previously experienced. . . . Individuals with low self-esteem lack the capacity to define and to deal with their environment, but they may learn to do so more rapidly and efficiently if they are exposed to persons who are themselves confident and effective. (p. 263)

Although these serve as helpful guidelines for working with persons with low self-esteem, research on interventions in this area suffer from the same problems as those in self-concept. That is, when one is working with clients with problematic self-esteem, how should one go about improving it? Again, one could argue that Bandura's (1977) approach to enhancing self-efficacy may lead to increases in self-esteem. This is dealt with in the next section.

## SELF-EFFICACY THEORY

Albert Bandura's (1984) concept of self-efficacy refers to a person's perception of his or her ability to perform at a level to meet situational requirements. A person must continually make decisions about what types of activities to engage in, how much effort to invest in them, and how long to continue them. According to Bandura (1977), the decision to engage in an activity is based on *perceptions* of what one is capable of doing (i.e., self-efficacy perceptions). It is important to note that self-efficacy perceptions may be different from what one actually *is* capable of doing. If a person is confident of his or her ability to perform a certain task, that person will utilize his or her skills effectively. However, if one is doubtful of one's skills one may behave ineffectually even if one does know what to do (Bandura, 1987). In other words, one may have the ability to complete a task, but an individual who doubts that ability (who has insufficient self-efficacy) may fall short of what he or she is capable of doing.[1] Bandura (1982) also points out: "Because acting on misjudgments of personal efficacy can produce adverse consequences, accurate appraisal of one's own capabilities has considerable functional value" (p. 123).

Bandura (1986) has argued that people who judge themselves to have a high sense of self-efficacy—that is, who are confident of their abilities—think, feel, and behave differently than do those who perceive themselves as inefficacious. People with low self-efficacy reduce their efforts and give up quickly when confronted with difficulties (Bandura, 1987). On the other hand,

> People who believe strongly in their capabilities attribute failure to insufficient effort, which supports a success orientation. They approach threatening situations with assurance that they can exercise control over them. As a result, they experience low stress. Such an efficacious outlook produces performance accomplishments, reduces stress, and lowers vulnerability to depression. (Bandura, 1987, p. 48)

It is important to distinguish between *efficacy expectations* and *response-outcome expectancies*. A person's estimate that a certain behavior will lead to certain outcomes is an outcome expectancy, whereas the conviction that one can perform successfully to produce the outcomes is an efficacy expectation. The reason for differentiating outcome and efficacy expectations is to emphasize that one may understand what behavior will lead to what consequences, but if one does not perceive oneself as having the capability to perform the necessary activities, knowledge of how to get from point A to point B may not influence one's actual behavior (Bandura, 1977). Therefore, it is not necessarily true that people with high self-efficacy have more knowledge about how to handle a particular situation than do those with lower perceived self-efficacy. Instead, those with higher self-efficacy perceive themselves as having the ability to achieve certain ends.[2]

Expectations of personal mastery can influence whether or not an individual will even engage in a particular activity. If a person judges the needs of a situation to exceed his or her ability to perform at a required level or to cope with the situation, that individual will fear and tend to avoid the situation. If, on the other hand, one assesses one's abilities as capable of matching the challenges of the task, then the individual will attempt to take on the situation (Bandura, 1977). Perceived self-efficacy can also influence how much effort one will expend and how long one will persist in an activity. The stronger the perceived self-efficacy, the more effort one will expend and the longer one will persist. Those who persist in activities they perceive to be threatening but are actually relatively safe may gain corrective experiences that change their sense of efficacy. If, however, they terminate an activity prematurely, they may reinforce their self-perceptions of inefficacy (Bandura, 1977).

According to Bandura (1977, 1982), people's perceptions of self-efficacy are based on four major sources of information: performance accomplishments, vicarious experience, verbal persuasion, and physiological states.[3] Bandura (1982) argued that performance accomplishments are the most influential of these, citing a number of studies showing that they produce higher, stronger, and more generalized increases in coping efficacy. According to Bandura, successful experience will raise one's mastery expectations,[4] where a failure will lower them. Once strong efficacy expectations are developed, through repeated successes, an occasional failure is less likely to be detrimental. If, however, the failures occur early in the course of events, they could have greater impact (Bandura, 1977, 1982). As the increased sense of self-efficacy becomes more established in one area, it may generalize to other areas. (Bandura, Adams, & Beyer, 1977; Bandura, Jeffery, & Gajdos, 1975; Smith, 1989; Williams, Kinney, & Falbo, 1989).

Watching others model threatening activities without adverse consequences (also advocated by Coopersmith), though not as powerful as performance, can also increase one's sense of self-efficacy. Bandura (1977) has cautioned, however, that:

> Vicarious experience, relying as it does on inferences from social comparison, is a less dependable source of information about one's capabilities than is direct evidence of personal accomplishments. Consequently, the efficacy expectations induced by modeling alone are likely to be weaker and more vulnerable to change. (p. 197)

With verbal persuasion, people are led into believing they can cope successfully with something they initially believed was overwhelming. This can contribute to the successes achieved through performance accomplishments. The aim of verbal persuasion is to *convince* a person that he or she possesses the capabilities to master a difficult situation. However, verbal persuasion does have important limitations. Efficacy expectations raised through the use of verbal persuasion are not as strong as expectations raised through personal experience (Bandura, 1977). Further, if one persuades a person to engage in an activity but does not ensure a positive outcome, it may undermine the credibility of the persuader and may undermine the recipient's perceived self-efficacy (Bandura, 1977).

Emotional arousal is the final source of influence on one's perceived self-efficacy. "Because high arousal usually debilitates performance, individuals are more likely to expect success when they are not beset by aversive arousal than if they are tense and viscerally agitated" (Bandura, 1977, p. 198). Feelings of fear can also feed upon themselves, generating self-debilitating statements that further elevate one's anxiety. The increase in arousal may then interfere with functioning, possibly resulting in failure and further lowering one's sense of self-efficacy (Bandura, 1977).

With regard to these different types of information, Bandura (1977) has pointed out that it is important to distinguish between information in the environment and information as it is "processed and transformed" by the individual (p. 200). The impact of information on efficacy expectations depends on the individual's cognitive appraisal.[5] If, for example, a person ascribes his or her success to situational factors rather than to his or her own personal competencies, the success experience is likely to have little effect on the person's level of self-efficacy. Successes, Bandura (1977) has explained, "are more likely to enhance self-efficacy if performances are perceived as resulting from skill than from fortuitous or special external aids" (p. 201). Also, challenging tasks that one is successful at providing much more evidence for one's ability to cope than does a task that is perceived as easy, and will subsequently enhance one's sense of self-efficacy to a greater degree (Bandura, 1977).

## RESEARCH EVALUATING SELF-EFFICACY THEORY[6]

Bandura's (1986) social cognitive theory posits that it is mainly one's perception of inefficacy in coping with a potential threat that results in fearful expectations and avoidance of that situation. It is not the fear itself that results in avoidance behavior;

rather, people avoid situations because they believe they are unable to manage them safely.

Cervone and Peake (1986) looked at the impact of *artificially altered* perceptions of efficacy on the amount of motivation exhibited in attempting to complete a task; that is, subjects were tricked into setting their efficacy expectations high or low. Subjects picked what they believed to be a random number from a bag. In the "high anchor" condition the "randomly chosen" number was 18; in the "low anchor" condition the number was 4. The subjects were then asked how many problems they believed they could complete: less than, more than, or equal to that number (i.e., 18 or 4). This set up their self-efficacy expectations artificially high or low. The results of this experiment showed that those in the high anchor condition reported that they believed they could solve more problems than did those in the low anchor condition (i.e., they demonstrated higher levels of perceived self-efficacy) and subsequently persisted longer on the unsolvable problems than the low anchor subjects did. In other words, if people can be convinced that they are capable of doing something, they will attempt to act accordingly.

Kavanagh and Wilson (1989) used group cognitive therapy with clinically depressed volunteers. The cognitive treatment consisted of a variety of techniques including identifying negative cognitive distortions and irrational beliefs, examining the validity of automatic negative thoughts, developing and using positive counterstatements, and so on. They found that not only were improvements in the level of the subjects' depression associated with self-efficacy, but also that posttreatment self-efficacy scores could predict subjects who relapsed over a 12 month period.

Bandura, O'Leary, Taylor, Gauthier, and Gossard (1987) demonstrated that through cognitive coping strategies, designed to enhance one's sense of self-efficacy, subjects were able to withstand and reduce pain compared to subjects in a placebo condition and a control condition. Results showed that although the cognitive coping group did better overall than the placebo group, regardless of what condition they were in, the greater the subjects' sense of self-efficacy, the longer they could withstand the pain stimulation. Bandura, Reese, and Adams (1982) reported a similar finding:

> The higher the level of induced self-efficacy, the higher were the subjects' performance attainments . . . Subjects executed successfully tasks that fell within their enhanced range of self-efficacy but

failed those that exceeded their perceived coping capabilities. (p. 19)

As with the Shavelson model of self-concept, the virtues of Bandura's self-efficacy theory are that it is very comprehensive (i.e., a number of assessment tools and intervention strategies have been developed from self-efficacy theory), and it has been soundly supported by a great deal of research, both by Bandura and by independent researchers.

## ASSESSING SELF-EFFICACY

In order to assess a person's self-efficacy, Bandura suggested providing the person with a list of performance tasks. The person is then to rate how *certain* he or she feels of being able to complete each task. A 100-point scale ranges in 10-unit intervals, from highly uncertain one could complete a task to completely certain one could complete the task. This, Bandura argued, measures one's perceived self-efficacy to complete each of the tasks (Bandura et al., 1982).

Sherer, Maddux, Mercandante, Prentice-Dunn, Jacobs, and Rogers (1982) have developed a more standardized way of assessing a person's self-efficacy. Responders rate 23 items on a 14-point likert scale from "strongly agree" to "strongly disagree." A factor analysis of their Self-Efficacy Scale revealed two subscales: general and social. The Cronbach alpha reliability scores were .86 for the general scale and .71 for the social scale. This scale has also been shown to have good criterion validity (Sherer et al., 1982)—that is, the general scale predicted past success in vocational, educational, and military areas—as well as good construct validity (Sherer & Adams, 1983; Sherer et al., 1982).

For children, Wheeler & Ladd (1982) developed the Children's Self-Efficacy for Peer Interaction Scale (CSPI) to assess children's social self-efficacy in peer situations. Each item on the CSPI consists of a statement describing a social situation, followed by an incomplete statement. The incomplete statements require the child to evaluate his or her ability to use a persuasive verbal skill by choosing one of four response choices: HARD!, hard, easy, EASY! Alpha coefficients for internal consistency were .85 for the total scale, and test–retest coefficients were .9 for boys and .8 for girls over a two-week period. They also reported evidence for convergent validity and "some preliminary evidence of discriminant validity" (Wheeler & Ladd, 1982, p. 803).

## PROPOSED INTERVENTION STRATEGIES FOR INCREASING SELF-EFFICACY

To change one's sense of self-efficacy, Bandura (1986) prescribes the use of mastery experiences. Mastery experiences develop an individual's coping skills and provide the individual with experience in demonstrating that he or she can stay in control even in the face of potential threats (Bandura, 1987). However, Bandura does not endorse the use of easy success experiences, which can set up the expectation that if the person does not achieve results quickly, he or she will not achieve them at all. "A resilient sense of efficacy requires experience in overcoming obstacles and meeting difficult challenges through perseverant effort" (Bandura, 1987, p. 42).

Bandura suggests the use of a participant modeling approach as the "primary vehicle of psychological change" (Bandura, 1977, p. 196). Because an individual is not about to engage in an activity he or she fears, the therapist must structure the environment to ensure success regardless of the person's incapacities. To do this, Bandura has suggested the use of a variety of response induction aids (Bandura, Jeffery, & Wright, 1974). First, the fear activities are modeled to show the clients how to cope with potential adversities they may encounter. "Having a serviceable coping skill at one's disposal undoubtedly contributes to one's sense of personal efficacy" (Bandura, 1977, p. 196). Modeling also helps to disconfirm any catastrophizing the person might engage in (also see Schunk, 1986, for an excellent review of vicarious influences on self-efficacy). The coping tasks are broken down into a series of subtasks that can be easily mastered by the person. At each step, the person is asked to do what he or she feels capable of doing, along with some extra effort in order to ensure success. Joint performance, in which the client and therapist engage in the activity together, the use of graduated time (i.e., increase time engaged in task after each performance trial), and modulating the severity of the threats can also help to develop a sense of coping efficacy. Finally, Bandura (1982) advocates the use of desensitization treatment, where people visualize threatening scenes while relaxed until they no longer experience any anxiety.

As treatment progresses, self-directed mastery experiences are encouraged and the protective aids are withdrawn. This is done to help the person verify that his or her ability to cope with the situation stems from enhanced efficacy rather than from reliance on the mastery aids. Bandura (1977) argued that independent performance can enhance efficacy expectations in a number of ways. First, the person gains additional exposure to a formerly feared situation, which gives the individual more evidence that he or she is no longer adversely aroused by it. The reduced emotional arousal will help confirm the individual's increased coping ability. This contention of Bandura, however, must be viewed with some caution. Barrios (1983), working with heterosocially anxious males, found that although motoric and self-report measures matched efficacy ratings at the posttest, physiological measures did not. A possible conclusion is that even when self-report and behavioral measures may indicate success, the individual may still be physiologically aroused.

The second way independent performance may enhance efficacy expectations is by affording the person a chance to perfect his or her coping skills, which may reduce the individual's vulnerability to stress. Third, the individual will (one hopes) have more success experiences, which serve to reinforce expectations of self-competency (Bandura, 1977). Finally, the repeated exposure will help to strengthen and *generalize* the individual's sense of coping efficacy to other situations (Bandura et al., 1975). For example, Williams, Kinney, and Falbo (1989) demonstrated the generalization of self-efficacy in a study using agoraphobics. They reported that agoraphobics who received brief treatment for some of their phobias experienced enduring generalized improvements in other phobias that were not treated. Smith (1989) also reported success in generalizing the effects of self-efficacy. Using structured coping skills training with test-anxious college students, Smith demonstrated that not only was there a significant reduction in test anxiety, which was "significantly correlated with improvements in test performance and increases in general self-efficacy" (p. 231), but that there was also a "significant reduction in general trait anxiety" (p. 231).

It is important to emphasize at this point that, according to Bandura (1977), mere exposure to a threatening event is not the crucial ingredient in changing someone's sense of self-efficacy. For example, phobics benefit more from seeing a model overcome his or her own difficulties than from watching a model perform a task without obstacles (Kazdin, 1973; Meichenbaum, 1971). It is important for the person not only to watch the model struggle, but also to observe how the model copes with the situation. It is "the modeling of effective coping strategies and socially comparative indicants of capability that constitute the critical influences" (Bandura, 1987, p. 39). Similarly, in verbal persuasion, it

is not the actual verbalizations that are important but, instead, the social power and credibility of the persuader that convince people (Bandura, 1987).

Bandura (1982) gives an example of how one would use this treatment process with postcoronary patients:

> The heart heals rapidly, but psychological recovery is slow for patients who believe they lack the physical efficacy to resume their customary activities. . . . Enactive efficacy information is compellingly conveyed through the strenuous treadmill exercises. Vicarious efficacy information is provided by enlisting the aid of former patients who exemplify active lives. Persuasive efficacy information is furnished by informing patients about what they are capable of doing. A heart attack is apt to give rise to overattentiveness to cardiac activity and misattribution of fatigue to an impaired heart. The meaning of physiological efficacy information is explained to ensure that patients do not misread their physiology, for example, by interpreting cardiac acceleration as portending a reinfarction. (p. 131)

Finally, Bandura (1982) advocated the use of positive incentives to increase self-efficacy. This involves the person setting personal standards against which to evaluate his or her performance. This self-motivation is best sustained by using attainable subgoals that lead to large future ones. His argument is that proximal subgoals provide immediate incentives and guides for action, whereas distal goals are too far removed in time to be effective. Bandura (1982) commented that "Without standards against which to measure their performance, people have little basis for judging how they are doing or for gauging their capabilities," (p. 134). This echoes Coopersmith's (1967) contention. Bandura (1982) supported this by citing a study conducted with children who exhibited deficits and disinterest in mathematical tasks (Bandura & Schunk, 1981). Using proximal subgoals, distal goals, or no reference to goals they found that where distal goals produced no effects, the use of proximal subgoals resulted in rapid progress, mastery in mathematical operations, and development of a strong sense of self-efficacy in solving arithmetic problems.

## CONCLUSIONS REGARDING INTERVENTIONS FOR SELF-EFFICACY, SELF-CONCEPT, AND SELF-ESTEEM

The focus of self-efficacy theory on performance seems to lend itself to a more developed and integrated treatment plan than either self-concept and self-esteem (i.e., it is more concrete). However, one could easily interpret Bandura's treatment plan for enhancing self-efficacy in terms of improving self-concept and self-esteem. For example, if a therapist was working with an adolescent who had poor social skills, the therapist could: (1) use role-playing to teach the client and allow the client to practice new skills (e.g., approaching others, initiating and maintaining a conversation, coping with adversity, etc.); (2) use a model to demonstrate the skills and coping strategies; (3) use verbal persuasion techniques such as rational-emotive therapy (Ellis, 1984) to appraise their situation accurately, and (4) use desensitization procedures to decrease his or her arousal level. If these techniques are effective in increasing these persons' level of self-efficacy, their belief that "Yes, I can accomplish this task," or "I am good at meeting new people and making a good impression," it might follow that they would begin to see themselves as doing well in social situations (i.e., increased *social* self-concept) and begin to feel better about themselves with regard to their social skills (i.e., increased *social* self-esteem).

A good argument can be made that if one simply follows Bandura's guidelines for increasing self-efficacy and emphasizes the impact of feeling more capable in situations, this may lead to improvement in how individuals will view themselves (i.e., self-concept) and how they will feel about themselves (i.e., self-esteem). However, as pointed out by Bandura (1977), "people can gain competence through authentic means but, because of faulty appraisals of the circumstances under which they improve, will credit their achievements to external factors rather than to their own capabilities," (p. 201). This point has been made several times throughout this chapter: People don't just absorb information in a simple "objective" fashion. It is important to be aware of how the client is appraising his or her situation. Not only must the therapist be aware of and confront irrational beliefs, as suggested by Ellis (1984), but he or she also must be aware of other related processes, such as internal and external attributions. For example, Ickes (1988) reviewed research demonstrating that individuals with high self-esteem are more likely to use information in a positive way (e.g., attributing success internally and failure externally), whereas persons with low self-esteem do the opposite.

Finally, in a related vein, an argument could be made that sometimes it is a good idea to appraise one's situation inaccurately. This follows from the study by Alloy and Abramson (1979). In this experiment, subjects estimated the degree of contingency between their responses and an environmental outcome. Results showed that depressed subjects were accurate in discerning whether or not the outcome was contingent on their response. Nondepressed subjects, however, reported a contingency between their response and the outcome even when there wasn't such a relationship. That is, nondepressed subjects are more likely to distort reality than depressed subjects. This could be interpreted with respect to self-concept. Those with good self-concept may distort reality sometimes in order to give themselves a sense of control in a way that is very adaptive and serves to maintain their positive self-concepts. Although there can be some negative implications of this process (discussed by Miller & Porter, 1988), it is important to be aware that attempting to persuade clients to have completely accurate perceptions of reality in order to improve their self-concept or self-esteem may not be the best strategy.

## SOCIAL COMPARISON: THEORY AND RESEARCH

A related field of research that deserves some attention is that of social comparison. Social comparison seems to be an integral part of all three of the previous theories: People compare themselves to others when describing themselves, deciding how they will evaluate their abilities (or themselves as individuals), and deciding whether they are able to accomplish certain tasks.

One of the most influential theorists in social comparison was Leon Festinger. Festinger (1954) asserted that people have a "drive" (p. 117) to evaluate their abilities. They prefer to use objective standards for this evaluation process, but when these do not exist they use other people in their environment. For example, Schwarzer, Jerusalem, and Lange (1983), cited in Marsh (1990b), looked at the effects of moving students from unstreamed primary schools to streamed secondary schools.[7] Students who went into the higher ability schools had higher academic self-concepts than did those entering the lower ability schools. By the end of the first year at the new school, however, there was no difference in self-concept between these two groups; "The most able students in the low-ability schools were less able but had much higher academic self-concept than the least able children in the high-ability schools," (Marsh, 1990b, p. 125). Marsh (1990b) interpreted this as follows:

When a reasonably bright student first attends a higher-ability school, the student is confronted quickly with the reality that he/she is no longer one of the brighter students—in fact may not even be in the top half of the school. Although there may be many ways of dealing with this realization, one of the most common appears to be readjusting academic self-concept so as to reflect more accurately the student's relative standing within this new academic environment. (p. 132)

Similar results have been reported by Coleman (1983). He compared normal children, mildly handicapped children in special education classes, and children with academic difficulties who remained in regular classes. He found that the handicapped children had comparable levels of self-concept to those of normal children, and he hypothesized that this resulted from the children interacting in homogeneous classroom settings. In addition, he found that children who were experiencing academic difficulties but remained in regular classrooms had lower self-concepts than did children in the other groups.

Building on Festinger's (1954) theory, Wills (1981) proposed the process of "downward comparison." According to Festinger (1954), social comparison occurs for the purpose of self-evaluation. Wills (1981), however, argued that, in addition to this, social comparison occurs for self-enhancement. He maintained that persons experiencing negative emotion use others less fortunate than themselves to enhance their subjective well-being. Wills (1981) pointed out that "the favorable comparison between the self and the less fortunate other enables a person to feel better about his or her own situation" (p. 245). In addition, Wills (1981) pointed out that: (1) under ordinary conditions people do not like observing negative affect in others, and (2) persons who are low in self-esteem are more likely to engage in downward comparison.

Gibbons and Gerrard (1989), in agreement with Wills (1981), focused on the self-esteem dimension of this theory. In this study, subjects were given information that a fellow student had experienced some problems since arriving at the university. This student was described either as having difficulty dealing with their problems (i.e., downward comparison), or adjusting well to their problems (i.e., upward comparison). Results of the study indicated that the mood of subjects with low self-esteem improved when they heard that others were having problems coping, whereas this information had no effect on high self-esteem subjects. The authors concluded,

then, that persons with low self-esteem are more likely to engage in downward comparison for self-enhancement.

Buunk, Collins, Taylor, VanYperen, and Dakof (1990) disagreed with Wills (1981). They argued that affective consequences (i.e., feeling better or worse) depend on how one interprets information.[8] In other words, downward or upward comparisons can be interpreted either positively or negatively, depending on how one uses the information. They also pointed out that those with high self-esteem are better able to make use of either upward or downward comparison information (i.e., to perceive such information as self-enhancing) than are those with low self-esteem. The results of their study (Buunk et al., 1990) showed that cancer patients low in self-esteem were more likely to see both upward *and* downward comparison information as having negative implications for themselves. This was also found with individuals with high marital dissatisfaction and with those who felt uncertain about their marital relationship. In partial agreement with Wills (1981), Buunk et al. (1990) demonstrated that, overall, individuals who perceived themselves or their situation as negative did make more downward comparisons, but these comparisons did not necessarily result in positive consequences (i.e., self-enhancement).

Finally, focusing more on upward than on downward comparisons, Testa and Major (1990) proposed that perceived control is an important variable in this process. Subjects in this experiment wrote two essays. After writing the first one, they were informed they had failed. They were then told either that it was very likely they could improve their test score on the second essay because scores on these two essays were only modestly correlated (high perceived control), or that it was very unlikely they would be able to improve their scores because scores on these two essays were highly correlated (low perceived control). Next, they were exposed to information indicating that others either had done better or had done worse than them on the first test. They found that subjects in the low control condition reported greater depressive and hostile emotion and persisted for a shorter period of time on the second test. The results of this study appear to have important implications for using models. Testa and Major (1990) argued that if individuals feel they have control over a situation, exposure to upward comparison information (i.e., a coping model) is more likely to motivate behavior than to cause distress. If, however, they feel they cannot control the outcome of a situation, upward comparison information will likely be debilitating rather than helpful.

## CONCLUSIONS

In what situations would a therapist want to focus on how clients describe their "self" (or the more specific aspects of their "self"); how they feel about their "self"; or what they believe their "self" is capable of? How do these self-constructs relate to the psychological problems (e.g., anxiety, substance abuse, depression) that the clients are experiencing? A reasonable argument seems to be that one of the primary determining forces in why people seek the help of mental health professionals is because of problems with their "self." That is, if a person has a good self-concept and good self-esteem, there is little chance that he or she will seek help. Therefore, a more direct approach in dealing with clients' selves seems warranted. Other points to keep in mind with regard to the "self," which have been outlined in this chapter, include: the multifaceted nature of "self," the importance of subjective appraisal of information, and the crucial role of being active in one's environment (i.e., doing or watching) for achieving change.

However, much important information is missing about how to assess accurately and intervene effectively with problems relating to inaccurate self-concept and self-esteem. More work has been done with self-efficacy, and this may serve, at least on a preliminary basis, as a heuristic for future research on self-concept and self-esteem. However, it must also be countenanced that these areas will require their own unique models and heuristics.

## NOTES

1. This is reminiscent of descriptions of persons with low self-esteem or poor self-concept.

2. Again, this could refer to persons with a good self-concept or high self-esteem.

3. Keep in mind that these probably relate to self-concept and self-esteem, also.

4. Or possibly self-concept, or self-esteem.

5. Again, in agreement with Coopersmith (1967).

6. Empirical support for Bandura's theory is presented in both this section and the section on proposed interventions for raising one's sense of self-efficacy.

7. Streamed classes are classes in which children are placed together on the basis of similar levels of academic achievement.

8. Again, this points to the importance of paying attention to how people interpret information.

## REFERENCES

Alloy, L. B., & Abramson, L. Y. (1979). Judgment of contingency in depressed and nondepressed students: Sadder but wiser? *Journal of Experimental Psychology—General, 108,* 441–485.

Allport, G. (1955). *Becoming: Basic considerations for a psychology of personality.* New Haven: Yale University Press.

American Psychiatric Association. (1987). *Diagnostic and statistical manual of mental disorders,* 3rd ed., revised. Washington, DC: American Psychiatric Press.

Bandura, A. (1977). Self-efficacy: Toward a unifying theory of behavioral change. *Psychological Review, 84,* 191–215.

Bandura, A. (1982). Self-efficacy mechanism in human agency. *American Psychologist, 37,* 122–147.

Bandura, A. (1984). Recycling misconceptions of perceived self-efficacy. *Cognitive Therapy and Research, 8,* 231–255.

Bandura, A. (1986). *Social foundations of thought and action: A social cognitive theory.* Englewood Cliffs, NJ: Prentice-Hall.

Bandura, A. (1987). Perceived self-efficacy: Exercise of control through self-belief. In J. P. Dauwalder, M. Perrez, and V. Hobi (Eds.), *Annual series of European research in behavior therapy.* Lisse (NL): Swets & Zeitlinger.

Bandura, A., Adams, N. E., & Beyer, J. (1977). Cognitive processes mediating behavioral change. *Journal of Personality and Social Psychology, 35,* 125–139.

Bandura, A., Jeffery, R. W., & Gajdos, E. (1975). Generalizing change through participant modeling with self-directed mastery. *Behaviour Research and Therapy, 13,* 141–152.

Bandura, A., Jeffery, R. W., & Wright, C. L. (1974). Efficacy of participant modeling as a function of response induction aids. *Journal of Abnormal Psychology, 83,* 56–64.

Bandura, A., O'Leary, A., Taylor, C. B., Gauthier, J., & Gossard, D. (1987). Perceived self-efficacy and pain control: Opioid and nonopioid mechanisms. *Journal of Personality and Social Psychology, 53,* 563–571.

Bandura, A., Reese, L., & Adams, N. E. (1982). Microanalysis of action and fear arousal as a function of differential levels of perceived self-efficacy. *Journal of Personality and Social Psychology, 43,* 5–21.

Bandura, A., & Schunk, D. H. (1981). Cultivating competence, self-efficacy, and intrinsic interest through proximal self-motivation. *Journal of Personality and Social Psychology, 41,* 586–598.

Barrett, T. E. (1985). Clinical application of behavioral social skills training with children. *Psychological Reports, 57,* 1183–1186.

Barrios, B. A. (1983). The role of cognitive mediators in heterosocial anxiety: A test of self-efficacy theory. *Cognitive Therapy and Research, 7,* 543–554.

Beck, A. T. (1976). *Cognitive therapy and the emotional disorders.* New York: International University Press.

Beck, A. T., Steer, R. A., Epstein, N., & Brown, G. (1990). Beck self-concept test. *Psychological Assessment: A Journal of Consulting and Clinical Psychology, 2,* 191–197.

Bedeian, A. G. (1976). Relationship of need achievement to self-esteem: Evidence for validity of Form B of Coopersmith's Self-Esteem Inventory. *Perceptual and Motor Skills, 43,* 1219–1220.

Bedeian, A. G., Teague, R. J., & Zmud, R. W. (1977). Test–retest reliability and internal consistency of short-form of Coopersmith's Self-Esteem Inventory. *Psychological Reports, 41,* 1041–1042.

Bedeian, A. G., & Zmud, R. W. (1977). Some evidence relating to convergent validity of Form B of Coopersmith's Self-Esteem Inventory. *Psychological Reports, 40,* 725–726.

Buunk, B. P., Collins, R. L., Taylor, S. E., VanYperen, N. W., & Dakof, G. A. (1990). The affective consequences of social comparison: Either direction has its ups and downs. *Journal of Personality and Social Psychology, 59,* 1238–1249.

Byrne, B. M. (1983). Investigating measures of self-concept. *Measurement and Evaluation in Guidance, 16,* 115–126.

Byrne, B. M., & Shavelson, R. J. (1986). On the structure of adolescent self-concept. *Journal of Educational Psychology, 78,* 474–481.

Cervone, D. & Peake, P. K. (1986). Anchoring, efficacy, and action: The influence of judgmental heuristics on self-efficacy judgments and behavior. *Journal of Personality and Social Psychology, 50,* 492–501.

Coleman, J. M. (1983). Self-concept and the mildly handicapped: The role of social comparisons. *The Journal of Special Education, 17,* 37–45.

Cooley, E., & Ayres, R. (1988). Cluster scores for the Piers-Harris Children's Self-Concept Scale: Reliability and independence. *Educational and Psychological Measurement, 48,* 1019–1024.

Coopersmith, S. A. (1967). *The antecedents of self-esteem.* San Francisco: Freeman.

Craven, R. G., Marsh, H. W., & Debus, R. L. (1991). Effects of internally focused feedback and attributional feedback on enhancement of academic self-concept. *Journal of Educational Psychology, 83,* 17–27.

Ellis, A. (1984). Expanding the ABCs of RET. *Journal of Rational-Emotive Therapy, 2,* 20–24.

Fairbairn, W. R. D. (1952). *An object relations theory of personality.* New York: Basic Books.

Festinger, L. (1954). A theory of social comparison processes. *Human Relations, 7,* 117–140.

Fleming, J. S., & Watts, W. A. (1980). The dimensionality of self-esteem: Some results for a college sample. *Journal of Personality and Social Psychology, 39,* 921–929.

Freud, S. (1948). In J. Strachey (Ed.), *The standard edition of the complete psychological works of Sigmund Freud.* London: Hogarth Press.

Gibbons, F. X., & Gerrard, M. (1989). Effects of upward and downward social comparison on mood states. *Journal of Social and Clinical Psychology, 8,* 14–31.

Gibbons, F. X., Smith, T. W., Ingram, R. E., Pearce, K., Brehm, S. S., & Shroeder, D. J. (1985). Self-awareness and self-confrontation: Effects of self-focused attention on members of a clinical population. *Journal of Personality and Social Psychology, 48,* 662–675.

Harter, S. (1979). *Manual: Perceived Competence Scale for Children.* Department of Psychology, University of Denver.

Hope, D. A., Rapee, R. M., Heimberg, R. G., & Dombeck, M. J. (1990). Representations of the self in social phobia: Vulnerability to social threat. *Cognitive Therapy and Research, 14,* 177–189.

Hughes, H. M. (1984). Measures of self-concept and self-esteem for children ages 3–12 years: A review and recommendations. *Clinical Psychology Review, 4,* 657–692.

Ickes, W. (1988). Attributional styles and the self-concept. In L. Y. Abramson (Ed.), *Social cognition and clinical psychology: A synthesis.* New York: Guilford Press.

Ingram, R. E., & Kendall, P. C. (1987). The cognitive side of anxiety. *Cognitive Therapy and Research, 11,* 523–536.

James, W. (1890, 1950). *The principles of psychology* (Vol. 1). New York: Dover.

Johnson, B. W., Redfield, D. L., Miller, R. L., & Simpson, R. E. (1983). The Coopersmith Self-Esteem Inventory: A construct validation study. *Educational and Psychological Measurement, 43,* 907–913.

Kavanagh, D. J., & Wilson, P. H. (1989). Prediction of outcome with group cognitive therapy for depression. *Behaviour Research and Therapy, 27,* 333–343.

Kazdin, A. E. (1973). Covert modeling and the reduction of avoidance behavior. *Journal of Abnormal Psychology, 81,* 87–95.

Kelly, G. (1955). *A theory of personality: The psychology of personal constructs.* New York: Norton.

Kohut, H. (1977). *The restoration of the self.* New York: International Universities Press.

Marsh, H. W. (1986). Global self-esteem: Its relation to specific facets of self-concept and their importance. *Journal of Personality and Social Psychology, 51,* 1224–1236.

Marsh, H. W. (1988). *The Self Description Questionnaire (SDQ): A Theoretical and Empirical Basis for the Measurement of Multiple Dimensions of Preadolescent Self-Concept: A Test Manual and Research monograph.* San Antonio, TX: Psychological Corporation.

Marsh, H. W. (1990a). Confirmatory factor analysis of multitrait–multimethod data: The construct validation of multidimensional self-concept responses. *Journal of Personality, 58,* 661–692.

Marsh, H. W. (1990b). A multidimensional, hierarchical model of self-concept: Theoretical and empirical justification. *Educational Psychology Review, 2,* 77–172.

Marsh, H. W. (1990c). The structure of academic self-concept: The Marsh/Shavelson model. *Journal of Educational Psychology, 82,* 623–636.

Marsh, H. W., Byrne, B. M., & Shavelson, R. J. (1988). A multifaceted academic self-concept: Its hierarchical structure and its relation to academic achievement. *Journal of Educational Psychology, 80,* 366–380.

Marsh, H. W., & Hocevar, D. (1985). Application of confirmatory factor analysis to the study of self-concept: First- and higher order factor models and their invariance across groups. *Psychological Bulletin, 97,* 562–582.

Marsh, H. W., & Peart, N. D. (1988). Competitive and cooperative physical fitness training programs for girls: Effects on physical fitness and multidimensional self-concepts. *Journal of Sport and Exercise Psychology, 10,* 390–407.

Marsh, H. W., Relich, J. D., & Smith, I. D. (1983). Self-concept: The construct validity of interpretations based upon the SDQ. *Journal of Personality and Social Psychology, 45,* 173–187.

Marsh, H. W., & Richards, G. E. (1988). The Outward Bound Bridging Course for low achieving high-school males: Effect on academic achievement and multidimensional self-concepts. *Australian Journal of Psychology, 40,* 281–298.

Marsh, H. W., Richards, G. E., & Barnes, J. (1986a). Multidimensional self-concepts: A long-term follow-up of the effect of participation in an Outward Bound program. *Personality and Social Psychology Bulletin, 12,* 475–492.

Marsh, H. W., & Shavelson, R. (1985). Self-concept: Its multifaceted hierarchical structure. *Educational Psychologist, 20,* 107–123.

Marsh, H. W., Smith, I. D., & Barnes, J. (1983). Multitrait–multimethod analyses of the Self Description Questionnaire: Student–teacher agreement on multidimensional ratings of student self-concept. *American Educational Research Journal, 20,* 333–357.

Mathews, A. & MacLeod, C. (1987). An information-processing approach to anxiety. *Journal of Cognitive Psychotherapy, 1,* 105–115.

Mboya, M. M. (1989). The relative importance of global self-concept and self-concept of academic ability in predicting academic achievement. *Adolescence, 24,* 39–46.

Meichenbaum, D. H. (1971). Examination of model characteristics in reducing avoidance behavior. *Journal of Personality and Social Psychology, 17,* 298–307.

Meicher, B. (1986). Moral reasoning, self-identity, and moral action: A study of conduct disorder in adolescence. Doctoral Dissertation, University of Pittsburgh.

Miller, D. T., & Porter, C. A. (1988). Errors and biases in the attribution process. In L. Y. Abramson (Ed.), *Social

cognition and clinical psychology: A synthesis.* New York: Guilford Press.

Nisbett, R. E., & Wilson, T. D. (1977). Telling more than we can know: Verbal reports on mental processes. *Psychological Review, 84,* 231–259.

Piers, E. V. (1984). *Piers-Harris Children's Self-Concept Scale: Revised Manual.* Los Angeles: Western Psychological Services.

Preyer, W. (1889). *The mind of a child.* New York: Appleton-Century-Crofts.

Rogers, C. R. (1951). *Client-centered therapy.* Boston: Houghton Mifflin.

Rosenberg, M. (1965). *Society and the adolescent self-image.* Princeton, NJ: Princeton University Press.

Scheirer, M. A., & Kraut, R. E. (1979). Increasing educational achievement via self-concept change. *Review of Educational Research, 49,* 131–149.

Schunk, D. H. (1986). Vicarious influences on self-efficacy for cognitive skill learning. *Journal of Social and Clinical Psychology, 4,* 316–327.

Segal, Z. V., & Vella, D. D. (1990). Self-schema in major depression: Replication and extension of a priming methodology. *Cognitive Therapy and Research, 14,* 161–176.

Shavelson, R. J., & Bolus, R. (1982). Self-concept: The interplay of theory and methods. *Journal of Educational Psychology, 74,* 3–17.

Shavelson, R. J., Hubner, J. J., & Stanton, G. C. (1976). Self-concept: Validation of construct interpretations. *Review of Educational Research, 46,* 407–441.

Sherer, M., & Adams, C. H. (1983). Construct validation of the Self-efficacy scale. *Psychological Reports, 53,* 899–902.

Sherer, M., Maddux, J. E., Mercandante, B., Prentice-Dunn, S., Jacobs, B., & Rogers, R. W. (1982). The Self-Efficacy Scale: Construction and validation. *Psychological Reports, 51,* 663–671.

Skinner, B. F. (1953). *Science and human behavior.* New York: Free Press.

Smith, R. E. (1989). Effects of coping skills training on generalized self-efficacy and locus of control. *Journal of Personality and Social Psychology, 56,* 228–233.

Spatz, K. C., & Johnston, J. O. (1973). Internal consistency of the Coopersmith Self-Esteem Inventory. *Educational and Psychological Measurement, 33,* 875–876.

Testa, M., & Major, B. (1990). The impact of social comparisons after failure: The moderating effects of perceived control. *Basic and Applied Social Psychology, 11,* 205–218.

Wheeler, V. A., & Ladd, G. W. (1982). Assessment of children's self-efficacy for social interactions with peers. *Developmental Psychology, 18,* 795–805.

Williams, S. L., Kinney, P. J., & Falbo, J. (1989). Generalization of therapeutic changes in agoraphobia: The role of perceived self-efficacy. *Journal of Consulting and Clinical Psychology, 57,* 436–442.

Wills, T. A. (1981). Downward comparison principles in social psychology, *Psychological Bulletin, 90,* 245–271.

Woolfolk, R. L., Sass, L. A., & Messer, S. B. (1988). Introduction to hermeneutics. In S. B. Messer, L. A. Sass, & R. L. Woolfolk (Eds.), *Hermeneutics and psychological theory: Interpretive perspectives on personality, psy-* *chotherapy, and psychopathology. Rutgers symposia on applied psychology* (Vol. 2, pp. 2–26). New Brunswick, NJ: Rutgers University Press.

Zorich, S., & Reynolds, W. M. (1988). Convergent and discriminant validation of a measure of social self-concept. *Journal of Personality Assessment, 52,* 441–453.

# CHAPTER 9

# ACADEMIC SKILLS

Julie S. Vargas
Deborah Shanley

When a teacher paddles a student so strenuously that the student requires hospitalization, the public rightfully demands immediate action. But when a school fails to provide youngsters with academic skills, change is slower in coming. Yet children who are not taught basic reading and math skills are harmed as surely as those who are paddled, and the harm reaches far into their futures. A student with weak reading and math skills is four times as likely to be dependent on public assistance as one with strong basic skills, and eight times as likely to have a child out of wedlock. Between 1973 and 1984 those who did not complete high school could expect a 42% reduction in what they could earn in their twenties (Schorr, 1989). Deficits in basic skills also appear in those who graduate from high school. In mathematics, for instance, over half of the graduating seniors in the United States cannot solve problems involving decimals, percentages, fractions, and simple algebra. Yet, once out of school, these young adults will encounter interest on credit cards and loans, discounts, taxation, insurance policies, and other situations requiring those computations. Shockingly, 23% of high school seniors could not even correctly tally the cost of buying three items on a simple menu (National Assessment of Educational Progress [NAEP], 1990, pp. 1, 2, 10).

Calls for reform abound. Critics suggest many possible solutions: more time in school, smaller student-teacher ratios, higher teacher salaries, and letting parents choose the schools for their children. As a few writers have pointed out (e.g., Greer, 1992; Keller, 1978; Skinner, 1983), however, these "solutions" do not get to the heart of the problem—ineffective teaching. More hours of the same merely perpetuates the status quo. Higher teacher salaries and smaller class sizes, though helpful, require additional resources. Vouchers for schools, like busing a decade before, will shift students from one school to another but will not help teachers teach more effectively. In fact, because resources depend on student numbers, support of private schools drains resources away from those public schools most in need. It also segregates students from different backgrounds, as experience in the Netherlands shows (Louis & van Velzen, 1991).

Teachers need help. They will need even more help as increasing numbers of students become "mainstreamed.'' No teacher deliberately plans classroom environments so that students become discipline problems or fail to learn. Teachers, like the students with whom they work, are caught in a web of ineffective educational practices perpetuated from classroom generation to classroom generation. Those practices are based on an outmoded view of teaching as a process of ''communicating ideas'' with the teacher presenting and the student absorbing information. When a student fails to ''absorb,'' this view often holds the student accountable and labels him or her with terms like ''unmotivated,'' ''learning disabled,'' or ''attention deficit disordered.'' Attention and responsibility are thus shifted away from instructional techniques and what we know about learning. It is as though a science of behavior did not exist.

## THE SELECTIONIST PARADIGM AND ITS IMPLICATIONS FOR TEACHING

Since the publication of Skinner's *Behavior of Organisms* (1938), we have had a science that explains how behavior changes through selection by consequences. Originally known as ''The Experimental Analysis of Behavior'' the field published its first journal, the *Journal of the Experimental Analysis of Behavior,* in 1958. As the applications of the science grew, the phrase *behavior analysis* came to stand for both the science and its applications. The *Journal of Applied Behavior Analysis* began in 1968; the Association for Behavior Analysis was founded in 1974; and its journal, *The Behavior Analyst,* started publication in 1978. Not all behavior analysts adhered to Skinner's selectionist paradigm, however, so in 1988 the term *behaviorology* was proposed to refer to the science that studies behavior change through selection by consequences (E. A. Vargas, 1991). A year later, the International Behaviorology Association was incorporated.

Behavior evolves over the lifetime of the individual through the moment-to-moment interactions that individual has within his or her environment. The way in which some behaviors are selected and others die out involves contingencies of reinforcement and punishment—the precise relations in a given setting between each action and the events immediately following that action. The selection process works continually. Within a single conversation, reactions of a listener affect verbal behavior over the course of a few moments. When contingencies are ''tight''— that is, when consequences are immediate and consistent—behavior changes rapidly and predict-

ably. A person writing by hand, for example, quits moving his pen when it suddenly runs out of ink. The consequence of marks-on-paper provides part of the contingencies maintaining writing behavior.

All environments either maintain or shift the behavior of those acting within them. Note that *environment* in a behaviorological sense means more than the overall attributes of one's world. It refers to details of one's interactions within the physical world (such as marks from a pen) as well as the contingencies provided by other people. It includes not only the consequences following a given behavior but also the kinds and amounts of consequences for alternative behaviors (Martens, Lochner, & Kelly, 1992; Martens, 1992). A particular family or a classroom setting thus provides very different ''environments'' for each child or student living within it.

## IMPLICATIONS OF SELECTIONISM FOR PRINCIPLES OF EFFECTIVE SKILLS TRAINING

The fluid nature of behavior permits us to change behavior by changing contingencies. All approaches to teaching recommend attention to objectives, to measurement, to instructional materials, and to evaluation; but a behaviorological approach analyzes each component in terms of the selection paradigm. The following sections elaborate and give case histories illustrating the following main points:

1. Because a selection process begins with an existing repertoire, we must know exactly what each student can and cannot do at all times. Daily, curriculum-based measures of rate of behavior provide the best information for teaching basic skills.
2. Because one can select behaviors only when students are behaving, a high rate of student activity is required for optimal skill development.
3. To make sure that students respond to the critical aspects of a problem—that they ''understand'' what they are doing, rather than going through motions by rote—one must find out just what aspects of problems determine how students respond.
4. Behaviors are selected through consequences: The more immediate and more natural, the better. Criteria for performance must also be raised as students improve.
5. For teachers to adjust so that they become increasingly effective, they too need to see the conse-

quences of their actions. Student progress can serve as feedback to teachers to help identify what works best with each individual student.

Although the interaction of each student within the physical and social world is a continual process that incorporates all of these features, each topic will be discussed separately.

## CURRICULUM-BASED DAILY MEASURES OF BEHAVIOR

Just as genetic evolution only selects from individuals already existing, so behavioral selection must operate on behavior already in the repertoires of students. Frequent and accurate assessment of what students can and cannot do is therefore a cornerstone of good educational practice. One sensitive and easy assessment procedure for basic skills is the use of one-minute timed drills. Simple one-minute timings of performance also correlate well with performance on standardized tests (Deno, Mirkin, & Chiang, 1982). They give a quick measure of rate of performance.

### The Importance of Rate

*Competence* and *mastery* carry implications of rate of performance. Competent students not only can do things their less prepared peers cannot, they also do them more fluently—that is, faster, at a higher rate. A reader who pronounces words slowly will find it difficult to grasp the meaning of an entire sentence and will not enjoy reading as much as one who reads more rapidly. Anyone who has studied a foreign language knows how difficult it is to understand a selection when you must pause over every few words. In fact, all so-called higher order skills depend on basic skills (Bloom, 1974). Students cannot create freely when they cannot control their bodies or the materials with which they work. No one would expect a jazz musician to be able to improvise well without having spent hours in repetitive practice on runs and scales. A dancer who has not done daily stretches and exercises cannot express an idea as easily as one who can move effortlessly. How much better, in art, to be master of the brush than to see it leave unintended blotches. ''Freedom of expression'' in composition includes freedom from having to concentrate on forming grammatically correct sentences, on spelling, or on finding the right word to express one's ideas. In order to think, a student has to have a basic repertoire with which to think. By building basic skills to a high degree of

fluency, one removes the constraints of having to concentrate on mechanics and provides the flexibility required for creative behavior.

Fluency has other benefits. Students who have achieved high rates of behavior show better retention and work for longer periods of time (Binder, Haughton, & Van Eyk, 1990). With the frequent diagnosis of attention deficit disorders, the latter point is particularly important for counselors. The fluency research suggests that it is possible to address so-called attention deficit by attacking *skill* deficits rather than working on attention span itself. Teaching a child to pay attention (even when bored) does not improve his fluency in working. In contrast, by helping the child gain high rates in basic skills, one not only improves academic performance but attention span as well.

There are times, of course, when rapid behavior is dysfunctional. Certain dance steps require a slow execution. We may wish students to slow down when reading so they will have more time to reflect or to appreciate the nuances of what they are reading. Such concerns do not negate the importance of rate: Slowing down behavior involves rate just as much as speeding up performance. The point is not that fast is always good but, rather, that the speed or frequency at which behaviors occur is a fundamental characteristic with which we need to be concerned.

Rate is a sensitive measure of behavior. It shows differences where number or percentage correct fall short. A student may complete 20 problems and score 100% for five days in a row, showing no change. By taking speed into account, however, one sees variations in performance. Perhaps by the end of the week the student is completing the problems in half the time it took her at the beginning of the week. She has actually doubled her performance. Without measuring rate, however, neither she nor her teacher can see that impressive improvement.

The simplicity of one-minute timings permits frequent assessment. By measuring daily, both students and teachers keep in touch with progress. They can adjust instruction before wasting a week or more with ineffective procedures. Daily rate measures can even reveal health or emotional problems. In laboratory research with psychotic adults and children, rate has been found to be from 10 to 100 times more sensitive than percentage in picking up the effects of drugs and different reinforcers on behavior (Lindsley, 1960).

The sensitivity of rate was made apparent to the first author (JSV) when working with inmates in an educational setting in a correctional institution. The students earned points by completing reading exercises. Their rate correct and incorrect was graphed each day. One new student showed an unusual jump in rate when he was given more difficult material to read. Upon checking, the teacher discovered that the student had "faked bad" on the placement test in order to get easy lessons to complete for points. He was clever enough to make realistic mistakes on each lesson, but he could not create realistic rates. Because of the sensitivity of the daily measurement system, we were alerted to a misplacement that we would never have seen with traditional measures.

### Rate of Behavior versus "Paying Attention" and "Time on Task"

In addition to its sensitivity, measuring rate emphasizes productivity. Ironically, many behavior analysts promote student passivity rather than activity by working to get students to "pay attention." In practice, "pay attention" usually means "sit still and watch the teacher talk." Increasing "time on task" is rarely better. The contingencies may encourage students to look busy, but not necessarily to learn better. In fact, promoting time on task may actually slow down student behavior because, by spreading a ten-minute task over a half hour, students need work only one-third as hard for the same credit. Worse, a student may be counted as being on task without working at all. It is difficult to tell whether or not a student facing an open book is reading. Even a student who is moving a pencil may be copying over numbers and words rather than actively thinking about an assignment.

Goals such as "time on task" and "paying attention" have an additional disadvantage. They encourage a teacher-centered style of classroom control rather than promoting a student-centered environment in which students work independently (see the section on "Sources of Control").

Behavior analysts who set up systems to reinforce paying attention and time on task may have the mistaken impression that they are following in the tradition established by Skinner. Not so. Skinner emphasized *rate* (also called *frequency*) as the basic datum of his science. It is impossible to extract a rate of behavior out of data on paying attention or from time on task.

## Research Case History: Precision Teaching in Great Falls, Montana

One of the greatest proponents of high rates in education is Ogden Lindsley, a former student and colleague of Skinner's. In the 1960s he founded a method called Precision Teaching. With Precision Teaching, Lindsley sought to introduce "(1) rate of response with (2) standard (3) direct (4) continuous, and (5) self-recording to public school classrooms" (Lindsley, 1990, p. 7). In actuality, Lindsley's system is more precision measurement than precision teaching, in that it has little to say about teaching per se, other than urging teachers to try something different for a student if he or she is not progressing satisfactorily. But the recording method provides the means by which both students and teachers can see progress.

Precision Teaching has been used widely in the United States. The method was validated by the National Diffusion Network of the U.S. government when that agency was first set up and has been continually validated ever since. One of the first Precision Teaching demonstration projects, conducted in the Sakajawea Schools in Great Falls, Montana, produced such spectacular results in standardized test performance that it is described in detail here.

The Sakajawea school in Great Falls, Montana, had 325 students and 19 teachers serving kindergarten through sixth grade. All teachers were trained in Precision Teaching methods and used them for at least three basic skill areas (math, spelling, and reading). Teachers constructed a sequence of one-minute quiz sheets with problems like those in workbooks, each sheet a bit more difficult than the last. The Materials Bank, as the series of sheets was called, contained about 6,000 practice sheets in reading, math, spelling, handwriting, map skills, and language arts. A math sheet might contain 143 single-digit times single-digit multiplication problems, all on multiplying by 3. The idea was to have more problems than a student could complete in one minute, so that no rates would be restricted by a student running out of problems to do.

At the start of a period each child would get whatever sheet he or she was working on out of the Materials Bank file, place it face down on his or her desk, and wait for the signal. When the teacher said, "Go," students turned over their sheets and completed as many problems as they could in one minute. After the "Stop" signal, students corrected their own papers and charted their rates of correct and incorrect answers (see Figure 9.1 for an example of the graph). When a student met a predetermined criterion (e.g., copying numbers at a rate of 100 a minute), he or she went on to the next sheet in the series. The timing, correcting, and charting took about 10 minutes to complete.

**Figure 9.1.** A Precision Teaching graph similar to those used in the project that, in four years, increased classwide average percentiles in reading and math on the Iowa Test of Basic Skills from the school district average to 20 to 40 percentile points above the rest of the school district. The data on this graph show seven weeks of a typical undergraduate's spoken responses to flashcards. The front of the cards gave definitions or simple problems, and the student had to supply the term defined or answer to the problem. On this student's best day (the second to last set of points), she gave correct answers at a rate of 30 times a minute with no errors.

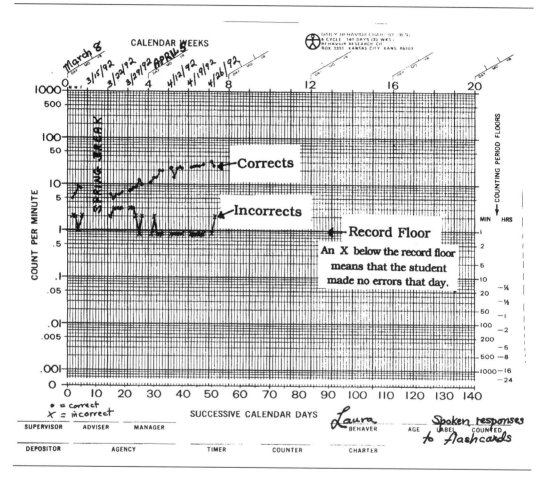

Teachers and students used the chart to make instructional decisions. The teachers were given a lot of freedom in designing instructional strategies. The only requirement was that they do something for a student who was not progressing satisfactorily. At the end of each year, the Iowa Test of Basic Skills was given throughout the school district.

Despite the fact that the Precision Teaching part of the curriculum consisted only of drill in basic skills, students in the Sakajawea School pulled ahead of their peers in all sections of the yearly standardized tests, including reading comprehension and problem solving in math. Before Precision Teaching was used, the Sakajawea students scored at the average for the school district. By the end of their third year in the project (now as fourth graders), the average of Sakajawea students' reading scores had reached the 96th percentile, compared with a percentile of 77 for the total school district. The average math score of students in the Precision Teaching fourth grade were even more impressive: They scored at the average percentile of 87, whereas the average percentile for the whole school district was only 43 (Beck, 1979). (Statisticians will be quick to point out that since

Sakajawea's scores were included in the district averages, the district averages would have been even lower without them.) Clearly, the educational practices were superior—so superior, in fact, that property values rose for houses within the Sakajawea School district boundaries (Lindsley, 1985).

The procedures involved in Precision Teaching require only materials readily available in U.S. schools, and the procedures can be used with any subject. They have been used with populations from first graders to advanced graduate students and with approaches to education as diverse as the Language Experience Approach (Peterson, Scott, & Sroka, 1990), flash cards in college instruction (McDade & Olander, 1990), and Direct Instruction (Lindsley, 1992). The procedures do require training in the use of a special "standard celeration chart" (shown in Figure 9.1) designed especially for showing changes in rate (see Bates & Bates, 1971, or Pennypacker, Koenig, & Lindsley, 1972, for an explanation of how to chart). But the dramatic results achieved in the Great Falls schools far exceed the kinds of effects typically found with educational innovations.

Precision Teaching features high rates of behavior during, typically, one-minute timings in each subject each day, providing an accurate, up-to-date assessment of progress and concentrated practice. Instead of taking nearly the whole period for a page of assigned problems (the usual procedure in schools), precision teachers pack the drill into the first ten minutes of each period, freeing the rest of the time for activities in which students can apply basic principles, analyze or formulate problems, solve problems, or engage in creative work. Thus, not only does the method help establish the skills that make possible activities such as reading for pleasure, reflecting on ideas, creating, designing, or researching, it also provides class time for the projects and activities that develop more complex repertoires.

Even when speed of answering is not important, we seek high rates of student involvement. The excited student talks, moves, even thinks more rapidly than one uninterested in a topic. *Motivation* is often defined as energizing students—that is, getting them to behave at higher rates. When "reflecting," a student covertly runs through ideas, asks herself questions, thinks of answers, accepts or discards notions. Of course, being able to perform rapidly does not mean one *must* perform rapidly, but fluidity is an important component of the basic skills in any field. The principles of selection by consequences require behavioral variation from which certain behaviors are reinforced. Higher rates of behavior provide more opportunities for selection—and thus permit more rapid shifting of skill levels. In Precision Teaching, students (and teachers) get feedback daily, and this helps to strengthen their better responses. The next step is to incorporate high rates of behavior into the learning process as well as assessment.

## A HIGH RATE OF STUDENT ACTIVITY

No one disputes the importance of providing many opportunities to respond in physical skills. In tennis, for example, where budgets permit, instructors use baskets full of balls so that students can hit more times during a lesson than they could if they had to chase after balls. No one would expect a clear presentation of how to serve to "communicate" the skills involved in playing a game. However, when teaching academic skills (when the goal is for student to talk, write, solve problems, reason, or think effectively), educators talk of "transferring ideas" as though some "content" were passed from teachers to students without the need for any behavior other than watching and listening. But talking, writing, problem solving, reasoning, and thinking are themselves behaviors. To shape them, teachers must ask students to do more than sit, watch, and listen. One way to improve teaching, then, is to increase the rate of relevant student responding.

Most students do not do much in a typical class period. Even in one-on-one instruction, the number of times a tutee responds can be too low to produce the kind of progress needed. A study of student speech therapists working one-on-one with clients in a speech clinic found that the actual number of times the clients practiced their difficult sounds varied between 2 and 17 responses per minute (Cowling-Reed, 1982). To increase the response rate, Cowling-Reed gave the therapists flash cards with pictures on them for their clients to name and recorded the data on client rate of pronunciations of sounds. Using these procedures, Dr. Cowling increased by a factor of four the number of sounds per minute that the clients practiced.

In a school setting, highly speeded timed practice can be used remedially without disrupting a student's day. A counselor in an elementary school in Iowa set up a computer-assisted math drill for students recommended by their teachers as needing additional practice in multiplication. Students came individually into the counselor's office, typed in their names and a number based on their typing speed (which set the speed at which problems were presented), and worked on problems presented rapidly by the computer. After the first few sessions, the counselor found he could leave the office and, by reviewing results at the end of the day, could check that each student set the parameters correctly and completed the drills. All students more than doubled their performance in a matter of a few days to a couple of weeks (Humphrey, 1983).

Many educators reject high rates of behavior as "mindless drill" or "rote learning." But a high degree of repetition does not preclude critical thinking. The benefits of practice improve when students constantly evaluate their own behavior, as Howard (1991) has pointed out. The speech therapist asks clients to evaluate their own sounds as well as giving feedback. The violinist practicing a difficult run improves fluency best when constantly evaluating: "That note was a bit flat. Third finger must be placed a bit higher. Think of the perfect fifth from three notes back to get it exactly on pitch . . ." In fact, critical thinking may occur more readily when fluency is high, because then the performer or student can concentrate on expression rather than on the mechanics of production.

To achieve fluency, a student must have time for practice. Private tutoring, of course, provides ample opportunity for a student or client to respond. But where school budgets do not permit a low student-teacher ratio, how can one increase relevant student activity? One solution has been developed by the Juniper Gardens Children's Project in Kansas City, Kansas, in working with children and teenagers in areas of high poverty. In 1982, the project was nationally recognized by a presidential commission as one "that works" (Hall, Schiefelbusch, Hoyt, & Greenwood, 1989). A key component of the project involved arranging for high rates of participation by all students.

## Research Case History: The Juniper Gardens Project

The Juniper Gardens Children's project began in 1965. A group of researchers at the University of Kansas decided to work with the schools as a way to attack "academic failures and behavior problems that lead to early school dropouts, delinquent behavior, early pregnancies and/or unstable marriages" (Hall et al., 1989, p. 301). One of the first problems the researchers addressed was the problem of low activ-

ity rates by students. To guarantee that *every* student in the class would respond a respectable number of times in each class period, a system of classwide peer tutoring (CWPT) was developed. The tutoring process is highly structured by the teachers, who train student tutors to provide (1) many opportunities to respond to curriculum-based materials, (2) strategies to ensure increased levels of active responding, (3) feedback for each response, and (4) correction of errors (Delquadri, Whorton, Elliott, & Greenwood, 1982).

To assess the academic benefits of classwide peer tutoring, Greenwood, Delquadri, and Hall (1989) conducted a longitudinal investigation over four years and four grade levels. Ninety-four teachers and 416 students began the project, although four years later only 182 of the original students remained because of the high number of students who moved out of the schools participating in the project. The students were randomly assigned to a teacher-designed instructional program using a traditional basal text, with lecture-discussions and seatwork assignments, or to the CWPT program. Teachers were trained with a CWPT program manual and by working directly with a consultant who helped them prepare curriculum materials and implement the program. The classwide peer tutoring procedures were introduced as part of spelling, mathematics, and reading. For 30 minutes each day in each subject, teachers used peer tutoring. The program started with a weekly chart in each classroom that announced the tutor pairs and their team membership. In spelling and math, the teacher set a timer for 10 minutes, and the designated tutor presented the word to be spelled or the problem to be solved. The tutee then wrote and orally stated the answer, gaining two points if correct. If incorrect, the tutor provided the correct answer and the tutee had to write it correctly three times, gaining one point. A five-minute period at the end of the tutoring time was allotted to record publicly the total number of points earned by the individual team members and to record the team totals. After statistically controlling for first-grade group differences (achievement and IQ), the average student performance on the Metropolitan Achievement Test (Basic battery) of those in the classwide peer tutoring program exceeded that of the controls by .5 to 1.4 grade equivalents (9 to 13 percentiles on the various subtests) after four years in the program.

Other investigators have used the original 1983 classwide peer tutoring program with adaptations. For example, Maheady and Harper (1987) demonstrated an immediate jump in performance when the classwide peer tutoring model was introduced in spelling with 70 third and fourth graders. They introduced the procedures one class at a time in a multiple-baseline ABAB design across classrooms. Each Monday, each student drew a red or blue tag out of a box to determine team membership. The teacher then randomly paired the students into tutoring pairs. From Monday through Thursday for five minutes a day, each tutor dictated words to his or her tutee, who wrote and orally spelled each of the 18 spelling words. Incorrectly spelled words were written three times correctly. Two points were awarded for correct words, one for corrected words. A pair continued through the list as many times as possible within the five-minute session, then reversed roles for a second five minutes. On Friday, the teacher gave the weekly spelling test in the usual fashion.

Maheady and Harper (1987) reported immediate and systematic increases in the students' weekly spelling test performance when the tutoring was introduced into each classroom. During baseline conditions, a mean of 79% accuracy was obtained across the four target classrooms. This increased to a mean of 93% when the CWPT program was instituted. Another indication of the improvement in performance can be seen in the students' spelling grades. Before peer tutoring, only half of the students were earning "A" grades on the Friday tests. When peer tutoring was introduced, this jumped to 81% for the third graders and 93% for the fourth graders.

The Juniper Gardens projects all involved a timing feature to keep the rates of responding high. Students work harder when they have a limited time. Whatever method is used, however, the point is to increase activity rates of each student to provide enough behavior so the selection process can work effectively.

High activity rates do not guarantee that students will gain from the exercises they complete, as the term *busy work* implies. Not all exercises are created equal. To benefit students, exercises must ask students to do something meaningful and must be designed with appropriate antecedent stimulus control. Otherwise, the behavior selected may not be useful in the real world of home and work.

## RELEVANT RESPONDING AND THE DESIGN OF EXERCISES

In the preceding sections, we have assumed that what students are doing at a high rate is relevant to what they are to learn. To make sure that exercises

are truly helpful, and not just busy work, one must consider not only what students do, but what part of the printed material is controlling their behavior. To help students respond correctly, some exercises let students get the right answers for the wrong reasons—a situation behaviorologists call inappropriate antecedent stimulus control. For example, if a teacher asks, "This is a bivalve, isn't it?," a student can answer "yes" whether or not she has ever heard of bivalves (and, in fact, without even seeing the specimen). "Isn't it?" gives away the answer.

The design of exercises so that students respond meaningfully has been addressed by nonbehavioral writers as well as behavioral ones. Wertheimer, in his book *Productive Thinking* (1959), described how students, in calculating the area of a parallelogram, responded by rote to the height-times-base formula. When the parallelogram was drawn vertically, standing on a point rather than on a base, the students did not know what to do. Wertheimer's solution was to teach students to talk about how many unit squares would fit inside the figure. He had students cut and reassemble irregular figures so that those squares could be counted. Students thus were brought under stimulus control of number of unit squares (the definition of area) rather than of vertical and horizontal lines. A more recent article (Schoenfeld, 1988) criticizes the repetitive nature of math exercises that encourage "solving" in a routine and nonthinking way. The author mentions how subtraction problems with the key word *left* give away what to do with the numbers, so that students can do the problems without reading the rest of the words and without understanding the situation those words describe. Similar inappropriate stimulus control in workbooks is described in the behavioral literature (J. S. Vargas, 1984). First- and second-grade exercise books in reading, for example, often contain such good pictures that students can answer so-called reading comprehension questions without reading at all. Yet these exercises are intended (according to the teachers' manuals) to teach students to read to develop conclusions. In English and grammar exercise books, highlighting often tells the student the words they are supposed to copy, so that they can complete the exercises without even knowing what the exercises are about. In math, word problems that are supposed to help students learn to apply mathematical processes to daily life (that is, to visualize whether quantities are being combined, separated, etc.) can often be done without reading a single word of the problems. Titles like "Word Problems in Multiplication" or a preceding page of division problems give away the process to be used. No wonder students have trouble when they are not told whether a word problem requires them to add, subtract, multiply, or divide. In some high school science texts, key concepts are highlighted or are summarized in figures or margin captions, so that students can answer the questions at the ends of the chapters without reading the content that those very questions are designed to make sure that they read. These poorly designed exercises keep students busy without helping them learn. Students can answer correctly without thinking and without paying attention to the content they are supposed to be learning.

## Research on Antecedent Stimulus Control: The Blackout Technique

An early systematic investigation of antecedent stimulus control was conducted in the 1960s and 1970s with research on programmed instruction.[1] James Holland and his colleagues, in a series of studies, examined the relationship between the design of individual frames and the behavior of students responding to them. In one study, for example, Doran and Holland (1971), tracked eye movements of students as they went through programmed instruction. They discovered that students read only those parts of a frame that were needed to fill in the blanks. An error analysis would not have revealed this behavior. It was necessary to watch students to see where they looked when answering questions.

To determine the sections of materials to which students responded, Holland and his colleagues developed the blackout technique (Holland, 1967). If students could respond correctly with portions of a problem physically blacked out, clearly the removed sections were not needed in order to respond. The higher the blackout ratio, the more extraneous material was included and the less programmed the lesson: Programming required a high density of student overt responding with only enough material present to prompt the correct response. Using the blackout index, Holland and his colleagues made sense of the contradictory results of studies comparing programmed instruction to reading. Only when blackout ratios were low—that is, when nearly everything in a frame was needed for responding—did it make a difference whether or not students wrote down answers or merely read through the content. Not only *how* students answered but also what parts of an

exercise controlled their responding were thus the critical factor.

It would be difficult for counselors or classroom teachers, with their busy schedules, to try out various versions of worksheets with different amounts blacked out. Nevertheless, by visualizing what an exercise would look like with certain parts covered, a teacher can guess where antecedent stimulus control probably lies. Can the student respond to pictures or set phrases so that he or she does not need to read the question? Can answers to questions at the ends of chapters be found in highlighted text or in figures, so that a student does not need to read the chapter? Can a student copy words without understanding what the words mean? When the answer is yes, then students can answer correctly without learning the basic skills that those exercises are intended to teach. Selection by consequences may be occurring in these worksheets, but the shortcut behaviors being strengthened will not help students solve the problems they will encounter in daily life.

## MOTIVATION: SHAPING THROUGH APPROPRIATE AND IMMEDIATE CONSEQUENCES

You have assessed your students. You have set up learning activities with high rates of responding, and you have made sure that the exercises require students to respond to the critical features of problems. Now, how will you get students to work? How can you select behavior that does not yet exist? The first task is typically called one of *motivation*. The second involves shaping. They are intertwined but will be addressed separately here.

Most educators approach motivation as a problem in antecedent control; that is, they look at what *precedes* responding by students. Teachers are encouraged to inspire students through their own enthusiasm or to explain to them how important it is to learn about a subject. As we all know, even the most enthusiastic teacher does not inspire all students, and knowing how important it is to learn to read or to stay in school does not necessarily produce the behaviors required. This is not to discourage enthusiasm or exhortations about the importance of education but, rather, to point out that, since the primary mechanisms controlling behavior lie in selection, the heart of motivation lies in arranging postcedent events.

If a student is not working, consequences need to be redesigned. The kind of consequences used and the behaviors they follow determine how effectively they motivate students. First, one needs to find consequences that strengthen behavior. Most people think of incentives or rewards when looking for ways to strengthen behavior, but they are only a small set of the consequences available.

## Nature of Consequences: Reinforcement

A *reward* is a tangible object or activity. Unlike reward, *reinforcement* is defined as any event that selects or strengthens the behavior it follows. Reinforcement may occur when a second person delivers a tangible object or gives access to an activity, but most reinforcement occurs less conspicuously in the form of facial expressions, body movements, or utterances. Much reinforcement does not even require the presence of a second person. The reinforcement for behaviors such as walking, doodling, humming, or scratching an itch follows directly from the behavior itself. Reinforcement is going on all the time whether or not people are aware of it. To say "Reinforcement doesn't work" is as naive as saying "Gravity doesn't work" when watching snow drift upward in the air.

Reinforcement is defined operationally, not by how a consequence appears. In one of the earliest published studies of the deliberate arrangement of contingencies with children, teachers were trying to get a 3-year-old called Dee to stand up and participate in nursery school activities. They noticed that Dee's withdrawal behavior drew the attention of a teacher, although Dee usually cringed and drew away when a teacher approached. Few people would have called the proximity of a teacher "reinforcement." Yet, in the study that followed, teacher approach was shown to reinforce Dee's behavior (Harris, Johnston, Kelley, & Wolf, 1964). Criticism, likewise, may actually increase rather than decrease the behaviors the criticizer intends to discourage (Becker, 1986). No one would call criticism—or the line that comes out of a pen—a reward. Yet these kinds of natural consequences—not the tangible "rewards" that are consciously added by others—control most of our daily behavior.

Rewards are given to people, but reinforcement selects and strengthens behavior. Statements such as "I reinforced Sarah for completing her homework" reveal a misunderstanding of the processes at work. One would not say, "I selected Sarah," or "I

strengthened Sarah." Incorrect statements about reinforcement raise more than just semantic questions. They involve what is probably the most critical feature in reinforcement, timing.

## Timing and Frequency of Consequences

A consequence strengthens the behavior going on at the time it occurs. To know what teachers are doing thus does not tell us much about what they are teaching. We need to know the contingencies they are setting up for *students.* Yet this datum is often ignored. A study of day care in Bermuda involving almost the entire population of 2- and 3-year-olds could not find consistent relationships between caregiver attention in day care and later aggressiveness of the children as kindergartners (Philips, McCartney, & Scarr, 1987). The researchers did not, however, collect data on the timing of teacher attention. For example, they did not distinguish between attention following grabbing and attention following sharing. Yet those data are needed to determine what behaviors are strengthened from among all the actions of each preschooler. Few early childhood teachers realize the power in their hands or recognize what behaviors they are drawing out through the timing of their attentions. No wonder some highly attentive caregivers in the Bermuda study shaped up aggressive behaviors while other highly attentive teachers did not.

Teacher attention generally has a greater effect on the behavior of younger students than on older ones. Nevertheless, small consequences have pronounced effects for high school students, too, when contingencies are tight—that is, the consequences are immediate and consistent. Take video games, for example. Apart from social approval of an audience, it makes no difference in a student's life whether one of those animated video characters gets to a new level or gets destroyed. Yet because of the frequency and timing of consequences, players work with tremendous intensity even when no peers are there to see their success. The power lies in the contingencies built into the games—the timing and frequency of consequences.

How then can a teacher or counselor motivate students? The task is to set up immediate consequences for as many behaviors as possible. We have mentioned the use of rate in assessment. Timing students, in addition to providing an accurate measure, sets up contingencies for working rapidly. Give a page of problems, untimed, and what student rushes to begin? But when timed, most students begin concentrating immediately, particularly when it makes a difference how they do, as when plotting progress on a graph. If that is not enough, other consequences can be added.

In the classroom, it is difficult to provide immediate consequences for all the actions desired of students. When only one student responds at a time, teachers can react to each contribution, but no teacher can personally give immediate feedback for most of what a student does. Take worksheets, for example. Even if a teacher grades papers as soon as a student is finished, the student does not get feedback from one problem soon enough to help with the next problem on the worksheet. As far back as the 1920s and 1930s, Sidney Pressey and his students demonstrated the superiority of a "testing machine" that gave feedback after each response rather than only at the end of a sequence of problems (Little, 1935; Pressey, 1926).

The fact that one teacher cannot personally provide feedback for all of each student's behavior may be good news, however, because too much teacher-centered control runs counter to the goals of education in a democracy.

## Sources of Control

In order to produce "education for life," the kinds of behaviors occurring in the classroom must continue once students leave the school grounds. Student behavior, therefore, cannot be dependent on consequences personally provided by teachers. Even during the school years, it is better for reinforcement to follow automatically from a student's actions than to depend on a teacher. Teachers recognize this when they stress "working independently" or "taking an interest in a subject." The problem with teacher-dispensed consequences is that they depend on factors over which students have no control—on the teacher's mood, on whether he or she happens to notice a behavior, or even on prejudices and personal likes and dislikes. The same problem occurs with "on-task behavior," where consequences depend on teacher judgment, not just on student behavior. Contingencies are not tight when an action may or may not count. In contrast, consequences produced by student behavior follow automatically from what students do, not on factors over which they have no control. Natural contingencies thus provide real "student empowerment."

One consequence that depends on student behavior and not on a teacher's opinion or good will is a student's own progress. Most students enjoy beating their own records—a fact not lost on the designers of the arcade and computer games already mentioned. Progress can only function as a reinforcer, however, if it can be seen, and that requires keeping precise records on individual performance. The charts kept by students in Precision Teaching fulfill that function —no doubt one reason for the success of that method. When teachers emphasize individual improvement, even the slowest students can reap rewards, because they, too, will beat their own records. This contrasts starkly with the usual competitive situation, in which only the best students get social approval—exactly those students who least need encouragement. Procedures to encourage individual progress can be adopted even in unlikely subjects. In one secondary school, swim coaches set a policy of cheering students whenever they beat their own records, regardless of how well they did competitively. At one swim meet, students from other schools were astonished to see teammates rushing to congratulate the swimmer who had come in last. That student (who had just started with the swim team) had beaten her own record, even though she was nowhere near competitive levels. What could have been a failure for her was turned into a success because of accurate recording and emphasis on individual progress.

In addition to records of progress, some instruction itself can be designed to incorporate natural consequences. By thinking of the natural consequences for behavior, one can sometimes design activities to incorporate those consequences. Take, for example, communicating through writing. What are the consequences for writing? The main one is the reaction of a reader. In a second-grade and a sixth-grade classroom, ten minutes each day were set aside. Students were not allowed to talk, but they could pass notes (without leaving their seats). In the furious passing back and forth of notes, students received natural consequences for what they wrote. If they did not express themselves well, the recipient looked confused or wrote back, "What?" Contrast such feedback with the usual consequences for writing in schools. Not only are the comments on "corrected" papers mainly negative (thus decreasing rather than increasing the tendency to write—a possible cause of "writer's block"), they address formal aspects of writing rather than responding to what a student is trying to express. If the only response we got for learning to talk was similar ("unclear," "split infinitive," "needs transition," etc.) none of us would talk any better than we write. Because writing was designed to have its natural consequences, students were eager to write: One sixth grader wrote a note to the teacher (who also communicated only through writing) that said, "Don't stop us." Of course, at some point students need to do more than write notes to their friends, but the principles of building in natural consequences can be extended throughout a writing curriculum (Vargas, 1978).

One way for students to generate their own feedback is through automation. Consequences delivered by computer can occur immediately for each response, and they can be made contingent solely on relevant student behavior—assuming that the program asks for some behavior other than "press the arrow to continue."

## Research Case History: Programmed Instruction on Computer

The kind of attention to contingencies described above can be illustrated by the computer-assisted instruction (CAI) produced by the New Century Education Corporation.[2] Schools purchase a system that includes everything from the design of the learning space to personnel support. Typically, a school sets aside one classroom for the learning center. Carrels are brought in, each of which contains a computer keyboard and screen. The center is stocked with materials for reading, math, or both. Training for center personnel involves sending teachers and administrators to a center in operation so that they can experience what they will be doing. By the end of two weeks, the newcomers run the existing center without help. They are then ready to go back to their own schools to run their own centers.

Most centers are at least partially funded with Chapter 1 funds, so in any given class period, students arrive from several different classrooms. They go to their assigned carrels, sign on to the system, and begin where they left off the last time they were in the center. Because the system is individualized, it is rare to see two students working on the same lesson. Also, because the teacher must check each lesson and approve the next one to be taken, even the sequence of lessons differs from student to student.

The most distinctive part of the learning centers, however, is not the administrative details but the nature of the individual lessons. They are designed to teach new material, not just to provide practice on skills already learned. Every screen asks for students to respond in a meaningful way, with prompting at

the beginning of sequences. To take a simple example, a new term might be defined at the top of a screen. At the bottom of the screen, the student is given several items, only some of which exemplify the new term, and is asked to pick out those examples. Later in the sequence, the definition would no longer be provided. Feedback to the student includes a running total of items completed and attempted, with points awarded for high accuracy (80%–90% correct). Points, in turn, buy certificates of achievement (paper certificates printed with colored filigree and the student's name). Several certificates led to a photograph of the student holding his or her latest certificate. In many schools, the photographs are posted on bulletin boards before being taken home. The students express a great deal of pride in the certificates they have earned.

In the design of the materials, stimulus control was carefully considered. Writers sat and watched individual students go through drafts of each lesson. Many changes were made by seeing where, on the screen, students were looking and what kinds of things they said as they typed in their answers (see the next section on "Cybernetic Evaluation").

Because of the many special features of the centers, it is difficult to identify which of them is mainly responsible for the success of students going through them. The combination of features, however, works well. Across the country, students gain, on the average, 1.6 months of reading performance on standardized tests for each month in which they attend a center for one class period a day. Since, to qualify for Chapter 1 programs, students must be at least two grades behind, 1.6 months growth represents a doubling in the rate of progress for most of the students in the program. Because one center can serve a large number of students, the centers are also cost-effective compared with other remedial programs (Weinstock, 1984).

## CYBERNETIC EVALUATION: THE TEACHER OR COUNSELOR AS RESEARCHER

We have been talking about contingencies for students. What about the contingencies for the teacher or counselor? To become sensitive to student needs and to what is or is not working with a particular student, the teacher or counselor becomes a researcher, trying out procedures and assessing their effects (Greer, 1991). Teachers and counselors need feedback in order to see what factors affect student behavior. The system becomes cybernetic; students adapt to the contingencies set by teachers and counselors, and the latter adjust their procedures according to how students respond. Cybernetic evaluation is a system in which the teacher gets information on student progress, and that information determines both the next instructional step and revisions of the original material.

Fortunately, the procedures described in the preceding sections provide just the kind of measurement that allows teachers and counselors to assess the effectiveness of programs they develop. The daily rates obtained in Precision Teaching show individual progress. Problems can be caught and strategies adjusted before a student becomes seriously behind. Precise daily measures of rate also show jumps or accelerations when a strategy is helping a particular student.

A cybernetic system focuses on what students are doing and why. Teachers look at behavior, not just at completed assignments. By watching students while they are solving problems in class, a teacher or counselor sees the strategies a student uses and can help improve problem-solving behaviors. In the development of worksheets or of other instructional materials (such as computer lessons), the developer watches students take each draft version of a lesson, rather than looking only at final scores. Sitting by a student while he or she works at a lesson can be quite informative. In the development of reading comprehension lessons, the senior author noticed students first looking down at the bottom of the screen at the questions and then searching back through the paragraph they were supposed to read. Students were getting the items correct, so a review of lesson results would not have revealed the fact that students were not reading through the selections. Because the author was watching, the students' behavior changed the behavior of the author, the essence of a cybernetic system. Lessons were rewritten to present one sentence of the paragraph at a time, with a choice of words embedded at the end. When a student selected the correct word, the incorrect choice disappeared. After the student read and responded to each sentence, the paragraph was complete. Not only did students read all of the text, they responded overtly at much higher rates. Unlike the case of the usual comprehension items, with one or two questions per paragraph, students continually responded to the meaning of what they read. Their rate of responding on the keyboard was over four times that in the original design. What students did altered what the instructional designer did, which, in turn, altered how students would respond to future editions of the lessons. A cybernetic measurement system thus evaluates not only the student, but the instructional procedures as well.

## SUMMARY: A STUDENT-BEHAVIOR CENTERED APPROACH

Few Americans are happy with the general quality of our educational system today. Reforms such as changing class size, lengthening the school day, and increasing teacher salaries may help; but only a major improvement in the effectiveness of teaching itself will produce the needed results. To produce such a change requires attention to pedagogy. In this chapter, we discussed principles of behavioral change through selection by consequences and the implications of this process for effective teaching.

The principles discussed operate continually. When understood, they explain many of our educational successes and some of our failures. They enable us to see why even concerned teachers and counselors and loving parents often fail with those they wish to help. By understanding that teaching is a process of skillfully selecting certain actions of each student, rather than a process of ''communicating'' content, educators focus on student behavior. Instead of attending to presentation, or to enthusiasm, or to the clarity of explanation, all of which are teacher-centered, the focus of instruction shifts to students and what they are doing. In the selection process, accurate and precise measures of student performance become important. Selection requires high rates of meaningful behaviors, with exercises designed so that students must attend to the relevant features of problems rather than responding by rote to irrelevant cues. Selection also requires immediate and frequent feedback. In most cases, the kinds of consequences generated by a student's own behavior are preferable to rewards added by teachers. Frequent and immediate signs of progress are usually sufficient both to motivate problem solving and to improve basic skills.

It often takes a long time for discoveries to become established practice. The relationship between eating citrus fruits and prevention of scurvy was convincingly demonstrated around 1600 and again in 1747. Typically, as many as half of the British sailors on a ship died of scurvy on long journeys. Yet it took forty-six years after the second demonstration for the British Navy to carry citrus fruits routinely and thus to eliminate scurvy. In the mercantile marine, it took even longer—118 years (Mosteller, 1981). The solution to the scurvy problem was neither difficult nor expensive, but it took many years for those who could have solved the problem to take action. We hope it will not take as long for counselors and educators to use what we know about selection by consequences to improve the teaching of the basic skills so critical for the success of our students.

## NOTES

1. In programmed instruction, content is broken into "frames," each of which requires a response by the student. Because programmed instruction was designed to introduce new skills, the first frames in each sequence provide prompts for the student. These prompts are reduced until the student responds, unaided, to the problem situation. See Vargas and Vargas (1991) for an analysis of programmed instruction. For a history of the movement, see Vargas and Vargas (1992).

2. The senior author of this chapter (JSV) has worked as consultant and author for New Century Education Corporation off and on since 1975. The data cited, however, were gathered by independent researchers.

## REFERENCES

Bates, S., & Bates, D. (1971, Spring). ". . . and a child shall lead them": Stephanie's chart story. *Teaching Exceptional Children,* 111–113.

Beck, R. (1979). *Report for the Office of Education Joint Dissemination Review Panel.* Submitted by Great Falls Public Schools, Great Falls, Montana.

Becker, W. (1986). *Applied psychology for teachers: A behavioral cognitive approach.* Chicago: Science Research Associates, pp. 47–49.

Binder, C., Haughton, E., & Van Eyk, D. (1990, Spring). Precision Teaching attention span. *Teaching Exceptional Children,* 24–31.

Bloom, B. S. (Ed.). (1974). *Taxonomy of educational objectives.* New York: McKay.

Cowling-Reed, K. (1982). *Measurement using one-minute Precision Teaching drills in articulation therapy.* Unpublished dissertation, West Virginia University, Morgantown, pp. 66–78.

Delquadri, J., Whorton, D., Elliott, M., & Greenwood, C. R. (1982, May). *Peer and parent tutoring programs: A comparative analysis of the effects of packages on opportunity to respond, reading performance, and achievement scores of learning disabled disadvantaged children.* Paper presented at the Convention of the Association for Behavior Analysis.

Deno, S. L., Mirkin, P. K., & Chiang, B. (1982). Identifying valid measures of reading. *Exceptional Children, 49,* 36–45.

Doran, J., & Holland, J. G. (1971). Eye movements as a function of response contingencies measured by the blackout technique. *Journal of Applied Behavior Analysis,* 411–416.

Greenwood, C. R., Delquadri, J., & Hall, R. V. (1989). Longitudinal effects of classwide peer tutoring. *Journal of Educational Psychology, 81,* 371–383.

Greer, R. D. (1991). The teacher as strategic scientist: A solution to our educational crisis? *Behavior and Social Issues, 1,* 25–41.

Greer, R. D. (1992). L'enfant terrible meets the educational crisis. *Journal of Applied Behavior Analysis, 25,* 65–69.

Hall, R. V., Schiefelbusch, R. L., Hoyt, R. K. Jr., & Greenwood, C. R. (1989). History, mission, and organization of the Juniper Gardens Children's Project. *Education and Treatment of Children, 12,* 301–329.

Harris, F. R., Johnston, K., Kelley, D. S., & Wolf, M. W. (1964). Effects of positive social reinforcement on regressed crawling of a nursery school child. *Journal of Educational Psychology, 1,* 35–41.

Holland, J. G. (1967). A quantitative measure for programmed instruction. *American Educational Research Journal, 4,* 87–101.

Howard, V. A. (1991). And learning drives me mad; or, the drudgery of drill. *Harvard Educational Review, 61,* 80–87.

Humphrey, J. (1983). *A comparison of how paced and unpaced problems affect learning during CAI math drills.* Unpublished dissertation, West Virginia University, Morgantown.

Keller, F. S. (1978). Instructional technology and educational reform: 1977. *The Behavior Analyst, 1,* 48–53.

Lindsley, O. R. (1960). Characteristics of the behavior of chronic psychotics as revealed by free-operant conditioning methods. *Diseases of the Nervous System,* monograph, supplement, *21,* 66–78.

Lindsley, O. R. (1985, May). *Quantified trends in the results of behavior analysis.* Presidential address to the Convention of the Association for Behavior Analysis.

Lindsley, O. R. (1990, Fall). Our aims, discoveries, failures, and problem. *Journal of Precision Teaching, 7,* 7–17.

Lindsley, O. R. (1992). Precision teaching: Discoveries and effects. *Journal of Applied Behavior Analysis, 25,* 51–57.

Little, J. K. (1935). An investigation by means of special test-scoring and drill devices of the effect of certain instructional procedures on learning in educational psychology. *Abstracts of Doctors' Dissertations, 16,* Ohio State University Press, pp. 113–123.

Louis, K. S., & van Velzen, B. A. (1991). A look at choice in the Netherlands. *Educational Leadership, 48,* 66–72.

Maheady, L., & Harper, G. (1987). A classwide peer tutoring program to improve the spelling test performance of low-income, third- and fourth-grade students. *Education and Treatment of Children, 10,* 120–133.

Martens, B. K. (1992). Contingency and choice: The implications of matching theory for classroom instruction. *Journal of Behavioral Education, 2,* 121–137.

Martens, B. K., Lochner, D. G., & Kelly, I. Q. (1992). The effects of variable-interval reinforcement of academic engagement: A demonstration of matching theory. *Journal of Applied Behavior Analysis, 25,* 143–151.

McDade, C. E., & Olander, C. P. (1990, Fall). SAFMEDS design: A comparison of three protocols. *Journal of Precision Teaching, 7,* 69–73.

Mosteller, F. (1981). Innovation and evaluation. *Science, 211,* 181–211.

NAEP (1990): *The state of mathematics achievement: Executive summary of NAEP's 1990 Assessment of the Nation and the Trial Assessment of the States.* Education Information Branch Office of Educational Research and Improvement. Washington, DC: U.S. Department of Education.

Pennypacker, H. S., Koenig, C. H., & Lindsley, O. R. (1972). *Handbook of the standard behavior chart.* Kansas City, KS: Precision Media.

Peterson, S. K., Scott, J., & Sroka, K. (1990, Spring). Using the language experience approach with precision. *Teaching Exceptional Children,* 28–30.

Phillips, D., McCartney, K., & Scarr, S. (1987). Child care quality and children's social development. *Developmental Psychology, 23,* 537–543.

Pressey, S. L. (1926). A simple apparatus which gives tests and scores—and teaches. *School and Society, 23,* 373–376.

Schoenfeld, A. H. (1988). When good teaching leads to bad results: The disasters of "well-taught" mathematics courses. *Educational Psychologist, 23,* 145–166.

Schorr, L. B. (1989). *Within our reach: Breaking the cycle of disadvantage.* New York: Anchor Press/Doubleday.

Skinner, B. F. (1938). *The behavior of organisms: An experimental analysis.* New York: Appleton-Century-Crofts. Reprinted (1990) by the B. F. Skinner Foundation, Box 825, Cambridge, MA 02238.

Skinner, B. F. (1983). The shame of American education. *The American Psychologist, 38,* 239–244.

Vargas, E. A. (1991). Behaviorology: Its paradigm. In W. Ishaq (Ed.), *Human behavior in today's world* (pp. 139–147). New York: Praeger.

Vargas, E. A., & Vargas, J. S. (1991). Programmed instruction: What it is and how to do it. *The Behavioral Educator, 1,* 235–252.

Vargas, E. A., & Vargas, J. S. (1992). Programmed instruction and teaching machines. In R. P. West & L. A. Hamerlynck (Eds.), *Designs for excellence in education: The legacy of B. F. Skinner* (pp. 33–69). Longmont, CO: Sopris West.

Vargas, J. S. (1978, Spring). A behavioral approach to the teaching of composition. *The Behavior Analyst, 1,* 16–24.

Vargas, J. S. (1984). What are your exercises teaching? An analysis of stimulus control in instructional materials. In W. L. Heward, T. E. Heron, D. S. Hill, & J. Trap-Porter (Eds.), *Focus on behavior analysis in education* (pp. 126–141). Columbus, OH: Merrill.

Weinstock, R. (1984, May). A Title I tale: High reading/math gains at low cost in Kansas City, Kansas. *Phi Delta Kappan,* 632–634.

Wertheimer, M. (1959). *Productive thinking.* New York: Harper & Row.

CHAPTER 10

# PARENTING SKILLS: A REVIEW AND DEVELOPMENTAL ANALYSIS OF TRAINING CONTENT

Deborah R. Barclay
Arthur C. Houts

## PARENTING SKILLS: AN ANALYSIS OF TRAINING CONTENT

"Parent training" has become a familiar slogan in both popular and professional literatures. Numerous popular books offer do-it-yourself advice on how to be a good parent (e.g., Clark, 1985). In the published literature of mental health professionals, "parent training" has become a standard treatment intervention for childhood problems that range from stealing to making poor grades. This parents as co-therapists approach grew out of social learning theory, with the idea that the most direct route to behavior change in children is through effective environmental design. Such change logically begins in the home and through the influence of parents. Thus the parent training literature has typically assumed that changing the behavior of parents toward their children results in a changed child. Reviews of treatment out-come research have suggested that using parents as agents of change is indeed a highly successful endeavor, at least with respect to changing certain undesirable child behaviors (Breiner & Beck, 1984; Dembo, Sweitzer, & Lauritzen, 1985; Dumas, 1989; Moreland, Schwebel, Beck, & Wells, 1982; O'Dell, 1974; Reisinger, Ora, & Frangia, 1976; Sallis, 1983; Wells & Forehand, 1980).

The general efficacy of parent training is typically not disputed. However, researchers have begun to question whether parent training is adequately meeting all the needs of parents and children who seek such interventions (e.g., Lutzker, McGimsey, McRae, & Campbell, 1983; Robertson, 1984; Sapon-Shevin, 1982). The purpose of this chapter is to review the recent parenting literature in an effort to determine the content of training presented to parents and its adequacy to meet what researchers consider a major goal of parenting: raising a socially independent,

Partial support for this research was provided by a Centers of Excellence grant from the state of Tennessee to the Department of Psychology at Memphis State University and also by a National Institute of Health Grant (R01 HD21736–04) to Arthur C. Houts.

The authors thank Robert Cohen, Sam Morgan, and Jim Whelan for helpful comments on an earlier draft of this chapter.

healthy child. A brief introduction to questions and concerns regarding current parenting interventions is followed by an extensive review of the parenting literature arranged by developmental age of the child. The content of these interventions is then interpreted according to two areas of development that have a great impact on the child's socialization: attachment and self-regulation or self-control. These widely studied areas of development directly involve the parents and their relationship with the child and have a significant impact on the child's social development (Maccoby & Martin, 1983). The chapter concludes with a summary of the limitations of current parent training approaches and directions for future research.

## THE SCOPE OF PARENT TRAINING

*Parent training* encompasses a variety of parent skills, different child populations, and different goals for intervention. Three main areas of skills are taught to parents. The first, child management skills, is what is most often meant by "parent training." Within this area, parents are taught basic principles of learning and conditioning, such as identifying antecedents and consequences that may be changed to manage children's behavior. The second area is teaching adult–child interaction skills, such as communication and problem-solving procedures. The third area focuses on parent teaching skills, whereby parents are taught how to be educators to improve their child's academic performance.

Parent training has been used with different populations and defined by different problem areas. It has been a dominant mode of intervention for children with behavior problems such as noncompliance, oppositional defiant disorders, conduct disorders, and severe antisocial behaviors (Dumas, 1989; Griest & Wells, 1983; Sallis, 1983). Children with physical handicaps, developmental disorders, and learning disabilities have also been treated through parent training (Breiner & Beck, 1984; Cunningham, 1985; Hornby & Singh, 1983). Mothers of infants with low birth weights and/or prematurity (Patteson & Barnard, 1990) and abusive and neglectful parents have been treated through parent training (Guadin & Kurtz, 1985; Smith, 1984). Parent training programs have been used in conjunction with early intervention programs for disadvantaged preschoolers (Lowry & Whitman, 1989). Furthermore, parent training has been used with parents of all socioeconomic levels and all intellectual levels.

Finally, some researchers have attempted to make a distinction between parent training and parent education in terms of goals such as remediation or prevention. According to this distinction, parent *training* is defined as any attempt to resolve serious childhood behavior problems, whereas parent *education* is defined as any attempt to prevent the development of these dysfunctional behaviors (Schaefer & Briesmeister, 1989). In the empirical literature and in national program efforts, however, the boundaries between these two are often blurred in that they often teach the same things to many of the same populations. Thus, the terms often are used interchangeably. In actual practice, parent training and parent education are not two distinct types of interventions; rather, one is subsumed under the other. Parent education is generally considered to be the more general term, whereas parent training, subsumed under parent education, is a process involving one component of education, teaching specific skills (Dembo, Sweitzer, & Lauritzen, 1985).

## Focus of Previous Reviews

Because of the confusion in terminology, the different types of skills taught, and the variety of populations trained, any attempt to define, describe, and understand parent training in general can be frustrating and confusing. Nevertheless, attempts have been made to review the parent training literature; and, as evidenced by the complexities involved in defining parent training, such reviews have had different emphases. For example, previous reviews have evaluated the effectiveness of different parent training programs (Dembo et al. 1985) and the effectiveness of parent training as a treatment method for specific problems (Wells & Forehand, 1980). Earlier reviews have also examined where parent training research is published and who does the research (Wiese & Kramer, 1988). Other reviews have focused specifically on behavioral parent training as therapy (Moreland, Schwebel, Beck, & Wells, 1982).

Despite the difficulties in defining, describing, and understanding what makes up parent training, outcome evaluations and literature reviews continue to argue that parent training is an effective intervention for at-risk populations and populations already experiencing problems (Atkeson & Forehand, 1978; Berkowitz & Graziano, 1972; Moreland, Schwebel, Beck, & Wells, 1982). However, no treatment is without problems. An entire paper could be devoted to discussing problems in parent training research methodology, as well as other issues such as dropout rates, adequate training criteria, and experience level of parent trainers. Furthermore, researchers are just beginning to explore problems with outcomes due in part to other interpersonal problems of the parents, such as marital discord (Dadds, Schwartz, & Sanders, 1987) and mother insularity (Wahler, 1980). Nevertheless, there seem to be at least two other areas that parent training research has not addressed despite past researchers' attempts to highlight these and other mental health researchers' work in the areas.

## Focus of This Review

The areas of parent training neglected by previous reviews are the use of parent training with the parents of ordinary children and the incorporation of research from developmental psychology into parent training programs. Many people persist in the belief that parenting is instinctual and that well-functioning families do not need help or outside intervention. However, the popularity of do-it-yourself parent training books and the outpouring of child care books, magazines, and videos attest to the fact that there is a general demand for information that can help parents raise a physically and emotionally healthy child. Parents of all children, whether referred for problem behavior or not, are responding to a social climate in which pressure on today's families is greater than in the past because of such factors as more mothers being in the work force, geographic mobility, decreased extended family support, higher divorce rates, and economic uncertainties (Powell, 1986). Yet, the field of parent training has been slow to meet the needs of "normal" parents to learn parenting skills (Wiese & Kramer, 1988). Instead, parent training largely ignores parents of ordinary children by narrowly focusing on parents of children who are already experiencing problems. In addition, the broader field of parent education, though purporting to be preventive in nature, still focuses primarily on at-risk populations. This may be due in part to the general inclination of clinical science to be concerned first with conditions that urgently demand alleviation (e.g., antisocial behavior in a child) before turning attention to more positive themes (e.g., the promotion of positive or prosocial behavior) (Eisenberg & Mussen, 1989).

Of course, one could contend that we do not know how to train "normal" parents to be more effective (Wiese & Kramer, 1988). This may be true in part; yet we do have information that could be used to train

such parents. Research in the area of developmental psychology has achieved what research in clinical psychology has not. Developmental research of the healthy, appropriate development of the child has examined parent–child relationships in both deviant and nondeviant families. Thus, whereas most previous parent training has been narrowly focused on teaching skills to parents to stop child behavior problems, developmental psychologists have been working in areas that could provide information on a much broader form of parent training that could be used with both "normal" parents and parents of children referred to clinics.

Should the goal of parent training be to teach parents a general skill such as how to obtain their child's compliance, or should the goal be to teach parents how to foster a developmentally healthy child? The goal in any intervention should be to promote the most psychologically healthy environment for all involved. In parent training, this would involve all aspects of the parent–child relationship, and the aim would be to promote optimal development of the child within this important relationship.

Researchers have criticized the most popular form of parent training, behavior modification or child management skills training, as being almost exclusively concerned with undesirable behaviors. Contrary to the intentions of the founders of behavior modification, such an emphasis on undesirable child behaviors may have caused programs to have a negative or punishment orientation and also to neglect basic aspects of the parent–child relationship, including appropriate developmental expectations (Sapon-Shevin, 1982). It may be that this knowledge about parent–child relationships and child development is what parents want. But those often involved in parent training have had little to offer in this area (Lutzker, McGimsey, McRae, & Campbell, 1983). Thus, not only are parent trainers failing to meet the needs of "normal" parents, they may not even be meeting all of the needs of parents referred for clinical services.

Lutzker et al. (1983) have called for an analysis of parenting that would include differences between activities, affection, and emotional support in deviant and nondeviant families. They emphasize that these variables must be examined in order to offer a comprehensive therapy to deviant families. We contend that the same comprehensive therapy could be useful to nondeviant families as well, and that one place to start understanding these factors is the literature on developmental psychology and what that field has to say about the "normal" development of the child.

## THE CONTENT
## OF PARENT TRAINING

We surveyed the content of literature published between 1983 and early 1991 that has focused on the training of parents either in a context of problem remediation or problem prevention. *Psych Info,* a computerized edition of *Psychological Abstracts,* was searched using the terms *parent training* and *parenting skills.* From this search, reports were included if they: (1) empirically evaluated a program designed to teach parents skills or reviewed empirical research on such programs, (2) evaluated more than one parent or set of parents (i.e., no case studies), and (3) stated clearly the age of the child. Our focus was on children not yet experiencing major problems. We excluded parent training programs that had as their focus children with severe behavioral problems such as conduct disorders and antisocial behaviors. Several excellent reviews of these programs already exist (Atkeson & Forehand, 1978; Berkowitz & Graziano, 1972; Dumas, 1989; Moreland et al., 1982). To narrow further the focus of our review, we concentrated on "normal" children and interventions bearing on social development. Therefore, reports were also excluded if the children had special problems such as developmental delay, autism, mental retardation, language impairment, or learning disabilities, or if the focus of the research was on improving the child's intellectual development.

Our content review is organized by age group of the child. This was done to examine any changes in the content of programs associated with the child's age. The age groups were defined as *infancy* (birth to 2 years old), *early childhood* (3 to 6 years old), *middle childhood* (7 to 12 years old), and *adolescence* (13 to 18 years old). Each report is summarized in six areas. Our organization by age is then used in the second part of this chapter to interpret the content of parent training in light of some major developmental dimensions of "normal" social development of children. We can thus examine the attention or lack of attention to developmental information in this sample of parenting skill interventions.

## Parent Training Interventions During Infancy

### Subjects and Design.

The literature for parents of infants consisted of 13 studies involving training conducted primarily by nurses, pediatricians, or professionals associated with mental health agency programs. These are summarized in Table 10.1. The settings for the training were primarily hospitals or homes. Training typically fell into one of two categories, with the first characterized by brief training (one to three sessions) and the second characterized by long-term training (home visits extending over periods of months to years). Experimental and control group sizes for seven studies ranged from 10 to 54, while for four studies there were 4 or fewer subjects. Two larger scale programs had 380 subjects (Pfannenstiel & Seltzer, 1989), and 1,413 subjects (Showers, 1989), respectively. Five studies focused specifically on special populations, such as parents of low-birth-weight infants or adolescent mothers; in all but one study, mothers were the subjects of the training. Although we will continue to use the term *parents,* it should be noted that this usually refers to mothers. Eight of the 13 studies used experimental designs with more than one group, six of which included a control group. Other designs included multiple-baseline (Dachman, Alessi, Vrazo, Fuqua, & Kerr, 1986; Feldman, Case, Rincover, Towns, & Betel, 1989; Mathews, Friman, Barone, Ross, & Christophersen, 1987) pretest and posttest single-group (Showers, 1989), and posttest-only single-group (Pfannenstiel & Seltzer, 1989).

### Content and Outcome of Training

Table 10.2 summarizes the parenting behaviors most often taught to parents of infants. Prevention was the stated purpose for the majority of these parent training efforts. This was more obvious in those studies with parents of low-birth-weight infants, teenage parents, and parents with intellectual deficits where the focus was prevention of child abuse and neglect or prevention of developmental delays in the child. Studies involving "normal" parents, however, were also preventive in that the studies argued that the mother–infant relationship has an impact on the child's later development (e.g., Pfannenstiel & Seltzer, 1989). Nevertheless, the content of the programs, whether the subjects were special populations or "normal," was very similar. The teaching of maternal responsiveness and sensitivity was the most common tenet in these programs, and increasing the quality of parent–infant interaction was often the goal. In general, the goal of such programs is to increase appropriate parent responses to infant cues rather than simply increasing parent responsiveness as such. Programs with this goal most often were taught either in the home or hospital. Only rarely was the content of a program concerned with behavioral management of the infant.

**Table 10.1.**  Parent Training Programs for Parents of Infants

| STUDY | SUBJECTS | DESIGN | TREATMENT | TRAINING | OUTCOME MEASURES |
|---|---|---|---|---|---|
| Anderson & Sawin (1983) | 30 mothers of normal children | 3-group comparison: observed Brazelton, Brazelton explained, placebo control | Provided with information on infant capabilities; goal to enhance responsiveness | One 45-minute session | Direct observation of mother–infant interaction |
| Barrera, Rosenbaum, & Cunningham (1986) | 59 mothers of preterm infants E1 = 16, E2 = 22, C1 = 21  24 mothers of full-term infants, C2 | 3-group comparison: developmental intervention, parent–infant interaction, no-treatment control | Parents received either information on development and how to assess it or training in skills to enhance parent–infant interaction. | 1- to 2-hour home visits: weekly/ 4 mo., biweekly/ 4 mo., monthly/ 4 mo. | Infant cognitive, motor, & temperament characteristics  Experimenter assessment of home physical and social environment  Direct observation of parent–child interaction |
| Baskin, Umansky, & Sanders (1987) | N not given; adolescent mothers | 2-group comparison: treatment vs. no-treatment control | Two-phase intervention: I. Accurate observation II. Appropriate interaction; preventive focus | Weekly home visits from birth to 4 mo. | Direct observation of mother–infant interaction  Maternal adaptation  Child cognitive development and temperament |
| Belsky (1985) | 67 families, mother and father of normal infants | 4-group comparison: passive exposure to Brazelton (M & F), passive exposure to Brazelton (M only), active exposure (M & F), active exposure (M only) | Passive or active exposure to Brazelton  Neonatal behavior assessment | 1 session | Direct observation of mother–infant interaction and mother–father–infant interaction |
| Dachman, Alessi, Vrazo, Fuqua, & Kerr (1986) | *Expt. 1:* 3 fathers with no experience in infant care  *Expt. 2:* 3 fathers with varying degrees of experience in infant care | Multiple-probe across fathers | Taught infant care skills and infant stimulation activities | 2–3 sessions per subject | Direct observation of father behavior  Consumer satisfaction questionnaire |
| Feldman, Case, Rincover, Towns, & Betel (1989) | 3 mothers of normal children | Multiple-baseline across-subjects & within-subject  multiple-baseline across-skills | Taught appropriate affection, praise, & imitation | Weekly home visits for unspecified length of time | Direct observation of both mother and child behavior  Infant intellectual performance |
| Lambermon & van Ijzendoorn (1989) | 35 families (M & F) of normal infants | 2-group comparison: videotape & brochure vs. brochure-only | Parents received interaction training videos and brochures through the mail | One set of materials by mail per week for four weeks | Direct observation of mothers' behavior  Direct observation of home environment |

*Continued*

Table 10.1 continued

| STUDY | SUBJECTS | DESIGN | TREATMENT | TRAINING | OUTCOME MEASURES |
|---|---|---|---|---|---|
| Mathews, Friman, Barone, Ross, & Christoph-ersen (1987) | 4 mothers of normal infants | Multiple-baseline across-subjects | Taught to increase positive interactions, and taught behavior management for dangerous behaviors | Mean total instruction time of 90 minutes | Direct observation of infant behavior<br><br>Parent satisfaction |
| Nurcombe et al. (1984) | 74 mothers of low-birthweight infants: E = 34 C1 = 40 and 41 mothers of normal birthweight infants (C2) | 2-group comparsion: treatment vs. placebo control | Taught sensitivity and responsiveness to babies' physiological and social cues | 7 hospital sessions and 4 home sessions | Infant temperament and cognitive development<br><br>Maternal role satisfaction, attitudes to child-rearing, self-confidence, and psychopathology |
| Pfannenstiel & Seltzer (1989) | 380 first-time parents in four school districts | Quasi-experimental, posttest-only single-group | Taught accurate observation; provided with child development information; provided with information on promoting child's motor, social, intellectual, and language development | Regular home visits and monthly group meetings from birth to 3 years | Child's cognitive and language ability, and social development<br><br>Parent knowledge of child development |
| Riesch & Munns (1984) | 108 mothers of term infants (E = 54, C = 54) & 32 mothers of preterm infants (E = 16, C = 16) | 2-group comparison: treatment vs. no-treatment control | Mothers were informed about infant capabilities and how they could enhance and support the infants' behavior | Single session; given audiotape and text | Direct observation of mother and infant behavior<br><br>Maternal self-report of behavior |
| Showers (1989) | 1,413 parents | Pretest/posttest single-group | Provided with behavior management cares during visits to pediatrician | Given 18 cards total | Parental knowledge of information provided and self-report of behavior |
| Whitt & Casey (1982) | 32 mothers of normal infants | 2-group comparison: treatment vs. attention control | Focus was to enhance parent–child interaction: taught normal patterns of infant development and how to enhance the infant's behavior | 6 sessions | Direct observation of infant behavioral frequencies and mother–infant interaction<br><br>Experimenter ratings of affective relationship qualities |

**Table 10.2.** Parenting Skills Taught to Parents of Infants

PARENT BEHAVIORS TAUGHT

Attending to baby's physical needs and responding to baby's signals for help
(sensitivity and responsiveness)

Providing physical affection and praising the infant

Responding reciprocally to match the actions of baby (e.g., smiling, cooing, vocal
imitation)

Responding contingently in exchange for certain behaviors of the baby (e.g.,
feeding)

Stimulating the baby through activity such as play, positioning, stroking, rocking,
gazing

Talking to the baby with clear language

When training responsiveness and sensitivity, the emphasis was on the parent responding to child-initiated behaviors rather than having the parent direct the activity (Baskin, Umansky, & Sanders, 1987). One example of how this was taught was a study with adolescent mothers by Baskin et al. (1987). Their home-based two-phase approach began by teaching mothers activities designed to help them become accurate observers of their baby's behavior and to determine appropriate responses to the baby's cues. The second part of training focused on teaching parents to use play as a means for learning the infant's engagement and disengagement cues. Emphasis also was placed on using clear language and allowing the infant to learn new tasks without adult intervention. This study, like the majority of these studies, evaluated the effects of training through direct observation of the mother–infant interaction, with specific emphasis on the mother's behavior. Other methods of evaluation included the child's cognitive development and temperament and measures of maternal adaptation such as confidence, role satisfaction, and attitude toward child rearing. The results indicated that mothers who participated in the intervention became more responsive to their infants than the comparison group mothers. As a whole, increases in the infant's intellectual ability and/or temperament were also seen, and treated mothers were more satisfied and confident as mothers after treatment.

These interventions aimed to foster and increase parent–infant interaction and did so primarily through the teaching of observational skills and appropriate responses to infant cues. Parents were taught to change their behavior to match that of the baby and to change their behavior only when the baby's behavior changed. Training included teaching parents the value of maintaining eye contact, face-to-face positioning, and vocal imitation through pediatric well-child visits to the home (Whitt & Casey, 1982). Other skills taught in the home included increasing physical affection and praising the infant (Feldman et al., 1989). One program, which started in the hospital and continued through home visits, attempted to help parents differentiate between social and physiological cues (Nurcombe et al., 1984). Many programs trained parents to consider normal developmental patterns of infant behavior as social communicative efforts. For example, Whitt and Casey (1982) described crying to parents as a developmental milestone that changes within a day and over months. Parents were taught that crying takes on a different communicative intent at different times. Appropriate responsiveness to crying was addressed, and relationships between trainers and parents served to enhance parents' feelings of competence.

All three of these studies found positive effects from their interventions. Feldman and his colleagues (1989) found that mothers quickly increased their affection, praise, and imitation of child vocalizations. Further, the changes in mothers' behavior were associated with increases in the child's cognitive development. In contrast to this finding, Nurcombe and colleagues (1984) found no effects on infant cognitive development. Yet Nurcombe and colleagues (1984) did find that mothers who took part in their intervention were more satisfied and confident as mothers and perceived their infants as less temperamentally difficult. Finally, Whitt and Casey (1982), through the use of observations of behavioral frequencies, chains of interactive behavior, and ratings of the affective relationship characteristics, found increases in infant-initiated chains of responsive maternal behaviors, frequencies of infant movement, and maternal smiles for trained mothers compared to controls.

One home-based intervention used individualized programs based on specific parent–infant interaction situations such as feeding and bedtime (Barrera, Rosenbaum, & Cunningham, 1986). Through the assessment of infant behaviors, the home environment, and parent–child interactions, this program found significant effects for increased maternal responsiveness and increased infant verbal independent play. Another program aiming to increase maternal responsiveness focused solely on specific interaction situations, yet provided the information in a less involved manner (Lambermon & van Ijzendoorn, 1989). This parent training program involved sending parents videotaped information and brochures of written material and photographs through the mail. The specific topics covered in the information were maternal reaction to infant's crying, interaction during bathing, talking with the infant, and stimulating play with the infant. These investigators reported increases in appropriate parent–child interaction and, in the process, found that parent education based on brochures can be as effective as videotaped information.

Programs similar to these home visit programs were sometimes initiated in the hospital before the mother and baby went home. One such study involved nurses providing mothers with audiotapes that described a neonate's ability to demonstrate protective reflexes; to habituate to sound, light, or motion; to self-quiet through touch, and to attend to objects (Riesch & Munns, 1984). Mothers then were told how they could elicit or support such behavior through such actions as positioning, stroking, rocking, and gazing. From direct observations and mothers' self-reports, the researchers found that mothers in the treated group were able to report more neonatal behavioral cues than nontreated mothers, and they were more aware of their own behaviors.

Other interventions taking place in the hospital just days after the baby's birth aimed to enhance the parent–infant relationship by having the parents either watch the administration of the Brazelton Neonatal Assessment Scale or administer the scale themselves. Again, increasing maternal responsiveness was the goal of such administrations (Anderson & Sawin, 1983). Researchers have posited that parents cannot increase their responsiveness and interact reciprocally with their infant if they are unaware how caregiver stimulation affects the infant. Anderson and Sawin compared "tell only" and "show and tell" groups of parents. "Tell only" meant the scale was administered to the infant, and the parent was only told the results, whereas the "show and tell" group also got to watch the administration. The investigators found, from direct observations of mother–child interactions, that "show and tell" mothers reliably enhanced their responsiveness.

A minority of parent training interventions addressed parental management of the behavior of their infants. One example of this type of intervention was a program designed to decrease dangerous infant behaviors by instructing parents in the use of time out for unsafe behavior, positive attention for safe behavior, and child-proofing the home (Mathews et al., 1987). Mothers were taught such skills as describing and praising their infant's appropriate behavior and using the playpen for time out for potentially dangerous behavior. This program indirectly evaluated the training of parent behaviors by observing the number of dangerous infant behaviors before and after training. Infants of trained mothers decreased their dangerous behaviors. Other researchers have reported the use of child management skills with infants, but their use has not been evaluated (Porterfield, Herbert-Jackson, & Risley, 1976) or not evaluated adequately (Powers & Shapieski, 1986).

One other study indirectly taught behavior management skills by providing parents with behavior management cards during their regular pediatric visits (Showers, 1989). The purpose of this study was again preventive in that the author cited data showing that unrealistic expectations of children's behavior are related to child abuse and that providing parents with information about appropriate developmental and behavioral expectations of children and about nonviolent approaches to child behavior management might prevent such abuse. Parents of infants and toddlers were given eighteen cards that covered topics such as toilet training, tantrums, bedtime problems, fighting, and biting. Results indicated that although a majority of the participants began with accurate information, there was a gain in knowledge for those who started out with inaccurate information. Further, those who started the study with accurate information said that the cards helped by validating how they felt about what they were already doing.

Finally, some programs offered to parents of infants have provided more than just training in responsiveness and sensitivity. Often such programs had as their goal improved development in all areas for the child, including intellectual, language, social, and motor skills development. These programs defined their purpose as prevention and often followed the parent and child for several years (Affholter, Connell, & Nauta, 1983; Nudd, 1989). These programs typically began in infancy but may have followed the family into the child's preschool and school-age years. In the past, these programs were designed primarily for use with disadvantaged populations (Greenspan & White, 1985). Many have been considered early intervention programs because they address populations with specific problems, such as multiproblem mothers (Booth, Mitchell, Barnard, & Spieker, 1989) and developmentally delayed infants (Lowry & Whitman, 1989).

A recently evaluated program in Missouri was designed to reflect the growing realization that such programs could be beneficial for all socioeconomic levels (Pfannenstiel & Seltzer, 1989). This program, called the New Parents as Teachers Project, followed families during the child's first three years, during which home trainers provided age-appropriate information on child development; helped parents increase their skills as observers of their child; and provided guidance in promoting the child's intellectual, language, social, and motor development. Children who participated in this program consistently scored higher than both the nationally normed group and the comparison group on measures of intelligence and language ability. Further, the children were more likely to distinguish a self-identity, to have positive adult relations, to have coping capabilities, and to engage in social play. Finally, participating parents were more knowledgeable about the importance of physical stimuli in their child's development, about appropriate discipline, and about knowledge of child development for children age 3 and younger.

Interventions such as this are obviously a very special type of comprehensive parent training that first gained attention with the advent of Head Start Programs (Greenspan & White, 1985). These programs are often based in schools. An example of a school-based early intervention program for children and parents is the Brookline Early Education Project in Massachusetts (Pierson, Walker, & Tivnan, 1984). This program followed the child from infancy to kindergarten and was designed primarily to provide support to parents. The program provided parents with developmental information and helped them recognize strengths in their children. This program, like other programs funded through local school sources

and national educational advocates, lacked the funds for research and evaluation and therefore was unable to make generalizable statements about its efficacy.

*Summary*

The majority of parent training efforts directed toward parents of infants have been focused on educating caregivers about their infants' abilities and training parents to be more responsive and sensitive to their infants' cues. Approximately half of the studies used a control group, and the majority used multiple assessment techniques. Outcomes were typically positive across all measures. The basic training protocol was used in the home setting, hospital settings, and child development centers; yet most were performed in the home. The training, primarily designed for preventive purposes, has been used with populations including parents of low-birth-weight and premature babies, parents with intellectual deficits, and adolescent parents. Less frequently, the training protocol has been used with middle class parents as well. Parents in these programs were primarily mothers. Efforts to train fathers in parent–infant interaction skills like those described are rare but have been shown to be effective when targeting fathers (Dachman, Alessi, Vrazo, Fuqua, & Kerr, 1986).

## Parent Training Interventions During Early Childhood

*Subjects and Design*

As shown in Table 10.3, the literature involving parents of preschool children consisted of 12 studies conducted primarily by psychologists in academic or medical center settings. The parents trained were most often mothers, with only 4 studies training both mothers and fathers. Eight studies had fewer than 10 parents per group, one study had 16 parents (Sloane, Endo, Hawkes, & Jenson, 1990), and three studies had 30 to 45 parents per group (Esdaile & Sanderson, 1987; Mischley, Mischley, & Dush, 1985; Strayhorn & Weidman, 1989). Most parents were trained in a group format consisting of 3 to 10 sessions. Only one study specifically identified the children of the parents as being "normal" (Packard, Robinson, & Grove, 1983), whereas in three others this was assumed because no problems were mentioned (Esdaile

**Table 10.3.**   Parent Training Programs for Parents of Children in Early Childhood

| STUDY | SUBJECTS | DESIGN | TREATMENT | TRAINING | OUTCOME MEASURES |
|---|---|---|---|---|---|
| Esdaile & Sanderson (1987) | 30 mothers of nonproblem children | Pretest/ posttest single-group | Toy-making workshop to promote interaction | 3 two-hour sessions | Parent self-report of expectations, experiences, and attitudes |
| Dadds, Sanders, Behrens, & James (1987) | 4 two-parent families with a problem child | Multiple-baseline across families | Child management training with planned activities and partner support training | 5–8 one-hour sessions | Marital satisfaction<br><br>Maternal perception of child behavior<br><br>Direct observation of parent–parent and parent–child interaction<br><br>Parents' problem solving |
| Green, Hardison, & Greene (1984) | 4 two-parent families with nonproblem children | Various within-group designs | Use of table-talk placemats during meal times; to enhance family interaction | Unspecified number of meal times | Direct observation of family interaction<br><br>Consumer satisfaction questionnaire |
| Knapp & Deluty (1989) | 49 mothers with problem child; 22 middle-SES & 18 lower-SES | 4-group Comparison<br><br>Lower-SES— role-play<br><br>Lower-SES— discussion<br><br>Middle-SES— role-play<br><br>Middle-SES— discussion | Behavioral Parent Training based on Forehand & McMahon (1981) | 8 sessions | Direct observation of child and parent behavior<br><br>Maternal perception of child behavior<br><br>Maternal perception of parenting stress<br><br>Child's perception of changes in maternal behavior |
| Lutzer (1987) | 9 mothers of children at risk | Quasi-experimental<br><br>posttest only<br><br>single-group | Parent education and peer support group; taught stress reduction, assertiveness, & behavior modification skills | 4 sessions | Parental self-report of interests, attitudes, & feelings of self-efficacy |
| Mischley, Stacy, Mischley, & Dush (1985) | 72 mothers and fathers of nonproblem children<br><br>E = 423, C = 30 | 2-group comparison: treatment vs. delayed-treatment control | Prevention program including interaction training and behavior management | 5 two-hour group sessions and 2 home visits | Direct observation of parent behavior<br><br>Direct observation of home environment<br><br>Child social competency |
| Packard, Robinson, & Grove (1983) | 18 mothers with nonproblem children; E1 = 7, E2 = 4, C = 7 | Follow-up of 3-group comparison: manual only, manual & coaching, placebo control | Relationship building<br><br>Skills training | Two 90-minute to 2-hour sessions | Direct observation of parent behavior<br><br>Parental perception of child behavior<br><br>Parental perception of self-competency and efficacy<br><br>Parental satisfaction |

| STUDY | SUBJECTS | DESIGN | TREATMENT | TRAINING | OUTCOME MEASURES |
|---|---|---|---|---|---|
| Sanders & Christensen (1985) | 20 mothers and fathers | 3-group comparison: child management (CM), CM + planned activities, no-treatment control | Behavioral child management training with planned activities | Two 90-minute sessions followed by twice weekly home visits for 7 weeks | Direct observation of mother–child interaction<br><br>Consumer satisfaction questionnaire |
| Sanders & Dadds (1982) | 5 families (M & F) with problem child | Multiple-baseline across-subjects | Child management training and planned activities | Home training; unspecified length of time | Direct observation of parent and child behavior |
| Scaife & Frith (1988) | 6 mothers with problem children | Pretest/posttest single-group | Behavior management training and relaxation training | Ten 90-minute sessions | Parent perception of child behavior<br><br>Parent attitudes<br><br>Parental knowledge of techniques |
| Sloane, Endo, Hawke, & Jenson (1990) | 16 families with mild behavior problem children | Multiple-baseline | Self-instructional behavioral parent training booklets | 8–12 weeks allowed for studying material | Parental perception of child behavior<br><br>Program fidelity<br><br>Parent satisfaction |
| Strayhorn & Weidman (1989) | 89 families<br><br>E = 45, C = 44 | 2-group comparison treatment vs. minimal-treatment | Behavioral parent training and parent–child interaction training | Not specified | Parent Practices Scale<br><br>Direct observation of parent and child behavior<br><br>Parent self-report of depression<br><br>Parent & teacher perception of child behavior<br><br>Consumer satisfaction |

& Sanderson, 1987; Green, Hardison, & Greene, 1984; Mischley et al., 1985). Thus, the majority of the studies identified the children as experiencing behavior problems including oppositional behavior and/or noncompliance, or the children were considered at risk for behavior problems. For those studies that clearly stated how the parents were recruited, most recruited parents from advertisements or clinic referrals. Parents self-selected for the program. Finally, experimental designs ranged from multiple-baseline designs (Dadds, Sanders, Behrens, & James, 1987; Sanders & Dadds, 1982; Sloane et al., 1990) to multiple-group comparisons (Knapp & Deluty, 1989; Mischley et al., 1985; Packard et al., 1983; Sanders & Christensen, 1985; Strayhorn & Weidman, 1989).

Two studies used pretest and posttest single-group designs (Esdaile & Sanderson, 1987; Scaife & Frith, 1988), one used within-group designs (Green et al., 1984), and one used a quasi-experimental, posttest-only single-group design (Lutzer, 1987).

## Content and Outcome of Training

Table 10.4 summarizes the content of parent training interventions among parents of preschool children. Programs in this section were assigned to one of four categories: prevention programs, behavioral programs, behavioral programs with relationship skills components, or programs focused solely on improving interaction.

**Table 10.4.** Parenting Skills Taught to Parents of Children in Early Childhood

PARENT BEHAVIORS TAUGHT

Reflective listening

Planned activities training: providing structured activities, discussing rules for community settings, and rehearsing and coaching appropriate behavior

Problem-solving skills

Assertively stating and enforcing rules (proper statement and use of commands)

Communicating approval through tone of voice and facial expression and showing excitement about positive behaviors of child

Providing explanations and information about rules

Active involvement with child through play and other activities (e.g., taking the child places, reading to child)

Providing structure through contingent consequences (e.g., praise and reinforcement for appropriate behavior, time out, ignoring, (and removal of privilege) for inappropriate behavior

Modeling prosocial interaction

Interacting during play: nondirectively verbalizing the child's play behavior without issuing commands, asking questions, or making criticisms; labeling and praising appropriate play and social behavior

Providing physical affection

As with parent training for infants, some programs were designed to follow the child from infancy through preschool or school-age years, and their purpose was to prevent potential behavioral and academic problems. Thus, parents of preschool children, like parents of infants, often received training as a means of prevention for some potential problem. These parent education and prevention programs seemed to be the only ones that actually provided services to parents for an extended period of time. Unfortunately, these programs often were not evaluated because of lack of funds.

An exception to this was the Midland Parent Education Project for low-income families (Mischley et al., 1985). Not only did this program differ from others in that it was formally evaluated, but it also began when the child was of preschool age rather than an infant. The program consisted of five two-hour group training modules covering the following topics: play experiences that involved interaction with the parent; listening and problem-solving skills; behavior management techniques (positive reinforcement, mild social punishment, ignoring and time out); building positive strengths (self-concept, responsibility taking, and independence); and helping parents determine which skills to use in different situations. Using outcome measures of the child's social competency, the parents' skills, and an observation of the home environment, these researchers found major gains in both parenting skills and child social compe-

tency for treated subjects as compared to controls. These effects persisted or increased across the follow-up period of six months.

Another smaller scale prevention program consisted of a four-session educational and peer support parenting group for mothers of children at risk for behavior disorders (Lutzer, 1987). In this program, mothers who rated their preschool child's behavior as "abnormal" attended sessions that focused on identification, acceptance, and methods of dealing with stress; assertiveness; techniques of behavior modification and reflective listening; and discussions of general areas of concern such as friendships, sex education, and television watching. During all sessions, information about normal development was presented. Evaluations of the program were based solely on parents' reports of how they felt the program had helped them. It is therefore unclear if their behaviors changed or if there was any effect on the child.

The parents of preschool children, in contrast to parents of infants, often are taught child behavior management skills. However, the focus on the parent–child relationship is also observed in preschool parenting approaches. This was evidenced by the addition of different skills to basic behavioral packages, by interventions focusing solely on the relationship, and by the inclusion of direct observation of both parent and child behaviors as an outcome measure for many of the preschool parenting interventions.

Some examples of behavioral parent training used with parents of preschool children have shown that these methods were used primarily for children already experiencing behavioral problems. This was most likely due to the fact that the child was capable of intentionally misbehaving or performing behaviors interpreted by parents as intentional misbehavior. Knapp and Deluty (1989) taught lower and middle-class parents through either role-play and modeling or readings and discussion. Specific skills taught concerned the appropriate use of contingent reinforcement, including praise, reward, ignoring, and time out. The program was based on that described by Forehand and McMahon (1981). Scaife and Frith (1988) taught parents how to observe children's behavior accurately and to use contingent reinforcement. These researchers also attempted to address parents' life stresses by teaching parents relaxation techniques. Both of these studies reported that, whether or not direct observations indicated changes in children's behavior, parents often perceived decreases in problem behavior in children. Further, Scaife and Frith found that, after treatment, parents demonstrated an increase in comprehension of behavior techniques.

Behavioral parent training programs for parents of preschoolers have been directed toward children with general problems of noncompliance or have targeted a specific behavior such as fighting (Sloane et al., 1990). Often, behavioral parent training programs have been designed in such a way that the efficacy is assumed and the question concerns what form the training should take. For example, Knapp and Deluty (1989) compared a modeling and role-play format to readings and discussion, and, through measures of changes in parent behavior, found that lower class mothers demonstrated the skills more often if they were trained through modeling and role-play.

Additions to basic behavioral packages directed toward parents of preschool children have included such components as specific training in "planned activities" and the inclusion of parent–child interaction training. Examples of the former are studies by Sanders and Dadds (1982); Sanders and Christensen (1985); and Dadds, Sanders, Behrens, and James (1987). In addition to basic behavioral child management skills, Sanders and Dadds (1982) trained parents to employ a planned activities procedure to engage children in activities over a range of potentially problematic settings such as shopping. Specifically, planned activities training involved teaching the parent how to select and arrange suitable activities for the child, how to discuss with the child rules regarding the situation, and how to rehearse and coach the child in the correct behavior for the situation. Sanders and Christensen (1985) expanded the planned activities training to include how to encourage and extend the child's interest in activities by incidental teaching procedures, how to select and apply incentives for motivating children's desired behavior, how to select practical consequences for inappropriate behavior in the specific situations, and how to hold feedback discussions with the child after the desired or undesired behavior. Dadds, Sanders, Behrens, and James (1987) used a multiple-baseline design with four families and taught general behavioral principles including the use of praise and other contingent consequences. After feedback sessions on the use of behavioral techniques, the families were instructed in planned activities training as described in Sanders and Dadds (1982). They found that, overall, the child management training including planned activities produced significant reductions in deviant child behavior. Dadds and colleagues (1987) did not examine the specific effects of the planned activities addition.

Planned activities training typically has been added to behavior parent training in an effort to improve the generalizability of training. Sanders and Dadds (1982) sequentially exposed five families to child management training and planned activities. Of the five families, four experienced improved child behavior using the child management training. Observations of parent behavior revealed that there were decreases in the parents' aversive behaviors in all settings but no real increases in parents' positive behaviors. Thus, the authors concluded that changes in aversive parent behaviors generalized more readily to nontraining settings than did positive parent behaviors. Sanders and Christensen (1985) randomly assigned 20 parents to either a child management training condition or a combined child management plus planned activities condition. Observations of parent and child behaviors in five home settings showed decreased oppositional behavior in children, decreased aversive behavior in parents, and increased positive behavior in parents for both groups. In interpreting the lack of differences between the two treatment groups, the authors concluded that planned activities training may produce greater effects in community settings than in home settings. Therefore, as this study examined only home settings, planned activities provided no additional effects beyond those of the child management training.

Strayhorn and Weidman (1989) added parent–child interaction training to behavioral parent training administered via videotapes and handouts and compared this intervention to what they considered a minimal treatment condition of the videotapes and handouts alone. The interaction training consisted of teaching parents specific behaviors for facilitating a positive relationship with their preschool child. Some of these behaviors included communicating approval through tone of voice and facial expression, showing excitement about positive behaviors of the child, modeling prosocial interaction with toys, "tracking and describing" (nondirectively verbalizing the child's play behavior during play with the child), and avoiding attribution of negative traits to the child when speaking to the child. This training also included directions and modeling of appropriate play with children. Outcome measures included parent self-report and blind observations of parent and child behavior. Results favored the intervention that included interaction training by finding that parents in this condition rated their children more favorably and had better interactions with their children. Interestingly, changes in parents' ratings of children's behavior was positively correlated with change in the observer's ratings of parents' behavior.

One study focused solely on relationship-building skills, specifically the attending skills of the mother (Packard, Robinson, & Grove, 1983). This study was a follow-up comparison of Grove's (1982) dissertation comparing self-administered versus trainer-assisted procedures in teaching mothers to use differential social attention. Mothers received a manual focused on nondirective attending that taught the parent to describe the ongoing play of the child without issuing commands, asking questions, or making criticisms. The parent also was taught to use social reinforcement by clearly labeling and praising the child's constructive play or appropriate social behavior, engaging in positive physical contact, and ignoring the child if he or she misbehaved. Mothers who were coached during interactions with their child continued to make gains in nondirective skills after training. They issued more descriptive statements and fewer indirect commands, and they displayed less negative behavior than did control mothers who read a placebo manual and practiced independently. Those mothers in the self-instruction-only group did not differ at follow-up from placebo controls. This suggests that maintenance of relationship-building skills was enhanced by the coaching. These differences were based on direct observational data.

In addition to early education prevention models, behavioral approaches, and behavioral approaches with additions, a variety of other interventions were found that fall under the general category of promoting interaction between parent and child. One example of this is Esdaile and Sanderson (1987), who presented developmental information and taught parenting skills through toy-making workshops. The primary objectives of this program included the intent to enhance child development through the provision of the toys made and to enhance family relationships through play involving these toys. Yet another unusual and indirect way of teaching appropriate parent–child interaction involved using placemats in restaurants designed to enhance family interaction (Green et al., 1984). The authors presented this intervention as a means of improving interaction during a common but often troublesome situation. This is related conceptually to the planned activities training described earlier.

*Summary.*

Overall, parent training interventions for parents of preschool children have as their focus some attempt to train parents how to manage their children behaviorally, to interact in a more positive manner with their preschool child, or both. The programs themselves vary from prevention programs with at-risk populations to basic behavioral training programs to such unusual training formats as toy-making workshops. Mothers were most often trained, and the majority of parenting approaches for this age group were directed toward children either at risk for behavior disorders or already displaying some problem behaviors. Finally, whereas evaluations of parenting programs for parents of infants focused primarily on child cognitive development and parenting behaviors, parents of preschool children were observed in interaction with their child in laboratory, home, and community settings and were often asked to report on changes in their child's behavior through questionnaires.

## Parent Training Interventions During Middle Childhood

*Subjects and Design*

When confined to studies of "normal" children or children with minor problems, the parent training literature for school-aged children was limited, as can be seen in Table 10.5. Eight studies were found that

**Table 10.5.** Parent Training Programs for Parents of Children in Middle Childhood

| STUDY | SUBJECTS | DESIGN | TREATMENT | TRAINING | OUTCOME MEASURES |
|---|---|---|---|---|---|
| Forehand & Long (1988) | 21 parents with problem children and 21 control parents with nontreated children | Follow-up of pretest/posttest single-group design adding a control group | Behavioral parent training | Twice weekly individual family sessions | Parental perception of child behavior |
| | | | | | Parent and child self-report of family communication & conflict |
| | | | | | Children's self-reported depression |
| | | | | | Child's perception of cognitive and social competence |
| | | | | | Teachers' perception of child competence |
| | | | | | Parents' perception of parenting competence |
| | | | | | Parents' self-reported depression |
| | | | | | Marital adjustment |
| | | | | | Direct observation of mother–child interaction |
| Graybill (1986) | 26 mothers & 6 fathers | Pretest/posttest single-group | Taught active listening skills | 6 two-hour sessions | Parental attitudes |
| | | | | | Parental knowledge of techniques |
| | | | | | Children's attitudes |
| | | | | | Teachers' perception of child behavior |
| Huhn & Zimpfer (1989) | 18 mothers of normal children | Pretest/posttest single-group | Survival training for parents program based on Adlerian principles | Six 2½-hour sessions | Parental attitudes |
| | | | | | Children's self-esteem and manifest anxiety |
| Kanigsberg & Levant (1988) | 34 parents of problem children, (9 F, 25 M); E1 = 15, E2 = 7, C = 12 | 3-group comparison: Behavioral skills, Communication skills, No-treatment control | Taught either behavioral child management skills or client-centered communication skills | 8 two-hour weekly sessions | Parental attitudes |
| | | | | | Parents' perception of children's behavior |
| | | | | | Children's self-concept |
| Lewis (1986) | 20 mothers with a problem child (E = 10, C = 10) | 2-group comparison: treatment vs. no-treatment control | Behavioral parent training with some reflective techniques | 6 six-hour training sessions | Parent and experimenter perception of child's behavior |
| | | | | | Parent and child perception of intrafamily adjustment |
| Lorber, Felton, & Reid (1984) | 27 families | 3-group comparison: child abusive, distressed-nonabusive, nonproblem | Behavioral management skills taught for purpose of prevention | Individual sessions with mean length of treatment = 23.6 hours | Direct observation of family interaction |

*Continued*

Table 10.5 continued

| STUDY | SUBJECTS | DESIGN | TREATMENT | TRAINING | OUTCOME MEASURES |
|-------|----------|--------|-----------|----------|-------------------|
| Rickert et al. (1988) | 8 parents, (6 M, 2 F) of problem children | Multiple-baseline across-skills | Taught instruction-giving skills and time-out skills | 2 one-hour didactic presentations & 6 two-hour training sessions | Direct observation of parent and child behavior<br><br>Parent perception of child child behavior<br><br>Parent attitudes<br><br>Consumer satisfaction |
| Wells & Egan (1988) | 24 mothers with a problem child | 2-group comparison: social learning parent training vs. systems family therapy | Behavioral training based on Forehand & McMahon (1981) or systems family therapy | 8–12 therapy sessions | Direct observation of parent–child interaction<br><br>Maternal emotional adjustment & marital satisfaction |

focused specifically on parents of this age group, and in five of these the children were experiencing some behavior problems. Parent training programs provided during middle childhood, like early childhood programs, often make use of behavioral methods.

Parents were trained primarily in a group format for 6 to 8 weeks of one- to two-hour sessions. Many programs were open to both mothers and fathers, but the majority of participants were mothers. Group sizes were generally small, with five studies having 15 or fewer parents in a group. The remaining three had group sizes of 18, 21, and 32. Parents usually responded to advertisements or were referred from clinics. Finally, five studies used a multiple-group comparison design, four of which used control groups, while two studies used pretest and post-test single-group designs (Graybill, 1986; Huhn & Zimpfer, 1989). One study used a multiple-baseline-across-skills design (Rickert et al., 1988).

### Content of Training

Table 10.6 summarizes the content of parent training interventions for parents of school-aged children. Tavormina (1974, 1975) grouped parenting approaches into two basic models: reflective counseling and behavioral counseling. This grouping apparently has not changed over the years, especially with this age group. Interventions were typically based on behavior therapy or on one of two reflective counseling approaches: Parent Effectiveness Training or Adlerian therapy. Even if the training was not a packaged program, the skills taught tended to fall within one of these three basic models.

The format of behavioral parent training varies considerably, but the concepts taught are typically the same. Dembo, Sweitzer, and Lauritzen (1985) summarized behavioral approaches as including "an overview of basic behavioral concepts, the nature and use of social reinforcers, the manner in which children shape the behavior of their parents, observations and recording procedures, and techniques for weakening undesirable behavior and strengthening desirable responses" (p. 158). Specific skills most often taught as part of such programs were specific delineation of target behaviors, ignoring inappropriate behavior, use of positive social reinforcement for appropriate behavior (i.e., praise, attention, reward), giving clear and concise commands and instructions, not repeating commands, and use of punishment for noncompliance (i.e., time out, overcorrection).

Programs were often based on books including such popular volumes as *Living with Children* (Patterson & Gullion, 1971), *ABCs for Parents* (Rettig, 1973), *Families: Application of Social Learning to Family Life* (Patterson, 1975), *Parents Are Teachers* (Becker, 1971), and *Helping the Noncompliant Child* (Forehand & McMahon, 1981). Some behavioral parent training interventions have included behavioral components without including all the aforementioned skills. For example, Rickert and his colleagues (1988) taught only instruction-giving and time-out skills. The results of their specific program showed that six of the seven parents achieved or exceeded a 90% skill proficiency.

Wells and Egan (1988) compared Social Learning Parent Training (SLPT) based on the behavioral program developed by Forehand and McMahon (1981)

**Table 10.6.**  Parenting Skills Taught to Parents of Children in Middle Childhood

### PARENT BEHAVIORS TAUGHT

Providing structure through contingent consequences, such as positive social reinforcement for appropriate behavior (praise, reward, attention), and use of mild punishment for inappropriate behavior (time out, overcorrection, and removal of privilege)

Positive and specific delineation of target behaviors

Ignoring inappropriate behavior where possible

Giving clear and concise commands and instructions; not repeating commands

Understanding and accepting the child's feelings: active listening, using I-messages

Recognizing dysfunctional patterns of communication such as interruptions, threats, accusations and unwarranted or global generalizations

Recognizing parents' and child's rights: listen empathically to other person's view and express own views in assertive fashion; arrive at problem resolutions after consideration of both viewpoints

Modify destructive self-talk, such as "This isn't going to work"

Applying natural and logical consequences

to systems family therapy. The program was divided into two phases. In the first phase, the parent was taught to be a more effective reinforcing agent and was trained in the use of rewards contingent on compliance and other appropriate behaviors. The parent also was taught to decrease commands, questions, and criticisms. In the second phase, the parent was trained to use appropriate commands and time out to decrease noncompliant behavior. Forehand and Long (1988) implemented the same treatment with parents of school-aged children and reported follow-up data from four years after the intervention as compared to a control group that did not receive the intervention (a nonclinic "normal" sample). These researchers considered the program to be preventive in the sense that noncompliance can lead to more serious antisocial behaviors. Follow-up results indicated that the families that had previously participated in the parent training were functioning well relative to the nonclinic "normal" sample.

Parent Effectiveness Training (PET) is a packaged parent education program developed by Thomas Gordon (1975) using the work of Carl Rogers (1951). The format of PET is structured and typically is taught in eight weekly three-hour sessions. This program was designed to improve parent–child relations, and training focuses on learning such skills as the use of active listening, sending "I-messages," and a problem-solving technique whereby conflicts are resolved through negotiation. The main thrust of this program is promoting democratic interactions through communication skills.

Like some behaviorally based approaches, some parenting interventions with this age group have used only a part of the PET program, such as teaching the skill of active listening. An example is the study conducted by Graybill (1986) in which 26 mothers and 6 fathers were trained in active listening and the importance of understanding and accepting children's feelings. The program was designed specifically for parents who believed that their children lacked self-confidence. Outcome measures included measures of parental attitudes, measures of parents' knowledge of how to respond to children's feelings and of active listening skills, and measures of children's attitudes and behaviors. Results indicated that parents who received the intervention became less anxious about their parenting skills and demonstrated knowledge of active listening and appropriate response to children's feelings. There were no changes in children's attitudes or behavior.

Other studies have included a training condition in "communication skills," which is usually at least partially based on PET philosophy. Kanigsberg and Levant (1988) compared behavioral contingency management to communication skills and problem-solving training. The communication skills taught to parents by Kanigsberg and Levant were adapted from a client-centered communication skills program entitled "Skills Training for Parents: A Personal Developmental Program" by Levant and Haffrey (1981). This group focused on the skills of empathy and genuineness and their application to problem-solving situations. Specific sessions covered: listening to your child, listening to how your child feels, becoming aware of your own feelings, speaking assertively, communicating rules, and resolving conflicts. Both these studies reported improvements in the children's behavior for those parents who participated in the behavioral intervention. Further, Kanigsberg and Levant reported improvements in children's self-concept for both behavioral and communication treatment groups. Lewis (1986) taught parents behavioral principles including positive reinforcement, consistency, extinction, and time out, with the addition of communication skills such as negotiations, feedback, and message sending. Lewis found that both parent and child rated family adjustment (attitudes toward family members) as improved after their behavioral plus reflective techniques training.

The third approach on which many parenting interventions were based is the Adlerian approach. This approach stems from the writings of Adler (1927, 1930) and has been translated into specific programs by Dreikurs and Soltz (1964) and Dinkmeyer and McKay (1976). The approach emphasizes social variables and has as its goal to help parents understand children, how children think, and what motives underlie their actions. The program outlined by Dinkmeyer and McKay (1976) is known as Systematic Training for Effective Parenting (STEP) and includes some PET approaches such as active listening and I-messages. Thus, again, a major tenet of this program is the learning of communication skills, and the program teaches discipline through natural and logical consequences, a method its proponents assert develops responsibility.

Some parenting interventions with children in middle childhood are preventive in their focus. Prevention of child abuse is one goal (Lorber, Felton, & Reid, 1984). In addition, some programs have recognized that this age group is at risk for drug abuse (Johnston, Bachman, & O'Malley, 1981). Arguments have been made that parent training programs could, through the improvement of parent–child relations and child self esteem, subsequently prevent drug abuse (Cohen, 1982; Coombs, Santana, & Fawzy, 1984).

Despite such sweeping claims, the parenting skills being taught in these preventive programs still fall within the basic programs already discussed. For example, Lorber et al. (1984) taught accurate parental monitoring of prosocial and aversive child behavior, consistent and contingent parental reinforcement of prosocial child behavior, and consistent and contingent parental application of a nonphysical punishment technique (time out) to reduce child abuse episodes. Behavior observations of family interaction used to assess the effects of treatment showed a significant reduction in abusive mothers' aversive behavior directed toward their children.

Huhn and Zimpfer (1989) used an Adlerian approach to teach parents mutual respect and understanding, natural and logical consequences, and communication skills to improve children's self-esteem and to reduce anxiety in an effort to prevent future drug abuse. The rationale for the program was based on parents improving their understanding of their children, which in turn would cause the children to feel better about themselves; experience less anxiety; and ultimately have fewer emotional problems and be less likely to resort to alcohol, drug abuse, or irresponsible sexual behavior. The program taught and modeled an accepting home atmosphere with a focus on positive behavior and a democratic approach to parenting. Parents also were provided with information about adolescent development and the typical problems of emerging adolescents. Compared to a wait-list control group, parents in the experimental condition had greater confidence in themselves and in their abilities to be responsible parents to their children and placed a higher value on communication with the child and the need to understand the child. No differences were found on child measures of self-esteem and manifest anxiety.

*Summary*

Parenting skills training approaches used with children aged 6 to 12 years old have been based on behavioral principles, PET principles, or Adlerian principles and conducted with small groups of parents. For the most part, training was done with parents who reported some behavior problems with their children. Training given to parents of nonproblem children did not differ significantly from that offered to parents of children with behavioral problems. Outcomes often were evaluated by direct observation of parent and child behavior, parent perception of child behavior, parent attitudes, and child variables such as self-esteem and depression. Even if the parent's behavior was measured through observations, however, when discussing results, researchers focused on the changes made by the child rather than the parent. Measurement of whether the parent had actually acquired the skills taught was indirect in reflective counseling interventions and at times suspect in the behavioral interventions.

## Parent Training Interventions During Adolescence

### Subjects and Design

As shown in Table 10.7, we located only four empirical studies that specifically trained parents of adolescents. One additional descriptive article is discussed here because of its implications for training parents of adolescents experiencing minor problems.

Of the four empirical studies, two trained parents who had adolescents who were experiencing problems (Hall & Rose, 1987; Raue & Spence, 1985), whereas the other two did not clearly state if the children had problems (Bredehoft & Hey, 1985; Klein & Swisher, 1983). Three of the four studies included mothers and fathers in the training, and in the fourth study participants were referred to merely as ''parents'' (Klein & Swisher, 1983). Klein and Swisher (1983), whose program was designed to pre-

vent drug abuse, had a large sample ($N = 286$), whereas the other studies had 8 to 14 parents per group. Parents were either referred by clinics or volunteered for the programs. Only Bredehoft and Hey (1985) included the adolescent in treatment. Experimental designs were either two- or three-group comparisons, with all four studies using a no-treatment or delayed-treatment control group.

### Content of Training

Table 10.8 summarizes the content of what was taught to parents in the four studies.

Adolescence is generally considered one of the most difficult periods in development for both the adolescent and the parent. As for parents of school-aged children, parent training approaches focusing on parents of ''normal'' adolescents were rare. Parenting interventions dealing with severely behaviorally disturbed teens (those with conduct disorders or anti-

**Table 10.7.** Parent Training Programs for Parents of Adolescents

| STUDY | SUBJECTS | DESIGN | TREATMENT | TRAINING | OUTCOME MEASURES |
|---|---|---|---|---|---|
| Bredehoft & Hey (1985) | 13 treatment families & 14 control (M & F in both) | 2-group comparison: treatment vs. no-treatment control | *Self-Esteem: A Family Affair* program (Similar to PET and Adlerian approaches) | Both parents and adolescent attended 8 two-hour sessions | All individuals' perception of the family system, perception of parent–adolescent conflict, and self-concept |
| Hall & Rose (1987) | 24 families, half with problem children (M & F) | 3-group comparison: experimental treatment, best alternative treatment, delayed-treatment control | Experimental: cognitive-behavioral training package; best alternative: communication skills | 5 sessions | Direct observation of parent–adolescent interaction<br><br>Parent perception of adolescent behavior<br><br>Adolescent perception of parent behavior |
| Klein & Swisher (1983) | 286 parents (E = 138, C = 148) | Post-test only 2-group comparison: treatment vs. delayed-treatment control | Communication and behavioral skills substance abuse education program | 9 two-hour sessions | Parental acceptance of child as individual<br><br>Parent perception of family climate<br><br>Parents' sensitivity to children |
| Raue & Spence (1985) | 26 parents of problem children (2 F) | 3-group comparison: individual-treatment, group-treatment, wait-list control | Communication skills and increasing positive interactions | Both groups: 4 1.5 hour sessions | Parent observation and perception of child behavior<br><br>Parental attitudes<br><br>Child perception of parent behavior<br><br>Parent and child perceptions of family environment |

**Table 10.8.**  Parenting Skills Taught to Parents of Adolescents

| PARENT BEHAVIORS TAUGHT |
| --- |

Providing structure through contingent consequences (e.g., praise and reinforcement for appropriate behavior, removal of privilege for inappropriate behavior)

Communication: futility of blaming, value of praise over criticism, management of angry or intense feelings through active listening, empathic responding (verbal and nonverbal), I-messages

Setting limits: presenting limited options rather than negotiation, environmental control, advance planning, and alternative seeking

Clarifying values: modeling positive attitudes and behaviors, modeling responsible use of substances

Use of appropriate request-making procedures and appropriate expression of annoyance

Regular discussion of positive events

Structured problem solving and behavioral contracting

---

social behavior) are more common. The scarcity of programs for parents of ''normal'' teens is disconcerting given the expressed desire for such programs from parents themselves (Cohen & Irwin, 1983; Hall & Rose, 1987).

One possible explanation for the scarcity of parent training programs for parents of adolescents is that trainers are simply unaware of parental desires for information concerning guidance with teenagers as well as younger children. Cohen and Irwin (1983) apparently have favored this explanation, as they assert that only in the past few years (i.e., the 1980s) have health professionals become aware of parents' needs for information and guidance with their adolescents. In response to parental distress involving this developmental period, which they characterize as ''a complex process involving the interaction and synthesis of many factors, including those of a physical, psychological, social, and familial nature,'' Cohen and Irwin (1983, p. 196) developed a parent education program called Parent-Time. The goal of this program, which was not empirically evaluated, was to increase parental knowledge of adolescent development while decreasing parental anxiety. It was directed toward parents who were troubled by changes they saw in their children but did not need major psychological or psychiatric intervention. The program presented information on adolescent development; and taught general communication techniques with adolescents, including the futility of blaming, the value of praise over criticism, and the management of angry or intense feelings through the use of attentive listening. Parents were also taught ways to set limits and clarify values and were made aware of the dangers and problems of the adolescent's environment. Parents indicated that the follow-ing were most helpful: the definition of what is normal, the knowledge that adolescence is a process similar to other known developmental stages, increased feelings of self-confidence, understanding of the need to listen and set limits, and the ability to share concerns with other parents.

Another program for parents of adolescents focused on the prevention of some of the potential dangers and problems facing adolescents, specifically drug abuse (Klein & Swisher, 1983). Over the past decade, with the increasing drug abuse problem, statewide campaigns to teach parenting skills for the purpose of preventing drug abuse in teens have been conducted. An example of this type of program is the Communication and Parenting Skills (CAPS) substance abuse education program in Pennsylvania. Klein and Swisher (1983) evaluated this program, which focused on parental modeling of positive attitudes and behaviors and the establishment of effective family communication patterns. Topics for the nine-session program were: importance of family relationships, listening skills, empathic responding (verbal and nonverbal), I-messages, structuring (environmental control, advance planning, and alternative seeking), positive guidance (through logical consequences, rule setting, and encouragement), substance abuse applications (modeling responsible use of substances), and parental values about substance abuse. Using measures that included a rating of subjective parental responses, a measure of the parent's acceptance of the child as an individual, and a measure of the social climate within the family, Klein and Swisher (1983) found that treated parents used significantly less destructive responses (e.g., evaluative or moralizing remarks) after treatment than did control parents.

Another parent training package used with parents of teens taught several of these skills with the purpose of decreasing parent–adolescent conflict. Hall and Rose (1987) evaluated a cognitive-behavioral training package that included teaching parents the following skills: active listening, pinpointing the problem (behavioral specificity), structured problem solving, assertive feedback (praise and criticism), management of stress and anger, and modification of irrational beliefs. As measured by observed interaction and parent evaluation of the adolescent's behavior, the results indicated that the frequencies of positive behaviors increased for treated parents and the frequencies of negative behaviors decreased for both treated parents and adolescents. Despite positive results, these researchers proposed enhancing treatment effectiveness by including the adolescent directly in the training.

Raue and Spence (1985) did just that. The focus of their training was on reducing dysfunctional communication and increasing more appropriate interaction. Training included the development of reciprocal positive reinforcement through regular discussion of positive events and efforts to increase the level of noncontingent reinforcement. Communication skills such as giving of compliments and appreciations, making requests appropriately, and expressing annoyance appropriately were also trained. Finally, families were trained in the use of behavioral contracts and positive practice procedures for dealing with repeated misbehavior. The researchers evaluated the training with measures of observational data collected by parents, parent attitudes, parent ratings of child behavior, child perception of parent behavior, and a measure of the quality of relationships within the family. Results indicated that parents rated their children's behavior as better after treatment, children rated their parents' behavior as better, and quality of family relationships was higher. There were no changes in parental attitudes.

The final study involving parents of adolescents was conducted by Bredehoft and Hey (1985) and evaluated the program based on *Self-Esteem: A Family Affair* (Clarke, 1978). This program followed a democratic model similar to the PET and Adlerian approaches discussed previously. No specific listing of skills was provided, but the goals of the program were to teach and strengthen the following areas: self-esteem, family togetherness and flexibility, and conflict resolution. Bredehoft and Hey (1985) assessed outcome with a measure of family cohesion and adaptability, a parent–adolescent conflict rating,

and a self-concept scale. They found that treated fathers demonstrated a significant increase in adaptability, treated families averaged more family empathy, but treated families did not differ from controls in actual parent–adolescent conflict. Nevertheless, both treated mothers and treated adolescents perceived a lower amount of conflict and dissonance. The authors concluded that the program was successful.

*Summary*

Parenting skills training with adolescents has not been used as often as skills training for parents of younger children. Training programs for parents of adolescents taught a combination of skills taken from the three basic programs described earlier. For parents of adolescents, there was a greater emphasis on communication skills and problem solving, and behavioral contracting was introduced. More emphasis was placed on both parents participating in training for parents of adolescents, and at this age programs also have included the adolescent in the program. Again, as with other age groups, there was a prevention focus in some of these skills-training programs, but the prevention addressed children at risk for problems occurring outside the family environment. Three of the four studies evaluating these programs had relatively small sample sizes, so conclusions regarding efficacy are premature.

## Summary and Comparison of the Content of Parent Training

Examination of the parenting literature according to the age of the child demonstrated some interesting patterns and comparisons. As compared to other age groups, in infancy it has been considered more important to focus on providing the parent with developmental information and promoting the parent–child relationship. This emphasis was carried over into preschool interventions but began to be balanced with an emphasis on providing parents with behavior management skills. In infant programs, the teaching of behavior management skills was rare. Interventions with parents of older children often were based on behavior therapy, and therefore more time has been spent teaching parents to manage behavior. Some emphasis on the parent–child relationship with children in middle childhood was evidenced by the inclusion of such topics as communication skills training, and programs based on PET or Adlerian principles that tend to focus more on the interaction between parent and child. These programs have received the least amount of outcome research. For parents of adolescents, the relationship between parent and child has been emphasized more than in the school-aged years, with more importance placed on communication and problem-solving skills.

Interestingly, the widest range of skills seemed to be taught during the preschool years, especially through the early intervention and prevention programs. In infancy, the range of skills has been limited primarily to the teaching of maternal responsiveness and sensitivity. Parents of children in the middle years have been taught skills directly linked to the three programs of behavioral training, PET, and Adlerian principles, with the greatest emphasis on child management. Thus, in the preschool years, there has been more variety in what has been taught and more variety in the format of training. Further, infant and adolescent interventions were similar in that more developmental information has been provided during these periods than in early childhood or middle childhood. Even so, developmental information has not been presented nearly as often as the desires of parents would dictate (Anderson & Nuttall, 1987).

A point of continuity across age groups was a focus on training mothers. In infancy, only one study was found that trained fathers. All others focused on the mother–child relationship. In the preschool years, the majority opened training to mothers only; and although in middle childhood training was open to fathers, primarily the mother was the attending parent. The continuity breaks in adolescence, where some investigators required fathers to participate. This focus on mothers has implications for training focusing on the parent–child relationship because an exclusion of fathers ignores a significant relationship in the child's life.

Finally, there also were differences across the age groups concerning how the programs were evaluated. For interventions with parents of infants, the most common outcome measure by far was changes in the mother's behavior and/or knowledge. No other age group had such a strong bias toward this form of outcome evaluation. This could be due in part to the fact that infancy interventions rarely focused on managing the behavior of the child and therefore did not measure outcome by changes in the child's behavior. This is supported by examining the one study that did train mothers to manage the behavior of their children (Mathews et al., 1987) because their evaluation emphasized changes in the child's behavior. Beginning

in the preschool years, more emphasis was placed on observation of interactions and parent perceptions of children's behavior. Only in the preschool age range was there a study that evaluated the program in terms of the child's social competency (Mischley et al., 1985). Despite the fact that in the preschool and middle childhood periods there was an emphasis on measures of observed interaction between parent and child, more often than not, the discussion of the results focused on the observed changes in the child's behavior. Beginning in middle childhood, measures of parent attitudes and child self-esteem were used more often. This was most likely an outgrowth of PET and Adlerian approaches that have as their goals changes in these areas. Further, only in adolescence was there a study that included a measure of the child's rating of the parent's behaviors, which is an interesting, albeit indirect, way to measure changes in parents' behavior. Finally, it is interesting to note that no studies located for this review attempted to measure the overall style of parenting along such dimensions as authoritative, authoritarian, and permissive.

## SOCIAL DEVELOPMENT OF THE CHILD

A key problem noted in this parent training literature is the lack of the incorporation of findings from the child and family development literature (Robertson, 1984). Parent trainers, in their focus on treating problem behaviors and at-risk populations, have often lost sight of the ultimate goal of parenting: successful socialization of the child. Parenting, of necessity, assumes a knowledge of child development and how parent behaviors influence such development. Some researchers have speculated that this information is neglected because of inconsistencies in findings regarding the effects of parental behaviors on child behavior (Griffore, 1980). Kagan (1984) has noted that the omission of parental behavior as an influence on the child's experience is due to the fact that most experiences are not fixed but depend on the child's interpretation. Extensive research has indicated that within the parent–child relationship, reciprocal processes are constantly at work (Bell & Harper, 1977). This bidirectionality in the parent–child relationship has made it difficult to isolate parental effects on child behavior. Although developmental psychologists have not arrived at ''the'' prescription for raising ''good'' children, and tremendous diversity exists in the knowledge that is available, ignoring what information does exist is not reasonable (Robertson, 1984). Furthermore, parent training interventions can be an excellent method for studying the socialization process—that is, how changing parent behavior affects child development and what aspects of development are most amenable to change (Clarke-Stewart, 1988). Thus, parenting studies can bring researchers one step closer to a theoretical model of what effective parenting entails.

In attempts to evaluate the influence of the family on the child, psychologists have selected a few child qualities from the large array of potential characteristics that are related to adaptation in U.S. society: intellectual skills, a secure attachment to parents; sociability with peers; reasonable conformity to authority; and autonomy in making decisions (Kagan, 1984). The two most widely studied developmental dimensions in the socialization process are attachment and the self-regulation of behavior, which takes into account both conformity to authority and autonomy in making decisions. These two dimensions also represent developmental processes that epitomize the paradox on which social development is built: that at the same time we are both social and individual beings (Damon, 1983).

Before examining these dimensions and their potential benefit to the field of parent training in more detail, an understanding of social development and its paradoxical goals is necessary. Social development comprises two complementary functions: socialization and individuation (Damon, 1983). Damon has described socialization as the *integrating* function of social development and individuation as the *differentiating* function of social development. Although these functions may appear contradictory, in actuality they work together to contribute to a person's successful social adaptation, what we have called previously "normal, healthy social development." Socialization includes "all of one's tendencies to establish and maintain relations with others, to become an accepted member of society-at-large, to regulate one's behavior according to society's codes and standards, and generally to get along well with other people" (p. 2). On the other hand, individuation includes "the development of one's sense of self and the forging of a special place for oneself within the social order" (p. 2). Thus, though not contradictory, these functions create a tension in the development of the child, and this tension is represented in both attachment and self-control. In attachment, the tension involves the child's desire to be in close proximity with the parent as well as the child's realization that comes with motoric independence that he or she

also desires to be away from the parent. Self-control brings tension as children begin to learn the rules of society that restrict behavior but also realize they are capable of other behaviors.

Hartup (1989) has described the parent's role in the socialization process as a vertical relationship, an attachment to an individual who has greater knowledge and social power than the child, within which children are provided with a safe, secure environment for the time needed until they can "make it on their own." Within this vertical relationship with parents, children learn basic social skills, and the relationship follows a specific pattern of behavior regulation. This pattern begins with the regulation of children's behavior solely by the parent, moves to co-regulation in which the parent begins to understand that children are capable of regulating some of their own behaviors, and finally ends in children's total self-regulation. This process continually changes in its balance in the social development of the child. In other words, in a particular developmental stage, parents may totally regulate some behaviors, co-regulate others, and let the child self-regulate yet other behaviors. The balance of this regulation will change, although all three types of regulation can be occurring in any one stage. Nevertheless, the ultimate goal is for the child to learn total self-regulation of behavior, at which time the successful balance of socialization and individuation will have been achieved. Stated simply, parents are educators of their children in that they teach their children the skills needed to operate successfully in society as well as how to inhibit those behaviors that are deemed inappropriate by society (Maccoby & Martin, 1983). Thus, parents try to teach their children how to function autonomously in a social world.

Grusec and Lytton (1988) have summarized the tasks and goals of human socialization as: "provision of nurturance and protection; induction into the values and demands of society, including the internalization of moral norms; acquiring a concept of the self in broadening social experiences; increasing autonomy" (p. 162). Developmentalists believe that parents are aware of these goals. Baumrind (Lamb & Baumrind, 1978) believes parents want to produce instrumentally competent children who show a combination of social responsibility and independence. Kagan (1984) has stated that most U.S. parents "try to balance a promotion of the child's autonomy and separateness from others with encouragement of a desire to be with, rather than apart from, people and a commitment to aiding the welfare of others" (p.

248). A problem occurs when professionals involved in parent training interventions lose sight of these goals and fail to address them in their interventions.

## Attachment

*Attachment* has been defined as the child's tie to a caregiver and has a long history in developmental psychology. What is known about attachment fills books (Ainsworth, Blehar, Waters, & Wall, 1978; Bowlby, 1971; Bowlby, 1973). Attachment has been studied by examining the kinds of behavior associated with the relationship between baby and caregiver (Hall, Lamb, & Perlmutter, 1986). Bowlby (1971) segmented the attachment process into four stages. During the first, which lasts until the infant is approximately 2 months old, babies have no social preferences. From 2 to 7 months, infants prefer familiar people but do not protest when either parent leaves, and the child can be comforted by others. Around 7 to 12 months, the infant begins to show a preference for one or two persons, and separation causes distress. The final stage occurs around 30 months of age. The child begins to understand the caregiver's feelings and motives, and a partnership develops in which parent and child can work toward shared goals. The attachment remains strong, but distress at separation greatly decreases. Bowlby (1971) further specified two kinds of mediating behavior for attachment in humans. These are signaling behavior, which brings the mother to the infant (e.g., crying, smiling, babbling, and calling) and approach behavior, which takes the infant to the mother (e.g., following, clinging, and sucking).

Ainsworth (1973) focused her research on individual differences in the quality of the attachment relationship that develops between the infant and the caregiver. Through her "strange situation" laboratory paradigm (Ainsworth, Blehar, Waters, & Wall, 1978), she identified three different types of attachment: avoidant, secure, and ambivalent (or resistant). Children in the secure category were distressed by their mother's absence and sought her proximity when she returned. Children in the avoidant category avoided rather than sought the mother's proximity upon her return, and children in the ambivalent category both sought her proximity and, at the same time, resisted contact with the mother when it was offered.

Ainsworth noted a connection between a mother's style of caring for her baby and the baby's attachment, claiming that a secure attachment resulted when mothers were responsive and sensitive to their baby's cries, smiles, and other signals. Mothers of securely attached infants have been found to be more affectionate, more effective in soothing, and in general less intrusive and more sensitive to their baby's needs than mothers of babies in the other categories (Ainsworth et al., 1978). The quality of the child's attachment represents the child's adaptation to the developmental tasks of infancy, and evidence abounds that good adaptation in infancy predicts good adaptation to other developmental tasks that lie ahead (Arend, Gove, & Sroufe, 1979; Londerville & Main, 1981; Pastor, 1981).

This relationship between attachment security and maternal sensitivity has been supported by research of the following maternal behaviors: prompt responsiveness to distress (Crockenberg, 1981); moderate, appropriate stimulation and responsiveness observed at home (Belsky, Rovine, & Taylor, 1984); warmth, involvement, and responsiveness on the Home Observation for Measurement of the Environment Scales (Bates, Maslin, & Frankel, 1985); ratings of observed warmth, responsiveness, and happiness (Gaensbauer et al., 1985); and sensitivity and acceptance inferred from interviews (Benn, 1986). All these behaviors seem to reflect an underlying dimension of maternal sensitivity (Clarke-Stewart, 1988).

Secure attachment in infancy is generally considered to predict later positive social relations, competence, and self-confidence (Arend et al., 1979; Londerville & Main, 1981; Pastor, 1981). Nevertheless, attachment is not only important in infancy. Hartup (1989) has described attachment as a key foundation for social development throughout childhood and well into adolescence. He contends that attachment sets the stage for subsequent self-regulation and control because it fosters security and trust. This enables parents to begin teaching children how to regulate and control their own behavior.

## Self-Regulation and Self-Control

There appear to be two processes involved in the development of self-control and self-regulation (Grusec & Lytton, 1988). First, the child must internalize a value that emphasizes the importance of self-control. Activities that must be valued include: delay of gratification, impulse control, resistance to temptation, high standards of achievement, and nonaggressive reactions to frustration. Second, the child must acquire skills that allow him or her to adhere to these internalized values of appropriate behavior.

When addressing the internalization of values, researchers typically turn to the parent–child relationship, specifically the parenting style. Reward, punishment, modeling, the use of inductive reasoning, and a warm, nurturing relationship with the parent are all considered important for promoting the appropriate acceptance of societal standards for self-control. Physical punishment is typically linked to hostility and low impulse control (Lytton, 1980; Powers & Shapieski, 1986). The use of psychological rewards —approval and praise—tends to promote social responsibility and internalization of standards (Baumrind, 1973; Lytton, 1980). Inductive reasoning, defined as the use of explanations, appears valuable for raising autonomous children who have internalized moral standards independent of external control (Feshbach, 1974). Finally, a nurturing relationship characterized by expressions of caring, support, and feelings of love and acceptance (both contingent and noncontingent on the child's behavior) is related to good social adjustment (Daniels, Dunn, Furstenberg, & Plomin, 1985).

All of these behaviors that encourage internalization of societal standards and foster healthy social adjustment characterize the authoritative parenting style as researched and described by Baumrind (1971, 1973) and Maccoby and Martin (1983). Three parenting styles have emerged from the work of these researchers: authoritarian, permissive, and authoritative. Authoritarian parents primarily value obedience and restrict the child's autonomy in their efforts to achieve strict obedience. These parents do not encourage verbal give and take. Permissive parents are typically passively accepting of any behavior that does not threaten the child's physical survival. There is an absence of restraint. Authoritative parents set standards for conduct and expect compliance with reasonable rules. Yet, these parents also respect the child's autonomy and individuality. This authoritative parenting style is most commonly associated with positive outcomes in children, including greater social responsibility and independence, the ability to control aggression, greater self-confidence, and high self-esteem (Baumrind, 1971, 1973).

The second process involved in self-regulation is the acquisition of skills. When discussing the skills involved in self-control, a brief introduction to some of the developmental antecedents of self-regulation is helpful. Kopp (1982) has described a series of phases through which the young child passes, each involving a qualitative change in functioning, which provide the foundation for self-regulation. In the first phase,

neurophysiological modulation, the emphasis is simply on maturation, and the infant is protected from stimulation that is too strong by various physiological mechanisms. During the second phase, sensorimotor modulation, infants can engage in voluntary motor behavior and can adapt their behavior to changes in the environment, thus enabling them to differentiate their own actions from those of others.

The third phase, external control, begins around the first year of life, when the child is able to comply with commands from the caregiver. Behavior can be goal-directed, and children become increasingly aware that they are different from the rest of the world. The phase of self-control brings compliance, delaying a task on request, and displaying appropriate behavior in the absence of external monitoring. These abilities are possible because children of this age have developed representational thought and now have a good understanding of their identity. Thus, these children, if motivated, can engage in self-control. According to Kopp (1982), self-regulation differs from self-control only in degree. Self-regulation involves greater flexibility in adapting to changes.

As for the skills necessary to control one's behavior, researchers have focused most in the areas of verbal self-regulation and the employment of effective attentional strategies, specifically in the areas of helping children resist temptation and to delay gratification. Research in the area of verbal regulation has focused on such paradigms as teaching children to use self-instructions in an effort to reduce impulsive behavior. In an early study by Meichenbaum and Goodman (1971), the most effective training included a progression of instruction from adult instruction to overt self-instruction, and finally to covert self-instruction.

Hence, research has demonstrated that the skill of self-instruction helps children learn self-control. However, the form of the training in self-instruction changes as the child grows older (Carter, Patterson, & Quasebarth, 1979; Hartig & Kanfer, 1973; Toner & Smith, 1977; Miller, Weinstein, & Karniol, 1978). Preschoolers are better able to resist temptation and to delay gratification if they talk to themselves and if the content of the talk is irrelevant or focuses directly on the tempting objects. In other words, saying "I must not turn and look at the toy" and counting are equally effective. Speaking directly about the appealing characteristics of the tempting object is not helpful in encouraging self-control. For older children, focusing on the appealing characteristics of an object is also detrimental to self-control. For these children, however, overt verbalizations are not heard as often as for younger children, perhaps because older children use self-instruction covertly. If verbalizations are used with older children, they must be relevant to the temptation situation. These may be useful because they serve to focus attention on completing the task at hand. This leads to the next area of research on attention.

Mischel and his colleagues have done extensive research on attentional processes and self control. We know that what children say to themselves is important, but what about the focus of their attention? Does this make delay of gratification more tolerable? Mischel's studies (Mischel & Ebbesen, 1970; Mischel, Ebbesen, & Zeiss, 1972; Mischel & Moore, 1973) typically involved asking children to choose one of two possible rewards. The children were then told that the reward they had not selected was the one they could have right away, but they would have to wait to receive their chosen reward. They were told that the experimenter had to leave the room, and when the experimenter came back, they could have the chosen reward. If they changed their minds about the reward they wanted, they could summon the experimenter, who would then immediately give them the reward they had not chosen. Three important facts were discovered from these studies. First, being left alone with the reward in the room produced less self-control than if the rewards were not present. Similarly, the ability to delay gratification was greater when children only saw pictures of rewards than when they saw the actual rewards. Finally, being told to think about "fun things" promoted self-control more than thinking about the rewards. Thus, distraction from thinking about the reward was an important variable in delaying gratification.

Mischel reasoned that rewards have informational and motivational properties. The former help the child remember the pleasant things that can result from waiting; the latter serve only to frustrate the child and make delay more difficult to endure. Thus, knowledge of the reward not in the room and the picture of a reward provide information, whereas the actual reward itself, especially if left in the room, has a motivational impact. Overall, how one pays attention is important. One should focus on qualities of a reward that are less arousing rather than on exciting qualities.

There are developmental issues involved in attentional processes. The development of several cognitive processes may be necessary for children to divert their attention successfully from a reward, distract themselves, remember what they are doing, and imagine the outcome (Grusec & Mills, 1982). Representational thought is necessary. As in verbal self-regulation, it appears that younger children have more difficulty automatically engaging in attentional strategies that would help them delay gratification. Children under 7 years of age seemed to prefer looking at the actual reward, a counterproductive choice (Yates & Mischel, 1979). Furthermore, when offered the chance to view an irrelevant item instead, these children still chose to view the reward.

One final consideration in the development of self-control is the role of expectation. Efforts at self-control can result in either success or failure, and how children react to this affects their expectations about future attempts at self control. This, then, has an effect on the child's motivation to try to control his or her own behavior in the future. Therefore, feelings of efficacy are important in the domain of self-control (Grusec & Mills, 1982). Parents' role in teaching the skills of self-control, therefore, should include not only a knowledge of the skills involved and attempts to help the child acquire such skills, but also efforts to encourage the child so that motivation will be maintained.

## REFLECTION OF DEVELOPMENTAL ISSUES IN PARENTING LITERATURE

We can now address the question: To what extent does the parenting literature show that parent trainers incorporate the aforementioned knowledge about healthy social development of children? In the following sections, we examine the literature along the developmental dimensions described. Ideally, if parent training interventions adequately incorporate developmental information, the skills being taught to parents should reflect both a consideration of the dimension and the impact of the parent on the development of that dimension.

### Attachment

To the credit of parent training interventions, information on the child's development of attachment does appear to have had an impact on the skills taught to parents of infants. Maternal behaviors of responsiveness and sensitivity, behaviors Ainsworth (1973) found were important for secure attachments, were the most common parenting behaviors taught to new mothers. The studies reviewed had a common theme in their introductions: that the teaching of these behaviors was important for the child's subsequent development. Lambermon and van Ijzendoorn (1989) specifically addressed their attempt to base their intervention on attachment theory stating the importance of tying caregiving information to infant development information. Many cited research about the association between these maternal behaviors and optimal social development (e.g., Anderson & Sawin, 1983; Feldman, Case, Rincover, Towns, & Betel, 1989; Pfannenstiel & Seltzer, 1989; Whitt & Casey, 1982).

Skills taught to parents of infants closely matched those supported by research on fostering a secure attachment in the infant. For example, parenting interventions taught mothers to observe their infants accurately and respond to the baby's cues (e.g., Baskin et al., 1987). Parent trainers responded to Ainsworth's findings by teaching parents to increase physical affection (e.g., Feldman et al., 1989), to respond appropriately to crying (e.g., Whitt & Casey, 1982), and to respond to child-initiated behaviors rather than having the parent direct all activity (e.g., Baskin et al., 1987).

In addition, the majority of these interventions were designed for prevention of child abuse and neglect or to prevent developmental delays in at-risk children, but a considerable number also used ordinary mothers and their normal infants (e.g., Anderson & Sawin, 1983; Belsky, 1985; Lambermon & van Ijzendoorn, 1989; Pfannenstiel & Seltzer, 1989; Riesch & Munns, 1984; Whitt & Casey, 1982). Thus, with parents of infants, there was a realization that interventions can be beneficial for nonreferred populations as well as for problem populations.

Parent training interventions in the older age groups made no mention of attachment or of behaviors such as responsiveness and sensitivity. This is actually in keeping with developmental research because little or no research with older children exists in that area on attachment per se. However, developmental psychologists have emphasized that attachment to one's caregivers still exists for older children even though the behavioral expression of the relationship changes (Hartup, 1989). This suggests that there should be a parallel continuity in the quality of parental practices necessary for the development of attachment in order to maintain that attachment. Hence, such parental behaviors as responsiveness and sensitivity should not stop just because the child is no longer a baby, nor does the research suggest that if these behaviors were not practiced during infancy,

exhibiting them later in the child's life will have no effect on development. Nevertheless, the same terminology was not used when considering older children.

Some of the parent behaviors described by Baumrind (1967, 1971) in her typology of parenting styles reflect what one could assume are skills that maintain attachment to the caregiver. Specifically, in her description of the authoritative style, Baumrind (1971) has explained that these parents nurture their children in that they display warmth and an active involvement in their child's activities. Grusec and Lytton (1988) consider terms such as *acceptance, nurturance,* and *responsiveness* to be synonyms for what is basically the same construct. Research suggests that responsiveness, which influences attachment, is positively related to infant social development (e.g., Arend et al., 1979), and that parental warmth is related to good social adjustment (Daniels et al., 1985). So, if we assume that *responsiveness* and *warmth* are terms describing the same construct, we can assume that attempts to increase a parent's warmth or nurturance by generally improving the parent–child relationship could be indicative of attempts to maintain or establish a healthy attachment response in older children.

Although this is based on deduction rather than empirical evidence, it allows us to assume that parent trainers are not totally unaware of the value of the quality of the parent–child relationship. Regardless, there is a difference between being aware and including the information in an intervention. Unfortunately, few parent training interventions designed for parents of children older than 3 to 5 years of age specifically addressed the quality of the parent–child relationship. Interventions for parents of preschool children tended to include a component with the goal of improving the parent–child relationship more often than did interventions for parents of school-aged children or adolescents. Such components typically centered around play and encouraged the parent to play with the child in appropriate ways for this specific age group (Esdaile & Sanderson, 1987; Mischley et al., 1985; Strayhorn & Weidman, 1989) and to plan activities that can prevent coercive parent–child interchanges (Green, Hardison, & Greene, 1984; Sanders & Christensen, 1985; Sanders & Dadds, 1982). Consequently, parents of preschoolers have approximately an equal opportunity of receiving parent training that addresses the quality of the parent–child relationship as they have of receiving interventions that do not. If the child is at risk for some developmental delay or potential behavior problem, the odds increase in favor of receiving interaction training.

For parents of school-aged children and adolescents, the opportunities sharply decrease. At these ages, the focus is more often on fixing problems that have already developed. Thus skills taught are more likely to center around behavior management. Some specific package treatments do place more emphasis on parent–child relations through the teaching of various communication skills such as Gordon's (1975) Parent Effectiveness Training. Such communication training is most likely related to the quality of attachment between older children and their parents. However, evaluations of this particular program rarely appeared in the published literature (Dembo, Sweitzer, & Lauritzen, 1985); therefore, some may question the evidence for its effectiveness. Further, a study was done comparing communication skills training to behavioral training (Kanigsberg & Levant, 1988), but the discussion seemed to focus on how changes in the child's behavior were achieved more often by the behavioral group rather than on the effects of the communication training. Further, this study did not attempt to compare a combined behavioral and communications group. Such a group might better address the broader goal of social development and enhancing self-regulation in the child, rather than the limited goal of behavior programs to improve immediate behavior.

## Self-Regulation and Self-Control

Parenting interventions, across the age groups, seemed to address the first process in the development of self-control and self-regulation, that of the internalization of values. The interventions did not directly educate the parents about this process, but, through the training of behavioral techniques and communication skills, they may have instilled a parenting style that closely approximates that of the authoritative parent. The use of contingent consequences, mild punishment, active involvement with the child, acceptance of the child's feelings, and providing explanations for rules are all behaviors that are associated with authoritative parenting. Again, it should be pointed out that the behaviors that enhance the parent–child relationship often were excluded from strict behavioral parent training.

As for the child's acquisition of skills necessary for self-regulation and self-control, parenting interven-

tions fall short. No parent training program included training parents in how to help their child acquire the skills for self-regulation. It is possible that we excluded any such programs when excluding programs that focused on training parents to teach their children academic skills. Therefore, we attempted to examine a sample of these studies in order to determine if parents were being taught anything resembling the cognitive strategy training children need for self-control. This search revealed that the category of parent training in which parents are taught to teach their children some skill is reserved primarily for parents of children with problems such as learning disabilities, mental retardation, and developmental delays. These studies did indeed include some attempts to train parents in how to teach their children cognitive strategies to enhance problem solving in behavioral and social situations (i.e., Orlando & Bartel, 1989). Yet, such skills are not being taught to parents of "normal" children or children with minor behavioral problems. Nevertheless, these children need to acquire these skills also. A good way to help parents with such topics would simply be to provide them with developmental information in order to help clarify their expectations for the child and to help them know when their child could be expected to have varying degrees of self-control.

## LIMITATIONS OF PARENT TRAINING APPROACHES

### Developmental Void

Parenting is one of the most important roles in society, and yet it is the role for which most people are the least well prepared. This is especially true with the increased stresses modern families face, including breakdowns in cultural traditions, the changing status of women in society, increased mobility, and lack of extended family support. Whereas in the past it may have been adequate for parent training approaches to focus narrowly on the treatment of specific problems, the current practice of parent training needs to provide more. There needs to be a shift in the focus to a broader treatment of the parent–child relationship and the complexities therein. One way to begin addressing this shift is to provide parents with what they need and desire: general information on child development and the application of this information to their skills as parents (Anderson & Nuttall,

1987; Lutzker, McGimsey, McRae, & Campbell, 1983; Robertson, 1984).

The research reviewed here reflects the most recent approaches to parent training, and there is a definite void in the provision and utilization of developmental information. Training approaches focusing on mothers and infants have realized the importance of providing parents with information regarding their infant's development, and some approaches with parents of adolescents have begun to find that these parents need information on adolescent development. Otherwise, only rarely is developmental information provided to parents. Even what is presented in some approaches now is lacking because it fails to provide pertinent information beyond the age of the child at the time of intervention.

Researchers are beginning to see the need for such information. Turley (1985) asserted that mothers do not innately have sufficient knowledge about their infants to understand them and build a relationship with them. She goes on to note that research is beginning to show that new parents need information, and society is attempting to remedy this. However, research is not following up on this by evaluating attempts to provide parents with this information. In the area of preventing child abuse and neglect, the need also is emphasized. Schmitt (1987) has stressed the fact that difficult developmental phases can be overly stressful for parents if they are not prepared for them by way of both having adequate information and having the skills to deal with normal changes. Indeed, Anderson and Nuttall (1987) found that parents of children of different ages have different concerns and questions. For example, parents of infants want to know about transitional tasks such as weaning and toilet training, whereas parents of preschoolers express a need for help with toy selection and dealing with emotional responses.

Many prevention programs have been incorporating developmental information. An increasing awareness that there are no systematic ways for people in our culture to learn how to become good parents may be the reason for the incorporation of this information (Nudd, 1989; Rowland, 1989). If parents have unrealistic expectations of their child's abilities and thus make unreasonable demands on the child, the results could range from acting-out behaviors on the part of the child and frustration on the part of the parents to child abuse and a pattern of aversive interaction (Showers, 1989; Swetnam, Peterson, & Clark, 1983). Yet, parent training programs rarely assess the parents' knowledge of child development. Thus, professionals could be teaching parents how to get compliance from a child who is not able to comply with the parents' demands.

Finally, there is the question of the goal of parent training: Should it be to teach parents a general set of skills for gaining child compliance, or should it be to teach parents through a broad range of skills and information how to foster a socially independent, healthy adult? If we choose the broader goal, an incorporation of developmental information is imperative. Parents are the child's only continuous source of guidance, and as such they need a broad understanding of child development that encompasses the period from birth through adolescence (Strom, 1985). The ideal broad-based program would include behavior management skills to remedy existing and potential behavior problems, developmental information to guide expectations, and communication skills and specific interaction training to enhance the parent–child relationship (Swetnam et al., 1983).

## Emphasis on Problem Populations

Another limitation in present parenting interventions is the lack of attention given to parents with ''normal'' children. Only in infancy were the importance and benefits of training *all* mothers emphasized. The need to train parents of normal children is based in part on the same arguments used for the inclusion of developmental information. Specifically, being a parent is one of the most important and difficult roles any person can attempt to fulfill; yet most people rely only on the techniques their own parents used, which may or may not have been adequate. Choosing to intervene in parenting only after a serious dysfunctional behavior has developed ignores the greater need of parents to raise a socially responsible child from birth. Surely it would be easier to foster a good parent–child relationship, in which serious problems might not occur.

In the past, a common assumption has been that ''normal'' parents of ''normal'' children would not benefit from parent education, but at least one recent study casts doubt on this. Harris and Larsen (1989) evaluated a mandatory parent education class based out of a university preschool program. The sample of parents were middle class and educationally advantaged. There was a high percentage of intact families, nonworking mothers, and a religious orientation toward high-quality family life. Nevertheless, these parents significantly increased their one-on-one activities with the child and had more positive interactions. That such a unique group of parents could benefit from parent training underscores the potential for training all parents. Further, middle-class parents often exert undue pressure on their children to achieve in skill areas for which they may not be ready (Elkind, 1986). Thus, providing a basic understanding of child development and developmentally appropriate practices for these parents could moderate inappropriate pressures placed on the child.

## Focus on Children's Behavior over Parents' Behavior

Finally, despite outcome evaluations based on observations of parent–child interaction, there is still an overwhelming emphasis on change in the child's behavior. Typically, only in studies that specifically incorporated parent–child interaction training was there adequate evaluation of changes in parents' behavior (Strayhorn & Weidman, 1989). Further, it is rare to find researchers who directly examine the relationship between changes in the child's behavior and changes in the parent's behavior. Also rare is an evaluation of whether the child perceives a change in the parent's behavior. Generally, it is assumed that if the child's behavior changed, then the parent's behavior must have changed as well. Thus, many studies lack an investigation of treatment integrity— that is, whether the parent learned the skills as evidenced by use.

In conclusion, it is time to reexamine what is being offered as parent training. Attempts are needed to broaden these successful interventions to foster not just immediate change in a child's behavior but optimal social development for the child. Robertson (1984) has called for a comprehensive theoretical model of parent education that incorporates research on life span and family development. Perhaps we do not know at present what such a model would comprise. Nevertheless, parent training interventions provide an excellent research paradigm to explore such a model (Clarke-Stewart, 1988). Clarke-Stewart (1988) has emphasized the need for training programs for normal parents and children in order to assess how effective such programs are in changing parents' behavior and children's development. There is a need to know which aspects of a child's development are most amenable to influence and what in the training leads to changes in parents' behavior. Further, researchers are beginning to show that parents' social-

ization strategies are linked to their knowledge, beliefs, and attributions about child development (Sigel, 1985). Thus, what is needed in programs is the provision of information to increase the parents' knowledge and beliefs about general child development (Clarke-Stewart, 1988), in addition to behavior management skills, communication skills, and parent–child interaction training.

## REFERENCES

Adler, A. (1927). *Understanding human nature.* New York: Greenberg.

Adler, A. (1930). *The education of children.* New York: Greenberg.

Affholter, D. P., Connell, D., & Nauta, M. J. (1983). Evaluation of the child and family resource program: Early evidence of parent–child interaction effects. *Evaluation Review, 7,* 65–79.

Ainsworth, M. D. S. (1973). The development of infant–mother attachment. In B. Caldwell & H. Ricciuti (Eds.), *Review of child development research* (Vol. 3, pp. 1–94). Chicago: University of Chicago Press.

Ainsworth, M. D. S., Blehar, M. C., Waters, E., & Wall, S. (1978). Patterns of attachment: A psychological study of the strange situation. Hillsdale, NJ: Lawrence Erlbaum.

Anderson, S. A., & Nuttall, P. E. (1987). Parent communication training across three stages of childrearing. *Family Relations, 36,* 40–44.

Anderson, C. J., & Sawin, D. B. (1983). Enhancing responsiveness in mother-infant interaction. *Infant Behavior and Development, 6,* 361–368.

Arend, R., Gove, F., & Sroufe, L. A. (1979). Continuity of individual adaptation from infancy to kindergarten: A predictive study of ego-resiliency and curiosity in preschoolers. *Child Development, 50,* 950–959.

Atkeson, B. M., & Forehand, R. (1978). Parent behavioral training for problem children: An examination of studies using multiple outcome measures. *Journal of Abnormal Child Psychology, 6,* 449–460.

Barrera, M. E., Rosenbaum, P. L., & Cunningham, C. E. (1986). Early home intervention with low-birth-weight infants and their parents. *Child Development, 57,* 20–33.

Baskin, C., Umansky, W., & Sanders, W. (1987). Influencing the responsiveness of adolescent mothers to their infants. *Zero to Three, 8,* 7–11.

Bates, J., Maslin, C., & Frankel, K. (1985). Attachment security, mother–child interaction, and temperament as predictors of behavior-problem ratings at three years. In I. Bretherton & E. Waters (Eds.), *Growing points of attachment theory and research* (pp. 167–193). *Monographs of the Society for Research in Child Development, 50* (1–2, Serial No. 209).

Baumrind, D. (1967). Child care practices antedating three patterns of preschool behavior. *Genetic Psychology Monographs, 75,* 43–88.

Baumrind, D. (1971). Current patterns of parental authority. *Developmental Psychology Monographs, 4* (1, Pt. 2).

Baumrind, D. (1973). The development of instrumental competence through socialization. In A. Pick (Ed.), *Minnesota Symposia on Child Psychology* (Vol. 7, pp. 3–46). Minneapolis: University of Minnesota Press.

Becker, W. C. (1971). *Parents are teachers.* Champaign, IL: Research Press.

Bell, R. O., & Harper, L. V. (1977). *Child effects on adults.* Hillsdale, NJ: Lawrence Erlbaum.

Belsky, J. (1985). Experimenting with the family in the newborn period. *Child Development, 56,* 407–414.

Belsky, J., Rovine, M., & Taylor, D. G. (1984). The Pennsylvania Infant and Family Development Project, III: The origins of individual differences in infant–mother attachment: Maternal and infant contributions. *Child Development, 55,* 718–728.

Benn, R. K. (1986). Factors promoting secure attachment relationships between employed mothers and their sons. *Child Development, 57,* 1224–1231.

Berkowitz, B. P., & Graziano, A. M. (1972). Training parents as behavior therapists: A review. *Behaviour Research and Therapy, 10,* 297–317.

Booth, C. L., Mitchell, S. K., Barnard, K. E., & Spieker, S. J. (1989). Development of maternal social skills in multiproblem families: Effects on the mother–child relationship. *Developmental Psychology, 25,* 403–412.

Bowlby, J. (1971). *Attachment and loss: Attachment* (Vol. 1). London: Pelican Books.

Bowlby, J. (1973). *Attachment and loss: Separation* (Vol. 2). London: Hogarth.

Bredehoft, D. J., & Hey, R. N. (1985). An evaluation study of *Self-Esteem: A Family Affair. Family Relations, 34,* 411–417.

Breiner, J., & Beck, S. (1984). Parents as change agents in the management of their developmentally delayed children's noncompliant behaviors: A critical review. *Applied Research in Mental Retardation, 5,* 259–278.

Carter, D. B., Patterson, C. J., & Quasebarth, S. J. (1979). Development of children's use of plans for self-control. *Cognitive Therapy and Research, 4,* 407–413.

Clark, L. (1985). *S.O.S! Help for Parents.* Bowling Green, KY: Parents Press.

Clarke, J. L. (1978). *Self-esteem: A family affair.* Minneapolis, MN: Winston Press.

Clarke-Stewart, K. A. (1988). Parents' effects on children's development: A decade of progress. *Journal of Applied Developmental Psychology, 9,* 41–84.

Cohen, S. J. (1982). Helping parents to become the "potent force" in combating and preventing the drug problem. *Journal of Drug Education, 12,* 341–345.

Cohen, M., & Irwin, C. E. (1983). Parent-time: Psychoeducational groups for parents of adolescents. *Health and Social Work, 8,* 196–202.

Coombs, R., Santana, F., & Fawzy, F. (1984). Parent training to prevent adolescent drug use: An educational model. *Journal of Drug Issues, 14,* 393–402.

Crockenberg, S. B. (1981). Infant irritability, mother responsiveness, and social support influences on the security of infant-mother attachment. *Child Development, 52,* 857–865.

Cunningham, C. (1985). Training and education approaches for parents of children with special needs. *British Journal of Medical Psychology, 58,* 285–305.

Dachman, R. S., Alessi, G. J., Vrazo, G. J., Fuqua, R. W., & Kerr, R. H. (1986). Development and evaluation of an infant-care training program with first-time fathers. *Journal of Applied Behavior Analysis, 19,* 221–230.

Dadds, M. R., Sanders, M. R., Behrens, B. C., & James, J. E. (1987). Marital discord and child behavior problems: A description of family interactions during treatment. *Journal of Clinical Child Psychology, 16,* 192–203.

Dadds, M. R., Schwartz, S., & Sanders, M. R. (1987). Marital discord and treatment outcome in behavioral treatment of child conduct disorders. *Journal of Consulting and Clinical Psychology, 55,* 396–403.

Damon, W. (1983). *Social and personality development. Infancy through adolescence.* New York: Norton.

Daniels, D., Dunn, J., Furstenberg, F. F., & Plomin, R. (1985). Environmental differences within the family and adjustment differences within pairs of adolescent siblings. *Child Development, 56,* 764–774.

Dembo, M. H., Sweitzer, M., & Lauritzen, P. (1985). An evaluation of group parent education: Behavioral, PET, and Adlerian programs. *Review of Educational Research, 55,* 155–200.

Dinkmeyer, D., & McKay, G. (1976). *Systematic training for effective parenting.* Circle Pines, MN: American Guidance Service.

Dreikurs, R., & Soltz, V. (1964). *Children: The challenge.* New York: Hawthorn.

Dumas, J. E. (1989). Treating antisocial behavior in children: Child and family approaches. *Clinical Psychology Review, 9,* 197–222.

Eisenberg, N., & Mussen, P. H. (1989). *The roots of prosocial behavior in children.* New York: Cambridge University Press.

Elkind, D. (1986). Formal education and early childhood education: An essential difference. *Phi Delta Kappan, 67,* 633–636.

Esdaile, S., & Sanderson, A. (1987). Teaching parents toy making: A practical guide to early intervention. *British Journal of Occupational Therapy, 50,* 266–271.

Feldman, M. A., Case, L., Rincover, A., Towns, F., & Betel, J. (1989). Parent education project III: Increasing affection and responsivity in developmentally handicapped mothers: Component analysis, generalization, and effects on child language. *Journal of Applied Behavior Analysis, 22,* 211–222.

Feshbach, N. D. (1974). The relationship of child-rearing factors to children's aggression, empathy and related positive and negative social behaviors. In J. DeWit & W. W. Hartup (Eds.), *Determinants and origins of aggressive behavior* (pp. 427–436). The Hague: Mouton.

Forehand, R., & Long, N. (1988). Outpatient treatment of the acting out child: Procedures, long term follow-up data, and clinical problems. *Advances in Behaviour Research and Therapy, 10,* 129–177.

Forehand, R., & McMahon, R. J. (1981). *Helping the Noncompliant Child: A Clinician's Guide to Effective Parent Training.* New York: Guilford Press.

Gaensbauer, T. J., Harmon, R. J., Culp, A. M., Schultz, L. A., Van Doorninck, W. J., & Dawson, P. (1985). Relationships between attachment behavior in the laboratory and the caretaking environment. *Infant Behavior and Development, 8,* 355–369.

Gordon, T. (1975). *P.E.T.: Parent effectiveness training.* New York: American Library.

Graybill, D. (1986). A multiple-outcome evaluation of training parents in active listening. *Psychological Reports, 59,* 1171–1185.

Green, R. B., Hardison, W. L., & Greene, B. F. (1984). Turning the table on advice programs for parents: Using placemats to enhance family interaction at restaurants. *Journal of Applied Behavior Analysis, 17,* 497–508.

Greenspan, S. I., & White, K. R. (1985). The efficacy of preventive intervention: A glass half full? *Zero to Three, 5,* 1–5.

Griest, D. L., & Wells, K. C. (1983). Behavioral family therapy with conduct disorders in children. *Behavior Therapy, 14,* 37–53.

Griffore, R. J. (1980). Toward the use of child development research in informed parenting. *Journal of Clinical Child Psychology, 9,* 48–51.

Grove, D. C. (1982). *Self-administered vs. trainer assisted procedures in teaching mothers to use differential social attention.* Unpublished doctoral dissertation, University of Oregon.

Grusec, J. E., & Lytton, H. (1988). *Social development: History, theory, and research.* New York: Springer-Verlag.

Grusec, J. E., & Mills, R. (1982). The acquisition of self-control. In J. Worell (Ed.), *Psychological development in the elementary years* (pp. 151–183). New York: Academic Press.

Guadin, J. M., & Kurtz, D. P. (1985). Parenting skills training for child abusers. *Journal of Group Psychotherapy, Psychodrama, and Sociometry, 38,* 35–54.

Hall, E., Lamb, M., & Perlmutter, M. (1986). *Child psychology today,* 2nd ed. New York: Random House.

Hall, J. A., & Rose, S. D. (1987). Evaluation of parent training in groups for parent-adolescent conflict. *Social Work Research and Abstracts, 23,* 3–8.

Harris, J. D., & Larsen, J. M. (1989). Parent education as a mandatory component of preschool: Effects on middle-class, educationally advantaged parents and children. *Early Childhood Research Quarterly, 4,* 275–287.

Hartig, M., & Kanfer, F. (1973). The role of verbal self-instructions in children's resistance to temptation. *Journal of Personality and Social Psychology, 25,* 259–267.

Hartup, W. W. (1989). Social relationships and their developmental significance. *American Psychologist, 44,* 120–126.

Hornby, G., & Singh, N. N. (1983). Group training for parents of mentally retarded children: A review and methodological analysis of behavioural studies. *Child Care, Health and Development, 9,* 199–213.

Huhn, R. P., & Zimpfer, D. G. (1989). Effects of a parent education program on parents and their preadolescent children. *Journal of Community Psychology, 17,* 311–318.

Johnston, L. D., Bachman, J. G., & O'Malley, P. M. (1981). *Student drug use in America 1975–1981.* Rockville, MD: National Institute on Drug Abuse.

Kagan, J. (1984). *The nature of the child.* New York: Basic Books.

Kanigsberg, J. S., & Levant, R. F. (1988). Parental attitudes and children's self-concept and behavior following parents' participation in parent training groups. *Journal of Community Psychology, 16,* 152–160.

Klein, M. A., & Swisher, J. D. (1983). A statewide evaluation of a communication and parenting skills program. *Journal of Drug Education, 13,* 73–82.

Knapp, P. A., & Deluty, R. H. (1989). Relative effectiveness of two behavioral parent training programs. *Journal of Clinical Child Psychology, 18,* 314–322.

Kopp, C. B. (1982). Antecedents of self-regulation: A developmental perspective. *Developmental Psychology, 18,* 199–204.

Lamb, M. E., & Baumrind, D. (1978). Socialization and personality development in the preschool years. In M. E. Lamb (Ed.), *Social and personality development* (Chap. 13). New York: Holt, Rinehart and Winston.

Lambermon, M. W. E., & van Ijzendoorn, M. H. (1989). Influencing mother-infant interaction through videotaped or written instruction: Evaluation of a parent education program. *Early Childhood Research Quarterly, 4,* 449–458.

Levant, R. F., & Haffrey, N. A. (1981). *Skills training for parents: A personal developmental program.* Boston: Personal Developmental Program.

Lewis, W. M. (1986). Group training for parents of children with behavior problems. *Journal for Specialists in Group Work, 11,* 194–199.

Londerville, S., & Main, M. (1981). Security of attachment, compliance and maternal training methods in the second year of life. *Developmental Psychology, 17,* 289–299.

Lorber, R., Felton, D. K., & Reid, J. B. (1984). A social learning approach to the reduction of coercive processes in child abusive families: A molecular analysis. *Advances in Behaviour Research and Therapy, 6,* 29–45.

Lowry, M. A., & Whitman, T. L. (1989). Generalization of parenting skills: An early intervention program. *Child & Family Behavior Therapy, 11,* 45–65.

Lutzer, V. D. (1987). An educational and peer support group for mothers of preschoolers at-risk for behavior disorders. *Journal of Primary Prevention, 7,* 153–161.

Lutzker, J. R., McGimsey, J. F., McRae, S., & Campbell, R. V. (1983). Behavioral parent training: There's so much more to do. *Behavior Therapist, 6,* 110–112.

Lytton, H. (1980). *Parent–child interaction: The socialization process observed in twin and singleton families.* New York: Plenum Press.

Maccoby, E. E., & Martin, J. A. (1983). Socialization in the context of the family: Parent–child interaction. In E. M. Hetherington (Ed.), *Handbook of child psychology: Vol 4. Socialization, personality and social development* (pp. 1–102). New York: Wiley.

Mathews, J. R., Friman, P. C., Barone, V. J., Ross, L. V., & Christophersen, E. R. (1987). Decreasing dangerous infant behaviors through parent instruction. *Journal of Applied Behavior Analysis, 20,* 165–169.

Meichenbaum, D., & Goodman, J. (1971). Training impulsive children to talk to themselves: A means of developing self-control. *Journal of Abnormal Psychology, 77,* 115–126.

Miller, D. T., Weinstein, S. M., & Karniol, R. (1978). Effects of age and self-verbalization on children's ability to delay gratification. *Developmental Psychology, 14,* 569–570.

Mischel, W., & Ebbesen, E. B. (1970). Attention in delay of gratification. *Journal of Personality and Social Psychology, 16,* 329–337.

Mischel, W., Ebbesen, E. B., & Zeiss, A. (1972). Cognitive and attentional mechanisms in delay of gratification. *Journal of Personality and Social Psychology, 21,* 204–218.

Mischel, W., & Moore, B. (1973). Effects of attention to symbolically presented rewards upon self-control. *Journal of Personality and Social Psychology, 28,* 172–179.

Mischley, M., Stacy, E. W., Mischley, L., & Dush, D. (1985). A parent education project for low-income families. *Prevention in Human Services, 3,* 45–57.

Moreland, J. R., Schwebel, A. I., Beck, S., & Wells, R. (1982). Parents as therapists: A review of the behavior therapy parent training literature—1975 to 1981. *Behavior Modification, 6,* 250–276.

Nudd, M. E. (1989). Parents as teachers project. *Prevention in Human Services, 6,* 67–70.

Nurcombe, B., Howell, D. C., Rauh, V. A., Teti, D. M., Ruoff, P., & Brennan, J. (1984). An intervention program for mothers of low-birthweight infants: Preliminary results. *Journal of American Academy of Child Psychiatry, 23,* 319–325.

O'Dell, S. (1974). Training parents in behavior modification: A review. *Psychological Bulletin, 81,* 418–433.

Orlando, J. E., & Bartel, N. R. (1989). Cognitive strategy training: An intervention model for parents of children with learning disabilities. *Journal of Reading, Writing, and Learning Disabilities International, 5,* 327–344.

Packard, T., Robinson, E. A., & Grove, D. C. (1983). The effect of training procedures on the maintenance of parental relationship building skills. *Journal of Clinical Child Psychology, 12,* 181–186.

Pastor, D. L. (1981). The quality of mother–infant attachment and its relationship to toddlers' initial sociability with peers. *Developmental Psychology, 17,* 326–335.

Patterson, G. R. (1975). *Families: Application of social learning to family life.* Champaign, IL: Research Press.

Patterson, G. R., & Gullion, M. E. (1971). *Living with children.* Champaign, IL: Research Press.

Patteson, D. M., & Barnard, K. E. (1990). Parenting of low birth weight infants: A review of issues and interventions. *Infant Mental Health Journal, 11,* 37–56.

Pfannenstiel, J. C., & Seltzer, D. A. (1989). New Parents as Teachers: Evaluation of an early parent education program. *Early Childhood Research Quarterly, 4,* 1–18.

Pierson, D. E., Walker, D. K., & Tivnan, T. (1984). A school-based program from infancy to kindergarten for children and their parents. *The Personnel and Guidance Journal, 62,* 448–455.

Porterfield, J. K., Herbert-Jackson, E., & Risley, T. R. (1976). Contingent observation: An effective and acceptable procedure for reducing disruptive behavior of young children in a group setting. *Journal of Applied Behavior Analysis, 9,* 55–64.

Powell, D. R. (1986). Parent education and support programs. *Young Children, 41,* 47–53.

Powers, T. G., & Shapieski, M. L. (1986). Childrearing and impulse control in toddlers: A naturalistic investigation. *Developmental Psychology, 22,* 271–275.

Raue, J., & Spence, S. H. (1985). Group versus individual application of reciprocity training for parent–youth conflict. *Behaviour Research and Therapy, 23,* 177–186.

Reisinger, J. J., Ora, J. P., & Frangia, G. W. (1976). Parents as change agents for their children: A review. *Journal of Community Psychology, 4,* 103–123.

Rettig, E. B. (1973). *ABCs for parents: An educational workshop in behavior modification.* Van Nuys, CA: Associates for Behavior Change.

Rickert, V. I., Sottolano, D. C., Parrish, J. M., Riley, A. W., Hunt, F. M., & Pelco, L. E. (1988). Training parents to become better behavior managers: The need for a competency-based approach. *Behavior Modification, 12,* 475–496.

Riesch, S. K., & Munns, S. K. (1984). Promoting awareness: The mother and her baby. *Nursing Research, 33,* 271–276.

Robertson, S. E. (1984). Parent education: Current status. *Canadian Counsellor, 18,* 100–105.

Rogers, C. R. (1951). *Client-centered therapy.* Boston: Houghton Mifflin.

Rowland, L. (1989). Pierre the pelican. *Prevention in Human Services, 6,* 117–122.

Sallis, J. F. (1983). Aggressive behaviors of children: A review of behavioral interventions and future directions. *Education and Treatment of Children, 6,* 175–191.

Sanders, M. R., & Christensen, A. P. (1985). A comparison of the effects of child management and planned activities training in five parenting environments. *Journal of Abnormal Child Psychology, 13,* 101–117.

Sanders, M. R., & Dadds, M. R. (1982). The effects of planned activities and child management procedures in parent training: An analysis of setting generality. *Behavior Therapy, 13,* 452–461.

Sapon-Shevin, M. (1982). Ethical issues in parent training programs. *Journal of Special Education, 16,* 341–357.

Scaife, J., & Frith, J. (1988). A behaviour management and life stress course for a group of mothers incorporating training for health visitors. *Child Care, Health, and Development, 14,* 25–50.

Schaefer, C. E., & Briesmeister, J. M. (Eds.). (1989). Handbook of parent training: Parents as cotherapists for children's behavior problems. New York: Wiley.

Schmitt, B. D. (1987). Seven deadly sins of childhood: Advising parents about difficult developmental phases. *Child Abuse and Neglect, 11,* 421–432.

Showers, J. (1989). Behaviour management cards as a method of anticipatory guidance for parents. *Child: Care, Health, and Development, 15,* 401–415.

Sigel, I. E. (1985). *Parental belief systems.* Hillsdale, NJ: Lawrence Erlbaum.

Sloane, H. N., Endo, G. T., Hawkes, T. W., & Jenson, W. R. (1990). Decreasing children's fighting through self-instructional parent training materials. *School Psychology International, 11,* 17–29.

Smith, J. E. (1984). Non-accidental injury to children: I. A review of behavioural interventions. *Behaviour Research and Therapy, 22,* 331–347.

Strayhorn, J. M., & Weidman, C. S. (1989). Reduction of attention deficit and internalizing symptoms in preschoolers through parent–child interaction training. *Journal of American Academy of Child and Adolescent Psychiatry, 27,* 888–896.

Strom, R. D. (1985). Developing a curriculum for parent education. *Family Relations, 34,* 161–167.

Swetnam, L., Peterson, C. R., & Clark, H. B. (1983). Social skills development in young children: Preventive and therapeutic approaches. *Child and Youth Services, 5,* 5–27.

Tavormina, J. B. (1974). Basic models of parent counseling: A review. *Psychological Bulletin, 81,* 827–835.

Tavormina, J. B. (1975). Relative effectiveness of behavioral and reflective group counseling with parents of mentally retarded children. *Journal of Consulting and Clinical Psychology, 43,* 22–31.

Toner, I. J., & Smith, R. A. (1977). Age and overt verbalization in delay-maintenance behavior in children. *Journal of Experimental Child Psychology, 24,* 123–128.

Turley, M. A. (1985). A meta-analysis of informing mothers concerning the sensory and perceptual capabilities of their infants: The effects on maternal–infant interaction. *Maternal Child Nursing Journal, 14,* 183–197.

Wahler, R. G. (1980). The insular mother: The problems in parent–child treatment. *Journal of Applied Behavior Analysis, 13,* 207–219.

Wells, K. C., & Egan, J. (1988). Social learning and systems family therapy for childhood oppositional disorder: Comparative treatment outcome. *Comprehensive Psychiatry, 29,* 138–146.

Wells, K. C., & Forehand, R. (1980). Child behavior problems in the home. In S. M. Turner, K. Calhoun, & H. E. Adams (Eds.), *Handbook of behavior therapy.* New York: Wiley.

Whitt, J. K., & Casey, P. H. (1982). The mother–infant relationship and infant development: The effect of pediatric intervention. *Child Development, 53,* 948–956.

Wiese, M. R., & Kramer, J. J. (1988). Parent training research: An analysis of the empirical literature 1975–1985. *Psychology in the Schools, 25,* 325–330.

Yates, B. T., & Mischel, W. (1979). Young children's preferred attentional strategies for delaying gratification. *Journal of Personality and Social Psychology, 37,* 286–300.

# CHAPTER 11

# SEXUAL INTERACTION SKILLS

Steven R. Gold
Elizabeth J. Letourneau
William O'Donohue

In this chapter, sexual behavior and interactions will be examined from the framework of the interrelated constructs of sexual skills, sexual performance, and sexual competence. *Sexual skills* refers to the specific abilities required for competent performance in a sexual situation. *Sexual performance* refers to the behavior that is emitted when a sexual skill is executed. Thus, the distinction embodied in the terms *sexual skills* and *sexual performance* parallels the learning–performance distinction in conditioning (Catania, 1992). *Sexual competence* denotes the evaluation of the sexual performance and the effects of the performance. D'Augelli and D'Augelli (1985, p. 172) have defined *sexual competence* as "the ability to meet one's own and others' goals for sexual activity." (The reader is referred to O'Donohue and Krasner (Chapter 1, this volume) for a more detailed treatment of the skills–performance–competence distinction).

Although viewing sexual behavior and its problems from this perspective is not without precedent (e.g., D'Augelli & D'Augelli, 1985), it is admittedly somewhat unorthodox. Therefore, we will attempt to present considerations that we believe suggest that

viewing sexual behavior in this manner not only provides a heuristically useful paradigm for the understanding of the origin and treatment of sexual problems but also potentially can help in understanding and resolving some of the major obstacles and problems in contemporary sex therapy.

We believe that this sexual skill/performance/competence paradigm is plausible and useful for a variety of reasons:

1. Although there is a wide agreement that sexual behavior is influenced by physiological factors, there is also wide agreement even within the biological research community that it is not completely determined by biological variables (e.g., Money, 1983). The question becomes: "How, more precisely, is this nonbiological, sexual plasticity to be understood?" One possibility is that sexual behavior can be learned. This view is common to the majority of contemporary theories of human sexuality (Geer & O'Donohue, 1987). For example, anthropological and sociological accounts of sexual behavior usually claim that individuals learn the range of permissible, and even possible, sexual behavior through a variety of societal

and cultural mechanisms (Davenport, 1987; De-Lamater, 1987). Gagnon and Simon's (1973) influential scripting account of sexual behavior posits that sexual behavior is learned entirely through scripts in which the culture specifies the sequencing and content of sexual behavior. Developmentalists often address critical stages in the learning of sexual behavior and the correlations of age with what is being learned sexually (Serbin & Sprafkin, 1987). Feminist accounts of sexuality often emphasize that men learn through a variety of mechanisms in a patriarchal and misogynist society to become sexually aroused to women being battered, dominated, and infantilized (MacKinnon, 1987). Thus, it seems reasonable to claim that sexual behavior undergoes relatively enduring changes as a function of experience—that is, it is also influenced by learning (e.g., McConaghy, 1987; O'Donohue & Plaud, in press).

Thus, any approach such as skills training (Goldstein, 1981; O'Donohue & Krasner, Chapter 1, this volume), which utilizes the concept of learning in understanding the origin and modification of changeworthy behavior, has prima facie relevance and plausibility. In this view, sexual abilities (or skills) can be missing or poorly learned as a result of faulty learning histories. Given that sex is often private, that sexual information is often distorted or simply suppressed, and that sex is surrounded by a number of myths including the idea that it is "bad" and "dirty," it is not surprising that the sexual learning is often problematic. Therefore, although biological therapies are undoubtedly an important treatment modality, an approach that asks, "What learning problems caused this sexual competence deficit, and what behavior needs to be taught to produce a competent response?" appears to be plausible to the extent that sexual behavior is learned or can be relearned.

2.   Most sexual behavior is not entirely reflexive but, rather, consists of instrumental behavior—that is, behavior that is purposive and influenced by feedback and consequences (Masters & Johnson, 1970; McConaghy, 1987; Skinner, 1988; O'Donohue & Plaud, in press). Moreover, instrumental behavior varies in its effectiveness in producing desired consequences. The ability to make jump shots or to cook an appetizing meal varies across people, times, and situations. Similarly, sexual performance can vary in its degree of competence. Sexual behavior may be evaluated on complex sets of competency criteria that include factors such as duration, frequency, degree and kind of pleasure and/or pain, degree of novelty, morality, spontaneity, amount and kind of risk, athleticism, affiliativeness, romance, and a host of other factors.

3.   An individual may have learned relevant sexual skills but may not be able to perform these in a competent manner because of factors that influence the execution of a behavior that, under more ideal conditions, the person is capable of performing well. Among the most important factors inhibiting the skilled performance of behavior are (with commonly prescribed therapies): (a) anxiety (relaxation skills, desensitization, sensate focus); (b) interfering, irrational cognitions such as misinformation, myths, and problematic self-efficacy beliefs (sex education, cognitive restructuring); (c) inappropriate selective attention, or distraction (sensate focus); (d) lack of knowledge regarding when to apply certain skills (direct instruction, sex surrogates, modeling, role playing); and (e) lack of, or problematic, feedback (sexual communication training). Thus, an individual may have the requisite sexual skills for performing competently in some sexual situations, but the individual's performance may not be competent because of one or a combination of these interfering and inhibiting factors. Much of contemporary sex therapy (particularly for secondary as opposed to primary problems) has been based on the premise that the individual has the requisite sexual abilities to meet his or her goals but that one of these factors is inhibiting effective performance.

4.   Competence evaluations regarding sexuality are value-based judgments of performance in a situation (McFall, 1982) and are a function of two major factors. First, who is the judge of competence—the client, the sexual partner, the therapist, others, or some combination of these? Problems in sexuality can arise when there are disagreements between appropriate judges (e.g., client and partner), when there are inappropriate judges (e.g., locker room buddies), or when there are problematic worries about who the judge will be (e.g., parents). Second, by what criteria and values will the performance be judged? Problems in generating standard definitions of sexual dysfunction that are generally applicable (e.g., American Psychiatric Association, 1985) have much to do with controversies and difficulties in identifying generic competency criteria. For example, what is a generally applicable definition of *premature ejaculation?* Should it be given in terms of the percentage of orgasms reached by the partner and, if so, exactly

what percentage? Is such a percentage too variable? Might a low percentage of orgasm confound ejaculatory latency with a possibly problematic orgasmic potential of the partner? Moreover, criteria for evaluating sexual behavior might be somewhat relative and ideographic. In the example of premature ejaculation, the question might be better phrased: "What goals and values are held by this particular pair of partners for their sexual interactions, and, given these, what latency to orgasm in the male seems to be premature and what latency sufficient to attain these goals?" If we were to accept the current definition in the *Diagnostic and Statistical Manual of Mental Disorders,* third edition, revised (DSM-III-R; American Psychiatric Association, 1987), do we simply tell women who are dissatisfied with a 51% rate of orgasm that the American Psychiatric Association has decided that such a rate is sufficient and that therefore their unrealistically high expectations seem to be the problem? Thus, problems in delimiting generic criteria for sexual dysfunction in the various editions of the DSM can be understood from the lack of proper emphasis given to the ideographic nature of competence evaluations (McFall, 1982).

Moreover, problems in sexual functioning also may arise because competency criteria are unclear or poorly understood by the couple. Many individuals would be perplexed if asked: "What needs to occur before you and/or (preferably and) your partner would rate your sexual performance as competent?" However, this might be a very important question clinically, as it explicates a critical factor in defining the problem, and therefore clarifying this might in and of itself be therapeutic. Perceived problems in sexuality also can be understood as due to the use of inappropriate criteria; for example, in order for a man to be sexually competent, his female partner must experience an orgasm every time they have intercourse.

An important implication of this approach is that sexual incompetence is seen as a mismatch between the individual's performance and the situational demands. As McFall (1982) has stated:

> This discrepancy can be described, alternatively, as being due either to a deficit in skills, or to excessive performance demands. Psychological problems grow out of this imbalance between abilities and demands in the person–environment system; therefore, the reduction of psychological problems, which involves establishing a balance in the system, can be achieved either through increasing the person's abilities or through decreasing the environmental task demands imposed on the person. (p. 22)

Thus, adjusting performance demands or competency criteria also can result in problem resolution.

5.   Schlundt and McFall (1985) have claimed that competence judgments are judgments about an episode of behavior within a context, not about some enduring characteristic of a performer. This analysis can be helpful in that it can allow for the variability across time and situations commonly seen in sexual behavior—for example, why some women have problems having an orgasm in some situations (intercourse with husband) but not in others.

6.   Sexual behavior and interactions are associated with a variety of different demands and skills. Competent sexual expression often involves social skills (sometimes of a high level to create, sustain, and enhance intimacy), communication skills, assertion skills, relaxation skills, cognitive skills, and specific skills regarding sexuality. Thus, sex therapy may also need to address problems in these skills if they have an impact on sexual competence. For example, Spiess, Geer, and O'Donohue (1984) found that premature ejaculators as compared with normal controls had longer periods of abstinence from ejaculation. Although these data are correlational, these data might be construed to suggest that one path for the development of premature ejaculation (particularly for individuals who do not masturbate) might be: social competence problems → social isolation → less frequent orgasm → premature ejaculation.

Moreover, sexual skills themselves are multifaceted. D'Augelli and D'Augelli (1985) suggest that:

> Sexual competence includes knowledge of sexual functioning of men and women; an understanding of both one's own personal attitudes, values, and expectations regarding sexuality and the origins of this sexual ideology; the ability to make personally congruent decisions about sexual matters; the ability to assert one's sexual interests and their meanings to others; the ability to act in sexually satisfying ways to meet one's own and one's partner's needs; and the ability to discuss with others one's sexuality and its development over time. (p. 172)

7.   Sex therapy can be viewed as an educational experience in which goals are identified and evaluated (e.g., on whether they conflict with other goals or how realistic they are); assessment is conducted to ascertain the extent to which goals are not being met because of a lack of skills in certain situations, factors that interfere with performance, or problematic competence evaluations on the part of either the client or

his or her partners. Therapy becomes an educational experience in which clients participate in direct, active training in order to learn or relearn sexually competent behavior. For example, Masters and Johnson (1970) have defined their approach to sex therapy as largely educative.

Thus, in sum, the skills paradigm provides a framework to understand the origin of sexual problems (problematic learning), as well as providing a justification for nonbiological, "talk" therapies (new learning). It is largely consistent with many of the major forms of current sex therapy, as Masters and Johnson (1970), LoPiccolo (1978), and others (Annon, 1976), have emphasized the educative nature of their interventions. In fully explicating the skills model, however, several important factors are given clear emphasis:

1. It provides a structure to encompass situational variability in sexual behavior.
2. It provides a framework in which sexual skills are embedded in larger tasks and contexts, such as creating and sustaining an intimate relationship.
3. It takes sexual competence to be a complex matter involving numerous subskills that often need to be performed in a spontaneous, coordinated, but still somewhat controlled manner.

Finally, it also provides an explanation of problems in constructing standard, universally applicable definitions of sexual problems (lack of recognition of the situational specificity and ideographic nature of competency evaluations).

As Wiseman (1976) has maintained, much of human sexual behavior is a complex intrapersonal and interpersonal process in that it simultaneously requires a focus on one's own sexual pleasure in relation to another's and, concomitantly, requires the ability to make this process fairly spontaneous. In this chapter, therefore, we will review cognitive and intrapersonal sexual skills that have an important impact on sexual performance and competence. In the next section, we will discuss the important role of competent cognitive skills such as sexual fantasizing in eliciting and maintaining sexual desire and arousal, as well as in understanding sexual preferences. We will then review sexual interpersonal skills.

## COGNITIVE SKILLS

The brain is the primary sex organ and also the primary source of sexual problems. Perhaps more than any other behavior, sexual functioning is influenced both positively and negatively by cognitive processes (Barlow, 1986; Geer & Fuhr, 1976). Graber (1981, p. 485) illustrates some of the ways cognitive skills impact sexual performance:

> Sexual functioning is a psychomotor skill that may be compared to other psychomotor acts such as riding a bicycle. Both require attention and awareness to bodily functioning and a feedback mechanism for utilizing information as the body perceives it in order to perform the motor act. As with riding a bicycle, once the psychomotor skill is learned it becomes essentially automatic, and the learned nature of it fades from consciousness. Most of us do not remember how we learned to control our ejaculation. If for some reasons we did not learn how to ride a bicycle as a child, we can learn to do it as an adult. Having not learned the psychomotor function at the critical period when it was easiest to do, this is often a more difficult but not impossible task.

The cognitive foundation is laid by the communication between parent and child (Serbin & Sprafkin, 1987). There is very little direct verbal communication between parents and children related to sexuality, but a great deal of restrictive information is communicated indirectly (Darling & Hicks, 1983). Beginning with sex education in the family that consists of a list of restrictions and "don'ts," and reinforced by cultural sex-negative messages, many people grow up with their sexual knowledge consisting of some accurate information mixed with a large dose of myths, misinformation, and unrealistic and unattainable expectations and goals. In the set of possible sexual behaviors, most are defined by the sex-negative society as in some way "bad;" often, the complement of this "bad" subset is regarded as an underwhelming "not bad," rather than in a more positive light. There is no easy way to separate fact from fiction when open communication about sexuality is absent. Eventually, individuals realize there is a lot they don't know, but they don't know what it is they don't know or whom to ask to find out. With this problematic cognitive foundation, it is not surprising that sexual problems often begin before any sexual interpersonal interaction occurs. It is a thesis of this chapter that attention to intrapersonal sexual skill development is a precursor to establishing satisfying sexual interaction with another person.

There is an extensive body of literature describing the predominant sexual messages boys and girls receive as they mature (Allgeier & Allgeier, 1991; Warshaw & Parrot, 1991). Despite the sexual revolution, boys still get the message that they should take the lead in all sexual encounters; always be on the lookout for sexual opportunities; and always be ready to perform, go as far as they can, and never accept the first "no" as final. As in sports, winning by "scoring" sexually enhances males' reputations among peers, earning them the label "stud." The emphasis on sexual success as a prerequisite for masculinity leads many men to engage in sexual activities when they do not actually wish to do so because of concerns about others' perception of their masculinity (Muehlenhard & Cook, 1988).

Girls must try to decipher ambivalent and contradictory sexual messages ("Be attractive but not too sexual," "Good girls don't") and apply these messages appropriately during sexual interactions. If males are socialized to be on the sexual offense, then females are left to play defense. Perhaps the best description of females' defensive strategy is taken from football: "Bend but don't break." As applied to both football and sex, this means it is acceptable for the offense to make some gains, but the objective is to prevent the offense from going all the way and scoring. The female must keep one part of her attention fixed on deciding the stopping point unless she wants to be scored on and experience the negative consequences that go with "losing"—loss of virginity, damage to reputation, and risk of pregnancy. It is important for females not to appear too interested in sex or they may be perceived as "loose" or "easy."

Likely consequences of this sports-oriented, antagonistic approach to sexual development are poor communication between the sexes and the high rate of sexual aggression in our culture during courtship and marriage (Allgeier & Allgeier, 1991). Both men and women learn about competitive gender role expectations at an early age, which impedes clear heterosexual communication (Tannen, 1990). Responding to gender-specific scripts and, at the same time, deciphering another's sexual messages can result in confusion and lead to aggression. Both males and females are trained to perceive the other in competitive and contentious ways—men as always after sex, and women as teases who deny sexual interest unless awakened by a "real" man.

Against the backdrop of sexual ignorance, misinformation, and competitive messages is the goal of achieving a mutually satisfying and intimate sexual relationship. The individual is often not directly aware of these background messages and therefore accepts them without critical examination. Therefore, an essential intrapersonal cognitive skill in achieving intimate sexual relationships is to learn to pay greater critical attention to sexual thoughts, sexual images, sexual fantasies, and sexual daydreams in order to become aware of what is often automatically processed and to increase control over the internal sexual messages that influence sexual behavior.

When people think about sex, they usually think that sex equals sexual intercourse and that sex begins in the bedroom with foreplay, a preliminary to the main event. This type of thinking may be more characteristic of males than of females, but it ignores the broader nonphysical context of human sexuality. Sexual thoughts and sexual fantasies make up part of the constant stream of consciousness occurring while awake. The content of the stream of consciousness is dominated by the individual's current concerns (Klinger, 1971). Current concerns represent goals that one has made some degree of commitment to pursuing but that have not been either achieved or abandoned. Current concerns are a motivating force, as behavior is designed to reach or satisfy goals. Klinger, Barta, and Maxeiner (1980) had subjects list seven things they had thought about and seven things they had not thought about. Subjects carried a beeper and, when they were signaled to report their thoughts, the two highest ranked concerns made up half of their total thinking time. Daydreams also reflect current concerns. Gold and Reilly (1985–1986) found that 66% of daydreams recorded over a two-week period reflected subjects' previously listed current concerns. The goals reflected in current concerns vary in terms of their valence and importance and whether they are short-term or long-term objectives. A number of current concerns can dominate the stream of consciousness, as well as night dreams, at any one time. A graduate student's current concerns can range from the positive and important goal of completing a dissertation or finding a strategy to help a seriously depressed client, to more mundane goals of finding a way to get in a five-mile run and a trip to the grocery store before attacking the journals once again.

Sexual fantasies and sexual thoughts are themes that are part of most individuals' streams of consciousness and current concerns. Sexual fantasy is now regarded as a normal aspect of human sexuality, serving a variety of adaptive functions (Brown & Hart, 1977; Hariton & Singer, 1974). Hariton and Singer view fantasy as a cognitive skill in which an individual engages to enhance a variety of situations, including sex. Sexual fantasies can be used to increase arousal during lovemaking, to bring new ideas to sexual activities, to blot out or alter negative aspects of reality and make them more positive, to rehearse future sexual behavior, to set a sexual mood, and to substitute for sexual experiences that might be stimulating but are avoided because of legal, moral, or personal constraints (Chick & Gold, 1987–1988; Heiman & LoPiccolo, 1988; Klinger, 1990).

Rather than serving as a way to improve on an unsatisfactory reality, as Freud suggested (1962), engaging in and attending to sexual fantasies is a means of enriching sexuality. One of the most commonly reported fantasy themes is reliving past sexual experiences (Davidson & Hoffman, 1986; Knafo & Jaffe, 1984; McCauley & Swann, 1980). Individuals with more sexual experience tend to have richer sexual fantasies (Carlson & Coleman, 1977; Gold & Chick, 1988). Carlson and Coleman defined *richness* by asking subjects to rate the vividness, color intensity, clarity, positive or negative feelings, amount of sexual arousal, and complexity of their sexual fantasies. Engaging in sexual fantasizing is also associated with more sexual satisfaction and more frequent orgasms (Klinger, 1990). Conversely, those who feel guilty about their sexuality tend to fantasize less and have shorter and less rich fantasies (Hardin & Gold, 1988–1989). The relationship between sexual experience and sexual fantasy can be described as a reciprocal interaction: Sexual experience increases the frequency and richness of sexual fantasy, and more sexual fantasy is associated with a more active sex life.

Whenever people are not engaged in tasks that require full and concentrated attention, a stream of thoughts and images passes through consciousness. These may be fragmentary, brief, and barely identifiable, or long, elaborate, familiar stories or fantasies, or any combination in between. Approximately 1% to 5% of this material is related to sex (Gold & Gold, 1982; Klinger, 1990), with a somewhat greater percentage related to sex during adolescence and the college years and less in middle and old age (Giambra & Martin, 1977). Individuals differ in the amount of attention they pay to their internal processes. The ability to attend to internal events such as daydreams has been associated with greater understanding of one's personality and more creative problem solving (Klinger, 1990; Singer & Pope, 1978), although excessive self-focused attention to the detriment of attending to important environmental input has been associated with a variety of clinical disorders (Ingram, 1990).

Although fantasizing is a part of the ongoing stream of consciousness, people differ in the attention they pay to their fantasies. With practice, people can become more attuned to their fantasies and become better at self-monitoring fantasy content (Teague & Gold, 1981). Therefore, learning to pay greater atten-

tion to sexual fantasies and to increase their frequency is the first intrapersonal skill identified. The second corollary skill is to become adept at maximizing the positive and minimizing the negative aspects of the sexual fantasies.

A brief hypothetical vignette of a dysfunctional family interaction will serve to initiate the description of the skill-building process.

> Roy returned home from an unsuccessful and tiring sales trip. His growled "hello" immediately tipped off his wife Clara and son Billy that he was in a foul mood. Clara smilingly asked about the trip and received a grunt in response. "Why didn't you pay the bills while I was gone? How many times do I have to remind you! And why is there ice cream in the freezer? Has another diet gone down the tube? If you don't have any more respect for yourself than . . ." At this point Clara and Billy left the room and retreated to the sewing room and basement respectively. Clara left thinking, "It sure didn't take long for Roy's homecoming to screw up. I guess my planned candlelight dinner, massage, and night of good loving is just a fantasy. He probably hates me! I just feel so useless and ugly!"

Roy did not plan to come home and alienate his family. His irritable, demanding, and generally aggressive behavior was not understood by Clara, Billy, or Roy himself, as they were all looking forward to a family reunion after four days of Roy's absence. The interaction between Roy and his family can be better understood by eavesdropping on Roy's fantasies as he drove home. Fantasies, like stories, have a theme, a mood, feelings, actions, and an outcome. The makeup of the fantasy can have a direct bearing on the potential for the fantasy to be acted on and the quality of any subsequent encounter. This process can be illustrated by Roy's stream of consciousness as he drove home after work. The reader needs to accept one premise about Roy: that he has a conscious desire to improve the quality and quantity of his sex life.

> "Damn, what a lousy day! Two hundred miles of driving and not one sale and now I'm stuck on a parking lot they call a highway. I wonder what's for dinner. It will be good to get home after four days on the road. I hope Billy remembered to mow the lawn. That song reminds me of the week Clara and I spent in Jamaica. I can see the two of us tanned, relaxed, out on the beach, sipping a large drink. I bet she forgot to pay the mortgage this month. That woman never remembers to pay bills if I don't tell her to. I've got to call the bank and see about refinancing. I need my back rubbed and my front could use some

handling too. I hope Clara is sticking to her diet. I hate flabby thighs. I told her before I left to get serious about losing weight. Boy, that turns me off to picture her fat and naked! I think she likes to be fat so she can avoid having sex with me. I don't think I turn her on any more. We argued about it four days ago and I want results or else. When is this traffic going to move?"

Words cannot fully describe a sexual fantasy, which consists mainly of images, but several features of Roy's thoughts and suggested images are worth noting. Roy is cognitively priming himself for interpersonal difficulties when he arrives home. He is dwelling on real and imagined negative and unpleasant experiences—the traffic, his son's and wife's negligence, and her less appealing physical characteristics. As Bower's (1981) network theory of memory proposes, once unpleasant memories are evoked, other associated negative memories and thoughts are activated. Roy is irritable and angry, and by anticipating problems at home he has increased the likelihood that he will react in an annoyed, bothered, and angry fashion when he arrives home. Within Roy's stream of consciousness is the beginning of a sexual fantasy. A song reminds him of a pleasant image of himself and his wife on a beach. If current concerns about bills and money had not intruded, Roy's desire for some physical contact, coupled with the beach imagery, could have resulted in an enjoyable and arousing sexual fantasy.

With two related cognitive skills, Roy could turn his upcoming evening and sex life around: first, the ability to attend to the sexual fantasy elements drifting through his consciousness and/or to increase the frequency of sexual fantasizing; and second, the ability to counter negative imagery and negative thoughts with positive, sexually arousing images and thoughts. These two processes are skills that can be increased with practice.

The strategies to be described to increase Roy and Clara's intrapersonal sexual skills are all aspects of cognitive behavior therapy (Cormier & Cormier, 1991). The basic assumption of cognitive therapy is that internal events such as thoughts, images, fantasies, attitudes and beliefs have a direct effect on feelings and behavior. Cognitive therapists believe that dysfunctional or disturbed behavior is a consequence of negative and distorted cognitive processes and that positive and adaptive behavior can be achieved by altering the faulty cognitive processes. All these procedures can be carried out by individuals alone or with the help of a therapist, and the pro-

cedures share common elements worth noting. Prior to carrying out the cognitive change techniques, a rationale for the procedure is provided. It is important for clients to understand how internal cognitive processes affect behavior so they are motivated to carry out the assignments. A second commonality is the use of homework assignments to practice new skills. Just as learning new physical skills such as skiing or learning to type requires practice, learning new cognitive skills also requires practice. Finally, alone or with a therapist, clients develop new skills more rapidly if they reinforce themselves for making steps toward their goal. Internal, reinforcing statements—"I'm improving," "This new way of coping is working," and so on—speed up the change process.

## Increasing Fantasy Awareness

Several strategies are available to improve awareness of sexual thoughts and fantasies and help achieve a desired level of sexual activity. Sexual fantasies can be classified into two types: planned versus unplanned or planned versus unbidden. *Planned sexual fantasies,* as the name suggests, are fantasies one deliberately creates. They may be fantasies that are experienced over and over because they are sexually arousing and pleasurable. Often the planned fantasy is like an old friend that can be called upon to deliver predictable results. *Unbidden fantasies* are those that just seem to pop into consciousness without any forethought or sense of choice. Unbidden fantasies may be either positive or negative and can be particularly useful for learning about oneself. These fantasies are determined by stable factors such as personality and by temporary influences such as current concerns and mood, but because they are one's own creation they can be examined for information about oneself. Since these fantasies are unplanned and unexpected, the material may provide data about sexuality available in no other way. By just popping into the mind, unbidden fantasies are less subject to conscious control or censorship. Roy's fantasy is unplanned and is an example of his stream of consciousness.

To improve his skill in recognizing and attending to sexual fantasies, Roy needs to improve his self-monitoring, the process by which clients observe and record things about themselves and their interactions with environmental situations (Cormier & Cormier, 1991). Thoresen and Mahoney (1974) suggest that self-monitoring is a major first step in any self-change program. To improve his skills at self-monitoring, Roy can keep a log or diary of his sexual fantasies. He should write down any sexual thoughts or images he experiences as soon as possible after they occur to be most accurate. Keeping a log is likely to have several desired outcomes. Attending to sexual fantasies should increase the frequency of their occurrence through the process of reactivity. When individuals are instructed to pay close attention to the frequency of a behavior, the frequency of that behavior tends to increase over baseline levels (Kazdin, 1974). This is especially true when positive or desirable events are monitored by motivated clients (Nelson, 1977). Before Roy can self-monitor effectively, it is essential that he be able to discriminate the event to be monitored—in this case, sexual thoughts and fantasies. Roy should record any thoughts, images, or daydreams that have a sexual content or result in increased or decreased sexual arousal. Roy's log should include information about the antecedents and consequences of the process being monitored, such as the time of day the fantasy occurred, what Roy was doing, where he was, his mood, his level of tension or relaxation, and changes in mood and sexual arousal after the fantasy. The additional information is recorded to provide cues to conditions that set off or are conducive to fantasizing. It is useful to learn what one's individual conditions are for engaging in and attending to sexual thoughts and fantasies. Once the relevant cues have been identified, the individual has greater control over the occurrence of the fantasies by having the ability to establish the appropriate conditions. Roy may need to take five minutes in the morning and in the middle of the afternoon to close his eyes, practice deep breathing or muscle tensing and relaxing to increase his sense of relaxation, and engage in a sexual fantasy. Beyond providing a pleasant interlude during the work day, the fantasy exercise can be a significant sexual learning experience. What can be learned from this exercise includes the favorable conditions for sexual fantasies and real sexual experiences, the ability to embellish and expand sexual fantasies to increase arousal, the ability to cope with unwanted or negative intrusions into the fantasy, the skill to cope with cognitive distractions, the ability to restructure or reframe sexually illogical beliefs, the ability to identify sexual needs, wants, and preferences, and the ability to give oneself permission to be sexual. Learning from fantasy has a strong tradition in scientific history as well as in behavior therapy techniques such as systematic desensitization and covert modeling. Practice through imagination makes carrying out the

actual behavior more likely. Let us examine the skill-building opportunities available through the fantasy exercises.

## Establishing Sexual Conditions

Zilbergard (1978) has written about the effect on male sexuality of trying to perform when conditions are not right. He describes men trying to live up to the myth that "real" men are always ready for sex and should be able to get an erection under any and all circumstances. There are conditions in which sex becomes less of a priority for everyone, such as when life is threatened, and there are conditions that are individualized "turn-offs." Stress at work, fatigue, anger toward one's partner, or being rushed are examples of conditions that, for some people, interfere with being sexual. Trying to live up to sexual myths or trying hard to accommodate and please a partner can result in losing touch with one's unique set of turn-off conditions. Attending to the conditions contained in one's sexual fantasies and including these conditions in the log can increase awareness of what one desires in one's sex life. For example, an individual may become aware that most of his or her sexual fantasies have a romantic motif—dim lights, soft music, and lacy undergarments—but that these conditions are never part of actual sexual experiences. Fantasized sexual encounters may take place in the morning or afternoon even though the fantasizer's real sexual experiences consistently occur late at night when energy is at a low level. With increased awareness comes the option of making a fantasy into reality. Of course, all fantasized conditions may not be able to be actualized, but fantasy can be used to increase awareness of preferred conditions and options that previously were outside of one's awareness, ignored, or not shared with a partner.

## Embellishing Sexual Fantasies

As previously noted, individuals vary in the attention they pay to internal processes, including sexual fantasy. There are a variety of reasons, both conscious and unconscious, for inhibiting or ignoring sexual fantasies. For example, sexual fantasies may contain disturbing and intrusive elements of previous sexual traumas (Gold, 1991). Fantasies may be inhibited because the fantasy is exciting and arousing but reminds the fantasizer that reality is sexually barren. If past expressions of sexuality have resulted in punishment, all sexual content may be repressed, or the fantasy may be inhibited because the individual believes that his or her sexual fantasies involve acts that violate social norms. Roy's stream of consciousness contained brief sexual thoughts and images, but the theme in his thoughts was quickly changed to match his irritable mood. Roy's sexual fantasy seems to have been inhibited by a more pressing current concern of dealing with traffic and a negative mood induced by a poor sales trip. Roy's homecoming could have been dramatically different if he had been able to embellish and expand the fragmentary sexual fantasy. The beach scene could have been developed into a sexual fantasy of making love on a deserted beach with the sound of the waves breaking on the shore and the feeling of the warmth of the sun adding to the sensuality of the fantasy. This embellished "romantic" fantasy is consistent with Clara's hopes for a romantic dinner and sexual experience. If Roy had attended to his sexual fantasy, he would have had the opportunity to embellish the fantasy and alter his mood and his evening.

Most people have one or two planned, familiar favorite sexual fantasies that reliably produce sexual arousal. For men, these often involve hours of sexual gymnastics with a beautiful stranger who cannot get enough of them—or, better yet, two or more such women. Women, on the other hand, spend more time creating romantic fantasies that take place on beaches or in front of a warm, glowing fire, and more often than for males the partner is someone familiar to them or an ideal man who has the potential to be an ideal husband (Chick & Gold, 1987–1988). For those less creative in generating fantasies, help is available. Several books of erotic fantasies and erotic short stories have been published that are recommended as material for building individualized, favorite sexual fantasies. Friday has collected sexual fantasies from women (1973, 1975) and men (1980) that sample a wide variety of sexual themes, and Barbach has several books of erotic short stories especially written for women (1984, 1986). These erotic stories for females broaden the choices available over the older, more hard-core pornography, which was aimed primarily at a male audience.

Therapeutic strategies are also available to help people become "better fantasizers." Many behavioral interventions, such as systematic desensitization, depend on the client's ability to engage in imagery or fantasy. Clients are often instructed to imagine scenes as clearly as they can in order to enhance relaxation or to practice new responses such as assertiveness or anger control. Some clients may be unable to picture vivid scenes clearly in their minds, but for most people this ability can be improved with practice. Kazdin (1976) suggests having the client narrate aloud the sequence of imagery events as they are experienced. After listening for a while, the therapist asks questions designed to elicit more detail from the client by inquiring about the colors, sounds, smells, or tactile sensations involved in the imagery. This probing can help clients become more involved in the imagery and can help train them to engage in more detailed imagery in the future. It may be difficult or embarrassing for a client to describe details of a sexual fantasy to a therapist, but the technique can be used without the therapist knowing the fantasy content. While the client sits with eyes closed and imagines a sexual fantasy, the therapist can make comments to enhance the sensual quality and richness of the fantasy, such as "Try to really feel his/her touch," "Picture his/her face as clearly as possible," or "Listen to the sound of your breathing, your heart racing" (for additional sources on the usefulness of imagery, see Klinger, 1990; Lazarus, 1977; Shorr, 1977).

## Coping with Negative Intrusions

Roy's negative concerns about money and his images of Clara's flabby thighs interfered with his sexual fantasizing. When such negative and sexually disruptive images intrude, they can be countered by refocusing on positive images and recreating favorable conditions. Trying to block, suppress, or inhibit intrusive thoughts and images may be effective in the short term, but there is a risk of a "rebound effect." Wegner (1989) has shown that when efforts are made to suppress a particular thought or image, such as the white bears in his research, increased thoughts of white bears occur when the attempt to suppress is lifted and free expression of thoughts is encouraged. Therefore, perhaps a more effective strategy is to experience the intrusive and unpleasant image but follow it with positive and sexually arousing images in order to return to the desired state.

Lazarus and Abramovitz (1962) were among the first to use emotive imagery as a therapeutic strategy. Emotive imagery involves having a person focus on positive thoughts and images after imagining discomfiting or anxiety-arousing situations. Lazarus and Abramovitz had school-phobic children imagine a fictional character who was afraid of school but was helped by the client acting in a protective, reassuring manner or by setting a good example. Roy can create sexually arousing images to counter immediately his negative image of Clara. For example, he can imagine how deep and blue her eyes are or how warm and gentle her touch feels, or he can think her thighs look great the way they are. The strategy uses imagery to block anxiety because it is difficult to feel both anxious or turned off and aroused at the same time.

The substitution of pleasing thoughts or images in place of distressing fantasy elements may necessitate considerable practice if the distressing fantasy is one that has been experienced for a long time, is highly arousing, or is the only sexual fantasy experienced. In such circumstances, changes in the fantasies may be accomplished gradually, in small steps if necessary. For example, persons distressed by the level of force in their sexual fantasies could write out the current force fantasy and also a new, noncoercive fantasy they would like to substitute for the force fantasy. The differences between the current and the desired fantasy are then broken down into several steps, much like developing a fear hierarchy for conducting systematic desensitization. The force in the fantasy is gradually decreased, and noncoercive arousing elements are added. Each step in the fantasy change process is reinforced by pairing the modified sexual fantasy with heightened sexual arousal through masturbation and/or sensate focus exercises. Although there is no empirical data available concerning the efficacy of making gradual changes in distressing sexual fantasies, it is hypothesized to be effective for fantasies that are distressing but not for fantasies that have been acted on and would merit the diagnosis of paraphilia. Such ''deviant'' fantasies are likely to require elimination rather than modification, although again research is lacking on such issues. Treatment strategies have been developed to alter or eliminate ''deviant'' fantasies by aversive conditioning (Marshall, 1979) or orgasmic reconditioning (Marquis, 1970).

## Coping with Cognitive Distractions

The example involving Roy deals with an individual whose sexual fantasies do not involve deviant acts but do interfere with his sexual arousal by focusing on negative characteristics of his partner or nonarousing thoughts of work. Research has been directed toward understanding the effects of anxiety and distraction on sexual arousal. This research is somewhat limited in generalizability because it is based primarily on males and relies on laboratory tasks to simulate sexual experiences.

Barlow and his colleagues have developed a model of the interaction of autonomic arousal and cognitive interference processes in determining sexually functional and sexually dysfunctional responding (Barlow, 1986). The model is based on five processes or dimensions, found through a series of studies that differentiate functional and dysfunctional sexual performance. Although Roy is not sexually dysfunctional, his pattern of cognitive activity, as previously described, if it continued to progress in a negative direction, would fit Barlow's model.

Barlow's first dimension suggests that, in responding to demands for sexual performance, functionals and dysfunctionals respond with different affect. Whereas functionals respond with more positive than negative affect, dysfunctionals' responses are characterized by the self-report of negative affect or uninterest (Beck & Barlow, 1986b). The second difference is that functional males tend to show either a high correlation between subjective (self-report) and objective (physiological recording of penile tumescence) measures of arousal (Sakheim, Barlow, Beck, & Abrahamson, 1984) or overestimate erection levels (Abrahamson, Barlow, Sakheim, Beck, & Athanasiou, 1985), whereas dysfunctionals show a tendency to underestimate their level of erection (Abrahamson et al., 1985). Third, when presented with nonsexual stimuli while attending to erotic stimuli, functionals show an inhibition or decrement in erection while dysfunctional males evidence no decrement in erection under these presumably distracting conditions (Abrahamson et al., 1985). Fourth, when functional subjects are presented with laboratory tasks designed to operationalize the constructs of performance demand and spectatoring, their sexual arousal is either unaffected or facilitated, whereas dysfunctionals' arousal is inhibited (Barlow, Sakheim, & Beck, 1983). Fifth, increases in autonomic arousal or anxiety result in either a lack of inhibition or even facilitation in functionals, but a decrement in penile tumescence in response to anxiety is found in dysfunctionals (Beck, Barlow, Sakheim, & Abrahamson, 1984).

The key mechanisms proposed to account for these findings is a cognitive distraction process (Cranston-Cuebas & Barlow, 1990; Geer & Fuhr, 1976). At least under laboratory conditions, sexually functional subjects attend to erotic cues, and anything that draws their attention away from the erotic stimulus or their sexual arousal decreases their erection. If functional males are also subjected to situations designed to increase autonomic arousal or anxiety, they tend to interpret or misattribute the increased autonomic activity to sexual arousal, thereby increasing their over-all level of arousal. Dysfunctional subjects seem to be dysfunctional because they do not focus on erotic cues or stimuli but distract themselves with other concerns, such as whether they are achieving an adequate erection or whether their sexual performance is pleasing their partner.

One implication of the Barlow model is that treatment strategies for dysfunctional subjects aimed at the elimination of anxiety through the reduction of physiological arousal are inappropriate because the key variable is the focus of attention, an intrapersonal cognitive activity (Cranston-Cuebas & Barlow, 1990). Individuals who have sexual problems because they are anxious and focus not on sexual feelings and pleasurable sensations, but on their performance concerns, were said to be "spectatoring" (Masters & Johnson, 1970). Masters and Johnson as well as Kaplan (1974) regard anxiety as the common pathway of sexual dysfunctions. It is clear from Barlow's work that anxiety can inhibit or facilitate sexual arousal depending on how it influences the allocation of attention and how the autonomic activation is interpreted. Even if the theory has now been modified, sensate focus, a treatment developed by Masters and Johnson, is still relevant for coping with distraction. Under sensate focus instructions, individuals are told to focus on the pleasurable physical sensations produced by the partner's touch. The technique seeks to eliminate all performance demands by proscribing any sexual activity other than touching. Gradually the touching moves from nongenital to genital areas, but the central task is to stay mentally focused on the sensations and stop the process if any performance or task-irrelevant concerns or demands intrude. Sensate focus is a strategy used extensively by sex therapists to decrease anxiety and increase sexual pleasure, although the exact mechanisms by which it works have not been evaluated systematically. At the very least, it is a useful first step in decreasing cognitive distractions.

The procedure described to increase awareness of sexual fantasies, a sexual fantasy log, can also be used to identify cognitive distractions. By writing the sexual fantasy in as much detail as possible, sexually irrelevant or nonarousing thoughts and images can be noted, and patterns of how, when, and where the distractions occur can be observed. Because it is difficult to remember and write all the thoughts contained in a sexual fantasy, individuals can audiotape sexual fantasies as they occur or soon after. Taping may result in less loss of data because talking is faster

than writing. By listening to the recorded fantasies, one can determine the frequency, type, and stimuli that result in sexually irrelevant material. Roy became distracted from his sexual thoughts by images of his wife's flabby thighs. Focusing on a partner's imagined or real negative qualities is characteristic of people with sexual dysfunction, particularly low or hypoactive sexual desire (Knopf & Seiler, 1990). By focusing on the negative whenever sexual fantasies begin, gradually sexual thoughts become extinguished. Roy can, however, change his focus by being aware of his negative images and distracting himself from those images when they occur by imagining an arousing planned fantasy or picturing positive qualities of his partner. The key to the suggested exercises is developing the skills to increase awareness of the occurrence and content of sexual fantasies, learn to identify distracting and negative images and thoughts, and develop positive and arousing images to counter the negative ones.

## Coping with Sexually Illogical Beliefs

Cognitive therapists believe that many types of dysfunctional behavior are due to holding irrational beliefs, negative thoughts, or unrealistic perceptions (Beck, 1976; Beck & Emery, 1979; Ellis, 1975). Once these irrational beliefs are identified, one technique to teach the skill of using alternative cognitions or perceptions is cognitive restructuring.

The first step in cognitive restructuring, after the rationale has been provided, is to identify the client's negative thoughts and then to contrast the negative thoughts with positive, self-enhancing alternative thoughts (Cormier & Cormier, 1991). Roy told himself that Clara was no longer attracted to him and would not lose weight because she knew her being overweight kept Roy less interested in sex. These negative thoughts have the effect of turning off Roy's sexual thoughts and fantasies. They are irrational because he is drawing conclusions with no data to support them. Roy will benefit by shifting from self-defeating thoughts to positive self-statements, such as "I know Clara loves me but I wonder how I can help her feel better about herself," "I guess it is very difficult for Clara to lose weight—maybe I could help prepare some meals so she would be less tempted to snack," or "Clara isn't petite; she's a big, healthy, sexy woman." Roy should also practice reinforcing himself after he shifts to positive self-statements. Internal statements like "I'm getting better at seeing the bright side of my life," or "I feel better when I don't put myself or Clara down,'' reinforce the shift in thinking.

Clara is still sexually interested in Roy and also would like to increase the quality and quantity of the couple's sex life. Returning to Roy's homecoming scene, Clara's thoughts as she left the room were, ''He probably hates me! I just feel so useless and ugly!'' Clara's stream of consciousness demonstrates how quickly she accepts responsibility for the spoiled reunion and how readily she interprets Roy's lack of closeness as hating her. She could shift the nature of the interaction by making a more positive interpretation, such as, ''Roy really has had a rough day. It must be tough to have to deal with aggravating people all day with no one to confide in. I'm glad Roy trusts that our relationship is strong enough to let him blow off some steam without serious repercussions. I think I'll let him rest for half an hour and then see if he wants to talk about what is bothering him.'' This new interpretation focuses on the strength and trust in the relationship and on Clara's usefulness as a sounding board, and returns the responsibility for Roy's irritability to him rather than assigning it to Clara and Billy. Clara's cognitive change is an example of *reframing* (Cormier & Cormier, 1991). Reframing is based on the view that every behavior can be defined as adaptive or positive, given the right context. Reframing helps clients relabel a previously negative or disturbing behavior by perceiving it in a new context or frame.

## Identifying Sexual Desires and Preferences

One of the advantages of sexual fantasy is that anything sexual that can be conjured up can be experienced with no negative consequences, except those consequences that are self-imposed, such as guilt. As has been proposed throughout the chapter, attending to sexual fantasies provides information and choice to the fantasizer. Clearly, it is not being suggested that everything that is fantasized should be embellished, enjoyed, and acted on.

Most people engage in sexual fantasies, such as rape fantasies, that they do not want ever to experience. Despite not wanting actually to engage in the behavior, a person may have fantasies about rape that provide positive feelings and that may help the fantasizer learn more about his or her sexual wants and preferences if the fantasy is not interpreted literally. For males, fantasizing about forcing a woman to have sex who begins by protesting but ends by enjoying

the sex, may make the male feel powerful, in control, and a great lover (Klinger, 1990). Fantasies about forced sex are also a very common theme in women's sexual fantasies (Hariton & Singer, 1974; Pelletier & Herold, 1988). Rape fantasies do not indicate a desire to be raped but may be a way to achieve a feeling of control over a feared event (Gold, Balzano, & Stamey, 1991; Bond & Mosher, 1986), may indicate a desire for a man who takes charge or indicate a wish to be irresistible to men, or may be a way to engage in wanton sexuality without feeling responsible. By identifying the sexual wants underlying the force fantasies, the fantasizer can seek ways to satisfy their desires. Everyone at some time seeks reassurance about his or her attractiveness and lovemaking competence. Recognizing a desire for reassurance is the first step in finding a way to gain it from a partner. Safe sex games can be enacted on the basis of the preferences identified in fantasy. If one partner expresses a desire to feel in control, he or she can orchestrate the sexual encounter. If a partner wants to feel desired and adored, this can be developed into a sexual script enacted prior to lovemaking. The task is to identify the wants in the sexual fantasy and find a mutually acceptable, safe way to satisfy the preferences.

## Giving Oneself Permission to Be Sexual

We live in a society with an extremely ambivalent attitude toward human sexuality. On one hand, the media are more and more sexually explicit, and sex is used to sell a wide range of products. On the other hand, despite the constant sexual stimuli in the environment, there is no indication that children and adolescents are being educated or prepared to deal with their sexuality, as evidenced by the alarming rate of teen pregnancy and the continued high rate of sexually transmitted diseases, especially among youth (Gordon & Gordon, 1989). The majority of sexual messages youth receive are sex-negative in tone and prescription. It is not surprising that many people have a sex life hampered by feelings of shame and guilt. To overcome early negative messages about sex, learned when they could not be critically and logically examined, requires giving oneself permission to have an enjoyable sex life. This means having the choice to engage in sexual activities such as masturbation, reading erotica, and viewing X-rated movies—and being equally free not to do so. The skill development described in this chapter presumes that increased sexual skills are deemed worthwhile and that it is good to attend to sexual thoughts and fantasies. Thoughts and fantasies are not problematic by themselves unless they actualize into behavior that is illegal, harmful to oneself or others, or forced on an unwilling person. Sexual fantasies can enhance lovemaking by increasing arousal, can create more sexually receptive moods, can stimulate ideas to bring to lovemaking, and can help one learn more about the self and one's sexuality if permission is given to be sexual.

## INTERPERSONAL SKILLS

Thus far, the discussion has focused on the *intrapersonal* skills considered important for initiating positive sexual experiences. However, once the interpersonal sexual interaction is begun, there are numerous points at which the experience may be improved or hindered. The successful completion of a sexual interaction (and this may range from a good-night kiss to multiple orgasms during a night of lovemaking) depends in large part on the interaction of the people involved.

It has been proposed that interpersonal—that is, social—skills are useful in initiating events that lead to sexual interactions (see Gambrill, Chapter 12, this volume). For example, good communication skills are useful for meeting and getting to know potential lovers. Taking the skills-oriented approach one step further is the viewpoint that *interpersonal* sexual skills are also necessary (or at least very useful) for satisfying sexual interactions to occur. Thus, it may be heuristic to look at sexual problems and dysfunctions, at least in part, as stemming from sexual interpersonal skills deficits.

An interpersonal sexual skills approach to sexual functioning and dysfunction is not common in the sex research literature, for several reasons. First, there has been little empirical research, if any, on the specific interpersonal skills that are used in interpersonal sexual interactions. This type of study would obviously be difficult to carry out. For example, in a direct observational study, reactivity would be a primary concern, possibly limiting the validity of any results from an empirical study of sexual interactions. Additionally, social desirability and other confounds may make it difficult for clients to be completely forthright during such an assessment. Nonetheless, a task analysis of satisfying sexual encounters may reveal a common subset of interpersonal sexual skills that are useful in these encounters. Cooper, Heron,

and Howard (1987) have described a task analysis as having three primary segments:

1. The behavioral sequence of the task is broken down into constituent units, after which its validity is assessed.
2. A baseline assessment is conducted of a client's ability to perform each constituent element.
3. The client is taught the behavioral chain.

A task analysis of satisfying sexual encounters would involve assessing behaviors that occur from the start of the sexual phase of the encounter to the end of that phase. Whether such analyses would provide primarily nomothetic or ideographic information is unknown. It is possible that sexual interactions are very specific to the partners involved in an encounter. It may also be, however, that a subset of behaviors exists that is emitted during sexual encounters of different people. Some of the skills hypothesized to be useful in satisfying sexual encounters include the following: (1) assessing consent of partners; (2) nonsexual caressing; (3) sexual caressing (i.e., of breasts and genitals); (4) romantic verbalizations; (5) nonverbal cues indicating pleasure; (6) verbal cues indicating pleasure; (7) ability to request specific behaviors from partner; (8) reciprocation/sharing of pleasure-giving behaviors; (9) introduction of novelty/excitement/adventure into the sexual encounter; and (10) assessment of partner's reactions to different aspects of the sexual encounter. The point is that there are numerous interpersonal skills that could enhance sexual encounters or, if they are deficient or absent, could distract from encounters.

There are several benefits in taking a skills-oriented approach to enhance understanding of sexual problems and dysfunctions. The first potential advantage is that this theory suggests specific etiological and maintaining factors. At least some sexual behaviors appear to be learned. People often modify their behaviors during sexual interactions as they become more experienced. Thus, sexual dysfunctions may be due to behaviors that once were adaptive but are not any longer. For example, it may have been adaptive for a male to ejaculate quickly early in his sexual encounters (perhaps to avoid discovery), whereas later sexual encounters may be unsatisfying because of this behavior. Another etiological factor predicated by a skills-oriented approach would be that an individual has not yet learned certain interpersonal sexual skills (as opposed to having learned a certain behavior inadequately). For example, an individual may not have learned to monitor accurately, understand, and react to a partner's nonverbal cues during sexual interactions.

A second benefit of a skills-oriented approach is that certain treatment methods are suggested. As mentioned earlier in this chapter, training or retraining in interpersonal sexual skills may be useful with clients diagnosed with sexual dysfunctions.

Third, a skills-oriented approach recognizes the interdependency of both partners during sexual experiences and does not suggest that only one member of the couple is necessarily to blame. For example, if one member of a couple is too rough (or too gentle) during lovemaking, this may not be a problem unless the other member has poor communication skills and is unable to convey how she or he would prefer to be touched.

Fourth, a skills-oriented approach allows for clear operationalization of the problem and treatment. Rather than focusing on possible psychological problems that "inhibit" individuals during sexual encounters, as does the DSM-III-R (American Psychiatric Association [APA], *Diagnostic and Statistical Manual of Mental Disorders,* third edition, revised; 1987), a skills-oriented approach focuses on overt behaviors (or lack thereof) that may have caused or are maintaining the problem. These skills then may be targeted for treatment.

## SEXUAL DYSFUNCTIONS FROM A SKILLS-ORIENTED APPROACH

In order to develop more fully the viewpoint that sexual dysfunctions may be due to interpersonal skills deficits, sexual dysfunctions (as defined in the DSM-III-R) will be reviewed. For each dysfunction, a skills-oriented approach will be suggested regarding etiological and/or maintaining factors.

1.  Hypoactive Sexual Desire Disorder involves absence of sexual fantasies and desires (APA, 1987). As noted previously, intrapersonal skills deficits (i.e., poor sexual fantasy skills) may play a primary role in this dysfunction. A lack of sexual fantasy and desire may also develop toward one's partner as a result of poor interpersonal skills. For example, partners may present themselves in an "unappealing" manner (e.g., poor hygiene) or may have other interpersonal deficits that mitigate pleasure during sexual interactions and lead to a lack of desire. During previous sexual interactions, the partner may have failed to notice cues that indicated pleasure or displeasure. In

more extreme cases, these deficits may lead to an aversion toward sexual interactions—for example, if one partner lacks monitoring skills to help determine whether the sexual stimulation was actually painful for his or her partner.

2.  Female Sexual Arousal Disorder involves failure to attain or maintain vaginal lubrication during sexual activities (APA, 1987). The inadequate (e.g., too rough or too light) skills of the partner during stimulation of the vaginal area may be of primary importance. This may be combined with poor interpersonal monitoring skills of the female such that she does not position herself for adequate vaginal stimulation.

3.  Male Erectile Disorder involves failure to attain or to maintain erection to completion of the sexual activity (APA, 1987). A partner may inadequately stimulate the male or may attempt vaginal insertion before he is ready. Likewise, the male may attempt vaginal entry before his partner is adequately lubricated, making it more difficult to maintain an erection.

4.  Inhibited Female Orgasm involves the inability to achieve orgasm after sexual excitement has been experienced, when this is not due to inadequate stimulation by the partner or does not occur during masturbation (APA, 1987). The argument that the usefulness and validity of the stipulation that inadequate stimulation may not be considered an etiological factor for excitation and orgasm disorders is unfounded. In fact, it seems that at least a subset of clients with this dysfunction may be receiving inadequate genital stimulation from their partners. Another possible interpersonal skills deficit may be the inability of the partner to convey (verbally and/or nonverbally) that he wants the female to achieve orgasm or is concerned about whether or not this happens.

5.  Inhibited Male Orgasm involves delayed or absent orgasm (APA, 1987). With this disorder, it is possible that the partner fails to monitor accurately which stage of arousal the male is in and may miss cues that indicate imminent orgasm. If this is the case, she may accidentally behave so as to decrease the stimulation of the male. Alternatively, the male may not position himself for adequate control during intercourse, thus lessening his ability to achieve orgasm. It is also possible that the male previously learned not to ejaculate inside the female as an early

method of birth control, and now finds it difficult to overcome this pattern in situations where intravaginal ejaculation is permissible and perhaps desired.

6.   Premature Ejaculation involves ejaculation before the individual or his partner so desires (APA, 1987). As suggested previously, it may be that the male learned to ejaculate quickly early in his sexual experiences. Additionally, the female may not adequately assess the male's level of arousal and may overstimulate him accidentally.

7.   Finally, Dyspareunia and Vaginismus may be due, in part, to the technique of both partners during intercourse. For example, a partner may thrust too hard or not wait for enough lubrication before entering his partner, thus causing her pain. Partners may also misread cues that indicate pain on entry and therefore may fail to modify their behavior accordingly.

## TREATMENT

These suggestions regarding skills deficits for particular dysfunctions lead directly to specific interventions (e.g., improving genital stimulation techniques, improving the ability to monitor accurately the partner's level of enjoyment, and communication skills). However, interpersonal sexual skills often may be overlooked during therapy because of difficulties inherent in teaching interpersonal sexual skills. Simple oral description from a therapist to a client couple may be an ineffective method for communicating interpersonal sexual skills such as monitoring partner's arousal levels. These types of interpersonal skills are likely to be complex and to consist of component skills that are difficult to describe adequately. Films and books may be more useful but also may not be specific to the needs of a particular client couple. Finally, sexual skills may be easier to learn in an apprenticeship mode than via oral or written communication. However, the use of sexual surrogates to teach sexual skills has been generally dismissed as unethical and possibly even abusive to both the client and the surrogate (Malatesta & Adams, 1986; Ruff & St. Lawrence, 1985).

Appropriate assessment of the problem is also a difficult task. It seems likely that reactivity would be high during initial assessment and that social desirability (e.g., a desire on the part of couples to show improvement) could undermine outcome assessment.

Despite these difficulties, Masters and Johnson (1970) devised treatments for different sexual dysfunctions that include development and modification of skills designed to enhance sexual interactions. Although Masters and Johnson specify different techniques depending on the primary sexual dysfunction being targeted, there is a sequencing of techniques that is similar across dysfunctions.

The initial component of the Masters and Johnson (1970) therapy is the inclusion of "sensate focus," where the partners are instructed to touch each other in a "nondemanding" manner (that is, with the focus not including the end goal of orgasm or ejaculation). During this time, partners are instructed to concentrate on either receiving or giving pleasure and to be specific about what type of touching they prefer. With this focus, couples can learn interpersonal skills such as communication about sexual matters and may develop the ability to recognize and respond to nonverbal cues given by their partner.

After a few sessions of nongenital sensate focus, contact with genitalia is permitted. At this point, the partner who is experiencing the sexual dysfunction receives stimulation from his or her partner and is instructed to be specific about the type of stimulation that is most pleasurable and to focus on the sensations engendered by stimulation of the genital areas. For example, with Premature Ejaculation, the female partner is instructed to stimulate the male until he is close to the point of ejaculation, at which point she squeezes his penis or just stops stimulation until erection is lost in order to reduce that urge. These methods may allow the male partner to learn when ejaculation is imminent and (coupled with other techniques) to control the timing of ejaculation, and may teach the female partner better ways of controlling the rate of her partner's sexual arousal.

After several sessions of manual stimulation, nondemanding intromission is incorporated into the treatment plan. Initially, there is simply containment of the penis in the vagina and then the woman on top moves slowly, stopping and/or using the squeeze technique when ejaculation is imminent. Eventually, the man begins to move with the woman, and orgasm is incorporated into the sexual interactions.

Although this is a very general outline of the Masters and Johnson (1970) treatment program, it illustrates the importance of interpersonal skills in developing and maintaining pleasurable sexual encounters. Further, it is these behavioral components of the Masters and Johnson (1970) program that have been frequently employed by other therapists, with generally beneficial results (Hawton, 1982; Kaplan, 1979; Knopf & Seiler, 1990; McCarthy, 1989). However, few if any therapists report "cure rates" of the magnitude reported by Masters and Johnson (1970) (see Zilbergeld & Evans, 1980, for a critique of Masters and Johnson). In addition, some "sexual dysfunctions" have only recently been identified in the DSM-III-R, and outcome research on these dysfunctions (i.e., Hypoactive Sexual Desire Disorder and Sexual Aversion Disorder) is generally lacking (Gold & Gold, in press; Letourneau & O'Donohue, in press). Nonetheless, extant research concerning the treatment of sexual dysfunctions does seem to point to the importance of including behavior (both intra- and interpersonal) skills training (Letourneau & O'Donohue, in press; Malatesta & Adams, 1986; O'Donohue, Letourneau, & Geer, in press) of both partners.

It may be necessary for the interpersonal and intrapersonal skills used in sexual encounters to be subjected to a task analysis in order to attain a better understanding of sexual functioning and dysfunctions. As stated before, these skills often are complex and may comprise several component skills of which there is little empirical knowledge. Again, there are difficulties inherent in gathering relevant data given the private nature of sexual encounters. Nonetheless, a skills-oriented approach to the problem of sexual dysfunction calls for more detailed assessment of sexual functioning than perhaps is the norm. This may provide information necessary to the further development of skills training in this area.

## REFERENCES

Abrahamson, D. J., Barlow, D. H., Sakheim, D. K., Beck, J. G., & Athanasiou, R. (1985). Effects of distraction on sexual responding in functional and dysfunctional men. *Behavior Therapy, 16,* 503–515.

Allgeier, E. R., & Allgeier, A. R. (1991). *Sexual interactions,* 3rd ed. Lexington, MA: D. C. Heath.

American Psychiatric Association (1985). *Diagnostic and statistical manual of mental disorders,* 3rd ed. Washington, DC: Author.

American Psychiatric Association (1987). *Diagnostic and statistical manual of mental disorders,* 3rd ed., rev. Washington, DC: Author.

Annon, J. S. (1976). *Behavioral treatment of sexual problems.* New York: Harper & Row.

Barbach, L. (1984). *Pleasures: Women write erotica.* New York: Doubleday.

Barbach, L. (1986). *Erotic interludes.* New York: Doubleday.

Barlow, D. (1986). Causes of sexual dysfunction. *Journal of Consulting and Clinical Psychology, 54,* 140–148.

Barlow, D. H., Sakheim, D. K., & Beck, J. G. (1983). Anxiety increases sexual arousal. *Journal of Abnormal Psychology, 92,* 49–54.

Beck, A. T. (1976). *Cognitive therapy and the emotional disorders.* New York: International Universities Press.

Beck, A. T., & Emery, G. (1979). *Cognitive therapy of anxiety.* Philadelphia: Center for Cognitive Therapy.

Beck, J. G., & Barlow, D. H. (1986a). The effects of anxiety and attentional focus on sexual responding—I. Physiological patterns in erectile dysfunction. *Behaviour Research and Therapy, 24,* 9–17.

Beck, J. G., & Barlow, D. H. (1986b). The effects of anxiety and attentional focus on sexual responding—II. Cognitive and affective patterns in erectile dysfunctions. *Behaviour Research and Therapy, 24,* 19–26.

Beck, J. G., Barlow, D. H., Sakheim, D. K., & Abrahamson, D. J. (1984). *A cognitive processing account of anxiety and sexual arousal: The role of selective attention, thought content, and affective states.* Paper presented at the annual convention of the American Psychological Association, Toronto.

Bond, S. B., & Mosher, D. L. (1986). Guided imagery of rape: Fantasy, reality, and the willing victim myth. *Journal of Sex Research, 22,* 162–183.

Bower, G. H. (1981). Mood and memory. *American Psychologist, 36,* 129–148.

Brown, J. B., & Hart, D. H. (1977). Correlates of females' sexual fantasies. *Perceptual and Motor Skills, 45,* 819–824.

Carlson, E. R., & Coleman, C. E. (1977). Experimental and motivational determinants of the richness of an induced sexual fantasy. *Journal of Personality, 45*(4), 528–542.

Catania, A. C. (1992). *Learning.* Englewood Cliffs, NJ: Prentice-Hall.

Chick, D., & Gold, S. R. (1987–1988). A review of influences on sexual fantasy: Attitudes, experience, guilt, and gender. *Imagination, Cognition, and Personality, 7,* 61–76.

Cooper, J. O., Heron, T. E., & Heward, W. L. (1987). *Applied behavior analysis.* Columbus, OH: Merrill.

Cormier, W. H., & Cormier, L. S. (1991). *Interviewing strategies for helpers,* 3rd ed. Pacific Grove, CA: Brooks/Cole.

Cranston-Cuebas, M. A., & Barlow, D. H. (1990). Cognitive and affective contributions to sexual functioning. In J. Bancroft, C. M. Davis, & D. Weinstein (Eds.), *Annual review of sex research,* (Vol. 1, pp. 119–162). Lake Mills, IA: Society for the Scientific Study of Sex.

Darling, C. A., & Hicks, M. W. (1983). Recycling parental sexual messages. *Journal of Sex and Marital Therapy, 9,* 233–243.

D'Augelli, A. D., & D'Augelli, J. F. (1985). The enhancement of sexual skills and competence: Promoting lifelong sexual unfolding. In L. L'Abate & M. A. Milan (Eds.)

*Handbook of social skills training and research* (pp. 170–191). New York: Wiley.

Davenport, W. H. (1987). An anthropological approach. In J. Geer & W. O'Donohue (Eds.), *Theories of human sexuality* (pp. 197–236). New York: Plenum Press.

Davidson, J. K., & Hoffman, L. E. (1986). Sexual fantasies and sexual satisfaction: An empirical analysis of erotic thought. *Journal of Sex Research, 22,* 184–205.

DeLamater, J. (1987). A sociological approach. In J. M. Friedman & D. R. Hogan, (1985). Sexual dysfunction: Low sexual desire. In D. H. Barlow (Ed.), *Clinical handbook of psychological disorders.* New York: Guilford Press.

Ellis, A. (1975). *Growth through reason.* North Hollywood, CA: Wilshire.

Freud, S. (1962). *The interpretation of dreams.* In The Standard Edition of the Complete Psychological Works, Vols. IV, V. London: Hogarth.

Friday, N. (1973). *My secret garden: Women's sexual fantasies.* New York: Pocket Books.

Friday, N. (1975). *Forbidden flowers: More women's sexual fantasies.* New York: Pocket Books.

Friday, N. (1980). *Men in love: Men's sexual fantasies— The triumph of love over rage.* New York: Delacorte.

Gagnon, J. H., & Simon, W. (1973). *Sexual conduct.* Chicago: Aldine.

Geer, J. H., & Fuhr, R. (1976). Cognitive factors in sexual arousal: The role of distraction. *Journal of Consulting and Clinical Psychology, 44,* 238–243.

Geer, J. H., & O'Donohue, W. (1987). *Theories of human sexuality.* New York: Plenum Press, pp. 237–256.

Giambra, L. M., & Martin, C. E. (1977). Sexual daydreams and quantitative aspects of sexual activity: Some relations for males across adulthood. *Archives of Sexual Behavior, 6,* 497–505.

Gold, R., & Gold, S. (1982). Sex differences in actual daydream content. *Journal of Mental Imagery, 6* (2), 109–112.

Gold, S. R. (1991). History of child sexual abuse and adult sexual fantasies. *Violence and Victims, 6,* 75–82.

Gold, S. R., Balzano, B. F., & Stamey, R. (1991). Two studies of females' sexual force fantasies. *Journal of Sex Education & Therapy, 17,* 15–26.

Gold, S. R., & Chick, D. A. (1988). Sexual fantasy patterns as related to sexual attitude, experience, guilt and sex. *Journal of Sex Education and Therapy, 14,* 18–23.

Gold, S., & Gold, R. (1993). Sexual aversion: A hidden disorder. In W. T. O'Donohue & J. H. Geer (Eds.), *Handbook of sexual dysfunctions.* Boston: Allyn and Bacon.

Gold, S. R., & Reilly, J. P. III. (1985–1986). Daydreaming, self-concept and academic performance. *Imagination, Cognition and Personality, 5,* 117–125.

Goldstein, A. P. (1981). *Psychological skill training.* New York: Pergamon Press.

Gordon, S., & Gordon, J. (1989). *Raising a child conservatively in a sexually permissive word.* New York: Simon & Schuster.

Graber, B. (1981). Demystifying "sex therapy." *American Journal of Psychotherapy, 35,* 481–488.

Hardin, K. N., & Gold, S. R. (1988–1989). Relationship of sex, sex guilt, and experience to written sexual fantasies. *Imagination, Cognition and Personality, 8,* 155–163.

Hariton, E. B., & Singer, J. L. (1974). Women's fantasies during marital intercourse: Normative and theoretical implications. *Journal of Consulting and Clinical Psychology, 2*(8), 50–56.

Hawton, K. (1982). The behavioral treatment of sexual dysfunctions. *British Journal of Psychiatry, 140,* 94–104.

Heiman, J. R., & LoPiccolo, J. (1988). *Becoming orgasmic.* Englewood Cliffs, NJ: Prentice-Hall.

Ingram, R. E. (1990). Self-focused attention in clinical disorders: Review and a conceptual model. *Psychological Bulletin, 107,* 156–176.

Kaplan, H. S. (1974). *The new sex therapy.* New York: Brunner/Mazel.

Kaplan, H. S. (1979). *Disorders of sexual desire.* New York: Brunner/Mazel.

Kazdin, A. E. (1974). Reactive self-monitoring: The effects of response desirability, goal setting, and feedback. *Journal of Consulting and Clinical Psychology, 42,* 704–716.

Kazdin, A. E. (1976). Assessment of imagery during covert modeling of assertive behavior. *Journal of Behavior Therapy and Experimental Psychiatry, 7,* 213–219.

Klinger, E. (1971). *Structure and functions of fantasy.* New York: Wiley.

Klinger, E. (1990). *Daydreaming: Using waking fantasy and imagery for self-knowledge and creativity.* Los Angeles: Jeremy P. Tarcher.

Klinger, E., Barta, S. G., & Maxeiner, M. E. (1980). Motivational correlates of thought content frequency and commitment. *Journal of Personality and Social Psychology, 39,* 1222–1237.

Knafo, D., & Jaffe, Y. (1984). Sexual fantasizing in males and females. *Journal of Research in Personality, 18,* 451–462.

Knopf, J., & Seiler, M. (1990). *ISD: Inhibited sexual desire.* New York: William Morrow.

Lazarus, A. (1977). *In the mind's eye.* New York: Rawson.

Lazarus, A. A., & Abramovitz, A. (1962). The use of "emotive imagery" in the treatment of children's phobias. *Journal of Mental Science, 108,* 191–195.

Letourneau, E. J., & O'Donohue, W. T. (1993). Assessment and treatment of Inhibited Sexual Desire Disorder. In W. T. O'Donohue & J. H. Geer (Eds.), *Handbook of sexual dysfunctions.* Boston: Allyn and Bacon.

LoPiccolo, J. (1978). Direct treatment of sexual dysfunction. In J. LoPiccolo & L. LoPiccolo (Eds.), *Handbook of sex therapy.* New York: Plenum Press.

MacKinnon, C. A. (1987). A feminist/political approach: Pleasure under patriarchy. In J. Geer & W. O'Donohue (Eds.), *Theories of human sexuality* (pp. 65–90). New York: Plenum Press.

Malatesta, V. J., & Adams, H. E. (1986). Assessment of sexual behavior. In A. R. Ciminero, K. S. Calhoun, & H.

E. Adams (Eds.), *Handbook of behavioral assessment,* 2nd ed. New York: Wiley.

Marquis, J. N. (1970). Orgasonic reconditioning: Changing sexual object choice through controlling masturbation fantasies. *Journal of Behavior Therapy and Experimental Psychiatry, 1,* 262–264.

Marshall, W. L. (1979). Satiation therapy: A procedure for reducing deviant sexual arousal. *Journal of Applied Behavior Analysis, 12,* 377–389.

Masters, W., & Johnson, V. (1970). *Human sexual inadequacy.* Boston: Little, Brown.

McCarthy, B. W. (1989). Cognitive-behavioral strategies and techniques in the treatment of early ejaculation. In S. Leiblum & R. Rosen (Eds.), *Principles and practices of sex therapy.* New York: Guilford Press.

McCauley, C., & Swann, C. P. (1980). Male and female differences in sexual fantasy. *Journal of Research in Personality, 12*(1), 76–86.

McConaghy, N. (1987). A learning approach. In J. Geer & W. O'Donohue (Eds.), *Theories of human sexuality* (pp. 287–334). New York: Plenum Press.

McFall, R. M. (1982). A review and reformulation of the concept of social skills. *Behavioral Assessment, 4,* 1–33.

Money, J. (1983). Sexology: Behavioral, cultural, hormonal, neurological, genetic, etc. *Journal of Sex Research, 9,* 3–10.

Muehlenhard, C. L., & Cook, S. W. (1988). Men's self-reports of unwanted sexual activity. *Journal of Sex Research, 24,* 58–72.

Nelson, R. O. (1977). Methodological issues in assessment via self-monitoring. In J. D. Cone & R. P. Hawkins (Eds.), *Behavioral assessment: New directions in clinical psychology* (pp. 217–254). New York: Brunner/Mazel.

O'Donohue, W., Letourneau, E. J., & Geer, J. H. (in press). Assessment and treatment of premature ejaculation. In W. T. O'Donohue & J. H. Geer (Eds.), *Handbook of sexual dysfunctions.* Needham Heights, MA: Allyn and Bacon.

O'Donohue, W., & Plaud, J. J. (in press). *The conditioning of human sexual arousal.* Archives of Sexual Behavior.

Pelletier, L. A., & Herold, E. S. (1988). The relationship of age, sex guilt, and sexual experience with female sexual fantasies. *Journal of Sex Research, 24,* 250–256.

Ruff, G. A., & St. Lawrence, J. S. (1985). Past research progress, future directions. *Clinical Psychology Review, 5,* 627–639.

Sakheim, D. K., Barlow, D. H., Beck, J. G., & Abrahamson, D. J. (1984). The effect of an increased awareness of erectile cues on sexual arousal. *Behaviour Research and Therapy, 22,* 151–158.

Schlundt, D. G., & McFall, R. M. (1985). New directions in the assessment of social competence and social skills. In L. L'Abate & M. Milan (Eds.), *Handbook of social skills training and research.* New York: Wiley.

Serbin, L. A., & Sprafkin, C. H. (1987). A developmental approach: Sexuality from infancy through adolescence. In J. Geer & W. O'Donohue (Eds.), *Theories of human sexuality* (pp. 163–196). New York: Plenum Press.

Shorr, J. E. (1977). *Go see the movie in your head.* New York: Popular Library.

Singer, J. L., & Pope, K. S. (Eds.) (1978). *The power of human imagination: New methods in psychotherapy.* New York: Plenum Press.

Skinner, B. F. (1988). The phylogeny and ontogeny of behavior. In A. Catania & S. Harnad (Eds.), *The selection of behavior: The operant behaviorism of B. F. Skinner* (pp. 382–400). Cambridge: Cambridge University Press.

Spiess, W. F. J., Geer, J. H., & O'Donohue, W. (1984). Premature ejaculation: An investigation of factors in ejaculatory latency. *Journal of Abnormal Psychology, 93,* 242–245.

Tannen, D. (1990). *You just don't understand.* New York: William Morrow.

Teague, R. G., & Gold, S. R. (1981). Increasing attention to daydreaming by self-monitoring. *Journal of Clinical Psychology, 37,* 538–541.

Thoresen, C. E., & Mahoney, M. J. (1974). *Behavioral self-control.* New York: Holt, Rinehart and Winston.

Warshaw, R., & Parrot, A. (1991). The contribution of sex role socialization to acquaintance rape. In A. Parrot & I. Bechhofer (Eds.), *Acquaintance rape: The hidden crime* (pp. 73–82). New York: Wiley.

Wegner, D. M. (1989). *White bears and other unwanted thoughts.* New York: Viking Press.

Wiseman, J. P. (1976). *The social psychology of sex.* New York: Harper & Row.

Zilbergeld, B. (1978). *Male sexuality: A guide to sexual fulfillment.* New York: Banton.

Zilbergeld, B., & Evans, M. (1980). The inadequacy of Masters and Johnson. *Psychology Today, 14,* 29–34.

# CHAPTER 12

# HELPING SHY, SOCIALLY ANXIOUS, AND LONELY ADULTS: A SKILL-BASED CONTEXTUAL APPROACH

Eileen Gambrill

Loneliness is a common problem. About 11% to 26% of individuals complain of loneliness (Peplau, Russell, & Heim, 1979). As much as 25% of the adult population in the United States report that they have felt intensely lonely during the past two weeks (Bradburn, 1969). These figures may be underestimates given that a reluctance to view oneself (or to be viewed by others) as having social problems may discourage candid reports of loneliness (Rook, 1990). Thus, some people who report few social contacts but claim they are content with the few they have may be misreporting their feelings about these few contacts. Loneliness has been linked with a variety of presenting problems, including depression, substance abuse, adolescent delinquency, aggressiveness, physical illness, and suicide (Asher & Cole, 1990; Peplau & Perlman, 1982a, 1982b; Lynch, 1977). This is not surprising given the many provisions of relationships, including (1) attachment, resulting in a sense of safety and security; (2) social integration (shared interests and concerns with others); (3) opportunities to nurture others; (4) reassurance of worth through acknowledgment of skills and abilities; (5) reliable alliance (can count on assistance); and (6) guidance (provision of advice and assistance) (Weiss, 1974) (see also Rook, 1984a). There also has been a great interest in the relationship between social support and a variety of stress-induced illnesses (see, e.g., Sarason, Sarason, & Pierce, 1990).

The experience of shyness is also common. About 90% of Americans report feelings of shyness sometimes, and 50% report that shyness is at times a significant problem (Zimbardo, 1977). About 36% of currently shy individuals report that they have been shy since early childhood (see Cheek & Melchior, 1990). Cultural values influence the prevalence of shyness, as well as whether shyness is viewed as a problem or as an asset. Zimbardo (1977) found that shyness was most widespread in Japan, Taiwan, and Hawaii and most infrequently found among Israelis and American Jews. The percentages of individuals from these different countries who considered themselves shy were 60%, 55%, 60%, 31%, and 24%, respectively. Here, too, as with loneliness, people may be reluctant to describe themselves as shy. A review of 636 letters received by a BBC television station following a program about shyness indicated that some people did not reveal their shyness because of fears about negative reactions (Harris, 1984). They felt that shyness was not a "genuine" problem and so concealed it from others as best they could. Most had adopted a self-help approach. Interpersonal problems reported by shy people include difficulty in meeting people and making friends, anxiety, depression, loneliness, and excessive self-consciousness (Zimbardo, Pilkonis, & Norwood, 1975).

Anxiety in social situations such as initiating conversations or speaking in public results in lost opportunities for positive exchanges and often interferes with success in work situations (Liebowitz, Gorman, Fyer, & Klein, 1985). Between 20% and 41% of people report that they experience some performance anxiety or discomfort in social situations. This anxiety often results in avoidance of such situations (Curran, 1977; Zimbardo, 1977). Individuals who experience generalized social anxiety report continuous rather than episodic physiological arousal. Social isolation is associated with psychopathology as well as with mortality due to suicide and alcoholism. Advice to the shy, lonely, and socially anxious in newspaper columns and the popularity of self-help books on these topics attests to the prevalence of these concerns (see, e.g., Phillips, 1989; Zimbardo, 1977; Zimbardo & Radl, 1983). Dating services, singles groups of various kinds, and the use of personal ads seem to be increasing as well. Here, too, as with shyness, cultural factors influence how given kinds of social anxiety are viewed. For example, Gilbert and Trower (1990) point out that declaring oneself a Type A person who neglects his or her emotional ties with others may be viewed as positive—that a "serious difficulty [lack of intimately relating to others] can be paraded as evidence of a positive self in a culture that is competitive . . ." (p. 171). These authors view a fear of compassion, love, and vulnerable desire as forms of social anxiety.

Research concerning shyness, lack of assertion, timidity, dating anxiety, public-speaking anxiety, communication avoidance and apprehension, social reticence, embarrassment, social anxiety, social phobia, social support, loneliness, and social isolation has proceeded fairly independently. *Reticence* has been defined as the avoidance of communication by people who believe they will lose more by talking than by remaining silent (Phillips, 1984, p. 52). Only recently has some of the research in the areas of social isolation, social support, social skills, and loneliness been pulled together (Hansson, Jones & Carpenter, 1984; Rook, 1984a, 1984c). Systematic research on loneliness is one of the newest entries into the field and has

resulted in a rich output of information relevant to helping clients (see, e.g., Hojat & Crandall, 1989; Jones, Rose, & Russell, 1990; Peplau & Perlman, 1982a). Research concerning shyness and social phobia has increased greatly over the past years (see, e.g., Heimberg, 1989; Jones, Cheek, & Briggs, 1986; Scholing & Emmelkamp, 1990). Some studies focus on clearly defined samples of social phobics. Others focus on self-selected samples, such as individuals who report a low frequency of dating. Indirect approaches used with people who are unlikely to participate in programs designed to increase social contacts may avoid labels such as shyness, loneliness, or social anxiety (see later discussion). Here, too, different areas of inquiry have often proceeded separately. For example, literature describing programs designed to decrease anxiety in dating situations has not been integrated with research describing programs designed to increase social contacts in nondating situations.

This chapter presents an overview of assessment and intervention guidelines for helping shy, socially phobic or anxious, and lonely clients. The chapter focuses on the role of skill development. Relevant terms are first clarified. Correlates of shyness, loneliness, social anxiety, social phobia, and social isolation are reviewed, and the interrelationships among these complaints are discussed. This is followed by an overview of personal and environmental factors related to the development and persistence of loneliness, shyness, and social anxiety. Assessment options are reviewed, followed by a description of intervention methods and evaluation measures.

## CLARIFICATION OF TERMS

Loneliness, shyness, and social anxiety have been variously viewed as transitory, emotional states as well as more enduring traits. They have been described as unitary constructs as well as constructs that can be divided into different subtypes (Jones et al., 1990). Buss (1986) distinguishes between an early-developing or fearful shyness (shyness that has a genetic component) and later-developing self-consciousness that starts in adolescence. The latter includes feelings of being awkward, foolish, and vulnerable rather than fearfulness. Transitory shyness is common and is situationally related. More enduring shyness may affect behavior across a range of situations. Many associations have been found among loneliness, shyness, and social anxiety, as discussed in a later section. Loneliness is a subjective experience: "the unpleasant experience that occurs when a person's network of social relations is deficient in some important way, either quantitatively or qualitatively" (Perlman & Peplau, 1981, p. 31). Rook (1984c) defines loneliness as "an enduring condition of emotional distress that arises when a person feels estranged from, misunderstood, or rejected by others and/or lacks appropriate social partners for desired activities, particularly activities that provide a source of social integration and opportunities for emotional intimacy" (p. 1391). Thus, there are different kinds of loneliness: "for some people a disturbing and persistent core of separateness from others is the core of loneliness; whereas for others loneliness arises from the repeated disappointment of having to forgo activities that depend on the participation of another person" (Rook, 1984c, p. 1391). However, as Rook points out, these kinds of loneliness may occur together—some people lack companions and also feel different from or misunderstood by others.

Social isolation is defined mainly in terms of time spent with others. Social isolates have been defined as individuals who have few social contacts and who are happy with the few they have. Weiss (1973) distinguishes between emotional isolation loneliness (one does not have companionship with another person) and social isolation loneliness (a feeling of not belonging; of not being a member of a social network). Thus, it is generally agreed that loneliness results from inadequacies in social relationships; in particular, it is related to the quality of social contacts rather than the sheer frequency of contacts. Each individual has an optimal level of social contact that may vary at different times over the life cycle. When this falls below a certain level, loneliness may be experienced. Loneliness should be distinguished from social isolation; one can be socially isolated (have a low frequency of social contacts) but not be lonely.

Social anxiety (discomfort in social situations) has been investigated under many different terms, including "dating anxiety," "stage fright," "shyness," "social phobia," and "communication apprehension." Shyness is indistinguishable from social anxiety on a measurement level and is broader than more specific kinds of anxiety such as stage fright and dating anxiety (Anderson & Harvey, 1988). Most investigators consider shyness to be one form of social anxiety, along with audience anxiety, embarrassment, and shame (Edelman, 1987). Shyness is characterized by a reluctance to initiate social exchanges and a subjective experience of anxiety in

social situations with resultant awkward behavior (see Jones, Cheek, & Briggs, 1986). It has been viewed as both a state and a trait. There is an inhibition in the presence of others as well as discomfort related to self-focused attention, especially the possibility of negative evaluation. Shyness is related to other kinds of social anxiety such as embarrassment, shame, and audience anxiety (anxiety while speaking or performing in front of a group of spectators). Some writers use the terms *shyness* and *social anxiety* synonymously. Others distinguish between these and emphasize the behavioral-inhibition aspect of shyness. Buss (1980) argued that all these states share an origin in the experience of acute public awareness. A performance is (or was) expected, and there is (or was) a discrepancy in relation to what occurs (or has occurred). Embarrassment and shame are considered to be temporary uncomfortable reactions that arise when there is a discrepancy between one's self-presentation and one's standards (Crozier, 1990). Correlations between measures of shyness and measures of audience anxiety are about .45. Leary (1986) defines *shyness* as "an affective-behavioral syndrome characterized by social anxiety and interpersonal inhibition that results from the prospect or presence of interpersonal evaluation" (p. 30). Others argue that this definition fails to distinguish between three components of shyness: (1) *somatic anxiety* (upset stomach, pounding heart, sweating, trembling, and blushing, which are experienced by only some shy people); (2) *cognitive symptoms* (e.g., worry about negative evaluations); and (3) *awkward social behavior* (Cheek & Watson, 1989). Not all shy people avoid social situations; they may be anxious performers (Gambrill & Richey, 1975). An everyday-language definition of shyness as a trait is "the tendency to feel tense, worried, or awkward during social interactions, especially with strangers" (Cheek, Melchior, & Carpentieri, 1986). The greater the sociability (the degree of interest in interacting with others), the more discomfort may result from shyness because of conflicting motivation (approach and avoidance) (Cheek & Melchior, 1990). As with all behaviors, the distinction between learning and performance is relevant. That is, people may have the skills to succeed in a situation but may not use these skills because of a variety of factors, such as high anxiety.

A multi-response view of anxiety includes cognitive, affective, physiological, and behavioral components (Eifert & Wilson, 1991). Some investigators, such as Bandura (1986), believe that inclusion of cognitive and behavioral indicators in the definition of anxiety confounds the perceived causes and effects of anxiety. He defined *anxiety* as a state of anticipatory apprehension concerning possible negative consequences. The term *social phobia,* unlike the term *social anxiety,* has a fairly rigorous definition. According to the *Diagnostic and Statistical Manual of Mental Disorders,* third edition, revised (DSM-III-R; 1987), seven of the following criteria must be met to receive a diagnosis of social phobia:

1. A persistent fear of one or more situations in which the person is exposed to possible scrutiny by others. Essential is the fear to act in a way that will be embarrassing or humiliating.
2. The fear may not have any relation to another Axis I or III disorder (if present). This criterion states that fear of trembling caused by Parkinson's disease is not social phobia. In case panic disorder is also present, the fear of having a panic attack in social situations is not diagnosed as social phobia.
3. Exposure to the phobic stimulus almost invariably provokes an anxiety response.
4. Mostly, the situation is avoided or, if that is not possible, is endured with intense anxiety.
5. As a consequence of the avoidance behavior, problems exist in occupational functioning or in usual social relationships.
6. The individual has to recognize his or her fears as unreasonable or excessive.
7. If the person is under 18, the disorder does not meet criteria for avoidant disorder of childhood/adolescence (American Psychiatric Association, 1987, p. 243).

Anxiety when being observed by others while performing a task (e.g., talking in public, participating in a conversation) is a hallmark of social phobia (Marks, 1969). There is a fear of being evaluated and criticized by others. Social anxiety distracts attention away from performance, often hampering success (Heimberg & Barlow, 1988). Social phobias may be generalized or limited to a few situations (Heimberg, Hope, Dodge, & Becker, 1988). Examples of common social phobic situations include the following (Holt, 1992). Items were selected from the Liebowitz Social Phobia Scale (Liebowitz, 1987).

*Formal speaking and interaction:*
  Acting, performing or giving a talk in front of audience
  Giving a report to a group

  Speaking up at a meeting
  Participating in small groups
*Informal speaking and interaction:*
  Trying to pick up someone
  Going to a party
  Giving a party
  Meeting strangers
  Calling someone you don't know very well
*Assertive interaction:*
  Talking to people in authority
  Expressing a disagreement or disapproval to people you don't know very well
  Returning goods to a store
  Resisting a high pressure salesperson
*Observation of behavior:*
  Working while being observed
  Writing while being observed
  Eating in public places
  Drinking in public places

Estimates of the prevalence of social phobia in the general population runs from 1% to 15% (Barlow, 1988). Thus, social phobias have a much lower prevalence than do other forms of social anxiety such as shyness. Interestingly, both shy and nonshy individuals agree on the rank ordering of shyness-eliciting situations, and most individuals who do not describe themselves as shy report some shyness in these situations (Crozier, 1982). It has been suggested that attributional processes distinguish people who are dispositionally shy from those who are situationally shy (Pilkonis & Zimbardo, 1979, p. 141). The former blame themselves for social anxiety and label themselves as shy, whereas the latter blame anxiety on external situations and do not label themselves as shy.

Social phobia is distinguished from avoidant personality disorder, which is characterized by fear of negative evaluation, social discomfort, and timidity beginning in early childhood. Four of the following seven criteria must be met for a diagnosis of avoidant personality disorder.

1. Is easily hurt by criticism or disapproval.
2. Has no close friends or confidants (or only one other than first-degree relatives.
3. Is unwilling to get involved with people unless certain of being liked.
4. Avoids social or occupational activities that involve significant interpersonal contact (e.g., refuses a promotion that will increase social demands).

5. Is reticent in social situations because of a fear of saying something inappropriate or foolish, or of being unable to answer a question.
6. Fears being embarrassed by blushing, crying, or showing signs of anxiety in front of other people.
7. Exaggerates the potential difficulties, physical dangers, or risks involved in doing something ordinary but outside his or her usual routine (American Psychiatric Association, 1987, p. 353).

Some investigators suggest that the prime difference between people with social phobias and those with avoidant personality disorders is that avoidant individuals have accepted their life patterns, whereas social phobics continue to enter feared situations (Heimberg, Dodge, & Becker, 1987). Clients with avoidant personality disorders have more severe symptoms, are more disturbed in a wider range of situations, are not as socially skilled, and have higher scores on measures of social avoidance and distress than social phobics (see Barlow, 1988, for review).

## CAUSES OF LONELINESS, SHYNESS, SOCIAL ANXIETY, AND SOCIAL ISOLATION

Research to date indicates that both personal and environmental factors are related to the development of loneliness, shyness, social anxiety or phobia, and social isolation. These factors may influence both trait and state anxiety. Genetic factors influence "outgoingness" (see, e.g., Kagan, Reznick, & Snidman, 1988). Anxiety in social situations can be developed and maintained by unique individual learning histories. Some writers have emphasized the evolutionary roots of social anxiety. Gilbert and Trower (1990) argue that in "socially threatening situations we have innate tendencies to act as did our animal ancestors, with mixtures of aggression, anxiety, submission, flight/withdrawal, and so on" (p. 159) (for further detail, see Bailey, 1987). Social anxiety is viewed as arising "from the activation of evolved mechanisms for dealing with intra-species threat, which served a vital role in the evolution of social groups" (Trower & Gilbert, 1989, p. 19). These authors believe that "these inappropriately triggered mechanisms underlie the appraisal-coping processes in the socially anxious individual" (p. 19) such as the arousal defense system focused on potential harm. This focus distracts from the "hedonic mode," in which signals of reassurance and safety are sent by dominant participants. In their view, social anxiety

may represent a failure of reassurance. The adoption of submissive styles of behavior (e.g., shyness), serves as a protection from negative consequences. Support for such a position stems from a number of sources, including the finding that fear of high-status others is one factor found on the Social Reticence Scale (Jones et al., 1986). Some argue that angry faces are evolutionary fear-relevant stimuli (that we are prepared to fear angry, rejecting, or critical faces) (Ohman, 1986). Conditioned responses of fear to angry faces are much more resistant to extinction than are reactions to happy or neutral faces (Ohman & Dimberg, 1984). A certain degree of wariness in the presence of strangers and in unfamiliar situations is adaptive. Thus, it should not be surprising that social anxieties are so common. In fact, it is surprising that they are not more common. Barlow (1988) argues that to develop a social phobia, we must be biologically and psychologically vulnerable to anxious apprehension. In such cases, relatively minor events and/or stress from negative life events may set off an "alarm," which in turn may result in further anxious apprehension. Another pathway is through performance deficits; that is, one may not perform well in a situation and then anticipate failure in future similar situations. This apprehension in turn triggers further alarms.

Developmental experiences such as exposure to parental social models influence skill development and anxiety reactions. Parents of socially phobic individuals have been found to be significantly more socially fearful and preoccupied with what others think of them compared to parents of agoraphobics (Bruch, Heimberg, Berger, & Collins, 1987). Social confidence may be compromised by parental reactions. For example, parents may discourage their children's friendships by being overly critical. Lonely adolescents and college students describe their parents as rejecting and unsupportive (Brennan & Auslander, 1979; Sarason, Levine, Basham, & Sarason, 1983). Effects of divorce and separation may influence skill development and create a sense of rejection and fears about being different. Moving to a new area and leaving behind friends and relatives often results in loneliness; three-quarters of college students experience loneliness in their first year (Cutrona, 1982). Causes of loneliness identified by students include: leaving family and friends to attend college (40%); breakup of romantic relationships (15%); problems with a friend or roommate (11%); family events such as parental divorce, arguments with parents, or the marriage of a sibling (9%); difficulties with schoolwork (11%); and isolated living situation (6%). Fears of rejection, being shy, and not knowing how to start a conversation are frequently mentioned as causes of loneliness by chronically lonely students (Cutrona, 1982). A happy marriage may not make up for the loss of friends when a couple moves to a new location (Weiss, 1973). Different kinds of relationships fulfill different needs, and relationship interests may change over the life span. A past history of punishment in social situations may result in conditioned anxiety in such situations. Lack of positive consequences in social situations can contribute to anxiety. Thus, both conditioned cues for punishment and conditioned cues for lack of reinforcement may inhibit social behavior (Gray, 1982). People have different thresholds in relation to the level of frustrative nonreward that can be tolerated.

Certain personal characteristics predispose people to feelings of loneliness. A reluctance to take risks, low self-esteem, shyness, and inadequate social skills may decrease positive social relationships. Whether these characteristics are causes or outcomes of loneliness (or both) is not clear. Peplau and Perlman (1982) believe there are three ways in which such characteristics may contribute to loneliness: (1) They may decrease social desirability and decrease opportunities for social relationships; (2) they may affect how a person behaves in social situations and result in negative exchanges; and (3) ''personal qualities affect how a person reacts to changes in his or her actual social relations, and so influence how effective the person is in avoiding, minimizing or alleviating loneliness'' (p. 9). Coping strategies adopted to avoid criticism and rejection may in fact contribute to loneliness. The reinforcer profile is dysfunctionally balanced to avoid negative feedback rather than to seek positive social experiences. Shyness may serve a protective impression management function (protect an individual from negative consequences) (Arkin, Lake, & Baumgardner, 1986). This keeps social anxiety in check.

Cultural and situational factors influence loneliness. Opportunities to meet people differ in different cultures and situations. For example, it may be difficult for gay people in rural environments to meet other gay individuals. Living and working environments differ in the opportunities they provide for meeting people and maintaining relationships. Lack of transportation or money may limit opportunities for social contacts. Certain social roles such as that of caregiver may leave one prone to loneliness and/or social isolation. Although some environments, such

as college, may provide rich opportunities for a variety of social contacts, others may offer only a limited and unsatisfactory range of behavior settings that encourage valued social contacts (see, e.g., Wahler's (1980) descriptions of insular mothers). Cultures differ in the extent to which individualism and competition are stressed compared to cooperation and shared responsibilities. The vision of the lonely but independent American settler is a classic one, and many writers have commented on the loneliness of Americans (e.g., Slater, 1979; Reissman, 1950). Competitive climates in work and school may also decrease opportunities for friendship. Some writers suggest that allergens and physical irritants may influence shyness (Bell, 1992).

## CORRELATES OF SHYNESS, SOCIAL ANXIETY, AND LONELINESS

Affective, cognitive, and behavioral differences have been found between people who report that they are shy, socially anxious, or lonely and those who do not report this. People differ in the extent to which affective and/or cognitive changes associated with shyness or social anxiety bother them. The more bothersome such feelings and thoughts are, the more likely they are to result in self-focused attention and avoidance behaviors, which compromise social competence and diminish social rewards. There is an overlap in the correlates of shyness, loneliness, and social anxiety (see Table 12.1). As Peplau and Perlman (1982b) point out, ''it is at times difficult to distinguish among behavior that accompanies loneliness, behavior that leads to loneliness in the first place and behavioral strategies for coping with loneliness'' (p. 12). Being alone is not synonymous with loneliness, nor does being with other people necessarily prevent feelings of loneliness. Feelings of loneliness may be related to the lack of certain kinds of relationships. The type of deprivation is important to identify during assessment. One can be married and still be lonely or be in contact with many people and yet be lonely.

Determinants of loneliness include: (1) emotional threats to relationships such as arguments, (2) social isolation (e.g., being left out), (3) social marginality (being with strangers), or (4) romantic difficulties (breakups) (Jones, Cavert, Snider, & Bruce, 1985). Affective, cognitive, and behavioral responses are related to loneliness. Lonely compared to nonlonely people describe themselves as being less happy, less satisfied, more pessimistic, and more depressed

**Table 12.1.** Differences Between People Who Report That They Are Shy, Socially Anxious, or Lonely and Those Who Do Not

- Blame failure on unchangeable personal characteristics rather than lack of effort or use of incorrect strategies and attribute success to external factors (i.e., different attribution patterns).
- Have incorrect or inadequate information about relationships.
- Are less empathic to needs, concerns, and feelings of others; are more anxiously preoccupied.
- Have unrealistic expectations.
- Often expect to be negatively evaluated and to be inadequate.
- Dwell on their failures; have more negative and fewer positive self-statements.
- Have lower self-esteem.
- Are more depressed.
- Worry more about negative evaluations; selectively attend to negative information about themselves and their performance.
- Are less skilled in thinking of ways to solve interpersonal problems.
- Share their opinions less often; are cautious in how they present themsevles.
- Engage in less self-disclosure which results in others disclosing less to them.
- Ask fewer personal questions and refer less to others.
- Offer fewer social signals indicating liking.
- Respond more slowly.
- Date less and have fewer friends.
- Take fewer risks.
- Are less assertive.
- Conform more.
- Speak less and have greater latencies and more silences.
- Smile less.
- Initiate fewer conversations.
- Offer many ''disaffiliative'' behaviors (e.g., maintain distance from others, avoid eye contact).
- Like and trust others less, find others less attractive.
- Are dissatisfied with their social lives.
- Feel more uncomfortable and awkward in social situations.
- Are perceived as less friendly, less relaxed, and less competent by others.
- Underestimate their skills compared to observer ratings.
- Perceive the same feedback more negatively.
- Feel less intense positive affect when outcomes are positive and report greater negative affect in response to negative outcome.
- Feel less physically attractive and less well understood in communication settings.

*Sources:* See, for example, Daly and Stafford (1984); Jones, Hobbs, and Hockenbury (1982); and Peplau and Perlman (1982a).

(Perlman, Gerson, & Spinner, 1978). Young (1982) distinguishes between different types of loneliness: chronic, situational, and transient. Chronic loneliness occurs over many years as a result of not forming satisfactory relationships. Situational loneliness results from major life changes such as divorce or death of a significant other. Transient loneliness refers to short periods of loneliness. The affective dimensions of depletion, isolation, agitation, and dejection were reported as being associated with loneliness by a large group of college students (*n* = 763) (Scalise, Ginter, & Gerstein, 1984). Feelings when lonely reported by another sample included desperation, depression, impatience, boredom, and self-deprecation

(Rubenstein & Shaver, 1982). Lonely people may feel angry, empty, and awkward (Russell et al., 1986). Some lonely people have pessimistic and cynical attitudes. Hansson and colleagues (1984) conclude that such attitudes appear to be stable features of relational incompetence. The term *relational competence,* refers to characteristics of the individual that facilitate the acquisition, development, and maintenance of mutually satisfying relationships (p. 273). Correlations between depression and loneliness are substantial. As Peplau and Perlman (1982b) point out, however, although there is a relationship between depression and loneliness, these are not synonymous. Depression can be caused by a variety of changes. Low self-esteem is one of the most frequently reported correlates of self-reported loneliness (see review by Jones et al., 1990). Loneliness is also correlated with social anxiety. Loneliness may encourage or hinder motivation to pursue social contacts depending on how long it has lasted and on past successes in overcoming it.

There is a relationship between shyness, low social risk taking, and loneliness. Loneliness is positively related to sensitivity to rejection, measures of shyness, and social anxiety and is negatively related to measures of extraversion and sociability, likability, confidence, and skills involved in dating and conflict resolution (see review by Jones et al., 1990). Lonely college students compared to those who do not report that they are lonely are more self-conscious (Goswick & Jones, 1981) and thus may be less responsive to the feelings and concerns of others (Jones, 1982). Weiss (1972) suggests that loneliness encourages an oversensitivity to minimal cues and a tendency to misinterpret or to exaggerate hostile or affectionate intentions of others (Weiss, 1973). Lonely compared to nonlonely individuals view themselves more negatively and expect others to evaluate them negatively (Jones, Freeman, & Goswick, 1981). They often have cynical and pessimistic views about people and about relationships. They tend to violate normative social expectations (e.g., disclose too much or too little) (Solano & Batten, 1979). They evaluate themselves more negatively after brief social exchanges and make more self-statements, ask fewer questions of their partners, change the topic more often, and respond more slowly (Jones, 1982). Lonely compared to nonlonely males speak less both with strangers and with roommates and are less intimate, use simple attentiveness as a conversational mode more than nonlonely persons, and use familiarity modes less

(Sloan & Solano, 1984). Lonely people have different patterns of self-disclosure (either too much or too little), focus more on themselves, and are less assertive in social situations.

Attributions people offer for their loneliness influence how they deal with their loneliness. Peplau and colleagues (1979) believe that these attributions may function as precipitating reasons, maintaining causes, or anticipated solutions. If loneliness is attributed to unchangeable personal or environmental characteristics, greater negative affect is likely to occur. Feelings of hostility and anger may accompany loneliness if this is attributed to external factors such as being excluded by others. On the other hand, if loneliness is attributed to internal causes, shame, embarrassment, and guilt may occur. Depression is likely to result from loneliness only if loneliness is viewed as being a result of stable, unchangeable causes (Peplau et al., 1979). Reactions to lonely people are also influenced by attributions about causes. Rejection is more likely if loneliness is believed to result from personality dysfunction than if situational causes are assumed.

Some investigators confine their attention to the cognitive and affective components of social anxiety in the belief that these are primary (e.g., Leary, 1983; Schlenker & Leary, 1982). Social anxiety is associated with a reversal of self-serving attributional biases (Hope, Gansler, & Heimberg, 1989; Taylor & Brown, 1988). That is, in contrast to blaming lack of success on external factors and attributing success to personal characteristics, shy and socially anxious individuals tend to blame failures on personal characteristics and to attribute success on external factors. Offering an alternative explanation for shyness (e.g., high noise levels) resulted in a decrease in shy behavior, showing the importance of attributions for shyness (Brodt & Zimbardo, 1981). Socially anxious individuals compared to people who are not anxious are less assertive and have more negative self-statements (Halford & Foddy, 1982). Both loneliness and social anxiety are related to disruptive self-focused attention (see e.g. Jones et al., 1982; Melchoir & Cheek, 1990). Programs designed to redirect attentional focus to the task at hand have resulted in behavioral gains for both lonely and anxious clients (Jones et al., 1982). Cognitive components of social phobia include extreme or misdirected standards for performance, overprediction of negative consequences, and misperception of negative evaluation (see e.g. Heimberg, 1989; Lucock & Salkovskis,

1988; Stopa & Clark, 1993). People with high or moderate social anxiety interpret the same feedback as more negative than do people with low social anxiety and have a greater expectancy that others will evaluate them negatively (Smith & Sarason, 1975). Socially anxious men underestimate positive aspects of their performance and overestimate negative aspects compared to less socially anxious men (Valentine & Arkowitz, 1975). Some research suggests that socially anxious individuals have a more accurate memory for negative information and a less accurate one for positive information (O'Banion & Arkowitz, 1977), which is likely to be associated with negative self-evaluations as well as with infrequent self-reinforcement for social behaviors. Other reports do not suggest a memory bias (Rapee, McCallum, Melville, Ravenscroft, & Rodney, 1994). High-anxiety speakers in a public-speaking situation are likely to make statements to themselves such as ''I must be boring'' when they see two or three people leave while they are talking. The person low in speech anxiety is more likely to attribute people leaving to external circumstances. Social anxiety, however, is not necessarily reflected in behavior.

Behavioral correlates of social phobia include avoidance of feared situations, escape or early exit from feared situations, behavioral disruption (fidgeting, stuttering, and pacing), disaffiliative behaviors (such as averted gaze) and behavioral withdrawal (appearing shy, aloof, unnoticed) (Heimberg, 1990). Not all social phobics avoid social situations. Seeking out and tolerating anxiety in such situations distinguishes social phobics from avoidant individuals. Social anxiety may, however, result in a variety of subtle avoidance behaviors, such as not initiating conversations or introducing topics and leaving early (Butler, 1989). Physiological responses may include sweating, shaking, blushing, rapidly beating heart, rapid or shallow breathing, and difficulty in concentrating. Although global measures of behavior are often correlated with specific behavioral and self-report measures, the correlation is far from perfect (see Briggs & Smith, 1986, for a review). Correlations with self-rated behavior are also often modest. Specific behaviors assessed include number of gestures, head nods, utterances, and questions; amount of time spent talking to and looking at one's partner; time spent touching oneself; and amount of time needed to initiate conversations. The low correlations may be due in part to the specificity of the measures. It is often the pattern of behaviors that reveals anxi-

ety, not the presence of any one behavior (Briggs & Smith, 1986, p. 51). Arkowitz and his colleagues (Arkowitz, Lichtenstein, McGovern, & Hines, 1975) requested high and low dating subjects to interact with a female confederate and get to know her. They assessed the client's talk time, number of silences, number of verbal reinforcements, number of head nods, number of smiles, gaze time, and appropriate speech content. Few differences emerged between frequently and rarely dating subjects. The only differences found were in the number of silences and the higher rating in social skill received by the frequent daters. More recent studies investigating parameters such as ''timing'' have found differences between contrasted groups (see, e.g., Peterson, Fischetti, Curran, & Arland, 1981, as well as review by Hope & Heimberg, 1990). The unique influence of the two interactants on each other (dyadic dependency) is a problem in using this source of data.

Trower and Gilbert (1989) describe socially anxious and phobic individuals as being in a state of ''braced readiness''; ''the subordinate must remain constantly alert and on the ready to withdraw or send submissive, no-threat signals to those that have greater [resource holding potential]'' (p. 21). They view the socially anxious or phobic individual as caught in a primitive defense system in which attention is focused on a particular form of social comparison; outputs (social signals) are monitored and the potential for injury or put-down are checked out; appraisal is focused on the possibility that others can add to or subtract from one's status or prestige. Submissive gestures are offered to appease those perceived to be dominant. This differs greatly from the case of individuals who focus on what they can offer to others rather than how much they can threaten others (or be threatened by them).

Shy individuals differ from nonshy individuals in their affect, behavior, and thoughts. Detailed reviews of the shyness literature can be found in, for example, Jones, Cheek, and Briggs (1986). As with lonely individuals, there is an absence of normally expected social responsiveness. Here, too, the absence of expected social behaviors may be related not to behavior deficits but to interfering thoughts or arousal. As with loneliness and social anxiety, there are individual differences in the unique contribution of affective, cognitive, and behavioral correlates. Affective correlates associated with shyness include depression, hostility, fear, shame, alienation, self-consciousness, and communication apprehension. Shyness is often associated with physiological arousal, including blushing, rapid heartbeat, and dry mouth, as well as with various negative thoughts, such as considering how to escape from a situation, or feeling that one is doing poorly, as well as self-consciousness. Some people have viewed shyness as a handicapping strategy—that is, as a possible excuse for not doing well in a situation (Snyder & Smith, 1986). Shy males may not be able to interpret interpersonal cues as well as socially comfortable males and are more likely than nonshy people to expect rejection from others (Jones & Briggs, 1984). They rate others more negatively (as less friendly), expect to be rated negatively by others, and rate themselves as less friendly (Jones & Briggs, 1984). (See also Rapee & Lim, 1992; Stopa & Clark, 1993).

Shy people speak for less time, take longer to respond to others' comments, allow more uncomfortable silences to occur, and tend not to interrupt compared to nonshy individuals (Pilkonis, 1977). They tend to "play safe" and avoid social attention by offering minimum feedback responses such as "uh-hum," smiling, and nodding (see review in Arkin et al., 1986). Undergraduate males who describe themselves as confident "reported feeling less anxious than shy subjects when preparing to phone an unknown coed for a date and when interacting face-to-face with a "live" coed. They also tended to show less autonomic arousal when interacting with the women. In simulated heterosexual situations, they were less likely than shy subjects to avoid initiating interactions. Independent raters perceived confident subjects as being less anxious, more skillful, and more sustained in their interactions than shy subjects. Behavioral diary data indicated that confident subjects, in contrast to shy subjects, spent more time relating to more women in more situations" (Twentyman & McFall, 1975, p. 393).

Low self-esteem is related to shyness (about −.50) (Jones, Briggs, & Smith, 1986). There is a tendency to become anxiously self-preoccupied about social exchanges. As Cheek and Melchior (1990) point out, shy people have a low opinion of themselves. Shyness is related to the Turning Against Self scale of the Defense Mechanism Inventory (Foley, Heath, & Chabot, 1986). Those individuals who are high in both sociability and shyness may report greatest discomfort during social interactions. Cheek and Melchior (1990) emphasize the conflict experienced by such individuals. Shyness and depression correlated about .40 with self-reports of loneliness (Anderson & Arnoult, 1985). Socially anxious individuals

view themselves as less attractive compared to non-anxious people (Prisbell, 1982).

## THE INTERRELATIONSHIPS BETWEEN SHYNESS, LONELINESS, AND SOCIAL ANXIETY

Shyness, loneliness, social anxiety, and social phobia are related both conceptually and empirically. They all emphasize emotional discomfort related to social situations and they may all compromise social bonding (Rook, 1984c) and social support (Hansson et al., 1984). Jones et al., (1990) described empirical sources of convergence between loneliness and social anxiety:

1. Measures of loneliness are related to measures of social anxiety, especially shyness (correlations range from .40 to .51).
2. Both loneliness and shyness are related to unsatisfactory interpersonal relationships.
3. Both are similarly related to other constructs, such as depression, hostility, low self-esteem, and alienation.
4. Behavioral correlates of both loneliness and social anxiety indicate ineffective interpersonal behaviors.

The correlation between measures of these constructs, though high, is far from perfect, suggesting that these constructs are different. Many studies have found a relationship between social skills, social anxiety, shyness, and loneliness (Jones et al., 1986; Peplau & Perlman, 1982b). Dissaffiliative behavior on the part of shy people may lead others to view them as depressed, snobbish, or suspicious, which in turn will decrease approaches by others.

Shyness, social anxiety, and social phobia may result in loneliness in that they may decrease opportunities for enjoyable social exchanges. Jones et al. (1990) stated that there is some evidence from longitudinal studies that shyness preceeds loneliness. Unwanted social isolation may also result in loneliness. Thus, shyness, social anxiety, social phobia, and unwanted social isolation may be precursors to loneliness. Many individuals are anxious performers. For example, they may initiate conversations despite their anxiety. In this case, anxiety may compromise social effectiveness by encouraging disaffiliative behaviors such as gaze avoidance that decrease social success, which in turn results in loneliness due to inadequate social contacts. Although observers may not be able to detect social anxiety, socially anxious people often worry that their anxiety can be detected (McEwan & Devins, 1983). The greater the interest in being with people (the greater the sociability), the more intense may be the conflict caused by shyness and social anxiety and the greater the loneliness resulting from ineffective behavior and less than satisfactory social outcomes (see Jones et al., 1990, for a detailed discussion of the interrelationships between loneliness and social anxiety). The negative affective state that characterizes loneliness may increase shyness and social anxiety and encourage social isolation; it is difficult to be socially outgoing when feeling lonely and alone. Persistent loneliness or unwanted social isolation may result in a lowering of expectations for enjoyable social contacts as well as a number of other effects such as physical illness, depression, substance abuse, suicide, delinquency, and aggression.

The research concerning shyness, social anxiety, and loneliness shows that these are interrelated. Genetic predispositions toward shyness may interact with nonoptimal social environments in ways that encourage the development and maintenance of social anxiety and reticence in social situations. Environmental conditions in relation to social contexts provided affect the range of exchanges permitted and the extent to which individual potentials are realized (see, e.g., Jacobs, 1961).

## ASSESSMENT

An individually tailored assessment is a hallmark of behavioral practice. This provides guidelines for selection of intervention methods. Assessment should clarify desired outcomes, the behaviors required to achieve these and the situations in which these must occur, personal and environmental resources that can be drawn on to pursue goals and personal and environmental obstacles that may get in the way. Assessment involves discovering the unique meaning of loneliness, shyness, and social anxiety for each client. What does it mean when a client says, "I find it hard to make friends"? (Horowitz, Weckler, & Doren, 1983). What situations are of concern? Examples of situations identified by shy individuals include the following (Russell et al., 1986):

With a group of strangers
Giving a speech
Meeting a date's parents
Saying something stupid, tripping
Asking for a date, blind dates
Parties

Dates, being with opposite sex
New job, new school
Oral exams, interviews
High status, attractive others
Loud, intoxicated others
Crowded restaurants

Anxiety may interfere with use of social skills. The relative contribution of conditioned anxiety and anxiety arousing thoughts or beliefs should be identified and appropriate procedures selected based on this assessment. Social skills may not be used because of lack of self-management skills and lack of skills in arranging practice opportunities or because of interfering beliefs about social relationships and social behavior. These incorrect beliefs may interfere with acquisition and use of effective self-management and exposure skills. Assessment requires the distinction between social phobia and other problems such as depression. Otherwise, inappropriate intervention methods may be recommended. Social anxiety is related to many different problems, making the assessment task a challenging one (Rapee, Sanderson, & Barlow, 1987). Depressed individuals are often rejected by others, perhaps because of their tendency to disclose depressive affect. Such disclosures lead to rejection, devaluation, and discounting (Gurtman, 1987). Some clients are excessively sensitive to physiological reactions such as rapid heart rate in social situations. Some are excessively concerned about an imagined or actual body defect that may in fact not even be observable to other people.

Earlier research used a component model of social behavior in which attention was focused on normative component behaviors (nods, looks) or sequences (greetings) involved in social exchanges. Trower (1982) refers to these components as social skills. More recently, a process model of social behavior has been introduced (Argyle, Furnham, & Graham, 1981; McFall, 1982; Trower, 1982). Components of social competence in a process model include the following (Argyle, 1981): (1) accurate perception and translation of social cues; (2) the ability to take the role of others; (3) nonverbal communication of attitudes and emotions; (4) offering others clear reinforcement and rewards; (5) planning goals and altering behavior as required; (6) sending social signals that accurately present one's roles, status, and other elements of social identity; (7) skill in analyzing situations and their rules to adapt behavior effectively; and (8) verbal behavior that fits into the orderly sequence of social exchanges. *Social skill* is defined by Trower as "the process of generating skilled behavior directed toward a goal" (p. 418). *Social competence* refers to the capability of generating skilled behavior. This requires both social skills (the verbal and nonverbal behaviors related to success) and social skill. *Social performance* refers to the production of skilled behavior in specific situations (p. 419). These distinctions as well as related literature highlight the importance of attending to both acquisition and performance problems. Knowledge (information that reduces uncertainty about how to attain a desired outcome) as well as performance competencies are valuable (see Table 12.2). Cognitive, emotional, or behavioral excesses or deficits may interfere with acquisition and use of skills (Gambrill, 1977; Gresham, 1988). Low-frequency daters may have appropriate social skills but not display these for one or more of the following reasons: (1) conditioned anxiety in related encounters; (2) negative self-evaluations in such situations; (3) prior failures in related encounters leading to their avoidance; (4) lack of knowledge of when and how to display social skills; (5) misconceptions about and unrealistic fears of dating situations; and (6) a lack of exposure to dating situations. As discussed earlier, excesses or deficits may be related to genetic differences, evolutionary contingencies, or unique individual learning histories. Many function as self-handicapping conditions.

**Table 12.2.** Skill and Knowledge Related to Shyness, Social Anxiety/Phobia, and Loneliness

1. Social skills (verbal and nonverbal behaviors and behavior chains as well as established $S^Ds$)

2. Cognitive skills (e.g., setting realistic goals, attending to positive consequences; social problem solving)

3. Affect regulating skills

4. Self-presentation skills (physical attractiveness)

5. Access competencies (locating promising settings to meet people, creating new settings)

6. Self-management skills (setting goals and assignments including graduated exposure to feared situations, monitoring progress, prompting and reinforcing desired behaviors)

7. Content knowledge about behavior and how it can be altered

8. Content knowledge about social relationships, including norms

9. Content knowledge about personal characteristics that influence social exchanges

## Setting Goals

Setting goals is a critical part of assessment. What are expected outcomes? Outcomes pursued should be relevant to each client, clear, and attainable. Shy, lonely, or socially anxious clients often approach counseling with vague or unattainable goals ("never be anxious, shy, or lonely"; "have everyone like me"; "never make social blunders"; "meet a romantic partner next week"). Helping clients to select relevant, achievable short- and long-term goals is a key part of assessment (Gambrill & Richey, 1988). Focusing on specific goals increases the likelihood of attaining objectives of value to clients and facilitates evaluation of progress. Both short- and long-term personal and social goals should be considered (Nezu & D'Zurilla, 1979). Clients usually focus on negative goals such as decreasing anxiety and not getting rejected. That is, they focus on defensive goals such as avoiding making a poor impression rather than trying to create a favorable impression. In some programs designed to help clients increase enjoyable social contacts, there is a focus on positive goals (initiating more conversations) (see, e.g., Gambrill & Richey, 1988). The excessive attention shy, socially anxious, or lonely individuals devote to feelings of anxiety and potential negative consequences and their neglect of opportunities for positive experiences are highlighted. The importance of considering positive as well as negative goals is supported by research indicating the relative independence of negative and positive affect (Diener, 1984). Intermediate goals, such as having brief, pleasant conversations, are often dismissed as irrelevant. Clients are encouraged to view intermediate steps as valuable in their own right.

## Reviewing Knowledge and Beliefs about Social Relationships, Behavior, and Feelings

Knowledge and beliefs about emotions and behavior and how they can be altered, as well as about relationships and how they are formed and maintained, should be reviewed to identify views in need of correction. The view of social anxiety and social behavior as learned is quite new for many people. Many people believe they can change how they feel or what they do by resorting to "will power" (Furnham, 1988). A belief in mind power—the power to change solely by thinking different thoughts—is endemic to American culture, and therefore clients are likely to believe in this route to change and to over-look environmental causes and solutions (Weiss, 1969). This belief may get in the way of altering an unsatisfying social life. During assessment, clients are introduced to a skill-based approach to increasing comfort and success in social situations, which, un-like reliance on will power, offers concrete guidelines about how to achieve goals (Gambrill & Richey, 1988). Another potential obstacle is the belief that the best way to change behavior is to change feelings. The relationship between feelings, thoughts, and be-haviors often is not recognized, especially the rela-tionship between behavior and feelings (that feelings can be altered by changing behavior). A good exam-ple of this effect is the success of positively biased interactions in increasing social success (see later discussion).

Inaccurate beliefs about how relationships are formed and developed may interfere with enjoyable social exchanges. Examples include the belief that relationships that develop by chance are better than those that develop as a result of some planned activity and that it is best not to be persistent because of fear of offending people. Knowledge about how relation-ships are formed, deepened, and maintained has in-creased substantially, especially in the area of friend-ship (see, e.g., Duck, 1983). Relationships progress through different phases (initiating, developing, and deepening), and somewhat different skills are re-quired in these different stages. A client may have the skills required to do well in one stage of relationship formation but may have dysfunctional thoughts or incorrect beliefs and lack some of the required skills to do well in other stages. Incorrect rules may be used. Examples of rules related to friends include the following (Argyle & Henderson, 1985):

- Volunteer help in time of need.
- Respect the friend's privacy.
- Keep confidences.
- Trust and confide in each other.
- Stand up for the friend in his or her absence.
- Don't criticize each other in public.
- Show emotional support.
- Look him or her in the eye during conversation.
- Strive to make him or her happy while in each other's company.
- Don't be jealous or critical of his or her other relationships.
- Be tolerant of each other's friends.
- Share news of success.
- Ask for personal advice.

- Don't nag.
- Engage in joking or teasing with the friend.
- Seek to repay debts, favors, and compliments.
- Disclose personal feelings or problems to the friend.

## Reviewing Social Skills

Goals such as increasing social contacts require a variety of social skills, including timing and sequenc-ing skills. Some studies have found that socially competent and incompetent women differ in the tim-ing, placement, and distribution of their responses, but not in the frequency of their responses (Peterson et al., 1981). However, behavior in role-plays may not reflect behavior in real-life situations (see later discussion of the validity of role-plays). A review of each client's entering repertoire will indicate which skills are available and which behaviors will have to be increased, decreased, varied, or stabilized. For example, a client may use only one way to initiate a conversation and may benefit from broadening her repertoire. Cues that convey interest in dating include eye contact, smiling, asking questions, mentioning an activity that could be shared (e.g., a movie), offering minimal listening responses ("um-hum"), indicating that she/he) noticed him (her) in the past, laughing at the other person's jokes, and commenting on what the other person says (Muehlenhard, Koralewski, An-drews, & Burdick, 1986). Although high-frequency daters are not necessarily better cue readers com-pared to low-frequency daters, they are more certain of their ratings (Muehlenhard, Miller, & Burdick, 1983). Many clients report lack of skill in making small talk and do not understand the functions this serves. Lack of empirical data regarding skills re-quired for success in different social situations often makes it necessary to rely on "what seems obvious" with the inevitable effect that different people may select different skills which may or may not be re-lated to success. The skills required for success differ in different relationship stages. For example, in-creased disclosure is required to move a relationship to deeper levels (Chelune & Associates, 1979; Duck, 1983). Most applied research has focused on the initial relationship stages of meeting people. The de-velopment and maintenance of friendships that pro-vide companionship has been neglected (Rook, 1990). Training programs in which it is assumed that shyness, loneliness, social anxiety, and social phobia are mainly related to affective and cognitive variables often do not include assessment of each client's social skills relevant to desired outcomes and pay little or no attention to identification of social skills needed to enhance success in real-life settings (see later discussion).

## Reviewing Self-Presentation Skills

Many studies have found correlations between physical attractiveness and dating frequency (see review in Duran, 1989 as well as Calvert, 1988). Many physical characteristics are modifiable, and changes that can be made to enhance success should be pursued. Relevant questions include: Is manner of dressing compatible with social goals? Will this increase or decrease a client's chances of success? Posture and grooming should be reviewed to identify helpful changes. Some people believe that spending time on their appearance is a sign of lack of modesty and vanity. Here, too, a skill-based view can be emphasized. Selecting a hairstyle, dress, and makeup that increases social success are acquired competencies that can be enhanced by increasing relevant knowledge and skill.

## Reviewing Thoughts

Differences have been found in what shy, lonely, and socially anxious people say to themselves in social situations compared with people who do not report these complaints (see previous discussion). Private events such as thoughts and feelings can function as mediators that may assist or hamper social performance. Whether this role is viewed as causative is a key difference between behavioral and cognitive approaches. The varying results of cognitive methods in altering social anxiety argue against a causative role (see later discussion). Increased arousal in social situations may encourage the likelihood of negative thoughts, including irrational expectations. Many self-statements can be thought of as rules that facilitate (or hinder) effective behavior (Poppen, 1989). Rules and beliefs related to self-statements such as "I must never make mistakes" may be discovered during assessment. For example, a related belief may be "I am not a worthwhile person if I do make mistakes." Identification of such beliefs permits the possibility of challenging these (Safron & Greenberg, 1991). Negative self-statements may occur in anticipation of, during, or following encounters. For example, people who are socially anxious may have negative self-statements before, during, and after exchanges. Attributing an unsatisfactory

social life to stable personality characteristics may impede change efforts and increase depression (Peplau, Russell, & Heim, 1979). If dysfunctional thought patterns are found, intervention could include a focus on altering them. Or, successful experiences could be arranged resulting in a decrease in negative self-statements. Shy or socially anxious clients with excessive vigilance for negative reactions may benefit from decreasing their accuracy in observing negative social signals (Taylor & Brown, 1988).

Some clients do not believe they are worth knowing or believe they cannot be trusted. Poor self-regard is one of four groups of variables Hansson and colleagues (1984) relate to loneliness. The other three include negativistic attitudes (hostility, pessimistic attitude toward people, life, and society), inadequate social skills (e.g., shyness, low assertion), and emotional conflict and distress (e.g., depression, anxiety). Young (1982) identifies low self-concept as one of twelve reasons related to loneliness. Automatic thoughts include "I'm undesirable," "I'm dull and boring," and "I'm ugly." Other clusters identified by Young related to beliefs about oneself include sexual anxiety ("I'm not a good lover"), anxiety about emotional commitment ("I can't give enough to satisfy him/her"), and intimate rejection ("There's something wrong with me"; "I'd screw up any relationship"; "I won't risk being hurt again"). The belief that "There's something wrong with me" is one of the most common statements made by participants in classes on Taking Charge of Your Social Life (Gambrill, 1993). Butler (1989) identifies four kinds of concerns that may be associated with particular kinds of thoughts: (1) about developing intimate relationships, (2) about self-worth, (3) about contact with people in authority, and (4) about performance. She believes the common theme to be fear of negative evaluation (see also Schlenker & Leary, 1982).

## Reviewing Self-Management Skills

The role of self-management skills in decreasing shyness, social anxiety, and loneliness has not been systematically investigated. However, a number of sources suggest the importance of this skill cluster, including the finding that many shy, lonely, or socially anxious people have correct knowledge about social skills and when to use these but do not do so. They do not arrange for opportunities to use their skills or to overcome or diminish social anxiety by exposure to feared situations. For example, shy college students report that they engage in fewer social and extracurricular activities, are less willing to ask attractive people out, and spend more time by themselves because of fears about being rejected or making a social blunder (Zimbardo, 1977). The success of self-help programs in decreasing anxiety also suggests the role of self-management skills, as well as the importance of exposure to feared situations (see later discussion of self-help approaches). The majority of participants who have taken part in a minimal contact intervention program designed to increase social contacts do not use effective self-management skills to put their social skills to use to attain their objectives (Gambrill, 1993). Most of these individuals do not know how to: (1) select specific long-term and short-term goals or intermediate steps; (2) select clear, achievable, relevant assignments; (3) motivate themselves; (4) monitor their progress; or (5) take successful corrective steps based on degree of progress. Lack of a skill-based conceptualization of social comfort and success make it unlikely that self-management skills would be viewed as relevant to attaining social goals.

Socially anxious individuals often avoid social interactions (e.g., Dodge, Heimberg, Nyman, & O'Brian, 1987). Conditioned anxiety and excessive concern about negative reactions may be related to this avoidance, but there is also another possibility—lack of self-management skills that would provide exposure to avoided situations, resulting in a lessening of anxiety. The focus on the ''down'' side of client complaints (decreasing shyness, loneliness, and social anxiety) rather than on the ''up'' side (increasing enjoyable social contacts) has probably been partly responsible for overlooking and/or underplaying the role of self-management skills in attaining desired outcomes.

## Reviewing Access Competencies

The importance of access skills has been suggested in a number of studies (Gambrill, 1973; Lipton & Nelson, 1980). *Access competencies* refer to knowledge and behavior that increase the likelihood of gaining access to environments, situations, and interactions that are reinforcing and provide opportunities for additional skill acquisition and rewards (Hawkins, 1986). Even with excellent social skills, if clients do not seek out opportunities to use their skills, they will not achieve valued social goals. The importance of taking the initiative is shown by a study investigating the effectiveness of direct requests and hints on the

part of women who wanted to go out with men (Muehlenhard & McFall, 1981). If a man liked a woman, there was an 80% chance that he would accept a direct invitation and a 20% chance that he would reject it. If he liked a woman but was not thinking of dating women, there was only a 2% chance that he would ask her out. Self-management skills are required to gain access to promising environments (see previous discussion). In addition, knowledge of social ecology is important (i.e., knowledge about available social settings that would provide opportunities for pleasant social experiences).

Most people underestimate the importance of environmental variables in influencing the quality of their social life. They focus instead on personality characteristics. Environments differ in the number of behavior settings, the variety of roles within each, and the number of people available to fill them. Environmental pollutants such as noise, high crime rates, and crowding may decrease opportunities for positive exchanges. The availability of public spaces that offer contexts for positive exchanges has decreased in the United States (Schiller, 1989). Increasing enjoyable social contacts requires skill in arranging opportunities to meet people as well as skills in developing and maintaining positive relationships. Taking advantage of such opportunities will require skill in locating promising places as well as self-management skills to ensure that these situations are sampled. A major part of a minimal counselor contact program designed to help people increase social contacts involves enhancing skills in identifying and/or creating promising social settings (Gambrill & Richey, 1988). Participants complete an Activity Inventory to identify activities that they enjoy and that offer an opportunity to meet people. They are then coached how to scan their environment using informational aids such as newspapers to locate possible places to check out. It is surprising that more attention has not been devoted in research on shyness, loneliness, and social anxiety to a description of available behavior settings and the design of methods to enrich their variety. Opportunities to use social skills are dependent on settings that are available or that could be arranged.

## Reviewing Affect Management Skills

Excessive attraction, anxiety, or anger may interfere with enjoyable social exchanges. Some people do not distinguish between negative and positive arousal but react to both as unpleasant. Excessive self-attention may encourage a focus on physiological reactions that increases anxiety. Schlenker and Leary (1982) propose that whenever there is a self-presentation goal, an assessment process is triggered. People may become "frozen in the self-assessment phase," with the result that anxiety increases still further (Carver, 1979, p. 1266). The opposite problem may also occur; that is, some clients may not identify emotional cues and therefore may not have access to this source of information. Shy subjects have been found to have less intense positive affect in response to favorable outcomes but more intense negative affect in response to unfavorable outcomes compared to nonshy subjects (Teglasi & Hoffman, 1982). This affect bias encourages internal/stable attributions that may increase depression and social anxiety. Anxious apprehension concerning potential negative outcome will decrease risk taking and will increase the likelihood of "alarm" reactions that may further increase anxiety (Barlow, 1988).

## SOURCES OF INFORMATION

An individually tailored assessment is required to identify objectives as well as how these can be pursued most effectively. Sources of information include the behavioral interview, self-report measures, self-monitoring, physiological indicators, and observation in role-plays or real-life contexts. Some measures used with children, such as sociometric ratings, have not been used with adults.

## BEHAVIORAL INTERVIEWS

Self-report during behavioral interviews is used to obtain a description of specific situations of concern to each client, typical ways of reacting in each, outcomes that occur, and knowledge of how to handle situations more effectively. The specific kinds of social situations involved are described, including particular kinds of people (strangers, friends, acquaintances, other employees, etc.), how often problems occur, and the effect they have on the client's life. In addition, goals are clarified and personal and environmental factors related to presenting complaints are identified (Gambrill, 1977). Data are also collected about factors that lessen or aggravate problems. Reviewing a client's relationship history provides useful data about skills, obstacles and reinforcers. If clients have had rewarding social lives in the past, this suggests that needed skills are available unless the situations in which they find themselves

have altered and/or their social goals have changed, requiring development of new skills. If loneliness is a problem, is it chronic, transitory, or situational? Have there been recent changes such as retirement, moving to a new location, or loss of a significant relationship that may be related to complaints? Unemployment may significantly alter social relationships and also create changes that negatively affect social behavior (e.g., increase depression). What setting events influence acquisition and use of social skills? An interview guide developed by Arkowitz (1981) for assessing social inadequacy provides data about social behavior in twelve different areas, including same- and opposite-sex relationships, casual and intimate relationships, public speaking, and initiating and developing social exchanges. Clients estimate their skill level and their level of anxiety in each area.

Interview schedules developed to assess social phobia include the Avoidant Personality Disorder Examination adapted from the personality disorders examination (Heimberg et al., 1990). Respondents are rated in seven areas:

1a. Avoids social activities
2. Avoids occupational activities
3. No close friends/confidants
4. Must be certain of being liked
5. Reticent in social situations
6. Fears of being embarrassed
7. Easily hurt by criticism
8. Exaggerates difficulties/dangers

To receive a positive score, the behavior must occur at present (within the last year) and must be characteristic of long-term functioning (occurred over the past five years). At least one of the criteria must have had an onset prior to the age of 25 in order to meet a diagnosis. Respondents are asked to answer in terms of "what they are like most of the time." Answers are scored 0 (denied, infrequent, or not supported by examples), 1 (often avoids social activities outside of family and work that involve significant interpersonal contact), and 2 (almost always avoids social activities outside of family or work that involve significant social contact). The Anxiety Disorders Interview Schedule (ADISR)—Social Phobia includes 11 situations such as parties, meetings, using public rest rooms, writing in public, dating situations, and being assertive (refusing unreasonable requests; asking others to change their behavior; initiating and maintaining conversations) (DiNardo et al., 1985). Respondents indicate their degree of fear and avoidance on a scale ranging from none to very severe. They are also asked whether there are other pertinent situations that should be noted, and they indicate whether fears currently interfere with their lives on a scale from 0 (no interference) to 4 (extreme interference). At the end of the interview, the interviewer rates severity of social phobia on a scale ranging from 0 (absent) to 8 (very disabling). Depending on the answers given, a DSM-III-R primary diagnosis of social phobia is given.

## STANDARDIZED SELF-REPORT MEASURES

Measures designed to assess shyness, loneliness, social anxiety, and social phobia reflect assumptions about these constructs. Some investigators use one-item self-labeling measures of concepts such as shyness. Other scales assess presumed components of shyness or social anxiety (for more detailed reviews, including information on reliability and validity, see Briggs & Smith, 1986; Glass & Arnkoff, 1989; Peplau & Perlman, 1982a).

### Measures of Loneliness

The UCLA Scale of Loneliness is widely used to assess loneliness (Russell, 1982). Scores on this inventory are significantly related to social activities and relationships. Both 20-item and 4-item versions are available. The short version has a coefficient alpha of .75. The UCLA scale is a unidimensional scale. It does not distinguish between trait and state loneliness. Multidimensional scales include items tapping different kinds of social deprivation (intimate partner, feelings of abandonment), hopelessness, degree of permanence of loneliness and attributions (e.g., blaming others) (Jong-Gierveld & Raadschelders, 1982). Asher, Hymel, and Renshaw (1984) developed a loneliness scale for children. This includes 16 items related to feelings of loneliness and social dissatisfaction as well as hobbies and interests. The Young Loneliness Inventory (see Young, 1982) consists of 19 items related to kinds of relationships lonely clients often view as missing in their lives.

### Measures of Social Anxiety

The Social and Avoidance Distress Scale (Watson & Friend, 1969) consists of 28 true/false items that can be grouped into two categories (social approach/avoidance and social anxiety). Watson and Friend

(1969) also developed the 30-item Fear of Negative Evaluation Scale. This too has a True/False format. Items are included such as "I am often afraid that I may look ridiculous or make a fool of myself," "I feel very upset when I make a social error," and "I brood about the opinions my friends have about me." A brief (12-item) version has also been developed that correlates well with the longer version (Leary, 1983). Changes in fear of negative evaluation have been found to be a major predictor of clinical change in phobic severity and avoidance (Mattick, Peters, & Clarke, 1989). Schlenker and Leary (1982) argue that all social anxiety is due to a fear of negative evaluation, that when we expect to do well in a social situation, there will be no anxiety. Responses on these inventories do not offer specific information about particular situations of concern to clients.

A number of measures have been developed to assess social anxiety and social phobia. The Mattick Social Phobia Scale (SPS) assesses fears of public scrutiny (see Mattick, Peters, & Clarke, 1989). Twenty items are listed, such as "I am worried people will think my behavior is odd," "I feel awkward and tense if I know people are watching me," and "I get panicky that others might see me faint or be sick or ill." Respondents indicate their responses on a scale ranging from 1 (not at all) to 4 (extremely). The Mattick-SIAS (Social Interaction Anxiety Scale) lists 20 items, such as "I feel tense if I am alone with just one person," "I become tense if I have to talk about myself or my feelings," and "When mixing socially, I am uncomfortable." Respondents indicate their reactions on a 5-point scale (Mattick & Clarke, 1988). The Social Phobia and Anxiety Inventory (SPAI) was specifically developed to assess anxiety and fear (see, e.g., Turner, Beidel, Dancu, & Stanley, 1989). Rehm and Marston (1968) developed a Situation Questionnaire (SQ). Subjects rate their anxiety level in relation to a number of heterosexual situations. The 18-item Dating and Assertiveness Questionnaire (Levinson & Gottman, 1978) offers two measures: dating skills (conversational and initiating skills) and assertiveness. Respondents indicate their comfort and ability to handle each situation on a 5-point scale. The Self-Consciousness Scale (Scheier, 1985) contains 22 items, such as "I think about myself a lot," "I get embarrassed easily," and "Large groups make me nervous." A 4-point scale is used, ranging from 0 (not at all like me) to 4 (a lot like me). The Social Interaction Self-Statement Test (Glass, Merluzzi, Biever, & Larsen, 1982) consists of 15 positive and 15 negative self-statements. Attributions for social phobia are focused on in the SPA (Heimberg, 1990). Twenty-one possible reasons why a person might develop a social phobia are listed, such as "born that way," "low self-esteem," and "lack of social skills," and the respondent indicates degree of importance on a scale ranging from 0 (not at all important as a cause of social phobia) to 4 (one of the most important causes). Some investigators have explored the use of composite measures including behavioral performance measures, independent evaluator ratings, and self-report measures (Turner, Beidel, Long, Turner, & Townsley, 1993).

## Scales Measuring Shyness

The Social Reticence Scale (Jones & Russell, 1982) consists of 21 items (see also revised version, Jones, Briggs, & Smith, 1986). This is designed to assess seven aspects of dispositional shyness, including difficulty in meeting people or expressing opinions, anxiety, loneliness, distraction, inhibition, and feelings of isolation. The Shyness Scale developed by Cheek and Buss (1981) correlates between .75 and .87 with other major scales such as The Social Avoidance and Distress Scale and the Social Reticence Scale (Cheek & Melchior, 1990). Examples of items are: "I feel tense when I'm with people I don't know well," "I feel inhibited in social situations," and "I have trouble looking someone right in the eye." In a recent comparison of measures used to assess shyness, Briggs and Smith (1986) concluded that they all appear to measure the same construct despite the fact that some focus on affective and cognitive correlates of shyness and others on behavioral correlates. Measures of shyness and social anxiety have similar correlates except for their success in accurately predicting behaviors associated with shyness. Some reports indicate that shyness and social anxiety scales measure the same construct (Anderson & Harvey, 1988).

## Other Measures

Degree of control people believe they have over their lives may be assessed by the Locus of Control of Behavior Scale (LCBS) (Craig, Franklin, & Andrews, 1984). A one-item scale used to tap this dimension asks respondents to indicate how much control they feel they have over the quality of their social life on a scale ranging from 1 (none) to 4 (a great deal) (Gambrill, 1993). The Multidimensional Perfectionism Scale (see Frost, Martin, Lahart, & Rosenblate, 1990) includes 35 items such as "I set higher goals than most people," "I hate being less than the

best at things," and "Neatness is very important to me." Respondents answer using a 5-point scale of agreement. Setting excessively high performance standards has often been identified as a cause of social anxiety and social phobia. The Irrational Beliefs Test has been used to assess beliefs of anxious individuals (Deffenbacher, Zwemer, Whisman, Hill, & Sloan, 1986). D'Zurilla and Nezu (1990) developed a 70-item Social Problem Solving Inventory. Scales that are used to test for depression include the Beck Depression Inventory (Beck, Ward, Mendelson, Mock, & Erbaugh, 1961) and the Atypical Depression Scale. This scale also reviews whether respondents meet diagnostic criteria of schizophrenia, schizoaffective disorder, unspecified functional psychosis, or endogenomorphic depression. A scale to assess fear of intimacy has been designed by Descutner & Thelen (1991).

## Social Behavior and Skill Inventories

A number of self-report instruments have been developed to assess social behavior/competence. The Social Situations Questionnaire (SSQ; Bryant & Trower, 1974) lists 30 situations, including both casual and intimate interactions. Respondents rate both difficulty and frequency of occurrence of each. The Survey of Heterosexual Interactions (SHI; Twentyman & McFall, 1975) presents 20 situations, most of which involve the early stages of dating. Respondents indicate whether they would perform the behavior if called for on a 7-point scale. A similar version for women was developed by Williams and Ciminero (1978). The Social Competence Scale includes 24 behaviors (Gambrill, 1993). Clients rate their degree of competence using a 5-point scale (see Figure 12.1). Frequency of dates, range of dating patterns, and self-report of comfort and satisfaction with current dating behavior are tapped by the Social Activities Questionnaire (SAQ; Arkowitz et al., 1975).

## Self-Anchored Scales

Many studies use self-anchored scales. For example, in a study investigating the effectiveness of a minimum counselor contact program designed to increase social contacts, subjects indicated their degree of anxiety as well as their satisfaction with their response following each audiotaped role play on a 7-point scale (Gambrill, 1973). In a program offered in a class format for enhancing enjoyable exchanges, participants indicate degree of shyness, satisfaction with their social life, and degree of control they feel

**Figure 12.1.** Social Competence Scale

Indicate how competent you feel in each of the following areas by checking the appropriate value.

|  | NOT AT ALL | A LITTLE | SOMEWHAT | FAIRLY | VERY |
|---|---|---|---|---|---|
| Identifying friendly people to approach | | | | | |
| Offering friendly reactions | | | | | |
| Greeting people | | | | | |
| Initiating conversations | | | | | |
| Introducing interesting topics | | | | | |
| Listening (encouraging others to talk) | | | | | |
| Maintaining conversations | | | | | |
| Balancing talking and listening | | | | | |
| Sharing information about yourself | | | | | |
| Offering opinions | | | | | |
| Responding to criticism | | | | | |
| sharing your feelings | | | | | |
| Changing the topic of conversation | | | | | |
| Disagreeing with others | | | | | |
| Using humor | | | | | |
| Ending conversations | | | | | |
| Suggesting interesting activities to share | | | | | |
| Arranging future meetings | | | | | |
| Requesting behavior changes | | | | | |
| Refusing unwanted invitations | | | | | |
| Asking favors | | | | | |
| Responding to put-downs | | | | | |
| Refusing unwanted sexual overtures | | | | | |
| Making sexual overtures | | | | | |

*Source:* E. D. Gambrill, ''A Class Format for Helping People to Increase the Quality of Their Social Lives,'' paper presented at the 23rd European Congress on Behavior and Cognitive Therapies, London, 1993.

they have over the quality of their social life, on 4-point scales (Gambrill, 1993).

## Self-Monitoring

Clients can gather valuable information in real-life settings. In a minimal counselor contact program designed to increase social contacts developed by Gambrill and Richey (1988), clients keep track of social contacts on a Social Contacts Recording Form. They record the date, who was involved (stranger, acquaintance or friend, man or woman), where and when the exchanges occurred, who initiated the exchange, how long each contact lasted, how comfortable they felt, how much they enjoyed the exchange, and how the other person reacted to them (neutral, positive, negative). This provides data on number of social contacts with men or women; with strangers, friends, and acquaintances; range of different exchanges (number of different people involved); average duration of contacts; average anxiety and enjoyment ratings; number of different situations sampled; how other people responded; and percentage of exchanges initiated. This record provides baseline data as well as clues about how to increase enjoyable social contacts (e.g., initiate more conversations). Review of data often indicates that few efforts are made to initiate social contacts. Participants are also encouraged to select one positive and one negative exchange during the week and to note additional information that would be helpful in increasing success on future occasions. In the cognitive behavioral program designed to decrease social phobia developed by Heimberg and his colleagues (1990), clients keep a daily diary in which they record situations listed on their fear hierarchy as well as other situations in which they feel anxious. They record the date, briefly describe the situation, rate their anxiety, fear of evaluation, and adequacy of performance (using scales that range from 0 to 100), as well as the total number of minutes they experienced anxiety.

## Physiological Measures

Physiological measures such as heart rate, pulse rate, blood pressure, and pupil dilation have been used to assess social anxiety (see, e.g., Beidel, Turner, & Dancu, 1985). A portable Lafayette Heart Rate monitor was used to record subjects' heart rate before and during a conversation with a confederate (Neumann, Critelli, Tang, & Schneider, 1988). Often, there is a lack of correlation between self-report measures of shyness and physiological measures, even though some believe that shyness is characterized by involvement of the sympathetic branch of the autonomic nervous system (Buss, 1980; Izard & Hyson, 1986). One reason for this is the frequent combination of both positive and negative emotions in social situations; that is, "one of the distinguishing qualities of shyness may be the conflict between positive [interest] and negative social feelings" (Izard & Hyson, 1986, p. 153). Both normals and social phobics display increased physiological arousal right before performing a task (Barlow, 1988).

## Role Play

Observation in structured settings has been used to assess behavior of shy, socially anxious, and socially phobic individuals. Either trained confederates or na-

ive volunteers may be used as partners. Role plays may involve an "extended" interaction (5 to 10 minutes) or require brief responses to a number of discrete stimulus presentations. Videotape or audiotape may be used to present the scene and record responses. Each situation is described, and a voice (male or female as relevant) then offers a leading statement, such as "Hi, . . ." Subjects then offer their response. Rehm and Marston (1968) developed one of the earliest audiotaped role-play tests for heterosexual situations. Interactions may be observed by raters or videotaped for later rating. Decisions must be made about what code categories to use to review performance: Will these be global and/or specific? Who will rate them? Categories of behavioral components assessed include nonverbal behaviors (e.g., gaze, smiles, gestures), paralanguage (voice, loudness, latency), verbal behavior (e.g., asking questions, praise), and mixed components (e.g., timing). Coding systems developed include the Behavioral Referenced Rating System of Intermediate Social Skills (Wallender, Conger, & Conger, 1985) (for more detail, see Glass & Arnkoff, 1989). Subjects in a minimal counselor contact program designed to increase social contacts responded to 12 tape-recorded stimulus presentations before and after intervention. Situations included initiating conversations, ending conversations, refusing unwanted requests, initiating a new topic of conversation, and asking a person out (Gambrill, 1973). Responses were reviewed and coded for discomfort, latency, fluency, affect, content, and overall skill. Situations selected for role-plays should be related to client goals and to unique anxiety-producing situations. A Behavioral Approach Test (BAT) based on individually tailored items is often used to assess behavior. Criteria used to select items include the report by the subject that he or she would avoid the situation if given a choice (Mattick et al., 1989). "Generalization" scenes may be included to determine the extent to which new behaviors generalize to different settings.

The SUDS Scale (Wolpe, 1973), which ranges from 0 (no anxiety) to 100 (maximum anxiety), can be used by clients to rate anxiety during role-plays. Ratings can be obtained before and after each role-play as well as during the role-play at points at which the client is instructed to use task-focused thoughts to control anxiety. This provides opportunities for clients to see the relationship between their anxiety level and what they focus on. In the program developed by Heimberg and his colleagues (1990), a rating of 25 is viewed as mild anxiety that does not interfere with what the client is doing, 50 is rated as uncomfortable anxiety that affects concentration but does not disrupt behavior, and 75 is considered uncomfortable anxiety that is preoccupying (i.e., it is difficult to concentrate and the client has thoughts of leaving the situation). A rating of 100 is the highest anxiety ever experienced or that the client can imagine experiencing. A lack of correspondence between behavior in role-plays and behavior in real life has been found in a number of studies, calling into question the external validity of role plays (see Nay, 1986).

## Observation in Real-Life Contexts

Intrusiveness may prohibit observers from watching clients in real-life settings such as parties or dances, although more could be done along these lines. Social encounters are not necessarily planned, which also makes observation problematic. Some methods fall between observation in real life and role-plays, as does the phone call assessment method used by Glass, Gottman, and Shmurak (1976). Each subject was given names and phone numbers of two women and was asked to call and "practice" getting to know this person. The women called were told they were participating in an experiment on telephone conversations. They rated each subject on their degree of skill and reported which caller they would most like to meet. Observation in real-life contexts is a neglected resource both in research concerning social skills and in assessment of individual behavior (Boice, 1982).

## INTERVENTION OPTIONS

Selection of intervention methods should be informed by assessment. This will indicate the role of behavior deficits, interfering thoughts, excessively high performance standards, social anxiety, environmental obstacles, lack of self-management skills, and lack of social opportunities. Social anxiety is viewed here as a learned reaction that can be altered through new conditioning experiences and acquiring cognitive, behavioral, and affect regulation skills. Social skills training will not be the method of choice for all clients with the complaints discussed in this chapter. Studies that have found that cognitive-behavioral methods, or practice are just as effective as social skills training suggests the contrary. For example, Shelver and Gutsch (1983) found that self-administered cognitive therapy resulted in positive changes on self-report measures compared to a no-treatment control and an attention-placebo condition. Studies

finding social skill deficits among social phobics suggest the value of social skills training (Stopa & Clark, 1993). Some studies have found an enhanced effect of combining graduated exposure and social skills training (Cappe & Alden, 1986). Questions about the relative contribution of different methods to positive outcomes are complicated by the inclusion of similar components in different methods. For example, social skills training involves exposure of clients to feared situations.

Many people who describe themselves as shy, socially anxious, phobic, or lonely do have the social skills required to do well but, for a variety of reasons, do not use these skills. For example, socially anxious people often behave submissively even though they know how to be assertive (Alden & Safran, 1978; Arkowitz et al., 1975; Vitkus & Horowitz, 1987). Reasons for this discrepancy include interfering emotional reactions (e.g., conditioned anxiety) and/or disruptive thoughts (worry about being rejected). Emotional, cognitive, and behavior deficits that may interfere with use of social skills include a dislike of people, an absence of facilitating positive self-statements, and a lack of self-management skills. Clients may lack practice in using skills so that situations that should serve as cues for social behaviors do not serve this function. Low sociability may be a problem.

An overview of intervention options is provided in the sections that follow. A group context is often used. Some groups are quite large (White, 1993). Intervention methods that pay little or no attention to the systematic development of specific social skills include those that focus on exposure to feared or avoided situations, including practice dating and positively biased interactions, those that focus on cognitions, minimal counselor contact self-help programs, and indirect methods. Intervention may be offered individually or in a group setting. Some studies combine social skills training, exposure, and modification of self-statements (Stravynski, 1983). Evaluation of the results of studies exploring the effectiveness of different kinds of programs is hampered by methodological problems such as lack of clear description of individuals included and differences among studies in the kinds of individuals selected. It is not clear, for example, whether people included in some studies would be diagnosed as socially phobic, avoidant personality disorder, or socially inadequate. Often clients are not described in terms of their unique reactions to anxiety-provoking situations and their entering repertoire of cognitive, affective, and social skills. It is thus often unknown whether a given client's loneliness, shyness, or social anxiety involves an acquisition problem in relation to self-management and social skills or a performance problem (social skills as well as self-management skills are available but are not used).

Clear description of intervention procedures is often lacking—for example, number of practice experiences of each client, number of model presentations observed, and number of homework assignments given and percentage correctly completed. Further problems include lack of (1) control groups, (2) follow-up data, (3) real-life progress measures, and (4) clear specification of the independent variable (e.g., number and duration of exposure experiences). Most behavioral programs focus on shy, lonely, or socially anxious individuals. These include social skills training, cognitive-behavioral methods, anxiety management training, and minimal counselor contact programs. Rearranging environmental conditions to increase opportunities for positive social contacts has received less attention. Programs presented as self-help methods may in fact include considerable counselor involvement.

Much of the research on increasing social contacts has focused on heterosexual dating situations (Prisbell, 1989). Reviews of the literature on increasing dating behavior often make no mention of programs developed to increase friends even though there is an overlap in the skills required to make friends and to establish romantic relationships, and even though research indicates that we often meet partners through friends and that companionship offered by friends is a key source of life satisfaction (Rook, 1990) (for exceptions see, e.g., Gambrill, 1973; 1993; Gambrill & Richey, 1988). Most programs focus on initial relationship stages. The development and maintenance of relationships is often ignored despite the fact that many people have problems in these later stages. Research investigating the importance of tailoring intervention programs to each client's unique assessment profile has yielded inconsistent results. Some studies report that such tailoring enhances success (see, e.g., Ost, Jerremalm, & Johansson, 1981; Trower, Yardley, Bryant, & Shaw, 1978). Other studies do not (e.g., Mersch, Emmelkamp, Bögels, & van der Sleen, 1989; Schulte, Künzel, Pepping, & Schulte-Bahrenberg, 1992). No clear and consistent differences in effectiveness among various kinds of intervention have been found (e.g., Butler et al., 1984; Emmelkamp et al., 1985; Mattick & Peters, 1988; Mattick et al., 1989; Scholing & Emmelkamp, 1993). Both in vivo exposure and cognitive therapies

have been found to be useful (see reviews by Heimberg, 1989; Scholing & Emmelkamp, 1990). The effects of exposure may be dampened by relatively automatic negative thinking in social phobics that gets in the way of attending to how other people actually respond (Stopa & Clark, 1993).

## SOCIAL SKILLS TRAINING

A number of programs designed to decrease social anxiety, loneliness, and shyness and to increase enjoyable social contacts focus on developing the social skills required to achieve these objectives. Social skills training is designed to develop skills required to attain valued social goals. It has been compared with systematic desensitization, relaxation training, and cognitive-behavioral methods (for a review, see, e.g., Heimberg, 1989). Such training has been found to be more effective compared to relaxation training in enhancing dating skills of developmentally disabled clients (Mueser, Valenti-Hein, & Yarnold, 1987). Social skills training is useful when needed social skills are absent and when clients will participate in this kind of training (see later section on indirect methods) (see Table 5.3 in Chapter 5). Components of social skills training include clear descriptions of specific skills to be acquired, model presentation, rehearsal, coaching, feedback, programming of change, and homework assignments. A number of studies have found behavior rehearsal to be valuable (e.g., MacDonald, Lindquist, Kramer, McGrath, & Rhyne, 1975). More recent programs complement social skills training with cognitive skill training and exposure (see later section). Homework assignments are a component of most programs, but rarely is their contribution to the success of programs evaluated. Lack of data about percentage of assignments correctly completed makes it impossible to determine the value of assignments in contributing to outcome (Primakoff, Epstein, & Covi, 1986). Relatively little attention has been given to knowledge, values, and skills of trainers as this influences outcomes (values of professionals involved in assertion training have been explored by Wilson & Gallois, 1993).

### Reconceptualizing Concerns

Presenting a rationale for social skill training is a key part of the intervention. Most clients do not think of the quality of their social life as being partly skill-based. Rather, they usually have a variety of misconceptions about social behavior, most of which either offer no guidelines for positive change or provide misleading directions. Encouraging a "skill power" approach to increasing enjoyable social experiences is a key part of many programs and should be initiated during assessment. Anxiety in social situations is viewed as a learned reaction resulting from previous social experiences, which can be unlearned by corrective learning experiences (Wolpe, 1958). The influence the individual can have over the quality of his or her social life is emphasized. This conceptualization of social behavior is built directly into the titles of some programs, such as *Taking Charge of Your Social Life* (Gambrill & Richey, 1988). Data concerning the prevalence of shyness and social anxiety can be valuable in normalizing concerns. Clients are often surprised that 38% of individuals report anxiety when meeting someone for the first time (Arkowitz, Hinton, Perl, & Himadi, 1978).

## What Criteria Should Be Used to Select Social Skills?

Outcomes of concern to clients should be a key criterion in selecting social skills to address. Other criteria include research concerning effective and ineffective behavior in specific situations and the nature of each client's "entering repertoire" (What skills are available? What skills are missing?). Selection of skills is hampered by a lack of data describing the skills required to achieve certain social goals. Literature on nonverbal communication is often ignored (Siegman & Feldstein, 1987). Research using judges to identify skills of value may provide misleading data because the skills identified may not be related to success in real-life situations. That is, competency ratings may not indicate competence in real life. Different investigators have emphasized different skills and have used different criteria for selecting these. Some investigators have used a content approach; they observed behaviors of different groups and identified differences. Others have used a consequences approach; they focused on outcomes achieved (Arkowitz, 1981, p. 299). For example, Libet and Lewinsohn (1973) defined *social skill* as "the complex ability to emit behaviors which are positively reinforced and not to emit behaviors that are punished or extinguished by others" (p. 311). Both content and consequences should be considered. As Arkowitz (1981) noted, discovering that groups such as high and low dating women differ in certain ways of behaving does not ensure that differences reported or noted in role-plays are the most important ones.

However, many studies suggest specific skills that are helpful. For example, showing personal attention to others results in significantly higher ratings from conversational partners (Kupke, Calhoun, & Hobbs, 1979). Many other examples could be cited. Ideally, a task analysis would be conducted to determine what skills are required to attain certain outcomes in specific situations and training would focus on these skills. Task analyses would also reveal the range of responses (the operant class) that would be effective in attaining a specific goal.

## Kinds of Skills Addressed

The particular skills addressed will depend on the outcomes of interest, the skills required to attain these, and the behavior deficits or surfeits of each client. Examples of social skills often addressed in programs designed to increase positive social contacts can be seen in Figure 12.1. Valuable opportunities to meet others are often lost because of reticence or lack of skill in initiating conversations. A client may have appropriate skills for initiating conversations but may display these at the wrong time. Even though clients may know a variety of ways to initiate conversations, they may benefit from learning and practicing additional ones (see, e.g., Gambrill & Richey, 1988). Nonverbal behaviors that are important in initiating conversations include eye contact, pleasant facial expression, and body orientation toward the other person. Voice qualities such as loudness and a relative absence of hesitations and stammers may influence success. Vocal training may be needed to enhance delivery (Phillips, 1984). Negative thoughts related to a reluctance to initiate conversations include worries about rejection or the possibility of rude or hostile replies. Shy, lonely, or socially anxious individuals often focus on the risk of negative outcomes and overlook opportunities for positive outcomes. Listening as well as speaking skills are important in maintaining conversations, and both areas should be assessed. When listening, does the client look at the other person and offer occasional verbal and nonverbal feedback in the form of "Mm-hms" and head nods? Does she wait until others have finished speaking before starting to talk? Does she ask the other person questions, and do these match what the other person has been saying? Does she offer information about herself as well as pick up on information offered by others and use this as the basis for questions and comments? Does she speak too much or too little? Does she introduce interesting topics of conversation and change the topic when appropriate? Are elaborated opinion statements offered as well as brief yes and no replies? Is she prepared with a variety of topics to speak about? Not sharing opinions or introducing topics of conversation may be related to a client's belief that her opinions are not valuable or interesting. Increasing personal attention (e.g., topic continuation, asking questions, references to the other person) by use of modeling, practice, and feedback were found to decrease loneliness, self-consciousness, and shyness significantly compared to a no-treatment group and a practice-only group (Jones, et al., 1982).

It is important to know how to end conversations in a polite way. Difficulty in ending conversations will limit opportunities to meet a variety of people at social events. The client's repertoire can be examined to determine whether he has the skills to do this. Does he wait for a natural pause in the conversation? If a pause does not occur, can he politely interrupt the other person? Failure to interrupt a talkative person who does not offer natural pauses is often related to the belief that it is impolite to interrupt someone. Arranging future contacts is another needed skill. This may require use of the telephone as well as in-person planning. Elements that probably influence success include showing enthusiasm, suggesting interesting activities, and persisting if initial efforts are not successful. Opportunities for further contacts may be lost because of ineffective reactions to requests for future meetings (e.g., saying no instead of yes, putting a decision off, not knowing how to get in touch with the person again). Offering positive responses to welcomed overtures is important. Behaviors to be increased in such situations include smiles, eye contact, and answering questions with more than yes or no (e.g., asking questions of the other person (Muehlenhard et al., 1986).

The client's impact in personal encounters may be decreased by a failure to show appropriate signs of affection. He may be hesitant ever to touch someone when offering a positive comment or ever to hug someone when saying goodbye. This may be combined with distancing reactions in response to affection shown by others, such as becoming tense when touched. ''Rewardingness'' is considered a critical skill cluster (Argyle et al., 1981). Behaviors associated with a friendly attitude are shown in Table 12.3. Cultural and ethnic differences in behavior in specific social situations will have to be considered in making recommendations. Other skills included in training programs are giving and receiving compliments, refusing unwanted requests, requesting changes in annoying behaviors, handling silences, altering participation in conversations (talking more or less), and sharing feelings (Gambrill & Richey, 1988; Gambrill, 1993). Cappe and Alden (1986) compared graduated exposure to fear-provoking situations and training in other-focused skills with exposure alone and a wait-list control condition. Skills addressed in the interpersonal process training included active listening, empathic responding, communicating respect, and self-disclosure. After discussion and model presentation of each skill, each subject practiced his or her own problematic social situations and tried to adapt the skill to unique situations and individual style. Subjects then selected several situations to approach in real life to attempt to apply their skill, beginning at the bottom of their hierarchy. Subjects receiving a combination of exposure and interpersonal process

**Table 12.3.** Behaviors Associated with a Friendly Attitude

| NONVERBAL | VERBAL |
|---|---|
| • Touch (hand on arm) | • Compliments |
| • Forward body lean | • Agreeing with what others say |
| • Body oriented toward others | • Active listening (e.g., minimal verbal cues) |
| • Moderate relaxation | • Expressing interest in what others say (asking questions) |
| • ''Open'' body position (arms unfolded) | • Disclosures of similarity |
| • Frequent looks and eye contact | • Few speech disturbances |
| • Positive facial expressions (smiling, interest) | • Good timing (few interruptions) |
| • Affirmative head nods | |
| • Moderate amount of gesturing and animation | |
| • Fairly close distance (within 3 feet) | |

*Source:* See, for example, Trower, Bryant, and Argyle (1978).

training improved significantly more on measures of community functions and therapist ratings than did subjects receiving exposure alone or wait-list subjects. MacDonald et al., (1975) compared two skill-training programs involving behavior rehearsal with and without extrasession assignments with attention-placebo and wait-list control groups. Subjects in the training groups showed significant increases in social dating skill levels compared to the other two groups, but no differences were found in number of self-reported dates.

## EXPOSURE AS A KEY FACTOR

Many studies suggest the role of exposure to feared situations as a key factor in overcoming social anxiety (Barlow, 1988; Marks, 1987). Specific anxiety-provoking situations relevant to each individual are identified, and exposure to these situations is arranged. Exposure programs help clients to maintain contact with feared cues until anxiety decreases (habituation occurs). Most programs designed to decrease loneliness, shyness, social anxiety, and social phobia involve exposure to feared situations. In systematic desensitization, clients imagine or actually encounter feared situations. Programs designed to enhance coping skills that can be used to manage anxiety in any situation, such as anxiety management training (Suinn, 1990), also involve exposure. Cognitive methods involve thinking about feared situations. Cognitive-behavioral programs emphasize exposure. Other kinds of programs focus more squarely on exposure. These include self-exposure programs, arranging positively biased interactions, and practice dating. All involve minimal counselor contact. Programs based around a social activity also involve exposure (see, e.g., Leon & Gambrill, 1973).

### Self-Exposure

Marks (1987) argues that "most sufferers can complete live self-exposure successfully without a therapist having to be present, especially if it is systematized with the aid of an appropriate manual and diary" (p. 458). (For a recent meta-analysis of self-help treatment approaches see Gould & Clum, 1993.) Clients differ in the amount of counselor help required. Although it is clear that many clients can benefit from a self-exposure program involving minimal therapist time, failure to carry out recommended procedures is a key problem with others. Some studies comparing social skills training and exposure for decreasing social phobia have found comparable

effects (Wlazlo et al., 1990). Comparison of self-exposure with the aid of a self-help book (*Living with Fear;* Marks, 1978) with treatment by a psychiatrist or a computer indicated that all these groups improved markedly and equally up to six months' follow-up (Ghosh & Marks, 1987). Response induction aids help clients to initiate and complete exposure programs. These include keeping an exposure diary to record self-exposure homework and guidance by a manual. Other aids include carrying out exposure in small, manageable bits; trying difficult tasks briefly at first; engaging in rather than dissociating from the task, varying tasks until fear has decreased to all relevant cues; and fading out aids as confidence and competence are acquired. Long exposure periods are more effective than short periods (see Marks, 1987, for more detail). Problems that may arise with in vivo exposure include the unpredictability of most social situations, the brevity of some social exchanges, and lack of clear feedback about whether other people's reactions are positive or negative (Butler, 1985).

Self-help programs involving minimal counselor contact are ideally suited for individuals who do not have extremely high levels of social anxiety, who have the skills required to do well in social situations, and who are "motivated" to carry out recommended procedures. The results of some studies suggest that the addition of cognitive restructuring increases the effectiveness of exposure. The results of other studies indicate that cognitive approaches add little to the value of exposure (see Marks, 1987). Mattick et al. (1989) compared exposure, cognitive restructuring without exposure, a combination, and a wait-list trial in decreasing social phobia. The combination group was superior to the exposure group on two measures. The cognitive-restructuring group was inferior to both the exposure and combination groups on behavioral approach following treatment but showed continued improvement compared to the exposure group on this measure as well as other variables. Change in fear of negative evaluation accounted for most of the explained variance in effects found. Butler, Cullington, Munby, Amies, and Gelder (1984) compared exposure and exposure plus anxiety management for decreasing social phobia. Exposure was self-controlled. Clients practiced homework assignments for one hour a day. Subjects receiving anxiety management training learned to control the symptoms of anxiety. (Anxiety management training is a key part of the cognitive-behavioral program developed by Heimberg and his colleagues; see later discussion). Anxiety management training included relaxation, distraction, and rational self-talk. Both groups improved more compared to a wait-list group. Adding anxiety management training did not offer substantial gains. However, 40% of clients in the exposure group requested further treatment within a year, whereas no clients in the combined group did so.

McGovern, Arkowitz, and Gilmore (1975) compared a group required to read and discuss a dating manual with a group required to read the manual and rehearse situations described in the manual. Rehearsal did not result in any additional improvement. A manual was also used in a minimal counselor contact program designed by Gambrill (1973). Very brief (about 30-minute) group meetings were held with participants who were selected on the basis of a low frequency of social contacts. Respondents completed both self-report and behavioral measures before and after intervention and monitored daily social interactions. Comparison of a group receiving a self-help manual, a manual plus self-reinforcement group, an attention-placebo group, and a wait-list group showed that women in both training groups improved on self-report and self-monitoring measures and gains were maintained at a three-month follow-up in proportion of contacts initiated. Gains in a role-play test of social skill were found only for women who also received self-reinforcement training, and subjects in this group reported higher gains in confidence in social situations than did subjects in any other group. Considerable attention is given to self-management skills in this program, including monitoring progress, setting specific long-term and intermediate goals, selecting assignments, and prompting and reinforcing desired behaviors (see also Gambrill, 1993; Gambrill & Richey, 1988). Clients are encouraged to focus less on themselves and more on positive consequences—to be more concerned about lost opportunities for enjoyment than about getting rejected. As part of this rebalancing, they are encouraged to paint the worst and best scenarios. It is unlikely that a self-help format will provide sufficient guidelines for all people. Additional research is needed about what format would be most effective for particular clients.

## Positively Biased Interactions

Montgomery and Haemmerlie (1986) explored the effectiveness of positively biased interactions in decreasing heterosexual anxiety (see also Haemmerlie, 1983; Hammerlie & Montgomery, 1984). In two sessions given one day apart, each subject engaged in six 10- to 12-minute positively biased exchanges with an opposite-sex confederate. (Conversational partners were coached to be pleasant and warm.) This procedure was effective with both men and women on a variety of measures. Subjects reported that the experience was enjoyable, and gains were maintained on a six-month follow-up. Total treatment time was under three hours. These talks provide success experiences. As the authors note, it could be that social skills training programs succeed not because of reinforcement, modeling, and/or shaping of behavior and instructions but because subjects offer appropriate behavior. "Thus improvement may come more simply from the clients having observed that he or she is capable of performing the behavior deemed appropriate, rather than from the actual acquisition and reinforcement of these skills . . . nothing succeeds like success, and the perception of that success in the area where one has previously been unsuccessful" (p. 507). This research supports a behavior–attitude link; that one way to alter attitudes and beliefs is to change behavior (not to change internal states). Positively biased interactions also involve exposure to feared situations as well as vicarious modeling opportunities (watching how others act).

## Practice Dating

Lack of exposure to social situations may be responsible for an unsatisfactory quality and quantity of social contacts. Avoidance of social situations will maintain social anxiety because there is no opportunity for exposure and new learning experiences. Simply arranging a series of practice dates has been found to be successful in increasing the dating behavior of college students. Martinson and Zerface (1970) pointed to the lack of exposure that nondaters had to heterosexual social situations and to the presence of misconceptions and unrealistic fears about such situations. They explored the use of a series of five arranged interactions between male subjects and female volunteers who wished to improve their social skills, during which the couple was encouraged to discuss problems that might interfere with successful social interaction. This was more effective than eclectic counseling or no treatment. Christensen, Arkowitz, and Anderson (1975) explored the value of six practice dates between male and female subjects with and without feedback provided by each partner. Posttest results showed that both treatment groups improved more than a control group on self-report, self-monitoring, and behavioral measures. Offering clients practice in public speaking not only increased their comfort in this situation but also increased social contacts initiated even though no attention was given to increasing social contacts during intervention (Phillips & Sokoloff, 1979; Phillips, 1986). This suggests the generalization of effects from different kinds of practice opportunities. Encouraging participants to focus on accomplishing specific goals and focusing on observable achievements distracts them from focusing on internal feelings that may increase anxiety and compromise performance.

The success of minimal counselor contact programs involving guided self-exposure as well as practice dating and positively biased interactions support the value of exposure to feared situations in habituation to anxiety-provoking social events. The success of exposure experiences requires a minimal level of effective social skills.

## COGNITIVE METHODS

A variety of cognitive methods have been drawn on to alter shyness, loneliness, and social anxiety including rational emotive therapy and cognitive restructuring. Cognitive methods focus on altering thoughts in order to alter behavior. In contrast, exposure procedures alter avoidance on the assumption that cognitive and physiological changes will follow (Marks, 1987). "Unlike exposure, which encourages a direct approach to the stimulus that evokes fear in real life and fantasy until there is habituation of behavior, physiology, and thoughts, cognitive therapies attempt to change false beliefs in the hope that this will change behavior" (p. 486). As Marks points out, most cognitive methods involve some exposure to feared events.

Programs that focus on altering beliefs related to interpersonal situations have received increasing attention. Beck's cognitive methods have been drawn on by Young (1982) in helping lonely clients. It is assumed that interfering beliefs and self-statements are responsible for loneliness. Young (1982) emphasizes the importance of determining whether loneliness is a primary or secondary problem (whether other concerns such as depression and anxiety are present). A relationship history is used to determine these factors. This will indicate how long loneliness has lasted and what events result in loneliness. The program Young developed is for clients who have primary chronic or situational loneliness. Loneliness is viewed as a developmental process, and each client is viewed as entering counseling at a particular point.

Stages include being alone, forming casual friendships, engaging in mutual self-disclosure, meeting a potentially intimate partner, developing intimacy, and making a long-term emotional commitment. Major objectives for these six stages include the following.

1. To overcome anxiety and sadness about spending time alone
2. To engage in activities with a few casual friends
3. To engage in mutual self-disclosure with a trustworthy friend
4. To meet a potentially intimate, appropriate partner (usually of the opposite sex)
5. To begin to develop intimacy with an appropriate partner, usually though disclosure and sexual contact
6. To make an emotional commitment to an appropriate partner for a relatively long period of time (p. 391)

Clients complete the Young Loneliness Inventory (1982). This consists of 19 items asking clients about the nature of their relationships. Examples of items are "I have someone nearby who really understands me," "I can't trust anyone," "I have a lot in common with the people I know," and "When I want to do something for enjoyment, I can usually find someone to join me." Young and his colleagues believe that lonely clients can be divided into 12 different clusters that predispose them to loneliness, and they are developing intervention programs designed for each particular cluster. One is the "intimate rejection" cluster. Automatic thoughts that characterize this cluster include "I won't risk being hurt again," and "There's something wrong with me, I'd screw up any relationship." Other clusters include low self-concept (clients consider themselves undesirable), discontented being alone ("I don't want to go out by myself"), social anxiety, social awkwardness, mistrust (clients have a profound mistrust of others), constriction (difficulty with self-disclosure, belief that no one understands them), problems in partner selection (beliefs that there is nowhere to meet people, excessive restrictions in selection of partners), anxiety about emotional commitment, insecure passivity cluster (reluctance to express dissatisfaction), and unrealistic expectations.

Comparisons of systematic desensitization with social skills training and cognitive restructuring in relation to decreasing dating anxiety suggests that they are equally effective (see, e.g., Arkowitz, 1977; Curran, 1977). In their review of the dating anxiety literature, Hope and Heimberg (1990) concluded that all four treatments (practice dating, social skills training, systematic desensitization, and cognitive modification) appear to be effective. As they noted, methodological problems as well as lack of attention to individual differences in assigning subjects to groups limit conclusions that can be drawn. Some have argued that all four methods increase subjects' confidence that they can attain their goals, perhaps by making the goals more realistic or by enhancing self-efficacy beliefs. All four methods involve exposure to feared events.

## COGNITIVE-BEHAVIORAL PROGRAMS

Many programs combine cognitive and behavioral methods. Glass et al. (1976) compared a response acquisition treatment with a cognitive self-statement program, a combination program, and a wait-list control. Self-statement modification included identification of negative self-statements that occur before, during, and after social exchanges. These statements are then examined, focusing on helping clients to identify irrational, self-defeating, and self-fulfilling nature of their statements. Finally, more appropriate positive self-statements are identified and encouraged. Subjects trained in cognitive self-statement modification showed better performance in role-play situations for which they were not trained, made significantly more phone calls, and made a significantly better impression on the women compared to subjects in other groups. As the authors noted, "At least for subjects who already possess the necessary repertoire of dating skills, learning how to cope with negative self-statements appears to be a technique the individual can practice on his own and use in situations different from those practiced only in the program" (p. 525).

Heimberg and his colleagues have developed a cognitive-behavioral treatment program for working with socially phobic clients (Heimberg, 1989, 1990). Components of this program include exposure to simulated phobic events, cognitive restructuring of maladaptive thoughts, and homework assignments for self-directed exposure and cognitive restructuring between sessions. Applicants are carefully screened for the program. Two reviewers must assign a diagnosis of social phobia to a client. Clients must also meet a number of requirements for participation in a group (e.g., lacking profound disturbance, not too demanding of attention, motivated to participate, and

lacking hostility). Clients with depression or who are on tranquilizing drugs and refuse to stop taking these are excluded. Treatment takes place over 12 weekly two-hour sessions with 5 to 6 clients using a mixed-gender team of co-therapists. The major goal of this program is to arrange exposure of the client to anxiety-provoking social situations and provide practice in using cognitive coping skills to alter interfering negative thoughts. Cognitive-behavioral group therapy treatment components include (1) structured cognitive exercises, (2) exposure to simulated anxiety-provoking events, (3) cognitive restructuring before and after exposures, (4) behavioral homework assignments, and (5) cognitive homework assignments. Goals of structured cognitive exercises are to (1) determine the frequency of patients' maladaptive thinking and its relationship to anxiety, (2) to identify automatic thoughts as hypotheses rather than facts, (3) to identify the distorted reasoning in automatic thoughts, (4) to develop means of disputing automatic thoughts, and (5) to develop rational responses to automatic thoughts. Specific situations of concern to each client are identified, as well as stimulus variations that influence anxiety. A tripartite view of anxiety is described to clients, and clients are encouraged to identify physiological, cognitive, and behavioral components of their anxiety. Clients complete a number of assessment measures at each session, including the Beck Depression Inventory (Beck et al., 1961).

Practice is given in identifying negative thoughts in anxiety-arousing situations and in challenging these. The method used is a mix of rational-emotive therapy (Ellis & Grieger, 1977) and Beck's cognitive treatment (Beck, Emery, & Greenberg, 1985). Clients receive a list of the cognitive distortions developed by Beck and practice identifying these both during role-played exposure sessions and in structured homework assignments. Although a hierarchy is formed that may be drawn on in outside practice, this is not relied on in sessions. There is no effort to protect clients from high levels of anxiety during exposure (practice of behavior in anxiety-provoking situations). Clients rehearse cognitive coping strategies while they are experiencing anxiety. The key role of avoidance in maintaining social anxiety is emphasized and clients are encouraged to stay in anxiety-arousing situations using their arousal-lowering cognitive coping skills to stay in the situations until anxiety subsides. Comparison of this package with a credible placebo control showed that participants receiving the cognitive-behavioral program improved more at both posttest and follow-up than did participants receiving lecture-discussion and group support (Heimberg et al., 1990).

## PROVIDING INFORMATION

Social skills training programs with shy, lonely, or socially anxious clients differ in the extent to which there is a strong educational component. Topics of relevance include (1) relationships (how they develop, deepen, are maintained, and end); (2) social anxiety (its nature, etiology, and correlates); (3) shyness, loneliness, and social anxiety (their nature and interrelationships); (4) social and self-management skills of value; and (5) social ecology (how to identify and/or create opportunities for social contacts). Clients often have incorrect beliefs in all these areas that get in their way. Incorrect beliefs may be directly related to false information provided in the media, such as incorrect reports about the shortages of men (Faludi, 1991). In the minimal counselor contact program developed by Gambrill and Richey (1976, 1988), clients are requested to review their beliefs about the causes of unsatisfactory social experiences, and corrective information about behavior and social relationships is offered. The view of relationship development as a process with different stages is introduced, and participants are encouraged to develop skill in and find value in exchanges at all stages (Duck, 1983). Many clients do not value brief encounters with strangers because they are focused totally on their goal of making close friends or finding a romantic partner. This results in discounting intermediate steps such as meeting new people and having brief conversations. The program developed by Heimberg and his colleagues in working with socially anxious clients also contains an educational component. A cognitive-behavioral explanation of social phobia as well as a rationale for treatment effectiveness is offered. The acquired nature of social anxiety, as well as the rationale for exposure experiences, is part of self-administered exposure programs (see, e.g., Marks, 1987).

Provision of information in a class format offers a normalizing context for instruction. Preliminary analysis of pre–post questionnaires completed by men and women who participated in a course offered through the University of California at Berkeley Extension on *Taking Charge of Your Social Life* suggests that this format is effective with some individuals (Gambrill, 1993). Six weekly two-hour sessions are held, and participants carry out homework assignments between meetings. The presence of both men and women allows each group to see and empathize with the concerns of the other group. Women are often surprised that men are anxious when initiating conversations or requesting future meetings. This format has disadvantages also. One is lack of time to individualize each participant's program fully under expert supervision.

## NETWORK BUILDING

Many people are reluctant to describe themselves as lonely, shy, or socially anxious, perhaps even to themselves. One has to admit that he or she is shy, lonely, or socially anxious to enroll in programs focused on these concerns. Only a small proportion of shy, lonely, or socially anxious or phobic individuals seek treatment. Thus, programs designed specifically to decrease shyness, loneliness, or social anxiety may be shunned by many people who could otherwise benefit from them. For many people, simply rearranging opportunities for practice and contact provides the changes necessary to enhance social opportunities (see earlier discussion). Involvement in activities that are *not* focused on increasing social contacts has been effective in increasing valued social experiences. Rook (1984c) referred to this as network building. One project designed to establish supportive social networks for isolated senior citizens took place in an inner-city single-room occupancy hotel (Pilisuk & Minkler, 1980). A station was set up in the hotel lobby offering free blood pressure checkups. This offered residents opportunities to meet and identify shared interests. Within a year, they had formed a Senior Activities Club that became an ongoing support group. This project made creative use of an indirect approach (provision of free blood pressure checkups) to encourage contacts among isolated individuals (p. 395). As Rook (1984c) pointed out, such indirect approaches will be of special value in situations in which a sense of belonging and interacting with others is uncommon.

Combining participation in activities of interest (such as volunteer work, sports, hobbies, or recreational activities) with an interest in meeting other people is a key part of a program designed by Gambrill and Richey (1976, 1988). Participants complete an Activity Inventory and select activities that they enjoy, that are possible to pursue, and that offer opportunities to meet people. Strategies for locating promising places are reviewed, and activities discovered are shared with other participants. A checklist for reviewing behavioral settings is provided. Finding promising settings can be carried out in a buddy format in which participants accompany each other. This provides company and support during social reconnaissance adventures. Environmental conditions that are directly related to the development of loneliness, social anxiety, and shyness, such as few social contexts in which to meet people, should receive greater attention. Altering these to enhance the quality of social experiences and to prevent loneliness, social anxiety, and shyness may be difficult to achieve. Richey, Lovell, and Reid (1991) have explored the use of social skills training to increase the friendship networks of parents at risk of child maltreatment. Loneliness is a common complaint among women who maltreat their children (Polansky, 1986).

Enhancing the skills of lonely, shy, or socially anxious individuals will not necessarily result in desired changes in the quality of interpersonal relationships. Obstacles that may get in the way include an emphasis on competition and individualism rather than cooperation and sending reassurance signals, a lack of behavior settings that encourage positive exchanges, and a small pool of individuals who are open to forming new relationships. Public spaces that permit informal social exchanges are decreasing (Schiller, 1989). Given the uncertainty in arranging more rewarding social experiences for many people, Rook (1984c) recommends that increased attention be given to enhancing competencies for coping with unwanted solitude (such as learning to enjoy solitary activities) (see Table 12.4).

## GENERALIZATION AND MAINTENANCE

There are a number of steps that can be taken to increase the likelihood of generalization and maintenance of skills (Stokes & Osnes, 1989). Examples include the use of multiple training models and practice in a range of situations. The skill clusters related to increasing opportunities for social reinforcement (self-management, as well as those involved in identifying situations that offer opportunities for practice and social contact) should be helpful in maintaining behaviors. Maintenance of satisfying friendships will be especially challenging given the voluntary aspect of friendship and the contradictory pressures on such relationships (such as their voluntary nature and intimacy, which suggests expectations that should be fulfilled) (Wiseman, 1986).

## CONCLUSION

Loneliness, shyness, and social anxiety are common complaints and are implicated in a variety of other presenting problems. These are separate but interrelated concepts and experiences. Initially, the focus was on enhancing specific verbal and nonverbal behaviors believed to be of value in attaining valued objectives such as increasing enjoyable social contacts and decreasing anxiety in social situations. Recently, more attention has been devoted to programs that focus on interfering factors that hinder effective use of social skills such as conditioned anxiety and dysfunctional thoughts. Many shy, lonely, or socially anxious people have the social skills required to increase enjoyable social exchanges but do not use them. Different skills and experiences will be required for these performance problems compared to cases in which social skills must be developed.

An individualized assessment will indicate the particular goals and problems of each client, the specific situations involved, and variables that influence performance and success, including conditioned anxiety, interfering thoughts, lack of self-management skills, and limited environmental opportunities. Research concerning the role of negative thoughts, excessive physiological arousal, environmental obstacles, lack of self-management skills, and behavior surfeits such as aggressive reactions highlights the potential value of a careful assessment. A description of relevant behavioral, affective, and cognitive entering repertoires in situations of concern as well as cognitive, behavioral, and affective deficits and excesses that may interfere with the acquisition and use of social skills should aid in judicious selection of intervention programs.

Drawing conclusions about the effectiveness of different methods is hampered by a variety of methodological problems in studies conducted (see, e.g., Curran, 1977). Evaluation of effectiveness is sometimes hampered by lack of data about real-life changes including follow-up data. Even in studies purporting to examine the efficacy of matching intervention methods to individual characteristics, no assessment may be made of relevant entering repertoires and clients matched to intervention methods accordingly (see, e.g., McCann, Woolfolk, & Lehrer, 1987). Programs are often selected without careful review of a client's repertoire to determine if needed skills are available. Clients may be randomly distributed to different methods without any prior assess-

**Table 12.4.** Overview of Interventions for Loneliness

| GOAL OF INTERVENTION | INDIVIDUAL APPROACHES | | GROUP APPROACHES | | ENVIRONMENTAL APPROACHES | |
| --- | --- | --- | --- | --- | --- | --- |
| | SPECIFIC TO LONELINESS | RELEVANT TO LONELINESS | SPECIFIC TO LONELINESS | RELEVANT TO LONELINESS | SPECIFIC TO LONELINESS | RELEVANT TO LONELINESS |
| Facilitate social bonding | Cognitive; behavioral therapy for loneliness | Client-centered therapies Psychodynamic therapies | Social skills training for lonely college students and socially isolated children | Social skills training for dating anxiety Shyness groups Self-help groups | Network building (Intentional and unintentional) | Restructuring social settings (e.g. school classroom modification) |
| Enhance coping with loneliness | | Improving solitary skills (pleasurable activities scheduling) | Support groups for bereavement, divorce, and other social losses | | | |
| Prevent loneliness | | | Early intervention with high-risk groups (e.g., children of divorce) | | Community awareness and educational programs | Removing obstacles to social contact |

*Source:* K. S. Rook "Promoting Social Bonding: Strategies for Helping the Lonely and Socially Isolated." *American Psychologist, 39.* 1984. p. 1401. Reprinted by permission.

ment of social or cognitive skills (e.g., Rosenfarb, Hayes, & Linehan, 1989). No wonder results are often disappointing. Potential problems with reliance on programs in which intervention is not tailored to individual differences have been noted (Wolpe, 1986). Comparative studies as well as the effectiveness of minimal counselor contact programs such as practice dating, self-exposure, and positively biased exchanges support the importance of exposure. The success experiences provided by such methods may alter expectations, which in turn influence future behavior. The role of expectations is suggested by studies in which social behavior was altered by varying expectations. For example, interviewers who were told that an interviewee was extroverted asked different questions compared to interviewers who were told that the interviewee was introverted (Swann, Giuliano, & Wegner, 1982). Questions were asked that resulted in the kind of behavior expected. There is a behavioral confirmation tendency. Characteristics of the therapeutic relationship may influence outcome (Ford, 1978). These may be influential even in minimal counselor contact programs involved in self-exposure. A careful review of each client's repertoires related to situations of interest and inclusion of skill training to fill in the gaps may increase real-life success. Thus the question "How much change is possible?" is an important one.

There is no doubt that social skills training will have an important role to play in helping many shy, lonely, socially anxious, and phobic clients. This option is uniquely suited to developing a range of social skills that are required to do well in specific social situations. There is also no doubt that social skills training will not necessarily be the method of choice or the sole method used. The success of minimal counselor contact self-exposure programs indicates that this will not be the case. Social skills training focused on verbal and nonverbal skills will not be the method of choice for clients whose complaints are related to a lack of environmental settings that permit and encourage enjoyable social experiences, or to factors that interfere with use of social skills such as interfering thoughts or high anxiety. Indirect methods will be required to achieve success with some populations. Greater advantage could be taken of programmed instruction to increase knowledge and skills. Bullmer (1972) found that programmed self-instructional material was more effective than a required educational psychology class in increasing ability to perceive affect in others (see also Muehlenhard, Baldwin, Bourg, & Piper, 1988). The programmed text included content on interpersonal per-

ception, sources of error, identifying emotions, and identifying hidden meanings. It would be helpful if consumers had a guide to identify effective intervention options. One possibility would be an interactive computer-based assessment protocol that permits low-cost state-of-the-art assessment. Consumers could be directed to methods that are most likely to be effective at the least cost in terms of time, money, effort, and discomfort. People could determine if they can identify effective ways of acting in specific social situations and could observe varied ways to handle specific situations. It would even be possible to gather subjective anxiety ratings and/or physiological data at the same time that would facilitate the creation of avoidance hierarchies of value in planning practice experiences. Programs could guide users through a review of factors that may interfere with use of available skills, such as excessively high standards and environmental obstacles.

Identification of the skills required for success in specific situations is a high priority. What are the social operants in specific situations (the range of behaviors that would be successful in attaining a given outcome)? To date, there has been a lack of integration of the skills-training literature focused on children with that dealing with adults. Films and video modeling, as well as placing a child in a "leadership role" (pairing him or her with a younger child), have been found to decrease social isolation (Kendall & Morrison, 1984). Certainly, some methods that have been used with children will not be relevant to adults, but others will. The social skills-training literature with children shows that neglected children differ from rejected children. In the first case, there is a lack of positive reinforcement. In the latter, there may be a significant history of punishment. This difference is probably true of adults as well, but little attention has been given to the effect of these different histories of reinforcement on selection of intervention programs.

Although many obstacles can be avoided by a thorough, individually tailored assessment, this will not be true of all. It is not surprising that achieving success with all clients is still an ideal to be hoped for rather than a fait accompli. Shyness, loneliness, and social anxiety or phobia range from straightforward and simple in relation to causative factors and selection of intervention methods to highly complex and challenging, involving patterns of behaviors and associated beliefs that do not change easily if at all (Butler, 1989; Young, 1982). Social anxiety is associated with evolutionary causes that remain with us (Trower & Gilbert, 1989). Hostility toward others, not liking or trusting other people, and disliking oneself may require individual counseling to address these interfering characteristics. Often, little mention is made of people who really do not like other people. How can the reinforcing value of social exchanges be enhanced for such individuals? An individually tailored assessment should offer guidelines. Possible reasons include not seeking out people who would be liked and not planning enjoyable social activities. A basic mistrust of people or blaming others for an unsatisfactory social life may be related to a dislike of other people. Cultivating the view of social exchanges as a two-way street (a reciprocal influence process) may aid in altering such attitudes. Compliance in carrying out assignments and collecting data regarding progress is a common problem. Social situations are unpredictable, making it impossible to control the intensity of anxiety arousal. And we must not forget environmental obstacles: the inadequate range of social contexts for facilitating enjoyable social exchanges and life pressures such as overly busy work schedules that leave little room for social explorations. Environmental approaches are among three intervention approaches described by Rook (1984c) in her overview of interventions for loneliness (see Table 12.4).

The consequences to individuals as well as to society of reticence and anxiety in social situations are great. The results include unnecessary distress and lost opportunities as well as dysfunctional ways of handling these outcomes, such as substance abuse. There are losses for society as well: "The study of social anxiety provides more than an important insight into personal suffering. Social anxiety may also be apparent in the fear of acting morally, the fear of disobeying, shown in part in the preparedness to harm others, the fear of being shamed, and the avoidance of the truly social and compassionate life that is capable of seeking, finding, and giving reassurance" (Gilbert & Trower, 1990, p. 173). These consequences call for greater attention to the prevention of shyness, loneliness and social anxiety (Rook, 1984c). However, this public health model has not been popular.

## REFERENCES

Alden, L., & Safran, J. (1978). Irrational beliefs and non-assertive behavior. *Cognitive Research and Therapy, 4*, 256–364.

American Psychiatric Association. (1987). *Diagnostic and statistical manual of mental disorders,* 3rd ed., rev. Washington, DC: Author.

Anderson, C. A., & Arnoult, L. H. (1985). Attributional styles and everyday problems in living: Depression, loneliness and shyness. *Social Cognition, 3,* 16–35.

Anderson, C. A., & Harvey, R. J. (1988). Discriminating between problems in living: An examination of measures of depression, loneliness, shyness, and social anxiety. *Journal of Social and Clinical Psychology, 6*(3/4), 482–491.

Argyle, M. (1981). The contribution of social, interaction research to social skills training. In J. D. Wine & M. D. Smye (Eds.), *Social competence* (pp. 261–286). New York: Guilford Press.

Argyle, M., Furnham, A., & Graham, J. A. (1981). *Social situations.* Cambridge: Cambridge University Press.

Argyle, M., & Henderson, M. (1985). *The anatomy of relationships.* London: Heinemann.

Arkin, R. M., Lake, E. A., & Baumgardner, A. H. (1986). Shyness and self-presentation. In W. H. Jones, J. M. Cheek, & S. R. Briggs (Eds.), *Shyness: Perspective on research and treatment* (pp. 189–203). New York: Plenum Press.

Arkowitz, H. (1977). Measurement and modification of minimal dating behavior. In M. Hersen, Eisler, R. M., & P. Miller (Eds.), *Progress in behavior modification* (Vol. 5, pp. 1–61). New York: Academic Press.

Arkowitz, H. (1981). Assessment of social skills. In M. Hersen & A. S. Bellack (Eds.), *Behavioral assessment: A practice handbook,* 2nd ed. (pp. 296–327). New York: Pergamon Press.

Arkowitz, H., Hinton, R., Perl, J., & Himadi, W. (1978). Treatment strategies for dating anxiety in college men based on real-life practice. *The Counseling Psychologist, 7,* 41–46.

Arkowitz, H., Lichtenstein, E., McGovern, K., & Hines, P. (1975). The behavioral assessment of social competence in males. *Behavior Therapy, 6,* 3–13.

Asher, S. R., & Cole, J. D. (1990). *Peer rejection in childhood.* New York: Cambridge University Press.

Asher, S. R., Hymel, S., & Renshaw, P. D. (1984). Loneliness in children. *Child Development, 55,* 1457–1464.

Bailey, K. (1987). *Human paleopsychology: Application to aggression and pathological processes.* Hillsdale, NJ: Lawrence Erlbaum.

Bandura, A. (1986). *Social foundations of thought and action: A social cognitive theory.* Englewood Cliffs, NJ: Prentice-Hall.

Barlow, D. H. (1988). *Anxiety and its disorders: The nature and treatment of anxiety and panic.* New York: Guilford Press.

Beck, A. T., Emery, G., & Greenberg, R. (1985). *Anxiety disorders and phobias: A cognitive perspective.* New York: Basic Books.

Beck, A. T., Ward, C. H., Mendelson, M., Mock, J., & Erbaugh, J. (1961). An inventory for measuring depression. *Archives of General Psychiatry, 41,* 561–571.

Beidel, D. C., Turner, S. M., & Dancu, C. V. (1985). Physiological, cognitive and behavioral aspects of social anxiety. *Behavior Research Therapy, 23*(2), 109–117.

Bell, I. R. (1992). Allergens, physical irritants, depression and shyness, *Journal of Applied Developmental Psychology, 13,* 125–133.

Bellack, A. S., Hersen, M., & Lamparski, D. (1979). Role-play tests for assessing social skills: Are they valid? Are they useful? *Journal of Consulting and Clinical Psychology, 47,* 335–342.

Boice, R. (1982). An ethological perspective on social skills research. In J. P. Curran & P. M. Monti (Eds.), *Social skills training: A practical handbook for assessment and treatment* (pp. 374–396). New York: Guilford Press.

Bradburn, N. (1969). *The structure of psychological well-being.* Chicago: Aldine.

Brennan, T., & Auslander, N. (1979). *Adolescent loneliness: An exploratory study of social and psychological predispositions and theory* (Vol. 1). Washington, DC: National Institute of Mental Health, Juvenile Problems Division. (ERIC Document Reproduction Service No. ED 194822).

Briggs, S. R., & Smith, T. G. (1986). The measurement of shyness. In W. H. Jones, J. M. Cheek, & S. R. Briggs (Eds.), *Shyness: Perspectives on research and treatment* (pp. 47–60). New York: Plenum Press.

Brodt, J. E., & Zimbardo, P. G. (1981). Modifying shyness-related social behavior through symptom misattribution. *Journal of Personality and Social Psychology, 41,* 437–449.

Bruch, M. A., Heimberg, H. G., Berger, P., & Collins, T. M. (1987). *Parental and personal origins of social evaluative threat: Differences between social phobics and agoraphobics.* Unpublished manuscript cited in Barlow (1988).

Bryant, B. M., & Trower, P. E. (1974). Social difficulty in a student sample. *British Journal of Educational Psychology, 44,* 13–21.

Bullmer, K. (1972). Improving accuracy of interpersonal perception through a direct teaching method. *Journal of Counseling Psychology, 19,* 37–41.

Buss, A. H. (1980). *Self-consciousness and social anxiety.* San Francisco: W. H. Freeman.

Buss, A. H. (1986). A theory of shyness. In W. H. Jones, J. M. Cheek & S. R. Briggs (Eds.), *Shyness: Perspectives on research and treatment* (pp. 39–46). New York: Plenum Press.

Butler, G. (1985). Exposure as a treatment for social phobia: Some instructive difficulties. *Behavior Research and Therapy, 23,* 651–657.

Butler, G. (1989). Issues in the application of cognitive and behavioral strategies to the treatment of social phobia. *Clinical Psychology Review, 9,* 91–106.

Butler, G., Cullington, A., Munby, M., Amies, P., & Gelder, M. (1984). Exposure and anxiety management in the treatment of social phobia. *Journal of Consulting and Clinical Psychology, 52,* 642–650.

Calvert, J. D. (1988). Physical attractiveness: A review and reevaluation of its role in social skill research. *Behavioral Assessment, 10,* 29–42.

Cappe, R. F., & Alden, L. E. (1986). A comparison of treatment strategies for clients functionally impaired by extreme shyness and social avoidance. *Journal of Consulting and Clinical Psychology, 54*(6), 796–801.

Carver, C. S. (1979). A cybernetic model of self-attention processes. *Journal of Personality and Social Psychology, 37,* 1251–1281.

Cheek, J., & Buss, A. H. (1981). Shyness and sociability. *Journal of Personality and Social Psychology, 41,* 330–339.

Cheek, J. M., & Melchior, L. A. (1990). Shyness, self-esteem, and self-consciousness. In H. Leitenberg (Ed.), *Handbook of social and evaluation anxiety* (pp. 47–82). New York: Plenum Press.

Cheek, J. M., Melchior, L. A., & Carpentieri, A. M. (1986). Shyness and self-concept. In L. M. Hartman & K. R. Blankstein (Eds.), *Perception of self in emotional disorder and psychotherapy* (pp. 113–131). New York: Plenum Press.

Cheek, J. M., & Watson, A. K. (1989). The definition of shyness: Psychological imperialism or construct validity? *Journal of Social Behavior and Personality, 4*(1), 85–96.

Chelune, G. J., and associates (1979). *Self-disclosure: Origins, patterns and implications of openness in interpersonal relations.* San Francisco: Jossey-Bass.

Christensen, A., Arkowitz, G. H., & Anderson, J. (1975). Practice dating as treatment for college dating inhibitions. *Behavior Research and Therapy, 6,* 510–521.

Craig, A., Franklin, J. A., & Andrews, G. (1984). A scale to measure locus of control of behavior. *British Journal of Medical Psychology, 57,* 173–180.

Crozier, W. R. (1982). Explanations of social shyness. *Current Psychological Reviews, 2,* 47–60.

Crozier, W. R. (1990). Social psychological perspectives on shyness, embarrassment, and shame. In W. R. Crozier (Ed.), *Shyness and embarrassment: Perspectives from social psychology* (pp. 19–58). New York: Cambridge University Press.

Curran, J. P. (1977). Skills training as an approach to the treatment of heterosexual-social anxiety: A review. *Psychological Bulletin, 84*(1), 140–157.

Cutrona, C. E. (1982). Transition to college: Loneliness and the process of social adjustment. In L. A. Peplau and D. Perlman (Eds.), *Loneliness: A sourcebook of current theory, research and therapy* (pp. 291–309). New York: Wiley.

Daly, J. A., & Stafford, L. (1984). Correlates and consequences of social-communicative anxiety. In J. A. Daly & J. C. McCroskey (Eds.), *Avoiding communication: Shyness, reticence, and communication apprehension* (pp. 125–143). Newbury Park, CA: Sage.

Deffenbacher, J. L., Zwemer, W. A., Whisman, M. A., Hill, R. A., & Sloan, R. D. (1986). Irrational beliefs and anxiety. *Cognitive Therapy and Research, 10,* 281–292.

Descutner, C. J., & Thelen, M. H. (1991). Development and validation of a fear-of-intimacy scale. *Psychological Assessment: A Journal of Consulting and Clinical Psychology, 3,* 218–225.

Diener, E. (1984). Subjective well being. *Psychological Bulletin, 95,* 542–575.

DiNardo, P. A., Barlow, D. H., Cerny, J., Vermilyea, B. B., Vermilyea, J. A., Himadi, W., & Waddell, M. (1985). *Anxiety Disorders Interview Schedule—Revised (ADIS-R).* Albany: Phobia and Anxiety Disorders Clinic, State University of New York at Albany.

Dodge, C. S., Heimberg, R. G., Nyman, D., & O'Brien, G. T. (1987). Daily heterosocial interactions of high and low socially anxious college students: A diary study. *Behavior Therapy, 18,* 90–96.

Duck, S. (1983). *Friends for life: The psychology of close relationships.* Sussex: Harvester Press.

Duck, S. (Ed.). (1990). *Personal relationships and social support.* London: Sage.

Duran, R. L. (1989). Social communicative competence in adulthood. In J. F. Nussbaum (Ed.), *Life-span communication: Normative processes* (pp. 195–224). Hillsdale, NJ: Lawrence Erlbaum.

D'Zurilla, T. J., & Nezu, A. M. (1990). Development and preliminary evaluation of the social problem-solving inventory. *Journal of Consulting and Clinical Psychology, 2*(2), 156–163.

Edelman, R. J. (1987). *The psychology of embarrassment.* Chichester: Wiley.

Eifert, G. H., & Wilson, P. H. (1991). The triple response approach to assessment: A conceptual and methodological reappraisal. *Behavior Research & Therapy, 29,* 283–292.

Ellis, A., & Grieger, R. (1977). *Handbook of rational-emotive therapy.* New York: Lyle Springer.

Emmelkamp, P. M. G., Mersch, P. O., Vissia, E., & van der Helm, M. (1985). Social phobia: A comparative evaluation of cognitive and behavioral interventions. *Behavior Research and Therapy, 23,* 365–369.

Faludi, S. (1991). *Backlash: The undeclared war against American women.* New York: Crown.

Foley, F. W., Heath, R. F., & Chabot, D. R. (1986). Shyness and defensive style. *Psychological Reports, 58,* 967–973.

Ford, J. D. (1978). Therapeutic relationship in behavior therapy: An empirical analysis. *Journal of Consulting and Clinical Psychology, 46,* 1302–1314.

Frost, R. O., Martin, P., Lahart, C., & Rosenblate, R. (1990). The dimensions of perfectionism, *Cognitive Therapy and Research, 14,* 449–468.

Furnham, A. F. (1988). *Lay theories: Everyday understanding of problems in the social sciences.* New York: Pergamon Press.

Gambrill, E. D. (1973). *A behavioral program to increase social interaction.* Paper presented at the Seventh Annual Convention of the Association for Advancement of Behavior Therapy, Miami, December 1973.

Gambrill, E. D. (1977). *Behavior modification: Handbook of assessment, intervention and evaluation.* San Francisco: Jossey-Bass.

Gambrill, E. D. (1993). *A class format for helping people to increase the quality of their social lives.* Paper presented

at the 23rd European Congress of Behavior and Cognitive Therapies, London, September.

Gambrill, E. D., & Richey, C. A. (1975). An assertion inventory for use in assessment and research. *Behavior Therapy, 6,* 547–549.

Gambrill, E. D., & Richey, C. A. (1988). *Taking charge of your social life.* Berkeley, CA: Behavioral Options. [P.O. Box 8118, Berkeley, CA 94707]

Ghosh, A., & Marks, I. M. (1987). Self-directed exposure for agoraphobia: A controlled trial. *Behavior Therapy, 18,* 3–16.

Gilbert, P., & Trower, P. (1990). The evolution and manifestation of social anxiety. In W. R. Crozier (Ed.), *Shyness, embarrassment: Perspectives from social psychology* (pp. 144–177). New York: Plenum Press.

Glass, C. R., & Arnkoff, D. B. (1989). Behavioral assessment of social anxiety and social phobia. *Clinical Psychology Review, 9,* 75–90.

Glass, C. R., Gottman, J. M., & Shmurak, S. H. (1976). Response acquisition and cognitive self-statement modification approaches to dating skills training. *Journal of Counseling Psychology, 23,* 520–526.

Glass, C. R., Merluzzi, T. V., Biever, J. L., & Larsen, K. H. (1982). Cognitive assessment of social anxiety: Development and validation of a self-statement questionnaire. *Cognitive Therapy and Research, 6,* 37–55.

Goswick, R., & Jones, W. H. (1981). Loneliness, self-concept and adjustment. *Journal of Psychology, 107,* 237–240.

Gould, R. A., & Clum, G. A. (1993). A meta-analysis of self-help treatment approaches. *Clinical Psychology Review, 13,* 169–186.

Gray, J. A. (1982). *The neuropsychology of anxiety.* New York: Oxford University Press.

Gresham, F. M. (1988). Social skills: Conceptual and applied aspects of assessment, training and social validation. In J. C. Witt, S. N. Elliot, & F. M. Gresham (Eds.), *Handbook of behavior therapy in education* (pp. 523–546). New York: Plenum Press.

Gurtman, M. B. (1987). Depressive affect and disclosures as factors in interpersonal rejection. *Cognitive Therapy and Research, 11*(1), 87–110.

Haemmerlie, F. M. (1983). Heterosocial anxiety in college females: A biased interactions treatment. *Behavior Modification, 7,* 611–623.

Haemmerlie, F. M., & Montgomery, R. L. (1984). Purposefully biased interactions: Reducing heterosocial anxiety through self-perception theory. *Journal of Personality and Social Psychology, 47*(4), 900–908.

Halford, K., & Foddy, M. (1982). Cognitive and social skills correlates of social anxiety. *British Journal of Clinical Psychology, 21,* 17–28.

Hansson, R. O., Jones, W. H., & Carpenter, B. N. (1984). Relational competence and social support. In P. Shaver (Ed.), *Review of personality and social psychology* (Vol. 5, pp. 265–284). Beverly Hills, CA: Sage Publications.

Harris, P. R. (1984). The hidden face of shyness: A message from the shy for researchers and practitioners. *Human Relations, 37*(12), 1079–1093.

Hawkins, R. P. (1986). Selection of target behaviors. In R. O. Nelson & S. C. Hayes (Eds.), *Conceptual foundations of behavioral assessment* (pp. 331–385). New York: Guilford Press.

Heimberg, R. G. (1989). Cognitive and behavioral treatments for social phobia: A critical review. *Clinical Psychology Review, 9,* 107–128.

Heimberg, R. G. (1990). Material distributed at workshop presented at annual conference of the American Association for Advancement of Behavior Therapy, San Francisco, November.

Heimberg, R. G., & Barlow, D. H. (1988). Psychosocial treatments for social phobia. *Psychosomatics, 29,* 27–37.

Heimberg, R. G., Dodge, C. S., & Becker, R. E. (1987). Social phobia. In L. Michelson & M. Asher (Eds.), *Cognitive-behavioral assessment and treatment of anxiety disorders* (pp. 280–309). New York: Guilford Press.

Heimberg, R. G., Dodge, C. S., Hope, D. A., Kennedy, C. R., Zollo, L. J., & Becker, R. E. (1990). Cognitive behavioral group treatment for social phobia: Comparison with a credible placebo control. *Cognitive Therapy and Research, 14,* 1–23.

Heimberg, R. G., Hope, D. A., Dodge, C. S., & Becker, R. E. (1988). *DSM-III-R subtypes of social phobia: Comparison of generalized social phobias and public speaking phobias.* Manuscript submitted for publication.

Hojat, M., & Crandall, R. (Eds.). (1989). *Loneliness: Theory, research and applications.* Newbury Park, CA: Sage Publications.

Holt, C. S., Heimberg, R. G., & Hope, D. (1992). Situational domains of social phobia. *Journal of Anxiety Disorders, 6,* 63–77.

Hope, D. A., Gansler, D. A., & Heimberg, R. G. (1989). Attentional focus and causal attributions in social phobia: Implications from social psychology. *Clinical Psychology Review, 9,* 49–60.

Hope, D. A., & Heimberg, R. G. (1990). Dating anxiety. In H. Leitenberg (Ed.), *Handbook of social and evaluation anxiety* (pp. 217–246). New York: Plenum Press.

Horowitz, L. M., Weckler, D. A., & Doren, R. (1983). Interpersonal problems and symptoms: A cognitive approach. In P. C. Kendall (Ed.), *Advances in cognitive-behavioral research and therapy* (Vol. 2, pp. 81–125). New York: Academic Press.

Izard, C. E., & Hyson, M. C. (1986). Shyness as a discrete emotion. In Jones, W. H., Cheek, J. M., & Briggs, S. R. (1986). *Shyness: Perspectives on research and treatment* (pp. 147–160). New York: Plenum Press.

Jacobs, J. (1961). *The death and life of great American cities.* New York: Random House.

Jones, W. H. (1982). Loneliness and social behavior. In L. A. Peplau & D. Perlman (Eds.), *Loneliness: A sourcebook of current theory, research and therapy.* New York: Wiley.

Jones, W. H., & Briggs, S. R. (1984). The self-other discrepancy in social shyness. In R. Schwarzer (Ed.), *The self in anxiety, stress and depression* (pp. 93–107). Amsterdam: North Holland.

Jones, W. H., Briggs, S. R., & Smith, T. G. (1986). Shyness: Conceptualization and measurement. *Journal of Personality and Social Psychology, 51,* 629–639.

Jones, W. H., Cavert, C. W., Snider, R. L., & Bruce, T. (1985). Relational stress: An analysis of situations and events associated with loneliness. In S. Duck & D. Perlman (Eds.), *Understanding personal relationships* (pp. 221–242). London: Sage.

Jones, W. H., Cheek, J. M., & Briggs, S. R. (1986). *Shyness: Perspectives on research and treatment.* New York: Plenum Press.

Jones, W. H., Freeman, J. A., & Goswick, R. A. (1981). The persistence of loneliness: Self and other determinants. *Journal of Personality, 49,* 27–48.

Jones, W. H., Hobbs, S. A., & Hockenbury, D. (1982). Loneliness and social skills deficits. *Journal of Personality and Social Psychology, 42*(4), 682–689.

Jones, W. H., Rose, J., & Russell, D. (1990). Loneliness and social anxiety. In H. Leitenberg (Ed.), *Handbook of social and evaluative anxiety* (pp. 247–266). New York: Plenum Press.

Jones, W. H., & Russell, D. (1982). The social reticence scale: An objective instrument to measure shyness. *Journal of Personality Assessment, 46*(6), 629–631.

Jong-Gierveld, J. de, & Raadschelders, J. (1982). Types of loneliness. In L. A. Peplau & D. Perlman (Eds.), *Loneliness: A sourcebook of current theory, research and therapy* (pp. 105–119). New York: Wiley.

Kagan, J., Reznick, S., & Sniderman, N. (1988). Biological bases of childhood shyness. *Science, 240,* 167–171.

Kendall, P. C., & Morrison, P. (1984). Integrating cognitive and behavior procedures for the treatment of socially isolated children. In A. W. Myers & W. E. Craighead (Eds.), *Cognitive behavior therapy with children* (pp. 261–288). New York: Plenum Press.

Kupke, T. E., Calhoun, K. E., & Hobbs, S. (1979). Selection of heterosexual skills: II. Experimental validity. *Behavior Therapy, 10,* 336–346.

Leary, M. R. (1983). A brief version of the fear of negative evaluation scale. *Personality and Social Psychology Bulletin, 9,* 371–375.

Leary, M. R. (1986). Affective and behavioral components of shyness: Implications for theory, measurement and research. In W. H. Jones, J. M. Cheek, & S. R. Briggs (Eds.), *Shyness: Perspectives on research and treatment* (pp. 27–38). New York: Plenum Press.

Leon, S. & Gambrill, E. D. (1973). Behavior rehearsal as a method to increase heterosexual interaction. *Corrective and Social Psychiatry and Journal of Applied Behavior Therapy, 19,* 27–34.

Levenson, R. W., & Gottman, J. M. (1978). Toward the assessment of social competence. *Journal of Consulting and Clinical Psychology, 46,* 453–462.

Libet, J., & Lewinsohn, P. M. (1973). The concept of social skill with special references to the behavior of depressed persons. *Journal of Consulting and Clinical Psychology, 40*, 304–312.

Liebowitz, M. R. (1987). Social phobia. *Modern problems in pharmacopsychiatry, 22*, 141–173.

Liebowitz, M. R., Gorman, J. M., Fyer, A. J., & Klein, D. F. (1985). Social phobia: Review of a neglected anxiety disorder. *Archives of General Psychiatry, 42*, 729–736.

Lipton, D. N., & Nelson, R. O. (1980). The contribution of initiation behaviors to dating frequency. *Behavior Therapy, 11*, 59–67.

Lucock, M. P., & Salkovskis, P. M. (1988). Cognitive factors in social anxiety and its treatment. *Behavior Research and Therapy, 26*(4), 297–302.

Lynch, J. S. (1977). *The broken heart: The medical consequences of loneliness in America.* New York: Basic Books.

MacDonald, M. L., Lindquist, C. U., Kramer, J. A., McGrath, R. A., & Rhyne, L. D. (1975). Social skills training: Behavioral rehearsal in groups and dating skills. *Journal of Counseling Psychology, 22*, 224–230.

McGovern, K. B., Arkowitz, H., & Gilmore, S. K. (1975). Evaluation of social skills training programs for college dating inhibitions. *Journal of Counseling Psychology, 22*, 505–512.

Marks, I. M. (1969). *Fears and phobias.* London: Heinemann.

Marks, I. M. (1978). *Living with fear.* New York: McGraw-Hill.

Marks, I. M. (1987). *Fears, phobias and rituals: Panic, anxiety and their disorders.* New York: Oxford University Press.

Martinson, W. D., & Zerface, J. P. (1970). Comparison of individual counseling and a social program with nondaters. *Journal of Counseling Psychology, 17*, 36–40.

Mattick, R. P., & Clarke, J. C. (1988). *Development and validation of measures of social phobia, scrutiny, fear, and social interaction anxiety.* Manuscript submitted for publication.

Mattick, R. P., & Peters, L. (1988). Treatment of severe social phobia: Effects of guided exposure with and without cognitive restructuring. *Journal of Consulting and Clinical Psychology, 56*, 251–260.

Mattick, R. P., Peters, L., & Clarke, J. C. (1989). Exposure and cognitive restructuring for social phobia: A controlled study. *Behavior Therapy, 20*, 3–23.

McCann, B. S., Woolfolk, R. L., & Lehrer, P. M. (1987). Specificity in response to treatment: A study of interpersonal anxiety. *Behavioral Research and Therapy, 25*(2), 129–136.

McEwan, K. L., & Devins, G. M. (1983). Is increased arousal in social anxiety noticed by others? *Journal of Abnormal Psychology, 92*(4), 417–421.

McFall, R. M. (1982). A review and reformulation of the concept of social skills. *Behavioral Assessment, 4*, 1–33.

Melchoir, L. and Cheek, M. (1990). Shyness and anxious self-presentation during a social interaction, *Journal of Social Behaviour and Personality, 5*, 117–130.

Mersch, P. P. A., Emmelkamp, P. M. G., Bögels, S. M., & van der Sleen, J. (1989). Social phobia: Individual response patterns and the effects of behavioural and cognitive interventions. *Behaviour Research and Therapy, 27*, 421–434.

Montgomery, R. L., & Haemmerlie, F. M. (1986). Self-perception theory and reeducation of heterosocial anxiety. *Journal of Social and Clinical Psychology, 4*(4), 503–512.

Muehlenhard, C. L., Baldwin, L. E., Bourg, W., & Piper, A. M. (1988). Helping women "break the ice": A computer program to help shy women start and maintain conversations with men. *Journal of Computer Based Instruction, 15*, 7–13.

Muehlenhard, C. L., & McFall, R. M. (1981). Dating initiation from a woman's perspective. *Behavior Therapy, 12*, 682–691.

Muehlenhard, C. L., Koralewski, M. A., Andrews, S. L., & Burdick, C. A. (1986). Verbal and nonverbal cues that convey interest in dating: Two studies. *Behavior Therapy, 17*, 404–419.

Muehlenhard, C. L., Miller, C. L., & Burdick, C. A. (1983). Are high-frequency daters better cue readers? Men's interpretation of women's cues as a function of dating frequency and SHI scores. *Behavior Therapy, 14*, 626–636.

Mueser, K. T., Valenti-Hein, D., & Yarnold, P. R. (1987). Dating-skills groups for the developmentally disabled. *Behavior Modification, 11*(2), 200–228.

Nay, W. R. (1986). Analogue measures. In A. R. Ciminero, K. S. Calhoun, & H. E. Adams (Eds.), *Handbook of behavioral assessment.* New York: Wiley.

Neumann, K. F., Critelli, J. W., Tang, C. S. K., & Schneider, L. J. (1988). Placebo effects in the treatment of male dating anxiety. *Journal of Behavior Therapy and Experimental Psychiatry, 19*(2), 125–141.

Nezu, A., & D'Zurilla, T. J. (1979). An experimentation evaluation of the decision-making process in social problem solving. *Cognitive Research and Therapy, 3*, 269–277.

O'Banion, K., & Arkowitz, H. (1977). Social anxiety and selective memory for affective information about the self. *Social Behavior and Personality, 5*, 321–328.

Ohman, A. (1986). Face the beast and fear the face: Animal and social fears as prototypes for evolutionary analysis of emotion. *Psychophysiology, 23*, 123–145.

Ohman, A., & Dimberg, U. (1984). An evolutionary perspective on human social behavior. In W. M. Waid (Ed.), *Sociophysiology* (pp. 47–86). New York: Springer-Verlag.

Ost, L. G., Jerremalm, A., & Johansson, J. (1981). Individual response patterns and the effects of different behavioral methods in the treatment of social phobia. *Behavior Research and Therapy, 19*, 1–16.

Peplau, L. A., & Perlman, P. (1982a). *Loneliness: A sourcebook of current theory, research and therapy.* New York: Wiley.

Peplau, L. A., & Perlman, P. (1982b). Perspectives on loneliness. In L. A. Peplau & D. Perlman, *Loneliness: A sourcebook of current theory, research and therapy* (pp. 1–20). New York: Wiley.

Peplau, L. A., Russell, D., & Heim, H. (1979). The experience of loneliness. In I. H. Frieze, D. Bar-Tal, & J. S. Caroll (Eds.), *New approaches to social problems: Applications of attribution theory* (pp. 53–78). San Francisco: Jossey-Bass.

Perlman, D., Gerson, A. C., & Spinner, B. (1978). Loneliness among senior citizens: An empirical report. *Essence, 2,* 239–248.

Perlman, D., & Peplau, L. A. (1981). Toward a psychology of loneliness. In R. Gilmour & S. Duck (Eds.), *Personal relationships: 3. Personal relationships in disorder.* New York: Academic Press.

Peterson, J., Fischetti, M., Curran, J. P., & Arland, S. (1981). Sense of timing: A skill deficit in heterosocially anxious women. *Behavior Therapy, 12,* 195–201.

Phillips, G. M. (1991). *Help for shy people.* Englewood Cliffs, NJ: Prentice-Hall.

Phillips, G. M. (1984). Reticence: A perspective on social withdrawal. In J. A. Daley & J. C. McCroskey (Eds.), *Avoiding communication: Shyness, reticence and communication apprehension* (pp. 51–65). Newbury Park, CA: Sage Publications.

Phillips, G. M. (1986). Rhetoritherapy: The principles of rhetoric in training shy people in speech effectiveness. In W. H. Jones, J. M. Cheek, & S. R. Briggs (Eds.), *Shyness: Perspectives in research and treatment* (pp. 357–374). New York: Plenum Press.

Phillips, G. M., & Sokoloff, K. A. (1979). An end to anxiety: Treating speech problems with rhetoritherapy. *Journal of Communication Disorder, 12*(3), 385–397.

Pilisuk, M., & Minkler, M. (1980). Supportive networks: Life ties for the elderly. *Journal of Social Issues, 36,* 95–116.

Pilkonis, P. A. (1977). The behavioral consequences of shyness. *Journal of Personality, 45,* 596–611.

Pilkonis, P. A., & Zimbardo, P. G. (1979). The personal and social dynamics of shyness. In C. E. Izard (Ed.), *Emotions in personality and psychopathology* (pp. 133–160). New York: Plenum Press.

Polansky, N. A. (1986). *Treating loneliness in child protection.* Washington, DC: Child Welfare League of America.

Poppen, R. L. (1989). Some clinical implications of rule-governed behavior. In S. C. Hayes (Ed.), *Rule governed behavior: Cognition, contingencies and instructional control* (pp. 325–357). New York: Plenum Press.

Primakoff, L., Epstein, N., & Covi, L. (1986). Homework compliance: An uncontrolled variable in cognitive therapy outcome research. *Behavior Therapy, 17,* 433–446.

Prisbell, M. (1982). Heterosexual communicative behavior and communication apprehension. *Communication Quarterly, 30,* 251–258.

Prisbell, M. (1989). Dating competence among college students. In J. F. Nussbaum (Ed.), *Life-space communication normative processes.* Hillsdale, NJ: Lawrence Erlbaum.

Rapee, R. M., & Lim, L. (1992). Discrepancies between self-observor ratings of performance in social phobics, *Journal of Abnormal Psychology, 101,* 728–731.

Rapee, R. M., McCallum, S. L., Melville, L. F., Ravenscroft, H., & Rodney, J. M. (1994). Memory bias in social phobia. *Behaviour Research and Therapy, 32,* 89–99.

Rapee, R. M., Sanderson, W. C., & Barlow, D. H. (1987). *Social phobia symptoms across the DSM-III anxiety disorders categories.* Paper presented at the annual meeting of the Association for the Advancement of Behavior Therapy, Boston.

Rehm, L. P., & Marston, A. R. (1968). Reduction of social anxiety through modification of self-reinforcement. *Journal of Consulting and Clinical Psychology, 32,* 565–574.

Reissman, D. (1950). *The lonely crowd: A study of the changing American character.* New Haven: Yale University Press.

Richey, C. A., Lovell, M., & Reid, K. (1991). Interpersonal skill training to enhance social support among women at risk for child maltreatment. *Children and Youth Services Review, 13,* 41–59.

Rook, K. S. (1984a). The functions of social bonds: Perspectives from research on social support, loneliness and isolation. In I. G. Sarason & B. R. Sarason, *Social support: Theory, research and applications* (pp. 243–268). Boston: Martinus Nijholf.

Rook, K. S. (1984b). The negative side of social interaction: Impact on psychological well-being. *Journal of Personality and Social Psychology, 46,* 1097–1108.

Rook, K. S. (1984c). Promoting social bonding: Strategies for helping the lonely and socially isolated. *American Psychologist, 39,* 1389–1407.

Rook, K. S. (1990). Social relationships as a source of companionship: Implications for older adults' psychological well-being. In B. R. Sarason, I. G. Sarason, & G. R. Pierce (Eds.), *Social support: An interactional view* (pp. 219–250). New York: Wiley.

Rook, K. S., & Peplau, L. A. (1982). Perspectives on helping the lonely. In L. A. Peplau & D. Perlman (Eds.), *Loneliness: A sourcebook of current theory, research and therapy* (pp. 351–378). New York: Wiley.

Rosenfarb, I. S., Hayes, S. C., & Linehan, M. M. (1989). Instructions and experimental feedback in the treatment of social skills deficits in adults. *Psychotherapy, 26,* 242–251.

Rubenstein, C. M., & Shaver, P. (1982). The experience of loneliness. In L. A. Peplau & D. Perlman (Eds.), *Loneli-*

*ness: A sourcebook of current theory, research and therapy* (pp. 206–223). New York: Wiley.

Russell, D. (1982). The measurement of loneliness. In L. A. Peplau & D. Perlman (Eds.), *Loneliness: A sourcebook of current theory, research and therapy* (pp. 81–104). New York: Wiley.

Russell, D., Cutrona, C. E., & Jones, W. H. (1986). A trait-situational analysis of shyness. In W. H. Jones, J. M. Cheek, & S. R. Briggs (Eds.), *Shyness: Perspectives on research and treatment* (pp. 239–249). New York: Plenum Press.

Safron, J. D., & Greenberg, L. S. (1991). Affective change processes: A synthesis and critical analysis. In J. D. Safran & L. S. Greenberg (Eds.), *Emotion, psychotherapy and change* (pp. 339–362). New York: Guilford Press.

Sarason, R., Sarason, I. G., & Pierce, G. R. (1990). *Social support: An interactional view.* New York: Wiley.

Sarason, I. G., Levine, H. M., Basham, R. B., & Sarason, B. R. (1983). Assessing social support: The social support questionnaire. *Journal of Personality and Social Psychology, 44,* 127–139.

Scalise, J. J., Ginter, E. J., & Gerstein, L. H. (1984). A multidimensional loneliness measure: The loneliness rating scale (LRS). *Journal of Personality Assessment, 48*(5), 525–530.

Scheier, M. F. (1985). The self-consciousness scale: A revised version for use with general populations. *Journal of Applied Social Psychology, 15,* 687–699.

Schelver, S. R., & Gutsch, K. U. (1983). The effects of self-administered cognitive therapy on social evaluative anxiety. *Journal of Clinical Psychology, 39,* 658–666.

Schiller, H. I. (1989). *Culture, Inc.: The corporate takeover of public expression.* New York: Oxford University Press.

Schlenker, B. R., & Leary, M. R. (1982). Social anxiety and self-presentation: A conceptualization and model. *Psychological Bulletin, 92,* 641–669.

Scholing, A., & Emmelkamp, P. M. G. (1990). Social phobia: Nature and treatment. In H. Leitenberg (Ed.), *Handbook of social and evaluation anxiety* (pp. 269–324). New York: Plenum Press.

Scholing, A., & Emmelkamp, P. M. G. (1993). Cognitive and behavioral treatments of fear of blushing, sweating or trembling. *Behaviour Research and Therapy, 31,* 155–170.

Schulte, D., Künzel, R., Pepping, G., & Schulte-Bahrenberg, T. (1992). Tailor-made versus standardized therapy of phobic patients, *Advances in Behaviour Research and Therapy, 14,* 67–92.

Siegman, A. W., & Felstein, S. (Eds.). (1987). (2nd Ed.) *Nonverbal behavior and communication.* Hillsdale, NJ: Lawrence Erlbaum.

Slater, P. (1979). *The pursuit of loneliness: American culture at the breaking point.* New York: Beacon.

Sloan, W. W., & Solano, C. H. (1984). The conversational styles of lonely males with strangers and roommates.

*Personality and Social Psychology Bulletin, 10*(2), 293–301.

Smith, R. E., & Sarason, I. G. (1975). Social anxiety and the evaluation of negative interpersonal feedback. *Journal of Consulting and Clinical Psychology, 43,* 429.

Snyder, C. R., & Smith, T. W. (1986). On being "shy like a fox": A self-handicapping analysis. In W. H. Jones, J. M. Cheek, & S. R. Briggs (Eds.), *Shyness: Perspectives on research and treatment* (pp. 161–172). New York: Plenum Press.

Solano, C. H., & Batten, P. G. (1979). *Loneliness and objective self-disclosure in an acquaintenship exercise.* Unpublished manuscript, Wake Forest University (cited in Jones, 1982).

Stopa, L., & Clark, D. M. (1993). Cognitive processes in social phobia. *Behaviour Research and Therapy, 31,* 255–267.

Stravynski, A. (1983). Behavioral treatment of psychogenic vomiting in the context of social phobia. *Journal of Nervous and Mental Disease, 171,* 448–451.

Stokes, T. F., & Osnes, P. G. (1989). An operant pursuit of generalization. *Behavior Therapy, 20,* 327–356.

Suinn, R. M. (1990). *Anxiety management training.* New York: Plenum Press.

Swann, W. B., Giuliano, T., & Wegner, D. M. (1982). Where leading questions can lead: The power of conjecture in social interaction. *Journal of Personality and Social Psychology, 42,* 1025–1035.

Taylor, S. E., & Brown, J. D. (1988). Illusion and well-being: A social psychological perspective on mental health. *Psychological Bulletin, 103*(2), 193–210.

Teglasi, H., & Hoffman, M. A. (1982). Causal attributions of shy subjects. *Journal of Research in Personality, 16,* 376–385.

Trower, P. (1982). Toward a generative model of social skills: A critique and synthesis. In J. P. Curran & P. M. Monti (Eds.), *Social skills training* (pp. 399–427). New York: Guilford Press.

Trower, P., Bryant, B., & Argyle, M. (1978). *Social skills and mental health.* London: Methuen.

Trower, P., & Gilbert, P. (1989). New theoretical conceptions of social anxiety and social phobia. *Clinical Psychology Review, 9,* 19–35.

Trower, P., Yardley, K., Bryant, B., & Shaw, P. (1978). The treatment of social failure: A comparison of anxiety-reduction and skills acquisition procedures on two social problems. *Behavior Modification, 2,* 41–60.

Turner, S. M., Beidel, D. C., Dancu, C. V., & Stanley, M. A. (1989). An empirically derived inventory to measure social fears and anxiety: The social phobia and anxiety inventory. *Psychological Assessment: A Journal of Consulting and Clinical Psychology, 1,* 35–40.

Turner, S. M., Beidel, D. C., Long, P. J., Turner, M. W., & Townsley, R. M. (1993). A composite measure to determine the functional status of treated social phobics: The social phobia endstate functioning test. *Behavior Therapy, 24,* 265–275.

Twentyman, C. T., & McFall, R. (1975). Behavioral training of social skills in shy males. *Journal of Consulting and Clinical Psychology, 43,* 384–395.

Tyrer, P. (1986). The classification of anxiety disorder: A critique of DSM-III. *Journal of Affective Disorders, 11,* 99–104.

Valentine, J., & Arkowitz, H. (1975). Social anxiety and the self-evaluation of interpersonal performance. *Psychological Reports, 36,* 211–221.

Vitkus, J., & Horowitz, L. M. (1987). Poor social performance of lonely people: Lacking a skill or adopting a role? *Journal of Personality and Social Psychology, 52,* 1266–1273.

Wahler, R. G. (1980). The insular mother: Her problems in parent–child treatment. *Journal of Applied Behavior Analysis, 13,* 207–219.

Wallander, J. L., Conger, A. J., & Conger, J. C. (1985). Developmental and evaluation of a behaviorally referenced rating system for heterosocial skills. *Behavioral Assessment, 7,* 137–153.

Watson, D., & Friend, R. (1969). Measurement of social-evaluative anxiety. *Journal of Consulting and Clinical Psychology, 33,* 448–457.

Weiss, R. (1969). *The American myth of success: From Horatio Alger to Norman Vincent Peale.* New York: Basic Books.

Weiss, R. S. (1973). *Loneliness: The experience of emotional and social isolation.* Cambridge, MA: MIT Press.

Weiss, R. S. (1974). The provisions of social relationships. In Z. Rubin (Ed.), *Doing unto others: Joining, molding, conforming, helping, loving* (pp. 17–26). Englewood Cliffs, NJ: Prentice-Hall.

White, J. (1993). *A controlled comparative investigation of large group therapy for GAD: Process of change.* Paper presented at the 23rd European Congress of Behavior and Cognitive Therapies, London.

Williams, C. L., & Ciminero, A. R. (1978). Development and validation of a heterosocial skills inventory: The survey of heterosexual interactions for females. *Journal of Consulting and Clinical Psychology, 6,* 1547–1548.

Wilson, K., & Gallois, C. (1993). *Assertion and its social context.* New York: Pergamon Press.

Wiseman, J. P. (1986). Friendship: Bonds and binds in a voluntary relationship. *Journal of Social and Personal Relationships, 3,* 191–211.

Wlazlo, Z., Schroeder-Hartwig, K., Hand, I., Kaiser, G., & Munchau, N. (1989). Exposure in vivo vs. social skills training for social phobia: Long-term outcome and differential effects. *Behavior Research Therapy, 28*(3), 181–193.

Wolpe, J. (1958). *Psychotherapy by reciprocal inhibition.* Stanford, CA: Stanford University Press.

Wolpe, J. (1973). *The practice of behavior therapy,* 2nd ed. New York: Pergamon Press. (See also later editions, 4th ed., 1991.)

Wolpe, J. (1986). Individualization: The categorical imperative of behavior therapy practice. *Journal of Behavior Therapy and Experimental Psychiatry, 17,* 145–155.

Young, J. E. (1982). Loneliness, depression, and cognitive therapy: Theory and applications. In L. A. Peplau & D. Perlman (Eds.), *Loneliness: A sourcebook of current theory, research and therapy* (pp. 379–405). New York: Wiley.

Zimbardo, P. G. (1977). *Shyness: What it is and what to do about it.* Reading, MA: Addison-Wesley.

Zimbardo, P. G., & Radl, S. L. (1983). *The shyness workbook.* New York: McGraw-Hill.

Zimbardo, P. G., Pilkonis, P. A., & Norwood, R. (1975). The social disease called shyness. *Psychology Today, 8,* 68–72.

# CHAPTER 13

# COMMUNICATION AND SOCIAL SKILLS APPROACHES TO TREATING AILING MARRIAGES: A RECOMMENDATION FOR A NEW MARITAL THERAPY CALLED "MINIMAL MARITAL THERAPY"

John Gottman
Regina Rushe

## INTRODUCTION: SOCIAL SKILLS AND THE TASK ANALYSIS OF COMPETENCE

Early research in the Gottman laboratory in the 1970s followed a model of clinical research guided by a paper by Goldfried & D'Zurilla (1969). The Goldfried and D'Zurilla approach, called a "behavior-analytical approach to competence," was essentially an ethological view. The would-be designer of a therapy program, they argued, must study the natural variability in performance inherent in the population in performance. They would have us assume that the clinical problem is one of incompetence at some set of performances. One then finds a subset of the population that is competent at these performances (call it the "reference" population) and builds the intervention program from understanding both the precise nature of the deficits of the clinical population and the competencies of the reference population.

Goldfried and D'Zurilla's ideas had profound implications. For example, for a would-be designer of a therapy program for socially isolated preschool children, the skills might involve a child's ability to join another child in play. The reference population consists of other preschool children who are not isolated. One would first have to determine what they did to join other children at play and how it was different from the behavior of isolates. When Goldfried and D'Zurilla wrote their paper, this was not the common method for designing behavioral interventions. Instead, the therapy designer imagined an intervention and then tested it. For example, the preschool child might try to join another child by saying, "Hi, my name is Howard, can I play with you?" This would be taught to the child even though nonisolated children didn't join other children by introducing themselves.

The other profound implication of Goldfried and D'Zurilla's paper was that basic, descriptive research on both reference and clinical populations had to be done, and it had to go hand in hand with clinical research. Unfortunately, clinical research in marriage has largely not followed their prescription. Instead, the design of clinical interventions in marital therapy has, by and large, followed a haphazard route, very similar to that of the nonempirical clinical world.

Goldfried and D'Zurilla were, in part, responding to an influential book published by Mischel in 1968, which reviewed personality research and concluded that personality variables were poor predictors of behavior. A solution, Goldfried and D'Zurilla suggested, was to pay careful attention to both the situation and the behavioral performance required for competence in that situation. Their recommendations were similar to the idea of a task analysis proposed in the educational literature by Gagne (1965, 1977).

## MARITAL THERAPY: A SELECTED RECENT HISTORY

In the 1960s and 1970s a number of books and papers began appearing that sought to revolutionize marital therapy. In hindsight, it is clear that these books and papers were inspired by three distinct scholarly traditions. The first tradition was general systems theory, which had emerged in the mid-1950s (Bateson et al., 1956; Lederer & Jackson, 1968). The second tradition was behavior therapy, which began focusing on families during the decade of the 1960s (Patterson, 1974; Weiss, Hops, & Patterson, 1973). The third tradition was behavior exchange theory (Thibaut & Kelley, 1959). The general systems theory approach emphasized interpersonal communication and suggested that systems of interaction within relationships should be the unit of analysis. At that time, behavior therapy emphasized negative reinforcement (coercion) and positive reinforcement, social learning, and pinpointing changes that needed to be made in behavior. Behavior exchange theory proposed a reward/cost or "payoff" matrix that described the actual rewards and costs of behaviors exchanged between people. Gottman et al. (1976) later interpreted these rewards and costs to be perceived rewards and costs, and constructed a "talk table" for marital interaction, which permitted couples to rate the intent and impact of behaviors sent and received.

Implicit in these therapy approaches to ailing marriages is a theory of what has gone wrong in these marriages and what marriages need for things to go right. We will refer to each of these implicit theories as a *task analysis* of marriage. This term refers to the tasks that need to be competently accomplished (and the component skills that are part of this competence) to make a marriage run successfully. We will review a number of influential therapy approaches and summarize their task analyses of marriage. We will then review outcome research on marital therapy and sug-

gest that most therapies have steadily increased the complexity of their task analysis as they have encountered limitations in therapy outcome results.

Behavioral approaches to marital therapy began being invented and applied in the early 1970s (Azrin, Naster, & Jones, 1973; Weiss et al., 1973). Whether behavioral approaches will eventually prove right or wrong remains to be seen. However, a major contribution of the behavioral approach to marital therapy was its empirical epistemology. Before the early 1970s, the epistemology of marital therapy was the same as it is for all nonempirically based intervention methods: an epistemology based on clinical folklore, mutual support, accreditation standards, reputation, clinical case presentations, and ad hominems. This is not meant to be pejorative; many good ideas have emerged from this tradition, but there is, unfortunately, no way of sifting the wheat from the chaff without hard, objective criteria and the replicability criterion that scientific method brings with it.

The earliest paper in the behavioral tradition was one on contingency contracting in couples (Azrin et al., 1973). Here the assumption was that there was a deficit in ailing marriages, and that deficit was an inability to work out mutually satisfying reciprocal agreements, or implicit "contracts." The therapy and the outcome criterion were one and the same thing. The therapist helped the couple work out a contract, and then the therapy was successfully concluded.

Where did this assumption come from? Clearly, it had little to do with behavioral principles, nor did it have anything to do with empirical research. Instead, it followed very quickly on the heels of a popular book by Lederer and Jackson (1968) called *Mirages of Marriage*. In that book, Lederer and Jackson talked about the quid pro quo (literally, "something for something") behavior exchange view (Thibaut & Kelley, 1959) as the fundamental problem that needed to be rectified in ailing marriages. The method of therapy recommended was something akin to reciprocal contingency contracting. The other assumption of this early work on contingency contracting was that the therapist's role was that of a teacher, or perhaps a coach, in helping the couple acquire the appropriate social skills to be able to form a contract.

## The Roles of Love and Trust: Lederer and Jackson (1968)

*Mirages of Marriage* (Lederer & Jackson, 1968) was an important historical landmark in marital therapy. It began by listing seven false assumptions about marriage. First, these false assumptions involved a debunking of the role of love in marriage, particularly romantic love. Their false assumption #1 was "That people marry because they love each other" (p. 41). Instead, they suggested that "during courtship individuals lose most of their judgment" (p. 42), that they often marry because society expects it, and that there are other forces that impel people to marry that have nothing to do with romantic love (parental pressure, romantic fantasies, social hysteria, loneliness, fear for one's economic future, and other "neurotic" reasons). Their false assumption #2 was that most married people love each other; instead, they cynically suggested that married people "usually are not aware they are murdering their marriage and mangling their partners under the guise of love" (p. 47). False assumption #3 was that "Love is necessary for a satisfactory marriage." What Lederer and Jackson meant was that romantic love, or continually being "in love," which they described as "essentially selfish" (p. 54), is neither necessary nor good in a marriage.

This apparently cynical view of the role of romantic love was counteracted by their discussion of trust in marriage. They wrote, "Those couples who enjoy trust, who give trust to each other, probably are among the most fortunate people alive" (p. 109). By *trust* they meant a reciprocal giving, coupled with honest and clear communication. They wrote:

> The practice of honesty and clear communication in marriage is likely to result in an extra dividend, for it encourages spouses to be generous, comforting, and consoling. . . . Tolerance and generosity in relation to others' mistakes become easier when one learns that others can be generous in return. . . . We are able to give to people we trust because we have received from them and know that we will again; thus trust and generosity are both causes and results of a genuine give-and-take, or in our terms, quid pro quo.

The reader may also find it interesting to read the chapters on "how to drive your spouse crazy." In these chapters, the authors describe destructive interaction patterns they have observed in therapy and ways to counteract these patterns.

Lederer and Jackson noted that, to have a successful marriage, one must choose well, and they suggested choosing someone with whom one has a lot in common. Presumably, the idea is that therapy cannot be very effective when a couple is mismatched. Once one has chosen reasonably well, they suggest that

handling disagreements within a climate of respect and tolerance is the only other necessary ingredient of a successful marriage. In a short chapter, "The Major Elements of a Satisfactory Marriage," they list three necessary ingredients. The first is respect; they wrote, "each spouse finds some important quality or ability to respect in the other" (p. 198). Second, partners are tolerant of each other. Third, "the key ingredient in a successful marriage is the effort of the spouses to make the most of its assets and minimize its liabilities" (p. 198). In their view, this process is accomplished by "learning to communicate in order to negotiate quid pro quo's" (p. 199).

Lederer and Jackson also discussed differences in affiliative versus independent preferences and the need to find a match for the level of desired intimacy in the relationship. They avoided discussing possible gender differences in these preferences; in fact, one of their "false assumptions" (#4) was that "there are inherent behavioral and attitudinal differences between female and male, and that these differences cause most marital troubles." (p. 60) Denying that these "vast" gender differences exist, they claimed that the differences that do exist are small and arbitrary, vary greatly with culture, and hence are modifiable by the appropriate choice of sex roles.

To summarize, Lederer and Jackson emphasized the skill of being able to negotiate quid pro quo's within a climate of respect and tolerance. They also suggest that the basis of trust is the expectation that, if you give to your partner, you will also receive.

## Azrin, Naster, and Jones (1973)

Perhaps there is a Zeitgeist for new ideas, but the behavior therapy techniques of reciprocal contracting seem remarkably like Lederer and Jackson's recommendations. Thus, the Lederer and Jackson quid pro quo notion was either independently discovered or adopted wholeheartedly as a therapy technique by Azrin, Naster, and Jones (1973). What was interesting about the Azrin et al. paper was the implicit, perhaps logically circular, suggestion that the reciprocal contract was both the treatment method and the outcome measure of the treatment. In their view, all treatments in which the techniques was applied were, by definition, successful. Thus, we can see that Lederer and Jackson's task analysis of the necessary ingredients for a successful marriage had been accepted by behavioral therapy without an empirical test.

## Weiss, Hops, and Patterson (1973)

This remarkably creative paper, which appeared in a set of conference proceedings published in 1973 (Weiss, Hops, & Patterson, 1973), presented a more complex set of outcomes than did Azrin et al. as tests of the effectiveness of the marital therapy, change in marital satisfaction (self-reported by the Locke-Wallace; Locke & Wallace, 1959) and interaction behavior, as measured by the new Marital Interaction Coding System (MICS). The "technology" they proposed for altering marriages was somewhat more complicated than negotiating a reciprocal exchange agreement. Social skills began being introduced into the behavioral picture.

They were also quite explicit about their task analysis. They wrote:

> Oversimplifying, three main areas are of concern in a behavioral approach to marital dyads: (a) the partners exchange affectional behaviors, (b) they problem solve over a wide range of specifics including the division of resources, and (c) they engage in behavior-change attempts toward one another. At any given time, one or more of these dimensions may be salient so that a total rehabilitation program would necessarily provide training in skills germane to all dimensions. (p. 310)

Thus, this paper expanded the Lederer and Jackson task analysis. First, the negotiation skills beyond the quid pro quo were required to include problem solving, in general. Second, explicit mention was made that the partners must exchange affectional behaviors. Third, spouses must be skillful at changing each other's behavior in a direction desired by each. Toward the latter end, the Spouse Observation Checklist (SOC) and, later, the Areas of Change questionnaire were designed as both assessment devices and part of the therapy procedure (Weiss & Margolin, 1977; Weiss & Perry, 1979; Margolin, Christensen, & Weiss, 1975; Patterson & Hops, 1972; Weiss, Hops & Patterson, 1973).

## Jacobson and Margolin (1979)

Perhaps the most sophisticated and complex task analysis of marriage proposed to date was Jacobson and Margolin's behavioral-exchange model of relationship discord. Unlike those of their predecessors, Jacobson and Margolin's model is based on their thorough and thoughtful review of the research literature. They list the ingredients they suggest for a task

analysis of marriage. First, they discuss the requirement of a rich climate of positive reinforcement, including the ability to handle "reinforcement erosion," in which, inevitably, the attractiveness of reinforcers diminishes over time in a marriage. Second, they note that reciprocal positive exchange is no more characteristic of distressed than of nondistressed couples. They review the Gottman et al. (1976) "bank account model," in which couples invest in a relationship:

> which over time balance each other and thereby maintain the current rate of rewarding exchange. This aspect of reciprocity says nothing about any given interchange between a couple, nor does it preclude nonreciprocal exchanges at any given point in time. . . . Gottman's "bank account" model also explains this discrepancy between distressed and nondistressed couples. When the ratio of rewards to punishments in a relationship is low, as is the case with distressed couples, one is more apt to "balance the checkbook" regularly, to keep score. . . . It does appear that, in general, distressed couples are relatively dependent on immediate, as opposed to delayed, rewards and punishments (Jacobson, 1978e). Since happily married couples are accustomed to receiving a consistent, high rate of rewards from one another, nonreciprocal behavior or nonequitable exchanges can be tolerated in the short run, since their shared reinforcement history offers promise of long-term equality and continued rewards. Perhaps this freedom from control by a partner's immediate consequences is an operational definition of "trust." (Jacobson, 1978, p. 16)

Here, again, we have the notion of trust in a task analysis of marriage, but it seems to be quite the opposite of the definition Lederer and Jackson proposed. The situation Jacobson and Margolin propose to be the basis of trust is the *absence of contingency* or quid pro quo rather than its presence.

These authors noted that reciprocal *negative exchanges* are characteristic of distressed relationships, reciprocation far in excess of the higher base rates of negativity in distressed couples. However, this correct summary of the research literature does not seem to have led to any element of their task analysis.

Third, Jacobson and Margolin (1979) reviewed contributions from social exchange theory and suggested a modification. They wrote:

> It would be vastly oversimplified to suggest that each behavior in the repertoire of marital patterns is maintained by specific reinforcing stimuli from the spouse on a point-for-point basis. Rather, it seems

more realistic to posit a summation process such that classes of positive relationship behavior are maintained by a number of partner-initiated behaviors which are experientially summated by the receiver and integrated into an overall experience of the partner's behavior [pp. 18–19]. . . . The important point is that couples act in their marital environment to summarize and integrate the information provided by the partner, and that this cognitive processing affects the participant's subsequent responding, as well as his [or her] current evaluation of the quality of the marriage. (p. 20)

Fourth, they noted, as did Lederer and Jackson, that conflict is inevitable in a relationship, and, hence, the ability to manage that conflict is crucial. They also note (consistent with Weiss et al.) that the ability to change one's partner in a positive manner is also crucial. They single out coercive processes of influence as dysfunctional.

Fifth, they noted that all couples develop normative structures or "rules," which must be modified as necessary. They pointed out that some couples appear to have lacunae in their normative structure and, perhaps, an inability to modify rules as new situational demands arise that challenge the old rules.

Sixth, they noted, under a category they called "skill deficits," a long list of skills:

Spouses need to be able to express their feelings, both positive and negative. They need to provide support and understanding to one another (Weiss, 1978). In the sexual realm, they need skills to maintain a viable sex life, particularly after the initial novelty has ended. Various instrumental skills are also necessary, including child-rearing, household and financial management, and the like. (p. 26)

Later, they include the management of environmental stress as part of these skills.

Consistent with Lederer and Jackson, they discuss differences in affiliative versus independent preferences, and the need to find a match for the desired level of intimacy in the relationship.

## Emotionally Focused Marital Therapy: Greenberg and Johnson (1988)

Greenberg and Johnson (1988) described a new approach to marital therapy called emotionally focused therapy (EFT). They noted that other approaches to marital therapy give a secondary role to

emotion, emphasizing instead rational aspects of behavior such as the techniques the couples would use to negotiate agreements. They argued that what was needed in couples therapy was a direct approach to the emotions that were basic to the conflicts the distressed couple was experiencing.

They described two basic dysfunctional patterns of marital interaction (and their "variants"), the pursuer–distancer pattern (variants include mutual attack and mutual withdrawal) and the dominance–submission pattern (variants include mutual helplessness and mutual competitiveness).

Toward the end of their book they described a complex process of observational coding, with couples reviewing their own tapes for the construction of a task analysis of successful conflict resolution. This is a summary description of what couples who successfully complete EFT do during conflict resolution. They described four stages:

In the initial stage of the task, the partners are in conflict. The pursuer is engaged in blaming behavior and the withdrawer is either avoiding, protesting, or appeasing. The second component begins when either one of the partners openly discloses his or her feelings or needs, and the other partner responds with understanding, comforting, or helping behavior. One of the unexpected patterns that emerged, quite different from the hypothesized performance, was the third component, in which the pursuer temporarily reverted to blaming behavior, while the withdrawer did not revert to protesting or defending behavior but continued to affirm or understand the other partner. In each resolution event, the pursuers appeared to "test" their partners to see if their new, more understanding, behavior was genuine. If their partners held to their positive behavior, the couple proceeded to the next stage of resolution. In the fourth component, both partners trustingly disclosed feelings or needs while responding with empathic and affirming, protecting, or comforting behaviors. These four patterns were labeled escalation, deescalation, testing, and mutual openness. (p. 218)

The turning point, with the admission of vulnerability, is considered quite important by these authors. To accomplish this pattern of competent conflict resolution, the designers of EFT use a variety of techniques. They claim that some of these techniques are inspired by Gestalt therapy and some by client-centered therapy. The therapy combines interpersonal and intrapsychic perspectives. They encourage the exploration and expression of feelings and empathic responses. They wrote:

Major changes in interactional sequences can be brought about by reframing a negative interactional cycle in terms of the unexpressed aspect of the person's feeling and restructuring the interaction based on the need or motivation amplified by the emotional experience. A "pursue–distance" interaction can therefore be reframed in terms of the pursuer's underlying caring or fear of isolation and the distancer's fear or unexpressed resentment. (p. 45)

They view emotions as basic to concepts of the marriage and self:

Affect is very important in changing attitudes because affectively laden internal information appears to be closely linked to people's self-schemata and tends to override other cues and dominate the formation of meaning. (p. 46)

They believe that state-dependent learning suggests that it is essential to recreate the important emotions in therapy:

Certain core cognitions, cognitive-affective sequences, and complex meanings learned originally in particular affective states are much more accessible when that state is revived. Accessing these "hot cognitions" (Greenberg & Safran, 1984b, 1987a) can be particularly important in clarifying couples' interactions because key construals that induce certain behaviors in the interaction are often not readily available when the problem is being discussed coolly, after the fact, in therapy. Helping couples recreate the situation and relive the emotions in therapy often makes the cognitions governing these behaviors more available for inspection, clarification, and modification. (p. 47)

Greenberg and Johnson describe EFT as including nine steps:

1. Delineate the conflict issues.
2. Identify the negative interaction cycle.
3. Access unacknowledged feelings underlying interactional positions.
4. Redefine the problems in terms of underlying feelings.
5. Promote identification with disowned needs and aspects of self.
6. Promote acceptance by each partner of the other's experience.
7. Facilitate the expression of needs and wants to restructure the interaction.
8. Establish the emergence of new solutions.
9. Consolidate new positions.

# THE RESEARCH EVIDENCE ABOUT A TASK ANALYSIS

## Microanalysis of Conflict Resolution Skills: Research with the MICS

In the decade of the 1970s, psychologists began applying observational methods to the study of differences between happily and unhappily married couples. This was an exciting period, in which published papers revealed consistency across laboratories, and the findings had relative simplicity. What was this remarkable consistency that marital researchers were discovering by observing marital interaction? They were discovering two things. The first, was that the interaction of unhappily married couples was more negative than that of happily married couples, and that negativity was an absorbing state for unhappily married couples.

It may seem self-evident that unhappily married couples are more negative than happily married couples, but it is not. It is difficult even to arrive at that conclusion unless the behaviors observed are chosen very carefully. As an example, let us review the early research with one of the first observational systems of marriage, the MICS.

## A Careful Examination of the Obvious

Two major reviews of research have considered the question of which marital interaction patterns are related to marital satisfaction (Weiss & Summers, 1983; Schaap, 1984). Weiss and Summers restricted themselves to 45 studies (35 published, 10 unpublished) that employed the Marital Interaction Coding System (MICS). The MICS, one of the first observational systems of marital interaction, arose from a behavioral approach to marital therapy, in which the goal was to improve couples' problem-solving ability. It was a strange mixture of codes that tapped both negativity and the problem-solving skills the therapists were trying to teach their clients.

Of all the studies that Weiss and Summers reviewed, only 12 studies examined behavioral differences between satisfied and dissatisfied couples. Of these 12, one (Schaap, 1982) actually employed the content codes of the MICS and the affect codes of a second system, the Couples Interaction Scoring System (CISS), designed by Gottman, Notarius, and Markman in the early 1970s. We will delay discussing the Schaap study because of its special importance.

Of the remaining 11 studies reviewed by Weiss and Summers, 10 collapsed all the 32 MICS codes into an overall positive or an overall negative category, at times discriminating between verbal and nonverbal behaviors. The rules for combining codes varied inconsistently across studies. The authors of these studies usually computed mean summary scores (such as rates) for what were summarized as "positive" and "negative" behaviors over the whole interaction. In general, these studies found that negative interaction was more characteristic of dissatisfied than of satisfied couples. Without a neutral category, however, it is impossible to know if this result was due to less positive or more negative behavior on the part of the unhappily married couple. Some light on this question was shed by Margolin and Wampold (1981), who did have a neutral category. Surprisingly, in their analyses they did not find differences between satisfied and dissatisfied couples on either negative verbal or nonverbal behaviors. Thus, in these early studies of marital interaction with the MICS, it is not even clear that unhappily married couples are more negative than happily married couples when they attempt to resolve conflict.

Why should this be the case? Obviously, the answer has to do with the haphazard way in which codes of the MICS were combined into the global summary codes "negative" or "positive." One problem may be that the MICS codes are not purely measures of either problem solving or emotion but represent a rich and complex mixture of both.

Why would this prove to be a problem? Some codes are clearly negative (e.g., Put Down) and are considered negative in every study. In some studies, however, Disagreement, for example, was considered negative, whereas in other studies it was not. The same was true for other codes, such as Interruption. Perhaps better clarity would have been obtained if specific codes on the MICS were studied, rather than collapsing codes into global positive, negative, and neutral categories.

Unfortunately, we have only one study in which to seek an answer to this question. In the one MICS study that analyzed specific codes of the MICS, Haynes, Follingstad, and Sullivan (1979) found that members of satisfied couples were more likely to agree with their partners, less likely to criticize their partners, and more likely to be attentive listeners than members of dissatisfied couples. Indeed, this is a clear picture.

It seems that combining MICS codes on an a priori basis does not really work. Greater precision in the

analyses gives a clearer, more detailed picture, from which the general conclusions can emerge.

## Sequences of Negativity

With the MICS, specificity provides a clearer picture of the differences between happily and unhappily married couples than a more global approach to description. Perhaps an even clearer picture would emerge from these studies if the analysis of *sequences* of specific codes were employed.

Of the 10 studies with the MICS, only 2 employed sequential analyses. What were the results? Margolin and Wampold (1981) found that dissatisfied couples showed more negative reciprocity. Revenstorf, Vogel, Wegener, Hahlway, and Schindler (1980) also had a neutral category and found higher rates of negative interaction and negative reciprocity in dissatisfied compared to satisfied couples. Thus, in these early studies with the MICS, the reciprocation of negative codes seems more characteristic of unhappily married couples than does the amount of negativity.

From this research, it appeared that unhappily married couples were more likely than happily married couples to respond to a negative act of their partner with a negative act of their own. Hence, for unhappily married couples, negativity was likely to become an absorbing state.

## Microanalysis of Conflict Resolution Skills with the Couples Interaction Scoring System: Gottman (1979)

*Overview*

The Gottman (1979) book is a summary of nine studies of marital interaction conducted at Indiana University from 1972 to 1976, primarily with Clifford Notarius and Howard Markman. This work consisted largely of studies following the Goldfried and D'Zurilla (1969) strategy. In one study, unhappily and happily married couples were interviewed about areas of continuing disagreement. Two additional groups of couples, happy and unhappy, were presented with these problematic situations and asked to respond; their responses were coded. In several other studies, couples who were either happily or unhappily married were videotaped attempting to resolve a set of conflict situations; the situations varied from staged marital conflicts (improvisations) to nonmarital problems to attempts to resolve existing marital issues. Nonconflict, presumably more positive conversations were also sampled. Using a new observational coding system, called the Couples Interaction Scoring System (CISS), and applying lag-sequential analysis, happily and unhappily married couples (and clinic and nonclinic couples) were discriminated using characteristic sequences of behavior in what were described as three phases of a conflict discussion. Gottman (1979) had divided each marital discussion into thirds. In general, he found that there were three distinct phases to a conflict discussion. First was the "agenda-building phase," in which, among happily married couples, both people tended to present their views and feelings on a problem. The second phase was the "arguing phase," in which both people usually tried to persuade each other. The third phase was the "negotiation phase," in which compromise was the apparent goal.

A set of possible behavior exchange models was also studied. Using a device called a "talk table," couples were videotaped as they took turns at speech and rated the positivity/negativity of their intent for messages sent and the positivity/negativity of the impact of messages received.

On the basis of these studies, a therapy program was designed for unhappily married couples, and its effectiveness was evaluated in three studies. Both at-home transfer of training and longitudinal follow-up were included in the assessment. The results showed significant gains of the treatment, changes in both marital satisfaction and behavior, and transfer to the home environment. However, the data suggested a decrement of treatment gains over time. Although this decrement was not statistically significant, Gottman (1979) suggested that it probably would be if a long enough time period were employed.

The task analysis was summarized in the book *A Couple's Guide to Communication* (Gottman et al., 1976). We will review this book in some detail, as well as subsequent research that has attempted tests or replications of the findings.[1]

### Description of the Book

The book introduced the CISS and approaches to sequential and time-series analysis of interactional data. In several studies, the CISS was employed to differentiate satisfied from dissatisfied couples. Using the CISS, it recoded and reanalyzed data from the Raush, Barry, Hertel, and Swain study (1974) on the differences between their discordant and harmonious groups. New improvisations were then empirically developed and employed in a dissertation by Rubin (1977). This study made it possible to examine couples' differences in interaction on various specific issues, including a nonconflict issue called the "fun deck."

The book included studies with a device called the talk table, described previously, which operationalized couples' perceptions of the positivity of the intent of messages they sent and the impact of messages they received from their partners. This was an operationalization of behavior exchange theory (Thibaut & Kelley, 1959) as a perceptual theory.

The book also used the Goldfried and D'Zurilla (1969) approach to individual social competence assessment to demonstrate that there were social skill deficits in individuals, even when they were not interacting with their partners but merely imagining this interaction. With this approach, we could systematically vary the antecedent message and code the consequent. In a subsequent controlled study, Gottman and Porterfield (1982) showed that these deficits have to do with the unhappily married husband, but only in decoding his own wife's nonverbal messages, not those of another person's wife. They proposed that this particular deficit might have to do with male withdrawal from marital conflict. We will return to this theme later.

There were three intervention studies reported in the Gottman (1979) book, as well as a summary of Markman's impressive dissertation predicting longitudinal change in relationship satisfaction among couples planning to marry.

## Specific Methods and Results

We will review some themes that we have been exploring in current work.

### Three Phases of a Marital Conflict

The interactions of couples were divided into three phases. Then, lag-sequential analyses was employed to identify the sequences of each phase and to discover which sequences differentiated happily from unhappily married couples. Within each phase, specific sequences were found to discriminate satisfied from dissatisfied couples. Also, nonsequential frequencies of specific codes discriminated. On the basis of these analyses, the three phases were labeled (1) an agenda-building phase, (2) an arguing phase, and (3) a negotiation phase. Again, on the basis of the sequences, the task of the agenda-building phase appeared to be to air the issues. The task of the arguing phase appeared to be to find areas of common ground, to *persuade one another,* to argue for one's own point of view. This arguing phase was usually quite hot emotionally, and it is here that one saw codes and sequences designed to repair the interaction, such as metacommunication and feeling probe messages. Finally, in the negotiation phase, the goal appeared to be to come to a mutually satisfying resolution of the issue. We will review some important specific sequences here.

*Validation.* Some substantive results were reported from these analyses that suggested the pervasive role of various forms of agreement, validation, and acceptance in the interaction of satisfied couples. In general, we can suggest that in the agenda-building phase of the conflict discussion, satisfied couples followed descriptions of an issue with verbal or nonverbal signals that suggested agreement with the feelings being expressed—not that the partners agreed with the spouse's point of view but, rather, that it made sense to feel that way. The listener tended to be tracking and giving the usual backchannels, which could be as direct as occasional vocalizations ("Mmmhmmm," "Oh, yeah," "I see," "Yup," "O.K.," etc.) or as indirect as gaze toward the speaker, head nodding, and responsive facial movements. Dissatisfied couples, on the other hand, tended to respond to an expression of feelings about a problem with disagreement or a cross-complaint. The interspersed agreement was far less likely to be there.

*Repair and negative affect–absorbing states.* In the disagreement phase, two repair processes among satisfied couples were important: the *feeling probe* and *metacommunication.* Couples did not tend to discuss or ask about feelings directly. Instead, they used what the CISS called *mind-reading*—an attribution of feelings, motives, or past behaviors to the partner. For example, instead of asking her husband how he feels about going to dinner at her mother's house, a wife will say, "You always get tense at my mother's." Stems of "you always" or "you never" were found to be common in mind-reading. The feeling probe was a sequence of neutral-affect mind-reading followed by agreement and elaboration by the partner—for example:

W: You always get tense at my mother's (neutral affect).

H: Yeah, I do, and I think it's because she criticizes the way I discipline Jason.

If the mind-reading were delivered with negative affect, the sequence most common in dissatisfied couples, the response would be disagreement and elaboration—for example:

W: You always get tense at my mother's (neutral affect).
H: I don't *always* get tense at your mother's, but when I do I think it's because she criticizes the way I discipline Jason. And you never stand up for me.

The latter response is far more self-protective and defensive than the first.

Metacommunication was identified by the classic double-bind paper by Bateson et al. (1956). Metacommunication—a communication about communication—may qualify or change communication itself. A simple example is the statement "You're interrupting me." Metacommunication was equally likely for both satisfied and dissatisfied couples. However, satisfied couples used it often, with neutral affect, in short chains that ended with agreement—for example:

H: You're interrupting me.
W: Sorry. What were you saying?

In dissatisfied couples, the metacommunication was delivered with negative affect, and the chains were longer and led to countermetacommunication—for example:

H: You're interrupting me.
W: Maybe I wouldn't have to if I could get a word in edgewise.
H: Oh, now I talk too much.
W: You don't give me a chance to tell you how I feel.

Here, the metacommunication could not function as a repair mechanism because the negative affect from the interaction transferred to what was supposed to be a repair mechanism. This is how negative affect reciprocity works in *constricting the social processes available* to a couple in the course of trying to resolve an area of disagreement. That is the meaning of the term *negative affective absorbing state.* Although negative affect reciprocity occurs in all couples, it occurs more among unhappily than among happily married couples. To give another example, among happily married couples, if a message has both a repair component and a negative affect component (e.g., "You're making me mad. Quit interrupting me!"), it is the repair component that is most likely to determine the partner's response (i.e., "Quit interrupting me!"). Among unhappily married couples, however, the negative affect component will predominate in determining the partner's response (i.e., "You're making me mad.").

*Editing sequences.* Gottman (1979) explored the anatomy of this constriction in examining the linkages between the affective behavior of the listener and the subsequent behavior of that person when he or she became a speaker. These were called "editing sequences," and women performed this function in satisfied marriages. In dissatisfied marriages, women were far less likely to edit. Men performed an editing function only in satisfied marriages and in low-conflict situations.

*Negotiation.* A similar differentiation involving agreement was found in the negotiation stages of the discussion. Satisfied couples were more likely to enter into negotiation sequences, whereas counterproposals were more characteristic of the interaction of dissatisfied couples.

*Point graphs.* The book also classified couples by interactional deficits and strengths using a graphical transformation of the CISS categorical data into a "point graph" that plotted the cumulative sum of positive minus negative points earned by speaker and listener at each turn at speech. These curves are quite similar to Jacobson and Margolin's suggestion of an integrated summary of positivity minus negativity, but on a microanalytic level. The cumulated point graphs were good discriminators between happily and unhappily married couples. Positive slopes characterized the happily married couples, and flat or negative slopes characterized the unhappily married couples.

Using time-series analyses of the noncumulated curves, it was possible to find some support for the hypothesis that *husband dominance patterning was more characteristic of dissatisfied marriages. Dominance* was defined specifically as asymmetry in predictability in the point graphs. For example, if one could predict the wife's data better from the husband's than conversely, then the husband was said to be dominant in that interaction.

*Summary.* Several findings emerged from the observational studies reported in Gottman (1979). First, there was greater negative affect in the interaction of dissatisfied compared to satisfied couples, even when affect was coded separately from content and when a neutral affect code was employed. Second, there was greater negative affect reciprocity in the interactions of dissatisfied compared to satisfied couples. Third, there was evidence of negative affect turning normal social processes available to satisfied couples into a negative affect absorbing state for dissatisfied couples. It was as if they had no way of escaping this state once it was entered.

## Replications and Tests of Gottman (1979)

### Schaap (1982)

An ambitious dissertation by Cas Schaap in 1982 with Dutch couples sought to test the generality of both the studies that had employed the MICS and the observational studies and some of the analyses reported in Gottman (1982). Schaap employed the content codes of the MICS and the affect codes of the CISS in his analyses. He also computed the point graphs presented in Gottman (1979) but did no time-series analysis of the data. He did not divide the conversation into thirds, but he had two interactional tasks. He called the first a *habituation* phase, in which the couple discussed their courtship and early marriage. Schaap had three groups of couples, but we will review only the differences between the groups he called "distressed" and "nondistressed," respectively.

Schaap divided his results into *frequency* and *sequential.* He found that, in the habituation phase, dissatisfied couples laughed less often and used command and disagree codes more often than did satisfied couples. During the conflict discussion, dissatisfied couples showed less humor, laughter, agreement, approval, assent, and compliance. Dissatisfied couples also showed less negative solution (saying what they wanted to see less of in the marriage), issued more commands, disagreements, criticisms, making excuses, and put-downs (expressions of verbal contempt). Agreement-to-disagreement ratios also discriminated the groups. Schaap's ratios of agreement to disagreement were higher than those reported in Gottman (1979) for both satisfied and dissatisfied couples.

*Affect code frequencies.* Schaap found no significant differences between satisfied and dissatisfied couples on neutral codes, but his nondistressed couples were more positive and his distressed couples were more negative than those reported in Gottman (1979). This may be due, in part, to the fact that he asked couples to try to resolve two major issues in their discussion rather than only one, as in Gottman (1979). These instructions may generate a great deal more conflict in distressed couples. Schaap also found that wives delivered more codes with negative affect, whereas husbands delivered more codes with positive affect, a finding he noted was reminiscent of the gender differences reported by Raush et al. (1974).

*Listener withdrawal.* Schaap found that distressed couples also had significantly more "Listener Not Tracking" codes on the MICS, a code that assesses listener withdrawal. There were no gender effects on this code.

*Sequential analyses.* The results Schaap found with the sequential analyses are far too detailed to summarize completely here. We will mention only a few results. Schaap found greater likelihood of cross-complaining sequences with one sequential analysis but not with another (p. 75, note 3). He found a greater likelihood of validation sequences, which he necessarily defined somewhat differently than Gottman (1979) because of his use of the MICS. Validation sequences were defined as problem description followed by consenting, in which consenting included "accepts responsibility," "agrees," "assents," "approves," and "complies." Validation sequences were more common for nondistressed couples, which replicates Gottman (1979). The role of the nondistressed wife in validation was particularly salient in Schaap's data.

Schaap found a greater likelihood of reciprocated humor, especially for *distressed* couples. After joking by the husbands, validation sequences were likely. Humor increased the consequent probability of positive and decreased the consequent probability of negative affect. Contracting sequences were more likely for the nondistressed couples, which also replicate Gottman (1979). Schaap did not find evidence of the counterproposal sequences in distressed couples.

The dimension of *defensiveness,* defined as chains of dissenting (combines the MICS codes of Command, Deny Responsibility, Disagree, and Noncompliance), also emerged in Schaap's data. He summarized this as a "yes-but" sequence, but it appears more similar to a "no-no" sequence.

*Point graphs.* Schaap constructed point graphs differently than in Gottman (1979). Gottman had identified types of marital interaction from the shape of the point graphs. Schaap constructed his own typology of six groups, ranging from extremely negative to extremely positive. The shape of his curves generally related to marital satisfaction and agreement-to-disagreement ratios. Schaap's results do replicate the notion that more positive graphs are more likely to represent more positive sequences identified in Gottman (1979), such as contracting and validation (to a lesser degree), as opposed to cross-complaining and counterproposal sequences. Schaap also analyzed yes-but sequences and "yes dear" and "no deal" sequences between these groups. He did not replicate the Gottman (1979) results between flat-beginning and flat-end point graphs, but this failure to replicate is a reflection of the fact that there were no flat-beginning or flat-end couples in his sample, not that these patterns were not reflective of validation or negotiation deficits, as Gottman (1979) found. Schaap found the nonverbal data more useful in these discriminations than the verbal data.

*Summary.* In reviewing this complex dissertation, we may conclude that many, but not all of the observational results reported in Gottman (1979) were replicated. It is fair to conclude that the essential findings were replicated.

### Ting-Toomey (1983)

In a carefully executed study of 34 married couples, designed in part as an attempt to replicate the Gottman (1979) studies, Ting-Toomey (1983) designed a new observational coding system (the Intimate Negotiation Coding System, INCS) and conducted sequential analyses of two types, Markov model fitting to determine order and homogeneity, and lag-sequential analysis (see Gottman & Roy, 1990, for a discussion of these methods). Hers was a sophisticated and exemplary approach to sequential analysis.

Ting-Toomey divided her couples into three groups: low, moderate and high in marital satisfaction. She found that the interaction in the high marital satisfaction group could be characterized by "communication strings of coaxing, confirming and socioemotional questioning in a unilateral direction, while acts of task-oriented question and description were reciprocal or bilateral'' (p. 16, ms.). In the low marital satisfaction group, the interaction sequences could be described as *defensive.* One common sequence was the confront → defend → confront → defend → confront sequence, "with the sequential trend running toward complain and defend when confront was the criterion behavior" (p. 17, ms.). Another common pattern in the low marital satisfaction group was the complain → defend → complain → defend pattern, which "runs through lag 10 (10 events away from the criterion) when complain was used as the criterion behavior; and, (3) consequently, when defend was used as the criterion code, the sequential loop of defend → complain → defend → complain also runs through the entire ten lags" (p. 17, ms.). In the moderate satisfaction group, she found three patterns: (1) chains of questioning and agreement, when agreement was employed as the criterion code; (2) chains of confirm and agreement, when confirm was the criterion code; and (3) chains of coaxing, when coaxing was employed as the criterion code.

### Revenstorf et al. (1984)

Using the MICS, in a lag sequential analysis, these authors identified four patterns: (1) *distancing,* an alteration of negative responses; (2) *problem escalation,* an alternation of problem description and negative responses to it; (3) *acceptance,* problem description and positive responses in alternation; and (4) *attraction,* patterns of alternating positive responses. Distressed couples showed long chains of negative reciprocity before therapy. Distressed and nondistressed couples were distinguished by these sequences, and these authors found that marital therapy changed each of these patterns considerably.

### Schaap (1984) and Weiss and Heyman (in press)

The reader is referred to Schaap's (1984) review of the literature for additional conclusions about the relationship between concurrent marital satisfaction and marital interaction. An excellent recent review by Weiss and Heyman (in press) summarizes the marital interaction literature since the Schaap (1984) review. The reader is referred to that paper for another recent update of the marital interaction literature.

### Fitzpatrick (1989)

Fitzpatrick and Kalbfleisch studied 51 couples (Fitzpatrick, 1989). They employed the CISS content codes and performed lag-sequential analyses.

They concluded: "These results offer strong support for the importance of the conflict resolution sequences originally proposed by Gottman (1979) and found by Schaap, Buunke, and Kerkstra (1987)" (p. 152).

## Evaluation of Couples Therapy Programs to Date: Brief Review

As marital therapy based on a behavioral approach progressed, components were added to the original quid pro quo. As we have noted, implicit in this approach was the construction of a task analysis of successfully functioning marriages.

There have been a number of important reviews of the marital therapy literature to date (e.g., Baucom & Hoffman, 1986; Hahlweg & Markman, 1983; Jacobson & Addis, 1993). We will summarize their major conclusions here. Baucom and Hoffman noted that the skills usually taught by behavioral marital therapy (BMT) are (1) communication and problem solving and (2) behavior change using contracts (e.g., based on the quid pro quo). They distinguished these communication skills as problem solving in nature, as opposed to communication skill programs oriented toward the expression of emotions and listening skills. Baucom and Hoffman concluded that: (1) couples receiving BMT (compared to a waiting-list control group) improve significantly in negative communication and self-reports of problems (Jacobson's program was the only one to report improvements in positive communication); (2) BMT is superior to both nonspecific and attention control groups; (3) there are no major differences in the effectiveness of two components of BMT or in their order of administration. However, there is some evidence, reported by Jacobson et al. (1985; Jacobson, Schmaling, & Holtzworth-Munroe, 1987), that the communication/problem-solving (CO) training was superior to the behavior exchange (contracting) (BE) condition. Upon two-year follow-up, couples in the CO condition were most likely to be happily married and least likely to be separated or divorced. They also noted that, although statistically significant changes were obtained by BMT compared to a waiting-list (and other) control groups, "60–65% of the couples either remained somewhat distressed or failed to change during treatment" (p. 605).

In a more recent review, Jacobson and Addis (1993) reached similar conclusions to those of Baucom and Hoffman (1986). They estimate that about 50% of couples cannot be considered successes. They are considerably more pessimistic than Baucom and

Hoffman about the long-term effectiveness of BMT. They wrote:

> Little is known about these long-term effects because very few studies followed their couples beyond a few months after treatment termination. The BMT literature *has* produced evidence regarding the course of relationship functioning following termination. One two-year follow-up found that about 30% of those couples who recovered during the course of therapy had relapsed (Jacobson, Schmaling, & Holtzworth-Munroe, 1987). In another study, a four-year follow-up revealed a 38% divorce rate, based on the entire sample of couples who received treatment (Snyder et al., 1991). (p. 7, ms.)

Jacobson and Addis conclude that very little has been learned from so-called horse race studies, which compare "schools" of marital therapy, and note the effect (also noted by Baucom and Hoffman) that the relative outcome is strongly a function of the school to which the authors adhere. There are also problems in the purity of the treatments, particularly the least favored treatment. Jacobson and Addis note that therapy manuals at times will omit from the least favored treatment those ingredients that proponents of that school consider the active ingredients of that form of therapy. They also point out that the first study with a new method obtains the largest results and that there is a gradual decline of effectiveness upon replication.

Let us consider the two interesting findings of all this research. First, treatment gains are not generally maintained over time. Second, it does not seem to matter very much what one does in treatment; in general, the effect sizes are roughly the same, regardless of the exact nature of the intervention. This latter fact is remarkable in "dismantling" studies that are done within a school of thought (they have been done only in BMT). Rather than identifying an "active ingredient" of BMT, they suggest that any of the parts equals the whole. If this remarkable conclusion were true, it would suggest that a minimal marital therapy program may have success equal to that of a larger program. We now speculate about the conditions under which a minimal marital therapy program might be more effective than the total program.

## AN ALTERNATIVE MARITAL THERAPY: MINIMAL MARITAL THERAPY

We will explore one reason that these outcome results for the marital therapies may have been obtained, and will suggest an alternative model of marital therapy. We offer this alternative with humility

since we have no empirical data to support our suggestions. However, we hope to back up our speculations. One way to interpret the outcome results of marital therapy studies is that treatment effect sizes are relatively constant across schools of therapy and that, within schools, it makes very little difference which components are employed. Because it is well known that marital therapy is so aversive (particularly for men), unlike some forms of individual therapy, creating a minimal therapy may have some advantages, and at no cost of effectiveness.

Thus, we suggest that minimal marital therapy be created. Second, we suggest that the major reason for the lack of maintenance of effects over time may be that people do not have access to the learnings of therapy once they become physiologically aroused. Hence, we propose that there be a soothing component to the therapy and that the minimal skills be overlearned. The basic suggestion we will make is based on a concept called *diffuse physiological arousal*.

## Theoretical Foundation for Minimal Marital Therapy

We noted earlier that Greenberg and Johnson (1988) had stated that (1) emotions are basic to people's core concepts of the marriage and the self, and (2) state-dependent learning suggests that it is essential to recreate the important emotions in therapy "because key construals that induce certain behaviors in the interaction are often not readily available when the problem is being discussed coolly, after the fact, in therapy" (p. 47). Gottman (1990) suggested similar ideas and then also related them to a concept he called "diffuse physiological arousal."

*Diffuse physiological arousal* (DPA) means that more than one physiological system is activated to a significant degree above baseline levels (e.g., heart rate and blood velocity). It is well known in physiology that, as a negative stimulus becomes more intense and more aversive, more and more physiological systems become activated (see, e.g., Rowell, 1986). Thus, at first heart rate will increase as a result of vagal restraint, and then the sympathetic will become activated to bring the heart rate to higher levels. Blood flow to the gut and kidneys will drop dramatically. Then the adrenal will begin secreting epinephrine, and heart rate and myocardial contractility will increase. Next, the kidneys will begin secreting renin, the renin-angiotensin system will become engaged, and blood pressure will rise. In most instances of normal functioning, these systems function independently and are fairly uncorrelated. However, the body is capable of the defense response and other responses to emergency (such as the alarm response) in which different systems operate in concert. Gottman (1990) suggested that diffuse physiological arousal may accompany heated marital conflict discussions. He suggested that this physiological state could be created by multiple negative emotions in close temporal sequence, by constrained emotions, and by negative emotion blends. He also suggested that DPA is a highly unpleasant and aversive subjective bodily state.

*Implications of DPA for social interaction.* Gottman (1990) also suggested that DPA reduces the ability to process information, and that DPA makes over-learned behaviors and cognitions more likely than newly acquired behaviors and cognitions. This hypothesis, if true, would explain why it was difficult for marital therapy clients to have access to new learnings during times of heated controversy that resulted in DPA. Third, DPA increases the likelihood of the same behaviors that are engaged during fight or flight—that is, withdrawal and aggression. This would make sense as the result of past emotional conditioning; it states that, in effect, emotions that result in DPA become linked to the primitive fight or flight response. Fourth, sex differences may exist in recovery time from DPA: Males take longer than females. The clear-cut implications of this hypothesis are spelled out in Gottman and Levenson (1986). These implications are that males will be more likely than females to manage the level of negative affect in marital interaction and to take steps to keep it from escalating. In particular, males are more likely than females to inhibit the expression of emotion; they are more likely to appeal to rationality and compromise (see Raush et al., 1974) and more likely than females to withdraw or to aggress.

### Automatic versus Effortful Processing

*Emotionality, anxiety, arousal, and performance.* The most famous hypothesis in psychology in this area is the Yerkes-Dodson law (1908), the well-known inverted-U-shaped function between arousal and performance. There have been many methodological critiques of this law, including the difficulty of defining arousal in a unidimensional way and the difficulty of disproving the hypothesis. Kahneman (1973) showed that in general physiological arousal increases with task difficulty. There is no

evidence of a decline in task performance following this increased arousal. A review of the literature by Eysenck (1982) concluded that there is more evidence favoring the law when the increased arousal has been produced by aversive stimulation than by incentives (p. 48).

Kahneman, Tursky, Shapiro, and Crider (1969) suggested that the greater the processing demands, the larger the physiological effects. A series of digits presented to the subject had to be transformed by adding 0, 1, or 3 after a two-second pause. Three physiological measures (pupil diameter, heart rate, and skin conductance) all showed increases during the input and processing of the information, followed by a decrease. Pupil diameter grew steadily as task load (the number of serially presented digits) and task complexity (add 0, 1, or 3) increased. (see also Kahneman, 1973, for a review).

Obrist (1981) has shown that the illusion of control over aversive stimuli is adequate to create increases in heart rate *and* contractility. Actual control is sufficient but not necessary. Thus, actual control or the illusion of control over aversive stimulation is probably adequate to produce diffuse sympathetic arousal. We continue to encounter this notion that the avoidance of aversive stimuli is responsible for disruption of controlled attentional processes as well as being related to the sympathetic accelerator.

What do these results suggest about the efficacy of a minimal marital therapy program? They suggest that during marital conflict, vigilance and complex information processing should be kept to a minimum. Obrist's results also suggest that the sense of control that is usually part of vigilance will be adequate to create DPA; thus, perhaps somewhat paradoxically, subjects ought to enter a conflict discussion with a low sense of control. We say that this is paradoxical because therapy is usually thought of as providing people with a sense of control that comes with increased competence. The distinction between increased competence and lowered control and vigilance can be clarified somewhat by discussing effortful versus automatic information processing.

*Information processing.* Posner (Posner & Snyder, 1975a, 1975b) suggested that there are two kinds of information processing: automatic processes and those requiring conscious attention. Automatic processes involve parallel processing, whereas conscious processes involve serial processing. Research then began on the processing of information without awareness. In such priming experiments (see Eysenck's 1982 citation of Marcel), it was discovered that a priming effect could take place without awareness even at a high level of semantic meaning. Conscious performance was impaired somewhat when unexpected events occurred, but nowhere near as completely disrupted as when unexpected expectations were applied to automatic processes.

Schneider and Shiffrin (1977) suggested a similar distinction between automatic and controlled processes. They used a different paradigm, in which a small set of items is memorized and the subject has to find matches and mismatches in a set of serially presented items. Controlled processes are a linear function of the number of items in the memory set and involve serial comparisons, with each one occurring at the rate of 40 ms. Automatic processes were not hindered by capacity limitations on short-term memory and do not require attention. These authors found that controlled processes are slower but far more adaptable than automatic processes.

Triesman and Gelade (1980) modified this theory by suggesting that objects that are perceived and attended to have features. If the subject is asked to attend to a conjunction of two features (A and B), then the processing is controlled, or serial. When there is no conjunction, the processing is parallel and automatic. They found that even extensive practice with detection of a combination of features did not result in automatic processing.

What do these results suggest for the possible efficacy of a minimal marital therapy? They suggest the need for overlearning so that the skills taught in therapy will become automatic and will be less easily disrupted by diffuse physiological arousal. Combined with practical considerations of treatment, the possible need for overlearning also suggests the importance of teaching the couple only a minimal set of skills. We need to recall that the average number of sessions in BMT is about 14.

How can we rely on only a small set of skills? It could still be the case that the task analysis for marriage is quite elaborate and complex, but that the best way into the task analysis is to teach *entry-level skills* and then hope that a self-guided and self-correcting system will take over after that. Subsequent therapy could then be concerned with follow-ups and guiding the couples through the remainder of the task analysis.

## What Are These Entry-Level Skills?

At this point, the research evidence is equivocal about the selection of entry-level skills. The concept may even be wrong, and it may be arbitrary where one begins. However, we will assume that entry-level skills exist, and we will take a stab at suggesting what

these skills are. First, we suggest that all marital therapies need to be gender sensitive and take into consideration that during strong negative affect, men tend to withdraw and women tend to engage (Gottman & Levenson, 1986). Hence, the minimal set of skills may be different for men than for women. This has implications for *how* a therapist works with a couple. However, the minimal set of skills may need to be within the couple's interacting system, and hence would be somewhat symmetrical for both spouses.

We suggest that the skills are as follows: Soothing, Nondefensive Listening, and Validating. Details of these last two skills are given in *A Couple's Guide to Communication* (Gottman et al., 1976). We will not spend a great deal of space on them here. These skills are not new but are a part of almost all current marital therapy programs we have reviewed. We do not know the status of direct training in problem solving. We would suggest that at this entry level of skill, problem solving should be actively discouraged because it will lead to effortful information processing and vigilance. A commonly heard complaint from wives about men is that men rush in too soon to try to solve the problem without first hearing the wife's feelings and truly understanding her point of view. That is the goal of these entry-level skills. On the basis of our experience, we suggest that each marital interaction be preceded by a five-minute period of silence in which couples can gather their thoughts, followed by a conversation period of no longer than fifteen minutes.

Let us begin with the skill of soothing (this can be self-soothing, or the couple can soothe each other; eventually, it should not be the therapist who does this). The best methods for soothing physiological arousal are probably (1) withdrawing from the interaction—that is, taking a scheduled break (and scheduling a time to return, with a commitment to continue the discussion)—and (2) relaxation, either separately, or, even better, with each other.[2] There is some evidence that communications training of couples will reduce blood pressure reactivity (Ewart, Taylor, Kraemer, & Agras, 1984). We also have some unpublished evidence (Gottman, Rushe, Kiecolt-Glaser, Glaser, & Malarkey, 1992) that some positive affects, such as mutual humor and validation, are related to reductions in epinephrine secretion over time.

*Soothing and how to know if one is in a state of DPA.* Although research to date on the Yerkes-Dodson law would suggest that there are vast individual differences in the stimuli that create physiological arousal, there may be a simple, clear-cut, and inexpensive way to assess whether a client is in DPA. Rowell (1986), in his study of physical exercise, found that increases in heart rate above 100 beats per minute (BPM) seem to be an important cutoff for men. This cutoff marks the point at which sympathetic nervous system activation and the secretion of stress-related hormones become involved in regulating the heart increasing rate; this is one cutoff for heart rate that suggests the point at which physiological arousal may become DPA. Since the base heart rate is about 70 BPM for males and 80 BPM for females, this suggests that a critical cutoff of approximately 30 BPM increase will result in DPA. Our own research with violent marriages (conducted with N. Jacobson, and as yet unpublished) suggests that, during marital conflict, heart rate increases far less than this cutoff, and more on the order of 12 BPM, may create significant alterations in affective behavior.

If these initial results are true, they suggest that therapists should teach couples a soothing ritual during marital conflict. The soothing ritual for withdrawal should be instituted when heart rate gets above +10 BPM over baseline (80 for men, 90 for women). Heart rate can easily be monitored by having people use the first and second fingers of their right hand to count the pulses at the right side of the neck (carotid artery) for 15 seconds, and then multiply by 4 to get their heart rate. A baseline heart rate should be taken before the conversation begins during a short period when the subjects' eyes are closed and they are more or less relaxed. We suggest the frequent use of "Stop Action" interventions, which can be called by the couple at any time (see Gottman et al., 1976).

*Nondefensive listening.* Defensiveness involves self-protection and warding off a perceived attack. It includes whining, denying responsibility for a problem, rebutting mind-reading attributions made by one's spouse (e.g., *Spouse:* "You always do or feel X"; defensive rebuttal: "I do not always do or feel X"), and cross-complaining. Listening to one's partner's complaints needs to exclude a defensive response and substitute an affectively neutral (or, better yet, an empathic) response. The requirement that a person validate his or her spouse's feelings and viewpoint decreases the possibility of a defensive response, so that nondefensive listening and validation are part of the same constructive response.

*Validation.* Validation is actually a scale of responses. At the low point of the scale we have simply

providing listener backchannels that show that the listener is tracking (i.e., not stonewalling). These responses usually involve looking at the speaker, facial movement, occasional head nods, a nonrigid neck, relaxed breathing, and brief vocalizations (preferably assents such as "Yeah," "O.K.," "Mmhmm," and the like). These communicate to the speaker that the listener thinks what the speaker is saying could be valid and makes sense, that the listener could see things from the speaker's perspective. Validation at this lowest level on the scale does not necessarily imply that the listener agrees with the speaker. At the high end of the scale, we have the kind of empathic understanding that Greenberg and Johnson (1988) describe so ably.

*Organizing framework for couples: Knowledge of the corrosive cycle—The Four Horsemen of the Apocalypse.* In recent research from Gottman's laboratory (Gottman & Levenson, in press; Buehlman, Gottman, & Fainsilber-Katz, 1992; Gottman, in press a, b, c), a cycle of corrosive marital interaction processes can be identified that predicts marital dissolution over time. This cycle can be depicted as follows:

COMPLAIN → CRITICIZE →
DEFENSIVE → CONTEMPT → WITHDRAWAL

Complaining is not harmful to the long-term health of the marriage (Gottman & Krokoff, 1989). Although it starts the cycle, it is so common in discourse about a marital conflict that it would start constructive as well as corrosive cycles. The next four processes are the "Four Horsemen" (please ignore gender here). We believe that Listening and Validation combats Defensiveness, if the Validation is genuine and not mere mechanical paraphrasing (although this is often a start). Contempt and Withdrawal are so corrosive that they also need to be eliminated, and will be if Withdrawal is ritualized as previously discussed, and Listening and Validation follow complaints.

*Styles of persuasion.* *Persuasion* here is used in a limited way to mean a direct, overt attempt to convince one's partner that he or she is wrong and/or you are right. It need not be logical. Although, in general, persuasion occurs in the second third of the interaction, we have discovered three distinct styles of persuasion that are equally viable from the standpoint of marital stability (Gottman, 1993a). The three styles are called *validating, volatile,* and *avoiding.* The validating style listens for the first five minutes of the interaction and then begins attempts at persuasion. The volatile style begins persuasion attempts right away (usually with a lot of interspersed positive affect, like laughter). The avoiding style never engages in persuasion. The therapist needs to be sensitive to these differences in persuasive style. This typology is spelled out in detail in a forthcoming book titled *What Predicts Divorce?* (Gottman, 1994a).

## SUMMARY

The Goldfried and D'Zurilla task analysis approach to behavior change has been the implicit foundation of many forms of marital therapy. Although task analysis and social skills training have been effective when applied to marital enhancement and marital therapy, new approaches are in order. We advocate several changes. Quantitative descriptions of dysfunctional marriages that focus on overt behaviors (e.g., those that use the MICS) must provide more detailed accounts of specific behaviors as well as the specific type of dysfunctional marriage. Important progress has been made identifying patterns of positive, negative, and neutral behaviors, but further progress lies in the description of specific problem-solving strategies and specific emotions. We also advocate a shift in focus from the exclusive use of overt behaviors in social skills programs to an integration of physiological and attentional processes into existing behavior therapy technology. We challenge clinicians and researchers to perform more descriptive task analyses.

On the basis of a summary of what has been learned about the effectiveness of marital therapy, we recommend a new approach called *minimal marital therapy*. Therapy should focus on a minimal amount of material because, in outcome studies of marital therapy, the minimum seems to work as well as the full program. In short, the part is equal to the whole. We suggest that minimal marital therapy should last for a minimal amount of time because men, in particular, find the experience of marital therapy aversive and are often reluctant participants. Research on learning recommends overlearning so that clients will have access to new behaviors when they are in a state of DPA. Also, we suggest that ideally, under conditions of arousal, automatic versus controlled processing of information could operate so that soothing might proceed. During marital conflict, newly acquired adaptive responses must be made without conscious effort and performed under stress and arousal conditions. We believe the minimal approach should focus on the overlearning of a few basic skills; the selection of these skills is fairly arbitrary. We currently favor nondefensive listening, validating, and soothing; to us, these seem fundamental, although

much more data are required to justify this choice over others (such as contingency or good faith contracting).

Research by Gottman and his collaborators has had some success in predicting deterioration in marital satisfaction and progress toward marital dissolution, years before direct changes were observable. Our results have specific recommendations for implementing a new minimal marital therapy. We predict that the optimal physiological conditions for initial skills acquisition in therapy will exist when heart rate is not elevated above baseline. However, these skills need to be rehearsed and overlearned under all conditions of physiological arousal, including DPA. As part of the therapy, we suggest that couples learn to call a "Stop Action" and self-soothe (and/or soothe one another) once their heart rates exceed 10 beats per minute over their baseline rates. At approximately 100 beats per minute for men and 110 beats per minute for women, they are probably in DPA. Once the couple has calmed down, they need to practice listening nondefensively and validating one another.

In addition to gender differences, the social-skills marital therapist should also be sensitive to the couple's persuasion style. In stable marriages, spouses may attempt to influence each other at the beginning or middle of a conflict—or even not at all. A cascade model of marital dissolution is under development, starting with complaints and progressing to defensiveness, contempt, and ultimately withdrawal. New behaviors are expected to be acquired more easily at earlier stages of the model—that is, before there has been too much deterioration of positive marital processes.

## NOTES

1. The *Couple's Guide* (Gottman et al., 1976) is also a central component of Markman's prevention program (called PREP) with newlywed couples.

2. The reason that soothing is better in a couple context than it is separately involves the Gottman and Levenson escape conditioning model of how marriages change (Gottman & Levenson, 1986; Gottman, 1990). This model, which links the reduction of physiological arousal with the reinforcement of behavioral sequences, may be able to explain how marriages become either more or less satisfying over time. Escape conditioning moments during marital interaction are defined as occurring when both spouses make the transition from high to low levels of DPA. We expect that the behavior patterns that accompany these escape moments will be reinforced and increase in both unconditional probability and conditional probability (i.e., given ANS arousal).

This mechanism may provide natural change moments in marriages. The escape conditioning model can also be used as a model for how relationships could improve over time. What makes people feel better and restores calm could just as easily be an empathic, loving response as a negative response (see Gottman & Levenson, 1986, for an example). Then, according to the model, an empathic, loving response could also become more likely to be in the couple's repertoire as the response to upset.

## REFERENCES

Azrin, N. H., Naster, B. J., & Jones, R. (1973). Reciprocity counseling: A rapid learning based procedure for marital counseling. *Behavior Research and Therapy, 11,* 365–382.

Bateson, G., Jackson, D. D., Haley, J., & Weakland, J. (1956). Toward a theory of schizophrenia. *Behavioral Science, 1,* 251–264.

Baucom, D. H., & Hoffman, J. A. (1986). The effectiveness of marital therapy: Current status and application to the clinical setting. In N. Jacobson & A. Gurman (Eds.), *Clinical handbook of marital therapy.* (pp. 597–620). New York: Guilford Press.

Buehlman, K., Gottman, J., & Fainsilber-Katz, L. (1992). How a couple views their past predicts their future: Predicting divorce from an oral history interview. *Journal of Family Psychology, 5,* 281–304.

Ewart, C. K., Taylor, C. B., Kraemer, H. C., & Agras, W. S. (1984). *Behavior Therapy, 15,* 473–484.

Eysenck, M. W. (1982). *Attention and arousal: Cognition and performance.* Berlin: Springer-Verlag.

Fitzpatrick, M. A. (1988). *Between husbands and wives: Communication in marriage.* Newbury Park, CA: Sage Publications.

Gagne, R. M. (1965, 1977). *The conditions of learning.* New York: Holt, Rinehart & Winston.

Goldfried, M. R., & D'Zurilla, T. J. (1969). A behavioral-analytic model for assessing competence. In C. D. Spielberger (Ed.), *Current topics in clinical and community psychology* (Vol. 1, pp. 151–196). New York: Academic Press.

Gottman, J. M. (1979). *Marital interaction: Experimental investigations.* New York: Academic Press.

Gottman, J. M. (1982). Emotional responsiveness in marital conversations. *Journal of Communication, 32*(3), 108–120.

Gottman, J. M. (1990). How marriages change. In G. Patterson (Ed.), *New directions in family research: Depression and aggression.* Hillsdale, NJ: Lawrence Erlbaum.

Gottman, J. (1993a). Roles of conflict engagement, escalation, and avoidance in marital interaction: A longitudinal view of five types of couples. *Journal of Consulting and Clinical Psychology, 61*(1), 6–15.

Gottman, J. (1993b). A theory of marital dissolution and stability. *Journal of Family Psychology, 7*(1), 57–75.

Gottman, J. (1994). *What predicts divorce?* Hillsdale, NJ: Lawrence Erlbaum.

Gottman, J., Kiecolt-Glaser, J., Rushe, R., Glaser, R., & Malarkey, R. (n.d.). *Specific affects and recovery from plasma epinephrine secretion during marital conflict in newlywed couples.* Unpublished manuscript, available from the first author on request.

Gottman, J., & Krokoff, L. (1989). Marital interaction and satisfaction: A longitudinal view. *Journal of Consulting and Clinical Psychology, 57*(1), 47–52.

Gottman, J., & Levenson, R. (1992). Marital processes predictive of later dissolution: Behavior, physiology, and health. *Journal of Personality and Social Psychology, 63*(2), 221–233.

Gottman, J., & Levenson, R. (1986). Assessing the role of emotion in marriage. *Behavioral Assessment, 8*(1), 31–48.

Gottman, J., Notarius, C., Gonso, J., & Markman, H. (1976). *A couple's guide to communication.* Champaign, IL: Research Press.

Gottman, J. M., Notarius, C., Markman, H., Bank, S., Yoppi, B., & Rubin, M. E. (1976). Behavior exchange theory and marital decision making. *Journal of Personality and Social Psychology, 43,* 14–23.

Gottman, J., & Porterfield, A. (1983). Communicative competence in the nonverbal behavior of married couples. *Journal of Marriage and the Family, 43*(4), 817–824.

Gottman, J., & Roy, A. (1990). *Sequential analysis: A guide for behavioral researchers.* New York: Cambridge University Press.

Greenberg, L. S., & Johnson, S. M. (1988). *Emotionally focused therapy for couples.* New York: Guilford Press.

Greenberg, L., & Safran, J. (1984a). Integrating affect and cognition: A perspective on the process of therapeutic change. *Cognitive Therapy and Research, 8*(6), 559–578.

Greenberg, L., & Safran, J. (1984b). Hot cognition—Emotion coming in from the cold: A reply to Rachman and Mahoney. *Cognitive Therapy and Research, 8*(6), 592–598.

Greenberg, L., & Safran, J. (1987a). *Emotion in psychotherapy: Affect, cognition and the process of change.* New York: Guilford Press.

Hahlweg, K., & Markman, H. (1988). Effectiveness of behavioral marital therapy: Empirical status of behavioral techniques in preventing and alleviating marital distress. *Journal of Consulting and Clinical Psychology, 56*(3), 440–447.

Haynes, S. N., Follingstad, D. R., & Sullivan, J. C. (1979). Assessment of marital satisfaction and interaction. *Journal of Consulting and Clinical Psychology, 47,* 789–791.

Jacobson, N. (1978). A stimulus control model of change in behavioral couples' therapy: Implications for contingency contracting. *Journal of Marital and Family Therapy, 4*(3), 29–35.

Jacobson, N. S., & Addis, M. E. (in press). Research on couple therapy: What do we know? Where are we going? *Journal of Consulting and Clinical Psychology.*

Jacobson, N. S., Follette, V. M., Follette, W. C., Holtz-worth-Munroe, A., Katt, J. L., & Schmaling, K. B. (1985). A component analysis of behavioral marital therapy: One-year follow-up. *Behavior Research and therapy, 23,* 549–555.

Jacobson, N. S., & Margolin, G. (1979). *Marital therapy.* New York: Brunner/Mazel.

Jacobson, N. S., Schmaling, K., & Holtzworth-Munroe, A. (1987). Component analysis of behavioral marital therapy: Two-year follow-up and prediction of relapse. *Journal of Marital and Family Therapy, 13,* 187–195.

Kahneman, D. (1973). *Attention and effort.* Englewood Cliffs, NJ: Prentice-Hall.

Kahneman, D., Tursky, B., Shapiro, D., & Crider, A. (1969). Pupillary, heart rate and skin resistance changes during a mental task. *Journal of Experimental Psychology, 79,* 164–167.

Lederer, W. J., & Jackson, D. D. (1968). *Mirages of marriage.* New York: W. W. Norton.

Locke, H. J., & Wallace, K. M. (1959). Short marital-adjustment and prediction tests: Their reliability and validity. *Marriage and Family Living, 21,* 251–255.

Margolin, G., Christensen, A., & Weiss, R. L. (1975). Contracts, cognition and change: A behavioral approach to marriage therapy. *The Counseling Psychologist, 5,* 111–125.

Margolin, G., & Wampold, B. (1981). Sequential analysis of conflict and accord in distressed and nondistressed marital partners. *Journal of Consulting and Clinical Psychology, 49*(4), 554–567.

Mischel, W. (1968). *Personality and assessment.* New York: Wiley.

Obrist, P. (1982). *Cardiovascular psychophysiology.* New York: Plenum Press.

Patterson, G. R. (1974). A basis for identifying stimuli which control behaviors in natural settings. *Child Development, 45,* 900–911.

Patterson, G. R., & Hops, H. (1972). Coercion, a game for two: Intervention techniques for marital conflict. In R. E. Ulrich & P. Montjoy (Eds.), *The experimental analysis of social behavior* (pp. 424–440). New York: Appleton-Century-Crofts.

Posner, M. I., & Snyder, C. R. R. (1975a). Attention and cognitive control. In R. L. Solso (Ed.), *Information processing and cognition: The Loyola Symposium.* Hillsdale, NJ: Lawrence Erlbaum.

Posner, M. I., & Snyder, C. R. R. (1975b). Facilitation and inhibition in the processing of signals. In P. M. A. Rabbitt & S. Dornic (Eds.), *Attention and performance* (Vol. 5). London: Academic Press.

Raush, H. L., Barry, W. A., Hertel, R. K., & Swain, M. A. (1974). *Communication, conflict and marriage.* San Francisco: Jossey-Bass.

Revenstorf, D., Vogel, B., Wegener, C., Hahlway, K., & Schindler, L. (1980). Escalation phenomena in interaction sequences: An empirical comparison of distressed and nondistressed couples. *Behavior analysis and modification, 4,* 97–115.

Revensdorf, D., Hahlweg, K., Schindler, L., & Vogel, B. (1984). Interaction analysis of marital conflict. In K. Hahlweg & N. Jacobson (Eds.), *Marital interaction: Analysis and modification.* New York: Guilford Press.

Rowell, L. (1986). *Human circulation: Regulation during physical stress.* New York: Orford.

Rubin, M. E. (1977). *Differences between distressed and nondistressed couples in verbal and nonverbal communication codes.* Unpublished doctoral dissertation, Indiana University at Bloomington.

Schaap, C. (1982). *Communication and adjustment in marriage.* Lisse: Svets & Zeitlinger.

Schaap, C. (1984). A comparison of the interaction of distressed and nondistressed married couples in a laboratory situation: Literature survey, methodological issues, and an empirical investigation. In K. Hahlweg & N. Jacobson (Eds.), *Marital interaction: Analysis and modification.* New York: Guilford Press.

Schneider, W., & Schiffrin, R. M. (1977). Controlled and automatic human information processing: I. Detection, search and attention. *Psychological Review, 84,* 1–66.

Thibaut, J. W., & Kelley, H. H. (1959). *The social psychology of groups.* New York: Wiley.

Ting-Toomey, S. (1983). An analysis of verbal communication patterns in high and low marital adjustment groups. *Human Communication Research, 9*(4), 306–319.

Triesman, A. M., & Gelade, G. (1980). A feature-integration theory of attention. *Cognitive Psychology, 12,* 97–136.

Weiss, R. L. (1978). The conceptualization of marriage from a behavioral perspective. In T. J. Paolino & B. S. McCrady (Eds.), *Marriage and marital therapy: Psychoanalytic, behavioral, and systems perspectives.* New York: Brunner/Mazel.

Weiss, R. L., Hops, H., & Patterson, G. R. (1973). A framework for conceptualizing marital conflict: A technology for altering it, some data for evaluating it. In L. A. Hamerlynck, I. C. Handy, & E. J. Mash (Eds.), *Behavior change: The fourth Banff conference on behavior modification.* Champaign, IL: Research Press.

Weiss, R. L., & Margolin, G. (1977). Marital conflict and accord. In R. A. Ciminero, K. S. Calhoun, & H. E. Adams (Eds.), *Handbook for behavioral assessment.* New York: Wiley.

Weiss, R. L., & Perry, B. A. (1979). *Assessment and treatment of marital dysfunction.* Eugene: Oregon Marital Studies Program.

Weiss, R. L., & Summers, K. J. (1983). Marital Interaction Coding System III. In E. Filsinger (Ed.), *Marriage and family assessment.* Beverly Hills, CA: Sage Publications.

Yerkes, R. M., & Dodson, J. D. (1908). The relation of strength of stimulus intensity to rapidity of habit-formation. *Journal of Comparative and Neurological Psychology, 18,* 459–482.

# CHAPTER 14

# SKILLS TRAINING IN STRESS MANAGEMENT

Thomas W. Pierce

Over the last fifty years, health professionals have collected a substantial body of literature demonstrating the adverse effects of stress on human health. High levels of stress have been linked with increased risk for development of health-related problems, including but not limited to essential hypertension (Shapiro, 1978; Weiner, 1977), coronary heart disease (CAD) (Haney & Blumenthal, 1985), ulcer (Wolf, 1965), and headache (Henryk-Gutt & Rees, 1973; Howarth, 1965). The prevalence of stress-related disorders may be illustrated by findings showing that up to 70% of adults in the United States suffer from headaches and that 40% of these are tension headaches (Kashiwagi, McClure, & Wetzel, 1972) linked to the presence of stress (Bakal, 1975). Moreover, the financial costs to society of treating stress-related disorders can reach $4.8 billion a year, as in the case of hypertension (Weinstein & Stason, 1976).

Stress management, the specialty of treating and preventing stress disorders, has roots dating back to at least the beginning of the twentieth century. William Osler (1910), for example, commented on the detrimental effects of overly demanding life-styles on

health. In 1932, Walter Cannon described the physiological responses of the sympathetic nervous system to physical and emotional hardship. This activity of the autonomic nervous system (characterized by increased release of adrenaline and noradrenaline and by increases in heart rate, blood pressure, and skeletal muscle tone) has been termed the *stress response* (e.g., Everly, 1989; Feurstein, Labbe, & Kuczmierczyk, 1986). More recent lines of thought regarding stress can be traced to the work of Hans Selye (1956, 1976), who identified a pattern of physiological responses (decreased appetite, increased blood pressure, muscle weakness, and loss of ambition) that he characterized as the final "fatigue stage" in the body's struggle to adapt to unrelenting challenge.

In the last twenty years, the treatment of stress disorders has accelerated to the point where clinicians have a variety of treatment options available to them. Systematic training in specific skills for addressing stress-related problems is an important part of most stress management programs. Self-monitoring, problem solving, cognitive restructuring, relaxation, and biofeedback have all been shown to contribute to reductions in stress (Lehrer & Woolfolk, 1984).

The goals of this chapter are to present the rationale for skills training in a stress management setting and to describe these skills in detail. The chapter is organized as follows:

1. A theoretical framework for the concept of stress is presented.
2. Skills training in stress management is discussed, largely within the context of stress inoculation training (Meichenbaum, 1977, 1985; Meichenbaum & Cameron, 1983).
3. Empirical work regarding the application of skills training to stress management is briefly reviewed.

Emphasis is placed on skills for accurately appraising the significance of stressors as well as on skills for coping with sources of perceived stress. Since separate chapters in this book are devoted to relaxation (Chapter 2) and problem-solving skills (Chapter 7), the reader will be referred to these chapters for the specifics of instruction in these skills.

## THE CONCEPT OF STRESS

### The Difficulty of Defining Stress

When considering the introduction of a program in stress management, the first question might well be, "What exactly is *managed* in stress management?" Defining *stress* has not proved to be an easy task. As noted by a number of authors (e.g., Everly, 1989; Feurstein, Labbe, & Kuczmierczyk, 1986), stress has been referred to by various authors as (1) a *stimulus* that elicits unpleasant physiological and affective responses (Holmes & Rahe, 1967), (2) a *response* or constellation of responses to a demanding "stressor" (Selye, 1956, 1976), and (3) the result of a *transaction* between the demands that people face and the resources they possess to meet them (Cox & McCay, 1978; Lazarus, 1966). Although many models of stress have been proposed, to date, the transactional model of Lazarus (1966; Lazarus & Folkman, 1984) is widely viewed as the most comprehensive, accurate, and productive model of the origin of stress (e.g., Beck, 1984; Meichenbaum, 1985).

### The Transactional Model

The basic premise of the transactional model of stress is that stress occurs when perceived demands, internal or external, tax or exceed the resources that can be allocated to meet these demands. Stress, from this perspective, is viewed as neither a stimulus nor a response but, rather, the product of a transaction between demands (debits) and coping resources (credits). When credits (resources) exceed debits (demands) in this "stress equation," the present situation will be viewed as challenging—requiring mobilization of coping resources, but resolvable in a satisfactory manner. When debits exceed credits, the situation will be viewed as stressful with a high likelihood of an undesirable outcome. Although this model provides a reasonable explanation of the origin of stress, it may not provide a perfect fit for some situations in which stress is experienced even though sufficient coping skills appear to exist (as might be the case in driving a car in a snowstorm).

According to Lazarus (1966), the solution of the stress equation is based on two automatic appraisals of a given situation. A *primary appraisal* assesses the potential for the situation to result in a negative outcome. Primary appraisal provides an evaluation of the demands that must be met in a given situation and characterizes the degree of threat these demands impose. *Secondary appraisal* provides for evaluation of the coping resources currently available for meeting these demands. This process of appraisal, in which resources are compared with demands, is not seen as a purposive or static event but as a recognition of the extent to which demands do or do not exceed resources.

Within a transactional framework, stress can be reduced or prevented in one of two ways: Demands can be decreased or resources can be increased. The relative emphasis on these two avenues will vary depending on the context in which stress occurs. However, effective stress management will almost certainly contain at least an element of each.

### Settings for Stress Management

Stress management has been conducted within a number of contexts. For example, some clients may seek relief from physical conditions that they attribute to the presence of stress (e.g., chronic headache, muscle tension). Other clients may require training in coping skills to meet or alter unacceptably high demands imposed on them (e.g., career stress, caring for a chronically ill family member, chronic pain, anticipation of threatening medical procedures). In yet another setting, clients exhibiting the Type A behavior pattern may desire training in skills for reducing the demands they place on themselves. For descriptions of the etiology of specific stress disorders, see reviews by Everly (1989); Holroyd, Appel, & Andrasik (1983); and Weiner (1977).

## TREATMENT OPTIONS IN STRESS MANAGEMENT

The clinician may currently draw on a wide range of techniques for helping clients to manage the stresses they face. Treatment options for stress-related problems currently include meditation, hypnosis, biofeedback, autogenic training, progressive relaxation training, and cognitive-behavioral psychotherapy.

### Interventions at the Level of Physical Symptoms

*Progressive Relaxation Training*

The rationale for progressive relaxation training is that, because the health-threatening consequences of stress are mediated by an overactivation of physiological systems (e.g., exaggerated cardiovascular responsivity as a risk factor for development of hypertension; Drummond, 1983) to perceived threat, direct efforts to reverse these physiological effects will prevent the development of serious health consequences (e.g., heart disease in individuals with hypertension). Relaxation training helps clients learn to recognize the physiological processes associated with the stress response and to gain some measure of control over these systems. For some clients, the emphasis may be placed on gaining control over a specific physiological system, such as the cardiovascular system in the attempt to bring down blood pressure (e.g., Agras & Jacob, 1979). For others, a more general relaxation of the skeletal musculature may be deemed to be most beneficial.

In the original protocol for relaxation training, developed by Edmund Jacobson (1928), clients were instructed to tense and then to relax the muscles in a specific muscle group. In doing so, clients gradually learned to recognize muscle tension and to relax the muscles involved when they experienced this unwanted tension. Unfortunately, this original training program took place over the course of 50 sessions. More recently, a number of shorter training regimens have been developed (e.g., Bernstein & Given, 1984). In general, empirical research to date indicates that short duration relaxation training programs are as effective in reducing the physiological effects of stress as is the Jacobsonian procedure (Everly, 1989).

The scope of this chapter does not permit an involved discussion of the empirical literature regarding the use of relaxation training in a stress management setting. However, Lehrer and Woolfolk (1984) and Everly (1989), as well as Carlson and Bernstein (Chapter 2, this volume) provide reviews of the relevant literature.

### Biofeedback

Biofeedback takes advantage of technological advances in both the measurement and the presentation of physiological measures indicative of the activity of the sympathetic nervous system (e.g., muscle tension). With this information, clients can learn to recognize cues that signal increased activity in the system of interest. By learning to employ relaxation techniques when these cues are detected, clients can gain some measure of control over stress-related increases in physiological activity (Budzynski & Stoyva, 1984).

Although there are a variety of approaches to providing feedback regarding physiological activity, the basic protocol in biofeedback calls for clients first to observe the normal baseline fluctuations in the system under investigation. Then, while the client is trained in progressive relaxation, the effects on this system are observed. The goal of biofeedback is for clients to be able to gain control over the system in question—both to reduce overactivation of physiologic systems in demanding situations and to reduce the amount of time needed for these systems to return to baseline levels of activity.

Many authors have reported data attesting to the effectiveness of biofeedback in a number of settings, including the treatment of tension headache (e.g., Sharpley & Rogers, 1984) and muscle tension (e.g., Cannistraci, 1975–1976). However, other authors have not found biofeedback to be more effective than progressive relaxation training, which is less expensive (e.g., Burish, 1981).

### Other Intervention Strategies in the Treatment of Physical Symptoms

Both meditation (Benson, 1975) and hypnosis (Lehrer & Woolfolk, 1984) have been reported to elicit changes in physiological activity similar to those induced by relaxation training. These common outcomes have been described by Benson (1975) as a product of what he calls the *relaxation response*. This constellation of physiological responses, which include decreased muscle tone, lower blood pressure, slower heart rate, and decreased release of adrenaline and noradrenaline, is considered to be the opposite of the stress response. Everly (1989) also cites evidence that this relaxation response can be evoked by a wide range of activities, including the repetition of a simple prayer or phrase to oneself, exercise, and concentrating on one's own respiration.

Together, relaxation training, biofeedback, meditation, and hypnosis provide a set of stress management interventions intended to counteract directly the elicitation of the stress response. Research comparing these techniques against each other does not indicate that one is consistently more effective than another (Bruning & Frew, 1987; Lehrer & Woolfolk, 1984). However, the presence of more than one treatment option increases the likelihood that, given variations in client preferences and abilities, an acceptable and effective selection can be made.

## Cognitive-Behavioral Approaches to Stress Management: Addressing the Origins of Stress

The intervention strategies outlined in the previous section are mainly directed toward reducing or eliminating the physical symptoms of stress (e.g., headache, muscle tension). A cognitive-behavioral approach to stress management advocates developing an understanding of the sources of stress and generating a plan for how best to address these issues.

At present, the program of *stress inoculation training* (SIT) developed by Meichenbaum and Cameron (1983) provides the most flexible framework within which to apply the tools of cognitive-behavioral therapy to stress management. The flexibility and power of SIT derive from the fact that specific behavioral and cognitive techniques (e.g., progressive relaxation training, self-monitoring, cognitive restructuring) are easily incorporated into a treatment plan. This section will outline the basic structure and rationale for SIT and describe specific skills in which the client may be trained.

SIT is organized around three conceptually distinct phases (Meichenbaum & Cameron, 1983; Meichenbaum, 1985), although it is not meant to be conducted in a rigid, serial fashion. Some aspects of therapy may overlap, and some may be repeated or deemphasized, depending on the needs of the client. First, in a *conceptual phase,* the client is asked to participate actively in the collection of data relevant to understanding the stressors acting on that individual. In a *skills training and rehearsal phase,* the client is taught a variety of coping skills, which range from changing the patterns of thought concurrent with the onset or presence of a stressor to progressive relaxation. In this phase, clients are also trained in the proper execution of coping responses. In an *application and rehearsal phase,* clients apply their acquired skills to progressively more difficult situations. In this way, the current mastery level of coping skills is matched against fittingly demanding situations. In addition, clients are prepared to expect setbacks in the application of these skills and also to expect that the circumstances surrounding these failures can themselves provide valuable data.

One general principle consistent with the skills training approach of SIT is that people learn to deal with stress by *dealing with stress.* Application of skills in the most realistic settings possible is one of the best ways to ensure that effective use of coping skills can be transferred from the controlled conditions of therapy to unpredictable situations outside therapy. At any given stage in the skills acquisition process, however, clients are placed only in situations that evaluation of their present level of mastery suggests they can handle. Success in meeting challenges leads to increases in self-efficacy (Bandura, 1977) and the desire to acquire further mastery of coping skills. The following sections provide details regarding skills training within each phase of SIT.

### Conceptualization Stage

The primary goals of the conceptualization phase are (1) to collect a sufficient amount of information to enable both client and therapist to understand the nature of the client's stress-related problem(s) and (2) to train the client in skills for accurately appraising the nature of potential stressors. Progress in the conceptualization phase can be measured by the degree to which (1) clients demonstrate an understanding of why they feel and behave the way they do and (2) client and therapist identify a workable plan of action for reducing the perception of stress. In terms of skills training, the conceptualization phase addresses the stress equation primarily from the "demands" side of the stress transaction. Put simply, if perceived demands can be minimized, then fewer coping resources will be required.

*Data collection.* Because stress may be evidenced in a large number of distinctly different settings (e.g., on the battlefield, addressing an audience, working on an overdue manuscript) and for very different reasons (e.g., unreasonable demands, insufficient coping resources), there is little likelihood that a single diagnostic tool, or "assay," for stress will be found. Therefore, the data collection phase of stress inoculation training employs a variety of techniques and devices for gathering information about the occurrence of stress in the client's life.

This issue has recently been addressed by Lazarus (1990) who proposed a theoretical framework within which to organize the assessment of stress. His position is that stress, as the product of a transaction, is a multivariate construct that cannot be adequately captured by a single measure. Measures providing information concerning (1) the stimulus conditions preceding the onset of stress; (2) mediating factors such as the cognitive set and the effectiveness of coping skills; and (3) outcome, as related to affect, physiological activity, and long-term consequences can all provide useful information regarding the experience of stress and the events leading up to it. Data collection techniques commonly used in SIT provide information in each of these general areas.

*Interviews* with clients may provide information concerning the immediate antecedents of stress, the coping responses clients currently employ, and clients' views regarding the source or sources of stress in their lives. Other useful items of information that might be obtained include clients' thoughts both before and during the occurrence of stress and clients' views regarding the consequences of the stressor(s) in question and their responses to them.

As an extension of the interview process, clients may also be asked to *role-play* situations they describe as associated with stress. This affords the therapist the opportunity to observe a close approximation of clients' actual responses to perceived stressors. As another option, *image-based construction* may be used. Here, clients are asked to verbalize the factors and events leading up to their feelings of stress. This information may also prove useful in identifying cognitive distortions (e.g., Beck, Rush, Hollon, & Shaw, 1979) regarding clients' perceptions of the effectiveness of their own coping resources, as well as the immediate and long-term consequences of the stressor.

Clients may be asked to engage in *self-monitoring* in order to collect data regarding current stressful experiences. Advantages of self-monitoring include the following:

1. It allows measurement of the frequency, as well as the specific times during the day, in which stressors are encountered.
2. The client doesn't have to rely on memory for reports on specific events or behaviors.

3. It may afford an opportunity for the client to record the presence of factors that may induce or enhance the occurrence of stress.

One potential disadvantage of self-monitoring is that the quality of the data is largely a function of the clients' reliability and accuracy. To enhance compliance with self-monitoring procedures, Meichenbaum (1985) recommends that the therapist fully explain the rationale behind the exercise and make sure the client fully understands the requirements of the task. Options for self-monitoring include keeping open-ended diaries, recording the details of specific events during the day, or completing checklists regarding various moods or behaviors at specific intervals.

*Self-Report Measures of Stress*

The therapist can also ask clients to complete one of a number of self-report measures related to stress and factors that contribute to stress. Although these may not supply new information, they do provide a means of quantifying improvements in the frequency and severity of reported stress. Some clients may also provide written information that they would be less willing to discuss aloud.

Many questionnaire measures of stress have appeared in recent years. Some of the most popular of these measures are the following:

1. *The Daily Hassles Scale* (Kanner, Coyne, Schaefer, & Lazarus, 1981): This measure is designed to assess the extent to which everyday demands and irritations contribute to increases in stress. The rationale for collecting this information is that it is "the irritating, frustrating, distressing demands that to some degree characterize everyday transactions with the environment" (p. 3).

2. *The State-Trait Anxiety Scale* (Speilberger, Gorsuch, & Luchene, 1978): The "State" component of this scale contains 20 items regarding the presence of anxiety at the moment the scale is being completed. The "Trait" component contains 20 items regarding the degree to which anxiety is experienced on a regular basis.

3. *The Perceived Stress Scale* (Cohen, Kamarck, & Mermelstein, 1983): The PSS is a 14-item scale "designed to tap the degree to which respondents found their lives unpredictable, uncontrollable, and overloading" (p. 387).

4. *The Strain Questionnaire* (Lefebvre & Sandford, 1985): This scale consists of 48 items obtaining ratings regarding such things as "feeling out of control," whether people are "easily startled," and whether there is a perception that "things can't get worse." The Strain Questionnaire is designed to quantify the extent to which "physical, behavioral, and cognitive symptoms . . . are elicited . . . by environmental demands upon the individual" (p. 70).

5. *The Ways of Coping Checklist* (Lazarus & Folkman, 1984): The Ways of Coping Checklist is a 67-item scale designed to assess the degree to which coping strategies are employed.

Recent reviews concerning self-report assessment devices for stress-related issues and their psychometric properties may be found in Everly (1989) and Martin (1989).

### Physiological Measures

In recent years, it has become possible to obtain measurements of the activity of a number of physiological systems while clients engage in their regular activities. Measurement devices are available for continuous in vivo monitoring of blood pressure, heart rate, and muscle tension. One advantage of these devices is that readings are obtained automatically at regular intervals. Clients are not responsible for initiating measurement, although they are often required to note their activities at the time of measurement. Another advantage is that the activity of the autonomic nervous system (mediating the stress response) can be directly monitored. In cases of essential hypertension, physiological monitoring may be especially useful in that it can provide information about the times of day at which blood pressure is elevated and, used in conjunction with self-monitoring, can generate hypotheses about the environmental circumstances preceding elevations in blood pressure. One disadvantage of physiological monitoring is that the equipment needed is often expensive and noticeable to people with whom the client comes in contact.

### Skills Training in the Assessment of Stress

Data collection can and should be viewed as more than a series of exercises conducted only during the duration of the conceptualization phase. After clients gain a conceptual understanding of stress (e.g., stress as a transaction involving perceived demands and coping resources), they can continue to use skills acquired during the conceptualization phase to evaluate the sources of stress in their lives. If knowledge is indeed power, then data collection techniques provide the key to maintaining control over internal and external demands. In addition, since a number of authors report that merely engaging in data collection, regardless of the specific findings, can reduce the occurrence of undesirable behaviors (Hutzell, Platzek, & Logue, 1974; Jason, 1975), self-reported incidents of stress may be reduced also.

### Reconceptualization

After sufficient data have been collected, client and trainer should construct a model of the factors that contribute to the onset of stress. This model should be based on information collected by the client, and the client should be encouraged to participate in the process of hypothesis formation (Meichenbaum & Cameron, 1983). Meichenbaum (1985) states that reconceptualization:

1. Provides a means of integrating the various sources of information and a means of conveying the transactional nature of stress and coping (e.g., fostering an awareness of the role of the appraisal process);
2. Translates the client's symptoms (bodily complaints, thoughts, feelings, maladaptive behaviors) into specific difficulties that can be pinpointed as addressable problems rather than as overwhelming, hopeless, undifferentiated, and uncontrollable;
3. Recasts the client's stress into terms that are amenable to solutions, or that one can accept, or in which one can find meaning;
4. Proposes that the client's stress goes through various stages and is in part under his or her control;
5. Prepares the client for interventions contained within the treatment regimen. As the client views (or reframes) his or her stress from a transactional perspective, it leads naturally to the client's suggesting specific forms of intervention;
6. Creates a positive expectancy that the treatments being offered are indeed appropriate for the client's problems. (p. 47)

### Phase 2: Acquisition and rehearsal of coping skills

According to Meichenbaum (1985), the goal of the skills acquisition and rehearsal phase of SIT is "to ensure that the client develops the capacity to effectively execute coping responses" (p. 53). Work is directed toward (1) developing coping skills that are not currently part of the client's repertoire and (2) providing training in the appropriate mobilization of those coping skills the client already possesses.

Lazarus (1966) identifies two types of coping skills. *Instrumental coping skills* are problem- or issue-oriented. These skills are used to address current environmental demands. Information gathering, problem solving, communication and social skills, time management, life-style changes (reassessing priorities, mobilizing supports), and other direct action efforts are all examples of instrumental coping skills. *Palliative coping skills* serve to relieve the negative feelings surrounding the presence of a stressor. They can also help in redefining a given set of circumstances so that the likelihood of labeling it as a stressor is reduced. Examples of palliative skills include cognitive restructuring, diverting attention, expressing affect, and relaxation. A number of these skills will be described in detail in the remainder of this section.

### Relaxation Training in the Context of SIT

Meichenbaum (1985) presents guidelines for incorporating relaxation training into a stress management program. They include the following:

1. The therapist may refer to the physical tenseness that clients feel in order to convince them of the value of relaxation training. The reasoning is that if the tenseness itself adds to the stressfulness of a situation, then reducing the tenseness could remove one complicating factor.

2. Clients should be taught what it means to be relaxed and should be able to give themselves permission to relax.

3. Relaxation is treated as an active coping skill that must be practiced in order to become effective. Clients should be told not to expect results immediately but only over the course of weeks or months.

4. In collaboration, the client and trainer need to determine the context in which relaxation will be practiced. For example, are there times during the day at which relaxation might be effective in disrupting the stressor/mobilization cycle (e.g., before and after meeting with the boss)? Is it possible to practice at regular intervals throughout the day?

In SIT, relaxation is often selected as the first skill to be taught, because most people can develop some

degree of proficiency relatively quickly (Meichenbaum & Cameron, 1983). Early acquisition of an active coping skill is desirable because resulting increases in self-efficacy can facilitate training in other coping skills (Meichenbaum, 1985).

### Information Gathering

As mentioned previously, identifying the sources of stress in one's life may be considered an active coping skill that can and should be maintained after the conceptualization phase of SIT has been completed. Specific techniques for effective information gathering have already been outlined in the section describing the reconceptualization process.

### Problem-Solving Skills

The use of problem-solving skills constitutes a direct effort to cope with tangible, external demands. Training in problem-solving skills may prove especially valuable in the management of stress because of its emphasis on defining goals and acknowledging constraints on behavior (Meichenbaum, 1985). Moreover, the value of problem solving in a stress management setting is further illustrated by research showing that merely being in a position to engage in problem solving is associated with lower levels of stress (Jackson, 1983). For a detailed description of training in problem-solving skills, see Chapter 7 by O'Donohue and Noll in this volume.

### Cognitive Restructuring

Cognitive restructuring is an established technique in cognitive-behavioral therapy (Masters, Burish, Hollon, & Rimm, 1987). The rationale behind cognitive restructuring is that misinformation contained in thought or belief systems can result in, or contribute to, an imbalance between perceived demands and available coping resources. Although a variety of techniques have been introduced for correcting these mistakes, techniques based on Beck's cognitive therapy (1984) are often employed within the framework of stress inoculation training (Meichenbaum, 1985).

Beck (1984) describes the cognitive processes that lead to the stress response. He notes that initial appraisals of potentially stress-inducing situations are not "cool, deliberate computations, but are to a large degree automatic . . . [and] prone to considerable error" (p. 257). A cognitive model of the situation is constructed, or an existing cognitive set is activated. When this cognitive set mobilizes resources for action, a "behavioral inclination" is formed. According to Beck, stress results when a person is mobilized for action but no action occurs. The role of cognition in this process is explained by hypothesizing that the formation of the cognitive set is determined to a large degree by preexisting cognitive schemata. Expectations as to the meaning and consequences of an event determine the specific behaviors that are primed for initiation.

Under normal circumstances, this system matches effective responses against the current set of internal and external demands. However, Beck (1984) states that "the stress prone individual is primed to make extreme, one-sided, absolutistic, and global judgements" (p. 264). He notes that there are several sources of cognitive distortions that can lead to the mobilization of inappropriate responses in a particular situation. Examples of common types of cognitive errors taken from DeRubeis and Beck (1988) are as follows:

1. *Arbitrary inference* refers to the process of drawing a specific conclusion in the absence of evidence to support the conclusion or when the evidence is contrary to the conclusion.

2. *Selective abstraction* consists of focusing on a detail taken out of context, ignoring other more salient features of the situation and conceptualizing the whole experience on the basis of this fragment.

3. *Overgeneralization* refers to the pattern of drawing a general rule or conclusion on the basis of one or more isolated incidents and applying the concept across the board to related and unrelated situations.

4. *Magnification* and *minimization* are reflected in errors in evaluating the significance or magnitude of an event that are so great as to constitute a distortion.

5. *Personalization* refers to the client's proclivity to relate events to himself or herself when there is no basis for making such a connection.

6. *Dichotomous thinking* is manifested in the tendency to place experience in one of two opposite categories—flawless or defective, immaculate or filthy, saint or sinner. In describing himself or herself, the client selects the extreme negative categorization (DeRubeis & Beck, 1985, p. 276).

## Therapy

One basic assumption in applying cognitive therapy to the problem of stress management is that stress will be reduced if mistakes in cognitive appraisal can be reversed (Meichenbaum, 1977). Beck maintains that one of the most important skills for clients to learn is to recognize cognitive distortions when they occur and to construct an accurate cognitive model of the situation. Specific skills that can be brought to bear on this process include (1) the ability to recognize egocentrism, (2) the ability to increase objectivity and to gain perspective, and (3) the ability to change the cognitive set that would otherwise be activated automatically by the presence of stress-evoking cues.

1. *Recognizing egocentrism:* This skill involves the ability to recognize that many or most of the things that go on around us are not being done with us in mind at all. One example Beck (1984) uses is that of drivers who think that other drivers on the freeway are trying to pass *them*. In this type of thinking, clients interpret the essentially impersonal act of being passed on the freeway as a deliberate and personal attempt to "beat" them. This interpretation may lead to a mobilization of resources for responding to threat when, in fact, the threat was a product of the client's own distorted assumptions and expectations.

As a way of reducing cognitive distortions due to egocentric thinking, the client may be taught to ask him- or herself a number of questions such as, "Is it possible that I'm not really the center of events here?" "Are people really doing this with me in mind?" "Is this really a situation that's threatening to *me?*" Learning to question the basic assumptions of egocentric interpretations can help clients realize that the basis of stress in their lives can often be attributed to the *perception* of interpersonal challenge when no such challenge exists.

2. *Increasing objectivity:* According to Beck, objectivity "refers to the capacity of individuals to examine their thinking, motivations, and behavior as though they were disinterested observers" (Beck, 1984, p. 288). As with "recognizing egocentrism," objectivity refers to the ability to discriminate accurately between threatening and nonthreatening situations. By looking at events through the imaginary eyes of a neutral observer, one can perhaps bypass a set of faulty assumptions that have been built up over time. For example, a student may place a great deal

of emphasis on getting perfect grades in school be-cause to get anything less might lead to undesirable consequences, such as not getting into graduate school or having the instructor think that he or she isn't a good student. An objective appraisal of the situation might help to put the current situation in perspective. In this case, one might correctly assert that getting an occasional "B" probably isn't going to derail anyone's career completely. One option with clients prone to distortions of perspective is to train them to ask whether the outcome of the situation will have any bearing on their lives in two years.

3. *Shifting or damping cognitive set:* Beck (1984) defines a cognitive set as "the final product of the network of associated attitudes, expectations, memories, and meanings that are activated by a given situation" (p. 290). If it can be reasonably deter-mined that these attitudes and expectations are not based on fact, then it is desirable to reduce the likeli-hood that this cognitive set will be activated in that situation.

Beck (1984) suggests three options for shifting or damping a dysfunctional cognitive set. In the first, known as *environmental change,* the client simply avoids the cues associated with the activation of a stress-related cognitive set. For example, an em-ployee with an overly demanding boss may seek another job. Another person may avoid public speak-ing. In some cases, this may prove to be a satisfactory means of reducing stress. If this approach threatens career or personal goals, however, this change in environment may simply replace one stressor with another.

In *diversion,* a second option, the client attempts to divert attention away from the cognitive set activated in a given situation. The common technique of "counting to ten" before acting when angered is one example of diversion. Another is concentrating on pleasant imagery. *Relaxation,* the third option, is also cited as an effective means of altering cognitive sets. Concentration on the relaxation procedure is said to divert attention away from stress-engendering thoughts and weaken the link between the cognitive set and increases in physiological arousal.

## APPLICATION AND FOLLOW-THROUGH

Learning to gain an accurate sense of the nature of a demanding situation and acquiring effective coping skills are of limited value unless they are actually used in everyday life. The application and follow-through phase is designed to provide settings in which newly learned and mobilized coping skills can be practiced. One goal of this final phase of SIT is to ensure that clients allocate sufficient coping re-sources to meet those specific demands identified in the conceptualization stage. Another is to enable cli-ents to generalize the use of these skills so that they are applied in novel demanding situations.

The probability that coping responses will be used effectively is a product of whether a sufficient degree of self-efficacy (Bandura, 1977) regarding the use of these skills has been established (Cameron & Meichenbaum, 1982). Furthermore, according to Cameron and Meichenbaum (1982), "a sense of self-efficacy is likely to be strengthened if the therapist arranges for the client to engage in newly acquired coping responses in real-life circumstances in which there is a high probability both that the response will evoke the desired outcome and that the client can attribute success to personal capability rather than to emotional factors" (p. 707).

In order to maximize the likelihood that self-efficacy is established, clients are introduced to these stressors gradually. This approach provides an oppor-tunity to apply coping strategies to increasingly de-manding situations. In this way, coping skills can be practiced in settings that are challenging enough to test the limits of the clients' abilities, but not so demanding that they overwhelm those abilities. Sev-eral techniques have been used to introduce the im-plementation of coping skills in real life settings (Meichenbaum, 1985; Meichenbaum & Cameron, 1983). These techniques are discussed in turn next.

1. *Imagery rehearsal:* Based on a protocol de-scribed by Wolpe (1958), *imagery rehearsal* is intro-duced by having the client and trainer construct a hierarchy of scenes, ranging from least to most stress-ful. The information necessary to construct these scenes will likely be drawn from information col-lected during the conceptualization phase of SIT. As in systematic desensitization (Wolpe, 1958), the cli-ent is asked to imagine coping with progressively more threatening scenes while relaxed. In imagery rehearsal for stress inoculation training, however, the client is encouraged to continue to imagine coping in scenes which they report as stressful. Imagery train-ing gives clients the opportunity to recognize their own symptoms of distress. Once this is accom-plished, these distress cues can, in turn, be used to trigger the mobilization of coping responses.

2. *Role playing:* Role playing is another option for practicing coping skills. One way in which role playing can be used is to have the therapist take the part of a person engaged in some type of behavior with which the client must cope. For example, the therapist may take the role of a supervisor assigning an unreasonable amount of work. In this case, the client may be assigned the task of producing an effective response (e.g., tactfully suggesting that he or she already has as much work as one could reasonably be expected to handle). Alternatively, the client may be asked to take the role of the instructor in explaining how a particular situation might be interpreted and handled.

3. *Graduated in vivo exposure:* Skills training in coping skills is not complete until clients demonstrate the ability to reduce or eliminate stress in the same situations that brought them to therapy. Graduated in vivo exposure gives clients the opportunity to practice coping skills under conditions that are supervised, but that also closely approximate the stressors the client faces in real life. According to Meichenbaum and Cameron (1983), "successful application of coping skills in such situations enhances the client's confidence, . . . thereby nurturing positive expectations and increasing the probability a client will call on these skills in everyday situations" (p. 146). Graduated in vivo exposure allows newly acquired skills to be woven slowly into the everyday fabric of stressors (cues) and responses.

The selection of tasks to be assigned as "homework" (Beck, 1984) will be made easier if the client and therapist have already constructed a hierarchy of events or situations that have been ordered in terms of their ability to elicit stress. Initially, clients should be asked to demonstrate coping behavior under conditions toward the low-stress end of the hierarchy. Progression to more stressful conditions is made only after success in coping has been achieved several times (Turk, Meichenbaum, & Genest, 1983). Beck (1979) summarizes several factors that contribute to positive outcomes in the use of graduated in vivo exposure.

1. Problem definition. For example, the patient's belief that he (or she) is not capable of attaining goals that are important to him (or her).
2. Formulation of a project. Stepwise assignment of tasks (or activities) from simpler to more complex.
3. Immediate and direct observation by the patient that he (or she) is successful in reaching a spe-

cific objective (carrying out an assigned task). The continual concrete feedback provides the patient with new corrective information regarding his (or her) functional capacity.
4. Ventilation of the client's doubts, cynical reactions, and belittling of his achievement.
5. Encouragement of realistic evaluation by the patient of his actual performance.
6. Emphasis on the fact that the patient reached the goal as a result of his own effort and skill.
7. Devising new, more complex assignments in collaboration with the patient. (p. 132)

## Relapse Prevention

In order to maintain efforts to practice acquired coping skills, it is important to make it clear to the client that the management of stress is often a complicated and difficult process and that failures can and should be expected. Knowing that failures are a normal part of the learning process can reduce the likelihood of overestimating the importance of an individual failure. Clients also may be assigned the task of determining (1) why their coping efforts failed and (2) how the situation could be handled better next time. In fact, Marlatt and Gordon (1984) suggest that failures actually be rehearsed in order for clients to acquire a plan for handling these failures.

## Summary of The Role of Skills Training in SIT

Consistent with Lazarus's transactional model of stress and coping (1966; Lazarus & Folkman, 1984), stress inoculation training addresses the presence of stress with a multidimensional array of treatment options. It provides for training in specific skills for the relief of physical symptoms (e.g., relaxation training), accurate assessment of demands (e.g., cognitive restructuring), and the implementation of appropriate coping responses (e.g., problem-solving skills). SIT provides a flexible framework within which to tailor a stress management program that addresses the individual needs and abilities of the client.

## EMPIRICAL WORK REGARDING APPLICATIONS OF SIT

Stress inoculation training has been applied in a variety of settings, including the treatment of psychosomatic disorders (e.g., Holroyd & Andrasik, 1978), work site stress (e.g., Jones, Barge, Steffy, Fay, Kuntz, & Wuebker, 1988), and pain and chronic illness (e.g., Postlethwaite, Stirling, & Peck, 1986;

Puder, 1988). Material in this section does not represent an exhaustive review of the literature regarding the effectiveness of cognitive-behavioral treatments in stress management. Reviews may be found in Meichenbaum (1985), Holroyd et al. (1983), Turk et al. (1983), and Everly (1989).

Although the quality of stress research has increased steadily over the past twenty years, a number of authors (e.g., Auerbach, 1989; Ivancevich, Matteson, Freedman, & Phillips, 1990; Lehrer & Woolfolk, 1984) note weaknesses in the stress management literature. For example, there has been relatively little work to identify the types of clients that respond best to a given mode of therapy (Lehrer & Woolfolk, 1984; Meichenbaum, 1985), although notable contributions do exist (e.g., Martelli, Auerbach, Alexander, & Mercuri, 1987). There have been few studies employing ''process measures'' to assess the degree to which a treatment intervention works for the reasons the therapist thinks it does (Auerbach, 1989). Intervention strategies for stress management are often weakly grounded in theory (Auerbach, 1989; Ivancevich et al., 1990). In addition, there is still a great deal of work to be done to determine the skills or combinations of skills that produce the most optimal outcomes in specific stress management settings (Lehrer & Woolfolk, 1984).

Bearing in mind the work that still needs to be done, the remainder of this section describes empirical findings with regard to three common settings for stress management; headache, chronic pain and illness, and work site stress.

1. *Headache:* As mentioned earlier, relaxation training and biofeedback are commonly used in the treatment of migraine headache (Everly, 1989). However, cognitive-behavioral techniques have also been shown to elicit significant reductions in the frequency of both migraine headache (Mitchell & White, 1977) and tension headache (Holroyd & Andrasik, 1978).

Mitchell and White (1977) reported that a combination of self-monitoring and skills acquisition was associated with a significant reduction in the frequency of migraine headaches. These reductions took place over the course of a 48-week training period and were maintained at a 60-week follow-up. Self-monitoring alone was not associated with a reduction in headache activity. It should be noted that only 12 subjects took part in the study and only 3 received the full skills-training program.

Holroyd and Andrasik (1978) reported that two groups receiving cognitive self-training and a group participating in a discussion of the history of headache treatment displayed significant reductions in tension headache activity. One cognitive self-training group received training in both relaxation and in ''altering maladaptive cognitive responses.'' The other group received training only in altering cognitive responses. The frequency of reported headaches did not decrease in subjects assigned to a symptom-monitoring group. These results were interpreted as providing evidence that ''cognitive self-control procedures can provide an effective treatment for chronic tension headache'' (Holroyd & Andrasik, 1978, p. 1042). Improvements in the headache discussion group were explained by the results of a posttreatment interview in which subjects in the headache discussion group ''reported devising cognitive self-control procedures for coping with tension headaches'' (p. 1042).

2. *Pain:* A great deal of work has been done to apply the principles of stress inoculation training to clients experiencing chronic pain or to patients suffering from chronic illness. An extensive review of this literature may to be found in Turk et al. (1983). In a more recent study, Foley, Bedell, LaRocca, Scheinberg, and Reznikoff (1987) assigned patients with multiple sclerosis to either a stress inoculation training group or a current available care group. After training, SIT subjects reported lower levels of depression, anxiety, and emotional distress. Subjects in the SIT group also reported using problem-oriented coping strategies more often than did the current care group.

In another study (Puder, 1988), subjects receiving stress inoculation training displayed (1) increased ability to cope with chronic pain, (2) decreases in the degree to which pain interfered with daily activities, and (3) decreases in medication usage when compared against a wait-list group. No group differences were observed in ratings of pain intensity.

Postlethwaite, Stirling, and Peck (1986) also examined the effects of stress inoculation training on chronic pain patients. The authors did not find that stress inoculation training was associated with significant improvements in ratings of pain intensity, intake of pain medication, state anxiety, or depression. They speculated that the effects of stress inoculation training may not be powerful enough to alter the perception of severe chronic pain.

3. *Work site stress:* According to Ivancevich et al. (1990), there are ''relatively few methodologically

sound assessments of worksite stress management interventions'' (p. 252). Among the problems cited in conducting empirical work in this setting are the difficulty in obtaining appropriate comparison groups and the difficulty in controlling for stressors occurring outside the workplace. In one study employing appropriate comparison groups and outcome measures, Ganster, Mayes, Sime, and Tharp (1982) compared a cognitive training group and a wait-list control group on measures on anxiety, depression, somatic complaints, and amount of release of adrenaline and noradrenaline at work. The cognitive training group displayed lower levels of adrenaline and depression than control subjects both after eight weeks of treatment and at a four-month follow-up. However, the authors remained cautious about these results because (1) the size of the treatment effects were not large and (2) similar improvements were not seen for subjects in the control group when they subsequently received cognitive training.

In a more recent study, Bruning and Frew (1987) examined the effects of (1) training in management skills, (2) exercise, and (3) meditation on pulse rate, blood pressure, and galvanic skin response. Subjects were assigned either to one of these three types of intervention or to a wait-list control group. After an eight-week period, the stress intervention groups displayed significant reductions in pulse rate and systolic blood pressure when compared against the wait-list control group. Further analyses examining combinations of interventions did not reveal one combination to be more effective than any of the others.

To date, the results of empirical studies generally indicate that cognitive-behavioral interventions can significantly reduce stress in a variety of settings. Much remains to be learned from studies investigating (1) the techniques that might work best for a given client or in treating a given condition and (2) the theoretical basis for the effectiveness of stress reduction techniques.

## CONCLUSION

This chapter has attempted to provide a brief overview of the role of skills training in the treatment of stress-related problems. From this discussion, it should be evident that progress has been made in developing a theoretical framework within which to apply specific skills training regimens. It is also clear that a significant amount of effort has been directed toward applying stress reduction techniques to a wide variety of stress-related problems. However, the most

encouraging factor regarding the potential for skills training to be of value in stress management settings is the fact that these techniques will undergo continual modification and improvement. For example, it seems reasonable to expect that work in the future will focus on such areas as increased treatment compliance and long-term maintenance of reduced levels of stress. More work also remains regarding the relative effectiveness of the various stress reduction techniques for specific types of individuals and for specific stress-related problems.

In closing, skills training gives clients the opportunity to take some measure of control over the events and circumstances of their own lives. In doing so, cognitive-behavioral therapy for stress management holds out the possibility of replacing overwhelming demands with effective responses, and illness with health.

## REFERENCES

Agras, S., & Jacob, R. (1979). Hypertension. In O. F. Pomerleau & J. P. Brady (Eds.), *Behavioral medicine: Theory and practice.* Baltimore: Williams & Wilkins.

Auerbach, S. M. (1989). Stress management and coping research in the health care setting: An overview and methodological commentary. *Journal of Consulting and Clinical Psychology, 3,* 388–395.

Bakal, D. A. (1975). Headache: A biophysical perspective. *Psychological Bulletin, 82,* 369–382.

Bandura, A. (1977). Self-efficacy: Toward a unifying theory of behavioral change. *Psychological Review, 84,* 191–215.

Beck, A. (1984). Cognitive approaches to stress. In R. Woolfolk & P. Lehrer (Eds.), *Principles and practice of stress management* (pp. 255–305). New York: Guilford Press.

Beck, A., Rush, J., Hollon, S., & Shaw, B. (1979). *Cognitive therapy of depression.* New York: Guilford Press.

Benson, H. (1975). *The relaxation response.* New York: Morrow.

Bernstein, D. A., & Given, B. A. (1984). Progressive relaxation: Abbreviated methods. In R. L. Woolfolk & P. M. Lehrer (Eds.), *Principles and practice of stress management.* New York: Guilford Press.

Bruning, N. S., & Frew, D. R. (1987). Effects of exercise, relaxation, and management skills training on physiological stress indicators: A field experiment. *Journal of Applied Psychology, 72,* 515–521.

Budzynski, T. H., & Stoyva, J. M. (1984). Biofeedback methods in the treatment of anxiety and stress. In R. L. Woolfolk & P. M. Lehrer (Eds.), *Principles and practice of stress management.* New York: Guilford Press.

Burish, T. G. (1981). EMG biofeedback in the treatment of stress-related disorders. In C. K. Prokop & L. A. Bradley

(Eds.), *Medical psychology: Contributions to behavioral medicine.* New York: Academic Press.

Cameron, R., & Meichenbaum, D. (1982). The nature of effective coping and the treatment of stress-related problems: A cognitive-behavioral perspective. In C. Goldberger & S. Breznitz (Eds.), *Handbook of stress.* New York: Free Press.

Cannistraci, A. (1975–1976). *A voluntary stress release and behavior therapy in the treatment of clenching and bruxism* (Vol. 1) [cassette tape]. New York: Biomonitoring Applications.

Cannon, W. B. (1932). *The wisdom of the body.* New York: Norton.

Cohen, S., Kamarck, T., & Mermelstein, R. (1983). A global measure of perceived stress. *Journal of Health and Social Behavior, 24,* 385–396.

Cox, T., & McKay, C. (1978). Stress at work. In T. Cox (Ed.), *Stress.* Baltimore, MD: University Park Press.

DeRubeis, R. J., & Beck, A. T. (1988). Cognitive therapy. In K. S. Dobson (Ed.), *Handbook of cognitive behavioral therapies* (pp. 273–304). New York: Guilford Press.

Drummond, P. D. (1983). Cardiovascular responsivity in mild hypertension. *Journal of Psychosomatic Research, 27,* 291–297.

Everly, G. S. (1989). *A clinical guide to the treatment of the human stress response.* New York: Plenum Press.

Feurstein, M., Labbe, E., & Kuczmierczyk, A. (1986). *Health psychology: A biological perspective.* New York: Plenum Press.

Foley, F. W., Bedell, J. R., LaRocca, N. G., Scheinberg, L. C., & Reznikoff, M. (1987). Efficacy of stress-inoculation training in coping with multiple sclerosis. *Journal of Consulting and Clinical Psychology, 55,* 919–922.

Ganster, D. C., Mayes, B. T., Sime, W. E., & Tharp, G. D. (1982). Managing organizational stress: A field experiment. *Journal of Applied Psychology, 67,* 533–542.

Haney, T. L., & Blumenthal, J. A. (1985). Stress and the type A behavior pattern. In S. Burchfield (Ed.), *Stress: Psychological and physiological interactions.* New York: Hemisphere.

Henryk-Gutt, R., & Rees, W. C. (1973). Psychological aspects of migraine. *Journal of Psychosomatic Research, 17,* 141–153.

Holmes, T. H., & Rahe, R. H. (1967). The social readjustment rating scale. *Journal of Psychosomatic Research, 11,* 213–218.

Holroyd, K. A., & Andrasik. (1978). Coping and the self-control of tension headache. *Journal of Consulting and Clinical Psychology, 46,* 1036–1045.

Holroyd, K. A., Appel, M. A., & Andrasik, F. (1983). A cognitive-behavioral approach to psychophysiological disorders. In D. Meichenbaum & M. Jaremko (Eds.), *Stress reduction and prevention.* New York: Plenum Press.

Howarth, E. (1965). Headache, personality, and stress. *British Journal of Psychiatry, 111,* 1193–1197.

Hutzell, R. R., Platzek, D., & Logue, P. E. (1974). Control of Giles de la Tourette's syndrome by self-monitoring. *Journal of Behavior Therapy and Experimental Psychiatry, 5,* 71–76.

Ivancevich, J. M., Matteson, M. T., Freedman, S. M., & Phillips, J. S. (1990). Worksite stress management interventions. *American Psychologist, 45,* 252–261.

Jackson, S. E. (1983). Participation in decision making as a strategy for reducing job-related strain. *Journal of Applied Psychology, 68,* 3–19.

Jacobson, E. (1928). *Progressive relaxation.* Chicago: University of Chicago Press.

Jason, L. (1975). Rapid improvement in insomnia following self-monitoring. *Journal of Behavior Therapy and Experimental Psychiatry, 6,* 349–350.

Jones, J. W., Barge, B. N., Steffy, B. D., Fay, L. M., Kuntz, L. K., & Wuebker, L. J. (1988). Stress and medical malpractice: Organizational risk assessment and intervention. *Journal of Applied Psychology, 73,* 727–735.

Kanner, A. D., Coyne, J. C., Schaeffer, C., & Lazarus, R. S. (1981). Comparison of two modes of stress management: Daily hassles and uplifts versus major life events. *Journal of Behavior Medicine, 4,* 1–39.

Kashiwagi, T., McClure, J. N., & Wetzel, R. P. (1972). Headache and psychiatric disorders. *Diseases of the Nervous System, 33,* 659–663.

Lazarus, R. (1966). *Psychological stress and the coping process.* New York: McGraw-Hill.

Lazarus, R. S. (1990). Theory-based stress management. *Psychological Inquiry, 1,* 3–13.

Lazarus, R. S., & Folkman, S. (1984). *Stress, appraisal, and coping.* New York: Springer.

Lefebvre, R. C., & Sandford, S. L. (1985). A multi-modal questionnaire for stress. *Journal of Human Stress, 11,* 69–75.

Lehrer, P. M., & Woolfolk, R. L. (1984). Are stress reduction techniques interchangeable, or do they have specific effects? A review of the comparative empirical literature. In R. L. Woolfolk & P. M. Lehrer (Eds.), *Principles and practice of stress management* (pp. 404–477). New York: Guilford Press.

Marlatt, A., & Gordon, J. (1984). *Relapse prevention: A self-control strategy for the maintenance of behavioral change.* New York: Guilford Press.

Martelli, M. F., Auerbach, S. M., Alexander, J., & Mercuri, L. G. (1987). Self management in the health care setting: Matching interventions with patient coping styles. *Journal of Consulting and Clinical Psychology, 55,* 201–207.

Martin, R. A. (1989). Techniques for data acquisition and analysis in field investigations of stress. In R. W. J. Neufeld (Ed.), *Advances in the investigation of psychological stress* (pp. 195–234). New York: Wiley.

Masters, J. C., Burish, T. G., Hollon, S. D., & Rimm, D. C. (1987). *Behavioral therapy: Techniques and empirical findings,* 3rd ed. New York: Harcourt Brace Jovanovich.

Meichenbaum, D. (1977). *Cognitive-behavioral modification: An integrative approach.* New York: Plenum Press.

Meichenbaum, D. (1985). *Stress inoculation training.* New York: Pergamon Press.

Meichenbaum, D., & Cameron, R. (1983). Stress inoculation training: Toward a general paradigm for training in coping skills. In D. Meichenbaum & M. Jaremko (Eds.), *Stress reduction and prevention.* New York: Plenum Press.

Mitchell, K. R., & White, R. G. (1977). Behavioral self-management: An application to the problem of migraine headaches. *Behavior Therapy, 8,* 213–221.

Osler, W. (1910). The Lumleian lectures on angina pectoris. *Lancet, 1,* 696–700.

Postlethwaite, R., Stirling, G., & Peck, C. L. (1986). Stress inoculation for acute pain: A clinical trial. *Journal of Behavioral Medicine, 9,* 219–227.

Puder, R. S. (1988). Age analysis of cognitive-behavioral group therapy for chronic outpatients. *Psychology and Aging, 2,* 204–207.

Selye, H. (1956). *The stress of life,* New York: McGraw-Hill.

Selye, H. (1976). *Stress in health and disease,* Boston: Butterworth.

Sharpley, C. F., & Rogers, H. (1984). A meta-analysis of frontal EMG levels with biofeedback and alternative procedures. *Biofeedback and Self-Regulation, 9,* 385–393.

Shapiro, A. (1978). Behavioral and environmental aspects of hypertension. *Journal of Human Stress, 4,* 9–17.

Speilberger, C. D., Gorsuch, R. L., & Lushene, R. E. (1978). *Manual for the State-Trait Anxiety Inventory* (self-evaluation questionnaire). Palo Alto, CA: Consulting Psychologists Press.

Turk, D., Meichenbaum, D., & Genest, M. (1983). *Pain and behavioral medicine.* New York: Guilford Press.

Weinstein, M. C., & Stason, W. B. (1976). *Hypertension: A policy perspective,* Cambridge, MA: Harvard University Press.

Weiner, H. (1977). *Psychobiology of human disease,* New York: Elsevier.

Wolf, S. (1965). *The stomach.* Oxford: Oxford University Press.

Wolpe, J. (1958). *Psychotherapy and reciprocal inhibition.* Stanford, CA: Stanford University Press.

# CHAPTER 15

# CLINICAL PROBLEMS OF ANGER AND ITS ASSESSMENT AND REGULATION THROUGH A STRESS COPING SKILLS APPROACH

Raymond W. Novaco

Problems of anger are in the forefront of our attention. It is hard to avoid news reports of uncontrolled anger and aggression, and cinematic entertainment abounds in images of violence. Life in contemporary society can present a ongoing challenge to cope with anger and its aftermath. The shortcomings of institutional structures, intergroup conflict, economic frustrations, social policy failures, ever-present bureaucratic thwartings, and multiplicitous forms of human nastiness easily give rise to anger. As a transient emotional state, anger need not be problematic. Indeed, it can serve to mobilize our energy in the face of adversity and to fortify our sense of worth. As a recurrent state or disposition, however, anger does constitute a risk factor for impairments to personal health and to the well-being of others. Uncontrolled anger, being too easily transformed into destructive aggression, beckons for therapeutic intervention and self-regulation.

Aggression is an inevitably learned behavior because of its instrumental value. It functions in self-defense and in maintaining order in world affairs; yet it is always in need of regulation because of its capacity to erode the social fabric. If we glance at contemporary society, the view can be unflattering and suggestive of Hobbes's state of nature. Most probably, our world is no more violent now than it has been since preclassical times, but its present-day salience represents a threat to both personal and community well-being, and our scientific spirit and concern for humanity implore us to attenuate it. In that regard, anger control is indispensible to aggression control.

Because the occurrence of anger is such a common experience of contemporary life, certainly in the industrialized societies of the Western world, the need for its therapeutic regulation may not seem to be so pressing outside of its links to aggressive behavior.

Preparation of this chapter was supported by the John D. and Catherine T. MacArthur Foundation Research Network on Mental Health and the Law.

Indeed, anger is a normal emotion that has considerable adaptive value for coping with the adversities of a depersonalized social world and can facilitate perseverance in the face of frustration or injustice. Because anger can mobilize our psychological resources and can energize behaviors that take corrective action, we need a capacity for anger as a survival mechanism. In an increasingly bureaucratized world that diminishes the significance of the individual, anger is a psychological fortification for our sense of worth. Anger provides for personal resilience. It is a guardian of our self-esteem, it potentiates our ability to redress grievances, and it can boost determination to overcome obstacles to our happiness and aspirations.

Because anger has multiple functions (Novaco, 1976), both adaptive and maladaptive, the idea of anger control is less than straightforward. My own view of anger is an admixture of the philosophies of Seneca and Nietzsche, leaning strongly in the direction of the Roman Stoic. To the extent that anger is a positive force, interventions aimed at anger reduction are arguably misguided and perhaps might even be disparagingly viewed as totalitarian strategies to stifle the individual human personality. The term *anger management* might even suggest a control over our will to determine our own destiny. Yet, the aggression-producing, harm-doing capacity of anger is unmistakable, as is the adverse effect of high physiological arousal on prudent thought and on physical wellness. The research linking anger to coronary disease and to other stress-related disorders (Chesney & Rosenman, 1985; Johnson, Gentry, & Julius, 1992), as well as to aggression and violence (Berkowitz, 1990; Novaco, 1986), implores us to provide anger management treatments.

The concept of stress offers a number of useful perspectives for understanding anger as a problem condition. Anger can be viewed as a stress reaction, as an internal stressor, and as a component of stress coping style. These aspects of anger will be developed later. The assumption here is that the occurrence of anger embodies significantly more than the experience of a more or less unpleasant emotional state. Stress concepts have value in accounting for the problematic aspects of the activation, maintenance, and consequences of anger arousal.

In the realm of treatment, a small but significant body of research has shown the effectiveness of therapeutic interventions for anger problems. Much of this clinical research on anger has followed from a cognitive-behavioral model that began with Novaco (1975) and then was recast as a "stress inoculation" approach (Novaco, 1977a, 1977b, 1980), inspired by the ideas of Meichenbaum (1975). Other researchers, such as Deffenbacher (Deffenbacher, 1988; Deffenbacher, Story, Brandon, Hogg, & Hazaleus, 1988; Deffenbacher, Story, Stark, Hogg, & Brandon, 1987; Hazaleus & Deffenbacher, 1986) and Howells (Howells, 1989; Howells & Hollin, 1989) have extended the cognitive-behavioral approach to other populations and have employed additional techniques, such as social skills training. An overview of this body of treatment research will be provided, with suggestions for future directions.

At the outset, a basic theoretical view of anger will be given, followed by some ideas on anger with regard to human stress. These conceptual aspects are fundamental to fully understanding the treatment method, which takes a stress coping skills approach. Hence, clinically minded readers are urged to give careful consideration to these sections as blueprints for the therapeutic method. Knowing how to proceed in treatment hinges on understanding the conceptual base.

## THEORETICAL PERSPECTIVE

Anger can be understood as a subjective emotional state defined by the presence of physiological arousal and cognitions of antagonism. Anger arousal is marked by physiological activation in the cardiovascular, endocrine, and limbic systems, as well as other autonomic nervous system (ANS) and central nervous system (CNS) areas and tension in the skeletal musculature. It is also defined by the presence of antagonistic thoughts, and, at times, aggressive behavior. The "subjective affect" element of anger is a cognitive labeling of the emotional state as anger or something semantically proximate, such as "annoyed," "irritated," "enraged," or "provoked." The cognitive labeling is a highly automatized process, rather than being something deliberate or necessarily in tandem to the arousal. Implicit in this cognitive labeling process is an impulse to action. That is, it inherently involves an inclination to act in an antagonistic or confrontative manner toward the source of the provocation. These action impulses, which are learned responses, are incorporated in the cognitive labeling process.

The relationship of anger to aggressive behavior is that it is a significant activator of aggression and has a mutually influenced relationship with aggression, but it is neither necessary nor sufficient for aggression to occur. The "mutually influenced" idea is a bidirectional causality postulate (Konecni, 1975a, 1975b), which asserts that level of anger influences level of aggression and vice versa. Aggressive behavior can produce anger reduction by cathartic effects, as Konecni's meticulously performed experiments have demonstrated, but it can also be speculated that anger can be intensified by aggression when such behavior has not yet redressed the provocation. In the latter regard, acting aggressively pulls for the cognitive label *anger* and thereby serves to define one's emotional state as anger, which can in turn serve to justify acting aggressively. The "neither necessary nor sufficient" idea is simply that aggression occurs in the absence of anger and that it takes more than anger to produce aggression. Whether or not aggression occurs following provocation is a function of a number of social learning factors, such as reinforcement contingencies, expected outcomes, modeling influences, disinhibitory factors, and self-control capabilities (Bandura, 1983). When the infliction of injury or damage is expected to produce personal gain or when the aggressive act is a well-learned behavior, aggression may occur without anger. Elsewhere, I have elaborated this "neither necessary nor sufficient" postulate for both individual and collective violence (Novaco, 1986).

The arousal of anger is cognitively mediated. While so much psychological theorizing is now cognitively based, this viewpoint is ancient, receiving a full exposition in the writings of Lucius Seneca (41/1917), as part of his first-century treatise on morals. The central proposition, from both the classical and a contemporary cognitivist perspective (e.g., Ortony, Clore, & Collins, 1988), is that there is no direct relationship between external events and anger. The arousal and maintenance of anger is a function of our perceptions and of the way in which we process information.

The notion of *cognitive mediation* is often misunderstood. The term does not necessarily refer to an intermediary process interposed between the exposure to some stimulus and the resulting physiological and behavioral reactions. Cognitive mediation should be understood as an automatic and intrinsic part of the perceptual process, as well as explicit thinking or otherwise conscious operations that might be involved in an event–thought–reaction sequence. Cognitive mediational processes such as *appraisal* are intrinsic to perception. Philosophers of science such as Wittgenstein (1953) and Hanson (1969) have made precisely this point in elaborate and elegant accounts of the perceptual process. In the field of human aggression, Berkowitz (1983) has criticized the cognitive mediation view but fails to treat cognitive appraisal as anything other than an operation tandem to observing (cf. Novaco, 1986, for an elaboration of this argument). Furthermore, the selection of what receives attention and ultimately functions as a provocation is very much influenced by cognitive dispositions such as expectations, schemata, and scripts. More recently, Berkowitz (1990) proposed a "cognitive neoassociationist" model, which posits what could be called a fight-or-flight network of associations and reactions generated by negative affect. Ironically, his newer model incorporates tandem sequence premises about cognitive operations pertaining to the generation of anger. This position here is that cognitive appraisal of provocation is often a highly automatized process and that an intervening "negative affect" state is an unnecessary hypothetical condition.

In order to get angry about something, one must first pay attention to it—an idea that I attribute to William James, although the text has eluded my searches. *Attention* is relevant to anger with regard to the initial perception of provocation and the subsequent recall of it. The recollection may involve a ruminative replay of the event or intrusive thoughts. By paying attention to self-generated anger cues in recalling provoking events, anger is revivified and prolonged. Attention to situational cues is a function of dispositional and contextual variables. Dispositional states, such as needs, emotions, and expectations, influence cue value and our vigilance for particular stimuli. Contextual factors affect the salience of those cues, as exemplified by occurrences of anger and aggression on roadways (Novaco, 1991). A discussion of attentional cueing and perceptual matching as information-processing biases predisposing toward anger and aggression can be found in Novaco and Welsh (1989). Therapeutic interventions must help clients distract themselves from anger-engendering preoccupations. To direct their attention away from anger cues, clients must learn to become "task-oriented" in dealing with provoking circumstances, focusing on what is instrumental to achieving the desired resolution.

Two well-known concepts that are useful for understanding the cognitive determination of anger are *expectation* and *appraisal*. Elsewhere (Novaco, 1979, 1985), I have reviewed the psychological research and theory that establish the value of these concepts as cognitive structures for anger. The appraisal concept is familiar to anyone at all acquainted with the stress field since the landmark book by Lazarus (1966), and it remains a potent idea, as evidenced by the recent book on the cognitive structure of emotions by Ortony et al. (1988). The concept of expectation as a mediator of emotion is less well established. Expectations are viewed as determinants of anger in several ways that are linked with contextual conditions and that interface with appraisal structures:

1. When one's experience is discrepant from expectations, arousal accompanies the disturbance in equilibrium as the person seeks to adjust to the demands of the situation. The magnitude of the discrepancy between the expected and the observed will influence the level of arousal. The arousal is experienced as anger when there are contextual cues that signify thwarting or antagonism.

2. The expectation of aversive events, as a type of "mental set," can create a predisposition for anger. When one expects an antagonistic experience and when the prepotent appraisals for the events are anger-inducing, the expectation of annoyance can lead to selective perception of situational cues such that anger more readily occurs. When one confronts an antagonist, certain words and gestures can have a greater salience than they otherwise might, and anger occurs in conjunction with their appraisal as insulting, thwarting, or annoying.

3. The probability of anger is also increased when anger arousal is expected to be instrumental in achieving desired outcomes.

As discussed earlier, anger can be an adaptive emotional response to a conflict by energizing behaviors that confront the problem and seek to resolve it. The expectation of this service of anger may, of course, be misguided or illusory. While Martin Luther stated that anger quickened his temperament and sharpened his understanding and Walter B. Cannon thought that anger was the emotion "preeminently serviceable for the display of power," many times people will resort to anger as their only way to achieve control. In this regard, anger can be seen to occur because they have unnecessarily low expectations for resolving conflict by nonantagonistic means, and resort to anger or aggression because they lack the skills or the experience to do otherwise.

The physiological arousal components of anger have received extensive research attention. Although there was a considerable lag from the time of the early writings in the field of psychosomatic medicine (Alexander, 1939; Saul, 1939) and the pioneering laboratory studies of Ax (1953); Funkenstein, King, and Drolette (1957); Oken (1960); and Schachter (1957) to the contemporary research on the physiological correlates and sequelae of anger, the resurgence of this interest by those in the field of cardiovascular health is a welcomed movement. Indeed, this was presaged in the concluding chapter of Novaco (1975), which concerned extended applications of the anger control treatment and discussed the relationship of anger to hypertension as one topical area. Because the physiological correlates of anger are beyond the scope of this book, I will deal here with only one important element of anger physiology. This element comes from the work of Zillmann and is represented by his concept of *excitation transfer* (Zillmann, 1971, 1983; Zillmann & Bryant, 1974).

Zillmann made a major contribution to our understanding of anger, especially as it can be seen to pertain to stress-related conditions. His experiments showed that excitation residues from prior arousal can combine with excitatory responses evoked by some present event. This transfer of excitation enhances or intensifies the experience of anger, and thus fosters aggressive behavior in the immediate situation (when it is cognitively guided by cues for anger or aggression). Transfer effects are not hypothesized to occur when residual arousal is attributed to nonprovocation sources. This concept provides a theoretical and empirical basis for understanding how exposure to stressors, either acute or ambient, can predispose the person to respond angrily when faced with a minor provocation.

My understanding of anger is compatible with Averill's (1982) "constructivist" viewpoint, which was a major advance in theory about anger, not so fully appreciated by behavioristically minded psychologists. Averill views anger as a socially constituted syndrome, a transitory social role governed by social rules. His perspective emphasizes the idea that the meaning and function of emotions are determined primarily by the social systems in which they occur and of which they are an integral part. Thus, anger is a rule-governed syndrome, an idea consistent with my functional analysis of anger (Novaco, 1976), especially with regard to the dramaturgical or promotional dimension. Averill's exceedingly complex analysis does, however, remain confined to anger as a *normal* emotion. Because he does not address anger as a psychological disturbance, his very important perspective does not extend to therapeutic interventions.

## UNDERSTANDING ANGER IN TERMS OF HUMAN STRESS

The stress theory framework offers many advantages for understanding anger. Conventional emotion theory views (Izard, 1977; Plutchik, 1980) are intrapsychic models that have depth from the standpoint of the human personality and its development. Antiquated passion views of anger (cf. Averill, 1982), which have carried over to much contemporary aggression theory, overemphasize the negative aspects of anger and overlook its place as a normal human emotion; further, in addressing the negative side of anger, they give too much weight to its link to aggression and ignore its physical health implications. Averill's social constructivist approach is highly differentiated with regard to anger as a normal emotion but neglects the pathological aspects, both physiological and behavioral. Here, I am not putting forward a comprehensive perspective on anger but am only suggesting that stress theory and research have much to offer.

From a stress perspective, anger can be seen as an emotion–action complex with several stress-related dimensions: (1) it has properties of a stress reaction or response outcome of stressor exposure; (2) it is a component of a stress coping style with functional deficiencies; and (3) it operates as an internal stressor that causes wear and tear on the organic system. The stress-theoretic analysis is congruent with the stress inoculation therapeutic approach that has been shown to be effective in a number of independent investigations.

### Anger as a Stress Reaction

The adverse health and behavioral consequences of exposure to environmental demands or stressors are known as *stress reactions* and consist of physiological disturbances, negative affect, and impairments to cognitive and behavioral functioning. They vary in magnitude and extension, dimensions that determine their severity.

It is unquestionable that arousal is activated by exposure to environmental elements and conditions that are categorized as stressors, such as noise, heat,

traffic congestion, crowding, difficult tasks, and high-pressure job environments. Arousal that is induced by acute and prolonged exposure to such conditions can combine immediately with arousal from anger stimuli, or it can decay slowly. In the latter case, it leaves a residual that can transfer subsequently to other experiences having anger cues, following Zillmann's propositions presented previously. The residual arousal from stressors thus adds in a nontrivial way to arousal induced by subsequent events appraised in terms of anger. This then argues for addressing anger in terms of contextual conditions (Novaco, 1992), instead of merely examining the more conspicuously identifiable provoking event.

As a stress response to environmental demands, anger can be seen as a result of overload, reflecting a condition in which demands exceed resources for coping. Being a strong emotional reaction, it suggests that performance proficiencies or problem-solving capacities have been strained. However, it is unclear how to gauge this hypothetical performance impairment. Many highly creative individuals are known to have had a strong proclivity to become angry. For example, the composers Beethoven and Brahms both had enormous propensities for anger. Beethoven was notorious for storming out of dinner engagements in a fit of rage, even in the company of royalty, and his correspondence to friends who had offended him was blistering. His furious tearing of the title page of the *Eroica Symphony* (he had dedicated it to Bonaparte but then recognized him as a tyrant) displayed an anger rooted in idealism; but his many episodes of anger with regard to his nephew, Karl (who eventually shot himself in the head but fortunately survived), represented an anger of rigid expectations and a controlling personality. Yet, whatever unhappiness and distress was reflected in Beethoven's anger, who could possibly say that his performance was impaired as a result of these eruptions? Similarly, Brahms was described by his physician as a powder keg waiting to explode. Yet, who could listen to Brahms's *Requiem* or to Beethoven's quartets and not hear gentle, even heavenly, expressiveness? Certainly it is not difficult to see that the intensity of these men's personalities, which produced frequent episodes of anger, also produced magnificent achievements when combined with their artistic brilliance. Therefore, although I justify classifying anger as a stress response, I do so with some qualification and with the acknowledgment that the performance-impairing aspects of anger remain to be delineated.

## Anger as a Component of Stress Coping Style

It is generally assumed in the stress field that people actively respond to forces that impinge upon them (Pearlin & Schooler, 1978). However, coping with stress may involve dysfunctional behavior patterns, which can have anger as a dynamic component. Antagonistic responses to aversive events, impatience, low frustration tolerance, and unrealistic expectations of oneself and others can involve anger as a prominent feature. Anger may be a customary feature of a personality style that takes a combative orientation to perceived threats and challenges. Illustrations of anger involvement in stress coping could be given with regard to many clinical problems, such as child abuse, spouse abuse, paranoia, mania, alcoholism, and others. However, it is very well exemplified in the study of personality attributes presenting risk for coronary heart disease.

From the earliest observations of Type A behavior (Friedman & Rosenman, 1974), anger was recognized as a key ingredient of coronary proneness. When I saw Ray Rosenman conduct his structured interview assessment procedure, it was evident to me that this was partly a provocation procedure. An abundance of research soon developed on the anger theme in CHD studies, seeking to disentangle the empirical relationships and receiving major reviews in Diamond (1982) and in the Chesney and Rosenman (1985) volume. Unfortunately, the concept of anger became blurred by the interchangeable use of the terms *anger* and *hostility* in the field of psychosomatic medicine, especially by those studying cardiovascular disorders.[1]

This confusion of constructs, which occurred early in writings on essential hypertension (e.g. Alexander, 1939; Saul, 1939), has been perpetuated by the popularity of the Cook-Medley Hostility Scale in the assessment of a risk factor for coronary artery disease, as begun by Williams and his colleagues (Barefoot, Dahlstrom, & Williams, 1982; Williams et al., 1980). Although others have taken note of this mixing of terms, an important reason for this confusion has gone unnoticed; that is, research in psychosomatic medicine did not intersect with research on human aggression which also has been conducted, quite coincidentally, since 1939 (beginning with Dollard, Doob, Miller, Mowrer, & Sears, 1939). Ever since these terms were distinguished by Buss (1961), no serious aggression researcher would confuse *anger*

with *hostility*—and Williams and his colleagues (e.g., Williams, Barefoot, & Shekelle, 1985) do not confuse them. But because these research fields have proceeded with little intersection, elementary distinctions and conventions in the aggression field are not so uniform in the health psychology field.

Whereas anger is straightforwardly an *emotional* state, hostility is best understood as an attitudinal disposition. Thus, a person, group, or organization can be accurately described as being "hostile" toward some other entity, without necessarily being angry at them at a given time. This holds for nation-states as well as individuals. Knowing the existence of a hostile disposition, we can usefully predict the occurrence of anger or aggressive behavior between the hostile parties in situations of scarce resources, uncertainty, arousal activation, opportunity for retaliation, and so on.

The construct validity of the hostility component of coronary risk has received particular attention, notably by Smith and his colleagues (Allred & Smith, 1991; Pope & Smith, 1991; Pope, Smith, & Rhodewalt, 1990; Smith & Frohm, 1985; Smith, Sanders, & Alexander, 1990), and I will make no attempt at review here. Instead, I will briefly conjecture about how the functional properties of anger are linked to hostility, which is acknowledged as a prominent stylistic feature of coronary-prone behavior, but which has relevance to many other impairments of well-being.

Two important ways that anger affects behavior are through its "energizing" and "potentiating" functions (Novaco, 1976). Anger increases the vigor with which we act, energizing behavior and enabling us to persevere during times of distress. It also imparts a sense of potency, mastery, and control. The expression of anger is intuitively associated with taking charge of a problem situation. This may be illusory, in that very little problem solving might be accomplished, as the anger expression may only distance and alienate others. However, we can see these energizing and potentiating effects of anger among ardent members of social movements who seek to accomplish social change. Similarly, these functions of anger can be observed among Type A individuals who seek to overcome obstacles and to control their environments. Their "chronic struggle . . . against the opposing efforts of other things or persons" (Friedman, 1969, p. 84) is an enterprise imbued with anger. The concept of *control* emerged in Glass's (1977) analysis of Type A as a learned style of coping, and anger is quite serviceable in efforts to control events. The suggestion here is that anger often appears as a way to coerce a response from the environment to fit our expectations. As part of a chronic syndrome, it can be dysfunctional in stress coping.

## Anger as an Internal Stressor

The activation of anger is an internal stressor that causes wear and tear on bodily systems. Here I am not referring to the short-term disruptions that justify the classification of anger as a "stress reaction" but to the long-term impairments in well-being that can result from repeated evocation of anger. Cardiovascular health problems are the best exemplification of this aspect of anger from a stress perspective.

One defining property of anger is physiological arousal, and numerous experiments have demonstrated that anger provocation is accompanied by significant changes in cardiovascular arousal. Across many published experiments, significant increases of systolic and diastolic pressure have been reported in conjunction with anger arousal manipulations. Recovery time to baseline levels has also been found to be prolonged when anger is not expressed. Although suppressed anger has been linked with essential hypertension since the early days of psychosomatic research, the physiological mechanisms by which transient increases in blood pressure are converted to chronically elevated levels remain to be identified.

Physiological responsiveness to situations of challenge or threat has been thought to be an indicator of pathological processes associated with coronary artery disease and essential hypertension. The review by Krantz & Manuck (1984) concluded that, compared to Type Bs, Type As displayed larger elevations in blood pressure, heart rate, catecholamines, and cortisol when challenged or confronted by stressful tasks. The volume by Matthews et al. (1986) constituted an extensive analysis of cardiovascular disease on the reactivity theme, and although the involvement of anger was acknowledged, the psychological and physiological processes associated with anger were far from specified.

We need to understand the mechanisms whereby recurrent anger experiences have negative impacts on both physical and psychological health. The stress framework provides many useful ideas for analysis of the determinants and consequences of anger as a problem condition and can inform us about the extended and unanticipated costs of anger-proneness.

Stress models can improve our identification of the range of circumstances that engender anger and the varied impacts that anger can have on well-being. In this regard, an emerging feature of contemporary, environmentally oriented stress research is its "contextual" perspective (Stokols, 1987, 1988), which suggests ways of understanding anger not found in the intrapsychically focused approaches that dominate psychosomatic research. Some cursory ideas on a contextual view of anger are given in Novaco (1992).

Because the study of anger predominantly has concerned the personal experience of emotion, most existing assessment procedures have focused on the self-report of subjective states and, to some extent, on aggressive behavior connections. The assessment of attitudinal dispositions (hostility) has also been part of the study of anger. While the construct validation of anger assessment procedures should properly involve physiological and behavioral criterion measures, much of the measurement of anger has been confined to the realm of self-report. Within the scope of this chapter, a limited presentation of existing anger self-report instruments can be given.

## OVERVIEW OF ANGER SELF-REPORT MEASURES

Since anger is a subjective emotion, it is appropriate that anger has been studied primarily by self-report measures. For the most part, they have been developed ad hoc, "empirically" generated from interviews with convenience samples, or produced in a form parallel to previous measures of other constructs. The construction of anger measures, including one previously developed by me (Novaco, 1975, 1988), has conspicuously neglected theory—a shortcoming I have recently sought to address in developing a new measure (Novaco, in press). However, although we have learned a great deal about the nature of anger and its relationship to aggressive behavior, we are far from understanding the psychological deficits that cause anger disorders or how properly to target treatment interventions.

The normative study of anger from subjects' reports began with G. Stanley Hall (1899) and continued sporadically to the exemplary studies by Averill (1982). This body of research has concerned anger as a normal emotion; its procedures have ranged from introspection to daily diaries with rating scales and have often involved questionnaires and inventories. Recent studies have involved autobiographical narratives (Baumeister, Stillwell, & Wotman, 1990) and imagined scenarios (Ben-Zur & Breznitz, 1991). Experimental laboratory methodologies have entailed combinations of self-report, behavioral, and physiological measures, but this genre of research has almost exclusively involved college student samples and has been concerned with anger as a precondition to induce aggression. The anger measures, therefore, have typically been manipulation check assessments to establish the internal validity of procedures designed to provoke aggression. The exceptions to this generalization have been studies on "catharsis" and those in the field of psychosomatic medicine, where recent research on cardiovascular disorders has given attention to anger and hostility.

Perhaps the most widely known "anger" measure is the Buss-Durkee Hostility Inventory (Buss & Durkee, 1957), which has 75 items in true-false format, making up eight subscales (physical assault, indirect hostility, irritability, negativism, resentment, suspicion, verbal hostility, and guilt). Regarding the measurement of anger, the Buss-Durkee measure pertains to what people do when they become angry rather than the events that provoke anger or the degree of anger experienced. This instrument has been found to have good reliability (internal and test–retest from .70 to .80), but various validity studies have produced mixed results. Aside from college student studies, typically involving concurrent validity assessments with other instruments, significant relationships have been found between Buss-Durkee scores and ratings of patients' aggressiveness by doctors and nurses, though not consistently. This measure has been found to discriminate violent from nonviolent alcohol abusers (Renson, Adams, & Tinklenberg, 1978) and criminals (Selby, 1984). The Selby study involved a comparative analysis of instruments in discriminating violent male felons.

Originating in an attempt to validate the Buss-Durkee Inventory as applied to an Italian population, Caprara subsequently constructed several scales that he found to be related to aggressive behavior in psychological laboratory studies (Caprara, Cinanni, D'Imperio, Passerini, Renzi, & Travaglia, 1985; Caprara, 1986). These scales of "Irritability," "Emotional Susceptibility," and "Dissipation-Rumination" are 20 to 40 items in length and have six-point scales for response ratings of "completely true for me" to "completely false for me." Although the validational analyses have been performed on student samples in laboratory aggression experiments, the scale constructs are relevant to clinical problems.

In the 1950s, a number of MMPI scales of hostility and control were developed, but a cross-validational study of 12 such scales, conducted by Megargee and Mendelsohn (1962) found that these assorted scales did poorly in predictively discriminating violent from nonviolent and other criminal groups. In fact, it was found that extremely assaultive offenders were "overcontrolled" (rigid inhibitions), which led Megargee (1966) to develop an MMPI-derived overcontrolled hostility (OH) scale. This measure successfully discriminated extremely assaultive from less assaultive groups. The idea of overcontrolled hostility was buttressed by research by Blackburn (1968) with psychiatric offenders. Megargee did not articulate the psychological mechanisms involved in the overcontrol phenomenon, except to refer to psychodynamic concepts (repression, denial, displacement, and sublimation); there are more parsimonious interpretations than such psychodynamic ones regarding why someone not previously aggressive suddenly becomes a murderer, and these include anger, rumination, and disinhibition (cf. Novaco, 1986). Selby (1984) indeed found that the violent groups had significantly higher anger scores than did the nonviolent felons.

One of the MMPI scales examined by Megargee and Mendelsohn that did poorly in discriminating assaultiveness was the Cook and Medley Hostility Scale (Cook & Medley, 1954). This scale was originally developed with samples of teachers and, curiously, came to be used in studies of Type A behavior and heart disease (e.g., Barefoot, Dahlstrom, & Williams, 1982), as longitudinal research on hostility as a risk for heart disease mortality among physicians was made possible by their having been administered the MMPI in medical school and could then be followed up through American Medical Association (AMA) directories. Cook-Medley hostility scores have been found to be predictive of the incidence of heart disease and mortality in retrospective longitudinal studies. The scale has high test–retest reliability and good concurrent validity with other anger/hostility instruments. It has had extensive use in research in the health psychology area, for example, in construct validity analyses by Smith and his colleagues (Allred & Smith, 1991; Pope & Smith, 1991; Pope et al., 1990; Smith & Frohm, 1985; Smith et al., 1990) and in recent epidemiological studies (Barefoot et al., 1991; Scherwitz, Perkins, Chesney, & Hughes, 1991). With regard to aggressive behavior, Selby (1984) found this scale to significantly differentiate violent from nonviolent groups.

At present, one of the most commonly used anger measures is the Spielberger State-Trait Anger Scale (Spielberger, Jacobs, Russell, & Crane, 1983). Developed from Buss-Durkee items and other anger measures, the State Anger and Trait Anger scales each consist of 10 items rated on four-point scales. The instrument is designed in parallel to Spielberger's State-Trait Anxiety measures. Normative data were gathered on students, military recruits, and working adults. Internal reliability is high, and there is modest test–retest reliability (.50–.60). The Trait Scale has significant concurrent validity with other self-report anger/hostility measures. The Trait Anger Scale and the more recent Anger Expression (Ax) Scale (Spielberger et al., 1985) have been found to be related to blood pressure and hypertension, (Johnson & Broman, 1987; Spielberger, Crane, Kearns, Pellegrin, & Rickman, 1991), but their relationship to aggressive behavior has not been studied.

A variety of inventory measures have been developed, including the Reaction Inventory (Evans & Strangeland, 1971), the Anger Self-Report Inventory (Zelin, Adler, & Myerson, 1972), the S-R Inventory of Hostility (Endler & Hunt, 1968), the Novaco Provocation Inventory (Novaco, 1975, 1988), and the Multidimensional Anger Inventory (Siegel, 1986). These measures inventory various situations for their anger-arousing potential. Most of these instruments were developed with college students, and they typically have not been used with either violent or clinical populations. The Siegel measure is the most recent, and it attempts to build on the previous inventories, including the Buss-Durkee. Her Multidimensional Anger Inventory sought to assess aspects of anger relevant to cardiovascular disease. This measure gauges anger across the response dimensions specified by the present author (Novaco, 1980), plus hostile outlook and "range of anger-eliciting situations" (the rationale and operationalization of the latter category are puzzling). Developed on two samples of college students and factory workers, relatively small for the factor analysis conducted, this 30-item measure has good internal and test–retest reliabilities and modest to poor concurrent validities. Siegel's extraction of five factors (anger arousal, range of situations, hostile outlook, anger-in, and anger-out) is weakly supported by her validational measures.

The Novaco Provocation Inventory (NPI) is an 80-item self-report instrument for assessing anger responsiveness. The inventory consists of brief descriptions of situations of provocation, for which the respondent indicates the degree of anger. The ratings are performed on a five-point scale of arousal level. The NPI was first reported in Novaco (1975). The items were intuitively derived and partly based on interviews with subjects about situations of anger arousal. The instrument was found to have internal consistency ($r = .95$), but several items were replaced to incorporate more situations of home life. The resulting 80-item measure was then administered to a variety of clinical and nonclinical samples, including university students, industrial workers, police officers, military personnel, mental health workers, psychiatric patients, child abusers, and prison hospital inmates. Designed to gauge the range and intensity of anger responses, the NPI does not assess the frequency, duration, or mode of response parameters of anger problems (Novaco, 1980), nor does it differentially assess theoretically relevant psychological components of anger and aggression. It was developed for three purposes: (1) to provide a general index of anger responsiveness across a wide range of situations; (2) to serve as a guide for interview assessments; and (3) to generate an empirical basis for the content of laboratory provocation procedures used in Novaco (1975). The inventory provides information about the types of situations most likely to arouse anger and the overall magnitude of the respondent's proneness to provocation.

The principal index for the inventory is the total score, computed by summing the item intensity ratings. The mean for normal samples ranges from 230 to 255. This approximates endorsing the scale midpoint across the 80 items. The standard deviation is consistently about 45. Internal reliability coefficients are consistently high ($r = .93$) across samples. Test–retest reliabilities with university student samples have ranged from $r = .83$ ($N = 34$) for a one-month interval to $r = .89$ ($N = 39$) and $r = .90$ ($N = 69$) for one-week intervals. In Selby's (1984) study of 204 male felons, the NPI had a test–retest reliability of .74 over a one-month interval. Correlations with the Buss-Durkee Hostility Inventory (Buss & Durkee, 1957) range from .41 to .50.

One structure for the inventory is the intuitive categorization of the provocation items. Seven primary categories were identified: (1) annoying behavior of others, (2) humiliation/verbal insult, (3) personal injustice, (4) social injustice, (5) frustration, (6) personal clumsiness, and (7) physical assault. Items were sorted into these categories with a 94% rate of agreement between judges (Novaco & Robinson, 1984).

Factor analysis of the inventory has been performed with the undergraduate, industrial worker, military, and child abuse samples by means of principal axis analysis rotated to a Varimax solution. The factor solution was selected by the "scree" method. Across samples, three factors emerge consistently: injustice/unfairness, frustration/clumsiness, and physical affronts. One departure from this pattern is that for female undergraduates, humiliation/verbal insult emerges as the first factor.

Validational studies on the inventory have found it to be significantly related to laboratory self-report measures of anger (Novaco, 1975). Studies with military samples have found significant associations with the Jenkins Activity Survey measure of Type A behavior ($r = .34$, $N = 59$) and inverse relationships to job performance evaluations ($r = -.32$, $N = 59$). Selby (1984) found that a 25-item subset of the NPI discriminated between violent and nonviolent criminal offenders with 90% accuracy, which far exceeded that for several other alternative instruments. Regarding physiological arousal, Katz and Toben (1986) found that the NPI was significantly associated with blood pressure and heart rate reactivity to experimental challenge conditions. In contrast, for the Jenkins measure of Type A behavior, they found it to be significantly ($r = .42$) related to the NPI but unrelated to cardiovascular reactivity. Holroyd & Gorkin (1983) found NPI anger to be significantly related to essential hypertension.

A recent anger measure to appear in the literature is the Brief Anger-Aggression Questionnaire (BAAQ) developed by Maiuro, Vitaliano, and Cahn (1987). The BAAQ is indeed brief, consisting of six items judged to be representative of six Buss-Durkee subscales (assault, indirect hostility, irritability, negativism, resentment, and verbal hostility). Maiuro and his colleagues conducted four analyses with separate samples, which found high internal and test–retest reliabilities (.82 to .84), strong concurrent validity with the Buss-Durkee (.78), and significant criterion validity in discriminating violent from nonviolent cases. Although this measure would have value for certain mental health screening decisions, its scope and brevity limit its clinical assessment potential.

The neglect of theory in the development of existing anger assessment instruments, including the NPI, was disconcerting to me. Because anger is a rich theoretical construct, linked to aggression and to many physical and psychological disorders, an anger assessment instrument should seek to operationalize the construct. In this way, assessment data could,

hypothetically, be more readily utilized for purposes of treatment and be better suited for research questions pertaining to anger determinants, mediational processes, and consequences. To that end, an new instrument, the NAS (Novaco, in press) was developed, guided by a theoretical model, having specified theoretical dimensions. This new measure was developed primarily with hospitalized psychiatric patients in a hierarchical process of instrument construction and evaluation. The intention was to construct a measure that could be used with mentally disordered persons as well as with normal persons.

The NAS consists of two parts. Part A, which contains clinically oriented scales, is grounded in a conception of anger in terms of three principal domains with subdimensions: *cognitive* (attentional focus, suspicion, rumination, and hostile attitude), *arousal* (intensity, duration, somatic tension, and irritability), and *behavioral* (impulsivity, verbal antagonism, physical confrontation, and indirect aggression). Part B is an abbreviated improvement of the NPI, intended to provide an index of anger intensity and generality across a range of potentially provoking situations, having five subscales (disrespect, unfairness, frustration, annoying traits, and irritations). An innovative response scaling was constructed for Part A, and item construction throughout was done with an eye toward simplicity and clarity. Approximately 60% of the items are newly constructed to operationalize theoretical dimensions; the remainder are modifications of previously existing items from other scales of anger or hostility.

The hierarchical steps in the development of this new measure included a cataloging of the items of nearly all anger scales in the literature, analyses of archival data pertaining to state hospital patients regarding anger and aggression, extensive interviews with hospital clinicians and with angry/assaultive patients, pretesting of the measure with convenience samples, a reliability and validity study on the reconstructed measure with hospital patients, and then a further validity with the again reconstructed instrument (Novaco, in press).

The NAS was found to be highly reliable, with an internal consistency of .97 and a test–retest reliability of .86 over a two-week interval ($N = 158$ patients). Six other self-report scales (Buss-Durkee Hostility, Spielberger Trait Anger, Cook-Medley Hostility, Caprara Irritability, Caprara Rumination, and Barratt Impulsivity) were also studied for purposes of concurrent and discriminant validity and for comparisons in predictive validity analyses. The NAS was found to have high concurrent validity (having the highest intercorrelation among the comparison scales) and high subscale discriminant validity; that is, the highest correlations occur with other measures having the same focus, and there is less correlation with those of more distant relevance (e.g., the NAS Physical Confrontation scale was most strongly correlated, .73, with the Buss-Durkee Assault scale, with which no other comparison measure correlated higher than .58, and this NAS subscale has low correlations where expected).

Predictive validity was also established. Among the most important findings obtained with a sample of 142 patients involving retrospective criteria were that the NAS was significantly related to the number of convictions for violent crimes against persons (.34) and inversely with Axis 5 diagnosis (−.36), and more strongly than were the comparison anger instruments. In prospective analyses conducted with a different sample of 158 patients, the NAS and the Spielberger *Trait* Anger scale were contemporaneously administered (in counterbalanced order) as predictors of the Spielberger *State* Anger scale, which was administered as the criterion at two-week, one-month, and two-month follow-ups. The correlations of the NAS as predictor of the state anger criterion testings were highly significant (.37, .42, and .47, respectively), which was very similar to those found for the Spielberger Trait Anger scale as predictor (.32, .44, .50). Given the high degree of similarity between the Spielberger Trait and State measures in their scale structure and item wording, the results for the NAS are quite strong.

The new anger scale was developed to address the need for an instrument that improved on existing measures. Scale development was based on a conception of anger as a theoretical construct, and the scale was systematically generated through a hierarchical procedure that emphasized applicability to mentally disordered persons and to violence. It is hoped that the NAS will be useful not only for understanding violence risk but also for guiding and evaluating clinical treatment of anger and aggression. Through the identification of a patient's salient anger dimensions, treatment might fruitfully be targeted and orchestrated. Additionally, for research investigations, the new instrument should have value for screening decisions in the selection of patients for treatment research and in evaluating treatment effectiveness in a more differentiated manner than has been possible with previous measures.

## THE CHALLENGING TASK OF TREATING ANGRY CLIENTS

Therapeutic intervention with persons who are chronically angry presents special challenges for the clinician, not only in terms of the potentially refractory nature of the problem condition, but also with regard to the therapeutic relationship. Unique difficulties arise in the treatment of anger, owing to its very nature, which can thwart or derail the therapeutic process. Because anger is an activator of aggressive behavior, because it is a manifestation of intolerance for frustration, and because it has instrumental value as part of a learned style of coping with aversive events, there are some common obstacles and concerns for therapists.

A prevalent concern is personal danger. It is unsettling for therapists and counselors to work with persons who have explosive tendencies. In cases where there has been a history of violent behavior, the clinician's concern is easily aroused by the client's expressions of anger and by descriptions of experiences of anger accompanied by aggressive impulses. It is imperative that the therapist be at ease in encountering client anger, both as part of narrative accounts and as reproduced in the therapy room experience. Precautions for personal safety should always be in place, particularly in conjunction with treating mentally disordered patients who have been violent in the past.

Whereas on the one hand, anger imparts a sense of mastery, on the other, it can signify that one is out of control, and when it attains levels of intense arousal, it can be profoundly troubling to the person experiencing the anger. In this regard, the client needs the therapist to provide a sense of control and, in many ways, to serve as a role model for how to handle anger experiences (modeling of anger control coping skills is, in fact, an explicit part of the treatment procedure, as will be described later). Because the experience of strong anger and its implied loss of control can be anxiety-engendering for the client, it is imperative that the therapist not be unduly alarmed by exposure to anger. First, the admixture of fear might even intensify rage reactions. Second, the troubled individual might well wonder whether it is safe or useful to reveal matters of deep personal significance to someone who becomes unsettled upon hearing the disclosures.

Some clients who have anger problems may even test the therapist's acceptance of them by describing angry feelings, hostile fantasies, and violent behavior. These issues have often been salient, for example, in the treatment of Vietnam veterans suffering from combat posttraumatic stress disorder (PTSD; cf. Horowitz & Solomon, 1978). My present research with this PTSD patient group confirms the pervasiveness of anger reactions and the need for composure on the part of the therapist. More generally, when clients sense that their psychological realities alarm or disturb the therapist, the helping process can be undermined. The treatment of angry clients requires that clinicians master their own anxieties about assaultiveness.

A second difficulty in doing treatment with persons who are prone to provocation is that they are inherently impatient. Being in treatment often involves ambivalence, and some clients will have poorly defined or unrealistic goals for the course of therapy. They may thus become frustrated when desired treatment effects are not quickly forthcoming. As their impatience mounts, they may become inclined to disengage prematurely from therapy, the impulse for which may be activated by relatively minor events in their regular life or in conjunction with receiving treatment. Because angry people, by their own long-standing behavior, have raised the probability of exposure to aversive events, the therapist should be prepared for such occasions of client frustration and demoralization. It is imperative that the clinician exercise good coping skills when faced with client expressions of frustration, by viewing these as a manifestation of the clinical problem and not taking the reactions personally. Rather than making undue personal attributions about the client's reactions, the therapist can utilize the manifest crisis as an opportunity to teach anger control coping skills. Instead of merely providing reassurance and attempting redirection, the therapist can attempt to engage and explore the client's frustration and impatience. This also teaches the client something about how to communicate about anger and how to deal with conflict.

Given the general disposition of clients with anger problems, it is advantageous that a treatment program be clearly defined and structured in order to minimize the ambiguity and frustration that can result from vague expectations regarding treatment. Moreover, the proneness to frustration and impatience that are intrinsic to the problem constellation also dictates that treatment studies be thoughtfully designed, with control group conditions that do not activate anger responses. Waiting-list and placebo-control group conditions are likely to elicit anger, which is undesirable from both an ethical and a design standpoint. The absence of a plausible treatment can easily agitate clients, resulting in higher measured anger in control groups. Particularly when a treatment experiment involves a real clinical population (as opposed to psychology student samples in analogue studies), constructing comparison treatment conditions presents internal validity challenges in minimizing reactivity effects.

A third and very important complication in treating angry, aggressive people is that this action–emotion complex has instrumental value in dealing with aversive situations. Anger has a potentiating function, imparting a sense of mastery or control. One can overcome constraints and dispatch unwanted others by becoming angry and acting aggressively. Persons who are so disposed are reluctant to relinquish this sense of effectiveness. The propensity for anger reflects a combative orientation in responding to situations of threat and hardship, which, as an overgeneralized response, is clearly problematic; one does not, however, easily surrender this learned style of coping with stressful life demands.

If the clinician's presentation of ''anger control'' therapy suggests to the client that he will be robbed of his power, then the leverage for treatment is easily undermined. Clients need to understand that learning anger control skills will mean that they will become *more* powerful rather than less powerful. The stress inoculation approach indeed provides new coping strategies for handling provocation in an adaptive manner. To some extent, this involves skills in interpersonal communication and assertiveness, but many problems entailing anger cannot be resolved so straightforwardly. Hence, anger control must be approached in a preventive mode and in an arousal-regulatory mode, as well as by enhancing overt behavioral skills. Clients must learn to ask themselves not, ''What should I do when I get angry'' but, ''How can I not get angry in the first place; and, if I do get angry, how can I keep the anger at a moderate level of intensity?''

The anger control therapy involves interventions in the cognitive, somatic, behavioral, and environmental domains. The client is helped to restructure cognitions, to regulate arousal, to engage in problem-solving action, and to make changes in the environmental fields within which anger experiences occur. The treatment aims to promote anger self-regulation by developing coping skills by means of an approach that emphasizes collaboration with the client. This stress inoculation therapy for anger control is described next.

## TREATMENT INTERVENTION

Having set forth a view of anger in terms of stress, the key aspects of the stress inoculation treatment approach can be better understood. Unfortunately, scientific investigators and clinicians have implemented the stress inoculation treatment in a way that reflects only cursory attention to the concept of stress. For example, in some studies of anger and of anxiety interventions, the treatment has been operationalized as little more than the use of coping self-statements, preceded by brief didactics about the problem condition. There has been a tendency to ignore the environmental/contextual determinants of stress and the physiological arousal component of stress reactions. Although a key attribute of the treatment involves cognitive modification, the arousal reduction and behavioral coping skills components are prominent therapeutic elements that have been neglected for the sake of experimental expediency. From viewing anger in terms of stress, we can proceed to treat anger by a skills-training approach involving cognitive, somatic, and behavioral coping.

The stress inoculation approach to anger treatment is a therapeutic procedure based on principles of cognitive-behavioral intervention that began with Novaco (1975). The core components of the treatment consist of (1) cognitive modification techniques (attentional focus strategies, cognitive restructuring, problem-solving skills, and self-instruction); (2) arousal reduction procedures, primarily relaxation counterconditioning but also breathing regulation and imagery exercises; and (3) behavioral skills for dealing with provoking situations, modeled and rehearsed with the therapist. The stress inoculation approach is designed as a three-phase procedure of cognitive preparation, skill acquisition, and application training, first developed by Meichenbaum (1975) for problems of anxiety and then extended by me to anger disorders (Novaco, 1977a, 1977b, 1980). A thorough account of its application to anxiety, anger, pain, and a variety of other extensions can be found in Meichenbaum (1985). In addition to treatment, it also has use as a preventive intervention (Meichenbaum & Novaco, 1985).

The inoculation concept is a medical metaphor, and the treatment approach involves exposing the client to graduated dosages of a stressor that challenges but does not overwhelm coping resources. The client is taught a variety of cognitive modification, arousal reduction, and behavioral skills, which are then applied to conditions of provocation (stressor) exposure in a graduated, hierarchical procedure. Provocation is simulated in the therapeutic context by imagination and role-play of anger incidents from the life of the client, as directed by the therapist, in either an individual or a group therapy format. This is a graduated exposure to provocation based on a hierarchy of anger incidents produced by the collaborative work of client and therapist. This graduated, hierarchical exposure, done in conjunction with the teaching of coping skills (cognitive, somatic, and behavioral) is the basis for the ''inoculation'' metaphor.[2]

The anger treatment procedures have been found to be successful in over a dozen independent studies in the literature. Significant therapeutic gains have been achieved with adult outpatients, hospitalized psychiatric patients, adolescent delinquents (both institutionalized and noninstitutionalized), brain-damaged patients, mentally retarded adults, forensic patients, emotionally disturbed children, and college students. For some time, however, (see the postscript addendum in Meichenbaum & Novaco, 1985), I have been concerned that investigators and clinicians have implemented the stress inoculation approach in ways that do not reflect a full grasp of the stress concept. As stated previously, the tendency has been to operationalize stress inoculation training as primarily the use of brief didactics about the problem state followed by coping self-statements, while ignoring the environmental or contextual determinants of stress and the physiological arousal component of stress reactions. In anger treatment research, this has occurred primarily in studies done with college students, studied for the convenience of the investigator rather than because they had a serious problem with anger.

Regarding the neglect of the physiological arousal component of anger, to which the stress perspective has given great emphasis, anger treatment interventions ought to attach importance to *arousal reduction*. The arousal reduction component of the Novaco treatment is derivative of systematic desensitization and its use of relaxation training. Reciprocal inhibition by relaxation counterconditioning has been used in a number of anger treatment studies and has achieved modest support for its usefulness. Five controlled studies and three case studies are reviewed by

Warren and McLellarn (1982), whose summary indicates a range of 3 to 18 sessions. The brief versions (3 to 5 sessions) were two studies conducted with college students, although 15-session treatments were used in two studies with nursing students (Evans, Hearn, & Saklofske, 1973; Hearn & Evans, 1972). Evans (1971) successfully treated a male inpatient having anger problems with an 8-session reciprocal inhibition therapy, and Herrell (1971) treated a soldier with psychiatric problems (not PTSD), using systematic desensitization to eliminate excessive anger in response to being given orders. Herrell's treatment lasted for 18 sessions. Other behavioral therapies for anger problems have involved 10- to 14-session treatments—for example, that of Foy, Eisler, and Pinkston (1975), who used assertion training modeling to treat a case of explosive rages.

The recent work by Deffenbacher indeed gives attention to arousal reduction (Deffenbacher, 1988; Deffenbacher et al., 1987; Hazaleus & Deffenbacher, 1986). Although his client population has been college students, he and his colleagues have taken care to select high-anger subjects and to incorporate post-treatment follow-up testing in the research designs. On a variety of predominantly self-report measures, they have obtained significant anger reduction effects for cognitive-relaxation treatment that have been maintained at a 12-month and a 15-month follow-up in separate studies. Even more important than for these college student clients, when investigators work with patients who have physical health problems, concerted attention needs to be given to arousal reduction in anger treatment. Correspondingly, assessments of the effectiveness of therapy should incorporate physiological dependent measures.

With regard to seriously disturbed patients, the work of Howells (1989) superbly illustrates both a thorough grasp of the complexity of anger problems and proficient therapeutic method. He also insightfully discusses the limitations of the anger treatment procedures with seriously violent psychiatric patients. Howells and Hollin (1989) provides a valuable account of clinical approaches to violence, and it is stimulating to see this clinical research interest proceeding with great vigor outside the United States.

Another exemplary extension of the anger treatment approach is the work of Feindler and her colleagues (Feindler & Ecton, 1986; Feindler, Marriott, & Iwata, 1984). Feindler and Ecton (1986) emphasize a coping skills approach and make improvements in cognitive-behavioral treatments, refining methods of stress inoculation and social skills training for utiliza-

tion with a difficult client population. Their book gives a superb portrayal of a variety of assessment techniques, intervention strategies, and evaluative designs for both individual and group treatments. Among the strengths of their presentation is the anticipation of problems that might arise in treatment with regard to client resistance, inadequacies of assessment, and generalization of training. For clinicians dealing with adolescents in outpatient, inpatient, or residential facilities, they provide a clear sense of the complexities of treatment and guidance for dealing with difficulties.

Superb work on a skills-training approach to aggression that is particularly applicable to adolescents has also been done by Goldstein and Keller (1987). They adopt a structured learning approach to the training of prosocial skills, such as communication, negotiation, and contracts, and further utilize procedures to develop prosocial values. They incorporate a range of cognitive-behavioral methods, including some of the anger management procedures of the stress inoculation approach. Among the earliest treatments of problems of anger and aggression was that of Witmer (1908), whose approach is psychoeducational, and Goldstein and Keller's work ought to revitalize this neglected strategy. Another psychoeducational approach based in cognitive-behavioral principles toward the modification of aggressive behavior and the augmentation of prosocial behavior among schoolchildren can be found in the work of Dubow, Huesmann, and Eron (1987).

In the experimental studies and case reports in the literature that have used the Novaco anger treatment approach or its component procedures, the length of treatment has typically ranged from 5 to 12 sessions. The initial experimentally evaluated procedure was 6 sessions with outpatients (Novaco, 1975, 1976b) and then elaborated as a "stress inoculation" approach in an 8-session treatment in a case study with a hospitalized patient (Novaco, 1977b). The method was established as an 8- to 10-session procedure for use by probation counselors, and that training was shown to be successful in an experimental evaluation (Novaco, 1980); similarly, it was implemented as a group therapy by Feindler, Marriott, and Iwata (1984) in an intervention with adolescent delinquents, with significant effects found in self-report and behavioral observation measures. Schlichter and Horan's (1981) experimental study with institutionalized juvenile delinquents found significant effects on various measures of self-report and on role-play behavior ratings, implementing the stress inoculation treatment in 10 sessions. Saylor, Benson, and Einhaus (1985), as well, achieved significant results with this population.

The Novaco anger treatment procedures, implemented in 8 sessions, were used by Bistline and Frieden (1984) in a case (which produced stable reductions in aggressive behavior over a twelve-month follow-up) and by Spirito, Finch, Smith, and Cooley (1981) with an emotionally disturbed boy in very low levels in a one-month follow-up. The Novaco approach was used in a 12-session format by Lira, Carne, and Masri (1983) with a brain-damaged patient who then had significant reductions in anger outbursts during hospitalization and at a five-month follow-up.

In addition to these and other case reports, there have been experimental studies of this treatment approach with control and comparison groups. Benson, Rice, and Miranti (1986) used a 12-session modification of Novaco procedures to treat mentally retarded adults and achieved significant decreases in anger and aggression on multiple measures. In an experimental study with forensic patients, Stermac (1986) used a group treatment procedure of 6 sessions, producing changes in anger, impulsivity, and coping strategies. Moon and Eisler (1983) conducted a 5-session treatment in their experimental study with college students who had anger problems. Although they unfortunately omitted the arousal reduction component, they found significant outcome effects on self-ratings of anger, diary reports of anger incidents, behavioral ratings of aggression in role-play, and blood pressure. Hazaleus and Deffenbacher's (1986) study of cognitive and relaxation treatments with college students involved 6 group sessions, which produced many effects on ratings of anger and constructive coping that were maintained at one-month and one-year follow-ups.

The Benson et al. (1986) findings with mentally handicapped clients and the Stermac (1986) results with forensic patients have been buttressed by successful case studies. Recently, Black and Novaco (1993) evaluated the stress inoculation treatment of a mentally handicapped man with a long history of serious problems of anger and aggression and found significant reductions in aggressive behavior incidents and staff ratings of anger-related attributes over the course of treatment and throughout a five-month follow-up, leading to this patient's eventual discharge and successful community placement. Important results have also been obtained for modifying anger related to criminal violence, as multiple treatment gains are reported by Howells (1989) with forensic patients in England, using the stress inoculation therapeutic approach. Also, Bornstein, Weisser, and Balleweg (1985) found significant anger treatment gains with three institutionalized forensic patients in a multiple-baseline design study. Ratings of behavior in videotaped role-play, ward behavior ratings, and self-reported anger each improved significantly from pre- to posttreatment and were maintained over a two-month follow-up period.

## SUMMARY

Despite the advantageous qualities of anger, the occurrence of this emotional state often constitutes a problem at either the individual or the societal level. Both the experience and the expression of anger can pose risks for personal or collective well-being (Novaco, 1986). Such anger-induced impairments occur in the domains of physical health, psychological adjustment, social group relationships, organizational performance, and community safety. The experience of anger is a homeostatic disruption, and the physiological arousal and negative affect easily interfere with productive thought and action. The expression of anger, especially when it takes harm-doing forms, transparently has undesirable consequences that demarcate it as a problem condition.

Anger presents a risk for violent behavior because it constitutes an antagonistic state of motivated arousal that disrupts cognitive functioning and provides an impetus for impulsive actions. Anger that is high in frequency, intensity, or duration can override inhibitory control mechanisms, internal and external. Although anger is intrinsically human, its association with aggressive behavior is unmistakable. The assessment and treatment of this turbulent emotion, especially among mentally disordered persons, is a domain that merits concerted attention.

Considerable progress has been made in the psychological treatment of anger since the early work of Witmer (1908), who, despite his therapeutic wisdom, considered anger to be a product of mental and moral deficiency. Viewing anger in terms of human stress and approaching anger regulation in terms of stress coping skills has now been shown to be beneficial in remediating prevalent problems in human functioning. It is hoped that recent improvements in anger assessment will facilitate further gains in treatment effectiveness.

## NOTES

1. It must be said, however, that whatever clarity may exist about the anger-versus-hostility distinction at a conceptual level, much remains to be done regarding *operational* clarity. Although self-report scales exist for both conceptual variables, there is much to be resolved in their differentiation, as well as the study of their interrelationship and their bearing on both aggression and health impairments.

2. The anger control treatment manual can be obtained by writing to the author.

## REFERENCES

Alexander, F. (1939). Emotional factors in essential hypertension. *Psychosomatic Medicine, 1,* 173–179.

Allred, K. D., & Smith, T. W. (1991). Social cognition in cynical hostility. *Cognitive Therapy and Research, 15,* 399–412.

Averill, J. R. (1982). *Anger and aggression: An essay on emotion.* New York: Springer-Verlag.

Ax, A. F. (1953). The physiological differentiation between fear and anger in humans. *Psychosomatic Medicine, 15,* 433–442.

Bandura, A. (1983). Psychological mechanisms of aggression. In R. Geen & E. Donnerstein (Eds.), *Aggression: Theoretical and empirical reviews: I.* New York: Academic Press.

Barefoot, J. C., Dahlstrom, G., & Williams, R. B. (1982). Hostility, CHD incidence, and total mortality: A 25-year follow-up of 255 physicians. *Psychosomatic Medicine, 55,* 59–64.

Barefoot, J. C., Peterson, B. L., Dahlstrom, W. G., Siegler, I. C., Anderson, N. B., & Williams, R. B. (1991). Hostility patterns and health implications: Correlates of Cook-Medley Hostility Scale scores in a national survey. *Health Psychology, 10,* 18–24.

Baumeister, R. F., Stillwell, A., & Wotman, S. R. (1990). Victim and perpetrator accounts of interpersonal conflict: Autobiographical narratives about anger. *Journal of Personality and Social Psychology, 59,* 994–1005.

Benson, B. A., Rice, C. J., & Miranti, S. V. (1986). Effects of anger management training with mentally retarded adults in group treatment. *Journal of Consulting and Clinical Psychology, 54,* 728–729.

Ben-Zur, H., & Bresnitz, S. (1991). What makes people angry: Dimensions of anger-evoking events. *Journal of Research in Personality, 25,* 1–22.

Berkowitz, L. (1983). The experience of anger as a parallel process in the display of impulsive, ''angry'' aggression. In R. G. Geen & E. I. Donnerstein (Eds.), *Aggression: Theoretical and empirical reviews* (Vol. 1). New York: Academic Press.

Berkowitz, L. (1990). On the formation and regulation of anger and aggression: A cognitive-neoassociationistic analysis. *American Psychologist, 45,* 494–503.

Bistline, J. L., & Frieden, F. P. (1984). Anger control: A case study of a stress inoculation treatment for a chronic aggressive patient. *Cognitive Therapy and Research, 8,* 551–556.

Black, L., & Novaco, R. W. (1993). Treatment of anger with a developmentally handicapped man. In R. A. Wells & V. J. Giannetti (Eds.), *Casebook of the brief psychotherapies.* New York: Plenum Press.

Blackburn, R. (1968). Personality in relation to extreme aggression in psychiatric offenders. *British Journal of Psychiatry, 114,* 821–828.

Bornstein, P. H., Weisser, C. E., & Balleweg, B. J. (1985). Anger and violent behavior. In, M. Hersen & A. S. Bellack (Eds.), *Handbook of clinical behavior therapy with adults* (pp. 603–629). New York: Plenum Press.

Buss, A. (1961). *The psychology of aggression.* New York: Wiley.

Buss, A., & Durkee, A. (1957). An inventory for assessing different kinds of hostility. *Journal of Counseling Psychology, 21,* 342–349.

Caprara, G. V. (1986). Indicators of aggression: The dissipation–rumination scale. *Personality and Individual Differences, 7,* 763–769.

Caprara, G. V., Cinanni, V., D'Imperio, G., Passerini, S., Renzi, P., & Travaglia, G., (1985). Indicators of impulsive aggression: Present status of research on irritability and emotional susceptibility scales. *Personality and Individual Differences, 6,* 665–674.

Chesney, M. & Rosenman, R. (1985). *Anger and hostility in cardiovascular and behavioral disorders.* Washington, DC: Hemisphere.

Cook, W. W. & Medley, D. M. (1954). Proposed hostility and pharisaic-virtue scores for the MMPI. *Journal of Applied Psychology, 38,* 414–418.

Deffenbacher, J. L. (1988). Cognitive-relaxation and social skills treatments of anger: A year later. *Journal of Counseling Psychology, 35,* 234–236.

Deffenbacher, J. L., Story, D. A., Brandon, A. D., Hogg, J. A., & Hazaleus, S. L. (1988). Cognitive and cognitive-relaxation treatments of anger. *Cognitive Therapy and Research, 12,* 167–184.

Deffenbacher, J. L., Story, D. A., Stark, R. S., Hogg, J. A., & Brandon, A. D. (1987). Cognitive-relaxation and social skills interventions in treatment of general anger. *Journal of Counseling Psychology, 34,* 171–176.

Diamond, E. L. (1982). The role of anger and hostility in essential hypertension and coronary heart disease. *Psychological Bulletin, 92,* 410–433.

Dollard, J., Doob, L., Miller, N. E., Mowrer, O. H., & Sears, R. (1939). *Frustration and aggression.* New Haven: Yale University Press.

Dubow, E. F., Huesmann, L. R., & Eron, L. (1987). Mitigating aggression and promoting prosocial behavior in aggressive elementary schoolboys. *Behaviour Research and Therapy, 25,* 527–531.

Endler, N. S., & Hunt, J. McV. (1968). S-R inventories of hostility and comparisons of the proportions of variance from persons, responses, and situations for hostility and anxiousness. *Journal of Personality and Social Psychology, 9,* 309–315.

Evans, D. R. (1971). Specific aggression, arousal, and reciprocal inhibition therapy. *Western Psychologist, 1,* 125–130.

Evans, D. R., Hearn, M. T., & Saklofske, D. (1973). Anger, arousal, and systematic desensitization. *Psychological Reports, 32,* 625–626.

Evans, D. R., & Strangeland, M. (1971). Development of the Reaction Inventory to measure anger. *Psychological Reports, 29,* 412–414.

Feindler, E. L., & Ecton, R. B. (1986). *Adolescent anger control: Cognitive therapy techniques.* New York: Pergamon Press.

Feindler, E. L., Marriott, S. A., & Iwata, M. (1984). Group anger control training for junior high school delinquents. *Cognitive Therapy and Research, 8,* 299–311.

Friedman, M. (1969). *Pathogenesis of coronary artery disease.* New York: McGraw-Hill.

Friedman, M., & Rosenman, R. (1974). *Type A behavior and your heart.* Greenwich, CT: Fawcett Crest.

Foy, D. W., Eisler, R. M., & Pinkston, S. (1975). Modeled assertion in a case of explosive rages. *Behaviour Therapy and Experimental Psychiatry, 6,* 135–137.

Funkenstein, D. H., King, S. H., & Drolette, M. E. (1957). *Mastery of stress.* Cambridge, MA: Harvard University Press.

Glass, D. (1977). *Behavior patterns, stress, and coronary disease.* New York: Wiley.

Goldstein, A. P., & Keller, H. R. (1987). *Aggressive behavior: Assessment and intervention.* Oxford: Pergamon Press.

Hall, G. S. (1899). A study of anger. *American Journal of Psychology, 10,* 516–591.

Hanson, N. R. (1969). *Perception and discovery.* San Francisco: Freeman.

Hazaleus, S. L., & Deffenbacher, J. L. (1986). Relaxation and cognitive treatments of anger. *Journal of Consulting and Clinical Psychology, 54,* 222–226.

Hearn, M., & Evans, D. (1972). Anger and reciprocal inhibition therapy. *Psychological Reports, 30,* 943–948.

Herrill, J. M. (1971). Use of systematic desensitization to eliminate inappropriate anger. *Proceedings of the 79th Annual Convention of the American Psychological Association,* pp. 431–432.

Holroyd, K. A., & Gorkin, L. (1983). Young adults at risk for hypertension: Effects of family history and anger management in determining response to interpersonal conflict. *Journal of Psychosomatic Research, 27,* 131–138.

Horowitz, M., & Solomon, G. F. (1978). Delayed stress response syndromes in Vietnam veterans. In C. R. Figley

(Ed.), *Stress disorders among Vietnam veterans: Theory, research, and treatment* (pp. 268–280). New York: Brunner/Mazel.

Howells, K. (1989). Anger-management methods in relation to the prevention of violent behavior. In J. Archer & K. Browne (Eds.), *Human aggression: Naturalistic accounts.* London: Routledge.

Howells, K., & Hollin, C. R. (1989). *Clinical approaches to violence.* Chichester: John Wiley & Sons.

Izard, C. E. (1977). *Human emotions.* New York: Plenum Press.

Johnson, E. H., & Broman, C. (1987). The relationship of anger expression to health problems among Black Americans in a national survey. *Journal of Behavioral Medicine, 10,* 103–116.

Johnson, E. H., Gentry, W. D., & Julius, S. (1992). *Personality, elevated blood pressure, and essential hypertension.* Washington, DC: Hemisphere.

Katz, R. C., & Toben, T. (1986). The Novaco Anger Scale and Jenkins Activity Survey as predictors of cardiovascular reactivity. *Journal of Psychopathology and Behavioral Assessment, 8,* 149–155.

Konecni, V. J. (1975a). Annoyance, type and duration of postannoyance activity, and aggression: The "cathartic effect." *Journal of Experimental Psychology: General, 104,* 76–102.

Konecni, V. J. (1975b). The mediation of aggressive behavior: Arousal level versus anger and cognitive labeling. *Journal of Personality and Social Psychology, 32,* 706–712.

Krantz, D. S., & Manuck, S. B. (1984). Acute psychophysiological reactivity and risk of cardiovascular disease: A review and methodological critique. *Psychological Bulletin, 96,* 435–464.

Lazarus, R. (1966). *Psychological stress and the coping process.* New York: McGraw-Hill.

Levey, S., & Howells, K. (1991). Anger and its management. *Journal of Forensic Psychiatry, 1,* 305–327.

Lira, F. T., Carne, W., & Masri, A. M. (1983). Treatment of anger and impulsivity in a brain damaged patient: A case study applying stress inoculation training. *Clinical Neuropsychiatry, 4,* 159–160.

Maiuro, R. D., Vitaliano, P. P., & Cahn, T. S. (1987). A brief measure for the assessment of anger and aggression. *Journal of Interpersonal Violence, 2,* 166–178.

Matthews, K., Weiss, S., Detre, T., Dembroski, T., Falkner, B., Manuck, S., & Williams, R. (1986). *Handbook of stress, reactivity, and cardiovascular disease.* New York: Wiley.

Megargee, E. I. (1966). Undercontrolled and overcontrolled personality types in extreme antisocial aggression. *Psychological Monographs* (Whole No. 611).

Megargee, E. I., & Mendelsohn, G. A. (1962). A cross-validation of 12 MMPI scales of hostility and control. *Journal of Abnormal and Social Psychology, 65,* 431–438.

Meichenbaum, D. (1975). A self-instructional approach to stress management: A proposal for stress inoculation. In C. Spielberger & I. Sarason (Eds.), *Stress and anxiety* (Vol. 2). New York: Wiley.

Meichenbaum, D. (1985). *Stress inoculation training.* New York: Pergamon Press.

Meichenbaum, D., & Novaco, R. W. (1985). Stress-inoculation: A preventative approach. In C. Spielberger & I. Sarason (Eds.), *Stress and anxiety* (Vol. 10). Washington, DC: Hemisphere.

Moon, J. R., & Eisler, R. M. (1983). Anger control: An experimental comparison of three behavioral treatments. *Behavior Therapy, 14,* 493–503.

Novaco, R. W. (1975). *Anger control: The development and evaluation of an experimental treatment.* Lexington, MA: D. C. Heath.

Novaco, R. W. (1976). The functions and regulation of the arousal of anger. *American Journal of Psychiatry, 133,* 1124–1128.

Novaco, R. W. (1977a). A stress inoculation approach to anger management in the training of law enforcement officers. *American Journal of Community Psychology, 5,* 327–346.

Novaco, R. W. (1977b). Stress inoculation: A cognitive therapy for anger and its application to a case of depression. *Journal of Consulting and Clinical Psychology, 45,* 600–608.

Novaco, R. W. (1979). The cognitive regulation of anger and stress. In P. Kendall & S. Hollon (Eds.), *Cognitive behavioral interventions: Theory, research, and procedures.* New York: Academic Press.

Novaco, R. W. (1980). The training of probation counselors for anger problems. *Journal of Counseling Psychology, 27,* 385–390.

Novaco, R. W. (1985). Anger and its therapeutic regulation. In M. Chesney & R. Rosenman (Eds.), *Anger and hostility in cardiovascular and behavioral disorders.* Washington, DC: Hemisphere.

Novaco, R. W. (1986). Anger as a clinical and social problem. In R. Blanchard & C. Blanchard (Eds.), *Advances in the study of aggression* (Vol. 2). New York: Academic Press.

Novaco, R. W. (1988). Novaco provocation inventory. In M. Hersen & A. Bellack (Eds.), *Dictionary of behavioral assessment techniques.* New York: Pergamon Press.

Novaco, R. W. (1991). Aggression on roadways. In R. Baenninger (Ed.), *Targets of aggression and violence.* Amsterdam: Elsevier.

Novaco, R. W. (1992). A contextual perspective on anger with relevance to blood pressure. In E. H. Johnson, W. D. Gentry, & S. Julius (Eds.), *Personality, elevated blood pressure, and essential hypertension.* Washington, DC: Hemisphere.

Novaco, R. W. (in press). Anger as a risk factor for violence among the mentally disordered. In, J. Monahan & H. Steadman (Eds.), *Violence and mental disorder: Devel-

opments in risk assessment.* Chicago: University of Chicago Press.

Novaco, R. W., & Robinson, G. (1984). Anger and aggression among military personnel. In, R. M. Kaplan, V. J. Konecni, & R. W. Novaco (Eds.), *Aggression in children and youth.* The Hague: Martinus Nijhoff.

Novaco, R. W., & Welsh, W. (1989). Anger disturbances: Cognitive mediation and clinical prescriptions. In K. Howells & C. Hollin (Eds.), *Clinical approaches to violence.* Chichester: Wiley.

Oken, D. (1960). Experimental study of suppressed anger and blood pressure. *Archives of General Psychiatry, 2,* 441–456.

Ortony, A., Clore, G. L., & Collins, A. (1988). *The cognitive structure of emotions.* Cambridge: Cambridge University Press.

Pearlin, L. I., & Schooler, C. (1978). The structure of coping. *Journal of Health and Social Behavior, 19,* 2–21.

Plutchik, R. (1980). *Emotion: A psychoevolutionary synthesis.* New York: Harper & Row.

Pope, M. K., & Smith, T. W. (1991). Cortisol excretion in high and low cynically hostile men. *Psychosomatic Medicine, 53,* 386–392.

Pope, M. K., Smith, T. W., & Rhodewalt, F. (1990). Cognitive, behavioral, and affective correlates of the Cook and Medley Hostility Scale. *Journal of Personality Assessment, 54,* 501–514.

Renson, G., Adams, J., & Tinklenberg, J. (1978). Buss-Durkee assessment and validation with violent and non-violent chronic alcohol abusers. *Journal of Consulting and Clinical Psychology, 46,* 360–361.

Saul, L. (1939). Hostility in cases of essential hypertension. *Psychosomatic Medicine, 1,* 153–161.

Saylor, C. F., Benson, B. A., & Einhaus, L. (1985). Evaluation of an anger management program for aggressive boys in residential treatment. *Journal of Child and Adolescent Psychotherapy, 2,* 5–15.

Schachter, J. (1957). Pain, fear, and anger in hypertensives and normotensives. *Psychosomatic Medicine, 19,* 17–29.

Scherwitz, L., Perkins, L., Chesney, M., & Hughes, G. (1991). Cook-Medley Hostility Scale and subsets: Relationship to demographic and psychosocial characteristics in young adults in the CARDIA Study. *Psychosomatic Medicine, 53,* 36–49.

Schlichter, K. L., & Horan, J. J. (1981). Effects of stress inoculation on the anger and aggression management skills of institutionalized delinquents. *Cognitive Therapy and Research, 5,* 359–365.

Selby, M. J. (1984). Assessment of violence potential using measures of anger, hostility, and social desirability. *Journal of Personality Assessment, 48,* 531–544.

Seneca, L. A. (41/1917). *Seneca's morals.* New York: Harper & Brothers.

Siegel, J. M. (1986). The multidimensional anger inventory. *Journal of Personality and Social Psychology, 51,* 191–200.

Smith, T. W., & Frohm, K. D. (1985). What's so unhealthy about hostility? Construct validity and psychosocial correlates of the Cook and Medley Ho Scale. *Health Psychology, 4,* 503–520.

Smith, T. W., Sanders, J. D., & Alexander, J. F. (1990). What does the Cook and Medley Hostility Scale measure? Affect, behavior, and attributions in the marital context. *Journal of Personality and Social Psychology, 58,* 699–708.

Spielberger, C. D., Jacobs, G., Russell, S., & Crane, R. (1983). Assessment of anger: The State-Trait Anger Scale. In J. D. Butcher & C. D. Spielberger (Eds.), *Advances in personality assessment* (Vol. 2). Hillsdale, NJ: Lawrence Erlbaum.

Spielberger, C. D., Johnson, E. H., Russell, S., Crane, R., Jacobs, G., & Worden, T. (1985). The experience and expression of anger: Construction and validation of an anger expression scale. In M. A. Chesney & R. H. Rosenman (Eds.), *Anger and hostility in cardiovascular and behavioral disorders.* Washington, DC: Hemisphere.

Spielberger, C. D., Crane, R. S., Kearns, W. D., Pellegrin, K. L., & Rickman, R. L. (1991). Anger and anxiety in essential hypertension. In C. D. Spielberger & I. G. Sarason (Eds.), *Stress and emotion* (Vol. 14). New York: Hemisphere/Taylor & Francis.

Spirito, A., Finch, A. J., Smith, T. L., & Cooley, W. H. (1981). Stress inoculation for anger and anxiety control: A case study with an emotionally disturbed boy. *Journal of Clinical Child Psychology, 10,* 67–70.

Stermac, L. E. (1986). Anger control treatment for forensic patients. *Journal of Interpersonal Violence, 1,* 446–457.

Stokols, D. (1987). Conceptual strategies of environmental psychology. In D. Stokols & I. Altman (Eds.), *Handbook of environmental psychology.* New York: Wiley.

Stokols, D. (1988). Transformational processes in people-environment relations. In J. E. McGrath (Ed.), *The social psychology of time.* Newbury Park, CA: Sage Publications.

Warren, R., & McLellarn, R. W. (1982). Systematic desensitization as a treatment for maladaptive anger and aggression: A review. *Psychological Reports, 50,* 1095–1102.

Williams, R. B., Barefoot, J. C., & Shekelle, R. B. (1985). The health consequences of hostility. In M. Chesney & R. Rosenman (Eds.), *Anger and hostility in cardiovascular and behavioral disorders.* Washington, DC: Hemisphere.

Williams, R. B., Haney, T., Lee, K., Kong, Y., Blumenthal, J., & Whalen, R. (1980). Type A behavior, hostility, and coronary atherosclerosis. *Psychosomatic Medicine, 42,* 539–549.

Witmer, L. (1908). The treatment and cure of a case of mental and moral deficiency. *The Psychological Clinic, 2,* 153–179.

Wittgenstein, L. (1953). *Philosophical investigations.* New York: Macmillan.

Zelin, M. L., Adler, G., & Myerson, P. G. (1972). Anger self-report: An objective questionnaire for the measurement of aggression. *Journal of Consulting and Clinical Psychology, 39,* 340.

Zillmann, D. (1971). Excitation transfer in communication-mediated aggressive behavior. *Journal of Experimental Social Psychology, 7,* 419–434.

Zillmann, D. (1983). Arousal and aggression. In R. G. Geen & E. I. Donnerstein (Eds.), *Aggression: Theoretical and empirical reviews.* New York: Academic Press.

Zillmann, D., & Bryant, J. (1974). Effect of residual excitation on the emotional response to provocation and delayed aggressive behavior. *Journal of Personality and Social Psychology, 30,* 782–791.

# CHAPTER 16

# STRATEGIES AND TACTICS IN THE TREATMENT OF PERSISTENT PAIN PATIENTS

Dennis C. Turk
Thomas E. Rudy

Chronic pain is a major health problem in the United States, one that affects millions of people, causes great physical and emotional suffering, and costs society millions of dollars in health care and lost productivity. We can consider some bleak statistics to support the importance of the problem. Over 75 million Americans have some form of chronic pain, with back pain alone responsible for the permanent disablement of over 8 million, a figure that grows by an estimated 65,000 new cases each year (Bonica, 1986). Over the last ten years there has been a 1,300% increase in payments for pain-related disability in the United States (Osterweis, Mechanic, & Kleinman, 1987). The Social Security disability insurance program alone pays over $110 billion per year for pain-related disabilities, and Worker's Compensation insurance pays another $6 billion per year (Osterweis et al., 1987). According to a recent survey (Taylor & Curran, 1985), Americans lose 550 million days of work a year, including homemaking activities. Treatment for chronic pain, along with loss of work productivity, and compensation, is estimated to cost over $70 billion each year (Bonica, 1986). With such astronomical figures, it is easy to lose sight of the incalculable human suffering accompanying chronic pain for both the individual and his or her family.

In this chapter we present a multidimensional perspective on persistent pain and describe an assessment and treatment strategy that builds on this perspective. We also will discuss a range of tactics that have been used in helping those with chronic pain problems reduce the intensity of their pain and suffering, increase their physical capacities, and improve the quality of their lives; despite that, for many, the pain will not be completely eliminated.

Preparation of this chapter was supported in part by Grant 2R01 AR38698 from the National Institute of Arthritis and Musculoskeletal and Skin Diseases and Grant 2R01 DE07514 from the National Institute of Dental Research.

## UNIDIMENSIONAL SENSORY CAUSAL MODEL

Pain is essential for survival because of its signaling function. In acute pain states, nociception (sensation produced by activation of neural pathways that are responsive to potential tissue damage) acts as a signal that focuses attention and cues action (or inaction)—for example, escape from the source of physical damage or prevention of further damage. It is the perception of nociception and not nociception per se that constitutes the experience of pain. A multiplicity of psychological and physical factors determine the perception of pain. When pain persists for extended periods of time, the adaptive function of escape (prevention of nociception) and the recuperative function of inactivity may become problems in their own right (e.g., Osterweis et al., 1987).

One particularly frustrating aspect of chronic pain is its highly refractory nature with respect to conventional medical treatment. Despite advances in modern medicine, pain—specifically, pain that persists beyond the expected period of healing, that is the result of progressive disease, or that occurs intermittently—has remained a diagnostic and treatment puzzle (Hilgard, 1969; Melzack & Wall, 1983). A prime contributor to this puzzle is the conventional view that reports of pain are a by-product of physical pathology. As a corollary, it is assumed that there is a direct relationship between the report of pain and actual tissue damage. This view does not distinguish the initial *cause* of pain from those factors that maintain and exacerbate suffering. From this perspective, pain is viewed as primarily a sensory phenomenon, in the same way that hunger or thirst is viewed as a sensation.

The traditional *unidimensional causal sensory model of pain* adheres to a specificity concept whereby pain is viewed as a specific sensation and the pain intensity reported is seen as directly proportional to the amount of peripheral nociceptive input following from tissue damage. It is assumed that some form of tissue damage activates receptors that are specific to nociceptive stimuli and initiate pain-specific neural impulses that are transmitted along specific pain pathways to a pain center localized in the brain, where the sensory information is interpreted as pain.

Accumulating clinical and laboratory research evidence mitigates against the validity of this sensory-physiological model. Specifically, neurosurgical attempts to alleviate pain report by the blockage of sensory input from the nociceptors or its transmission along the spinal cord by surgical interference of nociceptive transmission frequently do not abolish pain but only eliminate pain for short periods of time or elicit new types of pain or noxious sensations—iatrogenic—that exacerbate the original problem (cf. Loeser, 1980). Also, this model cannot explain why individuals:

1. With the same objective amount of tissue pathology vary so widely in their report of pain intensity
2. With objective radiographic evidence of bony degenerative changes do not all report pain
3. With minimal objective physical pathology complain of severe pain
4. With the same physical diagnosis and identified tissue pathology treated with the same intervention respond in distinctly different ways.

## UNIDIMENSIONAL PSYCHOGENIC CAUSAL MODEL

Throughout the history of pain research, there have been attempts to distinguish between somatogenic and psychogenic pain (American Psychiatric Association, 1987; Engel, 1959). The diagnosis of somatoform pain disorder in the DSM-III-R is made by (1) either the lack of organic findings to explain the present report of pain or (2) a discrepancy of organic findings and pain complaints and the identification of psychological causation. The diagnostic criteria for somatoform pain disorder are problematic because they define the presence of psychological problems on the basis of the absence of somatic findings and of retrospective identification of psychological factors that putatively play an etiological role in motivating the report of pain. Moreover, there is no exact definition of the nature of the organic findings that would be expected, nor is consideration given to individual differences in sensory sensitivity. The psychogenic view also overlooks the possibility that factors related to causation may differ from those related to the maintenance and exacerbation of a pain problem.

The two causal models discussed, sensory and psychogenic, are implicitly taken to be mutually exclusive. That is, the cause of pain reports is treated as if it were dichotomous in that pain has either a physical *or* a psychological basis. From these perspectives, successful treatment of the cause of the pain, whether physically or psychologically based, should result in elimination of the report of pain. There are sufficient data in the literature demonstrating the inadequacy of the dichotomous sensory-psychogenic view to suggest that an alternative conceptualization of chronic pain is needed (e.g., Melzack & Wall, 1983; Turk, Meichenbaum, & Genest, 1983).

## OPERANT CONDITIONING MODEL OF THE MAINTENANCE OF PAIN

A radical departure from traditional conceptualizations of pain began with Fordyce's (1976) explication of the role of operant reinforcement in pain. Fordyce distinguished between the private, subjective pain experience and observable and qualifiable "pain behaviors." According to Fordyce, only the latter are amenable to assessment and treatment. The model proposes that acute pain behaviors such as limping to protect a wounded limb from producing additional nociceptive input may subsequently come under control of external contingencies of reinforcement and thus evolve into a chronic pain problem.

Pain behaviors (overt communications of pain, distress, and suffering—for example, complaining, avoidance of activity) may be positively reinforced by attention from a spouse or medical personnel. Pain behaviors also may be maintained by the escape from noxious stimulation with drugs or rest, or by avoidance of undesirable activities such as work (i.e., negative reinforcement). In addition, "well behaviors" (e.g., working) may not be sufficiently reinforcing. Finally, response costs can operate to decrease "well behaviors" when, for example, individuals are told by lawyers or employers that they risk loss of their pending litigation case if they are observed being active—jurisagenic problems caused by attorneys and the current legal system. Thus, the pain behaviors originally elicited by organic factors may be maintained in part or even totally in response to reinforcing environmental contingencies. In sharp contrast to the sensory-physiological model, the operant model suggests that pain behaviors can occur in the absence of—and may even be independent of—nociception.

Expression of pain behaviors may lead to secondary physical problems that can exacerbate existing sources of nociception or even create new ones. Reduction of activity invariably leads to decreased muscle strength, tone, and flexibility (physical deconditioning). Muscles that were involved in the original injury generally heal rapidly, but underuse of these muscles causes them to become weakened and subject to nociception when pressed into service. This nociception may induce further reduction in activity and greater physical deconditioning. Another example of the pernicious physical effect of pain behaviors is that of reinforcement (reduction of nociception) of an abnormal gait pattern (e.g., limping). Over time, altered muscle response patterns that develop may lead to new sources of nociception arising from myofascial syndromes associated with compensatory but maladaptive muscle activity that are a consequence of the distorted gait pattern.

Linton, Melin, and Gotestam (1985) have elaborated some aspects of the operant model. Specifically, they describe how, in escape learning, pain serves as a discriminative stimulus (SD) for actions that terminate pain, such as lying down, changing one's posture, or taking pain medication. Consequently, the punishing stimulus (S-) is removed. In avoidance learning, the patient does not approach the situation so that the noxious stimulus never occurs. For example, the patient may not even assume a posture that *might* cause pain. This process occurs later in the learning sequence when all the necessary associations have been made. Avoidance learning is particularly resistant to extinction. As SDs often are also conditioned stimuli, there may be negative reinforcement resulting from fear reduction that also may motivate further avoidance behaviors.

Several studies provide evidence supporting the underlying assumptions of the operant conditioning model. Cairns and Pasino (1977) and Doleys, Crocker, and Patton (1982) demonstrated that pain behaviors can be decreased by verbal reinforcement and the setting of exercise quotas. Block, Kremer, and Gaylor (1980) demonstrated that pain patients reported differential levels of pain behavior in an experimental situation depending on whether they were being observed by their spouses or by ward clerks. Pain patients with nonsolicitous spouses reported more pain when neutral observers were present as opposed to spouses. When solicitous spouses were present, pain patients reported more pain than in the neutral observer condition. Flor, Kerns, and Turk (1987) also found that chronic pain patients reported more intense pain and less activity if they indicated their spouses were solicitous. The latter two studies can serve as discriminative stimuli for the display of pain behaviors by chronic pain patients, including reports of pain intensity.

### Pain Behavior versus Malingering

It should be noted that the concept of *malingering*—that is, conscious fabrication of symptoms to achieve gain—can be inappropriately associated with the operant conditioning perspective. In malingering, it is suggested that the patient is consciously and *purposely* faking a symptom for some gain, usually financial. Many third-party payers believe that pain report in the absence of "sufficient" tissue pathology is an indication of outright fabrication motivated by financial gain. This view is analogous to the causal models of pain discussed previously that viewed pain in a dichotomous fashion, as either physical or psychological. Here, however, the psychological motivation is believed to be money rather than maladaptive traits or "psychopathology," as proposed by the psychogenic model. The operant conditioning model differs in that there is no suggestion of conscious deception but, rather, nonconscious performance of pain behaviors resulting from environmental reinforcement contingencies. There is little support for the contention that there is a high degree of outright faking of pain complaints for financial gain (e.g., Osterweis et al., 1987; Peck, Fordyce, & Black, 1978).

## Treatment Based on the Operant Conditioning Model

Operant treatments are usually conducted on an inpatient basis because this permits better control of the external reinforcement contingencies. Spouse participation is strongly encouraged because the spouse is probably the most important reinforcing agent and he or she can facilitate transfer of new behavioral patterns to the home environment. The methods of achieving these goals include withdrawal of attention for pain behaviors, and attention and reinforcement of well behaviors. Increased activity levels are promoted by establishing exercise quotas and reinforcing activity using time-contingent or task completion–contingent rest, rather than pain-contingent rest, as well as praise and attention for effort and goal accomplishments. The negative reinforcing properties of medications are eliminated by altering administration of medication from the usual prn (pain-contingent) to a fixed-interval (time-contingent) schedule. The quantity of medication is usually tapered according to a predetermined schedule (usually 10% to 20% per day).

Fordyce's operant conditioning model has generated an effective treatment approach for pain behaviors (cf. Keefe & Williams, 1989; Linton, 1986; Turner & Romano, 1984). The operant approach has, however, been criticized for its exclusive focus on motor pain behaviors and its failure to consider the

emotional and cognitive aspects of chronic pain (e.g., Schmidt, Gierlings, & Peters, 1989; Turk & Flor, 1989). A serious concern about operant treatment relates to the issue of maintenance following program termination and generalization to the patient's natural environment (Keeley, Shemberg, & Carbonell, 1976). This is a concern in treatment of pain as well. For example, Cairns and Pasino (1977) demonstrated that removal of positive reinforcement resulted in rapid return to baseline levels of activity, and the data reported by Doleys et al. (1982) and Dolce, Doleys, Raczynski, Lossie, Poole, and Smith (1986) suggest that positive reinforcement for one physical exercise does not transfer to other exercises that were not directly reinforced. These results raise the issue of the long-term efficacy of operant treatment programs conducted in a highly structured inpatient environment.

The large number of selection criteria for acceptance into operant treatment programs (see Turk & Flor, 1989) may limit the general utility of the operant model. There are also problems with the number of patients who are willing to enter inpatient treatment programs (Turk & Rudy, in press), and the level of patient satisfaction with the treatments received in programs based on the operant model (Kotarba, 1983).

## RESPONDENT CONDITIONING MODEL

Gentry and Bernal (1977) were the first to suggest that classical conditioning of pain and tension may occur in an acute pain state due to physical damage instilling a pain–tension–pain cycle. This model views pain both as a response to and an antecedent of specific autonomic activity. Lentham, Slade, Troup, and Bentley (1983) postulated that once an acute pain problem is present, conditioned fear of movement may develop, motivating avoidance of activity and thereby leading to immobilization. As noted earlier, individuals who suffer from acute pain, whatever the cause, may adopt specific protective and maladaptive behaviors (e.g., limping, reclining) to avoid pain and therefore may never obtain "corrective feedback" because they fail to perform more natural movements (Philips, 1987; Rachman & Lopatka, 1988).

Nonoccurrence of pain is a powerful negative reinforcer for reduction of activity, and thus the original respondent conditioning may be completed by an instrumental learning process by which the nociceptive stimuli and the associated responses need no longer be present for the avoidance behavior to occur. Thus, from a respondent conditioning perspective, the patient may have learned to associate increases in pain with all kinds of stimuli that were originally associated with nociceptive stimulation (i.e., stimulus generalization). Sitting, walking, engaging in cognitively demanding tasks, or even thinking about these activities may increase anticipatory anxiety and concomitant physiological and biochemical changes (Flor et al., 1990). Through a process of stimulus generalization, patients may display maladaptive responses to many stimuli and may reduce the frequency of performing of a variety of activities other than those that initially induced pain. As the pain symptoms persist, more and more situations may elicit anxiety and anticipatory pain because of the low rate of reinforcement obtained.

It is evident that the respondent and operant models are not mutually exclusive. Although the patient may develop a conditioned pattern of bracing, gait and postural disturbances, and anxiety through respondent means, it is important to note that these disturbances may then be maintained through operant conditioning. In this sense, the formulation is analogous to the two-factor theory of the development of phobias (Eysenck & Rachman, 1965; Mowrer, 1960). Two-factor theory states that a neutral situation, such as being in a market, is contingently paired with fear caused by an aversive unconditioned stimulus (UCS), such as fainting due to influenza (an unconditioned response, UCR); subsequently, the neutral situation serves as a conditioned stimulus (CS) eliciting fear. This classically conditioned fear elicited in the previously neutral situation does not extinguish, however, because the phobic individual is negatively reinforced with anxiety reduction for avoiding the situation and thereby effectively minimizing contact and acquisition of corrective feedback.

## GATE CONTROL MODEL

Multidimensional views of chronic pain differentiate nociception (sensation) from pain that is a perceptual phenomenon comprising the integration and modulation of many afferent and efferent processes (Melzack, 1986). The complex interplay of the action of receptors, spinal as well as supraspinal processes, contributes to the experience of pain, which need not be equated with peripheral stimulation. On the basis of this view, Melzack and Wall (1965; Wall, 1978) proposed the gate control theory of pain. They postulated the modulation of the nociceptive input by af-

ferent as well as efferent mechanisms, converging on the dorsal horn substantia gelatinosa within the spinal cord, which they suggested acted as a gate involving presynaptic and postsynaptic inhibitory mechanisms. Furthermore, Melzack and Casey (1968) differentiate three systems related to the processing of nociceptive stimulation—a motivational-affective, sensory-discriminative, and cognitive-evaluative dimension—that they hypothesize contribute to the experience of pain.

The conceptual model of the gate control theory emphasizes the modulation of pain by peripheral as well as central nervous system processes and thus provides a physiological basis for the role of psychological processes in chronic pain. Because it attributes the perception of pain to more than simply sensory stimulation, the gate control model explains why the surgical, electrical, or neurolytic ablation of pain pathways has not always been effective in eliminating pain. The gate control model provides a basis for treatments as diverse as nerve stimulation produced through transcutaneous electrical devices (e.g., Long & Hagfors, 1975; Wall & Sweet, 1967) or deep brain stimulation, anesthetic nerve blocks, heat, ice, vibration, massage, acupuncture (Gaupp, Flinn, & Weddige, 1989), and even psychological therapies (Melzack & Wall, 1983). Despite the initial cause of nociception, the gate control model postulates that multiple modalities may cause relief and, to this end, simultaneous treatment modalities are encouraged.

Although physiological details of the gate control model have proved to be problematic (cf. Nathan, 1976; Price, 1987), it has had a substantial impact on basic research and in generating a wide range of treatment interventions. However, the gate control theory was presented as a static cross-sectional view; consequently, it has not incorporated the role of reinforcement and learning factors that are salient if one takes a more dynamic, longitudinal perspective on pain.

## ROLE OF COGNITIVE FACTORS IN THE PAIN EXPERIENCE

As noted, health care providers have long considered pain to be synonymous with nociception *and* a symptom of pathology. It is important, however, to make a tripartite distinction between nociception, pain, and suffering. Pain, because it involves conscious awareness, selective abstraction, appraisal, ascribed meaning, and learning, is best viewed as a *perceptual process*. Suffering, which includes interpersonal disruption, economic distress, occupational problems, and myriad other factors associated with pain's impact on life functioning, is largely a *response* to the perception of pain.

Recently, the role of cognitive factors has been emphasized in the exacerbation and maintenance of pain (Turk et al., 1983). From the cognitive-behavioral perspective, people with chronic pain are viewed as active processors of information. They have negative expectations about their ability and responsibility to exert any control over their pain. Moreover, they view their situation as hopeless and are fearful of engaging in activities that they believe will either exacerbate their pain or lead to further injury. These negative, maladaptive appraisals of their situation and their personal efficacy may reinforce the experience of demoralization, inactivity, and overreaction to nociceptive stimulation (e.g., Biedermann, McGhie, Monga, & Shanks, 1987; Turk et al., 1983). These cognitive appraisals and expectations are postulated as having an effect on behavior leading to reduced effort and activity that may contribute to increased psychological distress (feelings of helplessness and hopelessness) and, subsequently to physical limitations. Because these cognitive factors have a prominent place in the cognitive-behavioral treatment of chronic pain, described later in this chapter, we will outline some research supporting their contribution.

## Direct Effects of Cognition on Physiology

A number of studies support cognitive-behavioral formulations. For example, Rimm and Litvak (1969) demonstrated that subjects exhibit physiological arousal when they only *think about* or imagine painful experiences. Barber and Hahn (1964) showed that subjects' self-reported discomfort and physiological responses (frontalis EMG, HR, SCR) were similar when they merely *imagined* taking part in a cold pressor test (i.e., immersion of a limb in a tank of circulating ice water) as compared to participating in it. In patients suffering from recurrent migraine headaches, Jamner and Tursky (1987) observed increases in skin conductance (i.e., arousal) related to the *processing of words describing* a migraine headache. And Flor, Turk, and Birbaumer (1985) and Rudy (1990) noted that the mere *discussion* or *imagination* of painful events produces increases in heart rate, skin conductance, and frontalis EMG in all subjects, and very pronounced increases in EMG levels at the af-

fected site of pain patients compared to healthy controls.

## Perceived Control

There are many laboratory studies demonstrating that controllability of aversive stimulation reduces its impact considerably (for reviews, see Averill, 1973; Thompson, 1981). In chronic pain patients, the perceived lack of personal control by patients is likely related to the ongoing but unsuccessful efforts to control their pain. Furthermore, uncontrollability augments the perception of pain intensity (Miller, 1981). This relationship has been demonstrated in a variety of chronic pain syndromes. Brown and Nicassio (1987) showed that active coping is related to better adjustment and passive coping is related to poorer adjustment in patients suffering from rheumatoid arthritis (RA). Recently, Flor and Turk (1988) examined the relationship between general and situation-specific pain-related thoughts, convictions of personal control, pain severity, and disability levels in chronic low back pain patients and RA patients. The general and situation-specific convictions of uncontrollability and helplessness were more highly related to pain and disability than disease status variables for both samples (see also Smith, Follick, Ahern, & Adams, 1986).

## Symptom Appraisal

The perception of bodily symptoms and stimuli leads to specific interpretations (conscious and subconscious) and serves as an impetus for action (Nerenz & Leventhal, 1983; Pennebaker & Epstein, 1983). In chronic illness, there is a special problem in that patients often adhere to the acute disease model with which they are familiar. Patients therefore continue to seek a tangible physical cause of the problem even if they have received evidence that the original injury has resolved. Moreover, patients may interpret symptoms as indicative of underlying disease processes, with persistent pain signifying progressive disease. Thus, they may do everything to avoid pain exacerbations, often by resorting to inactivity.

## Self-Efficacy

A central construct in the multidimensional model of chronic pain is self-efficacy (Bandura, 1977). A self-efficacy expectation is defined as a personal conviction that one can successfully perform certain required behaviors in a given situation. It has been suggested that, given sufficient motivation to engage in a behavior, it is an individual's self-efficacy beliefs that determine whether a given behavior will be initiated, how much effort will be expended, and how long effort will be sustained in the face of obstacles and aversive experiences. From this perspective, the occurrence of coping behaviors is conceptualized as mediated by the individual's beliefs that situational demands do not exceed coping resources. Individuals with weak efficacy expectancies are viewed as less likely than individuals with strong expectancies to emit coping responses and less likely to persist in the presence of obstacles and aversive consequences.

The interrelated role of fear avoidance and self-efficacy was illustrated in a study reported by Council, Ahern, Follick, and Kline (1988). They found that actual physical performances of back pain patients were best predicted by self-efficacy ratings, which appeared to be determined by pain response expectancies. The authors interpreted these results as suggesting that daily pain experience determines pain response expectancies for specific movements. Pain response expectancies appear to influence performance and associated pain behavior through their effects on efficacy expectancies. These findings also suggest that pain response expectancies associated with specific movements are based on generalized expectancies drawn from daily experiences and suggest that chronic pain patients have well-established ideas of how much pain they will experience in different situations.

## COGNITIVE-BEHAVIORAL PERSPECTIVE

Although the operant and respondent conditioning models described earlier differ in their views of pain, they may be complementary and contribute to a broader multidimensional perspective of chronic pain. The cognitive-behavioral perspective suggests that behavior and emotions are influenced by interpretations of events, rather than solely by characteristics of the event itself. The cognitive-behavioral model adopts a broad perspective on pain, one that focuses on the patient and not just the symptom. That is, persistent pain, like any chronic disease, extends over time and affects all domains of the patient's life—vocational, familial, marital, social, psychological, and physical. Rather than focusing on the contribution of cognitive and affective contributions to the perception of pain in a static fashion, as in the gate

control view, or exclusively on behavioral responses and environmental reinforcement contingencies, as in the operant model, a transactional view is used to emphasize the ongoing reciprocal relationships among physical, cognitive, affective, and behavioral factors.

According to the cognitive-behavioral model, it is the patient's perspective that interacts reciprocally with emotional factors, sensory phenomena, and behavioral responses. Moreover, the patient's behavior will elicit responses from significant others that can reinforce both adaptive and maladaptive modes of thinking, feeling, and behaving. Thus, a transactional, reciprocal, or synergistic model of pain is proposed.

## COGNITIVE-BEHAVIORAL ASSESSMENT

From the cognitive-behavioral perspective, assessment of the *patient* with persistent pain requires a more comprehensive strategy that examines a range of psychosocial and behavioral factors, in addition to the pathophysiology, subjective report of pain, and observable pain behaviors. Turk and colleagues (Turk & Meichenbaum, 1989; Turk & Rudy, 1989) have suggested that three central questions guide assessment:

1. What is the extent of the patient's disease or injury (physical impairment)?
2. What is the magnitude of the illness? That is, to what extent is the patient suffering, disabled, and unable to enjoy usual activities?
3. Is the illness behavior appropriate to the disease or injury, or is there evidence of amplification of symptoms for any of a variety of psychological or social reasons or purposes?

We have recently proposed a model of assessment of pain patients, labeled a multiaxial assessment of pain (MAP), which incorporates these three questions (Turk & Rudy, 1987). The MAP approach postulates that three axes are essential in the assessment of chronic pain patients: biomedical, psychosocial, and behavioral. From our perspective, each of these three general domains must be assessed with psychometrically sound instruments and procedures, and the results of the assessment of each axis must be combined into a meaningful taxonomy or classification system that will guide decision making and treatment planning. We suggest that operationalizations of these axes should include: (1) biomedical—quantification of laboratory and other diagnostic procedures; physical examination; and assessment of functional mobility, strength, and flexibility; (2) psychosocial— evaluation of patients' perceptions of their pain; affective distress; perceived control over their lives; and interference of pain with social, vocational, marital, recreational, and physical domains; and (3) behavioral—measurement of observable communications of pain, distress, and suffering; pain-related use of the health care system; medication use; activity levels; and responses of significant others.

A number of assessment instruments and procedures are available to measure each of the three MAP axes. Some that appear to be useful and to have good psychometric properties include the following:

1. *Medical-physical axis:* Medical Examination Diagnostic Information Coding System (MEDICS; Rudy, Turk, Brena, Stieg, & Brody, 1990); American Medical Association's Guides for Evaluating Permanent Impairment (Engelberg, 1988)
2. *Psychosocial axis:* Multidimensional Pain Inventory (MPI; Kerns, Turk, & Rudy, 1985); Sickness Impact Profile (Bergner, Bobbitt, Carter, & Gilson, 1981)
3. *Behavioral axis:* Pain Behaviors (Keefe & Block, 1982); UAB Pain Behavior Scale (Richards, Nepomuceno, Riles, & Suer, 1982).

A detailed examination of the range of assessment procedures is beyond the scope of this chapter, and we will not review them here (see Keefe & Williams, 1989; Karoly & Jensen, 1987; Turk, 1990; in press; Turk & Rudy, 1986). We will, however, note several tactics that have been used to illustrate assessment of different components of pain patients.

## Interview

When conducting an interview from the cognitive-behavioral perspective, the psychologist should focus on patients' and significant others' thoughts and feelings, and should observe specific behaviors as well as attempt to obtain other relevant information. Table 16.1 summarizes some areas covered.

During an interview, it is important to enter the patient's perspective (see Table 16.2). Patients' beliefs about the cause of pain, its trajectory, and what treatments will benefit them appear to have important influences on emotional adjustment and compliance with therapeutic interventions. A habitual pattern of maladaptive thoughts may contribute to a sense of

**Table 16.1.** Targets Covered in the Interview

- The history of the problem from the point of view of the patient.
- Patient's concerns about problem (e.g., degeneration, reinjury, paralysis)
- How the patient thinks about his or her problem and the health care system
- Cognitive and behavioral antecedents that are consistently associated wtih fluctuations in pain (e.g., when certain topics are discussed)
- Thoughts and feelings that precede, accompany, and follow exacerbation of pain
- Problems that have arisen because of pain
- How the patient expresses pain
- How others react to the patient's pain and disability
- What effect the patient believes the problem is having on others
- Activity patterns
- Learning history (prior history of pain or chronic illness)
- Marital relationship, including sexual functioning
- Current or recent life stresses
- Vocational history and goals for return to work
- Job satisfaction (employers, co-workers, job conditions)
- Compensation-litigation status
- Benefits from having pain and disability
- Patterns of alcohol and medication use
- Mental Status Examination, including anxiety and depression
- What the patient has tried to do to alleviate the pain
- Inconsistencies and incongruities between patient report and behavior or between patient's and significant other's reports
- Patient's and significant other's goals for treatment

hopelessness, dysphoria, and unwillingness to engage in activity. The psychologist should determine both the patient's and the spouse's expectancies and goals for treatment.

Attention should focus on the patient's reports of specific thoughts, behaviors, emotions, and physiological responses that precede, accompany, and follow target behaviors, as well as on the environmental conditions and consequences associated with the response. During the interview, the psychologist should attend to the temporal association of these cognitive, affective, and behavioral events—their specificity versus generality across situations, the frequency

**Table 16.2.** Enter the Patient's Perspective

- What do you think is wrong with you?
- Why do you think your pain started when it did?
- What do you think is happening to your body?
- What do you think of the explanations given to you by others you have consulted?
- Do you understand the explanation(s) and find it (them) acceptable?
- Do you have any fears about your pain?
- What are the main problems that your pain has caused you?
- What do your family, friends, and co-workers think about your pain?
- Do you have any ideas or opinions about how this type of pain is treated?
- What do you hope to gain from treatment?
- If your pain is not entirely relieved by the treatment, what will you do?

of their occurrence, and so forth—to elucidate the topography of the target behaviors, including the controlling variables. The interviewer seeks information that will assist in the development of potential alternative behaviors, appropriate goals for the patient, and possible reinforcers for these alternatives.

In addition to using interviews, psychologists have developed a number of assessment instruments designed to evaluate patients' attitudes, beliefs, and expectancies about themselves, their pain, and the health care system. Standardized assessment instruments have advantages over semistructured and unstructured interviews. They are easy to administer and less time-consuming (for the psychologist). Most important, they can be submitted to analyses that permit determination of their reliability and validity. These standardized instruments should not be viewed as alternatives to interviews but, rather, may suggest issues to be addressed in more depth during the interview. Space does not permit a detailed examination of all relevant instruments. Several recent papers have examined these instruments in more detail (see Karoly & Jensen, 1987; Keefe & Williams, 1989). One specific instrument and approach will be described as it illustrates a comprehensive strategy design to integrate assessment of psychological and behavioral factors associated with reports of pain and disability with physical pathology and medical diagnoses (Turk & Rudy, 1987).

## West Haven–Yale Multidimensional Pain Inventory (MPI)

Although there are a diversity of assessment instruments that can be used in the evaluation of patients with persistent pain, it is important to consider how the information gathered will be used. The most appropriate use of psychological evaluation for patients with persistent pain is to identify significant psychological and behavioral contributors to pain and disability and to use this information to aid in decision making and in the guidance of treatment planning.

In an attempt to assess the *chronic pain experience* in a comprehensive manner, Kerns et al. (1985) developed the West Haven–Yale Multidimensional Pain Inventory (MPI). This assessment instrument was designed to assess the impact of pain from the patient's perspective. That is, the MPI operationalizes psychological reactions to chronic pain, perceived responses of significant others, and activities interfered with because of pain. The MPI has demonstrated good internal consistency, test–retest reliability, and convergent and discriminant validity, and can be computer-scored (Rudy et al., 1990).

## Assessment of Operant Learning Factors

According to Fordyce (1976), pain behaviors include: (1) verbal complaints of pain and suffering; (2) nonlanguage, paraverbal sounds (e.g., moans, sighs); (3) body posturing and gesturing (e.g., limping, rubbing a painful body part or area, grimacing); (4) display of functional limitations or impairments (e.g., reclining for excessive periods of time—"downtime"); and (5) behaviors designed to reduce pain—for example, use of medication and use of the health care system. Because pain behaviors are overt, they are particularly susceptible to conditioning and learning influences. Such behaviors are subject to influence by consequences that follow their occurrence.

The most systematic approach to the quantification of pain behaviors is reflected in the work of Keefe and colleagues. Keefe and Block (1982) developed a coding system for the observation of five pain behaviors in back pain patients (grimacing, rubbing, bracing, guarded movement, sighing) that occur under static and dynamic movement conditions. Originally, patients were videotaped during the performance of each of a set of activities in both positions. The frequency of pain behaviors emitted during the specified activities is aggregated for each of the five categories under both conditions to create a total pain behavior score. Keefe and colleagues (Keefe, Wilkins, & Cook, 1984) have reported that their original categorical system can be used with observations during physical examination without the cumbersome requirement of videotaping patients.

A caveat is in order. There is evidence that frequency of pain behaviors during physical examination is positively correlated with the presence of organic pathology in patients presenting for neurosurgical evaluation. Thus, considerable caution needs to be exercised in interpreting the pain behaviors solely as a response to reinforcement contingencies (Turk & Flor, 1989). Moreover, the patient may believe that he or she has to convince the psychologist that pain is real and thus may exaggerate symptoms in the latter's presence. Therefore, the frequency of pain behaviors observed during an interview may not be related to the presence of these behaviors in the patient's usual environment.

## COGNITIVE-BEHAVIORAL TREATMENT

With the background provided here, we can now consider some specific components of the cognitive-behavioral intervention. It should be emphasized that appropriate treatment of patients with chronic pain requires involvement of a team consisting of physical therapists, occupational therapists, and physicians as well as psychologists (Turk & Stieg, 1987). We will focus only on the psychologist's role and provide some illustrative examples of the tactics available.

To understand the cognitive-behavioral approach to the treatment of chronic pain patients, it is important to understand that the techniques (tactics) employed are viewed as significantly less important than the more general cognitive-behavioral conceptualizations and orientation described earlier. These factors, which are often called somewhat dismissively the ''nonspecifics'' of treatment, are in reality the most important components of successful treatment. Although technical details of the tactics used are important, they will contribute to treatment efficacy only if they are embedded in a more strategic treatment framework (Turk & Holzman, 1986; Turk, Holzman, & Kerns, 1985).

### Strategic Overview

When patients come to a treatment program for chronic pain, they have received multiple evaluations and a range of treatments, some conventional (bed rest, analgesic medication, nerve blocks, TENS, physical therapy, surgery) and other less conventional (chiropractic manipulations, acupuncture). Patients ($N = 1,385$) treated in the pain program at the University of Pittsburgh have had a mean duration of pain of 5.37 (SD = 9.8) years, with some patients reporting pain for over 20 years. A common feature across all patients despite medical diagnosis is that the array of interventions did not adequately ameliorate their suffering. Table 16.3 displays the downward course in the natural history of chronic pain. Thus, it is not surprising that, when these patients are seen by a specialty pain clinic, they are demoralized and frustrated, and feel that their situations are hopeless, yet they continue to seek *the* cure for the cause of their suffering. This, then, is the background against which any therapeutic regimens that will be offered must be viewed.

Cognitive-behavioral therapy is designed to help patients identify, evaluate, and correct maladaptive conceptualizations and dysfunctional beliefs about themselves and their plight. Patients are encouraged to become aware of and to monitor the impact that negative pain-engendering thoughts and feelings play in the maintenance of maladaptive behaviors. Additionally, patients are taught to recognize the connections linking cognition, affect, and behavior with their combined consequences. Finally, patients are encouraged to test the effects of these cognitions and beliefs with selected homework assignments. The cognitive-behavioral therapist is concerned not only with the role that patients' thoughts play in contributing to disability and to the maintenance and exacerbations of nociception (directly and indirectly), but also with the nature and adequacy of the patient's behavioral repertoire. Detailed description of cognitive-behavioral treatment is beyond the scope of this chap-

**Table 16.3.** Natural History of Persistent Pain

- Awareness and interpretation of symptoms
- Help seeking
- Diagnostic uncertainty
- Patient—family—employer—health care provider—third-party payer frustration
- Preoccupation with symptoms
- Multiple costly, invasive diagnostic tests
- Suggestion of psychological causation and/or malingering
- Increased symptom reporting, pain behaviors, and help seeking
- Increased psychological distress

ter, and the interested reader is encouraged to see one of many publications that describe this approach in depth (e.g., Holzman, Turk, & Kerns, 1986; Turk et al., 1983).

A key component of a cognitive-behavioral intervention is to facilitate patients' reconceptualizations of their views of their plight. Patients inevitably come to pain clinics with the view that pain is a medical problem. They see their symptoms as overwhelming and as occurrences over which they have no personal control. The cognitive-behavioral approach is designed to be optimistic, emphasizing both the effectiveness of the rehabilitation approach and patients' abilities to alleviate much of their suffering. An important proviso is that the patient must be willing to work with the treatment team. That is, the treatment components included will only be effective if the patient accepts responsibility for a large part of the treatment with the guidance, supervision, and support of all treatment team members. This view stands in marked contrast to the usual medical approaches, which are designed to "do something to the patient," with the patient assuming a passive "sick role." The sick role allows patients to engage in a whole range of dependency behaviors while neglecting usual responsibilities.

Throughout the rehabilitation process, pain is reconceptualized so that the patient comes to view his or her situation as amenable to change by combined psychologically based and physically based approaches. The treatment program is designed to teach the patient a range of physical and psychological skills and to help him or her deal with maladaptive thoughts and feelings as well as noxious sensations that may precede, accompany, and follow the experience of pain or pain exacerbation and thereby escalate the patient's suffering.

More generally, the cognitive-behavioral approach is concerned with using environmental manipulations, similar to the operant conditioning approach, and gives attention to the potential stress-induced muscular reactivity as well as to fear-induced avoidance of activity, emphasized by respondent conditioning models. Many behavioral (reinforcement, exposure) as well as cognitive techniques (e.g., cognitive restructuring, problem-solving training, coping skills training) are used. In the cognitive-behavioral approach, however, techniques based on these models (e.g., biofeedback, extinction of pain behaviors, reinforcement of activity) represent feedback trials that provide an opportunity for the patient to question, reappraise, and acquire self-control over maladaptive thoughts, feelings, behav-

iors (including avoidance behaviors), and physiological responses.

The cognitive-behavioral treatment relies heavily on active patient participation and emphasizes a mutual problem-solving approach among the treatment team, the patient, and significant individuals in the patient's environment (spouse, friends, employer). We view the cognitive-behavioral approach as a collaborative endeavor that attempts to foster an increased sense of self-efficacy and intrinsic motivation. Even the most ideal treatment plan has little likelihood of success if the patient does not continue to engage in the prescribed behaviors once discharged from the treatment program. The likelihood of continued adherence to the self-care regimen is limited to the extent that the patient (1) does not learn the necessary skills; (2) does not feel competent to perform the recommended overt and covert behaviors on both a regular and an as-needed basis; (3) permits other factors to interfere with the performance of the adaptive behaviors; and (4) experiences no external or intrinsic motivation to persevere with the performance of the behaviors regularly and in the face of difficulties (Meichenbaum & Turk, 1987).

It is important to reiterate that comprehensive treatment of patients with persistent pain requires involvement of physicians, occupational therapists, physical therapists, and psychologists working as a team. It is essential that the entire treatment team, despite specialty, follow the same strategic perspective, with all efforts directed toward the same outcome, although tactics may vary (Turk & Stieg, 1987). Space does not permit discussion of how interdisciplinary treatment team members can direct their efforts toward the common goal of changing patients' conceptualizations of themselves and their situation from helpless and passive to resourceful and active (see Barrios, Turk, & Rudy, 1990).

## Assumptions of Cognitive-Behavioral Treatment

Five central assumptions characterize the cognitive-behavioral perspective of pain treatment (Turk & Meichenbaum, 1989, Turk & Rudy, 1988). The first assumption is that all *individuals are active processors of information rather than passive reactors.* Individuals attempt to make sense of the stimuli that impinge upon them from the external environment by filtering information through organizing templates derived from their prior learning histories and by using general strategies that guide the processing of information (e.g., Nisbett & Ross, 1980). Individuals' responses, both overt and covert, are based on these appraisals and subsequent expectations and are not totally contingent on the actual consequences of their behaviors (i.e., positive and negative reinforcements and punishments). Thus, from this perspective, the anticipated consequences are as important in governing behavior as the actual consequences.

A second assumption of the cognitive-behavioral perspective is that one's *thoughts* (appraisals, attributions, expectancies) can elicit or modulate affect and physiological arousal, both of which may serve as impetuses for behavior. Conversely, affect, physiology, and behavior can instigate or influence one's thinking processes. Thus, the causal priority depends on where in the cycle one chooses to begin. Causal priority may be less of a concern than the view of a transactional process that extends over time with the interaction of thoughts, feelings, physiological activity, and behavior (Lazarus & Folkman, 1984).

Unlike the operant conditioning model, which emphasizes the influence of the environment on behavior, the cognitive-behavioral perspective focuses on the reciprocal effects of the individual on the environment and on the unidirectional influence of environment on behavior. Individuals not only respond passively to their environment but also elicit environmental responses by their behavior. In a sense, individuals create their environments. The patient with back pain who seeks medical consultation evokes a set of circumstances different from those of the individual with back pain of the same intensity who does not choose to self-medicate. The third assumption of the cognitive-behavioral perspective, therefore, is that *behavior is reciprocally determined by both the environment and the individual* (Bandura, 1978).

A fourth assumption is that if individuals have learned maladaptive ways of thinking, feeling, and responding, then successful interventions designed to alter behavior should focus on each of these thoughts, feelings, physiology, as well as behaviors and not on one to the exclusion of the others with the expectancy (faith) that changing thoughts, feelings, or behaviors will necessarily result in the others following suit, as is true in radical operant (Rachlin, 1985) or exclusive cognitive treatment (Ciccone & Grzesiak, 1984) approaches.

The final assumption of the cognitive-behavioral perspective is that, in the same way as individuals are instrumental in the development and maintenance of maladaptive thoughts, feelings, and behaviors, *they can, are, and should be considered active agents of change of their maladaptive modes of responding.*

Patients with persistent pain, despite their common belief to the contrary, are not helpless pawns of fate. They can and should become instrumental in learning and carrying out more effective modes of responding to their environment.

Unfortunately, most of us have learned an acute model of illness whereby there is a specific physical cause for any symptom, there is an appropriate medical treatment, there is a specific time course (expected to be brief) for resolution of the symptoms, and there are socially sanctioned healers who will act upon the patient and whose ministrations will eliminate the symptoms. In this model, the "good" patient is the one who is passive, permits healers to do things to him or her, asks few questions, complies with the healers' orders, and as a result will get relief of symptoms. Most patients with chronic illnesses, especially patients with chronic pain, are confronted with challenges to the acute illness model and, not surprisingly, cause frustration for physicians who, like the patient, ascribe to the acute illness model.

Chronic pain patients often do not have sufficient objective evidence to account for the extent of their pain, despite what might seem an endless number of consultations and diagnostic tests. Many therapeutic interventions have been tried with only limited success, their pain extends over long periods of time, and there is little encouraging information that there is an end in sight. Despite the best efforts of the healers, the symptoms persist. Insurance companies, family, and friends may come to question the veracity of these patients' complaints, viewing them as "wimps" if not outright malingerers. Thus, it is hardly surprising that chronic pain patients become angry, frustrated, and demoralized. Combating demoralization is perhaps the essential feature of any treatment for this population (Turk & Holzman, 1986).

## Strategic Objectives of Cognitive-Behavioral Intervention

Given the description of the cognitive-behavioral perspective discussed previously, we can now consider the implications of this perspective for developing interventions for use with chronic pain patients. A strategic objective that has been addressed repeatedly is that of changing patients' view of their problem from overwhelming to manageable. A major component of any intervention, then, is to confront and overcome patients' maladaptive conceptualizations because these conceptualizations contribute to, exacerbate, and maintain the initial problem.

One way to change patients' conceptualizations is to persuade them that there are ways to address their problems adequately and that the skills the patient needs to respond more effectively are included in the therapist's armamentarium and can be transferred to the patient. Unfortunately, convincing patients through logic and disputing irrational beliefs is not an easy task; even if they believe in the efficacy of the proposed treatment regimen, they may not believe they are competent to learn these skills successfully and implement them as situations demand. Convincing patients of their ability is more likely if they are successful and their behavior becomes a positive reinforcer than if one relies exclusively on logic, rational arguments, and exhortation (Bandura, 1977). Specific goals and paced mastery (i.e., graded increase in the difficulty of task requirements, beginning at a level where patients have a good likelihood of succeeding) are primary tactics to employ in fostering patients' sense of confidence and competence. Only when they feel a sense of self-efficacy are patients likely to try more difficult tasks and goals and to persist in their efforts in the face of difficulties (Bandura, 1977).

Patients need evidence that they can exert more control over their bodies and their situation. It is all too easy to disregard successful behavior and goal attainment and to focus instead on failures. Moreover, unless individuals specifically attend to the impact of their thoughts, feelings, physiological responses, and behaviors on each other, they are likely to see little interrelationship. To accomplish the levels of awareness of successful goal attainment and the relationship among thoughts, feelings, physiological responses, and behavior requires focused, conscious effort. Thus, cognitive-behavioral therapists emphasize the tactical use of self-observation and self-monitoring. Specific use of charts and diaries of goals, effort, goal attainment, antecedents and consequences of maladaptive thoughts, feelings, and behaviors are employed.

Such self-monitoring can serve to bring maladaptive automatic models of responding into conscious awareness and, consequently, can become the focus of voluntary control. Self-monitoring of both overt and covert behaviors is an important tactic used in many behavioral and cognitive-behavioral interventions. A difference is that the cognitive-behavioral approach is much more concerned about patients' self-monitoring of their thinking as it relates to their appraisals, expectations, performance, and dysfunctional modes of responding.

An additional objective of cognitive-behavioral interventions involves teaching patients specific skills to employ that will foster more effective and adaptive modes of responding. A number of specific skills may be employed (and these are reviewed in other chapters of this volume), but some of the most frequently used include relaxation, problem solving, rational restructuring, and communications skills.

Teaching patients a specific set of skills is an important component of cognitive-behavioral interventions but skills training is not sufficient by itself. Patients need to know not only how to perform specific skills but when to perform them and how to access them from memory. Most people can learn to relax when they are not upset, but it is more difficult to learn how to be aware of stress and automatic maladaptive responding and how to execute these skills within one's natural environment. Moreover, factors that may interfere with the production of these skills need to be addressed. Skills training may lead to a diminution of a skills deficiency, but cognitive-behavioral interventions also emphasize production deficiencies—that is, the factors that inhibit the use of skills acquired (e.g., insufficient motivation, automaticity of maladaptive responding, affective distress, and maladaptive cognitions).

A final important objective of cognitive-behavioral interventions is the fostering of self-attribution of success. Much effort is given to encouraging patients to view themselves as *the* agents of improvement. To the extent that patients attribute improvement to their *own* skills and efforts, there is a greater likelihood that they will feel more competent and thus be more likely to expend greater efforts and to persist in the face of difficulties that *will* emerge (Bandura, 1977).

## Reconceptualization

The crucial element in the successful treatment of chronic pain is bringing about a shift in the patient's repertoire from well-established, habitual, and automatic but ineffective responses toward systematic problem solving and planning, control of affect, and behavioral persistence.

The reconceptualization process serves several essential functions. It translates patients' symptoms into difficulties that can be pinpointed as specific, addressable problems. It recasts problems in forms amenable to solutions and thus can foster hope, positive anticipation, and expectation of success. It creates a positive expectation that the treatment being offered is appropriate for the problem.

Reconceptualization goes on throughout treatment and involves reorienting the patient from his or her belief that pain is an overwhelming, all-encompassing sensory experience that results solely from tissue pathology and that he or she is helpless to do anything about; to a concept of pain as an experience that can be differentiated and systematically modified and controlled by the patient. The reconceptualization of the patient's maladaptive view of pain is the framework of cognitive-behavioral treatment, which provides validity and incentive for the development of proficiency with various coping skills employed in pain control.

Throughout treatment, it is important to listen to the patient, both to permit and to encourage him or her to express concerns, fears, and frustrations, as well as anger directed toward the health care system, insurance companies, employers, the social system, family, and perhaps themselves. Many patients have unspoken fears about progression of their condition, about injuring themselves by performing certain activities, and about people thinking their pain is not real. Patients' greatest fears appear to be that, following evaluation, the treatment team will: (1) find something serious that has been missed by others (e.g., cancer), (2) tell them that they have a degenerative condition, (3) find nothing wrong and label the problem as merely psychological, or (4) tell them that nothing can be done and they will just have to learn to live with the pain.

Many patients are reluctant or perhaps even unable to articulate these concerns. The therapist should assume these fears are present and should acknowledge them. It may be helpful to phrase a statement in such a way to let the patient save face, reduce defensiveness, or make explicit an underlying worry. For example, the therapist might state:

> *Some patients who come here are worried that we and other people don't think that their pain is real, that they are faking or have psychological problems. You might not have had this concern, but let me tell you that there is no question that the pain you report is real and there is no question that you are suffering. If we did not believe your pain was real, we would not consider treating you here. Let me explain what we know about your condition and your pain and relate this to current understandings of pain.*

The psychologist may employ a more didactic approach. The educational component of treatment consists of the presentation of the cognitive-behavioral perspective on pain and the control of pain (i.e., role of cognitions, affect, behavior, environmental factors, and physical factors). At the outset of treatment and continuing throughout, we attempt to discuss pain and its impact on the patient's life as well as how others in his or her life may be affected by the pain problem. The cognitive-behavioral psychologist tries to make use of patients' vocabularies and match examples, metaphors, and analogies to patients' experiences and understanding of their problems obtained during assessment. The emphasis is on the collaborative nature of the relationship between the therapist and patient. That is, the therapist conveys to patients that he or she will work *with* them to achieve the best possible outcome given the constraints imposed by any physical limitations, but that the therapist will not do anything *to* them. It is preferable to have this discussion with significant others present so that their misinformation, concerns, and fears can be identified and addressed.

The therapist should review the psychological test results acquired during the assessment and demonstrate to the patient and significant others how the patient's situation might be influenced by these factors. In this way, the process of reconceptualization is initiated. That is, it might be suggested that pain interferes with different areas of people's lives and that people respond to this in different ways. The therapist may ask the patient how these differential responses might affect how they think, feel, and do, as well as influence how others respond to them.

During the reconceptualization process, pain is explained briefly with a simplified explanation of the gate control model (Melzack & Wall, 1965). The gate control model is presented, not as a complex scientific theory, but to demonstrate to the patient the multidimensional aspect of pain. It is presented in a way the patient can understand using personally relevant examples. This model is contrasted with the unidimensional sensory physiological model commonly held by patients. Pain is described as a multidimensional experience having physiological, cognitive, affective, and behavioral features. The effects of situations on the pain experience are presented in a clear, understandable fashion.

The impact of anxiety and depression is examined and related to exacerbations of pain. In addition, patients are encouraged to review recent stressful episodes or circumstances and to examine the course their pain followed at that time. For example, a recent conflict with an insurance claims adjuster might be examined to determine whether the patient's getting upset had any effect on the pain experienced. This might be contrasted to the level of pain experienced when distracted by an involving movie. Information collected during the assessment is used to illustrate any personally relevant examples of negative, emotionally influenced aggravation of pain. The idea of thoughts and feelings opening and closing "the pain gate" is described when the gate control model is presented.

Imaginal presentation or recall of previous pain episodes can be especially useful at this juncture. Patients can be asked to recall not only the situation but also their thoughts and feelings. With the help of the therapist, they can then discover the impact of thoughts and feelings on the experience of pain. In this manner, the therapist engages patients in a dialogue. The patients' maladaptive thoughts and feelings should be used by the therapist to illustrate how such thinking may influence inappropriate behavior and exacerbate the problem.

In sum, the reconceptualization process serves at least five important functions:

1. It provides a more benign view of the problem than the patient's original view.
2. It translates patients' symptoms into difficulties that can be pinpointed as specific, addressable problems rather than problems that are vague, undifferentiated, overwhelming, and uncontrollable.
3. It recasts problems in forms that are amenable to solutions and in this way should foster hope, positive anticipation, and expectation of success.
4. It prepares patients for interventions contained within the treatment regimen that are directly linked to the conceptualization proposed.
5. It creates a positive expectation that the treatment being offered is appropriate for the patient's problems.

*Role of Homework*

An important component of the cognitive-behavioral approach is the active involvement of patients and significant others outside the therapy session and clinic. Homework assignments are established within the same consultative framework as all cognitive-behavioral therapy. Each homework task is targeted toward observable and manageable tasks, starting with those that are most readily achievable and progressing to more difficult ones. The purpose of graded tasks is to enhance patients' sense of competence and to reinforce their continued efforts (Table 16.4).

**Table 16.4.** Factors to Consider When Establishing Homework Assignments

- Customize intervention to individual's needs. Whenever possible, set tasks collaboratively.
- Design the tasks to be appropriate for the patient's level of education, gender, physical and psychological ability.
- Try to create a no-lose situation. Whenever possible, do what you can to make sure that the patient will succeed at the task.
- Explain the rationale for each homework task.
- Make homework assignments as specific, concrete, and measurable as possible.
- Ask the patient to write down each homework assignment and to read these back and explain the rationale.
- Ask the patient to consider what factors (including thoughts, feelings, and significant others) might be obstacles to the accomplishment of each homework task.
- Ask the patient what he or she can do and will do if impediments to successful task completion arise.
- Ask the patient for feedback on the successes and difficulties of task completion at the next session.

Mastery experiences gained through performance accomplishments are hypothesized to have the greatest impact on establishing and strengthening expectancies because they provide the most information about actual capabilities. Successful versus unsuccessful physical therapy may be distinguished by the presence versus the absence of changes in perceived self-efficacy with physical improvements in tolerance, strength, and endurance. Patients need to learn to make a distinction between *hurt* and *harm.* One group of pain patients may stop an activity when it hurts, often for fear of exacerbating the physical injury (they also stop because they wish to avoid the noxious sensations themselves).

A second group of patients, less frequently considered, continue to be overactive because they have unrealistic self-efficacy beliefs. These patients may continue to overdo their activities and subsequently feel even worse. They may continue to engage in this pattern in the belief that, when their pain levels decrease, they will be cured and able to return to their activities in an unmodified form. Unfortunately, this belief is a consequence of being exposed to and accepting an acute formulation of pain. Eventually, these patients come to believe that all activities are dangerous and that they cannot do any activity without experiencing what they erroneously label "reinjury," and they thus enter the ranks of underactive patients. The attitude of these patients is exemplified by their refusal to engage in physical therapy because it makes them "worse." Physical therapy and psychological counseling that emphasizes "working through" the pain and breaking the hurt–harm link will provide corrective feedback of capabilities and reinforce the patient's perceived self-efficacy and, subsequently, increased efforts.

Additionally, physical therapy and psychological approaches can help patients learn to pace activities better, to understand that increased pain is not reinjury necessitating total incapacitation, and to label and change thoughts that would make them susceptible to engaging in unrealistic behaviors (e.g., "If I don't go hunting, my friends will never respect me"). Thus, techniques that enhance mastery experiences (e.g., graded task accomplishments with both physical and verbal feedback) will, according to Bandura (1977), be powerful tools for bringing about behavior change. Moreover, patients' self-attribution of task accomplishment should enhance maintenance of improvements (Kopel & Arkowitz, 1975). In this way, cognitive variables are the primary determinants of behavior, but these variables are altered most effectively by performance-based accomplishments.

Homework, therefore, provides important feedback to both patients and therapists. Successful completion of homework assignments can be reinforced and maladaptive patterns identified and subsequently addressed.

### Cognitive Restructuring

As noted several times, the cognitive-behavioral perspective assumes that the way individuals perceive their circumstances determines their mood, perception of pain intensity, and subsequent behavior, including seeking medical attention (e.g., Flor & Turk, 1988). Also, affect and behaviors reciprocally affect cognitions, and all have an effect on physiological functioning (e.g., Flor, Birbaumer, & Turk, 1990). Cognitive restructuring focuses on identification of maladaptive appraisals and expectations and subsequent consideration of more appropriate alternative modes of interpretation.

Therapy, from the cognitive-behavioral perspective, should be viewed as a collaborative process by which the therapist carefully elicits patients' troublesome thoughts and concerns, acknowledges their bothersome nature, and then constructs an atmosphere in which patients can critically challenge the validity of their own beliefs. Rather than suggesting alternative thoughts, the therapist attempts to elicit competing thoughts from patients themselves and then reinforces the adaptive nature of these alternatives. Patients have well-learned and frequently rehearsed thoughts about their condition. Only after repetitions and practice in cueing competent interpretations and evaluations will patients come to change their conceptualizations. Significant others may be important, as they may contribute to unwittingly undermining patients' changing conceptualizations.

## Skills Acquisition

In all cases, it is essential for patients to understand the rationale for the specific skills being taught and the tasks they are being asked to perform. Unless patients understand the rationale for treatment components and have opportunities to raise issues and sources of confusions about them, they are less likely to persevere in the face of obstacles, benefit from therapy, or maintain therapeutic gains. Cognitive and behavioral treatment makes use of a whole range of techniques and procedures (many described in detail in other chapters in this volume) designed to bring about alterations in patients' perceptions of their situation, their mood, their behavior, and their abilities to affect these.

Techniques such as progressive relaxation training, problem-solving training, distraction skills training, and communication skills training, to name only a few, have all been incorporated with the general cognitive-behavioral framework. Several publications have described in detail some specific techniques used, and interested readers should consult these (e.g., Holzman & Turk, 1986; Kanfer & Goldstein, 1986; Turk et al., 1983). A number of specific skills have been reported to be useful in helping pain patients to cope with their symptoms. At this point, research does not permit selecting among these. We believe that more important than the specific tactics selected from those that have proved useful are the strategic goals of enhancing self-control and intrinsic motivation. The manner in which the various skills are described, taught, and practiced may be more important than the skills per se.

Again, it is essential for the therapist to keep in mind patients' perspectives and how they perceive each skill and assignment. The therapist's skills and the relationship that is established between the therapist and the patient becomes the oil that keeps the gears of treatment moving; without a satisfactory therapeutic alliance, treatment will grind to a halt

(Turk, Holzman, & Kerns, 1985). It is important to note that treatment should not be viewed as a rigid process with fixed techniques. There is a need to individualize the treatment program for each specific patient (Turk, in press).

*Relaxation*

We usually begin the skills-training phase of treatment with relaxation exercises. These techniques are particularly useful early because they can be readily learned by almost all patients and have acceptable face validity. The training of relaxation is designed not only to teach a response that is incompatible with muscle tension but also to help patients develop a behavioral coping skill that can be used in any situation in which adaptive coping is required. The practice of relaxation strengthens patients' beliefs that they can exert some control during periods of stress and pain and that they are not helpless or impotent.

Relaxation can be used for its direct effects on specific muscles, for reduction of generalized arousal, for its cognitive effects (i.e., as a distraction or attention diversion strategy), and for its value in increasing the patient's sense of control and self-efficacy. Relaxation skills are generic, and there are a wide range of different techniques (e.g., biofeedback, autogenic training, imagery) geared toward assisting patients to learn how to deal with stress and, in particular, how to reduce site-specific muscular hyperarousal. Moreover, relaxation also includes *active* efforts such as aerobic exercise, walking, and engaging in a range of pleasurable activities that are consistent with the patient's interests and physical limitations.

The rationale presented to the patients follows the same principles seen in the presentation of the treatment rationale. The goal is to develop and enhance motivation and participation. The manner in which the rationale is presented depends on the patient's particular way of thinking about his or her pain problem and life situation. The rationale is presented within a framework that sets high expectation for success, indicates that the treatment is clinically indicated, and assumes that it is within the patient's own competencies to achieve.

Furthermore, the relaxation procedure should be presented to provide patients with a demonstration of their ability to control their muscles (both increases and decreases in pain intensity; biofeedback may be used to reinforce this point). We chose initially to use muscle tension reduction procedures (Bernstein &

Borkovec, 1973) because (1) they have face validity; (2) they are concrete procedures and thus are easy to recall and practice at home; and (3) this approach is less prone to failure resulting from distraction by pain or cognitive intrusions. Slight pain exacerbations that often accompany muscle tensing clearly demonstrate to the patient the role of muscle activity in pain intensity and perception. If muscle tension results in increased pain, we can reason that the converse, muscle relaxation, will lead to pain reduction. Also, the results of even the first relaxation training session are often inherently reinforcing by reducing generalized arousal. The therapist can build on this experience to predict the potential beneficial treatment effects with extended practice.

Throughout the practice of relaxation, the therapist continues to take the collaborator's role. This is very important for developing the conceptualization of relaxation as a *self*-management skill, thereby facilitating self-control of pain. The therapist also should assume a role that fosters the patient's perception of success. Failure during the initial stages of treatment can seriously undermine patients' confidence and motivation. Patients should be encouraged frequently with statements about their progress. Similarly, all possible indications and reports of success by patients should be reinforced.

After patients have become proficient in relaxation, we have them imagine themselves in various stress or conflict situations and visualize themselves employing the relaxation skills in those situations. The therapist may describe coping versus mastery examples derived from other patients. That is, the therapist may describe how patients reported trying to relax, having problems, and then overcoming them. In this way, patients become aware that problems might arise, that when they have difficulties they can overcome them, and that they are not the only ones who have difficulties. Patients are told that relaxation is a skill and, like any skill, requires a good deal of practice.

*Attention Diversion*

Attention is a major factor in perception and therefore of concern in examining and changing behavior. Attention-diverting coping tactics have been employed probably for as long as humans have experienced pain. A great deal of research based on attentional focus has been conducted on the relative efficacy of various cognitive coping techniques (Fernandez & Turk, 1989).

Cognitive techniques consist of several different types of procedures, including cognitive distraction or attention diversion techniques. Patients are often preoccupied with their pain and bodily symptoms. Every new sensation is seen as an indication of deterioration or a new problem resulting from increased exercise and activity. Cognitive distraction techniques are best used during specific pain episodes where the patient experiences an exacerbation of his or her pain.

Prior to a description of different coping techniques, we briefly describe to patients how attention can influence perception. The therapist can suggest that people can fully focus their attention on only one thing at a time and that we can control, to some extent, what we attend to, although doing so may sometimes require a good deal of effort. The therapist might ask patients to close their eyes and focus attention on some part of their bodies. The therapist then notes some ambient sound such as the ventilation system and suggests that, while attending to their bodies, patients were unaware of the sound of the air conditioning. The therapist calls their attention to the sound of ventilation but reminds them that now they have stopped focusing on their bodies. The therapist also might call their attention to some part of the body they were not attending to, such as the buttocks pressing on the chair or the gentle pressure of their watch on their wrist. The point is that there is always some environmental input (internal and external) that is present but remains out of conscious attention until patients focus directly on it. For example, the therapist might note that, while one is doing one's income tax, a loud-playing radio in the next room may make concentration difficult. The objective is to communicate to patients that people commonly employ various methods to get some degree of control over the focus of their attention.

The therapist should make frequent use of analogies and metaphors throughout treatment. For example, we use the analogy of a television tuner: All the stations are present but an individual can focus on only one at a time. The therapist suggests that he or she will help patients learn how to redirect their attention away from discomfort.

To date, no one type of cognitive coping technique has proved universally effective (Fernandez & Turk, 1989; Turk et al., 1983). We suggest providing patients with training in the use of many different ones. A variety of cognitive coping images and attention-diverting tasks are discussed in an attempt to find several that are most appealing to individual patients.

*Assertiveness and Communication Skills Training.* Assertiveness training is often an important intervention for enabling patients to reestablish their roles, particularly within the family, and thus to regain a sense of esteem and adequacy. Through role playing of existing tension-producing interpersonal transactions, the patient and therapist can identify and modify maladaptive thoughts, feelings, and communication deficiencies underlying nonassertiveness, while practicing more adaptive responses. Patients may find assertiveness training useful in addressing reactions from family members and health care providers that may be implicitly opposing their own self-management objectives.

*Problem-Solving Skills Training.* Adopting a problem-solving perspective is particularly important for patients. That is, we try to help patients identify problems that may contribute to their pain and suffering, and we suggest that if problems can be identified then they can be solved. Specifically, we outline the following steps in problem solving:

- Define the source of distress or stress reactions as problems to be solved.
- Set realistic goals as concretely as possible by stating the problem in behavioral terms.
- Generate a wide range of possible alternative courses of action to reach each goal.
- Imagine and consider how others might respond if asked to deal with a similar problem.
- Evaluate the pros and cons of each proposed solution and rank-order the solutions from least to most practical.
- Rehearse strategies and behaviors by imagery, role reversal, or behavioral rehearsal.
- Try out the most feasible solution.
- Expect some failures, but reward oneself for having tried.
- Reconsider the original problem in light of the attempted solution.
- Recycle as needed.

We also tie the problem-solving steps to specific questions: problem identification (What is the concern?), goal selection (What do I want?), generation of alternatives (What can I do?), consideration of consequences (What might happen?), decision making (What is my decision?), implementation (Now do it!), evaluation (Did it work? If not, recycle).

## Skills Consolidation

During the skills consolidation phase of the cognitive-behavioral treatment, patients practice and rehearse the skills they have learned during the skills acquisition phase and learn to apply them outside the clinical context. The techniques employed include mental rehearsal, during which time patients imagine using the skills in different situations to handle and overcome difficulties. Role reversal, where the patient interacts with the therapist as if he or she were in a specific situation and needed to use specific skills, with the therapist assuming the role of patient, is also used (to be discussed). Specific details of these approaches are described later in this chapter and in more depth in Holzman et al. (1986) and Turk et al. (1983).

*Imagery Rehearsal*

One means of providing patients with opportunities to rehearse coping skills is to use imagery rehearsal. As in the use of systematic desensitization, patients are asked, while relaxed, to imagine themselves in various situations in which the intensity of pain or stress varies. Our view of imagery rehearsal presumes that when patients are instructed to imagine scenes, they are providing themselves with a model of their behavior. The closer the imagery comes to representing real experiences, the greater the likelihood of generalization. Through imagery, patients can mentally rehearse the specific thoughts, feelings, and behaviors they will use to cope with stress and pain.

To maximize the similarity between the image and real life, coping images are used as well as mastery images. Mastery images involve patients' viewing themselves as handling the problem situation successfully. Coping imagery, in contrast, involves patients' imagining themselves becoming anxious, beginning to experience pain, or having maladaptive thoughts, and then coping with these difficulties using approaches they have learned during treatment.

*Role Playing.* This is another tactic used to help patients consolidate the skills learned during the skills acquisition phase. We find role playing useful not only in rehearsing new skills but also in identifying potential problem areas that may require special attention. Most typically, patients are asked to identify and participate in a role-play situation indicative of a particular problem area.

*Role Reversal.* In a variation of role-play, role reversal, patients are asked to role-play a situation in which therapist and patient reverse roles. Patients are instructed that it will be their job to assume the role of the therapist and the therapist will assume the role of a pain patient who has not received the specific skills training. We know from research on attitude change that when people have to improvise, as in a role-playing situation, they generate exactly the kinds of arguments, illustrations, and motivating appeals that they regard as most salient and convincing. In this way, they tailor the content of their roles to fit their unique motives, predispositions, and preferences. In such a role-playing situation, they not only emphasize those aspects of the training that are most convincing but also focus on less conflicting thoughts, doubts, and unfavorable consequences.

In sum, these exercises contribute to self-convincing as well as permitting the therapist to determine areas of confusion and potential difficulties. Also, dissonance theory tells us that once an individual has expressed a particular point of view for little or no extrinsic reinforcement, he or she is more likely to uphold that view subsequently.

## Preparation for Generalization and Maintenance

To maximize the likelihood of maintenance and generalization of treatment gains, cognitive-behavioral therapists focus on the cognitive activity of patients as they are confronted with problems throughout treatment (e.g., failure to achieve specified goals, plateaus in progress on physical exercises, recurrent stresses). These events are employed as opportunities to help patients learn how to handle such setbacks and lapses, given that these are probably inevitable and will occur once treatment is terminated. Rehabilitation is not a cure.

In the final stage of treatment, discussion focuses on possible ways of predicting and avoiding or dealing with pain and pain-related problems following treatment termination. We have found it helpful to help patients anticipate future problems, stress, and pain-exacerbating events and to plan coping and response techniques before these problems occur. Marlatt and Gordon (1985) refer to this process as "relapse prevention."

Briefly, relapse prevention involves helping the patient, prior to completion of treatment, to learn to identify and cope successfully with factors that may otherwise lead to relapse. Patients are helped to identify high-risk situations and the types of coping and behavioral responses that may be necessary for successful coping.

In the final stage of treatment, discussion is focused on possible ways of predicting and avoiding difficult and problematic situations in general, as well as specific ones identified during treatment. Discussion of relapse must be done in a delicate manner. On the one hand, the therapist does not wish to convey an expectation of treatment failure; on the other hand, the therapist wishes to anticipate and assist the patient to learn how to deal with potential recurrences or likely problematic situations.

It is important to note that all possible problematic circumstances cannot be anticipated. Rather, the goal during this phase, as for the entire treatment strategy, is to enable patients to develop a problem-solving perspective whereby they believe they have the skills and competencies within their repertoires to respond appropriately to problems as they arise. Attempts are made to help patients learn to anticipate future difficulties, develop plans for adaptive responding, and adjust their behavior accordingly. Successful responses should further enhance patients' sense of self-efficacy and help to form a "virtuous circle" in contrast to the "vicious circle" created and fostered by inactivity, passivity, physical deconditioning, helplessness, and hopelessness that characterize people with chronic pain.

We have found it useful to have patients anticipate future stress- or pain-exacerbating events and to plan how they will deal with these. For example, one patient was anticipating his daughter's wedding soon after therapy termination. Using a future-oriented problem-solving approach, the patient could identify both expected and potential problematic situations (e.g., dancing at the wedding reception, poor service by the caterer). He was able to develop a plan to cope with such situation and with general, unanticipated problems and thereby to decrease the likelihood of relapse.

The generalization and maintenance phases serve at least two purposes: (1) They encourage the patient to anticipate and plan for the posttreatment period, when symptoms are greatly improved but not totally removed; and (2) They focus on the necessary conditions for long-term success. More specifically, relapse prevention gives the patient the understanding that minor setbacks are to be expected but that they do not signal total failure. Rather, these setbacks should be viewed as cues to use the coping skills at which patients are already proficient. It is important

for patients not to think of their responsibility as ending at termination of treatment but, rather, as entering a different phase of maintenance. Emphasis is placed on the importance of adhering to recommendations on an ongoing basis.

During the final sessions, all aspects of the treatment program are reviewed. Patients are engaged in discussion of what they have learned and how they have changed from the onset of treatment and recognition of how the patient's own efforts contributed to the positive changes. The therapist is also encouraged to use patient self-monitoring charts to reinforce accomplishments. The goal is to help patients realize that they have skills and abilities within their repertoires to cope with their circumstances without needing to contact their therapists and without becoming dependent on others. It is emphasized that change has been achieved and can be maintained only if patients continue to accept responsibility for their lives. People should no longer view themselves as "patients" but as competent people who happen to have some discomfort.

## CONCLUSION

From our perspective, patients' attitudes and beliefs have an effect on motivation and behavior. We believe that environmental contingencies can influence thoughts, feelings, and behaviors. Thus, we suggest that employing both cognitive and behavioral techniques can bring about direct changes in behavior provided by environmental contingencies and indirect changes following modification of cognitive factors. External reinforcement is important at the beginning of treatment; however, unless significant changes in intrinsic motivation occur following from direct operant techniques, treatment efficacy will not be maintained following the removal of direct environmental reinforcement (e.g., Cairns & Pasino, 1977). The literature on relapse in a diversity of problems lends support to our reservations regarding adherence and long-term maintenance following exclusively operant approaches in the management of chronic pain (Turk & Rudy, in press).

We have been unable to address all the nuances of cognitive-behavioral treatments; but we hope we have whetted the reader's appetite to consider more carefully the nature of his or her treatment strategy and tactics used when interacting with patients. As is obvious from even a cursory scanning of the literature, single-modality techniques imposed on passive pain patients seem of limited value for the complexity of problems inherent in chronic pain. The history of treatment of chronic pain is replete with technically elegant interventions that have proved to be failures (e.g., Flor & Turk, 1984; Melzack & Wall, 1983; Turk & Flor, 1984). We do not mean to suggest that there is no place for conventional medical and surgical modalities or simple psychological interventions; however, it is apparent that optimal treatment of the complex problem of persistent pain must extend beyond these simple approaches.

The efficacy of a variety of cognitive-behavioral techniques has been evaluated in a number of laboratory analogue and clinical pain studies. Laboratory studies have demonstrated the effectiveness of these techniques in the enhancement of tolerance for a variety of nociceptive stimuli (e.g., Fernandez & Turk, 1989). The clinical effectiveness of cognitive-behavioral interventions has been demonstrated with a wide range of acute, acute recurrent, and chronic non-cancer-related pain syndromes, including headaches (e.g., Bakal, Demjen, & Kaganov, 1981; Holroyd, Andrasik, & Westbrook, 1977), arthritis (Bradley et al., 1987; O'Leary, Shoor, Long, & Holman, 1988; Parker et al., 1988), low back pain (Turner & Clancy, 1988), and heterogeneous samples of chronic noncancer pain patients (e.g., Corey, Etlin, & Miller, 1987; Hazard et al., 1989; Moore & Chaney, 1985).

In this chapter, we have emphasized the strategy and some tactics of cognitive-behavioral therapy. We made use of many techniques borrowed from different types of therapy. According to Turk and Holzman (1986), durable change can only be expected if:

1. There is a fit between patients' conceptualizations of their problems and the rationale for the treatment being offered.
2. The expected value of more adaptive behaviors, for patients, is emphasized rather than the worth of these behaviors to the health care provider.
3. Patients have or can be provided with the necessary skills to carry out more adaptive responding.
4. Patients believe that the treatment components will be effective in alleviating their problems.
5. Patients believe that they are competent to carry out the skills learned beyond the therapeutic context.
6. There is sufficient intrinsic and extrinsic reinforcement for the maintenance and generalization of the skills incorporated within the treatment regimen following termination.

All of these are incorporated within the cognitive-behavioral treatment we have described. It is important to note in closing that, at this point in time, methodologically adequate process research has yet to identify the necessary or sufficient components of effective treatment of persistent pain patients. Consequently, the treatment strategy and tactics that we have elaborated in this chapter are based on our clinical experience rather than on empirical support for each component described.

## REFERENCES

American Psychiatric Association. (1987). *Diagnostic and statistical manual of psychiatric disorders,* 3rd ed., rev. Washington, DC: American Psychiatric Press.

Averill, J. R. (1973). Personal control over aversive stimuli and its relationship to stress. *Psychological Bulletin, 80,* 286–303.

Bakal, D. A., Demjen, S., & Kaganov, J. A. (1981). Cognitive-behavioral treatment of chronic headache. *Headache, 21,* 81–86.

Bandura, A. (1977). Self-efficacy: Toward a unifying theory of behavior change. *Psychological Review, 84,* 191–215.

Bandura, A. (1978). The self-system in reciprocal determinism. *American Psychologist, 33,* 344–359.

Barrios, F. X., Turk, D. C., & Rudy, T. E. (1990). Chronic pain. M. Herson & V. Van Hasselt (Eds.), *Psychological aspects of developmental and physical disabilities: A casebook* (pp. 94–109). Newbury Park, CA: Sage Publications.

Barber, T. X., & Hahn, K. W. (1964). Experimental studies in "hypnotic" behavior: Physiological and subjective effects of imagined pain. *Journal of Nervous and Mental Disease, 139,* 416–425.

Bergner, M., Bobbitt, R. A., Carter, W. B., & Gilson, B. S. (1981). The Sickness Impact Profile: Development and final revision of a health status measure. *Medical Care, 19,* 787–805.

Bernstein, D. A., & Borkovec, T. D. (1973). *Progressive relaxation training.* Champaign, IL: Research Press.

Biedermann, H. J., McGhie, A., Monga, T. N., & Shanks, G. L. (1987). Perceived and actual control in EMG treatment of back pain. *Behaviour Research and Therapy, 25,* 137–147.

Block, A. R., Kremer, E. F., & Gaylor, M. (1980). Behavioral treatment of chronic pain: The spouse as a discriminative cue for pain behaviors. *Pain, 9,* 243–252.

Bonica, J. J. (1986). Status of pain research and therapy. *Seminars in Anesthesia, 5,* 82–99.

Bradley, L. A., Young, L. D., Anderson, K. O., Turner, R. A., Agudelo, C. A., McDaniel, L. K., et al. (1987). Effects of psychological therapy on pain behavior of rheumatoid arthritis patients: Treatment outcome and six-month follow-up. *Arthritis and Rheumatism, 30,* 1105–1114.

Brown, G. K., & Nicassio, P. M. (1987). Development of a questionnaire for the assessment of active and passive coping strategies in chronic pain patients. *Pain, 31,* 53–64.

Cairns, D., & Pasino, J. A. (1977). Comparison of verbal reinforcement and feedback in operant treatment of disability due to low back pain. *Behavior Therapy, 8,* 621–630.

Ciccone, D. S., & Grzesiak, R. C. (1984). Cognitive dimensions of chronic pain. *Social Science in Medicine, 19,* 1339–1346.

Corey, D. T., Etlin, D., & Miller, P. C. (1987). A home-based pain management and rehabilitation program: An evaluation. *Pain, 29,* 219–230.

Council, J. R., Ahern, D. K., Follick, M. J., & Kline, C. L. (1988). Expectancies and functional impairment in chronic low back pain. *Pain, 33,* 323–340.

Dolce, J. J., Doleys, D. M., Raczynski, J. M., Lossie, J., Poole, L., & Smith, M. (1986). The role of self-efficacy expectancies in the prediction of pain tolerance. *Pain, 27,* 261–272.

Doleys, D. M., Crocker, M., & Patton, D. (1982). Response of patients with chronic pain to exercise quotas. *Physical Therapy, 62,* 1111–1114.

Engel, G. L. (1959). ''Psychogenic pain'' and the pain-prone patient. *American Journal of Medicine, 26,* 899–918.

Engelberg, A. L. (Ed.). (1988). *Guides for the evaluation of permanent impairment,* 3rd ed. Chicago: American Medical Association.

Eysenck, H. J., & Rachman, S. (1965). *The causes and cures of neurosis.* London: Routledge and Kegan Paul.

Fernandez, E., & Turk, D. C. (1989). The utility of cognitive coping strategies for altering perception of pain: A meta-analysis. *Pain, 38,* 123–125.

Flor, H., Birbaumer, N., & Turk, D. C. (1990). The psychobiology of chronic pain. *Advances in Behaviour Research and Therapy, 12,* 47–84.

Flor, H., & Turk, D. C. (1984). Etiological theories and treatments for chronic back pain: I. Somatic factors. *Pain, 19,* 105–121.

Flor, H., & Turk, D. C. (1988). Rheumatoid arthritis and back pain: Predicting pain and disability from cognitive variables. *Journal of Behavioral Medicine, 11,* 251–265.

Flor, H., Turk, D. C., & Birbaumer, N. (1985). Assessment of stress-related psychophysiological reactions in chronic back pain patients. *Journal of Consulting and Clinical Psychology, 53,* 354–364.

Flor, H., Kerns, R. D., & Turk, D. C. (1987). The role of spouse reinforcement, perceived pain, and activity levels of chronic pain patients. *Journal of Psychosomatic Research, 31,* 251–259.

Fordyce, W. E. (1976). *Behavioral methods in chronic pain and illness.* St. Louis: Mosby.

Gaupp, L. A., Flinn, D. W., & Weddige, R. L. (1989). Adjunctive treatment techniques. In C. D. Tollison (Ed.),

*Handbook of chronic pain management* (pp. 174–196). Baltimore: Williams & Wilkins.

Gentry, W. D., & Bernal, G. A. A. (1977). Chronic pain. In R. Williams & W. D. Gentry (Eds.), *Behavioral approaches to medical treatment* (pp. 173–182). Cambridge, MA: Ballinger.

Hazard, R. G., Fenwick, J. W., Kalisch, S. M., Redmond, J., Reeves, V., Reid, S., & Frymoyer, J. M. (1989). Functional restoration with behavioral support—A one-year prospective study of patients with chronic low-back pain. *Spine, 14,* 157–161.

Hilgard, E. (1969). Pain as a puzzle for psychology and physiology. *American Psychologist, 24,* 103–113.

Holroyd, K. A., Andrasik, F., & Westbrook, T. (1977). Cognitive control of tension headache. *Cognitive Therapy and Research, 1,* 121–134.

Holzman, A. D., & Turk, D. C. (Eds.) (1986). *Pain management: A handbook of psychological treatment approaches.* Elmsford, NY: Pergamon Press.

Holzman, A. D., Turk, D. C., & Kerns, R. D. (1986). The cognitive-behavioral approach to the management of chronic pain. In A. D. Holzman & D. C. Turk (Eds.), *Pain management: A handbook of psychological treatment approaches.* (pp. 31–50). Elmsford, NY: Pergamon Press.

Jamner, L. D., & Tursky, B. (1987). Syndrome-specific descriptor profiling: A psychophysiological and psychophysical approach. *Health Psychology, 6,* 417–430.

Kanfer, F. H., & Goldstein, A. P. (Eds.). (1986). *Helping people change: A textbook of methods.* Elmsford, NY: Pergamon Press.

Karoly, P., & Jensen, M. P. (1987). *Multimethod assessment of chronic pain.* Elmsford, NY: Pergamon Press.

Keefe, F. J., & Block, A. R. (1982). Development of an observation method for assessing pain behavior in chronic low back pain patients. *Behavior Therapy, 13,* 365–375.

Keefe, F. J., Wilkins, R. H., & Cook, W. A. (1984). Direct observation of pain behavior in low back pain patients during physical examination. *Pain, 20,* 59–68.

Keefe, F. J., & Williams, D. A. (1989). New directions in pain assessment and treatment. *Clinical Psychology Review, 9,* 549–568.

Keeley, S. M., Shemberg, K. M., & Carbonell, J. (1976). Operant clinical intervention: Behavior management or beyond? Where are the data? *Behavior Therapy, 7,* 292–305.

Kerns, R. D., Turk, D. C., & Rudy, T. E. (1985). The West Haven–Yale Multidimensional Pain Inventory (WHYMPI). *Pain, 23,* 345–356.

Kopel, S., & Arkowitz, H. (1975). The role of attribution and self-perception in behavior change. *Genetic Psychology Monographs, 92,* 175–212.

Kotarba, J. A. (1983). *Chronic pain: Its social dimensions.* Beverly Hills, CA: Sage Publications.

Lazarus, R. S., & Folkman, S. (1984). *Stress, appraisal, and coping.* New York: Springer-Verlag.

Lenthem, J., Slade, P. O., Troup, J. P. G., & Bentley, G. (1983). Outline of a fear-avoidance model of exaggerated pain perception. *Behaviour Research and Therapy, 21,* 401–408.

Linton, S. J. (1986). Behavioral remediation of chronic pain: A status report. *Pain, 24,* 289–294.

Linton, S. J., Melin, L., & Gotestam, K. G. (1985). Behavioral analysis of chronic pain and its management. In M. Hersen, R. Eisler, & P. Miller (Eds.), *Progress in behavior modification* (Vol. 7, pp. 1–38). New York: Academic Press.

Loeser, J. D. (1980). Low back pain. In J. J. Bonica (Ed.), *Research publications: Association for research on nervous and mental disease* (Vol. 58, pp. 363–377). New York: Raven Press.

Long, D., & Hagfors, N. (1975). Electric stimulation in the nervous system: The current status of electrical stimulation of the nervous system for relief of pain. *Pain, 1,* 109–123.

Marlatt, G. A., & Gordon, J. R. (1985). *Relapse prevention: Maintenance strategies in the treatment of addictive behaviors.* New York: Guilford Press.

Meichenbaum, D., & Turk, D. C. (1987). *Facilitating treatment adherence: A practitioner's guidebook.* New York: Plenum Press.

Melzack, R. (1986). Neurophysiological foundations of pain. In R. A. Sternbach (Ed.), *The psychology of pain,* 2nd ed. New York: Raven Press.

Melzack, R., & Casey, K. L. (1968). Sensory, motivational, and central control determinants of pain: A new conceptual model. In D. Kenshalo (Ed.), *The skin senses* (pp. 423–443). Springfield, IL: Thomas.

Melzack, R., & Wall, P. D. (1965). Pain mechanisms: A new theory. *Science, 150,* 971–979.

Melzack, R., & Wall, P. D. (1983). *The challenge of pain.* New York: Basic Books.

Miller, S. M. (1981). Controllability and human stress: Method, evidence, and theory. *Behaviour Research and Therapy, 17,* 287–304.

Moore, J. E., & Chaney, E. F. (1985). Outpatient group treatment of chronic pain: Effects of spouse involvement. *Journal of Consulting and Clinical Psychology, 53,* 326–334.

Mowrer, O. H. (1960). *Learning theory and behavior.* New York: Wiley.

Nathan, P. W. (1976). The gate control theory of pain: A critical review. *Brain, 99,* 123–158.

Nerenz, D. R., & Leventhal, H. (1983). Self-regulation theory in chronic illness. In T. Burish & L. A. Bradley (Eds.), *Coping with chronic illness* (pp. 13–37). Orlando, FL: Academic Press.

Nisbett, R., & Ross, L. (1980). *Human inference: Strategies and shortcomings of social judgment.* Englewood Cliffs, NJ: Prentice-Hall.

O'Leary, A., Shoor, S., Lorig, K., & Holman, H. R. (1988). A cognitive-behavioral treatment for rheumatoid arthritis. *Health Psychology, 7,* 527–544.

Osterweis, M., Mechanic, D., & Kleinman, A. (1987). *Pain and disability: Clinical, behavioral, and public policy perspectives.* New York: National Academy Press.

Parker, J. C., Frank, R. G., Beck, N. C., Smarr, K. L., Buescher, K., Phillips, L. R., Smith, E. I., Anderson, S. K., & Walker, S. E. (1988). Pain management in rheumatoid arthritis patients—A cognitive-behavioral approach. *Arthritis and Rheumatism 31,* 593–601.

Peck, C. J., Fordyce, W. E., & Black, R. G. (1978). The effect of the pendency of claims for compensation upon behavior indicative of pain. *Washington Law Review, 53,* 251–278.

Pennebaker, J. W., & Epstein, D. (1983). Implicit psychophysiology: Effects of common beliefs and idiosyncratic physiological responses on symptom reporting. *Journal of Personality, 52,* 468–496.

Philips, H. C. (1987). Avoidance behavior in headache sufferers. *Behaviour Research and Therapy, 25,* 273–279.

Price, D. (1987). *Neural and psychological mechanisms in pain.* New York: Raven Press.

Rachlin, H. (1985). Pain and behavior. *Behavioral and Brain Sciences, 8,* 43–83.

Rachman, S., & Lopatka, C. (1988). Accurate and inaccurate predictions of pain. *Behaviour Research and Therapy, 26,* 291–296.

Richards, J. S., Nepomuceno, C., Riles, M., & Suer, Z. (1982). Assessing pain behavior: UAB Pain Behavior Scale. *Pain, 14,* 393–398.

Rimm, D. C., & Litvak, S. B. (1969). Self-verbalization and emotional arousal. *Journal of Abnormal Psychology, 74,* 181–187.

Rudy, T. E. (1990). Psychophysiological assessment in chronic orofacial pain. *Anesthesia Progress, 37,* 82–87.

Rudy, T. E., Turk, D. C., Brena, S. F., Stieg, R. L., & Brody, M. C. (1990). Quantification of biomedical findings of chronic pain patients: Development of an index of pathology. *Pain, 42,* 167–182.

Schmidt, A. J. M., Gierlings, R. E. H., & Peters, M. L. (1989). Environment and interoceptive influences on chronic low back pain behavior. *Pain, 38,* 137–143.

Smith, T. W., Follick, M. J., Ahern, D. K., & Adams, A. (1986). Cognitive distortion and disability in chronic low back pain. *Cognitive Therapy and Research, 10,* 201–210.

Taylor, H., & Curran, N. M. (1985). *The Nuprin pain report.* New York: Louis Harris and Associates.

Thompson, S. C. (1981). Will it hurt less if I can control it? A complex answer to a simple question. *Psychological Bulletin, 90,* 89–101.

Turk, D. C. (in press). Evaluation of pain and dysfunction. *Journal of Disability.*

Turk, D. C., & Flor, H. (1984). Etiological theories and treatments for chronic back pain: II. Psychological factors. *Pain, 19,* 209–233.

Turk, D. C., & Holzman, A. D. (1986). Commonalities among psychological approaches in the treatment of chronic pain: Specifying the metaconstructs. In A. D. Holzman & D. C. Turk (Eds.), *Pain management: A handbook of psychological treatment approaches* (pp. 257–268). Elmsford, NY: Pergamon Press.

Turk, D. C., Holzman, A. D., & Kerns, R. D. (1985). Chronic pain. In K. A. Holroyd & T. L. Creer (Eds.), *Chronic disease: A handbook of self-management approaches.* New York: Academic Press.

Turk, D. C., & Meichenbaum, D. (1989). A cognitive-behavioural approach to pain management. In P. D. Wall & R. Melzack (Eds.), *Textbook of pain,* 2nd ed. London: Churchill Livingstone.

Turk, D. C., Meichenbaum, D., & Genest, M. (1983). *Pain and behavioral medicine: A cognitive-behavioral perspective.* New York: Guilford Press.

Turk, D. C., & Rudy, T. E. (1986). Assessment of cognitive factors in chronic pain: A worthwhile enterprise? *Journal of Consulting and Clinical Psychology, 54,* 760–768.

Turk, D. C., & Rudy, T. E. (1987). Assessment of chronic pain patients: Toward a multiaxial system. *Behaviour Research and Therapy, 25,* 237–249.

Turk, D. C., & Rudy, T. E. (1988). Toward an empirically derived taxonomy of chronic pain patients: Integration of psychological assessment data. *Journal of Consulting and Clinical Psychology, 56,* 233–238.

Turk, D. C., & Rudy, T. E. (1989). A cognitive-behavioral perspective on chronic pain: Beyond the scale and syringe. In C. D. Tollison (Ed.), *Handbook of chronic pain management* (pp. 222–236). Baltimore: Williams & Wilkins.

Turk, D. C., & Rudy, T. E. (in press). Neglected topics in the treatment of chronic pain patients—Relapse, noncompliance, and adherence enhancement. *Pain.*

Turk, D. C., & Stieg, R. L. (1987). Chronic pain: The necessity of interdisciplinary communication. *The Clinical Journal of Pain, 3,* 163–167.

Turner, J. A., & Romano, J. M. (1984). Evaluating psychologic interventions for chronic pain: Issues and recent developments. In C. Benedetti, C. R. Chapman, & G. Moricca (Eds.), *Advances in pain research and therapy* (Vol. 7, pp. 123–130). New York: Raven Press.

Turner, J. A., & Romano, J. M. (1988). Comparison of operant behavioral and cognitive-behavioral group treatment for chronic low back pain. *Journal of Consulting and Clinical Psychology, 56,* 261–266.

Wall, P. D. (1978). The gate control theory of pain mechanisms. *Brain, 101,* 1–18.

Wall, P. D., & Sweet, W. H. (1967). Temporary abolition of pain in man. *Science, 155,* 108–109.

# CHAPTER 17

# UTILIZING COGNITIVE STRATEGIES IN THE ACQUISITION OF EMPLOYMENT SKILLS

Frank R. Rusch
Carolyn Hughes
Philip G. Wilson

Direct instruction methods derived from the experimental analysis of behavior have been described extensively in the literature (cf. Rusch, Rose, & Greenwood, 1988). Underlying these procedures is the idea that systematic manipulation of antecedent (e.g., prompting) and consequent (e.g., differential reinforcement) events can be used to strengthen or weaken the probability that an individual will emit a particular response. These behavioral techniques have been utilized successfully to teach persons with diverse abilities to acquire employment skills in a variety of settings. For example, initial investigations of direct instruction among persons with mental retardation focused on the acquisition of behavioral chains required to complete relatively simple assembly tasks (cf. Bellamy, Peterson, & Close, 1975; Crosson, 1969; Gold, 1972, 1976). Using a task-analytic approach, Hunter and Bellamy (1976) taught people with severe mental retardation to assemble cable harnesses. This approach involved first analyzing the assembly task into its discrete components, then prompting each individual's appropriate responses in order to complete each task component in a sequential fashion.

Subsequent research targeted teaching social and vocational survival skills necessary for competitive employment (versus sheltered employment) (cf. Cuvo, Leaf, & Borakove, 1978; Rusch, 1979; Rusch, Connis, & Sowers, 1978; Schutz, Rusch, & Lamson, 1979). These investigations demonstrated that persons with disabilities could learn to engage in social behaviors and perform specific job tasks required for employment. For example, Rusch (1979) differentially reinforced rate of production and attention to task among individuals with mental retardation who were employed as bussers in a restaurant. Findings indicated that reinforcing producing and attending resulted in an increased rate of production and time spent attending to task, respectively. Reinforcing lower levels of attending to task resulted in a decreased rate of production, which illustrated the functional relation between attending and producing.

It is important to note that although settings have differed across investigations (i.e., sheltered versus competitive) over the past twenty years, training procedures utilized have been similar in that they have focused on the manipulation of environmental events by external change agents (e.g., floor supervisors or employment training specialists in sheltered workshops and competitive employment, respectively) in order to teach skill acquisition. The ability of individuals to perform valued employment skills, however, appears to require more than focusing on acquisition of specific behaviors. An employee must be capable of responding to variations in the workplace that are encountered over time (Rusch, Martin, & White, 1985). Often, these variations are not part of the instructional program and consequently may pose problems for long-term adjustment.

More recent investigations of work behavior have focused on teaching individuals to assume increasing responsibility for their own behavior. The primary reason for this shift from external to self mediation strategies most likely resulted from our realization that external change agents (i.e., floor supervisors and employment training specialists) could not control all relevant variables in an employee's work setting. Consequently, it remained entirely possible that these individuals would do well under circumstances that closely resembled training situations, but poorly when situations varied. Indeed, direct instruction methods typically introduced and monitored by employment training specialists in competitive employment have been criticized because they increase the likelihood that work behavior is performed in the presence of the specialist (Agran & Martin, 1987; Alberto, Sharpton, Briggs, & Stright, 1986). To illustrate, Rusch, Menchetti, Crouch, Riva, Morgan, and Agran (1984) demonstrated that the behavior of employees with disabilities was different when an employment training specialist was present than when the specialist was absent. Specifically, dishwashers with mental retardation spent more time working when employment training specialists were present than when these same specialists were absent from the workplace.

Because the employment specialist typically manipulates behavioral antecedents and consequences, employees may not learn to generalize their performance across other people, different tasks, and new situations (cf. Berg, Wacker, & Flynn, 1990). Martin, Mithaug, Agran, and Husch (in press) have argued that unless employment specialists implement instructional strategies that promote generalization, they cannot expect employees with disabilities to perform independently in their absence.

## GENERALIZATION AND MAINTENANCE

To address our failure to promote independent performance, two interrelated components of behavior, generalization and maintenance, have been the focus of interventions in integrated employment (Berg et al., 1990). *Generalization* of behavior is demonstrated when employees adjust their behavior to respond appropriately to novel stimuli encountered in the work environment (i.e., when they encounter new people, different tasks, and unique situations). For example, Berg and Wacker (1989) taught a woman with mental retardation who was deaf and blind to perform an envelope-stuffing task by matching tactile cues (numbers) in a book to corresponding tactile cues placed on a tray containing materials to guide her work behavior. Instruction resulted in generalization of performance to a different envelope-stuffing task and a packaging task. In addition, generalization to a novel set of tactile cues was established by substituting tactile cues in the shape of letters for the number-shaped cues used during training.

*Maintenance* of behavior refers to the continued demonstration of work behavior subsequent to instruction (i.e., over time). Sowers, Rusch, Connis, and Cummings (1980) used clocks in the workplace to teach food service employees to manage their time. Specifically, employees who could not tell time were taught to match clock faces displaying the times they should go to and from lunch and breaks. After instruction in how to use their specially designed cards with clock faces illustrating the correct times, these employees continued to match their card times to actual clocks prominently displayed in each of their work areas after direct instruction was withdrawn.

Reviews of strategies that promote generalization and maintenance of work behavior (cf. Agran & Martin, 1987; Berg et al., 1990; Gifford, Rusch, Martin, & White, 1984; Martin & Mithaug, 1986; Rusch, Morgan, Martin, Riva, & Agran, 1985) introduce alternatives to direct instructional strategies including, primarily, self-management (also referred to as self-regulation; Whitman, 1990). These alternative strategies are important because they focus on teaching employees to generate critical responses that promote generalized performance.

## SELF-MANAGEMENT PROCEDURES

Rusch, Martin, et al. (1985) reported four self-management procedures that have been shown to be effective in teaching employees to generalize or maintain their work performance: antecedent cue regulation, self-instruction, self-monitoring, and self-reinforcement. As applied in competitive employment, *antecedent cue regulation* usually consists of pictures that serve as visual cues and prompt the occurrence of a desired behavior (as in the time management example just provided). *Self-instruction* has resulted in employees using their own verbal behavior to guide their work performance. *Self-monitoring* has focused on employees observing their performance and then systematically reporting or recording that performance. *Self-reinforcement* (typically used in combination with self-monitoring) has resulted in employees reinforcing their own work behavior. For example, Connis (1979) taught food service workers with mental retardation to record their own work behavior using pictures of work tasks that needed to be performed throughout the workday. These pictures were displayed in the order in which they were to be performed. The workers were taught to observe the picture (antecedent cue), perform the task, record their completion of the specific task (self-recording), and then proceed to the next task (self-reinforcement). Self-recording in combination with pictures (antecedent cues) was shown to be effective in increasing independent task changes for all employees.

In addition to these four self-management procedures, verbal correspondence training has been used to produce generalization and maintenance (cf. Karlan & Rusch, 1982). Traditionally, *verbal correspondence* refers to the correspondence between an individual's verbal and nonverbal behavior, with emphasis upon the effects of the reinforcer, which typically is delivered contingent on accurate self-reporting. In employment contexts, correspondence training typically has been applied as a say–do paradigm in which individuals *state* that they will perform a target behavior and subsequently *perform* that behavior. For example, Rusch, Martin, Lagomarcino, and White (1987) taught a woman with mental retardation who was employed at a McDonald's to instruct herself to perform assigned job tasks. When this employee said her tasks in the sequence in which they were to be performed, she increasingly completed the tasks in the assigned order. Rusch, Martin, et al. (1987) demonstrated conclusively the relationship between saying and doing by reversing the verbal intent from a "say–do" to a "say not–do not" focus. The employee verbally mediated her own work behavior by saying that she was *not* going to complete certain tasks on designated days and then *not* performing those tasks. Reinforcement always followed work performance.

This chapter (1) reviews self-management investigations and (2) analyzes the effects of these self-management strategies on generalization across time, responses, and situations. Most important, the chapter describes a self-management model based on our critical analysis of existing research (including our own), which produces generalization and maintenance of work behavior.

## REVIEW OF SELF-MANAGEMENT INVESTIGATIONS IN INTEGRATED EMPLOYMENT

Table 17.1 lists 13 self-management studies that have been conducted in competitive employment—that is, in work that produces valued goods or services, at a minimum wage or more, in a setting that includes workers without disabilities and provides opportunities for advancement (Rusch, 1986). We make no attempt here to review similar research that has been reported in sheltered workshops. Readers are referred to Rusch and Schutz (1979) for an evaluative review of these studies. In short, internal and external validity issues would need to become a major focus of the present analysis in order to clarify the contributions of sheltered employment investigations to promoting independent performance. Studies are included in this review on the basis of four criteria: (1) The study was conducted in an integrated work setting, (2) the independent variable included a self-management procedure, (3) the subjects were individuals with mental retardation, and (4) the study was published in a refereed journal.

Selected studies were evaluated in terms of characteristics relevant to our instructional model, which included: (1) subjects, including number of and level of mental retardation; (2) settings, (3) dependent variables, (4) independent variables, and (5) any direct instructional strategies reported.

As can be seen from examining Table 17.1, subjects included in these 13 investigations were diagnosed with mild ($n = 4$), moderate ($n = 21$), and severe or profound ($n = 8$) mental retardation. A total of 33 subjects were instructed. The majority of these investigations were conducted in food service settings ($n = 9$); in addition, two studies took place in a warehouse setting, one study in a film center, one in a university vivarium, and one in hospital patient rooms. A wide variety of dependent variables have been the focus of these investigations. The majority of studies targeted variables associated with initiating, sequencing, and/or completing job tasks independently ($n = 8$). Other dependent measures included task completion, problem solving, time management, social skills performance, time on task, and accurate performance of steps constituting a larger task.

**Table 17.1.** Review of Self-Management Investigations in Competitive Employment

| STUDY | NUMBER OF SUBJECTS (LEVEL OF MENTAL RETARDATION) | SETTING | DEPENDENT VARIABLES | INDEPENDENT VARIABLES | | | | | DIRECT INSTRUCTIONAL STRATEGIES REPORTED | | |
|---|---|---|---|---|---|---|---|---|---|---|---|
| | | | | Antecedent Cue Regulation | Self-Instruction | Self-Monitoring | Self-Reinforcement | Correspondence Training | Preinstruction During Performance | Feedback During Performance | Additional Training |
| Agran et al. (1986) | 3 mild 1 moderate | Hospital patient rooms and kitchen | (a) Job task sequencing (%) (b) Task completion (%) (c) Task repetition (%) | | Yes | | | | | | Yes |
| Connis (1979) | 3 moderate 1 severe | University-operated restaurant kitchen | (a) Independent task change (%) | Yes | | Yes | | | | Yes | |
| Crouch et al. (1984) | 3 moderate | University dormitory kitchen | (a) Task duration in minutes (frequency) (b) Days in which tasks were started on time (%) | | | | | Yes | Yes | Yes | |
| Hughes & Rusch (1989) | 2 severe | Janitorial supply company warehouse | (a) Correct responses to untrained problem situations (frequency) (b) Self-instruction steps verbalized during training (frequency) (c) Correct responses to multiple examples of trained problem situations during training (frequency) | | Yes[a] | | | | | | |
| Lagomarcino & Rusch (1989) | 1 profound | Janitorial supply company warehouse | (a) Steps completed independently (frequency) | | | Yes | Yes | | Yes | Yes[b] | |

| Study | Classification | Setting | Dependent measures | | | | | | |
|---|---|---|---|---|---|---|---|---|---|
| Mank & Horner (1987) | 5 moderate 1 severe | 2 university-operated restaurants 1 commercially operated restaurant | (a) Work rate (%) | Yesc | | Yesd | Yes | Yes | Yes |
| | | | (b) Work units completed correctly (%) | | | | | | |
| | | | (c) Accuracy of self-recording | | | | | | |
| | | | (d) Minutes of instruction (frequency) | | | | | | |
| | | | (e) Trials to criterion (frequency) | | | | | | |
| | | | (f) Supervisor contacts (frequency and duration) | | | | | | |
| Rusch et al. (1988) | 1 severe | University-operated film center | (a) Appropriate requests when materials were not available (frequency) | | | Yes | Yes | Yes | Yes |
| | | | (b) Appropriate requests when materials ran out (frequency) | | | | | | |
| Rusch et al. (1987) | 1 moderate | Lobby and dining room of fast food restaurant | (a) Tasks completed independently and in sequence (%) | | | | Yes | Yes | Yes |
| | | | (b) Tasks said independently and in sequence (%) | | | | | | |
| Rusch et al. (1985) | 1 mild 1 moderate | University dormitory cafeteria | (a) On-task intervals (%) | | | Yes | | | |
| Sowers et al. (1985) | 3 moderate 1 severe | University cafeteria | (a) Independent task change (frequency) | | | Yes | Yes | Yes | |
| Sowers et al. (1980) | 3 moderate | University-operated public cafeteria | (a) Minutes early and late to work and breaks (frequency) | | | Yes | | Yese | |
| Wheeler et al. (1988) | 1 moderate | University vivarium | (a) Days clean shaven (%) | | | | | | |
| | | | (b) Following instructions correctly (%) | | | | | | |
| | | | (c) Inappropriate belches per day (mean frequency) | | | Yesf | Yes | Yes | |
| | | | (d) Occurrences discussed excessive drinking per day (mean frequency) | | | | | | |
| | | | (e) Occurrences of pouting per day (mean frequency) | | | | | | |
| | | | (f) Initiating social interactions (%) | | | | | | |
| | | | (g) Socially appropriate responses to others' greetings (%) | | | | | | |
| Wilson et al. (1987) | 1 severe | Family-owned restaurant | (a) Prompts delivered per five minutes (rate) | | | Yes | Yes | | |
| | | | (b) Steps of task analyses correct (%) | | | | | | |

aUsed in combination with teaching multiple exemplars.
bChanging criterion design implemented.
cUsed in combination with self-recruited feedback.
dCriterion setting implemented.
eInstructional feedback removed during final condition of study.
fIn combination with social skills training.

Five self-management strategies have been employed as independent variables, either singly or in combination. Self-management procedures included: (1) self-monitoring ($n = 6$), (2) antecedent cue regulation ($n = 5$), (3) self-instruction ($n = 4$), (4) correspondence training ($n = 2$), and (5) self-reinforcement ($n = 1$). The most commonly used combination of self-management procedures was antecedent cue regulation plus self-monitoring ($n = 3$). Self-monitoring plus self-reinforcement and self-instruction plus antecedent cue regulation were each used in one investigation. Self-management instruction was combined with teaching multiple exemplars in Hughes and Rusch (1989) and with social skills training in Wheeler, Bates, Marshall, and Miller (1988).

Several studies reported using direct instruction after self-management instruction to produce desired outcomes. Except for Wilson, Schepis, and Mason-Main (1987), performance feedback was used in all the studies utilizing self-monitoring and antecedent cue regulation (Connis, 1979; Lagomarcino & Rusch, 1989; Mank & Horner, 1987; Rusch, McKee, Chadsey-Rusch, & Renzaglia, 1988; Sowers et al., 1980; Sowers, Verdi, Bourbeau, & Sheehan, 1985; Wheeler et al., 1988). Rusch, McKee, et al. (1988) used self-instruction and antecedent cue regulation in combination with preinstruction and performance feedback. Additional external contingencies used after self-management instruction included criterion setting (Lagomarcino & Rusch, 1989; Mank & Horner, 1987) and teaching subjects to recruit performance feedback (Mank & Horner, 1987).

Self-instruction was used exclusively by Agran, Fodor-Davis, and Moore (1986) and by Rusch, Morgan, et al. (1985) to assist employees with mild mental retardation to guide their own behavior. In the Agran et al. (1986) study, however, additional training was required. Six studies included persons with severe or profound mental retardation. Only one of these studies (Hughes & Rusch, 1989) utilized self-instruction in combination with teaching multiple exemplars to produce generalized responding among individuals with severe mental retardation. Seven of the nine studies that included persons with moderate mental retardation reported using one self-management strategy to assist employees to guide their behavior. Specifically, two studies utilized self-instruction (Agran et al., 1986; Rusch, Morgan, et al., 1985), correspondence training (Crouch, Rusch, & Karlan, 1984; Rusch, Martin, et al., 1987), and self-monitoring (Mank & Horner, 1987; Wheeler et al.,

1988). Antecedent cue regulation was utilized in one study (Sowers et al., 1980). A combination of antecedent cue regulation and self-monitoring was utilized in two studies (Connis, 1979; Sowers et al., 1980).

In summary, self-instruction training has been used to assist persons diagnosed with all levels of mental retardation. Correspondence training has been applied exclusively to persons with moderate mental retardation ($n = 4$). Antecedent cue regulation and self-monitoring procedures, often used in combination, have been utilized with persons with moderate, severe, and profound mental retardation. Self-reinforcement was utilized in combination with self-monitoring in a study that included one young man with profound mental retardation (Lagomarcino & Rusch, 1989). Single self-management strategies have been applied most frequently with persons having mild or moderate mental retardation, whereas combined strategies are generally used to assist persons with severe or profound mental retardation.

Several conclusions may be drawn from this review of self-management strategy applications in competitive employment. First, self-management strategies have been used successfully by persons with all levels of mental retardation, suggesting that even persons with severe mental retardation can benefit from cognitively oriented procedures, as suggested by Rusch, Martin, et al. (1985). Table 17.1 shows that self-management strategies also have been applied to a wide variety of dependent variables, illustrating the versatility of self-management procedures in employment settings.

A combination of self-management strategies was used in 5 of 11 studies focusing on persons with moderate, severe, or profound mental retardation. The lack of component analyses makes it impossible to conclude whether such combinations were indeed necessary. Although limitations inherent in single-subject designs combined with practical considerations of conducting applied research may impede component analysis research, incorporation of existing technology such as the use of sequential withdrawals (Rusch & Kazdin, 1981) may provide useful information in the future.

Perhaps the most striking concern highlighted by Table 17.1 is that 10 of the 13 studies we reviewed included direct instruction in conjunction with self-management strategies during postintervention phases. This finding, by itself, does not pose a great problem if one accepts Bandura's (1969) suggestion that the purpose of external control procedures should be to establish internal control so that individuals can learn to control their own behavior. Except for Agran et al. (1986), however, direct instruction was not completely withdrawn in any of these 10 studies. The resultant combination of self-management and externally regulated control procedures poses both an experimental analysis question and, more important, an application dilemma. In the former case, it remains unclear to what extent self-management is responsible for controlling behavior compared to externally mediated procedures. In the latter case, reliance on externally mediated procedures does not lead to optimal worker autonomy and adaptability; that is, involvement by external change agents has been required to ensure that workers continue to utilize self-management strategies in order to maintain and generalize their behavior.

Three studies did not report use of direct instruction during postintervention phases (Hughes & Rusch, 1989; Rusch, Morgan, et al., 1985; Wilson et al., 1987). In the Rusch, Morgan, et al. (1985) study, self-instruction was used by two women with mild and moderate mental retardation, respectively, to increase their time spent working on assigned tasks. The procedure appeared to be both efficient and effective. However, there are several limitations in interpreting these data. First, the dependent measure did not measure the quality of the employees' work. Second, there was considerable overlap in the pre- and posttreatment data series for both subjects. Third, the durability of the self-management intervention was assessed for only four to five weeks, leaving questions about the long-term effectiveness of the procedure. Finally, there was no direct evidence reported that the self-management strategy was actually being used by the workers.

Wilson et al. (1987) taught a man with severe mental retardation to use antecedent cue regulation and self-monitoring to perform four restaurant tasks and to decrease his dependence on external prompting. The procedures were successful in teaching the employee to perform the targeted tasks. Not surprisingly, the level of external assistance decreased concomitantly. In this study, antecedent cues and self-monitoring were withdrawn using a sequential-withdrawal strategy (Rusch & Kazdin, 1981) and performance maintained within acceptable levels during a 16-month follow-up period.

Hughes and Rusch (1989) taught two persons with severe mental retardation, employed by a janitorial supply company, to use self-instruction in combination with teaching multiple exemplars to solve work-related problems. Using the combined strategy (i.e., self-instruction and multiple exemplars), the employees learned to respond correctly to five diverse problem situations that they were likely to encounter during their workday. Generalized use of the training components (i.e., self-instruction steps verbalized and correct responses to multiple examples of problem situations) was observed, as was generalized responding to five untrained problem situations. These findings are important because they suggest that persons with severe mental retardation can learn to use self-instructional statements to solve unique problems when these statements are learned with multiple examples.

## Effects of Self-Management Strategies on Generalization

Table 17.2 again lists the 13 self-management studies that have been conducted in competitive employment (see discussion of Table 17.1 for description). These studies were evaluated in terms of the effects of various self-management strategies on generalization across responses (tasks), situations, and over time. In addition, Table 17.2 lists direct instructional strategies reported.

In relation to employment training, generalization may be said to have occurred when acceptable performance of behaviors acquired under training conditions is demonstrated under actual work conditions (in which no training or substantially reduced amounts of training occurs). Stokes and Baer (1977) state that generalization takes place when desired behavior occurs within "non-training conditions (i.e., across subjects, settings, people, behaviors, and/or time) without scheduling of the same events in those conditions as had been scheduled in the training conditions. Thus, generalization may be claimed when no extra training manipulations are needed for extra training changes; or may be claimed when some extra manipulations are necessary, but their cost or extent is clearly less than that of the direct intervention" (p. 350).

In the past two decades, generalization has been widely recognized as the ultimate goal of educative and habilitative programming (Bandura, 1969; Barrett, 1977; Rusch & Schutz, 1981). Classifications of generalization ranging in complexity from two elements (Kazdin, 1975) to 16 elements (Drabman, Hammer, & Rosenbaum, 1979) have been proposed. For purposes of our analysis we have adopted the classification scheme proposed by O'Leary and

CHAPTER 17

**Table 17.2.**  Effects of Self-Management Strategies on Generalization Across Responses, Time, and Situations

| | ACROSS RESPONSES | ACROSS TIME | ACROSS SITUATIONS | DIRECT INSTRUCTIONAL STRATEGIES REPORTED |
|---|---|---|---|---|
| Agran et al. (1986) | Not assessed | Yes, for 31, 29, 20, and 4 consecutive sessions across subjects | Yes, job-task sequencing, generalized from training to work situations. | Yes, additional training for one subject and verbal prompts to self-instruct for three subjects required to maintain performance. |
| Connis (1979) | Not assessed | Yes, for up to 7 weeks | Yes, independent task changes generalized from training to work situation. | Yes, instructional feedback required to maintain performance. |
| Crouch et al. (1984) | Not assessed | Not assessed | Not assessed | Yes, preinstruction and feedback provided during performance. |
| Hughes & Rusch (1989) | Yes, correct responses generalized from trained to untrained problem situations. | Yes, for 6 months | Yes, correct responses across trained problem situations generalized from training to work situation. | No |
| Lagomarcino & Rusch (1989) | Not assessed | Yes, for approximately 50 days | Yes, steps completed independently generalized from training to work situation. | Yes, preinstruction and criterion setting required to maintain performance. |
| Mank & Horner (1987) | Not assessed | Yes, for approximately 10 weeks | Yes, work rate and accuracy generalized from training to work situation. | Yes, additional training for two subjects and criterion setting for all subjects required to maintain performance. |
| Rusch, McKee et al. (1988) | No, training appropriate requests when materials missing did not generalize to appropriate requests when not enough materials. | Not assessed, training lessened in intensity but never completely eliminated. | Yes, appropriate requests generalized from training to work situation. | Yes, preinstruction combined with instructional feedback during performance systematically lessened. |
| Rusch et al. (1987) | Not assessed | Not assessed | Not assessed | Yes preinstruction and feedback provided during performance. |
| Rusch, Morgan et al. (1985) | Not assessed | Yes, for 24 and 18 sessions across subjects | Yes, percentage of time spent working generalized from training to work situation. | No |
| Sowers et al. (1985) | Yes, use of picture cues generalized to novel pictures | Yes, for 2 of 4 subjects for 20 days | Yes, independent task changes generalized from training to work situation. | Yes, feedback given during performance |
| Sowers et al. (1980) | Not assessed | Yes, for 19, 33, and 50 sessions across subjects | Yes, on-time behavior generalized from training to work situation. | Yes, feedback provided during performance but removed during final condition of study. |

| | ACROSS RESPONSES | ACROSS TIME | ACROSS SITUATIONS | DIRECT INSTRUCTIONAL STRATEGIES REPORTED |
|---|---|---|---|---|
| Wheeler et al. (1988) | Not assessed | Yes, for 1–9 weeks across behaviors | Yes, trained behaviors generalized from training to work situation. | Yes, feedback provided during performance. |
| Wilson et al. (1987) | Not assessed | Yes, for 16 months | Yes, steps performed correctly generalized from training to work situation. | No |

O'Leary (1976), who conceptualized generalization composed of three basic elements: (1) generalization across time, (2) generalization across responses, and (3) generalization across situations. *Generalization across time* occurs when the individual continues to demonstrate acceptable performance of the target response after achieving acquisition. Generalization across time is often described as response maintenance. *Generalization across responses* occurs when, after acquisition of the target response, the worker performs a response not specifically trained with minimal or no additional training. *Generalization across situations* occurs when an individual trained to perform a response under one set of environmental variables (e.g., settings, persons present, stimuli) performs that response under environmental conditions that differ in regard to one of several of the environmental variables present during training.

Generalization across time was reported in 10 of the 13 studies we analyzed. Seven of those 10 studies used additional direct instructional procedures. Therefore, the effect of self-management on generalization across time is unclear. Only Hughes and Rusch (1989), Rusch, Morgan, et al. (1985), and Wilson et al. (1987) produced generalization across time without incorporating direct instruction procedures during performance. In the Wilson et al. (1987) study, the self-management package was withdrawn after training. Therefore, the role that self-management may have played in the observed generalization across time is not clear. Although generalization across time was assessed in the majority of studies we analyzed, only two studies, Hughes and Rusch (1989) and Wilson et al. (1987) conducted assessments of generalization for at least six months.

Assessment of generalization across responses was reported in only four of the studies we analyzed (Agran et al., 1986, Hughes & Rusch, 1989; Rusch, McKee, et al., 1988; Sowers et al., 1985). Except for Hughes and Rusch (1989), additional direct instructional strategies were used in combination with self-

management procedures. Agran et al. (1986) and Hughes and Rusch (1989) reported that subjects in their respective studies were able to generalize responding across untrained behaviors while utilizing self-management strategies. Rusch, McKee, et al. (1988) trained a worker to make appropriate requests when materials were missing. Subsequently, the same worker was assessed to determine if generalization to making appropriate requests when there were not enough materials would occur without additional training. Rusch, McKee, et al. (1988) reported that, in their study, generalization across responses did not occur without additional training. Sowers et al. (1985) reported that use of picture cues by subjects generalized to novel pictures. However, feedback was given during performance, which makes it difficult to assess the role self-management may have played in the generalization across responses.

Eleven of the 13 studies we analyzed reported assessment of generalization across situations. In each case, generalization from training to work (performance) was reported. All but three studies reported utilizing additional direct instructional strategies in combination with self-management strategies (Hughes & Rusch, 1989; Rusch, Morgan, et al., 1985; Wilson et al., 1987). None of the authors provided detailed descriptions of the difference(s) between training and work (performance) situations.

In summary, self-management strategies have resulted in both acquisition of employment skills and generalization across time, responses, and situations by workers with mental retardation. In the studies we analyzed, generalization across time was assessed in 10 studies, generalization across responses was assessed in 4 studies, and generalization across situations was assessed in 11 studies. Generalization across time and responses was assessed in three investigations (Agran et al., 1986; Hughes & Rusch, 1989; Sowers et al., 1985). Except for Hughes and Rusch (1989), additional direct instruction procedures were implemented in combination with self-management strategies in these studies. Ten studies reported assessment of generalization across time and situations (Agran et al., 1986; Connis, 1979; Hughes & Rusch, 1989; Lagomarcino & Rusch, 1989; Mank & Horner, 1987; Rusch, Morgan, et al., 1985; Sowers et al., 1980, 1985; Wheeler et al., 1988; Wilson et al., 1987). However, except for Hughes and Rusch (1989), Rusch, Morgan, et al. (1985), and Wilson et al. (1987), additional direct instruction procedures were utilized. Generalization across responses and situations was assessed in four studies (Agran et al., 1986; Hughes & Rusch, 1989; Rusch, McKee, et al., 1988; Sowers et al., 1985). Again, only Hughes and Rusch (1989) did not utilize additional direct instructional procedures in combination with self-management strategies. Finally, three studies assessed generalization across time, responses, and situations (Agran et al., 1986; Hughes & Rusch, 1989; Sowers et al., 1980). Only Hughes and Rusch (1989) assessed the effects of self-management strategies on all three types of generalization without utilizing additional direct instructional procedures.

As can be seen from Table 17.2, only Hughes and Rusch (1989) produced generalization across time, responses, and situations without direct instruction. On the basis of the limited demonstration of generalization across studies apparent from our analysis, we have concluded that multiple-component instructional strategies must be developed to facilitate generalization across novel stimuli. Consequently, we recommend that a problem-solving strategy be developed whereby employees with disabilities respond to novel situations in their work environment by approaching these novel situations utilizing a cognitive-processing procedure.

Carnine (1990) suggested that the process of solving a problem requires finding the "sameness" across situations or stimulus conditions. Likewise, Skinner (1953) suggested that the difficulty of "solving a problem" relates to the availability of the response that constitutes the solution. That is, the diversity or novelty of the problem-solving response in relation to previous responses made by an individual makes solving the problem more "difficult." A problem-solving strategy must allow an individual to find the similarity in a response required by a novel situation to past responses made by that individual in order to facilitate generalization. As a result of our understanding of self-management strategies that rely on the individual's ability to mediate problem situations, we recommend that these self-management procedures be combined with our emerging understanding of how to utilize examples representative of situations that require the individual to act independently.

## PROBLEM-SOLVING MODEL

On the basis of the empirical literature and our own research program, we have developed a model for teaching problem solving that combines multiple strategies that facilitate generalization. We propose a six-step cognitive-processing model for teaching problem solving to employees with diverse abilities that utilizes traditional self-instruction combined with multiple exemplars. The *multiple-exemplar* approach requires teaching more than one example of a desired response in order to produce a generalized response. For example, Horner, Jones, and Williams (1985) taught three individuals with mental retardation to cross streets independently. Initially, the individuals were taught to cross eight different types of intersections. After the initial training condition, ongoing training and assessment were conducted, during which generalization occurred across 20 untrained street intersections. Generalization was facilitated by utilizing multiple examples (exemplars) of a similar situation (i.e., intersections).

When applying *self-instruction,* individuals typically are taught to guide their performance using verbal prompts after being instructed by an external change agent to perform target behaviors. For example, Rusch, Morgan, et al. (1985) taught two women with mental retardation who served food in a cafeteria to increase their time spent working by verbalizing statements when performing their assigned tasks (i.e., wiping counters, checking supplies, restocking supplies). Verbal statements included, for example: (1) "What does the supervisor want me to do?" (identifying the problem); (2) "I am supposed to wipe the counter, then check the supplies, then restock the supplies" (stating the response); (3) "O.K., I need to wipe the counter" (guiding the response); and (4) I did that right; I am doing what I'm supposed to" (self-evaluating and self-reinforcing). As a result of self-instructing, both employees in the Rusch, Morgan, et al. (1985) study increased their time spent working while serving dinner and lunch, often exceeding the performance of their co-workers.

Figure 17.1 displays the major components of our cognitive-processing model. As can be seen, the model comprises the following steps (see Figure 17.1): (1) select an array of examples (responses) an individual is likely to be required to perform in an

**Figure 17.1.** Model for teaching self-instruction utilizing multiple exemplars.

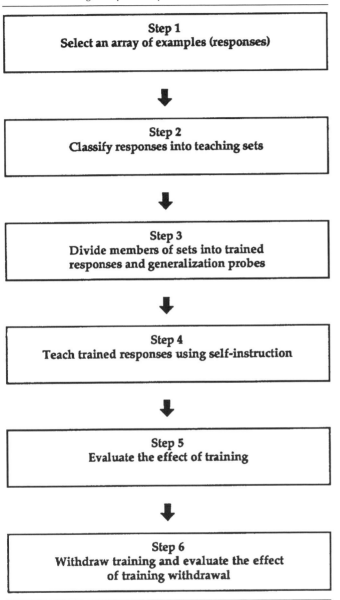

**Step 1**
**Select an array of examples (responses)**

**Step 2**
**Classify responses into teaching sets**

**Step 3**
**Divide members of sets into trained responses and generalization probes**

**Step 4**
**Teach trained responses using self-instruction**

**Step 5**
**Evaluate the effect of training**

**Step 6**
**Withdraw training and evaluate the effect of training withdrawal**

environment (step 1); (2) classify responses into teaching sets based upon a functional analysis (step 2); (3) divide members of each set into responses that will serve as training examples and those that will serve as generalization probes (step 3); (4) teach trained examples using self-instruction (step 4); (5) evaluate the effects of training on trained and untrained examples (i.e., generalization probes) as well as self-instructional statements verbalized (step 5); and (6) withdraw training based on performance criteria while evaluating the effect of withdrawal (step 6). This section analyzes the model by relating the processes and outcomes of each step to producing generalization and provides examples that demonstrate how each step of the model is implemented. Table 17.3 presents an analysis of the components of each of the six steps of the model.

## Step 1: Select an Array of Examples

Working in competitive employment requires that individuals with mental retardation respond independently to varying stimulus conditions in their environment. In order to determine the range (typically referred to as the *universe*) of conditions that an individual is likely to encounter in a particular work setting, the setting must be surveyed (Horner, Sprague, & Wilcox, 1982). Because it is impractical to attempt to teach singular responses to each of the myriad stimuli in an environment, representative examples of the universe of stimulus conditions and required responses are selected as teaching examples, based on setting surveys.

Hughes and Rusch (1989) asked a work supervisor in a company that packaged liquid soap to identify work-related problem situations that supported employees were likely to encounter throughout the workday, as well as correct responses to these problems. The work supervisor had observed that employees occasionally ran out of materials when working and that employees' work stations sometimes were blocked by obstacles. The supervisor reported that employees were expected to respond independently to these situations by obtaining required materials or removing obstacles; that is, they were to "solve the problems themselves." The array of problem situations identified by the supervisor (the survey) served as the "universe" of stimulus conditions to which employees were expected to respond. On the basis of the supervisor's survey of the work setting, 10 examples representative of the universe of identified responses then were selected to serve as teaching examples.

## Step 2: Classify Responses into Teaching Sets

After teaching several examples of related responses, one would expect generalized responding to occur across functionally related responses (Engelmann & Carnine, 1982; Haring & Laitinen, in press). For example, after teaching someone to turn on a fan and a lamp by plugging them in, you would expect the same individual to plug in a radio to turn it on, too (i.e., to generalize). Therefore, when generalized responding is the goal of the instruction, an instructional program should focus on teaching similar responses under similar stimulus conditions concurrently rather than in isolation.

In order to determine relatedness among responses (i.e., to classify responses into teaching sets), a functional analysis should be conducted to determine the response operations required to produce an effect on the environment (Haring & Laitinen, in press). Related responses then should be classified into teaching sets to enhance skill acquisition and generalized responding across functionally related skills. For example, Rusch, Morgan, et al. (1985) observed food service employees who worked in a university cafeteria to determine the range of task-related responses required throughout the workday. Observation revealed that specific responsibilities associated with working on the food-serving line included keeping the counter and other surfaces clean; checking supplies of plates, silverware, and glasses; replenishing condiments; and restocking bread, butter, and desserts. On the basis of the response requirements needed to perform these tasks, Rusch, Morgan, et al. (1985) classified responses into three teaching sets: wiping surfaces, checking supplies, and restocking supplies. The employees then were taught to self-instruct when performing responses representative of each of these teaching sets. Following training, the percentage of time spent working was found to increase across all assigned tasks throughout the workday.

## Step 3: Divide Members of Sets into Trained Responses and Generalization Probes

Because the goal of our model is to produce generalization, we must determine if similar responses that are acquired under similar stimulus conditions will occur under dissimilar stimulus conditions—that is, in the presence of nontrained stimuli. In order to provide an assessment of an individual's generalized responding across related but novel situations not encountered during training, members of teaching sets should be divided equally and assigned at random either to a group of responses to be trained or to a group of responses to serve as generalization probes (untrained) (Haring & Laitinen, in press). After teaching several trained responses, we expect individuals to respond correctly to generalization probes (i.e., untrained but similar stimuli).

**Table 17.3.** Analysis of Model for Teaching Generalized Problem Solving

| PROCESS | OUTCOME |
|---|---|
| *Step 1: Select examples.* | Teaching examples selected. |
| 1. Survey setting. | |
| 2. Determine range (universe) of stimulus conditions that individual is likely to encounter. | |
| 3. Determine correct responses to stimulus conditions. | |
| 4. Select representative examples from among available stimulus control. | |
| *Step 2: Classify examples into teaching sets.* | Teaching examples categorized in relation to response requirements. |
| 1. Conduct functional analysis of response requirements. | |
| 2. Determine relatedness among responses (common operations) based on functional analysis. | |
| 3. Classify related responses into teaching sets based on common operations. | |
| *Step 3: Divide members of sets into training and generalization probes.* | 1. Set of all possible responses identified to be utilized during training. |
| | 2. Set of examples requiring similar responses identified to test generalization |
| 1. Divide members of each testing set equally. | |
| 2. Assign members to group of responses to be trained or to serve as generalization probes (assignment should be random). | |
| *Step 4: Teach individual to self-instruct.* | Problem-solving strategy taught. |
| 1. Use training sequence: | |
| a. Teacher provides rationale for training and tells student to respond as if in response to instructional demands. | Common stimuli introduced. |
| b. Teacher models correct responses while self-instructing aloud, using multiple examples. | 1. Multiple examplars taught. 2. Generalization mediated. 3. Modeling provided. |
| c. Individual performs same responses while teacher instruct aloud. | 1. Opportunities for practice provided. 2. Modeling provided. |
| d. Individual performs same responses while self-instructing aloud. | 1. Opportunities for practice provided. 2. Generalization mediated. |
| e. Teacher provides corrective feedback and/or prompting if individual does not perform approximation of correct verbal or motor responses. | 1. Modeling provided. 2. Opportunities for practice provided. |
| f. Teacher reminds individual to self-instruct when presented with a problem situation. | Generalization mediated. |
| 2. Teach self-instruction statements: | |
| a. State problem (e.g., ''No spray''). | |
| b. State generic problem-solving response (e.g., ''Got to fix it''). | |
| c. State specific problem-solving response (e.g., ''Get more''). | |
| d. Self-report (e.g., ''Fixed it''). | |
| e. Self-reinforce (e.g., ''Good''). | |

*Continued*

Table 17.3 continued

| PROCESS | OUTCOME |
|---|---|
| *Step 4 continued* | |
| 3. Adjust training time: | |
|    a. Determine student disability level. | |
|    b. Adjust number and length of instructional sessions to student disability level. | |
| *Step 5: Evaluate effect of training* | Effect of training evaluated. |
| 1. Take repeated measures of self-instruction steps verbalized and responses to multiple exemplars made during training. | Point at which problem-solving strategy acquired isolated. |
| 2. Take repeated measures of self-instruction steps verbalized and responses to multiple exemplars made during performance (probe self-instructing if student does not verbalize overly). | Generalized use of problem-solving strategy across situations assessed. |
| 3. Take repeated measures of responses to untrained problems (generalization probes). | Generalized use of problem-solving strategy across tasks assessed. |
| 4. Take repeated measures of responses to problems presented by different teachers. | Generalized use of problem-solving strategy across people assessed. |
| *Step 6: Withdraw training and evaluate the effect of training withdrawal.* | Effect of training withdrawal on continued use of problem-solving strategy assessed (generalized over time). |
| 1. Establish range of acceptable behavior within setting. | |
| 2. Determine performance criteria. | |
| 3. When student is performing at criterion level, assess generalization over time (response maintenance of problem-solving strategy) using a partial-withdrawal of training. | |

As mentioned before, Hughes and Rusch (1989) selected 10 problem situations employees were likely to encounter throughout the workday. Responses to these situations then were assigned to one of three functionally related teaching sets, including plugging in appliances, finding missing items, and moving obstacles. Members of each set then were randomly assigned either to a group of five trained responses or five generalization probes (see Table 17.4). For example, because Problem Situation 1 (paper towel in drain of sink) and Problem Situation 2 (five pieces of trash on table) both required moving an obstacle, these two responses were assigned to different groups. As indicated in Table 17.4, trained responses for one employee (Myra) served as generalization probes for the other employee (Les). Conversely, trained responses for Les served as generalization probes for Myra.

Observation of the employees' performance during baseline revealed that Myra made no correct responses to either trained or untrained problem situations, and Les made only 4 correct responses out of a

total of 50 problem presentations (see the two upper panels of Figure 17.2). Correct responses to trained and untrained problems continued to be assessed after self-instruction training was introduced with the group of trained responses. Data indicated that self-instruction with multiple exemplars resulted in increased correct responding to trained problem situations for both employees, as well as increased generalized responding to untrained problems (generalization probes). Additionally, correct responding to both trained and untrained problems maintained for six months after daily, repeated observation and recording (see follow-up data, Figure 17.2).

## Step 4: Teach Trained Responses Using Self-Instruction

Teaching self-instruction in combination with multiple exemplars has been shown to produce generalized problem solving without the need for direct instruction. The success of procedures used to teach self-instruction appears to relate to three factors.

**Table 17.4.** Work-Related Problem Situations and Correct Responses

| PROBLEM SITUATION | INSTRUCTION | CORRECT RESPONSE |
|---|---|---|
| 1. Paper towel is in drain of sink; sink is full of water.[a] | Instructed by trainer to wring out rag in sink. | Remove paper towel; drain sink. (Move obstacle) |
| 2. 5 pieces of trash are on table[b] | Instructed by trainer to go to table to begin work. | Throw trash in basket located within 2 m of table. (Move obstacle) |
| 3. Radio is unplugged. | Instructed by trainer to turn on radio. | Plug in radio and turn on. (Plug in appliance) |
| 4. Box is on table next to soap dispensing machine. | Instructed by trainer to put tray on table. | Put box in proper place or seek assistance. (Move obstacle) |
| 5. Bundle is on table where work is to be conducted. | Instructed by trainer to begin working. | Put bundle in proper place. (Move obstacle) |
| 6. Tape dispenser is empty. | Instructed by trainer to get tape dispenser. | Find tape and fill tape dispenser. (Find missing item) |
| 7. Cardboard pad is in box with chip boards. | Instructed by trainer to get more chip boards. | Find pad and put in proper place. (Find missing item) |
| 8. Chair is in center of work room. | Instructed by trainer to hang rag by sink. | Put chair next to table. (Move obstacle) |
| 9. Puddle of soap is on table where work is to be conducted. | Instructed by trainer to begin working. | Wipe up soap with rag. (Move obstacle) |
| 10. Box containing hair nets is in wrong place. | Instructed by trainer to get hair net. | Find box and put in proper place. (Find missing item) |

[a]Trained responses for Myra; generalization probes for Les: 1, 3, 5, 7, 9.

[b]Trained responses for Les; generalization probes for Myra: 2, 4, 6, 8, 10.

*Source:* "Teaching Supported Employees with Severe Mental Retardation to Solve Problems" by C. Hughes and F. R. Rusch, 1989, *Journal of Applied Behavior Analysis,* p. 367. Adapted by permission.

These factors include: (1) training sequence used, (2) self-instruction statements taught, and (3) length of training time. Hughes and Rusch (1989) and Rusch, Morgan, et al. (1985) taught self-instruction using a variation of Meichenbaum and Goodman's (1971) training sequence (see Table 17.5).

Additionally, Hughes and Rusch (1989) taught two supported employees to verbalize the following statements in response to five problem situations: (1) stating the problem ("No soap"); (2) stating the response (e.g., "Find it"); (3) self-evaluating (e.g., "Fixed it"); and (4) self-reinforcing (e.g., "Good"). Myra and Les, the two employees, verbalized 92% and 81% of the self-instruction statements across all training sessions, respectively. The lower two panels of Figure 17.2 display the generalized use of the four trained self-instructional statements during work performance. Few verbalizations of self-instructions occurred for the employees during either baseline or self-instruction with multiple-exemplar training until requests for verbalizations were made by an experimenter during Session 24 for Myra and Session 29 for Les. When asked, "What are you doing?" after

the initiation of a correct response, the frequency of verbalization of all four self-instruction steps corresponded, with few exceptions, to frequency of correct responses for both Myra and Les. On only two occasions out of 85 did Myra fail to verbalize a self-reinforcement statement. Les failed to state the correct response twice and to self-evaluate three times out of 60 opportunities. On all other occasions, frequency of self-instruction steps corresponded identically to frequency of correct responses. This correspondence maintained throughout the 6 months of follow-up assessment. An important feature of the current model, based on the Hughes and Rusch study, is to request verbal verification of cognitive statements in order to determine if the employee is actually using the self-instructional statements (see later for elaboration).

Adjusting length of training time to subject disability level in combination with teaching four self-instruction statements has produced generalization without the need for further training. For example, a minimum of 15 half-hour training sessions was needed to produce generalization with individuals

**Figure 17.2.** Frequency of correct responses to trained problems and untrained problem situations(generalization probes) and frequency of self-instruction steps verbalized during performance. Broken lines indicate data missing as a result of employee absence.

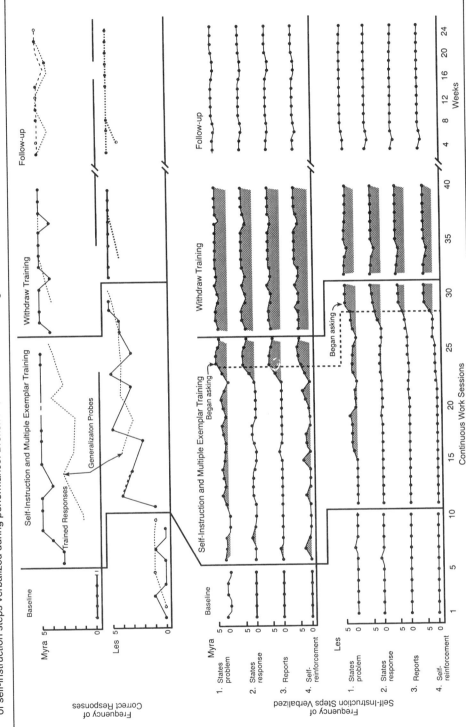

*Source:* From "Teaching Supported Employees with Severe Mental Retardation to Solve Problems" by C. Hughes and F. R. Rusch, Journal of Applied Behavior Analysis, 1989, p. 369. Reprinted by permission.

**Table 17.5.** Comparison between Current Model and Meichenbaum and Goodman's (1971) Training Sequence

| CURRENT MODEL | MEICHENBAUM AND GOODMAN (1971) | COMPARISON |
|---|---|---|
| 1. Trainer provides rationale for self-instruction training and tells subjects to respond as if in response to work demands. (Program Common Stimuli) | Trainer does not provide rationale or tell subjects to respond as if in response to work demands. | Different |
| 2. Trainer models multiple examples of tasks while self-instructing aloud. (Teach Sufficient Exemplars and Mediate Generalization) | Trainer models multiple examples of tasks while self-instructing aloud. (Teach Sufficient Exemplars and Mediate Generalization) | Same |
| 3. Subject performs tasks while trainer instructs. | Subject performs tasks while trainer instructs. | Same |
| 4. Subject performs tasks while self-instructing aloud. | Subject performs tasks while self-instructing aloud. | Same |
| 5. Subject does not perform tasks while whispering. | Subject performs tasks while whispering. | Different |
| 6. Subject does not perform tasks while self-instructing covertly. | Subject performs tasks while self-instructing covertly. | Different |
| 7. Trainer provides corrective feedback and prompting, if needed. | Trainer provides corrective feedback and prompting, if needed. | Same |
| 8. Trainer reminds subject in training to self-instruct when working. (Mediate Generalization) | Trainer does not remind subject to self-instruct when working. | Different |

with severe mental retardation (Hughes & Rusch, 1989). In contrast, only four 30-minute training sessions were required to produce similar results in individuals with mild to moderate mental retardation (Rusch, Morgan, et al., 1985).

## Step 5: Evaluate the Effect of Training

In order to isolate the point at which individuals learn to self-instruct, repeated measures of self-instructing while responding to multiple exemplars must be taken during training. Additionally, in order to assess generalization across situations and tasks, repeated measures of the use of the problem-solving strategy and of responses to untrained problems must be taken, respectively. For example, Rusch, McKee, et al. (1988) collected repeated measures of frequency of correct responding and self-instructing across all performance and training sessions. Data showed that self-instructing was being learned gradually during training; interestingly, all self-instruction statements were not acquired in training until corrective feedback during performance was provided. Thereafter, frequency of self-instructions and frequency of correct responses corresponded throughout the remainder of the study. Repeated measures obtained by Hughes and Rusch (1989) showed that

generalization of correct responding to untrained problem situations during performance occurred simultaneously with the acquisition of self-instruction during training. Their data also demonstrated that frequency of self-instructing corresponded with frequency of correct responding during performance.

## Step 6: Withdraw Training and Evaluate the Effect of Training Withdrawal

The decision about when to withdraw training should be based on frequency of correct responses during performance, because the ultimate test of an instructional strategy is whether an individual can perform desired responses in settings where training did not occur and under circumstances that are novel to the individual. Criterion performance is determined by establishing a range of acceptable behavior as determined by significant others within a setting (e.g., supervisors, employers, teachers) (Rusch, Chadsey-Rusch, & Lagomarcino, 1987). When an individual is performing at criterion level during performance observation sessions, an assessment of response maintenance can be obtained by using a partial withdrawal of training (Rusch & Kazdin, 1981). Individual training components can be withdrawn, or an entire training package can be withdrawn while performance measures continue to be taken. In Hughes and Rusch (1989), a performance criterion of 4 or 5 correct responses across three consecutive sessions (total possible = 5 responses per session) was established. Withdrawal of training sequentially across subjects resulted in maintenance of training gains throughout six months of follow-up evaluation without the need for direct instruction.

## Summary

We have proposed a six-step cognitive-processing model for teaching employees with diverse abilities to generalize their employment skill training across time, responses, and situations. This model utilizes traditional self-instruction combined with multiple exemplars. An important contribution made to traditional self-instruction includes the use of more than one example of a desired response in order to produce generalized performance. Six steps are proposed to accomplish this goal. These steps include selecting an array of examples (step 1), classifying responses into teaching sets (step 2), dividing members of sets into trained responses using self-instruction (step 3), teaching trained responses using self-instruction (step 4), evaluating the effect of training (step 5), and withdrawing training and evaluating the effect of training withdrawal (step 6).

## CONCLUSION

This chapter has focused on teaching generalized performance across time, responses, and situations. Most important, we reviewed available literature related to maintenance and generalization as well as procedures that focus on employees' use of self-management strategies. These self-management strategies include antecedent cue regulation, self-instructing, self-monitoring, and self-reinforcement. After a review of all the available research conducted in integrated employment settings that utilized self-management procedures, we assessed the effects of these self-management strategies on generalization. The problem-solving model we proposed is based on this existing literature and on our emerging understanding of how best to teach individuals with diverse abilities to be independent and autonomous in the workplace.

## REFERENCES

Agran, M., Fodor-Davis, J., & Moore, S. (1986). The effect of self-instructional training on job-task sequencing: Suggesting a problem-solving strategy. *Education and Training of the Mentally Retarded, 21,* 273–281.

Agran, M., & Martin, J. E. (1987). Applying a technology of self-control in community environments for individuals who are mentally retarded. In M. Hersen, R., Eisler, & P. Miller (Eds.), *Progress in behavior modification* (Vol. 14, pp. 108–115). Newbury Park, CA: Sage Publications.

Alberto, P. A., Sharpton, W. R., Briggs, A., & Stright, M. H. (1986). Facilitating task acquisition through the use of a self-operated auditory promoting system. *Journal of the Association for Persons with Severe Handicaps, 11,* 85–91.

Bandura, A. (1969). *Principles of behavior modification.* New York: Holt, Rinehart and Winston.

Barrett, B. H. (1977). Behavior analysis. In J. Wortis (Ed.), *Mental retardation and developmental disabilities, an annual review* (Vol. 9). New York: Brunner/Mazel.

Bellamy, G. T., Peterson, L., & Close, D. (1975). Habilitation of the severely and profoundly retarded: Illustrations of competence. *Education and Training of the Mentally Retarded, 10,* 174–186.

Berg, W. K., & Wacker, D. P. (1989). Evaluation of tactile prompts with a student who is deaf, blind, and mentally retarded. *Journal of Applied Behavior Analysis, 22,* 93–99.

Berg, W. K., Wacker, D. P., & Flynn, T. H. (1990). Teaching generalization and maintenance of work behavior. In F. R. Rusch (Ed.), *Supported employment: Models, methods, and issues* (pp. 145–160). Sycamore, IL: Sycamore Publishing Company.

Carnine, D. (1990). New research on the brain: Implications for instruction. *Phi Delta Kappan, 71,* 372–377.

Connis, R. T. (1979). The effects of sequential pictorial cues, self-recording, and praise on the job task sequencing of retarded adults. *Journal of Applied Behavior Analysis, 12,* 355–361.

Crosson, J. A. (1969). A technique for programming sheltered workshop environments for training severely retarded workers. *American Journal of Mental Deficiency, 73,* 814–818.

Crouch, K. P., Rusch, F. R., & Karlan, G. P. (1984). Competitive employment: Utilizing the correspondence training paradigm to enhance productivity. *Education and Training of the Mentally Retarded, 19,* 268–275.

Cuvo, A. J., Leaf, R. B., & Borakove, L. S. (1978). Teaching janitorial skills to the mentally retarded: Acquisition, generalization, and maintenance. *Journal of Applied Behavior Analysis, 11,* 345–355.

Drabman, R. S., Hammer, D., & Rosenbaum, M. S. (1979). Assessing generalization in behavior modification with children: The generalization map. *Behavioral Assessment, 1,* 203–219.

Engelmann, S., & Carnine, D. W. (1982). *Theory of instruction: Principles and applications.* New York: Irvington.

Gifford, J. L., Rusch, F. R., Martin, D. E., & White, D. M. (1984). Autonomy and adaptability in work behavior of retarded clients. In N. W. Ellis & N. R. Bray (Eds.), *International review of research in mental retardation* (Vol. 12, pp. 285–318). New York: Academic Press.

Gold, M. (1972). Stimulus factors in skill training of the mentally retarded on a complex assembly task: Acquisition, transfer, and retention. *American Journal of Mental Deficiency, 76,* 517–526.

Gold, M. (1976). Task analysis of a complex assembly task by the retarded blind. *Exceptional Children, 43,* 78–84.

Haring, T. G., & Laitinen, R. E. (in press). Extending complex repertoires of critical skills. In R. J. Gaylord-Ross (Ed.), *Issues and research in special education* (Vol. 2). New York: Teachers College Press.

Horner, R. H., Jones, D. N., & Williams, J. A. (1985). A functional approach to teaching generalized street crossing. *Journal of the Association for the Severely Handicapped, 10,* 71–78.

Horner, R. H., Sprague, J., & Wilcox, B. (1982). General case programming for community activities. In B. Wilcox & G. T. Bellamy (Eds.), *Design of high school programs for severely handicapped students* (pp. 61–98). Baltimore: Paul H. Brookes.

Hughes, C., & Rusch, F. R. (1989). Teaching supported employees with severe mental retardation to solve problems. *Journal of Applied Behavior Analysis, 22,* 365–372.

Hunter, J., & Bellamy, T. (1976). Cable harness construction for severely retarded adults: A demonstration of a training technique. *AAESPH Review, 1,* 2–13.

Karlan, G. R., & Rusch, F. R. (1982). Correspondence between saying and doing: Some thoughts on defining correspondence and future directions for application. *Journal of Applied Behavior Analysis, 15,* 151–162.

Kazdin, A. E. (1975). *Behavior modification in applied settings* (1st ed.). Homewood, IL: Dorsey Press.

Lagomarcino, T. R., & Rusch, F. R. (1989). Utilizing self-management procedures to teach independent performance. *Education and Training in Mental Retardation, 24,* 297–305.

Mank, D. M., & Horner, R. H. (1987). Self-recruited feedback: A cost-effective procedure for maintaining behavior. *Research in Developmental Disabilities, 8,* 91–112.

Martin, J. E., & Mithaug, D. E. (1986). Advancing a technology of self-control. *British Columbia Journal of Special Education, 10,* 93–100.

Martin, J. E., Mithaug, D. E., Agran, M., & Husch, J. V. (in press). Consumer-centered transition and supported employment. In J. L. Matson (Ed.), *Handbook of behavior modification with the mentally retarded,* 2nd ed. New York: Plenum Press.

Meichenbaum, D., & Goodman, J. (1971). Training impulsive children to talk to themselves: A means of developing self-control. *Journal of Abnormal Psychology, 77,* 116–126.

O'Leary, S. G., & O'Leary, K. D. (1976). Behavior modification in the school. In H. Leitenberg (Ed.), *Handbook of behavior modification and behavior therapy.* Englewood Cliffs, NJ: Prentice-Hall.

Rusch, F. R. (1979). A functional analysis of the relationship between attending and producing in a vocational training program. *Journal of Special Education, 13,* 399–411.

Rusch, F. R. (Ed.) (1986). *Competitive employment models, methods, and issues.* Baltimore: Paul H. Brookes.

Rusch, F. R., Chadsey-Rusch, J., & Lagomarcino, T. (1987). Preparing students for employment. In M. E. Snell (Ed.), *Systematic instruction for persons with severe handicaps* (3rd ed., pp. 471–490). Columbus, OH: Charles E. Merrill.

Rusch, F. R., Connis, R. T., & Sowers, J. (1978). The modification and maintenance of time spent attending to task using social reinforcement, token reinforcement and response cost in an applied restaurant setting. *Journal of Special Education Technology, 2,* 18–26.

Rusch, F. R., & Kazdin, A. E. (1981). Toward a methodology of withdrawal designs for the assessment of response maintenance. *Journal of Applied Behavior Analysis, 14,* 131–140.

Rusch, F. R., Martin, J. E., Lagomarcino, T. R., & White, D. M. (1987). Teaching task sequencing via verbal mediation. *Education and Training in Mental Retardation, 22,* 229–235.

Rusch, F. R., Martin, J. E., & White, D. M. (1985). Competitive employment: Teaching mentally retarded employees to maintain their work behavior. *Education and Training of the Mentally Retarded, 20,* 182–189.

Rusch, F. R., McKee, M., Chadsey-Rusch, J., & Renzaglia, A. (1988). Teaching a student with severe handicaps to self-instruct: A brief report. *Education and Training in Mental Retardation, 23,* 51–58.

Rusch, F. R., Menchetti, B. M., Crouch, K., Riva, M., Morgan, T., & Agran, M. (1984). Competitive employment: Assessing employee reactivity to naturalistic observation. *Applied Research in Mental Retardation, 5,* 339–351.

Rusch, F. R., Morgan, T. K., Martin, J. E., Riva, M., & Agran, M. (1985). Competitive employment: Teaching mentally retarded employees self-instructional strategies. *Applied Research in Mental Retardation, 6,* 389–407.

Rusch, F. R., Rose, T., & Greenwood, C. (1988). *Introduction to special education and behavior analysis.* Englewood Cliffs, NJ: Prentice-Hall.

Rusch, F. R., & Schutz, R. P. (1979). Non-sheltered employment of the mentally retarded adult: Research to reality? *Journal of Contemporary Business, 8,* 85–98.

Rusch, F. R., & Schutz, R. P. (1981). Vocational and social work behavior: An evaluative review. In J. L. Matson & J. R. McCartney (Eds.), *Handbook of behavior modification with the mentally retarded* (pp. 247–280). New York: Plenum Press.

Schutz, R. P., Rusch, F. R., & Lamson, D. S. (1979). Evaluation of an employer's procedure to eliminate unacceptable behavior on the job. *Community Services Forum, 1,* 4–5.

Skinner, B. F. (1953). *Science and human behavior.* New York: Macmillan.

Sowers, J., Rusch, F. R., Connis, R. T., & Cummings, L. E. (1980). Teaching mentally retarded adults to time manage in a vocational setting. *Journal of Applied Behavior Analysis, 13,* 119–128.

Sowers, J., Verdi, M., Bourbeau, P., & Sheehan, M. (1985). Teaching job independence and flexibility to mentally retarded students through the use of a self-control package. *Journal of Applied Behavior Analysis, 18,* 81–85.

Stokes, T., & Baer, D. (1977). An implicit technology of generalization. *Journal of Applied Behavior Analysis, 10,* 349–367.

Wheeler, J. J., Bates, P., Marshall, K. J., & Miller, S. R. (1988). Teaching appropriate social behaviors to a young man with moderate mental retardation in a supported competitive employment setting. *Education and Training in Mental Retardation, 23,* 105–116.

Whitman, T. L. (1990). Self-regulation and mental retardation. *American Journal on Mental Retardation, 94,* 347–362.

Wilson, P. G., Schepis, M. M., & Mason-Main, M. (1987). In vivo use of picture prompt training to increase independent work at a restaurant. *Journal of the Association for the Severely Handicapped, 12,* 145–150.

# CHAPTER 18

# COORDINATED MULTITARGETED SKILLS TRAINING: THE PROMOTION OF GENERALIZATION-ENHANCEMENT

Arnold P. Goldstein

As the social skills training movement has matured and relevant outcome evidence has accumulated, it has become clear that whereas skill acquisition is a reliable finding across both training methods and diverse populations, generalization is quite another matter. Both generalization to new settings (transfer) and over time (maintenance) have been reported to occur in only a minority of training outcomes. In this chapter, we will examine the alternative approaches that have been taken toward generalization and its enhancement, and propose that the embedding and delivery of social skills training within a broadly comprehensive psychoeducational curriculum—via which both social skills and an array of supportive psychological competencies are taught—has substantial potential for maximizing both transfer and maintenance of acquired social skills.

## INTERVENTION AS INOCULATION

Many traditional interventions—reflecting both a core belief in personality change as both the target and the outcome in effective treatment and their strong tendency to ignore environmental influences

on behavior—viewed successful intervention as a sort of psychological inoculation. The positive changes purported to have taken place within the individual's personality structure were supposed to arm the client to deal effectively with problematic events wherever and whenever they might occur. That is, transfer and maintenance were viewed as automatically occurring processes. With reference to the prevailing psychoanalytic view on this matter, Ford and Urban (1963) note:

> If the patient's behavior toward the therapist is modified, the changes are expected to transfer automatically to other situations. The conflicts involved in the neurosis all become directed toward the therapist during the "transference neurosis." They are not situation-specific. They are responses looking for an object to happen to. Thus, if they are changed while they are occurring in relation to the therapist, they will be permanently changed, and can no longer attach themselves to any object in their old form. No special procedures are necessary to facilitate the transfer from the therapist to other situations if the therapist has successfully resolved the transference pattern of behavior. (p. 173)

Such purported automatic maintenance and transfer, variously explained, also characterize the therapeutic positions of Adler (1924), Horney (1939), Rank (1945), Rogers (1951), and Sullivan (1953). In each instance, the view put forth is that, when the given therapy process results in positive intrapsychic changes in the patient, the patient is assumed to be able to "take these changes with him" and apply them where and when needed in the real-life environment. As Ford and Urban (1963) note, Rogers, like Freud,

> assumes that changes in behaviors outside of the therapy interview will follow automatically upon changes in the self-evaluative thoughts and associated emotions during the therapy hour. Changes in the self-evaluative thoughts and their emotional concomitants result in reduced anxiety; improved discrimination among situational events and responses, more accurate symbolization of them, and greater confidence in one's own decisions. These provide the conditions from which more appropriate instrumental and interpersonal responses will naturally grow. (p. 435)

This intervention-as-inoculation perspective was thus quite widespread among diverse approaches to psychological change throughout the 1950s. Because transfer and maintenance were held to occur inexorably as a consequence of within-treatment gains, no call emerged for the development of purposeful means for their enhancement.

## TRAIN AND HOPE

Psychotherapy research as a viable enterprise was initiated in the 1950s and grew in both quantity and scope during the 1960s and 1970s. Much of the outcome research conducted at the time included systematic follow-up probes, which sought to ascertain whether gains evident at the termination of formal intervention had generalized across settings and/or time. Stokes and Baer (1977) described this phase as one in which transfer and maintenance were hoped for and noted but not pursued. They comment as follows:

> Studies that are examples of Train and Hope across time are those in which there was a change from the intervention procedures, either to a less intensive but procedurally different program, or to no program or no specifically defined program. Data or anecdotal observations were reported concerning the maintenance of the original behavior change over the specified time intervening between the termination of the formal program and the postchecks. (p. 351)

The overwhelming result of these many investigations was that, much more often than not, transfer and maintenance of intervention gains did not occur. Treatment and training did not often serve as an inoculation; gains did not persist automatically; transfer and maintenance did not necessarily follow from the initial training and the hoped-for generalization of its effects (Goldstein & Kanfer, 1979; Hayes, Rincover, & Solnick, 1980; Karoly & Steffen, 1980; Kauffman, Nussen, & McGee, 1977; Kazdin, 1975; Keeley, Shemberg, & Carbonell, 1976). If such be the case, these several writers chorused, then transfer and maintenance must be actively sought. In fact, the failure of the inoculation model, as revealed by the evidence accumulated during the train-and-hope phase, indeed led to a third phase of concern with generalization—the energetic development, evaluation, and clinical use of a number of procedures explicitly designed to enhance transfer and maintenance of intervention gains.

## THE DEVELOPMENT OF TRANSFER AND MAINTENANCE ENHANCERS

The early call by ourselves and others for the development of transfer and maintenance enhancers also made explicit the belief that the enhancement that might result would have its roots in the empirical literature on learning and its transfer:

> A different assumption regarding response maintenance and transfer of therapeutic gains has in recent years begun to emerge in the psychotherapy research literature, especially that devoted to the outcome of behavior modification interventions. This assumption also rests on the belief that maintenance and transfer of therapeutic gain are not common events but, instead of positing that they should occur via an automatic process whose instigation lies within the procedures of the therapy itself, the position taken is that new maintenance-enhancing and transfer-enhancing techniques must be developed and purposefully and systematically incorporated into the ongoing treatment process. Thus, not satisfied that "behaviors usually extinguish when a program is withdrawn" (Kazdin, 1975, p. 213), or that "removal of the contingencies usually results in a decline of performance to or near baseline levels" (Kazdin, 1975, p. 215), a number of therapy practitioners and researchers are actively seeking to identify, evaluate, and incorporate into ongoing treatment a series of procedures explicitly designed to enhance the level of transfer which ensues. As we have stated elsewhere, the starting point in this search for effective gain maintenance and transfer-

enhancers is clear: We need specific knowledge of the conditions under which learning or other changes that take place in therapy will be carried over into extra-therapy situations. . . . We cannot assume that a behavior acquired in the therapy situation, however well learned, will carry over into other situations. Unquestionably the phenomena of therapy are orderly and lawful; they follow definite rules. We must, then, understand the rules that determine what responses will be generalized, or transferred, to other situations and what responses will not. As a first approximation to the rules obtained in psychotherapy, we suggest the knowledge gained from study of transfer of other habits. (Goldstein, Heller, & Sechrest, 1966, p. 244)

The effort to develop effective and reliable means for maximizing transfer and maintenance, though clearly still in progress, has been largely successful. A variety of useful techniques have been developed, evaluated, and incorporated into clinical practice. These several procedures, which collectively constitute the current technology of transfer and maintenance enhancement, are listed in Table 18.1 and are examined in detail in the remainder of this section.

**Table 18.1.**  Transfer- and Maintenance-
Enhancing Procedures

*Transfer*

1. Sequential modification
2. Provision of general principles (general case programming)
3. Overlearning (maximizing response availability)
4. Stimulus variability (training sufficient exemplars, training loosely)
5. Identical elements (programming common stimuli)
6. Mediated generalization (self-recording, self-reinforcement, self-instruction)

*Maintenance*

1. Thin reinforcement (increase intermittency, unpredictability).
2. Delay reinforcement.
3. Fade prompts.
4. Provide booster sessions.
5. Prepare for real-life nonreinforcement
   a. Teach self-reinforcement.
   b. Teach relapse and failure management skills.
   c. Use graduated homework assignments.
6. Program reinforcement.
7. Use natural reinforcers.
   a. Observe real-life settings.
   b. Identify easily reinforced behaviors.
   c. Teach reinforcement recruitment.
   d. Teach reinforcement recognition.

## Transfer-Enhancing Procedures

### Sequential Modification

Sequential modification refers to the utilization of an intervention in one setting (e.g., school, agency), testing for transfer in a second setting (e.g., home, playground), and—if transfer is not found to occur—implementation of the same intervention in that second (third, fourth, etc.) setting. Epps, Thompson, and Lane (1985) comment as follows:

Stokes and Baer (1977) refer to generalization as the occurrence of behavior under different, nontraining conditions without implementating the same behavior-change program in these conditions as was used in the original training environment. Technically, then, sequential modification is not really an example of programming for generalization because what was originally a nontreatment setting . . . becomes a treatment setting when the intervention is implemented there. . . . It is a frequently used technique that may help students demonstrate appropriate behavior under a variety of conditions. (p. 100)

We will not dwell at length on this approach to enhancing appropriate behaviors in real-world contexts because we agree that, formally, it is not a transfer-enhancing technique. It is identified here because both its frequency of use and its behavior-spread goals are identical to those sought by the transfer-enhancing techniques we will now consider.

### Provision of General Principles

Transfer of training may be facilitated by providing the trainee with the general mediating principles that govern satisfactory performance on both the original and the transfer task. The trainee can be given the rules, strategies, or organizing principles that lead to successful performance. This general finding—that mediating principles for successful performance can enhance transfer to new tasks and contexts—has been reported in a number of domains of psychological research, including studies of labeling, rules, advance organizers, learning sets, and deutero-learning. It is a robust finding indeed, with empirical support in both laboratory (Duncan, 1953, 1958; Goldbeck, Bernstein, Hellix, & Marx, 1957; Hendrickson & Schroeder, 1941; Ulmer, 1939) and clinical psychoeducational settings, the latter including the scripted roles in Kelly's (1955) fixed-role therapy; directives in Haley's (1976) problem-solving therapy; strategies in Phillips's (1956) assertion-structured therapy; principles in MacGregor, Ritchie, Serrano, and Schuster's (1964) multiple-impact therapy; problem-solving skills in Steiner, Wyckoff, Marcus, Lariviere, Goldstine, and Schwebel's (1975) radical therapy; and in many of the self-regulatory mediational interventions that lie at the heart of cognitive-behavioral therapy (Kanfer & Karoly, 1972; Kendall & Braswell, 1985).

## Overlearning

Transfer of training has been shown to be enhanced by procedures that maximize overlearning or response availability: The likelihood that a response will be available is very clearly a function of its prior use. We repeat and repeat foreign language phrases we are trying to learn, we insist that our child spend an hour per day in piano practice, and we devote considerable time practicing to make a golf swing smooth and "automatic." These are simply expressions of the response-availability notion—that is, the more we have practiced responses (especially correct ones), the easier it will be to use them in other contexts or at later times. We need not rely solely on everyday experience. It has been well established empirically that, other things being equal, the response that has been emitted most frequently in the past is more likely to be emitted on subsequent occasions. This finding is derived from studies of the frequency of evocation hypothesis and the spew hypothesis (Underwood & Schultz, 1960), preliminary response pretraining (Atwater, 1953; Cantor, 1955; Gagne & Foster, 1949), and overlearning (Mandler, 1954; Mandler & Heinemann, 1956). In all these related research domains, real-life or laboratory-induced prior familiarization with given responses increased the likelihood of their occurrence on later trials. Mandler (1954) summarizes much of this research as it bears upon transfer by noting that "learning to make an old response to a new stimulus showed increasing positive transfer as the degree of original training was increased" (p. 412). Mandler's own studies of overlearning are especially relevant to our present theme because it is not sheer practice of attempts at prosocially effective behaviors that is of most benefit to transfer, but practice of *successful* attempts.

Overlearning involves extending learning over more trials than would be necessary merely to produce initial changes in the individual's behavior. In all too many instances of near-successful training, one or two successes at a given task are taken as evidence to move on to the next task or the next level of the original task. This is a training technique error if one wishes to maximize transfer via overlearning. Mandler's (1954) subjects were trained on the study task until they were able to perform it without error (0, 10, 30, 50, or 100 consecutive times). As noted earlier, transfer varied with the degree of original learning. To maximize transfer through the use of this principle, the guiding rule should not be "practice makes perfect" (implying that one simply practices until one gets it right and then moves on), but "practice of perfect" (implying numerous overlearning trials of correct responses after the initial success).

## Stimulus Variability

In the previous section, we addressed enhancement of transfer by means of practice and repetition—that is, by the sheer number of correct responses the trainee makes to a given stimulus. Transfer is also enhanced by the variability or range of stimuli to which the individual responds. For example, Duncan (1958) has shown that, on paired-associates tasks, transfer is markedly enhanced by varied training. Training even on two stimuli is better than training on a single stimulus. Other investigators have obtained similar results in concept attainment tasks, showing more rapid attainment when a variety of examples is presented (Callantine & Warren, 1955; Shore & Sechrest, 1961). As we noted several years ago in response to such studies, "The implication is clear that in order to maximize positive transfer, training should provide for some sampling of the population of stimuli to which the response must ultimately be given" (Goldstein et al., 1966, p. 220). As Kazdin (1975) comments,

> One way to program response maintenance and transfer of training is to develop the target behavior in a variety of situations and in the presence of several individuals. If the response is associated with a range of settings, individuals, and other cues, it is less likely to be lost when the situations change. (p. 21)

Epps, Thompson, and Lane (1985) discuss stimulus variability for transfer enhancement purposes as it might operate in a special education context under the rubrics "train sufficient examples" and "train loosely." They observe that generalization of new skills or behaviors can also be facilitated by training students under a wide variety of conditions. Manipulating the numbers of trainers, settings, and response classes involved in the intervention promotes generalization by exposing the student to a variety of situations. (p. 26)

Stimulus variability has only a modest history of use in clinical and psychoeducational contexts thus far— for example, multiple-impact therapy for MacGregor et al. (1964); use of multiple therapists by Dreikurs, Schulman, and Mosak (1952); Hayward, Peters, and Taylor (1952); and Whitaker, Malone, and Warkentin (1966); round-robin therapy (Holmes, 1971); and rotational group therapy (Frank, 1973; Slavin, 1980). In the clinical realm of anger management, Feindler and Ecton (1986) urge the employment of stimulus variability (varied task training) for transfer enhancement purposes through the use of diverse role-play stimulus situations.

## Identical Elements

In perhaps the earliest experimental work dealing with transfer enhancement, Thorndike and Woodworth (1901) concluded that, when there was a facilitative effect of one habit on another, it was to the extent that, and because, the habits shared identical elements. Ellis (1965) and Osgood (1953) have more recently emphasized the importance for transfer of similarity between characteristics of the training and application tasks. As Osgood (1953) notes, "the greater the similarity between practice and test stimuli, the greater the amount of positive transfer" (p. 213). This conclusion rests on a particularly solid base of experimental support, involving studies of both motor (Crafts, 1935; Duncan, 1953; Gagne, Baker, & Foster, 1950) and verbal (Osgood, 1949, 1953; Underwood, 1951; Young & Underwood, 1954) behaviors.

In the contexts of psychotherapy and psychoeducational training, the principle of identical elements could be implemented by procedures that function to increase the "real-lifeness" of the stimuli (people, behaviors, places, events, etc.) to which the therapist or trainer is helping the target person learn to respond with effective, satisfying behaviors. There exist two broad strategies for attaining such high levels of veridicality between in-therapy and extratherapy stimuli. The first is to move the training or therapy out of the typical office setting and into the very

interpersonal and physical context in which the person's real-life difficulties are being experienced. Such in vivo interventions are, in fact, a growing reality; the locus of at least some approaches has shifted to homes, airplanes, bars, elevators, and other problem sites (Sherman, 1979; Sherman & Levine, 1979). To be sure, the several marital and family therapies are all examples of use of identical elements in the interpersonal sense in that the persons treated and the persons to whom they must apply their therapeutic learnings are one and the same.

The second broad approach to maximizing identical elements—or, as Epps et al. (1985) put it, *programming common stimuli*—is to remain in a training setting but to enhance its physical and/or interpersonal naturalness. We regularly follow this strategy in our prosocial skills training with aggressive adults and youth by creating role-play contexts (with each trainee's help) that appear and feel similar to "the real thing" (Goldstein et al., 1986). Transitional living centers and the systematic use of *barbs* (Epps et al., 1985) or *red flags* (McGinnis & Goldstein, 1984) in classroom contexts are each examples of promoting transfer by maximizing identical elements.

## Mediated Generalization

The one certain commonality, which by definition is present in both training and application settings, is the individual target trainee. Mediated generalization —mediated by the trainee, not by others—is an approach to transfer enhancement that relies on instructing the trainee in a series of context-bridging, self-regulation competencies (Kanfer & Karoly, 1972; Neilans & Israel, 1981). Operationally, it consists of instructing the trainee in self-recording, self-reinforcement, self-punishment, and self-instruction. Epps et al. (1985), working in a special-education setting, have structured these generalization-mediating steps as follows:

## Self-recording

1. The teacher sets up the data collection system— that is, selects a target behavior, defines it in measurable terms, and decides on an appropriate recording technique.
2. The teacher tries out the data collection system.
3. The teacher teaches the trainee how to use the data collection system.

4. The teacher reinforces the trainee for taking accurate data.

*Self-reinforcement*

1. The teacher determines how many points a trainee has earned, and the trainee simply records these.
2. The teacher tells the trainee to decide how many points should be awarded for appropriate behavior.
3. The trainee practices self-reinforcement under teacher supervision.
4. The trainee employs self-reinforcement without teacher supervision.

*Self-punishment* Self-punishment, operationalized in this example by response cost (taking away points), is taught in a manner directly parallel to that just described for self-reinforcement, in which the teacher employs the technique of fading.

*Self-instruction*

1. The teacher models the appropriate behavior while talking herself through the task out loud so that the trainee can hear.
2. The trainee performs the task with overt instructions from the teacher.
3. The trainee performs the task with overt self-instructions.
4. The trainee performs the task with covert self-instructions.

In recent years, as the cognitive behavior modification therapies, especially those relying heavily on self-instructional processes, have grown in popularity, self-mediated approaches to generalization have grown correspondingly in frequency of use.

## Maintenance-Enhancing Techniques

The persistence, durability, or maintenance of behaviors developed by diverse skills-training approaches is primarily a matter of the manipulation of reinforcement both during the original training and in the client's postintervention, natural environment. There are several specific means by which such maintenance-enhancing manipulation of reinforcement may proceed.

### Thinning of Reinforcement

A rich, continuous reinforcement schedule is optimal for the establishment of new behaviors. Maintenance of such behaviors will be enhanced if the reinforcement schedule is gradually thinned. Thinning of reinforcement will proceed best by moving from a continuous (every trial) schedule, to some form of intermittent schedule, to the level of sparse and infrequent reinforcement characteristic of the natural environment. In fact, the maintenance-enhancing goal of such a thinning process is to make the trainer-offered reinforcement schedule indistinguishable from that typically found in real-world contexts.

### Delay of Reinforcement

Resistance to extinction is also enhanced by delay of reinforcement. As Epps et al. (1985) note:

> During the early stages of an intervention, reinforcement should be immediate and continuously presented contingent on the desired response. . . . After the behavior becomes firmly established in the student's repertoire, it is important to introduce a delay in presenting the reinforcement. Delayed reinforcement is a closer approximation to reinforcement conditions in the natural environment. (p. 21)

Delay of reinforcement may be implemented, according to Sulzer-Azaroff and Mayer (1977), by (1) increasing the size or complexity of the response required before reinforcement is provided; (2) adding a time delay between the response and the delivery of reinforcement; and (3) in token systems, increasing the time interval between the receipt of tokens and the opportunity to spend them and/or requiring more tokens in exchange for a given reinforcer.

### Fading Prompts

Maintenance may be enhanced by the gradual removal of suggestions, reminders, prompts, or similar coaching or instruction. Fading of prompts is a means of moving away from artificial control (the trainer's) to more natural (self-) control of desirable behaviors. As with all the enhancement techniques examined here, fading of prompts should be carefully planned and systematically implemented.

### Booster Sessions

Notwithstanding the importance of fading of prompts, it may be necessary periodically to reinstate instruction in the specifics of given appropriate behaviors in order for those behaviors to continue in the natural environment. Booster sessions between trainer and trainee, either on a preplanned schedule or as needed, have often proved valuable in this regard (Feindler & Ecton, 1986; Karoly & Steffen, 1980).

### Preparation for Deficits in Reinforcement in the Natural Environment

Both trainer and trainee may take several energetic steps to maximize the likelihood that reinforcement for appropriate behaviors will occur in the natural environment. Nevertheless, on a number of occasions, reinforcement will not be forthcoming. Thus, it is important for maintenance purposes that the trainee be prepared for this eventuality. As described in our earlier examination of mediated generalization, self-reinforcement is one means of responding in a maintenance-promoting manner when the desirable behaviors are performed correctly but are unrewarded by external sources. When the trainee performs the behaviors incorrectly or inappropriately in the natural environment, he will respond best to any lack of reinforcement in the natural environment if he has earlier learned skills and cognitive interpretations for dealing with relapse and failure experiences. Kendall and Braswell (1985) have proposed specific means for implementing this suggestion.

A third way in which the trainee may be prepared for nonreinforcement in the natural environment, at least in the context of social skills training and similar interventions, is the use of graduated homework assignments. In our skillstreaming approach (Goldstein, 1973; Goldstein, Sprafkin, Gershaw, & Klein, 1980), for example, skills role-played successfully within group sessions are assigned as homework to be performed outside the group. The main actor's task is to perform the skills before the next session with the real-life parent, sibling, classmate, etc. portrayed by the co-actor in the role play. On occasion, it becomes clear as the homework is discussed that the real-life figure is too difficult a target, too harsh, too unresponsive, or simply too unlikely to provide reinforcement for competent skill use. When faced with this circumstance, with the newly learned skill still fragile and the potential homework environment looming as nonrewarding, we have recast the homework assignment toward two or three more benevolent and more responsive target figures. When the trainee finally does utilize the skill correctly with the originally skipped-over target figure and receives no contingent reinforcement, his or her string of previously reinforced trials help minimize the likelihood that the behavior will be extinguished.

### Programming for Reinforcement in the Natural Environment

The maintenance-enhancing techniques examined thus far are targeted toward the trainee himself—his reinforcement schedule, instruction, booster sessions, and preparation for nonreinforcing consequences. But maintenance of appropriate behaviors also may be enhanced by efforts directed toward others, especially those others in the trainee's natural environment who function as the main providers of the trainee's reinforcement. As Galassi and Galassi (1984) comment,

> Significant others can be trained to deliver the same or similar contingencies in the natural environment as occurred during treatment. Parents, peers, and teachers can be taught to apply reinforcement for appropriate behavior. . . . Perhaps even better than individuals being taught new behaviors in a treatment setting by professionals and later having significant others trained to insure transfer to the natural environment, is training significant others initially to conduct the entire training process in the natural environment. (p. 12)

Patterson and Brodsky (1966); Nay (1979); Tharp and Wetzel (1969); and Walker, Hops, and Johnson (1975) are among the several investigators who have repeatedly demonstrated the efficacy of this now generally employed approach to maintenance enhancement.

### Using Natural Reinforcers

A final and especially valuable approach to maintenance enhancement is the use of reinforcers that naturally and readily exist in the trainee's real-world environment. Stokes and Baer (1977) observe that

> perhaps the most dependable of all generalization programming mechanisms is the one that hardly deserves the name; the transfer of behavioral control from the teacher-experimenter to stable, natural contingencies that can be trusted to operate in the environment to which the subject will return, or already occupies. To a considerable extent, this goal is accomplished by choosing behaviors to teach that normally will meet maintaining reinforcement after the teaching. (p. 353)

Galassi and Galassi (1984) offer the following similar comment:

> We need to target those behaviors for changes that are most likely to be seen as acceptable, desirable,

and positive by others. Ayllon and Azrin (1968) refer to this as the "Relevance of Behavior Rule." "Teach only those behaviors that will continue to be reinforced after training." (p. 10)

Alberto and Troutman (1982) suggest a four-step process that facilitates effective use of natural reinforcers:

1. Observe which specific behaviors are regularly reinforced and how they are reinforced in the major settings that constitute the trainee's natural environment.
2. Instruct the trainee in a selected number of such naturally reinforced behaviors (e.g., certain social skills, grooming behaviors).
3. Teach the trainee how to recruit or request reinforcement (e.g., by tactfully asking peers or others for approval or recognition).
4. Teach the trainee how to recognize reinforcement when it is offered, because its presence in certain gestures or facial expressions may be quite subtle for many trainees.

The call in the 1960s for a technology of transfer and maintenance enhancement has been vigorously answered. That technology, examined in this section, is substantial and still growing. Its full employment in the context of social skills training is strongly recommended. Yet, we must not be overly enthusiastic here. In our own skills-training evaluation research program, as over the course of fifteen years we have systematically utilized and evaluated the outcome efficacy of these several transfer and maintenance enhancers, overall results combined to indicate a growth in effective generalization of skill competence from approximately 25% to approximately 50% of the skills taught to our (primarily adolescent) trainees (Goldstein, 1981). A cup-is-half-full perspective applauds such doubling of generalization effectiveness. A cup-is-still-half-empty viewpoint underscores the manner in which, for half of our trainees, the skills-training effort was of highly truncated value, with effectiveness limited to skills acquisition. Our fourth broad strategy for generalization-enhancement, coordinated multitargeted skills training, has sought to respond to this remaining, and difficult, challenge.

## COORDINATED MULTITARGETED SKILLS TRAINING

It is our basic contention that generalization of acquired skills will be promoted substantially if the trainee is concurrently taught an array of companion,

supportive psychological competencies.[1] As we have noted elsewhere:

> Growing evidence suggests that generalization of gain will be more likely when the psychological treatment offered is both broad and multichannel. Bandwidth in this context refers to the breadth or *number* of client qualities targeted by the treatment; multichannelness refers to the range of different *modes* of client response targeted, respectively, by the different components of the treatment. Our approach to chronically aggressive adolescents, Aggression Replacement Training, consisting of separate but integrated weekly sessions of prosocial skills training (the behavior-targeted components), anger control training (the affect-targeted component), and moral reasoning (the values-targeted component), is an example of such a broad band, multichannel treatment. Demonstrations of reductions in recidivism associated with this intervention are initial evidence of its generalization promoting efficacy. (Goldstein, 1990, pp. 31–33)

In 1988, we expanded Aggression Replacement Training (which itself was an earlier expansion of our social skills training approach, Skillstreaming) into a 10-course, prosocial competencies training program called The Prepare Curriculum (Goldstein, 1988). Although each course teaches competencies (empathy, cooperativeness, etc.) that are of value in their own right, a major goal and benefit of each course inheres in their intended generalization-promoting relationship to the curriculum's focal, skills-training course, Skillstreaming.

## Prepare Curriculum Course 1: Skillstreaming

Since 1970, we have sought to teach an array of interpersonal, prosocial competencies to withdrawn, aggressive, immature, developmentally delayed, and other skill-deficient youth and children (Goldstein, 1973, 1981; Goldstein, Carr, Davidson, & Wehr, 1981; Goldstein, Sprafkin, Gershaw, & Klein, 1980). In this approach, small groups of chronically skill-deficient youngsters with shared prosocial skill deficiencies are (1) shown several examples of expert use of the behaviors constituting the skills in which they are weak or lacking (*modeling*); (2) given several guided opportunities to practice and rehearse these competent interpersonal behaviors (*role playing*); (3) provided with praise, reinstruction, and related feedback on how well their role playing of the skill matched the expert model's portrayal (*performance feedback*); and (4) encouraged to engage in a series of activities designed to increase the likelihood that skills learned in the training setting will endure and be available for use when needed in the school, home, community, institution, or other real-world setting (*transfer training*).

By means of this set of didactic procedures, we have been able to teach such youngsters a 50-skill curriculum, organized into six groups:

A. *Beginning Social Skills:* "Starting a Conversation," "Introducing Yourself," "Giving a Compliment"

B. *Advanced Social Skills:* "Giving Instruction," "Apologizing," "Convincing Others"

C. *Skills for Dealing with Feelings:* "Dealing with Someone Else's Anger," "Expressing Affection," "Dealing with Fear"

D. *Skill Alternatives to Aggression:* "Responding to Teasing," "Keeping Out of Fights," "Helping Others"

E. *Skills for Dealing with Stress:* "Dealing with Being Left Out," "Responding to Failure," "Dealing with an Accusation"

F. *Planning Skills:* "Setting a Goal," "Arranging Problems by Importance," "Deciding What Caused a Problem"

Such Skillstreaming curricula now exist at the secondary (Goldstein et al., 1980), elementary (McGinnis & Goldstein, 1984), and preschool (McGinnis & Goldstein, 1990) age levels and are widely employed in hundreds of schools and agencies involving as trainees many thousands of adolescents and children.

In the remainder of this chapter, we wish to describe these Prepare Curriculum courses and, in each instance, specify the bases for their skill generalization–promoting potential. Because such potential has only recently begun coming under investigative scrutiny, the assertions that follow regarding the potentialing effect of each Prepare Curriculum course on the generalization of Skillstreaming skills are stated in the form of hypotheses.

• *Hypothesis I.* **Skill generalization will be promoted to the degree that the probability of competing responses is reduced.**

## Prepare Curriculum Course 2: Anger Control Training

Anger Control Training was developed by Feindler and her research group at Adelphi University (1979; Feindler & Ecton, 1986), and substantially modified

by us in separate programs involving disruptive elementary school children (Keller, Goldstein, Wynn, & Glick, in progress) and incarcerated juvenile delinquents (Goldstein, Glick, Reiner, Zimmerman, & Coultry, 1986; Goldstein, Glick, Irwin, McCartney, & Rubama, 1989). In contrast to the direct facilitation of prosocial behavior in Skillstreaming, Anger Control Training facilitates such skill behaviors indirectly, by teaching means for inhibiting anger and loss of self-control. Participating youngsters are taught, over a one-term span, how to respond to provocations to anger by: (1) identifying their external and internal triggers; (2) identifying their own physiological/kinesthetic cues that signify anger; (3) using reminders, which are self-statements designed to function in an opposite fashion to triggers (i.e., to lower one's anger-arousal level); (4) using reducers to lower anger further via deep breathing, counting backwards, imagining a peaceful scene, or contemplating the long-term consequences of one's anger-associated behavior; and (5) self-evaluation, in which one judges how adequately anger control worked and rewards oneself when it worked well.

## Prepare Curriculum Course 3: Stress Management

It has been demonstrated by Arkowitz (1977) and by Curran (1977) that individuals may possess an array of prosocial skills in their repertoires but may not employ them in particularly challenging or difficult situations because of anxiety. A youth may have learned well the Skillstreaming skill "Responding to Failure," but his embarrassment at receiving a failing grade in front of his teacher or at missing a foul shot in front of his friends may engender a level of anxiety that inhibits proper use of this skill. A young woman may possess the problem-solving competency to plan well for a job interview but may perform poorly in the interview itself as anxiety, as it were, "takes over." Such anxiety-inhibition as a source of prosocially incompetent and unsatisfying behavior may be especially prevalent in the highly peer-conscious adolescent years.

A series of self-managed procedures exists by means of which stress-induced anxiety may be substantially reduced. It is these procedures that form the contents of the Stress Management course. Participating youngsters are taught systematic deep muscular relaxation (Benson, 1975; Jacobson, 1938), meditation techniques (Assagioli, 1973; Naranjo & Ornstein, 1971), environmental restructuring (Anderson, 1978), exercise (Walker, 1975) and related means of management, control, and reduction of stress-induced anxiety.

• *Hypothesis II*. **Skill generalization will be promoted to the degree that the trainee's level of motivation for skill utilization is increased.**

## Prepare Curriculum Course 4: Moral Reasoning Training

In a long and pioneering series of investigations, Kohlberg (1969, 1973) demonstrated that exposing youngsters to a series of moral dilemmas, in a discussion group context that includes youngsters reasoning at differing levels of moral thinking, arouses an experience of cognitive conflict whose resolution will frequently advance a youngster's moral reasoning to that of the higher level peers in the group. Although such moral reasoning stage advancement is a reliable finding, as with other single interventions, efforts to utilize it by itself as a means of enhancing actual overt moral behavior have yielded only mixed success (Arbuthnot & Gordon, 1983; Zimmerman, 1983)—perhaps, we would speculate, because such youngsters did not have in their behavior repertoires either the actual skill behaviors for acting prosocially or those for successfully inhibiting the antisocial. Consistent with our curriculum development goal of course complementarity, we thus reasoned—and have in fact been able to show—that Kohlbergian Moral Education has marked potential for providing constructive directionality toward prosocialness and away from antisocialness in youngsters armed with the fruits of both Skillstreaming and Anger Control Training (Goldstein et al., 1986).

## Prepare Curriculum Course 5: Cooperation Training

Chronically aggressive and other skill-deficient youth have been shown to display a personality trait pattern that is often high in egocentricity and competitiveness, and low in concern for others and cooperativeness (Slavin, 1980). We offer here a course in Cooperation Training not only because enhanced cooperation among individuals is a valuable social goal in itself but also because of the several valuable concomitants and consequences of enhanced cooperation, such as heightened motivation to employ the prosocially oriented Skillstreaming skills. An extended review of research on one major set of approaches to cooperation training, namely "cooperative learning" (to be discussed) reveals outcomes of enhanced self-esteem, group cohesiveness, altruism, and cooperation itself, as well as reduced egocentricity. As long ago as 1929, Maller commented:

> The frequent staging of contests, the constant emphasis upon the making and breaking of records, and the glorification of the heroic individual achievement . . . in our present educational system lead toward the acquisition of competitiveness. The child is trained to look at the members of his group as constant competitors and urged to put forth a maximum effort to excel them. The lack of practice in group activities and community projects in which the child works with his fellows for a common goal precludes the formation of habits of cooperativeness. . . . (p. 163)

It was many years before the educational establishment responded concretely to this Deweyan challenge, but when it did, it created a wide series of innovative, cooperation-enhancing methodologies, each of which deserves long and careful application and scrutiny both in general educational contexts as well as, in our instance, with particularly noncooperative youth. We refer to the cooperative learning methods: Student Teams—Achievement Division (Slavin, 1980), Teams–Games–Tournaments (Slavin, 1980), Jigsaw Classrooms I (Aronson, Blaney, Stephen, Sikes & Snapp, 1978), Jigsaw Classrooms II (Slavin, 1980), Group-Investigation (Sharon & Sharon, 1976), and Co-op Co-op (Kagan, 1985). Using shared materials, interdependent tasks, group rewards, and similar features, these methods (applied to any content area—mathematics, social studies, etc.) have consistently yielded the several interpersonal, cooperation-enhancing, group and individual benefits noted previously.

In our course, not only do we make use of the many valuable features of the cooperative learning approaches noted here but, in addition—responding to the physical action orientation typical of many skill-deficient youth—in planning course content we rely heavily on cooperative sports and games. Such athletic activity, though not yet popular in the United States, does exist elsewhere in both action and written document (Orlick, 1978; Fluegelman, 1981). Collective score basketball, no-hitting football, cross-team rotational hockey, collective fastest time track meets, and other sports restructured to be what cooperative gaming creators term "all touch," "all play," "all positions," "all shoot," and cooperative in other playing and scoring ways may seem strange to typical American youth, weaned on highly competitive, individualistic sports, but it appears to us to be a valuable additional channel to be utilized with many skill-deficient youth in an effort to enhance both cooperation and skill generalization.

• *Hypothesis III*. **Skill generalization will be promoted to the degree that the trainee concurrently acquires strategies for determining which skills to employ [Course 6], and where, when, and with whom to use them [Courses 7 and 8].**

## Prepare Curriculum Course 6: Problem-Solving Training

Adolescents and younger children may, as Ladd and Mize (1983) point out, be deficient in such problem-solving competencies as "(a) knowledge of appropriate *goals* for social interaction, (b) knowledge of appropriate *strategies* for reaching a social goal, and (c) knowledge of the *contexts* in which specific strategies may be appropriately applied" (p. 130; emphasis in the original). An analogous conclusion flows from the research program on interpersonal problem solving conducted by Spivack, Platt, and Shure (1976). At early and middle childhood, as well as in adolescence, chronically aggressive youngsters were less able than more typical youngsters to function effectively in most problem solving subskills, such as identifying alternatives, considering consequences, determining causality, and engaging in means–ends thinking and perspective taking.

Several programs have been developed in an effort to remediate such problem-solving deficiencies with the types of youngsters of concern here (DeLange, Lanham, & Barton, 1981; Giebink, Stover, & Fahl, 1968; Sarason, Glaser, & Fargo, 1972). Such programs represent a fine beginning, but problem-solving deficiency in such youth is substantial (Chandler, Greenspan, & Barenboim, 1974; Selman, 1980; Spivack et al., 1976), and substantial deficiencies require substantial, longer term, more comprehensive interventions. The course described here seeks to provide just such an effort. In its pilot development, it is a longer term (then existing programs) sequence of such graduated problem-solving skills as reflection, problem identification, information gathering, perspective taking, identification of alternatives, consideration of consequences, and decision making. Our initial evaluation of this sequence with an aggressive adolescent population has yielded significant gains in problem-solving skills thus defined, substantially encouraging further development of this

course (Grant, 1987). These results give beginning substance to our assertion made earlier that

> Individuals can be provided systematic training in problem solving skill both for purposes of building general competence in meeting life's challenges and as a specific means of supplying one more reliable, prosocial alternative to aggression. (Goldstein, 1981)

Its potential value for purposes of enhancement of skill generalization seems high but remains untested.

## Prepare Curriculum Course 7: Situational Perception Training

Once armed with the interpersonal skills necessary to respond prosocially to others (Course 1); the problem-solving strategies underlying skill selection and usage (Course 6); and a fuller, empathic sense of the other person's perspective (Course 9), the chronically skill-deficient youngster may still fail to behave prosocially because he or she misreads the context in which the behavior is to occur. A major thrust in psychology of the past fifteen years has been this emphasis on the importance of the situation or setting as perceived by the individual in determining overt behavior. Morrison and Bellack (1981) comment, for example:

> . . . adequate social performance not only requires a repertoire of response skills, but knowledge about when and how these responses should be applied. Application of this knowledge, in turn, depends upon the ability to accurately "read" the social environment: determine the particular norms and conventions operating at the moment, and to understand the messages being sent . . . and intentions guiding the behavior of the interpersonal partner. (p. 70)

Dil (1972), Emery (1975), and Rothenberg (1970) have each shown that emotionally disturbed youngsters, as well as those "socially maladjusted" in other ways, are characteristically deficient in such social perceptiveness. Argyle (1981) observes:

> . . . It has been found that people who are socially inadequate are unable to read everyday situations and respond appropriately. They are unable to perform or interpret nonverbal signals, unaware of the rules of social behavior, mystified by ritualized routines and conventions of self-presentation and self-disclosure, and are hence like foreigners in their own land. (p. 37)

Argyle (1981) and Backman (1979) have emphasized this same social-perceptual deficit in their work with aggressive individuals. Yet, we believe that the ability to "read" social situations accurately can be taught, and we do so with this course. Its contents are responsive to the valuable leads provided in this context by Brown and Fraser (1979), who propose three salient dimensions of accurate social perceptiveness:

1. The setting of the interaction and its associated rules and norms
2. The purpose of the interaction and its goals, tasks, and topics
3. The relationship of the participants, their roles, responsibilities, expectations, and group memberships

## Prepare Curriculum Course 8: Understanding and Using Group Processes

The acute responsiveness to peer influences of adolescents and preadolescents is a truism frequently cited in both lay and professional literature on child development. It is a conclusion resting on a very solid research foundation (Baumrind, 1975; Field, 1981; Guralnick, 1981; Manaster, 1977; Moriarty & Toussieng, 1976; Rosenberg, 1975). As a curriculum designed to enhance prosocial competencies, it is especially important that Prepare include a segment giving special emphasis to group—especially peer—processes. Its title includes both "understanding" and "using" because both are clearly part of its goal. Participating youth will be helped to understand such group forces and phenomena as peer pressure, clique formation and dissolution, leaders and leadership, cohesiveness, imitation, reciprocity, in-group versus out-group relations, developmental phases, competition, within-group communication and its failure, and similar processes, with special emphasis on the manner in which these diverse processes are optimally initiated, responded to, or otherwise dealt with by particular Skillstreaming skills and skill sequences.

This course's instructional formal also relies heavily on group activities in which, experientially, participants can learn means for resisting group pressure effectively when one elects to do so, for seeking and enacting a group leadership role, for helping to build and enjoy the fruits of group cohesiveness, and so forth. Examples of specific activities of apparent value for such group-experiential learning include group simulations, structured experiences, and gam-

ing as "Assessment of Leadership Style," "Committee Meeting: Demonstrating Hidden Agendas," "Process Observation: A Guide," "Top Problems: A Consensus-Seeking Task," "Dealing with Shared Leadership," "Conflict Resolution: A Collection of Tasks," "Group on Group," "Line Up and Power Inversion," "Polarization: A Demonstration," "Not Listening: A Dyadic Role Play," "Towers: An Intergroup Competition," and "Peer Perceptions: A Feedback Experience" (Pfeiffer & Jones, 1974; Thayer & Beeler, 1975).

• *Hypothesis IV*. **Skill generalization will be promoted to the degree that the trainee concurrently acquires enhanced competence in assuming the perspective of the skill-use target person(s).**

## Prepare Curriculum Course 9: Empathy Training

Expression of empathic understanding can simultaneously serve as an inhibitor of negative interactions and a facilitator of positive ones. Evidence clearly demonstrates that

> . . . responding to another individual in an empathic manner and assuming temporarily their perspective decreases or inhibits one's potential for acting aggressively toward the other (Feshbach, 1982; Feshbach & Feshbach, 1969). Stated otherwise, empathy and aggression are incompatible interpersonal responses, hence learning to be more skilled in the former serves as an aid to diminishing the latter. (Goldstein et al., 1986, p. 309)

The notion of empathy as a facilitator of positive interpersonal relations stands on an even broader base of research evidence. Our recent review of the literally hundreds of investigations inquiring into the interpersonal consequences of empathic responding reveal such responding to be a consistently potent promoter of interpersonal attraction, dyadic openness, conflict resolution, and individual growth (Goldstein & Michaels, 1985). It is a most potent facilitator indeed.

This same review effort led us to define empathy as a multistage process of perception of emotional cues, affective reverberation of the emotions perceived, their cognitive labeling, and communication and, correspondingly, to develop a multistage training program—this Prepare Curriculum course—by which these four constituent components could be taught.

• *Hypothesis V.* **Skill generalization will be promoted to the degree that the trainee learns to construct, employ, and is rewarded for employing in his or her real-life environment skill sequences and combinations.**

## Prepare Curriculum Course 10: Recruiting Supportive Models

Aggressive youth quite typically are regularly exposed to highly aggressive models in their interpersonal worlds. Parents, siblings, and peers each are frequently chronically aggressive individuals themselves (Knight & West, 1975; Loeber & Dishion, 1983; Robins, West, & Herjanic, 1975). Simultaneously, there tend to be relatively few countervailing prosocial models available to be observed and imitated. When they are, however, such prosocial models can apparently make a tremendous difference in the daily lives and development of such youth. In support of this assertion we may turn not only to such community-provided examples of prosocial modeling as Big Brothers, Police Athletic League, Boy Scouts, and the like, and not only to the laboratory research consistently showing that rewarded prosocial behaviors (e.g., sharing, altruism, cooperation) are often imitated (Bryan & Test, 1967; Evers & Schwarz, 1973; Canale, 1977), but also to more direct evidence. For example, Werner and Smith (1982), in their impressive longitudinal study of aggressive and nonaggressive youth, *Vulnerable but Invincible,* clearly demonstrated that many youngsters growing up in a community characterized by high crime, high unemployment, high secondary school dropout rates, and high levels of aggressive models were indeed able to sail on through, as it were, and develop into effective, satisfied, prosocially oriented individuals if they had had sustained exposure to at least one significant prosocial model—be it parent, relative, or peer.

Because such models are often scarce in the real-world environments of the youth Prepare is intended to serve, efforts must be put forth to help these youth identify, encourage, attract, elicit, and at times perhaps even create sources and attachments to others who not only—as models—function prosocially themselves, but also can serve as sustained sources of direct support for the youth's own prosocially oriented efforts.

Our course contents for teaching such identification, encouraging, attraction, elicitation, and creation skills rely on both the teaching procedures and the interpersonal skills that constitute the Skillstreaming

skills training technology and curricula for adolescents (Goldstein et al., 1980) and younger children (McGinnis & Goldstein, 1984, 1990).

## SUMMARY

Over the past sixty-five years, the perspective of the helping professions on generalization of gain has progressed from inoculatory assumptions, to a train and hope stance, on to the proactive development and use of an array of transfer- and maintenance-enhancing techniques. Longer term outcomes have improved, but positive effects limited to the place and time of intervention still occur with considerable frequency. This mixed generalization outcome appears to characterize many helping interventions, including social skills training. We have in this chapter urged consideration, implementation, and evaluation of a fourth strategy—one that, it should be noted, is designed to be used in conjunction with, not as a replacement for, the generalization-enhancer strategy described previously. This fourth approach is the teaching of an array of companion psychological competencies, to be employed in a manner coordinated with and in potentiation of the social skills themselves. Our recently developed Prepare Curriculum exemplifies this approach. A partial test of its efficacy, involving simultaneous training in social skills, anger control, and moral reasoning, did in fact yield relatively long-term evidence of skill utilization (Goldstein et al., 1989). Such initial evidence combines with the status of generalization as *the* all-too-frequently unrealized yet central goal of all current psychological interventions to urge further implementation and, especially, evaluation of the generalization strategy we have proposed herein.

## NOTES

1. This generalization-enhancement strategy, emphasizing the attempt to increase the level of transfer and maintenance of gain by increasing the potency (breadth, mode, variety, intensity) of intervention provided the trainee, became especially attractive to us as we taught social skills to soon-to-be-decarcerated juvenile delinquents and sought, mostly in vain, for a great many of them, to reach out into their real-world environment in order to "bring on board" a peer, parent, teacher, sibling, or other to serve as our allies in the generalization effort. For a great many of these youths, no such person existed, or was available, or could be enlisted. We had no one in these instances to serve as real-world transfer and maintenance promoter but the youth himself or herself. Since this was the case—and since, as

noted, skills training alone too often failed to yield generalization effects—the strategy of seeking such effects via increased potency of the youth-directed intervention itself became compelling.

# REFERENCES

Adler, A. (1924). *The practice and theory of individual psychology.* New York: Harcourt Brace Jovanovich.

Alberto, P. A., & Troutman, A. C. (1982). *Applied behavior analysis for teachers: Influencing student performance.* Columbus, OH: Charles E. Merrill.

Anderson, R. A. (1978). *Stress power.* New York: Human Sciences Press.

Arbuthnot, J., & Gordon, D. A. (1983). Moral reasoning development in correctional intervention. *Journal of Correctional Education, 34,* 133–138.

Argyle, M. (1981). The experimental study of the basic features of situations. In D. Magnusson (Ed.), *Toward a psychology of situations: An interactional perspective.* Hillsdale, NJ: Lawrence Erlbaum.

Arkowitz, H. (1977). Measurement and modification of minimal dating behavior. In M. Hersen, R. M. Eisler, & P. M. Miller (Eds.), *Progress in behavior modification* (Vol. 5). New York: Academic Press.

Aronson, E., Blaney, N., Stephan, C., Sikes, J., & Snapp, M. (1978). *The jigsaw classroom.* Beverly Hills, CA: Sage Publications.

Assagioli, R. (1973). *The act of will.* New York: Viking Press.

Atwater, S. K. (1953). Proactive inhibition and associative facilitation as affected by degree of prior learning. *Journal of Experimental Psychology, 46,* 400–404.

Backman, C. (1979). Epilogue: A new paradigm. In G. Ginsburg (Ed.), *Emerging strategies in social psychological research.* Chichester: Wiley.

Baumrind, D. (1975). Early socialization and adolescent competence. In S. E. Dragastin & G. H. Elder (Eds.), *Adolescence in the life cycle.* Washington, DC: Hemisphere.

Benson, H. (1975). *The relaxation response.* New York: Avon.

Brown, P., & Fraser, C. (1979). Speech as a marker of situations. In K. Scherer & H. Giles (Eds.), *Social markers in speech.* Cambridge: Cambridge University Press.

Bryan, J. H., & Test, M. A. (1967). Models and helping: Naturalistic studies in aiding behavior. *Journal of Personality and Social Psychology, 6,* 400–407.

Callantine, M. F., & Warren, J. M. (1955). Learning sets in human concept formation. *Psychological Reports, 1,* 363–367.

Canale, J. R. (1977). The effect of modeling and length of ownership on sharing behavior of children. *Social behavior and personality, 5,* 187–191.

Cantor, J. H. (1955). Amount of pretraining as a factor in stimulus predifferentiation and performance set. *Journal of Experimental Psychology, 50,* 180–184.

Chandler, M., Greenspan, S., & Barenboim, C. (1974). Assessment and training of role-taking and referential communication skills in institutionalized emotionally disturbed children. *Developmental Psychology, 10,* 546–553.

Crafts, L. W. (1935). Transfer as related to number of common elements. *Journal of General Psychology, 13,* 147–158.

Curran, J. P. (1977). Skills training as an approach to the treatment of heterosexual-social anxiety: A review. *Psychological Bulletin, 84,* 140–157.

DeLange, J. M., Lanham, S. L., & Barton, J. A. (1981). Social skills training for juvenile delinquents: Behavioral skill training and cognitive techniques. In D. Upper & S. Ross (Eds.), *Behavior group therapy, 1981: An annual review.* Champaign, IL: Research Press.

Dil, N. (1972). *Sensitivity of emotionally disturbed and emotionally non-disturbed elementary school children to emotional meanings of facial expressions.* Unpublished doctoral dissertation, Indiana University.

Dreikurs, R., Schulman, B. H., & Mosak, H. (1952). Patient–therapist in multiple psychotherapy: Its advantages to the therapist. *Psychiatric Quarterly, 26,* 219–227.

Duncan, C. P. (1953). Transfer in motor learning as a function of degree of first-task learning and inner-task similarity. *Journal of Experimental Psychology, 45,* 1–11.

Duncan, C. P. (1958). Transfer after training with single versus multiple tasks. *Journal of Experimental Psychology, 55,* 63–72.

Ellis, H. (1965). *The transfer of learning.* New York: Macmillan.

Emery, J. E. (1975). *Social perception processes in normal and learning disabled children.* Unpublished doctoral dissertation, New York University.

Epps, S., Thompson, B. J., & Lane, M. P. (1985). *Procedures for incorporating generalization programming into interventions for behaviorally disordered students.* Unpublished manuscript, Iowa State University, Ames.

Evers, W. L., & Schwartz, J. C. (1973). Modifying social withdrawal in preschoolers: The effects of filmed modeling and teacher praise. *Journal of Abnormal Child Psychology, 1,* 248–256.

Feindler, E. L., & Ecton, R. B. (1986). *Adolescent anger control: Cognitive-behavioral techniques.* New York: Pergamon Press.

Feshbach, N. D. (1982). Empathy, empathy training and the regulation of aggression in elementary school children. In R. M. Kaplan, V. J. Konecni, & R. Novaco (Eds.), *Aggression in children and youth.* Alphen den Rijn, The Netherlands: Siuhogg/Noordhoff.

Field, T. (1981). Early peer relations. In P. S. Strain (Ed.), *The utilization of classroom peers as behavior change agents.* New York: Plenum Press.

Fluegelman, A. (1981). *More new games.* Garden City, NY: Dolphin.

Ford, D. H., & Urban, H. B. (1963). *Systems of psychotherapy.* New York: Wiley.

Frank, R. (1973). Rotating leadership in a group therapy setting. *Psychotherapy: Theory, Research and Practice, 10,* 337–338.

Gagne, R. M., Baker, K. E., & Foster, H. (1950). On the relation between similarity and transfer of training in the learning of discriminative motor tasks. *Psychological Review, 57,* 67–79.

Gagne, R. M., & Foster, H. (1949). Transfer to a motor skill from practice on a pictured representation. *Journal of Experimental Psychology, 39,* 342–354.

Galassi, J. P., & Galassi, M. D. (1984). Promoting transfer and maintenance of counseling outcomes. In S. D. Brown & R. W. Lent (Eds.), *Handbook of counseling psychology.* New York: Wiley.

Giebink, J. W., Stover, D. S., & Fahl, M. A. (1968). Teaching adaptive responses in frustration to emotionally disturbed boys. *Journal of Consulting and Clinical Psychology, 32,* 336–368.

Goldbeck, R. A., Bernstein, B. B., Hellix, W. A., & Marx, M. H. (1957). Application of the half-split technique to problem-solving tasks. *Journal of Experimental Psychology, 53,* 330–338.

Goldstein, A. P. (1973). *Structured learning therapy: Toward a psychotherapy for the poor.* New York: Academic Press.

Goldstein, A. P. (1981). *Psychological skill training.* New York: Pergamon Press.

Goldstein, A. P. (1988). *The Prepare Curriculum.* Champaign, IL: Research Press.

Goldstein, A. P. (1990). Generating transfer: Toward a technology of transfer and maintenance enhancement. In C. R. Snyder & D. Forsyth (Eds.) *Handbook of clinical-social psychology* (pp. 31–33). New York: Pergamon Press.

Goldstein, A. P., Carr, E. G., Davidson, W. S., & Wehr, P. (1981). *In response to aggression.* New York: Pergamon Press.

Goldstein, A. P., Glick, B., Irwin, M. J., McCartney, C., & Rubama, I. (1989). *Reducing delinquency: Intervention in the community.* Champaign, IL: Research Press.

Goldstein, A. P., Glick, B., Reiner, S., Zimmerman, D., & Coultry, T. (1986). *Aggression replacement training.* Champaign, IL: Research Press.

Goldstein, A. P., Heller, K., & Sechrest, L. B. (1966). *Psychotherapy and the psychology of behavior change.* New York: Wiley.

Goldstein, A. P., & Kanfer, F. H. (1979). *Maximizing treatment gains.* New York: Academic Press.

Goldstein, A. P., & Michaels, G. Y. (1985). *Empathy: Development, training and consequences.* Hillsdale, NJ: Lawrence Erlbaum.

Goldstein, A. P., Sprafkin, R. P., Gershaw, N. J., & Klein, P. (1980). *Skillstreaming the adolescent.* New York: Pergamon Press.

Grant, J. E. (1987). *Problem solving intervention for aggressive adolescent males: A preliminary investigation.* Unpublished doctoral dissertation, Syracuse University.

Guralnick, M. J. (1981). Peer influences on the development of communicative competence. In P. Strain (Ed.), *The utilization of classroom peers as behavior change agents.* New York: Plenum Press.

Haley, J. (1976). *Problem solving therapy.* San Francisco: Jossey-Bass.

Hayes, S. C., Rincover, A., & Solnick, J. V. (1980). The technical drift of applied behavior analysis. *Journal of Applied Behavior Analysis, 13,* 275–285.

Hayward, M. L., Peters, J. J., & Taylor, J. E. (1952). Some values of the use of multiple therapists in the treatment of psychoses. *Psychiatric Quarterly, 26,* 244–249.

Hendrickson, G., & Schroeder, W. H. (1941). Transfer of training in learning to hit a submerged target. *Journal of Educational Psychology, 32,* 205–213.

Holmes, D. S. (1971). Round robin therapy: A technique for implementing the effects of psychotherapy. *Journal of Consulting and Clinical Psychology, 37,* 324–331.

Horney, K. (1939). *New ways in psychoanalyses.* New York: Norton.

Jacobson, E. (1938). *Progressive relaxation.* Chicago: University of Chicago Press.

Kagan, S. (1985). Learning to cooperate. In R. Slavin, S. Sharan, S. Kagan, R. Hertz-Lazarowitz, C. Webb, & R. Schmuck (Eds.), *Learning to cooperate, cooperating to learn.* New York: Plenum Press.

Kanfer, F. H., & Karoly, P. (1972). Self-control: A behavioristic excursion into the lion's den. *Behavior Therapy, 3,* 398–416.

Karoly, P., & Steffen, J. J. (Eds.). (1980). *Improving the long term effects of psychotherapy.* New York: Gardner.

Kauffman, J. M., Nussen, J. L., & McGee, C. S. (1977). Follow-up in classroom behavior modification: Survey and discussion. *Journal of School Psychology, 15,* 343–348.

Kazdin, A. E. (1975). *Behavior modification in applied settings.* Homewood, IL: Dorsey.

Keeley, S. M., Shemberg, K. M., & Carbonell, J. (1976). Operant clinical intervention: Behavior management or beyond? Where are the data? *Behavior Therapy, 7,* 292–305.

Keller, H., Goldstein, A. P., Wynn, R., & Glick, B. (1987). *Aggression prevention training.* Unpublished manuscript, Syracuse University.

Kelly, G. A. (1955). *The psychology of personal constructs.* New York: Norton.

Kendall, P. C., & Braswell, L. (1985). *Cognitive-behavioral therapy for impulsive children.* New York: Guilford Press.

Knight, B. J., & West, D. J. (1975). Temporary and continuing delinquency. *British Journal of Criminology, 15,* 43–50.

Kohlberg, L. (1969). Stage and sequence: The cognitive-developmental approach to socialization. In D. A. Goslin

(Ed.), *Handbook of socialization theory and research*. Chicago: Rand-McNally.

Kohlberg, L. (Ed.) (1973). *Collected papers on moral development and moral education*. Cambridge, MA: Harvard University, Center for Moral Education.

Ladd, G. W., & Mize, J. (1983). A cognitive-social learning model of social skill training. *Psychological Review, 90,* 127–157.

Loeber, R., & Dishion, T. (1983). Early predictors of male delinquency: A review. *Psychological Bulletin, 94,* 68–99.

MacGregor, R., Ritchie, A. M., Serrano, A. C., & Schuster, F. P. (1964). *Multiple impact theory with families*. New York: McGraw-Hill.

Maller, J. B. (1929). *Cooperation and competition: An experimental study in innovation*. New York: Teachers College, Columbia University.

Manaster, G. J. (1977). *Adolescent development and the life tasks*. Boston: Allyn and Bacon.

Mandler, G. (1954). Transfer of training as a function of degree of response overlearning. *Journal of Experimental Psychology, 47,* 411–417.

Mandler, G., & Heinemann, S. H. (1956). Effect of overlearning of a verbal response on transfer of training. *Journal of Experimental Psychology, 52,* 39–46.

McGinnis, E., & Goldstein, A. P. (1984). *Skillstreaming the elementary school child: A guide for teaching prosocial skills*. Champaign, IL: Research Press.

McGinnis, E., & Goldstein, A. P. (1990). *Skillstreaming in early education*. Champaign, IL: Research Press.

Moriarty, A. E., & Toussieng, P. W. (1976). *Adolescent coping*. New York: Grune & Stratton.

Morrison, R. L., & Bellack, A. S. (1981). The role of social perception in social skills. *Behavior Therapy, 12,* 69–79.

Naranjo, C., & Ornstein, R. E. (1971). *On the psychology of meditation*. New York: Viking Press.

Nay, W. R. (1979). Parents as real-life reinforcers: The enhancement of parent-training effects across conditions other than training. In A. P. Goldstein & F. H. Kanfer (Eds.), *Maximizing treatment gains*. New York: Academic Press.

Neilans, T. H., & Israel, A. C. (1981). Towards maintenance and generalization of behavior change: Teaching children self-regulation and self-instructional skills. *Cognitive Therapy and Research, 5,* 189–195.

Orlick, T. (1978). *The cooperative sports and games book*. New York: Pantheon.

Orlick, T. (1982). *The second cooperative sports and games book*. New York: Pantheon.

Osgood, C. E. (1949). The similarity paradox in human learning: A resolution. *Psychological Review, 56,* 132–143.

Osgood, C. E. (1953). *Method and theory in experimental psychology*. New York: Oxford University Press.

Patterson, G. R., & Brodsky, G. A. (1966). A behavior modification program for a child with multiple problem behaviors. *Journal of Child Psychiatry, 7,* 277–295.

Pfeiffer, J. W., & Jones, J. E. (1974). *A handbook of structured experiences for human relations training*. (Vols. 1–5). La Jolla, CA: University Associates.

Phillips, E. L. (1956). *Psychotherapy: A modern theory and practice*. Englewood Cliffs, NJ: Prentice-Hall.

Rank, O. (1945). *Will therapy*. New York: Knopf.

Robins, L. N., West, P. A., & Herjanic, B. L. (1975). Arrests and delinquency in two generations: A study of black urban families and their children. *Journal of Child Psychology and Psychiatry, 16,* 125–140.

Rogers, C. R. (1951). *Client-centered therapy: Its current practice, implications, and theory*. Boston: Houghton Mifflin.

Rosenberg, M. (1975). The dissonant context and the adolescent self-concept. In S. E. Dragastin & G. H. Elder (Eds.), *Adolescence in the life cycle*. Washington, DC: Hemisphere.

Rothenberg, B. B. (1970). Children's social sensitivity and the relationship to interpersonal competence, interpersonal comfort, and intellectual level. *Developmental Psychology, 2,* 335–350.

Sarason, I. G., Glaser, E. M., & Fargo, G. A. (1972). *Reinforcing productive classroom behavior*. New York: Behavioral Publications.

Selman, R. L. (1980). *The growth of interpersonal understanding*. New York: Academic.

Sharon, S., & Sharon, Y. (1976). *Small-group teaching*. Englewood Cliffs, NJ: Prentice-Hall.

Sherman, A. R. (1979). In vivo therapies for phobic reactions, instrumental behavior problems and interpersonal communication problems. In A. P. Goldstein & F. H. Kanfer (Eds.), *Maximizing treatment gains*. New York: Academic Press.

Sherman, A. R., & Levine, M. P. (1979). In vivo therapies for compulsive habits, sexual difficulties, and severe adjustment problems. In A. P. Goldstein & F. H. Kanfer (Eds.), *Maximizing treatment gains*. New York: Academic Press.

Shore, E., & Sechrest, L. (1961). Concept attainment as a function of number of positive instances presented. *Journal of Educational Psychology, 52,* 303–307.

Slavin, D. R. (1967). *Response transfer of conditional affective responses as a function of an experimental analogue of rotational psychotherapy*. Unpublished doctoral dissertation, Northwestern University, Chicago.

Slavin, R. E. (1980). *Using student team learning*, rev. ed. Baltimore, MD: Johns Hopkins University Center for Social Organization of Schools.

Spivack, G., Platt, J. J., & Shure, M. B. (1976). *The problem-solving approach to adjustment*. San Francisco: Jossey-Bass.

Steiner, C., Wyckoff, H., Marcus, J., Lariviere, P., Goldstine, D., & Schwebel, R. (1975). *Readings in radical psychiatry*. New York: Grove Press.

Stokes, T. F., & Baer, D. M. (1977). An implicit technology of generalization. *Journal of Applied Behavior Analysis, 10,* 349–367.

Sullivan, H. S. (1953). *Conceptions of modern psychiatry.* New York: Norton.

Sulzer-Azaroff, B., & Mayer, G. R. (1977). *Applying behavior analysis procedures with children and youth.* New York: Holt, Rinehart & Winston.

Tharp, R. G., & Wetzel, R. J. (1969). *Behavior modification in the natural environment.* New York: Academic Press.

Thayer, L., & Beeler, K. D. (1975). *Activities and exercises for affective education.* Washington, DC: American Educational Research Associates.

Thorndike, E. L., & Woodworth, R. S. (1901). The influence of improvement in one mental function upon the efficiency of other functions. *Psychological Review, 8,* 247–261.

Ulmer, G. (1939). Teaching geometry to cultivate reflective thinking: An experimental study with 1,239 high school students. *Journal of Experimental Education, 8,* 18–25.

Underwood, B. J. (1951). Associative transfer in verbal learning as a function of response similarity and degree of first-list learning. *Journal of Experimental Psychology, 42,* 44–53.

Underwood, B. J., & Schultz, R. W. (1960). *Meaningfulness and verbal behavior.* New York: Lippincott.

Walker, H. M., Hops, H., & Johnson, S. M. (1975). Generalization and maintenance of classroom treatment effects. *Behavior Therapy, 6,* 188–200.

Werner, E. E., & Smith, R. S. (1982). *Vulnerable but invincible.* New York: McGraw-Hill.

Whitaker, C. A., Malone, T. P., & Warkentin, J. (1966). Multiple therapy and psychotherapy. In F. Fromm-Reichmann & M. Morens (Eds.), *Progress in psychotherapy.* New York: Grune & Stratton.

Young, R. K., & Underwood, B. J. (1954). Transfer in verbal materials with dissimilar stimuli and response similarity varied. *Journal of Experimental Psychology, 47,* 153–159.

Zimmerman, D. (1983). Moral education. In A. P. Goldstein (Ed.), *Prevention and control of aggression.* New York: Pergamon Press.

# GENERAL PSYCHOLOGY SERIES

*Editors:* **Arnold P. Goldstein,** Syracuse University
**Leonard Krasner,** Stanford University & SUNY at Stony Brook

---

*Out of print.

Vol. 36. GRAZIANO—*Child Without Tomorrow*
Vol. 37. MORRIS—*Perspectives in Abnormal Behavior*
Vol. 38. BALLER—*Bed Wetting: Origins and Treatment**
Vol. 40. KAHN, CAMERON & GIFFEN—*Methods and Evaluation in Clinical and Counseling Psychology*
Vol. 41. SEGALL—*Human Behavior and Public Policy: A Political Psychology*
Vol. 42. FAIRWEATHER et al.—*Creating Change in Mental Health Organizations*
Vol. 43. KATZ & ZLUTNICK—*Behavior Therapy and Health Care: Principles and Applications*
Vol. 44. EVANS & CLAIBORN—*Mental Health Issues and the Urban Poor*
Vol. 46. BARBER, SPANOS & CHAVES—*Hypnosis, Imagination and Human Potentialities*
Vol. 47. POPE—*The Mental Health Interview: Research and Application*
Vol. 48. PELTON—*The Psychology of Nonviolence**
Vol. 49. COLBY—*Artificial Paranoia—A Computer Simulation of Paranoid Processes*
Vol. 50. GELFAND & HARTMANN—*Child Behavior Analysis and Therapy, Second Edition*
Vol. 51. WOLPE—*Theme and Variations: A Behavior Therapy Casebook**
Vol. 52. KANFER & GOLDSTEIN—*Helping People Change: A Textbook of Methods, Fourth Edition*
Vol. 53. DANZIGER—*Interpersonal Communication**
Vol. 55. GOLDSTEIN & STEIN—*Prescriptive Psychotherapies*
Vol. 56. BARLOW & HERSEN—*Single-Case Experimental Designs: Strategies for Studying Behavior Changes, Second Edition*
Vol. 57. MONAHAN—*Community Mental Health and the Criminal Justice System*
Vol. 58. WAHLER, HOUSE & STAMBAUGH—*Ecological Assessment of Child Problem Behavior: A Clinical Package for Home, School and Institutional Settings*
Vol. 59. MAGARO—*The Construction of Madness: Emerging Conceptions and Interventions in the Psychotic Process*
Vol. 60. MILLER—*Behavioral Treatment of Alcoholism**
Vol. 61. FOREYT—*Behavioral Treatments of Obesity*
Vol. 62. WANDERSMAN, POPPEN & RICKS—*Humanism and Behaviorism: Dialogue and Growth*
Vol. 63. NIETZEL, WINETT, MACDONALD & DAVIDSON—*Behavioral Approaches to Community Psychology*
Vol. 64. FISHER & GOCHROS—*Handbook of Behavior Therapy with Sexual Problems. Vol. I: General Procedures. Vol. II: Approaches to Specific Problems**
Vol. 65. BELLACK & HERSEN—*Behavioral Assessment: A Practical Handbook, Third Edition*
Vol. 66. LEFKOWITZ, ERON, WALDER & HUESMANN—*Growing Up to Be Violent: A Longitudinal Study of the Development of Aggression*
Vol. 67. BARBER—*Pitfalls in Human Research: Ten Pivotal Points*
Vol. 68. SILVERMAN—*The Human Subject in the Psychological Laboratory*
Vol. 69. FAIRWEATHER & TORNATZKY—*Experimental Methods for Social Policy Research**
Vol. 70. GURMAN & RAZIN—*Effective Psychotherapy: A Handbook of Research**
Vol. 71. MOSES & BYHAM—*Applying the Assessment Center Method*
Vol. 72. GOLDSTEIN—*Prescriptions for Child Mental Health and Education*
Vol. 73. KEAT—*Multimodal Therapy with Children*
Vol. 74. SHERMAN—*Personality: Inquiry & Application*
Vol. 75. GATCHEL & PRICE—*Clinical Applications of Biofeedback: Appraisal and Status*
Vol. 76. CATALANO—*Health, Behavior and the Community: An Ecological Perspective*
Vol. 77. NIETZEL—*Crime and Its Modification: A Social Learning Perspective*
Vol. 78. GOLDSTEIN, HOYER & MONTI—*Police and the Elderly*
Vol. 79. MIRON & GOLDSTEIN—*Hostage*
Vol. 80. GOLDSTEIN et al.—*Police Crisis Intervention*
Vol. 81. UPPER & CAUTELA—*Covert Conditioning*
Vol. 82. MORELL—*Program Evaluation in Social Research*

# AUTHOR INDEX

# SUBJECT INDEX